INTERNATIONAL PROVERB SCHOLARSHIP
An Annotated Bibliography
Supplement II (1982–1991)

Wolfgang Mieder

GARLAND PUBLISHING, INC. • NEW YORK & LONDON
1993

Library of Congress Cataloging-in-Publication Data
(Revised for vol. 2)

Mieder, Wolfgang.
    International proverb scholarship, an annotated bibliography. Supplement.
    (Garland reference library of the humanities ; vol. 1230, vol. 1655)
    (Garland folklore bibliographies ; vol. 15, vol. 20)
    Includes indexes.
    Contents: v. 1. 1800–1981 — v. 2. 1982–1991.
    1. Proverbs—History and criticism—Bibliography. I. Title. II. Title:
International proverb scholarship. III. Series. IV. Series: Garland reference
library of the humanities ; vol. 1230, vol. 1655. V. Series: Garland folklore
bibliographies ; v. 15, v. 20.
    Z7191.M543   1990   PN6401   016.3989   90–3049
    ISBN 0–8153–1133–8 (v. 2 : alk. paper)

Printed on acid-free, 250-year-life paper
Manufactured in the United States of America

George B. Bryan
and
Kevin J. McKenna

colleagues—supporters—friends

CONTENTS

SERIES EDITOR'S PREFACE

Wolfgang Mieder, professor of proverbs, the doyen of *dicton*, has done it again! Just when folklorists and paremiologists thought that all known theoretical writings on the proverb and related forms had been ably surveyed by Mieder's extraordinary *International Proverb Scholarship: An Annotated Bibliography* (New York: Garland, 1982) and his equally impressive *Supplement I (1800–1981)* (New York: Garland, 1990) with a combined total of more than 3000 entries, they are now confronted with his compilation of a second *Supplement* with more than 1500 additional items. When one realizes that he is not including mere collections of proverbs, but rather only analytic discussions of some aspect of proverb study, his achievement becomes all the more remarkable.

So many students all over the world—and ranking scholars for that matter—carry out research on a subject in almost total ignorance of what has already been written on the same topic. This is as true in proverb scholarship as it is in any other branch of folkloristics, not to mention nearly all academic disciplines. In fairness, it must be noted that the burgeoning international growth of folklore study makes it well nigh impossible for any individual scholar in one particular country, especially with limited library resources, to keep up with the rapidly expanding universe of published knowledge. This is why there is simply no substitute for comprehensive annotated bibliographies. In this case, anyone with the slightest interest in any aspect of the proverb who has access to Professor Mieder's magisterial *International Proverb Scholarship* and *Supplements* will have no excuse whatsoever for "reinventing the wheel" as so often happens when naive students or scholars wrongly assume they are the first to consider a theoretical issue or problem.

Anyone who browses in this *Supplement II* will soon realize that far more than the proverb proper is covered. There are numerous essays, for example, concerned with the utility of employing proverbs as an aid to teaching foreign languages. Teachers of foreign languages will find many helpful suggestions in this volume. Still other references deal with the specific difficulties involved in translating proverbs from one language to another, part of the problem stemming from the culture-bound nature of some metaphors.

Perhaps the most exciting feature of *Supplement II* for English-language readers is the coverage of a field commonly called "Phraseology," a field not well known in Anglo-American academic circles. Phraseology incorporates verbal forms which fall between single items of folk speech, e.g., slang, and full-scale proverbs. Thus phraseology would include: folk similes (as blind as a bat), folk metaphors (to set [put] the cart before the horse), greeting and leave-taking formulas, twin formulas (kith and kin), emission traditions (uttered after sneezes, burps, farts, etc.), and a host of other idiomatic constructions. Incidentally, I prefer the term folk similes and folk metaphors to proverbial comparisons and proverbial phrases precisely because these items are *not* true proverbs. The adjective "proverbial" is in this instance simply a synonym for "folk" or "traditional."

Phraseology is an object of keen interest and a subject of much publication among scholars in France, Germany, Hungary, Romania, and Russia. Professor Mieder has done a great service by bringing a substantial portion of this lively literature to the attention of the worldwide community of proverb enthusiasts.

Although Professor Mieder's position as paramount paremiographer is well established wherever the proverb is seriously studied, it was only a question of time before this prolific scholar's incredible expertise became known to the general public. Richard Wolkomir's delightful essay, "A Proverb Each Day Keeps This Scholar at Play," which appeared in *Smithsonian, Volume* 23, number 6 (September, 1992), pp. 111–118 and which also features a full-page photograph (p. 110) of the proverbial hero, has brought Professor Mieder's lifelong preoccupation with the proverb into the public arena. Such national recognition is surely well deserved.

The wonderful part of Mieder's richly annotated set of more than 4500 references to proverb studies is that they will never cease to be of value. While there will undoubtedly be numerous investigations of proverbs in the future, those who make them will need to know what has been accomplished in the past. *International Proverb Scholarship* with its *Supplements,* its lucid annotations, and comprehensive indices makes knowing the past accomplishments a relatively easy task. If only there were comparable bibliographical aids for all the other genres of folklore! It is devoutly to be hoped that specialists in other genres will arise to take up the challenge to follow the Mieder.

Alan Dundes

INTRODUCTION

It is with much relief and the feeling of having served proverb scholars from around the world that I present this third bibliography of international proverb scholarship. The first volume with the title *International Proverb Scholarship: An Annotated Bibliography* (1982) contained 2142 entries of books, dissertations, monographs, and articles on proverbs that appeared between 1800 and 1981. This was followed by a second volume in 1990 with the same title and the additional statement *Supplement I (1800–1981)*. This bibliography lists 892 publications (nos. 2143–3034) that had come to my attention after the completion of the original volume. It is my sincere belief that these 3034 annotated publications represent the major paremiological scholarship from around the world that appeared in the 19th and 20th centuries through the year 1981. Now and then an additional publication will be found, and obviously they will be included in later supplements. Some of these have in fact been registered in my annual bibliographies that appear in *Proverbium: Yearbook of International Proverb Scholarship* (1984ff.) under the title of "International Proverb Scholarship: An Updated Bibliography." As the readers of this yearbook know, there is no space in this publication to add annotations to the bibliographical entries. They also lack, of course, the three indices of my book-length bibliographies, and it is for these reasons that a new supplementary volume needs to be published from time to time.

In the introduction to the first supplement that was published in 1990 I promised paremiologists and other scholars interested in proverbs that I would prepare a second annotated supplement as soon as possible for those publications that have appeared during the years 1982 to 1991. The present volume entitled *International Proverb Scholarship: An Annotated Bibliography. Supplement II (1982–1991)* fulfills this promise after many months of intensive labor. It contains 1565 new entries (nos. 3035–4599) of which about 95% were published in the past ten years. This represents indeed vast worldwide scholarship on proverbs and their related forms (i.e., proverbial expressions, proverbial comparisons, wellerisms, idioms, routine formulas, sententious remarks, slogans, etc.). I must admit that it is almost unmanageable for an individual scholar to cope with this wealth of studies, but I am proud to state that I have dealt with this challenge to the best of my abilities. The result is this third volume of my *International Proverb Scholarship* bibliography, and I am happy to report that I have already started to work on the fourth volume that will cover the next ten years. It is my hope that I will be able to put together one annotated volume every ten years. Perhaps I will have the strength, courage, and longevity to serve international scholars for two (or even?) three more decades in this fashion.

As already observed, it is amazing to see this large number of publications on proverbs during the short time span of ten years. This is primarily due to the fact that proverbs are of interest to so many scholars. While there are, of course, the paremiologists who dedicate most of their professional careers to the study of these traditional bits of wisdom, there are also dozens of scholars interested in proverbs who represent such varied fields as anthropology, art history, ethnology, folklore, history, law, linguistics, literature, mass communication, medicine, philology, psychology, religion, sociology, and others. They all study proverbs occasionally to explain their use and function in the most varied situations and contexts. There is no doubt that paremiology has become a well-established discipline that attracts scholars from many countries, languages, and backgrounds. Proverbs lend themselves to regional, national, and international investigations, and many of the publications indicate an interdisciplinary and culturally diverse approach to proverbs.

This global interest in proverbs is also reflected in the many languages and cultures represented in this volume. Once again it is true that English, German, and French publications comprise the major part of this book. However, there are also numerous entries that report on proverb publications written in Dutch, Hungarian, Italian, Polish, Rumanian, Russian, Spanish, etc. Admittedly, books and articles written in Asian languages are probably underrepresented, but those publications dealing with Asian proverbs that appeared in a major European language are included. This is also true for the many studies on African proverbs. Most African scholars publish in English or French, and their important scholarly contributions are registered in this volume. I can, therefore, state with some pride that this third volume of my bibliography does deserve to have the word "international" in its title.

The fact that such a large number of studies is presented here for the past ten years is, to be sure, also due to the rapid growth of two linguistic subfields, namely those of phraseology and lexicography. A regular explosion of publications has occurred in these two related areas. Numerous essay volumes containing between a dozen and over twenty essays each have appeared. While these articles do not deal primarily with proverbs, they certainly investigate the larger concern of fixed phrases or phraseological units. Almost all of them touch on proverbial questions as well, usually commenting on proverbial expressions and proverbial comparisons. In fact, phraseologists consider proverbs to be a subgenre of the larger field of phraseology, and it certainly behooves paremiologists and any other scholars interested in proverbs to be acquainted with their theoretical and pragmatic work. All of this is yet another clear indication of the global, interdisciplinary, and comparative nature of proverb scholarship.

As has always been the case, I have made my annotations as fair and objective as possible. The length of individual entries is not necessarily a reflection of their quality. Some of the shorter articles are sometimes more difficult to annotate than monographs. It all depends on the nature and complexity of the publication. In any case, most annotations are similar in length with the exception, of course, of the large books and essay volumes. In the case of the latter I have always listed all the authors and the complete titles of their essays with page references under the entry of the edited volume itself. This will enable scholars to see at one glance what such essay volumes contain. Each essay is, however, individually annotated under the author's name. For major literary or historical figures I have once again provided biographical dates. Publication dates are given for proverb collections and literary works mentioned in the annotations. All of this should help scholars who might not be that well acquainted with the cultural history of a certain region or nation. Some cross references have also been added again, but I have kept these to a minimum. After all, the two previous volumes and the present one do include three major name, subject, and proverb indices. Each entry is indexed under approximately a dozen or even more key-words, making this bibliography accessible to anybody with little opportunity to miss anything. Preparing these indices was no easy task, and I would like to thank Hope Greenberg, Lynne Meeks, and Kevin Turner from the Academic Computing Services at the University of Vermont for their invaluable help.

There have been times when the preparation of this third volume almost became too much to bear. Yet, there have always been people who were willing to help and encourage me. Scholars don't or shouldn't work in isolation, and my friendships with scholars from around the world have meant a great deal to me during the past few years. Many colleagues and friends have supplied me with publications, and I would like to thank the following individuals in particular: Shirley L. Arora (Los Angeles), Dan Ben-Amos (Philadelphia), Marinus A. van den Broek (Amsterdam), Pack Carnes (Berkeley), Raymond Doctor (Punee), Charles Clay Doyle (Athens/Georgia), Alan Dundes (Berkeley), Rainer Eckert (Berlin), Czaba Földes (Szeged), Iwona Frackiewicz (Wroclaw), Gabriel Gheorghe (Bucuresti), Peter Grzybek (Graz), Malcolm Jones (Derbyshire), G.L. Kapchits (Moscow), Iver Kjaer (Birkerød), Waclawa Korzyn (Krakow), Matti Kuusi (Helsinki), Sergei Mastepanov (Malokurgannyi), Hans-Manfred Militz (Jena), Constantin Negreanu (Drobeta-Turnu-Severin), Timothy C. Nelson (Engelberg), Gyula Paczolay (Veszprém), Christine Palm (Uppsala), Stanislaw Predota (Wroclaw), Lutz Röhrich (Freiburg), Robert Rothstein (Amherst), Ingrid Schellbach-Kopra (Helsinki), Danica Skara (Zadar), Dumitru Stanciu (Bucuresti), Anna Tothné Litovkina (Szekszard), Helmut Walther (Wiesbaden), Jürgen Werner (Leipzig), and Fionnuala Williams (Belfast). Numerous publications had to be obtained through the interlibrary loan office at the University of Vermont, and I would like to thank my colleagues Nancy Crane, Barbara Lambert, Patricia Mardeusz,

Linda MacDonald, Daryl Purvee, and Wei Xue for their efforts in getting many publications from abroad. The result of all of these labors by so many good people is that I now have a truly superb archive of proverb scholarship. I am the proud owner of the 4599 publications listed in the three volumes of my *International Proverb Scholarship* bibliography. This number does not include the hundreds of proverb collections that I have assembled, and there are, of course, already new studies that have appeared during 1992. Please continue sending me your own publications and those of your colleagues under the following address: Prof. Dr. Wolfgang Mieder, Department of German and Russian, 422 Waterman Building, University of Vermont, Burlington, Vermont 05405-0160, USA. This will enable me to make these bibliographies as comprehensive as possible while at the same time contributing to an archive that is intended to serve scholars everywhere.

Special thanks are also due my good friend Alan Dundes who as general editor of the Garland Folklore Bibliographies series has supported me for so many years. He is the person who keeps encouraging me to continue with this bibliographical project, and I owe him much gratitude for challenging me to commit myself to truly international scholarship. Were it not for his friendship and support, these three volumes might never have come into print.

I also need and want to thank my wife Barbara for putting up with me when the chores of this bibliography almost drove me (and her) "crazy." How wonderful to know that she understands my "workaholic" nature and that she supports me in my endeavors whatever they might be. Without her generous support this volume would also surely not have been completed.

Finally, I owe many thanks to two very close colleagues and special friends here at the University of Vermont. Prof. George B. Bryan from the Department of Theatre has helped me for years with his vast knowledge, interest, and support. Prof. Kevin J. McKenna from my own Department of German and Russian has provided much assistance with the many Slavic publications annotated in this volume. Both of them have become active proverb scholars by now, and I understand this to be a unique indication of our friendship. It is with much gratitude and appreciation that I dedicate this book to these two exceptional scholars and special friends.

Wolfgang Mieder
December 1992

International Proverb Scholarship
Supplement II (1982–1991)

A

3035. Adeeko, Adeleke. *Words' Horse, or The Proverb as a Paradigm of Literary Understanding.* Diss. University of Florida, 1991. 229 pp.

This valuable dissertation is a literary investigation of the use and function of proverbs contained in three modern African novels. Adeeko begins with four general chapters dealing with (1) the theory of metaphor and figurativeness as they relate to literature (pp. 11–53), (2) the integration of proverbs in African literature in general (pp. 54–79), (3) the interpretation of proverbs in literary works by philologists and anthropologists (pp. 80–108), and (4) the proverbs interpreted as a paradigm for literary understanding (pp. 109–139). The fifth chapter (pp. 140–168) investigates Chinua Achebe's (1931–) novel *Arrow of God* (1964), the sixth chapter (pp. 169–196) analyzes the novel *Devil on the Cross* (1981) by James Ngugi wa Thiong'o (1938–), and the seventh chapter (pp. 197–220) studies Femi Osofisan's (20th century) novel *Kolera Kolei* (1978) for the literary, social, and political significance and meaning of proverbs. Many contextualized examples are cited in each chapter to show the importance of proverbs as an effective literary device. A useful bibliography (pp. 221–228) is attached.

3036. Adkin, Neil. "Some Omissions in the *Thesaurus* and in Otto's *Sprichwörter.*" *Eranos*, 80, no. 2 (1982), 176–177.

A short note on five classical proverbs and proverbial expressions not having been referenced in standard proverb collections before. Adkin provides Greek, Latin and Biblical references. Philological and cultural explanations are included, but nothing is mentioned regarding the modern use of these obscure phrases. Adkin is more interested in etymological questions than actual proverbiality. Of most interest is the Latin proverb that "It is the business of the nurseryman to pluck the rose from among the thorns" ("lego . . . de concha margaritum" [ib. "de spinis rosas, de terra aurum"]).

3037. Agel, Vilmos. "Abgrenzung von Phraseologismen in einem historischen Text. Einige Indizien als Ergebnis einer historischen Valenzuntersuchung." *Beiträge zur Phraseologie des Ungarischen und des Deutschen.* Ed. Regina Hessky. Budapest: Lorand-Eötvös-Universität, 1988. 26–38.

The author deals with the complex problem of identifying phraseological units in historical texts, stressing in particular that frequency of appearance and specific lexical and idiomatic meaning must be established. A number of German and Hungarian examples are cited by comparing the similarities and differences in the verbal valences of these traditional expressions. The point is made that such valences have a definite influence on the semantic and syntactical aspects of phraseological units. A small bibliography (pp. 37–38) is attached.

3038. Ageno, Franca. "Un personaggio proverbiale: Il 'povero' Codro." *Lingua nostra,* 24, no. 1 (1963), 1–3.

Ageno presents an historical study of the Italian proverbial expression "Il povero Codro" (The pitiful Codrus). He explains that in Greek legend Codrus was the last king of Athens who came to Athens as a refugee. It was prophecied at the time of the Dorian invasion (11th century B.C.) that only the death of their king at the enemy's hands would ensure victory to the Athenians. King Codrus made his way disguised into the enemy's camp, where he provoked a quarrel and was killed. This sacrifice is commemorated in the proverbial expression, for which the author cites numerous historical references. He also shows the relationship between onomastics and paremiology, arguing that many of the older Italian proverbs and fixed phrases contain names from classical times.

3039. Airmet, Douglas Elliot. *The Saying: Snatches for a Poetic.* Diss. University of Iowa, 1985. 339 pp.

In this dissertation Douglas Airmet examines the saying (i.e., an unqualified assertion of truth) as a dimension of poetic language. He points out that in modernist poetry the universal claims of the saying, whether as proverb, aphorism, or maxim, are made problematic by the loss of the "classical" universal. In part one of his study Airmet differentiates between the proverb and the self-authorized saying, and he explains the changing role of the latter in the poetry of Robert Frost (1875–1963). The second part deals with William Stanley Merwin's (1927–) comments on the poetic potential of the saying. It is shown how the image—as the traditional constituent of the modern poetic—attempts to usurp the traditional role of the saying. Detailed interpretations of Frost's poem "Mending Wall" (1914) and Merwin's "Ballade of Sayings" (1973) are included in this literary study of the significance of sayings in modern American poetry.

3040. Akimova, T.M., V.K. Arkhangel'skaia, and V.A. Bakhtina. "Poslovitsy i pogovorki." In T.M. Akimova, V.K. Arkhangel'skaia, and V.A. Bakhtina. *Russkoe narodno poeticheskoe tvorchestvo.* Moskva: Vysshaia shkola, 1983. 125–136.

This is a major book chapter on Russian proverbs and proverbial expressions with many valuable bibliographical references. The authors start with the definition of these two genres and then present two lists of the most important paremiological and paremiographical publications in the Russian language. There is a special discussion of Vladimir Ivanovich Dal's (1801–1872) significant collection *Poslovitsy russkogo naroda* (1862), but the authors also deal with collections of earlier and later times, including those of the other languages of the Soviet Union. Sections on the poetic, stylistic and structural aspects are included, and as a final matter the authors treat the employment of proverbs and proverbial expressions in Russian literature.

3041. Alexander, Richard. "Fixed Expressions in English: Reference Books and the Teacher." *ELT Journal,* 38 (1984), 127–134.

Points out the importance of fixed expressions in the teaching and learning of the English language. The author differentiates among idioms, twin formulas, greeting formulas, proverbs, proverbial expressions, catch phrases, clichés, slogans, quotations, similes and allusions. He then reviews thirteen dictionaries and reference works to ascertain their coverage of such fixed expressions. An annotated bibliography (pp. 132–134) assesses the utility of selected reference works for both the teacher and learner. Special attention is paid to acquainting students of English as a second language with various fixed expressions in order to increase their active vocabulary. It is argued that such expressions definitely belong to the study of foreign languages and that more of them should be included in dictionaries of all types.

3042. Alexander, Richard. "Article Headlines in *The Economist*. An Analysis of Puns, Allusions and Metaphors." *Arbeiten aus Anglistik und Amerikanistik*, 11 (1986), 159–187.

Detailed analysis of the use of puns, allusions and metaphors in the headlines of four issues of the British weekly newspaper *The Economist*. These "foregrounding devices" are studied from a linguistic and functional point of view, including such stylistic aspects as homonymy, homophony, polysemy, phonological similarity or allusion, semantic allusion to idioms and metaphors, the literalization of metaphors and idioms, alliteration, assonance, rhyme as well as mimicry and style imitation. A number of proverbial headlines are discussed along these lines, and Alexander also includes a statistical analysis of the frequency of this type of headline.

3043. Alexander, Tamar, and Galit Hasan-Rokem. "Games of Identity in Proverb Usage: Proverbs of a Sephardic-Jewish Woman." *Proverbium*, 5 (1988), 1–14.

The two authors report on the important results of field research concerning the proverb competence of an individual. They studied the repertoire of a Sephardic-Jewish woman in her early sixties from Jerusalem, soliciting the proverbs from her through oral and written interviews. The informant provided them with thirty Judeo-Spanish proverbs which are cited with English translations. Detailed analyses of the content, meaning and function of the proverbs are included, stressing the importance of context for an actual understanding of proverbial speech. This study is particularly significant since it reports on the pragamatics and semantics of proverb performance in actual speech acts. A short bibliography (p. 14) touching on theoretical questions and Judeo-Spanish proverbs in particular is attached.

3044. Alexander, Tamar, and Galit Hasan-Rokem. "Yesodot shel makom b'fitgamim shel yehudey turkia: Haolam vehabayit." *Pe'amim: Studies in Oriental Jewry*, 41 (1989), 112–133.

The article argues that proverbs do not describe reality as such but that as verbal-artistic strategies they are rather means to create social realities and to form them. Limiting themselves to the semiotic subsystem of proverbs that relate to space or locality, the authors discuss proverbs that deal with the world and with the home. They are able to show that proverbs deal much more with social matters than myths and riddles. Proverbs are therefore anthropocentric in which people are seen as social beings. The home becomes an idiom for the inner world and reflects images of the self, while the world as such represents traditional society. Many "locality" proverbs of Turkish Jews with Hebrew translations are included, and there is also a very useful diagram (p. 115) illustrating the theoretical aspects of this study.

3045. Alexiades, Minas Al. "Demetrios S. Loukatos." *"Syndepnon." Timitiko aphieroma ston kathigiti Demetrio S. Loukato.* Ed. Minas Al. Alexiades et al. Ioannina: Panepistimio Ioanninon, 1988. 9–55.

An extremely important bibliographical essay on the leading Greek paremiologist and paremiographer Démétrios S. Loukatos (1908–). Following a short biographical sketch tracing the scholarly development of this internationally acclaimed folklorist, Minas Alexiades assembles a complete bibliography of Loukatos' many publications. Altogether there are 456 titles of books, articles, book reviews, obituaries, etc. His many paremiological publications are listed in the philological section (nos. 36–116). Obviously most of Loukatos' publications are in Greek, but he has also published widely in French on such varied topics as proverbs, wellerisms, folk narratives, folk songs, myths, etc. A picture (p. 11) of Démétrios Loukatos is included. For titles of his proverb publications see nos. 1104–1115 and nos. 3793–3794 below.

3046. Alfes, Henrike. *Sprachschätze. Wie eine Versicherung auszog, das "gesunde Volksvermögen" zu finden.* Siegen: Universität-Gesamthochschule Siegen, 1985. 50 pp.

In 1983 the German AM-Insurance Group started an advertising campaign which asked people throughout Germany to supply proverbs, proverbial expressions and short verses to well-known humorous drawings by Wilhelm Busch (1832–1908), Ludwig Richter (1803–1884) and Heinrich Hoffmann (1809–1894). The only stipulation was that these new picture captions had to deal somewhat with insurance matters. Based on a selection of 400 references out of a total of about 40000, Henrike Alfes has studied the use of proverbial materials in them. It is shown how proverbs due to their authority, currency and metaphors can easily be used for advertising purposes in their original or varied wording. Especially on pp. 15–19 the author presents significant statistical tables concerning the use of proverbs, literary quotations and slogans in advertisements. A useful bibliography (pp. 40–41) and a wealth of texts with 10 illustrations are included. An impressive study of the use of formulaic language in advertising.

3047. Alizade, Z.A. "O semanticheskom razvitii poslovits i pogovorok." *Izvestiia Akademii Nauk Azerbaidzhanskoi SSR, seriia literatury, iazyka i iskusstva,* no. 2 (1984), 68–71.

A short paper on the semantic development of proverbs and proverbial expressions from the Azerbaijan Soviet Socialist Republic of the Soviet Union on the Caspian Sea. Alizade points out that these texts comment on such aspects as everyday life, religion, worldview, etc. It is also shown that what is said about friendship, modesty, laziness, dishonesty, etc. is quite similar to the proverb content of other nationalities. The proverbs contain complex and multifaceted realia of life. In order to understand their meaning properly, paremiologists must conduct synchronic and diachronic studies. A Russian abstract (p. 71) is provided.

3048. Almqvist, Bo. "Siul an Phortain, Friotalfhocal agus Fabhalsceal (AT 276)." *Sinsear,* no volume given (1982–1983), 35–62.

A careful study of the Irish wellerism "'Siul direach, a mhic,' mar a duirt an seanphortan leis an bportan og" ("Walk straight, my son," as the old crab said to the young crab). Almqvist also deals with the possibility of an English origin of the text, stating that there is a striking lack of wellerisms in older Irish sources. The second part of the article studies the relationship of this text with a particular folk tale (AT 276). It might well be that the wellerism is a compressed form of this story. There definitely are connections to be studied between the genres of the folk tale and the wellerism. An English summary (pp. 59–62) is provided.

3049. Alster, Bendt. "Paradoxical Proverbs and Satire in Sumerian Literature." *Journal of Cuneiform Studies*, 27 (1975), 201–230.

An invaluable study of 44 Sumerian textual examples handed down on cuneiform tablets dating from approximately 2500 B.C. to 1100 B.C. Bendt Alster divides his materials into five groups, analyzing in each case aspects of paradox, humor and satire: (1) juxtaposition of incompatible words, (2) paradoxical proverbs, (3) wellerisms, (4) fables, and (5) mythological satire. It is particularly noteworthy that these early recorded texts already include wellerisms. For each example Alster cites the original text with an English translation, and he then provides detailed historical, cultural and linguistic explanations. It is shown that the humor and satire result primarily from paradoxical contradictions within these texts. A short bibliography (p. 227) and 3 illustrations of actual cuneiform tablets are included.

3050. Alster, Bendt. "Sumerian Proverb Collection Seven." *Revue d'assyriologie et d'archéologie orientale*, 72 (1978), 97–112.

The author starts with a reference to previous important work on Sumerian proverbs by Edmund I. Gordon (see nos. 550–556) and himself (nos. 27–28). Next he presents a very useful list of all published and unpublished Sumerian proverb collections known thus far and still extant on cuneiform tablets. This is followed by a precise transliterated edition of *Proverb Collection Seven* together with an English translation. The collection contains 113 proverbs, for which Alster provides extremely helpful cultural and linguistic notes.

3051. Alster, Bendt. "An Akkadian and a Greek Proverb. A Comparative Study." *Die Welt des Orients*, 10 (1979), 1–5.

An interesting article on an early Akkadian proverb of the Babylonians and Assyrians, dating most likely to around 1800 B.C. Bendt Alster refers to translation problems that other scholars have had with this text and then offers his own rendition as "The bitch, in its being in a hurry, gave birth to blind (puppies)." He is able to show that Aristophanes (445–385? B.C.) cites it in Greek as "The hasty bell-goldfinch bears blind (youngs)" in one of his comedies to create a ludicrous image. Realizing that several modern European languages do have the proverb "The hasty bitch brings forth blind whelps" (English proverb from 1556), Alster feels secure in stating that the Akkadian proverb is the oldest extant text. See also Y. Avishur (no. 3080).

3052. Alster, Bendt. "Sumerian Proverb Collection XXIV." *Assyriological Miscellanies*, 1 (1980), 33–50.

This time Alster presents the carefully edited Sumerian *Proverb Collection XXIV* in its transliterated original and with an English translation. He provides many comparative notes showing which of the 11 proverbs of this small collection also appear on other Sumerian cuneiform tablets. There are also once again detailed cultural and linguistic notes that help to explain the meaning of these ancient proverbial texts. With 2 illustrations.

3053. Alster, Bendt. "Sumerian Literary Texts in the National Museum, Copenhagen." *Acta Sumerologica*, 10 (1988), 1–15.

This somewhat imprecise title actually refers to the careful edition of two Sumerian cuneiform tablets. The first is an Old Babylonian tablet inscribed with an emesal lament, while the second text is a transliterated publication of *Sumerian Proverb Collection 23* (pp. 4–15). English translations are once again provided, and Alster also includes some cultural and linguistic notes. With 1 illustration.

3054. Alster, Bendt. "An Akkadian Animal Proverb and The Assyrian Letter ABL 555." *Journal of Cuneiform Studies*, 41 (1989), 187–193.

Alster cites a Neo-Assyrian manuscript which contains a reference to a fox and to a lion. The text is presented in transliterated form with an English translation, and the lines "The man who seized the tail of a lion sank in the river. / He who seized the tail of a fox was saved." The author interprets the lion as brute force and the fox as cunning and has no difficulty citing early Greek and Latin parallels. One Greek variant is "Where the lion's skin will not reach, one must sew on the fox's instead" and a second text would be "The fox drives the lion away." We have thus once again an ancient proverb that definitely predates classical antiquity.

3055. Alster, Bendt. "Väterliche Weisheit in Mesopotamien." *Weisheit: Archäologie der literarischen Kommunikation.* Ed. A. Assmann. München: Wilhelm Fink, 1991. 103–115.

In this German essay Bendt Alster gives a general picture of the proverbial wisdom contained in a major piece of Mesopotamian literature, namely *The Instructions of Suruppak. A Sumerian Proverb Collection.* Alster had edited this ancient example of wisdom literature in 1974 in Copenhagen (see no. 27), and he now gives his German readers an idea of the rich proverbial wisdom contained in this collection of a father's advice to his son. Many examples are cited in German translation, indicating that the proverbs deal with ethics, morality, family, society, love, etc. Many historical and cultural insights are provided, and Alster also includes an important bibliography (pp. 114–115) on Sumerian proverbs.

3056. Amali, Emmanuel. "Proverbs as Concept of Idoma Performing Arts." *Nigeria Magazine,* 53, no. 3 (1985), 30–37.

The author argues that it is extremely important that theatre managers, directors, and creative writers study and understand the importance of African proverbs for indigenous African dramatic performance. To illustrate this, he explains that proverbs are extremely important for the Idoma people of Benue State in Nigeria. In fact, since they view life as a stage, there are many proverbs which deal with the use of space, voice, dance, costume, etc. Amali cites many Idoma examples with English translations and adds useful ethnographic explanations. He closes his article with the legitimate plea that those involved in "academic theatre" in Nigeria should pay more attention to "conventional theatre" and its natural use of Idoma proverbs as part of performing arts.

3057. Andreesco-Miereanu, Ioana. "Souvenirs en proverbes." *Cahiers de littérature orale*, no. 13 (1983), 171–173.

An emotional and poetic remembrance of the proverbial wisdom of the author's elderly father. Several African proverbs are cited with French translations, and their didacticism and wisdom are made clear by placing them into a dialogue between the father and his child. While comments about the meaning and significance of the proverbs are added, this is not a scholarly article, but rather a touching testimony to the ageless truth and validity of proverbs in the modern world. The article also shows how an adult identifies certain proverbs with the person from whom he/she learned them, thereby being cognizant of the transmission of proverb texts from generation to generation.

3058. Andrei, Alexandru. "Semnificatii etice în paremiologia româneasca." *Proverbium Dacoromania*, 2 (1987), 13–17.

A small study of the ethical and figurative significance of traditional Rumanian proverbs. It is argued that the proverbs have taken on an epistemological value during their transmission from one era and reality to the other. Nevertheless, they can be utilized and adapted to new realities with their social structures and psycho-cultural concerns. Many Rumanian examples are cited, and the author has also provided a short French summary (p. 17).

3059. Andresen, Martha. "'Ripeness is All': Sententiae and Commonplaces in 'King Lear'." *Some Facets of "King Lear": Essays in Prismatic Criticism*. Eds. Rosalie L. Colie and F.T. Flahiff. Toronto: University of Toronto Press, 1974. 145–168.

This is a thorough literary investigation of the thematic and dramatic function of commonplaces, aphorisms and sententiae in William Shakespeare's (1564–1616) tragedy *King Lear* (1605).

The author discusses the commonplace "Ripeness is all" at great length by explaining its significance for the play as a whole. She also shows that many of Shakespeare's proverbial statements can be found in Renaissance emblems of which she includes two illustrations. It is shown that Shakespeare manages and disposes proverbial wisdom not to define any rigid system of truths but to affirm the simple truth that people and their community need to believe in some order if they wish to endure. Andresen also makes the valid point that the timeless appeal of this play lies at least in part in Shakespeare's use of *sententiae* as a vehicle for the archetypical theme of human temporality.

3060. Angenot, Marc. "'La lutte pour la vie': Migrations et usages d'un idéologème." *La locution. Actes du colloque international Université McGill, Montréal, 15–16 octobre 1984.* Eds. Giuseppe Di Stefano and Russell G. McGillivray. Montréal: Editions CERES, 1984. 171–190.

Fascinating article of the "ideologism" as a phraseological unit expressing a particular ideology. As his example Marc Angenot chose Charles Darwin's (1809–1882) idea "la lutte pour la vie" (struggle for life) which evolved into a slogan for Darwinism throughout Europe. He shows how Herbert Spencer (1820–1903) and above all Alphonse Daudet (1841–1897) in his French play *La lutte pour la vie* (1889) helped to popularize this concept. Other references are cited, and it is argued that this phrase is of greatest importance in the study of ideas.

3061. Angress, Ruth K. "The Epigram as a Genre." In R.K. Angress. *The Early German Epigram. A Study in Baroque Poetry.* Lexington/Kentucky: University Press of Kentucky, 1971. 19–40.

Starting with a clear definition of the epigram, Ruth Angress traces its history from its Greek origins through the Baroque age in Germany. She also discusses the theoretical thoughts about this genre by Martin Opitz (1597–1639), Gotthold Ephraim Lessing (1729–1781) and Johann Gottfried Herder (1744–1803). She then explains that the German epigram is above all a satirical genre, and she cites a number of examples from the late Middle Ages through the 17th century. There is also a section (see pp. 30–40) that discusses the use of folklore and in particular proverbs in these short epigrams. The point is made that while the epigram is a more sophisticated and more involved form to express certain human insights and ways, the proverb does the same in a much more traditional and basic form and language.

3062. Anido, Naiade (ed.). *Des proverbes . . . à l'affut.* Paris: Publications Langues'O, 1983 (=*Cahiers de littérature orale*, no. 13). 215 pp.

An important essay volume on various aspects of French, African, Brazilian, Mexican and Lebanese proverbs including Naiade Anido, "Homélie proverbiale" (p. 17); Lajos Nyéki, "Proverbes et opérations logiques" (pp. 19–32); Paulette Roulon and Raymond Doko, "La parole pilée: Accès au symbolisme chez les Gbaya 'bodoe de Centrafrique" (pp. 33–49); Françoise Ugochukwu, "Les proverbes igbos d'hier à aujourd'hui" (pp. 51–65); Jordanka Hristova Foulon, "Quand le proverbe se fait mémoire" (pp. 67–90); Perla Garcia-Ruiz, "La vie des proverbes mexicains" (pp. 91–108); Dominique Fadairo-Kedji, "Proverbes fòn du Bénin: une approche anthropologique" (pp. 109–126); Naiade Anido, "Le proverbe: clé de la sagesse et clé des champs de la société gaucha" (pp. 127–141); Lydia Gaborit, "Proverbes et dictons dans l'île de Noirmoutier" (pp. 145–150); Praline Gay-Para, "Le proverbe, parole de circonstance" (pp. 151–157); Michèle Chiche, "Proverbes . . . et mon enfance embaume ma mémoire" (pp. 159–161); Jacqueline Henry-Rebours, "Proverbes de Haute-Bretagne" (pp. 163–169); and Ioana Andreesco-Miereanu, "Souvenirs en proverbe" (pp. 171–173). The essays deal above all with the validity, universality, wisdom, tradition, function, transmission, structure, variation, meaning, content, worldview, context, language, form, collection, psychology, logic, definition, acquisition, interpretation etc. of proverbs. French and English abstracts are included for all essays on pp. 175–180. For annotations see nos. 3063, 4053, 4285, 4487, 3443, 3467, 3393, 3062, 3461, 3472, 3238, 3579, 3057.

3063. Anido, Naiade. "Homélie proverbiale." *Cahiers de littérature orale*, no. 13 (1983), 17.

An impressive short homily in poetic language which stresses the universality of proverbs. Anido talks of the great treasures of proverbs throughout the world which are so varied and different while at the same time being very similar due to the fact that they express common human experiences. While languages, people and civilizations change, the proverbs always remain and continue to be present in the oral and written communication of people of all walks of life. Even if the seemingly immutable proverbs do undergo changes, they are argued to be always inclusive and powerful as expressions of traditional wisdom.

3064. Anido, Naiade. "Le proverbe: clé de la sagesse et clé des champs de la société gaucha." *Cahiers de littérature orale*, no. 13 (1983), 127–141.

The article starts with a discussion of the definition of proverbs and then points out that the Gauchos of Rio Grande do Sul in Brazil have their own proverb tradition which is independent of Portuguese or Spanish proverbs. Next Anido analyzes the role and function of these proverbs in their Gaucho social context. She then describes a particular use of proverbs among the Gauchos, namely the "joute à clés", which is a proverb duel between two persons. Proverbial creativity, i.e. spontaneous improvisation on pre-existing models, goes on for lengthy periods of time during such duels. The Gaucho proverbs with French translations and comments of such a proverb duel are included, and so are 3 illustrations and a map. With an English summary (p. 180).

3065. Anikin, V.P., and Iu.G. Kruglov. "Poslovitsy i pogovorki." In V.P. Anikin and Iu.G. Kruglov. *Russkoe narodnoe poeticheskoe tvorchestvo.* Leningard: Prosveshchenie, 1983. 116–134 and 339–340.

This is a comprehensive book chapter on Russian proverbs and proverbial expressions dealing with most major paremiological issues. The authors start with a discussion of the definition and origin of proverbs and then move on to an analysis of their analogical use and function. This is followed by detailed comments regarding the popularity of proverbs in everyday speech, their polysemanticity, content, poetics, and structure. The authors also deal with the difference between proverbs and proverbial expressions, closing their informative chapter with some general remarks on phraseology.

3066. Anozie, Lynda. "Semantic-Pragmatic Analysis of an Igbo Metaphorical Proverb." *Phenomenology in Modern African Studies.* Ed. Sunday O. Anozie. Owerri: Conch Magazine, 1982. 73–81.

A theoretical analysis of Chinua Achebe's (1931–) African meta-proverb "Proverbs are the palm-oil with which words are eaten" which he used in his Nigerian novel *Things Fall Apart* (1958). Anozie argues that too many books on proverbs, especially proverb collections, do not address the problem of the meaning of proverbs. It is particularly difficult to understand the meaning of metaphorical proverbs of a foreign culture. Only after an interactional view of metaphor does the meaning of a proverb become clear. See also Bernth Lindfors (no. 1071) and Austin J. Shelton (no. 1725).

3067. Arkush, R. David. "'If Man Works Hard the Land Will not Be Lazy'. Entrepreneurial Values in North Chinese Peasant Proverbs." *Modern China*, 10, no. 4 (1984), 461–479.

By means of the content of numerous Chinese proverbs in English translation the author attempts to explain the worldview of Chinese peasants. Many proverbs refer to a hard life, poverty and dependence on the weather. Instead of resignation and fatalism, these proverbs teach hard work, frugality and self-reliance. Arkush concludes that Chinese peasants are well disposed towards petty rural entrepreneurship and capitalism. A useful bibliography on Chinese proverbs (pp. 477–479) is included.

3068. Arngart, Olof. "Durham Proverbs 17, 30, 42." *Notes and Queries,* 227, new series 29 (1982), 199–201.

Following Olof Arngart's major article (see no. 61) on 46 Latin and Anglo-Saxon proverbs contained in a Durham Cathedral manuscript from the 11th century, he now adds some additional etymological, grammatical and linguistic (problems of translation) comments. The three proverbs under discussion in English translation are: "He is blind of both eyes who does not look into, or know, his own mind" (no. 17), "He has no hope who does not care for home" (no. 30), and "The fuller the cup, the more evenly it should be carried" (no. 42). Additional parallels from Old English literature are also provided. For proverb no. 17 see also no. 3069 below.

3069. Arngart, Olof. "Durham Proverb 23, and Other Notes on Durham Proverbs." *Notes and Queries*, 228, new series 30 (1983), 291–292.

Yet another detailed note on one of the 46 Latin and Anglo-Saxon proverbs contained in an 11th century manuscript of the Durham Cathedral. The proverb in English translation is "A man shall not be too soon afraid nor too soon pleased" (no. 23). Again Arngart provides further etymological and grammatical explanations in his attempt to find the best possible English translation. He also comments briefly on "He is blind of both eyes who does not look into, or know, his own mind" (no. 17). For this proverb see no. 3068 above.

3070. Arnold, Katrin. "'Der Teufel ist den Sprichworten feind'." *Neue deutsche Literatur*, 31, no. 11 (1983), 155–158.

This is a short descriptive essay on the proverb collection which Martin Luther (1483–1546) put together for his own use. The manuscript contains 489 proverbs and proverbial expressions of which at least 392 appear in Luther's essays and sermons. Arnold points out that Luther enjoyed varying traditional phrases for didactic and satirical purposes, and he was also very well aware of the two large published proverb collections by Johannes Agricola (1494–1566) and Sebastian Franck (1499–1542). There is no doubt that these collections and proverbs as such played a major role in spreading the ideas of the Reformation through folk speech. Arnold cites 23 examples from Luther, but for a scholarly edition of his proverb collection see Ernst Thiele (no. 1917).

3071. Arora, Shirley L. "A Critical Bibliography of Mexican American Proverbs." *Aztlán*, 13 (1982), 71–80.

Extremely useful annotated bibliography surveying the compilations of Mexican American proverbs, describing each collection in terms of type and quantity of material included, presence or absence of interpretative comments or translations, sources, organization, and accuracy of presentation. Following a short introduction Arora presents 19 collections categorized regionally and chronologically: California (4 collections), New Mexico (6), Texas (6), and Mexico (3). This critical bibliography should serve as a model for other bibliographies of ethnic proverb collections. Such bilingual collections are of much importance for the sociolinguistic and ethnic study of proverbs.

3072. Arora, Shirley L. "Proverbs in Mexican American Tradition." *Aztlán*, 13 (1982), 43–69.

Based on field research in the area of Greater Los Angeles, California, the author discusses the use of proverbs among 304 Mexican Americans aged 16 to 85. Many of the documented proverbs belong to the common proverb tradition of Europe or are pan-Hispanic in their distribution, while only a few are truly Mexican or Mexican American. Arora points out that the proverbs are used for didactic purposes, for the regulation of social relationships, for child rearing, for cultural identification (ethnicity), and for the purpose of lending color to one's speech. In addition to this functional analysis the author also investigates proverb translations, loan proverbs and the sociolinguistic aspects of bilingual proverb use by Mexican Americans. Many proverb examples are cited in Spanish, some with English translations.

3073. Arora, Shirley L. "The Perception of Proverbiality." *Proverbium*, 1 (1984), 1–38.

Seminal article concerning the problem of what people perceive to be proverbs. Arora argues that proverbiality depends upon traditionality, currency, repetition, certain grammatical or syntactical features, metaphor, semantic markers (parallelism, paradox, irony, etc.), lexical markers (archaic words, etc.), and phonic markers (rhyme, meter, alliteration, etc.). The more a given statement possesses such markers, the greater are its chances of being perceived as a proverb. These theoretical considerations are followed by a discussion of a "proverb survey" consisting of 25 different texts which Shirley Arora presented to

46 Spanish-speaking residents of Los Angeles, California. The survey included 2 *bona fide* Spanish proverbs and 23 were *ad hoc* inventions (pseudo-proverbs) incorporating one or more of the identifying features mentioned. Arora presents statistical analyses of the responses and is able to prove her contention that statements with the most "proverbial" markers have a good chance to be perceived as actual proverbs. She concludes by stating that it is important for the scholar to know by what criteria a native speaker judges a statement to be a proverb. Detailed notes and a Spanish and English list of the "proverbs test" are also included in this significant study.

3074. Arora, Shirley L. "'No Tickee, No Shirtee'. Proverbial Speech and Leadership in Academe." *Inside Organizations. Understanding the Human Dimension.* Eds. Michael Owen Jones, Michael Dane Moore, and Richard Christopher Snyder. Newbury Park/California: Sage Publishers, 1988. 179–189.

A fascinating study showing that proverbs, proverbial expressions, proverbial comparisons and proverbial exaggerations do in fact play a considerable role in the oral communication among professors. Arora studied the use of proverbial language by 16 full professors during the many committee meetings that took place over a period of two years at the University of California at Los Angeles. She noted 159 texts during her unique "field research" and explains that the intellectually sophisticated professors used the proverbial texts for the purposes of instruction, persuasion, commentary, humor, and impression of familiarity. Obviously this paper is descriptive rather than prescriptive, but there can be no doubt that traditional proverbial language is very much alive and well in Academe.

3075. Arora, Shirley L. "On the Importance of Rotting Fish: A Proverb and Its Audience." *Western Folklore*, 48 (1989), 271–288.

An intriguing study of the role that the proverb "The fish rots from the head first" played during the American presidential campaign in the summer of 1988. The Democratic candidate Michael S. Dukakis (1933–) had used it to attack the policies of the Reagan administration, and the proverb became very current in the mass media (television, radio, newspapers, magazines, cartoons, etc.) during the next few weeks. Dukakis had labeled the proverb as being Greek at his original use of it, and Arora is able to substantiate this fact. She actually is able to show that the proverb is known in most European languages, one of its most important variants being "The fish begins to stink at the head." The author discusses the use, function and meaning of the proverb as a political metaphor and also describes its effectiveness among possible voters. With 1 illustration.

3076.   Arora, Shirley L. "Weather Proverbs: Some 'Folk' Views." *Proverbium*, 8 (1991), 1–17.

Taking her lead from Alan Dundes' provocative article "On Whether Weather 'Proverbs' Are Proverbs" (see no. 3338 below), Arora presents impressive documentation for the fact that the folk in general does consider the subgenres of weather and medical proverbs to be *bona fide* proverbs and not superstitions as Dundes has argued. She describes the use of weather proverbs as proverbs by an informant in Spain, but even more importantly she devised a "proverbs test" of 25 texts for her Spanish-speaking informants in the Los Angeles area. The result was that plenty of them considered the weather and medical texts to be true proverbs and not superstitions. While the result of this study does not completely negate Dundes' contention, it must be recognized that the folk does not appear to be bothered much by the academic interest in differentiating between proverbs and weather (medical) superstitions.

3077.   Arveiller, Raymond. "L'univers du vieux Monégasque, d'après les proverbes et les dictons." *Richesse du proverbe*. Eds. François Suard and Claude Buridant. Lille: Université de Lille, 1984. II, 139–154.

A detailed content analysis of numerous old proverbs from Monaco. Arveiller cites his examples in the Monaco dialect with French translations. Proverbs concerning God, faith, marriage, education, money, government, weather, etc. are cited, but the author only provides very short explanatory notes. Nevertheless, the proverbs reflect the way of life and worldview of the older Monaco society which has changed so quickly in modern times.

3078. Asmussen, Jes. P. "'Kamel'—'Nadelöhr'. Matth. 19:24, Mark. 10:25, Luk. 18:25." *Studia Grammatica Iranica. Festschrift für Helmut Humbach.* Eds. Rüdiger Schmitt and Prods Oktor Skjaervo. München: R. Kitzinger, 1986. 1–10.

This article concerns the well-known Biblical proverb "It is easier for a camel to go through the eye of a needle, than for a rich man to enter into the kingdom of God" (Matth. 19,24). However, the author does not concern himself as much with the text in the Bible but rather with its occurrence in the Koran, explaining how ideas of Christianity and Islam became intertwined in ancient Iran. Etymological explanations concerning this paradoxical metaphor are included. For a very detailed study of this proverb see Georg Aicher (no. 19).

3079. Attal, Robert. "Bibliographie raisonnée des proverbes arabes et judéo-arabes du Maghreb." *Studies in Bibliography and Booklore,* 17 (1989), 43–54.

Starting with a reference to the earlier "Critical Bibliography of Spoken Arabic Proverb Literature" by Charles A. Fergusson and John M. Echols (see no. 436), the author presents an important additional list of 102 bibliographical titles together with a seven item addendum. This annotated bibliography of studies and collections of the Maghreb area of North Africa is divided into four major sections: North Africa in general, Tunisia, Algeria, and Morocco. Together with the earlier bibliography this compilation represents an invaluable resource to scholars of Arabic and Judeo-Arabic proverbs.

3080. Avishur, Y. "Additional Parallels of an Akkadian Proverb Found in the Iraqi Vernacular Arabic." *Die Welt des Orients,* 12 (1981), 37–38.

Referring to Bendt Alster's previous study of the Akkadian proverb "The bitch in her haste gives birth to blind pups" (see no. 3051), Avishur is able to show that this proverb and variants of it are also current to this day in the Mesopotamian area. Alster had cited Greek and other European parallels, and Avishur now quotes the variant "The cat in her haste kittens blind kittens" from a modern Arabic collection of proverbs from Baghdad. He also cites the Judeo-Arabic proverb from Iraqi Jews that he has collected himself from oral use: "The bitch in her hurry whelps blind pups." Avishur closes his article with the observation that this ancient proverb was translated from the original Akkadian text into Aramaic and from Aramaic into Arabic.

3081. Axnick, Margarete. *Probleme der deutschen Sprichwortübersetzungen aus Miguel de Cervantes' "Don Quijote"—eine vergleichende sprachliche und literarische Untersuchung.* M.A. thesis University of Bonn, 1984. 139 pp.

This thesis presents a short introduction to the proverb in Spanish literature and then discusses the function and the users of proverbs in Miguel de Cervantes Saavedra's (1547–1616) novel *Don Quijote* (1605/1615). Its major value lies in the analysis of the German translations of the proverbs used by Don Quijote and Sancho Panza by the translators Dietrich Wilhelm Soltau (1801/1802), Ludwig Tieck (1810/1816), anonymous (1837/1838, revised by Konrad Thorer), Ludwig Braunfels (1884), and Anton Rothbauer (1964). Axnick gives detailed comparative judgments of the different translation attempts and also discusses the problem of translating proverbs as such, presenting at the end guidelines for literary proverb translations. An index lists the various translations for 139 proverbs, and a useful bibliography (pp. 135–139) concludes this study which includes theoretical and pragmatic aspects of the difficulty of proverb translations.

3082. Ayerbe-Chaux, Reinaldo. "*El libro de los proverbios* del conde Lucanor y de Patronio." *Studies in Honor of Gustavo Correa.* Eds. Charles B. Faulhaber, Richard P. Kinkade, and Theodore A. Perry. Potomac/Maryland: Scripta humanistica, 1986. 1–10.

Treats the importance of the medieval Spanish book of fables and didactic stories *El conde Lucanor o El libro de Patronio* (1335) by Don Juan Manuael (1282–1348). Parts of this book comprise *El libro de los proverbios* which Ayerbe-Chaux analyzes in some detail. He discusses its publication history, its content and structure as well as its significance as a moralistic and didactic work. A number of maxims and proverbs are cited and analyzed as medieval wisdom.

B

3083. Baba, Stanislaw. *Twardy orzech do zgryzienia czyli o poprawnosci frazeologicznej*. Poznan: Wydawnictwo Poznanskie, 1986. 106 pp.

An important book comprised of thirty-one short chapters studying etymological, historical and cultural aspects of Polish proverbial expressions. In the first part of the book (pp. 8–50) Baba discusses theoretical concerns of phraseology. He deals with definition problems, variants, structure, innovative changes in proverbial expressions used in modern Polish, and the correct use of phraseological units. An index of the phrases, a list of theoretical terms of the field of phraseology and a selected bibliography (pp. 101–104) of Polish scholarship help make this a valuable study of frequently used Polish expressions.

3084. Babcock, Robert G. "The 'proverbium antiquum' in Acca's Letter to Bede." *Mittellateinisches Jahrbuch*, 22 (1987), 53–55.

This is a short philological study of the versified medieval Latin proverb "In mare quid pisces quid aquas in flumina mittas? / Larga sed indiguis munera funde locis" (Placing fish into the ocean or water into the rivers is but pouring great gifts into unworthy places). The author shows that it appears in a letter of Bishop Acca (died 740 A.D.) to The Venerable Bede (673–735) and again in two Latin manuscripts of the nineth and tenth centuries. Babcock refers to various Latin proverb collections of the Middle Ages and proves that this proverbial distich is in fact a text known to early religious writers.

3085. Baer, Florence E. "Wellerisms in *The Pickwick Papers*." *Folklore* (London), 94 (1983), 173–183.

This literary study of wellerisms in Charles Dickens' (1811–1870) novel *Pickwick Papers* (1837) starts with definition problems and a short survey of wellerism scholarship. Baer then investigates the various functions of wellerisms by quoting and discussing numerous examples of Sam Weller's proverb parodies. Wellerisms were used by Dickens primarily for educational purposes since they bring about an ironic detachment and a new awareness of social conditions. They are also employed to criticise class distinctions or class pretensions and to comment on entertainment, marriage, politics, fear, punishment and war. Baer explains that the wellerisms incorporate socially acceptable utterances and belligerent, destructive acts, often embodying the conflict and the resolution in an ironic twist. Altogether a superb paper on the function of wellerisms on literary, social and psychological levels. The notes include useful bibliographical references to the genre of wellerisms.

3086. Baird-Smith, David. "One Shrewd Wife in All the World." *Moreana: Bulletin Thomas More*, 21, nos. 83–84 (1984), 93–94.

This is a short note on Sir Thomas More's (1478–1535) use of the proverb "There is but one shrewd wife in the world, but he saith in deed that every man weeneth he hath her." A parallel Spanish text by Miguel de Cervantes Saavedra (1547–1616) is also cited to indicate that this misogynous proverb had currency beyond the English language and literature. Both references are cited and discussed in their literary context.

3087. Bakladzhiev, Samuil. "Khiperbola—litota v bulgarskite poslovitsi i pogovorki." *Problemi na bulgarskija folklor*, 7 (1987), 194–197.

This is a short study of hyperboles and litotes (understatements in which an affirmative is expressed by the negative or the contrary) as found in Bulgarian proverbs and proverbial expressions. Bakladzhiev cites a few examples and presents stylistic and structural explanations of how these stylistic devices function in this type of proverbial folk speech. It is shown that these poetic devices play a major role in Bulgarian literary works of the 19th and 20th centuries in which authors use traditional forms of communication like proverbs.

3088. Balavoine, Claudie. "Les principes de la parémiographie Érasmienne." *Richesse du proverbe.* Eds. François Suard and Claude Buridant. Lille: Université de Lille, 1984. II, 9–23.

A highly significant essay on various aspects of Erasmus of Rotterdam's (1469–1536) paremiographical publications. Balavoine discusses different editions of the *Adagia* (1500ff.) and comments in detail on the following points: the concept of the proverb in antiquity, Erasmus of Rotterdam's definition and understanding of the proverb, his methodology in his philological, cultural and historical studies on individual proverbs and proverbial expressions, his classification system, and the impressive variety of expressions in this large scholarly proverb collection. A number of examples are discussed, and the entire article offers a clear and precise introduction to this extremely important work concerning the rich tradition and reception of classical proverb lore.

3089. Balemans, Will, and Caspar van de Ven. "Automatisering binnen het project *De Brabantse Spreekwoorden* van de Hein Mondosstichting te Waalre." *Mededelingen van de Nijmeegse Centrale voor Dialect- en Naamkunde,* 21 (1987–1988), 69–79.

The two authors present a detailed report on the computerization of a large archive of Brabant proverbs which were collected between the years 1926 to 1978 in Belgium. The collection has now been published with the title *De Brabantse Spreekwoorden* (Waalre: Hein Mandosstichting, 1988) by Hein Mandos and Miep Mandos- van de Pol, representing one of the best modern dialect proverb collections. The authors discuss the computer hard- and software needed to archive hundreds of proverbs, proverbial expressions and proverbial comparisons according to key-words. They also present nine sample entries to indicate how a computer program can deal with the problem of alphabetization, variants, etc. Since proverb archives and the publication of large proverb collections rely more and more on the use of computers, this article should definitely be consulted as a major resource based on a successful publication project.

3090. Balint, Sandor. "Szeged müvelödéstörténete a varos szolashagyomanyaiban." *Magyar Nyelvör*, 83 (1959), 471–479.

Balint presents an interesting cultural history of Szeged, a city in southern Hungary, by citing many proverbs that relate to the town and its environment. The author cites early proverb collections and discusses in particular texts from the 16th to 19th centuries. The article shows the importance of city names in proverbs, indicating the close relationship between onomastics and paremiology. While large studies exist on major cities mentioned in proverbs (see for example the study on Rome by Marco Besso [no. 162]), it is interesting to note that other less known cities and their history can be studied by analyzing proverbs and proverbial expressions that include their names.

3091. Bambeck, Manfred. "Wenn einen der Teufel reitet." *Muttersprache*, 92 (1982), 185–195.

Detailed historical and cultural study of the German proverbial expression "Ihn plagt (reitet) der Teufel" (The devil has gotten to him, or: The devil has gotten hold of him). Bambeck traces the expression back to early ecclesiastical traditions and shows how Latin references to it were translated through Christian writings into German, French, English and Italian. Especially German examples, including some from Martin Luther (1483–1546), are cited which reflect the image of the devil "riding" on a person as a counterpart to Christ.

3092. Bambeck, Manfred. "'Weder Kuh noch Kalb'. Zu einem Exempel bei Johannes Pauli." *Archiv für das Studium der neueren Sprachen und Literaturen*, 221 (1984), 130–132.

Traces the German proverbial expression "Weder Kuh noch Kalb" (Neither cow nor calf, i.e. absolutely nothing) back to medieval Latin sources of the French preachers Jacques de Vitry (died 1240) and Etienne de Bourbon (died c. 1261). The German expression found in Johannes Pauli's (1455?–1530?) collection of anecdotes and tall tales *Schimpf und Ernst* (1522) is, therefore, much older than the 16th century and is most likely a loan translation from the Latin.

3093. Bambeck, Manfred. *Das Sprichwort im Bild. "Der Wald hat Ohren, das Feld hat Augen." Zu einer Zeichnung von Hieronymus Bosch.* Wiesbaden: Franz Steiner, 1987. 64 pp.

Following four previous discussions of the proverb picture "Der Wald hat Ohren, das Feld hat Augen" (in Dutch: "Het veld heeft ogen, het bos heeft oren", i.e. "The field has eyes, the forest has ears") by Hieronymus Bosch (1450?–1516), Manfred Brauneck now presents his own detailed and exemplary monograph of this fascinating drawing. He analyzes in great detail the seven eyes in the field, the major tree in the picture and the seven trees in the background, the fox and the rooster under the tree, the owl sitting in the trunk of the tree, the two birds on the tree, and the other birds in the picture. In addition there are also many references to Biblical symbols and parallel citations from many literary sources. Bambeck concludes that Bosch intended this drawing as an allegorical religious statement. With 2 illustrations. See Otto Benesch (no. 140), J.B.F. van Gils (no. 529), D. Roggen (no. 1567), and Paul Vandenbroeck (no. 2968).

3094. Baranov, A.N. "Aksiologicheskie strategii v strukture iazyka (paremiologiia i leksika)." *Voprosy iazykoznaniia,* no. 3 (1989), 74–90.

The author presents a highly theoretical analysis of the axiological strategy in the structure of language with special emphasis on the relationship between paremiology and lexicology. The first part of the essay deals exclusively with axiological aspects of language as such, while the second part considers the value system expressed in proverbs through certain words. Baranov draws his many examples from Vladimir Ivanovich Dal's (1801–1872) important Russian proverb collection *Poslovitsy russkago naroda* (1862), stressing that axiological strategies are of great importance in understanding the worldview expressed in the language of proverbs.

3095. Baranov, A.N., and Dmitrij Dobrovol'skij. "Kognitive Modellierung in der Phraseologie: Zum Problem der Aktuellen

Bedeutung." *Beiträge zur Erforschung der deutschen Sprache*, 10 (1991), 112–123.

This is a highly theoretical and linguistic article on semantic aspects of German phraseological units. The two authors start with a review of international scholarship, and they then present various models of understanding fixed phrases as signs. They talk especially about a structural-semantic model, but they also explain a conceptual model for the cognition of proverbial expressions. Numerous German examples are cited throughout this complex paper, and the result is a typological structure that will help in the comprehension of phraseological units. Two tables illustrating the function and typology of fixed phrases are included, and a useful bibliography (pp. 122–123) is also attached.

3096.   Barbazza, Marie-Catherine. "La femme dans le *Vocabulaire de Refranes* de Correas: Un discours d'exclusion?" *Imprévue*, 1 (1986), 9–27.

Taking Gonzalo de Correas' (1571–1631) important proverb collection *Vocabulario de refranes y frases proverbiales* (1626) as an historical document and source, Barbazza investigates the role that women play in these early Spanish proverbs. Not surprisingly she discovers that most proverbs relating to women are misogynous, having primarily negative things to say about widows, old women and prostitutes. It is shown that these proverbs marginalize women by attaching all kinds of stereotypical falsehoods and vices to them. Many examples in Spanish without French translations are cited, and what emerges is a very negative view of women.

3097.   Bardakhanova, S.S. "Khudozhestvennye osobennosti buriatskikh poslovits." *Traditsionny i fol'klor buriat.* Eds. E.N. Kuz'mina and A.I. Ulanov. Ulan-Ude: Buriatskii Filial, 1980. 110–126.

The author presents a detailed analysis of the poetic features of the proverbs from the Buriat Autonomous Soviet Socialist Republic. Basing her statements on numerous Buriat proverbs, Bardakhanova touches on such matters as structure, metaphor, style, and irony. She also includes comments on the use of alliteration, rhyme, tautology, allegory and mnemonic devices in these proverbs from the southeastern part of the Soviet Union. Due to their poetic language these proverbs are clearly marked as traditional wisdom and differentiated from normal speech patterns.

3098. Bardakhanova, S.S. "Poslovitsy—on'hon ugenuud." In S.S. Bardakhanova. *Malye zhanry buriatskogo fol'klora.* Ulan-Ude: Buriatskoe knizhnoe izdatel'stvo, 1982. 21–76.

This book chapter is an excellent example of the strong interest of Soviet paremiologists and paremiographers in the proverbs of the many ethnic and national minorities in the vast Soviet Union. In this case Bardakhanova presents a detailed discussion of Buriat proverbs from the Buriat Autonomous Soviet Socialist Republic in Asia. She deals with questions of origin, structure, form, language, poetics, and worldview. While the author emphasizes the proverbs from older periods, she also treats the expression of class differences in proverbs. The chapter closes with an analysis of the proverbs of the Soviet period, citing many examples throughout and also including valuable bibliographical information.

3099. Bárdosi, Vilmos. "'Un ange passe': Contribution à l'étymologie d'une locution." *Europhras 88. Phraséologie Contrastive. Actes du Colloque International Klingenthal-Strasbourg, 12–16 Mai 1988.* Ed. Gertrud Gréciano. Strasbourg: Université des Sciences Humaines, 1989. 7–16.

The author points out that many studies of individual proverbs and proverbial expressions deal primarily with morphological, syntactical and semantic questions. Bárdosi feels that more attention should be paid to etymological matters, and as an example he traces the origin of the common European expression "Un ange passe" (An angel passes) which is employed when there is a sudden silence during a conversation. The article establishes the fact that this phrase goes back to classical mythology and that it was loan translated from Greek into Latin and then into the vernacular languages.

3100. Barley, Nigel. "Strukturnyi podkhod k poslovitse i maksime."
       Paremiologicheskie issledovaniia. Ed. Gregorii L'vovich Permiakov.
       Moskva: Nauka, 1984. 127–148.

       This is a Russian translation of Nigel Barley's valuable study
       "A Structural Approach to the Proverb and Maxim with Special
       Reference to the Anglo-Saxon Corpus" (1972, see no. 86). The
       author presents a structural approach to the proverb and its
       relationship to riddles, maxims, proverbial expressions and
       wellerisms. According to Barley, "a proverb may be taken as a
       standard statement of moral or categorical imperatives in fixed
       metaphorical paradigmatic form. It deals with fundamental
       logical relationships." Barley also touches upon problems of
       translation of proverbs, the importance of context, values
       expressed in proverbs, variations, metaphors, meaning and
       function. Several diagrams are included and many English
       examples (now with Russian translations) are cited.

3101. Barna, Gabor. "Szolasok és közmondasok." *Barand története és
       neprajza.* Ed. Ivan Balassa. Barand: Uj Elet Mgtsz, 1985. 412–417.

       A general article on the proverb lore from Barand in
       Hungary. The author starts with some introductory comments on
       proverbs and proverbial expressions collected in this city and its
       environment. This is followed by a more detailed discussion of
       the historical and cultural significance of these texts. The essay
       thus presents primarily a content analysis of common phrases
       current in this particular Hungarian region.

3102. Barnard, P.J., N.V. Hammond, A. MacLean, and J. Morton.
       "Learning and Remembering Interactive Commands in a Text-
       Editing Task." *Behaviour and Information Technology,* 1 (1982), 347–
       358.

       Investigates how task and vocabulary differences affect initial
       learning and subsequent memory for commands used in a simple
       word processing task. Four groups of subjects were shown a
       distorted proverb on a computer terminal (i.e. sti tch in a time
       xpqy aves nine) and were told to produce the correct proverb
       (i.e. A stitch in time saves nine) on the computer by issuing a
       sequence of commands. Command names were general for two

groups and more specific for the other two groups. Systems with semantically specific terms were learned no more quickly than systems with semantically general terms. But users of the specific vocabulary appeared to take more time actively considering options before deciding to consult the "help" command option. With an English abstract (p. 347).

3103. Barnes, Daniel R. "Boswell, Johnson, and a Proverbial Candlestick." *Midwestern Journal of Language and Folklore*, 8, no. 2 (1982), 120–122.

Analyzes a passage in James Boswell's (1740–1795) biography *The Life of Samuel Johnson* (1791/1799) which contains an allusion to the English proverb "Tace is Latin for candle." Barnes argues that by not understanding the proverb correctly, Boswell unwittingly created an instance of wanton cruelty in his account of Johnson's school days. Boswell contends that the teacher would ask children "Latin for a candlestick" and not getting an answer, he would beat the pupils.

3104. Barnum, Erika. *Translating Shakespeare's Proverbs: A Study of Seven German Versions of "Much Ado about Nothing."* Honors Thesis University of Vermont, 1989. 100 pp.

Realizing that William Shakespeare's (1564–1616) comedy *Much Ado about Nothing* (1598) contains many proverbs, Erika Barnum investigates how seven German translators from the 18th to the 20th centuries have dealt with the difficult task of rendering 65 proverbial texts into German. The seven translations are by Christoph Martin Wieland (1765), Heinrich Graf Baudissin (Schlegel-Tieck, 1830), Philipp Kaufmann (between 1830–1836), Karl Simrock (between 1839–1866), Hans Rothe (between 1923–1962), Richard Flatter (between 1938–1955), and Erich Fried (about 1970). The author interprets the use and function of the proverbs in the play, she deals with Shakespeare's interest in proverbial language, and she analyzes the difference among the translations of several of the proverbs. The second part of the thesis consists of a "Proverb Translation Index" (pp. 49–92) that lists the seven translations for all 65 proverbial texts, thus clearly indicating the wide range of attempts at translating Shakespeare's proverbs. A useful bibliography (pp. 93–100) is included.

3105. Barras, Christine. *Les proverbes dans les patois de la suisse romande.* Diss. Université de Neuchâtel, 1984. Sierre: J. Périsset, 1984. 997 pp.

A massive and erudite dissertation consisting primarily of a significant collection of 5344 patois proverbs of the Rhaeto-Romanic linguistic area of southern Switzerland. Each text is cited in dialect form followed by a French translation, short explanatory comments and the written source. In the introduction (pp. 1–24) Barras explains her methodology and reviews previous collections. Of major importance is the second part (pp. 707–915) of this study which analyzes the corpus linguistically, touching on such matters as vocabulary, syntax, variability, grammar, context, content, form, style, etc. A number of diagrams and charts are also provided to summarize the findings. A major bibliography (pp. 916–921) and a most useful key-word index (pp. 929–993) are included, making this the standard work on these dialect proverbs.

3106. Barrick, Mac E. "El 446. refran de *Celestina.*" *Celestinesca: Boletin Informativo Internacional,* 7, no. 2 (1983), 13–15.

Referring to José Gella Iturriaga's article "444 refranes de 'La Celestina'" from 1977 (see no. 516) which actually lists 445 (!) Spanish proverbs out of the tragedy *La Celestina* (c. 1499), Barrick is able to add yet another proverb: "A buen comer o mal comer, tres veces beber" (To eat well or eat poorly, drink three times). He cites many references from Spanish proverb collections and also includes variants from literary sources, quoting them in their actual context.

3107. Barrick, Mac E. "'No Soap'." *Western Folklore,* 44 (1985), 41–44.

Starting with a reference to Archer Taylor's (see no. 1877) earlier attempt to discuss the origin and meaning of the American proverbial expression "No soap" (i.e. nothing doing), Barrick proposes that "soap" might in fact be a slang term for "money." Thus "no soap" might have meant originally "no chance, because there's no money for it." He also cites numerous references of the expression from anecdotes, jokes and American literary sources.

3108. Barrick, Mac E. "'Welcome to the Clothes': Changing Proverb Function in the Spanish Renaissance." *Proverbium,* 2 (1985), 1–19.

Barrick starts his important essay on proverbs in Spanish literature with a discussion of the relationship between an anecdote of wide-spread international distribution and its reduction to the Spanish proverb "Eu honrro aquella que me honrrou" (I honor that which honors me) in the 14th century. He argues that proverbs began to replace tales, fables and exempla at this historical juncture. Proverbs gained much importance in the Spanish Renaissance in and of themselves. This is indicated by such early collections as the *Seniloquium* (15th century), *Refranes glosados* (c. 1490), and Inigo Lopez de Mendoza's (1398–1458) *Refranes que dizen las viejas tras el fuego* (printed c. 1490). While these collections reflect didactic intentions, later collections of the 16th century like Hernán Núñez' (1472–1553) *Refranes o proverbios en romance* (1555) and Juan de Mal Lara's (1527–1571) *Philosophia vulgar* (1568) were put together because of an interest in the proverb's value as a rhetorical and stylistic device. They also clearly show the influence of Erasmus of Rotterdam's (1466–1536) *Adagia* (1500ff.). Important bibliographical notes (pp. 11–17) and two reproduced pages of the *Refranes glosados* are included.

3109. Barrick, Mac E. "'Where's the Beef'?" *Midwestern Journal of Language and Folklore,* 12 (1986), 43–46.

An essay dealing with the interrelationship of advertising slogans and proverbs. In particular Barrick states that the American phrase "Where's the beef?" was introduced in January of 1984 in a Wendy's fast food television commercial developed by Cliff Freeman of the Dancer Fitzgerald Sample agency. Barrick cites many references and variants in the form of headlines, cartoons and graffiti. He also refers to this new proverbial interrogative on T-shirts.

3110. Barulin, A. "Russkii paremiologicheskii minimum i ego rol'
prepodavanii russkogo iazyka." *Paremiologicheskie issledovaniia.* Ed.
Grigorii L'vovich Permiakov. Moskva: Nauka, 1984. 264–265.

A short summary of a lecture which Barulin delivered in
1973 in Varna (Bulgaria), stating the importance of teaching
proverbs, proverbial expressions and clichés to students studying
Russian as a foreign language. Anybody wanting to communicate
or read in Russian must have a passive or better yet an active
knowledge of close to 1000 expressions of various kinds. These
fixed phrases will also help the student to grasp grammatical
rules, and they should be considered as a serious pedagogical
tool by teachers. The learning and active oral and written use of
such a paremiological minimum should be part of all foreign
language instruction.

3111. Barz, Irmhild. "'Gefährliche' Redewendungen." *Sprachpflege,* 34,
no. 12 (1985), 181–182.

General note on the importance of phraseological units in
journalism. Barz argues that while such expressions add a lot to
the metaphorical style of a newspaper, they become even more
effective if they are varied. She discusses four German examples
in context explaining how the traditional phrases have been
modified to increase their expressiveness. The importance of
their lexicographical inclusion in dictionaries is also mentioned.

3112. Basgöz, Ilhan. "Proverbs about Proverbs or Folk Definitions of
Proverb." *Proverbium,* 7 (1990), 1–17.

Basing his significant study on 124 proverbs about proverbs
which he found in Selwyn Champion's *Racial Proverbs. A Selection
of the World's Proverbs Arranged Linguistically* (London: George
Routledge, 1938) and adding 10 such definitions from Turkey
and 5 from Luganda in an appendix (pp. 16–17) to them, Ilhan
Basgöz presents a detailed analysis of these meta-proverbs from
44 cultural and linguistic areas. He establishes the following
categories for these folk definitions of proverbs: (1) definition by
means of content, (2) definition in relation to speech and
discourse, (3) definition by means of origin, (4) definition by
means of transmission and diffusion in time and space, (5)

definition by means of prestige and power, (6) definition by means of form, and (7) definition by means of function. Many examples are cited in English translation, and it is argued that paremiologists trying to define proverbs should pay more attention to what the people have said about them.

3113. Bassin, Alexander. "Proverbs, Slogans and Folk Sayings in the Therapeutic Community: A Neglected Therapeutic Tool." *Journal of Psychoactive Drugs*, 16 (1984), 51–56.

A short discussion of the effective use of proverbs, slogans and folk sayings as therapeutic tools for drug addicts and alcoholics. It is pointed out that such expressions promote the cohesiveness and behavior code of a group of patients, and as such, may well provide a major therapeutic intervention. The author reports on lists of such phrases used by various treatment centers in the United States, some examples being: "There is no free lunch," "The journey of a thousand miles begins with the first step," "Pride comes before a fall," "What goes around comes around," "When the going gets tough, the tough get going," "You are what you think you are," "Honesty is the key" and "No gain without pain." Bassin attributes a high value to such proverbial slogans in the folk psychotherapy of various addicts.

3114. Basso, Keith H. "'Wise Words' of the Western Apache: Metaphor and Semantic Theory." *Meaning in Anthropology*. Eds. Keith H. Basso and Henry A. Selby. Albuquerque/New Mexico: University of New Mexico Press, 1976. 93–121. A shortened version (pp. 96–107) has appeared in *Folk Groups and Folklore Genres: A Reader*. Ed. Elliott Oring. Logan/Utah: Utah State University Press, 1989. 291–301.

This is one of the regrettably very few essays on the metaphorical speech of Native Americans, in this case of the residents of Cibecue, a Western Apache speech community located on the Fort Apache Indian Reservation in east central Arizona. Basso is able to show that these Apaches employ metaphors as similes and that quite a number of them might be termed "wise words." They follow the basic structure of "subject + predicate + verb" and form a distinctive speech genre associated with adult men and women who have gained a reputation for balanced thinking, critical acumen, and extensive cultural knowledge. Some of them appear to be proverbial comparisons, as for example "Lightning is a boy" or "Butterflies are girls." Basso cites eight such wise words in the Apache language with English translations and provides detailed ethnographic explanations based on field research with native informants. At the end of his significant essay he presents a theory of metaphor for this Indian language that proves once and for all that Native Americans do communicate with proverbial metaphors. It is of utmost importance that anthropologists, linguists and folklorists study the hitherto rarely recorded proverbial speech of the Native Americans (see Wolfgang Mieder, no. 3921).

3115. Baumann, Michael L. "The Question of Idioms in B. Traven's Writings." *German Quarterly*, 60 (1987), 171–192.

The many Americanisms, from individual words to idioms and proverbial expressions, in Bruno Traven's (pseud. Traven Torsvan and Ret Marut, 1890–1969) German prose are being analyzed in order to show that the original manuscripts were written in English by an American. Such an American must have written at least the narrative and dialogue parts of the original manuscripts in English. Traven's knowledge of American English remained poor over the period of his forty-five-year residence in Mexico, but he did write the reflexive passages in correct German. Many examples are cited in their literary context in this literary detective work on behalf of Michael Baumann.

3116. Baur, Rupprecht S., and Peter Grzybek. "Untersuchungen zu einem parömischen Minimum im Deutschen." *Interkulturelle Kommunikation. Kongreßbeiträge zur 20. Jahrestagung der Gesellschaft für Angewandte Linguistik.* Ed. Bernd Spillner. Bern: Peter Lang, 1990. 220–223.

This is a short statistical report on an experiment that the two authors undertook in Germany to establish a reliable way of finding out which proverbs are the most frequently used and best known among German speakers. They established statistical figures for 275 German proverbs by testing their knowledge among 100 German citizens between the ages of 19 and 84. The authors warn that their findings are not conclusive because of the smallness of their sample, but it is important to note that this type of analysis will eventually lead to the establishment of so-called paremiological minima. This in turn will be of greatest importance for lexicographers in their preparation of dictionaries. On the even more pragmatical level it can be argued that paremiological minima will be of greatest importance in the instruction of foreign languages. See also Grigorii L'vovich Permiakov (no. 2737).

3117. Bautier, Anne-Marie. "Peuples, provinces et villes dans la littérature proverbiale latine du Moyen Âge." *Richesse du proverbe.* Eds. François Suard and Claude Buridant. Lille: Université de Lille, 1984. I, 1–22.

An article filled with numerous examples of blasons populaires of the Romance languages of the Middle Ages. Bautier discusses a number of medieval Latin proverbs which contain ethnic slurs and stereotypes about people, geographical areas and cities. She also explains that such questionable comments on national characteristics were quite widespread at that time. The second half of the article presents many Latin examples with French translations about certain traits of the French, Germans, Spaniards, etc. Unfortunately these old proverbial misconceptions are still being quoted today and add to the racial and ethnic prejudices of the world. The notes (pp. 19–22) include important bibliographical references to the entire field of stereotypical expressions.

3118. Bebermeyer, Renate. "'Ich bin dazu geboren, das ich mit rotten und teufeln mus kriegen'. Luthers 'Teufel'-Komposita." *Muttersprache,* 94 (1983–1984), 52–67.

A philological essay discussing Martin Luther's (1483–1546) frequent use of the word "Teufel" (devil) in his writings. Many curses are cited, but there is also a section (pp. 54–56) that deals with proverbs containing the devil as the key-word. Bebermeyer discusses the cultural, historical and psychological significance of Luther's obsession with the devil. At the end there is a comprehensive list of all the noun-composita based on the devil which Luther used repeatedly in order to express himself in the folk speech of his time.

3119. Bebermeyer, Renate. "'Geflügelte Zitate'—gestern und heute." *Sprachspiegel,* 40 (1984), 66–70.

In these few pages Bebermeyer commemorates Georg Büchmann (1822–1884) and his famous German book of literary quotations *Geflügelte Worte* (1864ff.). She discusses a number of old and new quotations and also points out that the difference between a quotation and a proverb is not always entirely clear. Especially quotations from the Bible and Friedrich Schiller (1759–1805) have long become proverbial. But some recent quotations by politicians, coaches, comedians and aphoristic writers also are on their way to becoming proverbs. The question that remains is who will decide to enter them into new editions of "Büchmann" or new proverb collections and when will this take place.

3120. Bebermeyer, Renate. "'Der knarrende Baum steht am längsten'." *Sprachspiegel,* 41 (1985), 38–41.

Based on many German examples, Bebermeyer presents an overview of the image of the tree in proverbs. Karl Friedrich Wilhelm Wander (1803–1879) in his *Deutsches Sprichwörter-Lexikon,* 5 vols. (Leipzig: F.A. Brockhaus, 1867–1880; rpt. Darmstadt: Wissenschaftliche Buchgesellschaft, 1964) lists 300 proverbs that pertain to trees. Many of the trees symbolize mankind, and they refer to youth, age, growth, character, appearance, life, and knowledge. The content of "tree" proverbs is thus definitely related to human existence and its rites of passage.

3121. Bebermeyer, Renate. "'Wie ein Pferd, das die Grammatik nicht beherrscht, keineswegs unglücklich ist . . .' Zum 450. Todestag des Erasmus von Rotterdam." *Sprachspiegel,* 42 (1986), 109–112.

This is a short essay commemorating the 450th recurrence of the year of Erasmus of Rotterdam's (1469–1536) death. Bebermeyer mentions some of his major works and comments especially on the *Adagia* (1500ff.). It is pointed out that Erasmus popularized much classical wisdom through his philological, cultural and historical comments on Greek and Latin proverbs. The author also mentions the use and function of proverbs in Erasmus' satirical work *The Praise of Folly* (1511).

3122. Bebermeyer, Renate. "Nomen est omen—Name ist stilmitteltaugliche Vorbedeutung." *Sprachspiegel,* 44 (1988), 7–9.

A somewhat essayistic comment on the Latin phrase "Nomen est omen" (The name is omen). Bebermeyer explains that this common expression goes back to Titus Maccius Plautus (250?– 184 B.C.) who actually stated "Nomen atque omen" (Name and omen). She presents a number of examples where the name of a person actually indicates his/her character, profession, etc., and she also explains that the classical phrase is often used in German advertisements.

3123. Bebermeyer, Renate. "Das gegenwärtige Comeback des Sprichworts." *Sprachspiegel,* 45 (1989), 105–110.

Based on numerous examples of German proverbs which the author located in the mass media, it is argued that there is a definite "comeback" of proverbial language in modern communication. They express common sense, basic truths, and above all authority. Little wonder that journalists use them in newspaper headlines, advertisements contain them as catchy slogans, and politicians employ them to manipulate the opinions of voters. Bebermeyer also notices that often foreign proverbs in German translation are cited to add credence to a report or a statement about another country and its culture. Proverbs are definitely not "dead" in the modern technological German society, and there are even some signs that people enjoy using them in oral and written communication with higher frequency than some decades ago.

3124. Becker, A.L. "Biography of a Sentence: A Burmese Proverb." *Text, Play, and Story: The Construction and Reconstruction of Self and Society.* Eds. Stuart Plattner and Edward M. Bruner. Washington/D.C.: The American Ethnological Society, 1984. 135–155.

This intriguing article offers much more than a normal analysis of an individual proverb. The first half deals with theoretical questions of how proverbs fit into the performance of speech acts. Becker explains that there are six contextual situations that must be analyzed when studying the function and meaning of a particular proverb: (1) structural relations of parts to wholes, (2) generic relations of text to prior text, (3) medial relations of text to medium, (4) interpersonal relations of text to participants in a text-act, (59) referential relations of a text to Nature, the world one believes to lie beyond language, and (6) silential relations of a text to the unsaid and the unsayable. Several English proverbs are cited to illustrate these points. In the second part Becker studies the Burmese proverb "There are three kinds of mistakes: those resulting from lack of memory, from lack of planning ahead, or from misguided beliefs" along these lines.

3125. Beckman, Gary. "Proverbs and Proverbial Allusions in Hittite." *Journal of Near Eastern Studies*, 45 (1986), 19–30.

Points out the difficulty of deciding what text might be a proverb in a language like Hittite that is not spoken anymore. Beckman lists four criteria to judge possible proverbiality: (1) a saying is included in a collection, (2) a saying is explicitly cited as such, (3) a saying is found in the same shape in different texts, and (4) a saying, if interpreted literally, appears out of place in its context. The author then discusses fourteen texts in Hittite and English translation, placing them in their literary context and providing important annotations. A general section (pp. 26–30) on Hittite wisdom literature is also included. The article represents a significant step towards a deeper understanding of ancient Hittite proverbs.

3126. Bellmann, Werner. "'Cacatum non est pictum'—Ein Zitat in Heines 'Wintermärchen'." *Wirkendes Wort*, 33 (1983), 213–215.

A short analysis of Heinrich Heine's (1797–1856) use of the Latin proverb "Cacatum non est pictum" (Shitting is not [the same as] painting) in his long satirical poem *Deutschland. Ein Wintermärchen* (1844). Bellmann explains that Heine probably found this originally only German proverb in a dramatic sketch byJakob Michael Reinhold Lenz (1751–1792), but he also adds that the expression stems from the 16th century. The Latin translation of the German dialect text "Geskizzen wor nit gemohlen" was used by Lenz's editor as well as Heine to weaken its obvious scatological implication and to strengthen its satirical literary function.

3127. Belo, Fernando. "Analyse des logiques d'un corpus proverbial." *Richesse du proverbe.* Eds. François Suard and Claude Buridant. Lille: Université de Lille, 1984. II, 25–36.

Discusses a methodology of analyzing the logical structures of a corpus of proverbs. Having separated the proverbs from proverbial expressions and maxims, Belo proposes to group them according to semantic structures. He cites a number of French examples, also discussing problems of polysemy, metaphors and variability. Surprisingly there is no mention of Matti Kuusi's (no. 975) and Grigorii L'vovich Permiakov's (no. 1428) significant international work along these lines.

3128. Benet, Diana. "Herbert's Proverbs: The Magic Shoe." *Like Season'd Timber. New Essays on George Herbert.* Eds. Edmund Miller and Robert DiYanni. Bern: Peter Lang, 1987. 139–150.

Following James Thorpe's (see no. 2948) earlier article on George Herbert's (1593–1633) English proverb collection *Outlandish Proverbs* (1640), Diana Benet investigates not so much the collection itself but rather the way in which its proverbs influenced Herbert's poems. She points out that this collection was a personal thesaurus of wisdom for its compiler. This "sourcebook" was used in many instances to add a certain didactic character to his poems. Several examples are discussed in their literary context, and it is in this innovative use of "his" proverbs that Herbert proves that "All feete tread not in one shoe." Obviously he was much more interested in the effective use of proverbs than in their compilation into a collection.

3129. Benjafield, John, and Eleanor Carson. "The Image-Arousing Potential of Proverbs as a Function of Source and Mode." *British Journal of Social Psychology*, 25 (1986), 51–56.

A central hypothesis of this study is that anonymous proverbs are higher in imagery than authored proverbs. Someone who is known as the author of a proverb is likely to have belonged to an educated class. Members of an educated class possess the communicative skills and resources to both make and be remembered for an abstract proverb (i.e. quotation), while anonymous sayings will tend to attain widespread use only if a high imagery value makes them easy to remember. Based on a proverb list of 203 texts, the authors are able to show that negative proverbs warn against widely held beliefs, and these texts are higher in imagery than their affirmative counterparts. This socio-psychological phenomenon suggests that anonymous negative proverbs are of a social origin. An English abstract (p. 51) and a bibliography (p. 55) are included.

3130. Berezov, Jack Lewis. *Single-Line Proverbs: A Study of the Sayings Collected in Proverbs 10–22:16 and 25–29.* Diss. Hebrew Union College, 1987. 164 pp.

In his dissertation Jack Berezov investigates certain chapters of the Biblical Book of Proverbs and the single-line proverbs that they include. He starts with a review of previous work by scholars of Form Criticism and states his own research goals (pp. 1–32). In chapter two (pp. 33–80) he analyzes the characteristic features of the single-verse sayings in Proverbs, stressing in particular the construction of individual proverbs, their syntax, function and intended message. Chapter three (pp. 81–118) investigates the broad patterns of arrangement and specific compositional techniques, arguing that these sections of the Book of Proverbs do not consist of earlier independent proverb collections. In the fourth chapter (pp. 119–134) the differences between the sentences in Proverbs and their appearance in other Biblical texts are explained, and the fifth chapter (pp. 135–142) summarizes the findings and calls for more detailed study of this wisdom literature. A useful bibliography (pp. 144–149) and an appendix (pp. 150–164) in Hebrew of the types of expressions under study are included.

3131. Berger, P.-R. "'Zum Huren bereit bis hin zu einem Rundlaib Brot': Prov. 6,26." *Zeitschrift für die Alttestamentliche Wissenschaft,* 99 (1987), 98–106.

Discusses various translation and interpretation attempts of the Biblical proverb "Eine Hure bringt einen ums Brot" (Prov. 6,26; A harlot may be hired for a loaf of bread). Martin Luther's (1483–1546) and several other German translations are analyzed in great detail, providing much etymological, historical and cultural information concerning the meaning of this obscure proverb. Yet another example of the complexity of traditional wisdom literature in the Old Testament.

3132. Berman, Louis A. "Using Proverbs to Test Readiness for College Composition." *Proverbium,* 7 (1990), 19–36.

The author starts his important article with a review of the use of proverbs for mental testing and argues successfully that proverbs can also be used for the assessment of writing skills. He then reports on an English composition placement test that he developed for the University of Illinois at Chicago. It includes a proverb-interpretation section which helps to establish the level of writing skills of both typical American students and students for whom English is a second language. The test contains 24 common proverbs and is designed to test proverb recognition and interpretation. It is a useful tool to place native and foreign students into the correct level of English courses. Six statistical tables and a useful bibliography (p. 36) are included.

3133. Bernath, Béla. *A szerelem titkos nyelvén. Erotikus szolasok és egyéb folklorszövegek magyarazata.* Budapest: Gondolat, 1986. 350 pp.

A scholarly book of twenty-five chapters studying a wealth of erotic proverbs and proverbial expressions from Hungary. Bernath includes many etymological, historical and cultural explanations, showing that erotic aspects play a major role in verbal folklore. Parallel texts and variants from other European languages are cited, and each chapter contains numerous bibliographical notes. An extensive bibliography (pp. 331–335) and an important subject index are included. The book is of particular interest to cultural historians and folklorists, and some

of the highly comparative chapters like the one on the expression
"Kosarat kap" (He got a basket; i.e. He was refused by a woman
[chapter 13, pp. 192–199]) deserve to be translated.

3134. Bernath, Csilla. "Phraseologische Neubildungen." *Beiträge zur
Phraseologie des Ungarischen und des Deutschen.* Ed. Regina Hessky.
Budapest: Lorand-Eötvös-Universität, 1988. 39–49.

Bernath deals with the problem of innovative changes of
phraseological units in the modern German language. She starts
with some theoretical considerations and then presents seven
examples of proverbial expressions, quotations, advertising
slogans, book and song titles, etc. that she has located in the
newspaper *Die Zeit* and the two magazines *Der Spiegel* and *Bunte
Illustrierte.* She also includes variants of these texts to illustrate
how fixed phrases get changed for a number of reasons. Some
changes are purely linguistic while others subsitute words or
entire segments depending on the message that the journalist or
copy writer has in mind. But even with these changes the original
text appears to remain recognizable. The text is reduced to a
formula whose variables can be changed as needed for specific
communicative results.

3135. Binotto, Armin. *Sprichwörter und Redensarten im Unterricht.*
Hitzkirch: Comenius-Verlag, 1983. 56 pp.

An interesting educational pamphlet for students and
teachers to study German proverbs and proverbial expressions.
Many examples are cited in 17 short chapters dealing with such
matters as body expressions, variants, structure, archaic
expressions, form, style, content, parody, validity, dialect texts,
wellerisms, literature, proverbs in art (Pieter Brueghel [1520–
1569] and Emil Zbinden [1908–]), variations, semantics, Bible,
national stereotypes, geographical distribution, etc. The book is
written in the form of a workbook with many exercises, and the
answers to the many questions are given in the back. Eleven
illustrations and an introductory bibliography (pp. 52–54) are
included in this useful teaching aid on proverbs for school
children.

3136. Bitterling, Klaus. *"The Proverbs of Alfred* and the *Middle English Dictionary." Neuphilologische Mitteilungen,* 84, no. 3 (1983), 344–346.

This is a small note on some linguistic questions regarding *The Proverbs of Alfred* (13th century) as they relate to the *Middle English Dictionary.* The etymology and meaning of the verbs "alothen" (to make odious), "coveren" (to succeed, be successful, prevail), and "forleren" (to learn falsely, to forget) are explained in their proverbial context, citing in each case the pertinent lines out of this Middle English proverb collection. These comments are ample proof of the important interrelationship of historical lexicography and paremiography.

3137. Bizzarri, Hugo Oscar. "Nuevo fragmento del *Libro de los buenos proverbios* contenido en el manuscrito BNMadrid 9428." *Incipit,* 8 (1988), 125–132.

In this note Hugo Bizzarri reports on a new fragment of the early Spanish proverb collection *Libro de los buenos proverbios* (14th century) which he discovered in the National Library of Spain in Madrid. He gives a small introduction to the manuscript history of this important collection and then prints the manuscript fragment (pp. 125–132). For earlier studies see Manuel Ariza Viguera (no. 59) and Frances Morgan (no. 1317) as well as Harlan Sturm's critical edition of the collection (no. 2921).

3138. Bizzarri, Hugo Oscar. "Un testimonio mas papa tres capitulos del *Libro de los cien capitulos." Incipit,* 9 (1989), 139–146.

Bizzarri presents a philological proof for the fact that the *Flores de Filosofia* (13th century) contain a selection of three chapters of the *Libro de los cien capitulos* (13th century). The latter is a book of hundred chapters containing moral advice in the form of sententious remarks and proverbs. The author shows that there are clear grammatical, lexical, and structural parallels between these two works, and he reprints the three chapters which have been copied by an anonymous writer. It is explained that these texts include many early references for medieval Spanish proverbs.

3139. Bizzarri, Hugo Oscar. "Consideraciones en torno a la elaboración de *El libro de los doze sabios.*" *La Corónica,* 18, no. 1 (1989–1990), 85–89.

In this paper Bizzarri offers a textual and philological analysis of the structure of *El libro de los doze sabios* (c. 1237). This book of the twelve wise men contains much advice on how to behave properly at the court, how to be a good warrior, how to govern with justice, etc. It contains didactic sententious remarks and also some folk proverbs. This book of moral instruction was quite popular in medieval Spain, and Bizzarri reports that five manuscripts of it are known (the latest from the 14th/15th century). The author cites a few examples, but his major interest is the structural organization of this educational book.

3140. Bizzarri, Hugo Oscar. "Es posible alcanzar una definicion precisa del 'refran' medieval?" *Studia Hispanica Medievalia.* Eds. Rosa E. Penna and Maria A. Rosarossa. Buenos Aires: Jornadas de literatura española medieval, 1990. II, 65–69.

Bizzarri begins his theoretical article with a review of various attempts at defining proverbs, mentioning in particular the work of Bartlett Jere Whiting (see no. 2060), Alan Dundes (no. 378), Otto Blehr (no. 167), and George Milner (nos. 1291 and 1293). He then wonders if these theoretical definitions are applicable to Spanish proverbs of the Middle Ages and into the 16th century. He cites literary, rhetorical, and philosophical works of that time to establish what early writers thought about the possible definition of proverbs. He also explains that it is quite difficult at times to distinguish between a sententious remark or maxim and a proverb. This is especially true for the modern scholar for whom it is difficult to establish the frequency and oral currency of such seemingly traditional statements. The 21 notes (pp. 68–69) contain useful bibliographical references.

3141. Bleton, Paul. "C'est juste une façon de parler: les locutions métalinguistiques." *La locution. Actes du colloque international Université McGill, Montréal, 15–16 octobre 1984.* Eds. Giuseppe Di Stefano and Russell G. McGillivray. Montréal: Editions CERES, 1984. 3–18.

An interesting survey of French proverbial expressions which contain the words "dire" (to say), "parler" (to speak) and "mot" (word). Bleton names this particular sub-class of expressions "louction métalinguistique" (metalinguistic expression) and cites numerous examples. He also deals with definition problems, the metaphorical nature of these phrases, and their figurative meaning. Some comments concerning the origin and worldview of these expressions dealing with human speech and communication are included as well.

3142. Bloc-Duraffour, Catherine. "Traitement de la logique des rôles narratifs dans les proverbes italiens." *Richesse du proverbe.* Eds. François Suard and Claude Buridant. Lille: Université de Lille, 1984. II, 37–49.

Based on the theoretical work of Grigorii L'vovich Permiakov (see esp. nos. 1424–1433) and Aleksandr K. Zholkovskii (no. 2132), the author investigates the treatment of logic in the narrative components of Italian proverbs. Bloc-Duraffour wants to show in particular the relationship of the realia mentioned in proverbs and their semiotic significance. She also looks at proverbs as "micro-récit" (micro-narrative) and studies their logico-semantic aspects, their structure and theme (content). The Italian examples are cited with French translations and complicated linguistic formulas are also provided to illustrate the logical relationships.

3143. Blondel, Jacques. "Les *Proverbes d'Enfer* de William Blake." *Études Anglaises*, 40, no. 4 (1987), 448–454.

This is a literary study of William Blake's (1757–1827) poem "Proverbs of Hell" (1790) which is part of his work *The Marriage of Heaven and Hell* (1790). Blondel presents a background to this important work by Blake, arguing that the poem can be understood only in the context of the entire book. The major part of the essay deals with the structure of the proverbial aphorisms contained within the poem. The fact that many of them come from the Biblical Book of Proverbs is explained, and there are also comments regarding the evil and passion expressed in these proverbs. For two other studies on this poem see Randel Helms (no. 2457) and Michael Holstein (no. 2478).

3144. Bluhm, Lothar. "'Er ist ihr zu dick, er hat kein Geschick'. Zu einem Spruch in Annette von Droste-Hülshoffs *Westphälische Schilderungen aus einer westphälischen Feder* und den *Kinder- und Hausmärchen* der Brüder Grimm." *Wirkendes Wort*, 37 (1987), 181–183.

Discusses the proverbial nature of a short German verse in Annette von Droste-Hülshoff's (1797–1848) prose work *Westphälische Schilderungen aus einer westphälischen Feder* (1842). The proverb "Kurz und dick hat kein Geschick" (Short and fat has no skill [ability]) already appears in Friedrich Petri's (or: Peters, 1549–1617) Baroque proverb collection *Der Teutschen Weissheit* (1604/05) and is also included in the Grimm fairy tale "König Drosselbart" (KHM 52). Since Droste-Hülshoff was in close contact with the Brothers Grimm, it is argued that the proverb might have found its way into the fairy tale via this author.

3145. Bluhm, Lothar. "Sprichwörter und Redensarten bei den Brüdern Grimm." *Sprichwörter und Redensarten im interkulturellen Vergleich.* Eds. Annette Sabban and Jan Wirrer. Opladen: Westdeutscher Verlag, 1991. 206–224.

Referring to previous books on proverbs in the *Haus- und Kindermärchen* (1812 and 1815) of the Brothers Grimm by Wolfgang Mieder (no. 3892) and Heinz Rölleke (no.), Bluhm summarizes their findings and then discusses in particular the proverbs and proverbial expressions in the fairy tale "Der Jude im Dorn" (KHM 110). He also gives a summary of his article on a proverb in the fairy tale "König Drosselbart" (KHM 52; see no. 3144 above), and then provides a few additional comments on how especially Wilhelm Grimm (1786–1859) added proverbial language during later editions of the fairy tales. A valuable bibliography (pp. 221–224) is attached, making this an important contribution to the interrelationship of folk narrative research and paremiology.

3146. Boateng, Felix. "African Traditional Education: A Tool for Intergenerational Communication." *African Culture: The Rhythms of Unity.* Eds. Molefi Kete Asante and Kariamu Welsh Asante. Westport/Connecticut: Greenwood, 1985. 109–122.

The author argues that Western formal eduction in Africa did not consider traditional cultural transmission as a goal of the educative process for Africans. There is a call for a return to more traditional education in Africa, including in particular the rich heritage of oral literature. Boateng points out the cultural and educational importance of fables, myths, legends, folk tales, and proverbs. In the section on African proverbs (pp. 117–118) it is stated that the educative and communicative power of proverbs in African societies lies in their use as validators of traditional ethics, procedures and beliefs. A few examples of proverbs that are especially important in the normal education of children are cited.

3147. Boeder, Winfried. "La structure du proverbe géorgien." *Revue des études géorgiennes et caucasiennes*, no. 1 (1985), 97–115.

An important structural analysis of 40 proverbs and their variants from the Georgian Soviet Socialist Republic in the Transcaucasus of the Soviet Union. Each proverb is cited in transliterated Georgian with a French translation, some cultural and historical explanations, and references to earlier Georgian proverb collections. Boeder also addresses the nature (both content and language) of Georgian proverbs as well as the difference between a quotation and a proverb. Next he deals with the questions of context, realia and semantic structure, basing his analysis on the previous linguistic and semiotic work of Grigorii L'vovich Permiakov (see nos. 1424–1428). A significant bibliography (pp. 113–115) is attached.

3148. Boeder, Winfried. "Struktur und Interpretation georgischer Sprichwörter aus Chewßuretien." *Sprichwörter und Redensarten im interkulturellen Vergleich.* Eds. Annette Sabban and Jan Wirrer. Opladen: Westdeutscher Verlag, 1991. 139–161.

This is an expanded German version of the previous article (see no. 3147), this time analyzing 68 Georgian proverbs. Every text is cited in transliterated Georgian with German translations, to which Boeder adds extremely important linguistic, etymological and cultural explanations. His major goal in this article is once again to investigate the interrelationship of structure and meaning in proverbs. He also deals with problems of definition and tries to differentiate between the proverb and the quotation, stressing in particular the metaphorical nature of proverbs. At the beginning of the article is also a short review of several major Georgian proverb collections.

3149. Bondarenko, V.T. "Ispol'zovanie poslovichnykh i pogo-vorochnykh vyrazhenii v roli chlenov predlozheniia." *Russkii iazyk v shkole,* 72, no. 4 (1985), 86–89.

Interesting paper on the use of Russian proverbs and proverbial expressions as parts of sentences in a literary or journalistic text. Bondarenko shows that proverbs and expressions can be viewed as signs of events and situations functioning in the particular text as syntactic units with all of the constructive features of a sentence. As communicative units they are also part of sentences, especially if they are integrated only partially into the prose. The author quotes numerous examples out of Russian literature and from newspapers like *Pravda.*

3150. Bonnet, Doris. *Le proverbe chez les Mossi du Yatenga (Haute-Volta).* Paris: Société d'études linguistiques et anthropologiques de France, 1982. 193 pp.

A highly significant linguistic and anthropological monograph on 130 proverbs of the Mossis of Yatenga in Africa. Each text is followed by a French lexical list and an attempt of a French translation. Detailed lexical, ethnographic and cultural explanations concerning the life of this sub-Saharan desert population follows. Bonnet also provides one or two situations in which the proverbs can actually be employed or which were given to her as interpretations (i.e. imaginary stories and tales). But there are also important chapters on paremiology as well as definition and classification problems (pp. 23–32), on Mossi words for "proverb" (pp. 33–37), and the situational use of proverbs (pp. 39–42). Following the actual proverb corpus is a fascinating chapter on various strategic functions of these proverbs (pp. 175–185). A valuable bibliography (pp. 187–189), a map, and a word/subject index conclude this study. French, English, Spanish and German abstracts (pp. 7–8) are provided as well.

3151. Borbély, Mária. "Phraseologische Spiele mit Sprichwörtern." *Beiträge zur Phraseologie des Ungarischen und des Deutschen.* Ed. Regina Hessky. Budapest: Lorand-Eötvös-Universität, 1988. 50–68.

The author found 55 German proverbs in such magazines as *Stern, Der Spiegel, Brigitte,* and *Bunte Illustrierte,* and she observes that most of them appear in an intentionally varied form. Journalists obviously enjoy the "play" with traditional proverbs whose textual stability is quickly changed to suit various manipulative goals. Many of the proverbs appear in headlines of articles or advertisements. But even though the proverbs show much variability, the original text always seems to be present as a contrast in the reader's mind. It is exactly this juxtaposition of traditional and varied proverb texts that makes such journalistic play with proverbs so effective. Many examples are cited in context, and there are also two statistical tables.

3152. Bornstein, Valerie. "A Case Study and Analysis of Family Proverb Use." *Proverbium,* 8 (1991), 19–28.

An interesting study in which the author investigates several French and Italian proverbs which her European mother used during a weekend in Dallas, Texas. The author cites her texts in context and differentiates between general proverbs on the one hand and family sayings on the other. The former are proverbs known to most members of a given society, while the latter are unique to just a family unit. There appears to be a middle ground on this spectrum which Bornstein labels family proverbs. Having cited examples for each group she also discusses the authoritative and didactic use of proverbs by her mother. For another study of family proverbs see Dennis Folly (no. 3433 below).

3153. Böttger, Walther. "Die 'Grillen' in bildlichen Ausdrücken." *Sprachpflege,* 32, no. 4 (1983), 53–56.

Presents the etymolgy of the German word "Grille" (cricket) and then explains the figurative meaning of it in various German proverbial expressions. Of particular significance are "Sich mit Grillen plagen" or "Grillen fangen" (To be low-spirited or in low spirits, To have a bee in one's bonnet, To worry unnecessarily) and "Ein Grillenfänger sein" (To be a grumpy dog, capricious person, crank, pessimist). Many references from German literature are cited, including Martin Luther (1483–1546), Sebastian Franck (1499–1542), Johann Fischart (1546–1590), Johann Wolfgang von Goethe (1749–1832), and Wilhelm Busch (1832–1908).

3154. Bouchard, Chantal. "La locution: problème de traduction." *La locution. Actes du colloque international Université McGill, Montréal, 15–16 octobre 1984.* Eds. Giuseppe Di Stefano and Russell G. McGillivray. Montréal: Editions CERES, 1984. 19–27.

Starts with a general discussion of the difficulty of translating proverbs, proverbial expressions, and clichés. The major translation problem lies in the metaphorical nature of these expressions. Bouchard then analyzes how two different (English and American) translators of Gustave Flaubert's (1821–1880) *Dictionnaire des idées reçues* (Paris: L. Conard, 1911) have dealt with 102 expressions taken from that work. It is shown that many of them were translated literally, but for some of the phrases the translators found identical or equivalent metaphorical expressions. The translatability of some expressions from French to English is also discussed by giving various possibilities.

3155. Bourel, Claude. "Les travaux et les jours en pays de Penthièvre à travers dictons et proverbes." *Langue et littérature orales dans l'Ouest de la France.* Eds. Michel Bonneau and Georges Cesbron. Angers: Publication de l'Université d'Angers, 1983. 144–153.

The author comments on so-called "weather proverbs" or meteorological superstitions collected in the Penthièvre area of the Bretagne in France. Bourel divides his French textual materials into four sections of winter, spring, summer, and autumn. Most of the proverbs refer to agricultural work and the weather or to specific calendar days and their saints as prognostic weather signs. Since many texts are cited in dialect form, some etymological, linguistic and cultural explanations as well as a map are included.

3156. Bowden, Betsy. "[Like a Rolling Stone]." In B. Bowden. *Performed Literature. Words and Music by Bob Dylan.* Bloomington/Indiana: Indiana University Press, 1982. 77–80 and 193–195 (text).

These pages contain short comments on the fact that lines from rock songs have functioned like proverbs among the youth subculture. Bowden mentions in particular that the line "When you ain't got nothing, you got nothing to lose" out of Bob Dylan's (1941–) famous song "Like a Rolling Stone" (1965) has definitely passed into proverbial usage. She also gives a keen interpretation of this song with its obvious link to the traditional English proverb "A rolling stone gathers no moss." Bowden explains different meanings of this proverb, emphasizing its significance in the African American tradition. In the appendix she records textual variants of this popular American proverb song. For proverbs in popular music see also Wolfgang Mieder (no. 3910).

3157. Braet, Herman. "'Cucullus non facit monachum': Of Beasts and Monks in the Old French *Renart* Romance." *Monks, Nuns, and Friars in Mediaeval Society.* Eds. Edward B. King, Jacqueline T. Schaefer, and William B. Wadley. Sewanee/Tennessee: The Press of the University of the South, 1989. 1616–169.

The author presents a general discussion about animals and religious life in the medieval French epic *Roman de Renart* (1165/1205). He explains that the fox and the wolf play a major role, and he also shows how monks and nuns are depicted in both positive and negative ways. The article contains some comments on the medieval Latin proverb "Cucullus non facit monachum" (The cowl doesn't make the monk). Braet also mentions that this literary work is filled with cultural information concerning the Middle Ages. Proverbs and proverbial expressions are used for didactic and also for satirical purposes, and this folk speech is of great importance for the understanding of this epic.

3158. Braff, David L., Ira D. Glick, and Peggy Griffin. "Thought Disorder and Depression in Psychiatric Patients." *Comprehensive Psychiatry*, 24 (1983), 57–64.

Using among other standard tests the Donald R. Gorham proverbs test (see no. 557), the authors studied the critical relationship of level of depression and general psychopathology to thought disorder and the level of depression in schizophrenic versus depressive patients. Results indicate that both schizophrenics and depressives had decreased abstraction ability compared with controls. Schizophrenics also had a dramatic, but not pathognomonic, increase in idiosyncratic abstractions. Increased abstraction disorder significantly correlated with increased level of general psychopathology but not with the level of depressive symptoms. A 23–item bibliography (pp. 63–64) is attached, but there is a lack of references to folklore studies concerning proverb interpretation and meaning.

3159. Brandt, Gisela. "Feste Wendungen." In Erwin Arndt and G. Brandt. *Luther und die deutsche Sprache.* Leipzig: VEB Bibliographisches Institut, 1983. 215–219.

The author gives an overview of Martin Luther's (1483–1546) interest in and use of German proverbs, proverbial expressions and idioms. Brandt refers to Luther's proverb translations in the Bible and his satirical writings. She also explains that many texts became proverbial only in the wording which Luther gave them. Luther also used numerous proverbs in his fables, helping to popularize the proverbial expression of the "Wolf im Schafskleid" (Wolf in sheep's clothing). Luther's frequent proverb use is typical for the Reformation of the 16th century, as can be seen in the writings of such contemporaries as Johann Eck (1486–1543), Johannes Agricola (1494–1566), Hieronymus Emser (1478–1527) and Ulrich von Hutten (1488–1523).

3160. Bratu, Ion I. "Contributii la bibliografia paremiologiei românesti." *Proverbium Dacoromania*, 2 (1987), 47–52; and 3 (1988), 28–32.

The first part of this invaluable bibliography lists 14 Rumanian publications from the 18th to the 20th centuries. In each case Bratu gives the precise bibliographical information and provides detailed annotations and page references where proverbs or proverbial expressions are treated. Among the books are grammars, dictionaries, folklore collections, manuscript catalogues, bibliographies of almanacs, etc. They all represent sources for Rumanian proverbs which would be difficult to locate. In the second part Bratu lists 61 additional sources, many of which are literary works that happen to have proverbs as their titles. Here too he provides very precise bibliographical references, including the name of the author, genre of literary work, place and date of publication, and page numbers.

3161. Braun, Peter, and Dieter Krallmann. "Inter-Phraseologismen in europäischen Sprachen." *Internationalismen. Studien zur interlingualen Lexikologie und Lexikographie.* Eds. P. Braun, Burkhard Schaeder, and Johannes Volmert. Tübingen: Max Niemeyer, 1990. 74–86.

The two authors argue convincingly that the various European languages actually have a lot of proverbs and proverbial expressions in common. This leads them to speak of a certain internationality of proverbial language for which they coin the linguistic term "inter-phraseologism." To prove their point they have put together an impressive list of proverbial expressions referring to body parts (head, heart, and eye). For each German phrase they also list the English, French and Italian parallels. A discussion of the syntactical and semantic structure of these expressions is included, and as a last point the authors do mention that there are, of course, also expressions that are quite unique to individual languages.

3162. Breuillard, Jean. "Proverbes et pouvoir politique: Le cas de l'U.R.S.S." *Richesse du proverbe.* Eds. François Suard and Claude Buridant. Lille: Université de Lille, 1984. II, 155–166.

Important article on the frequent use of proverbs not only in Russian literature but also in modern Soviet publications. Proverbs to this day play a major role in the oral and written communication in the Soviet Union. Breuillard points out that this is particularly true for the language of politics. Vladimir Ilich Lenin (1870–1924) and especially Nikita Khrushchev (1894–1971) used proverbs a great deal, and the same is true for today's politicians. It is also stated that the rich Russian proverb heritage is preserved in the large collection *Poslovitsy russkogo naroda* (1862) by Vladimir Ivanovich Dal' (1801–1872) from which Breuillard quotes many examples in French translation. A few modern parodistic "pseudo"-proverbs or slogans reflecting on societal problems are cited as well.

3163. Briggs, Charles L. "The Pragmatics of Proverb Performances in New Mexican Spanish." *American Anthropologist,* 87, no. 4 (1985), 793–810. See also the expanded version with the title "Proverbs" in C. Briggs. *Competence in Performance. The Creativity of Tradition in Mexicano Verbal Art.* Philadelphia: University of Pennsylvania Press, 1988. 101–135 and 380 (notes).

A fascinating anthropological study of oral proverb performance based on field research carried out in Córdova, a community of about 700 inhabitants located in the mountains of northern New Mexico in the United States. Briggs registers two proverb performances by transcribing his recorded conversations in Spanish with English translations. He then analyzes eight features of the actual proverb use in much detail: (1) tying phrase, (2) identity of owner, (3) quotation-framing verb, (4) proverb text, (5) special association, (6) general meaning or hypothetical situation, (7) relevance to context, and (8) validation of the performance. Two major sections interpreting the function of the proverbs in their context are added, and a significant bibliography (pp. 808–810) as well as an abstract (p. 793) are also included, making this a truly seminal study. The revised version of this essay in Charles Briggs' book adds more transcribed texts and also expands some of the discussion on contextualization of proverbs in actual speech acts.

3164. Broek, Marinus A. van den. "'Ein gut wort eine gute stat findet'. Sprichwort und Redensart in Sigismund Suevus' *Spiegel des menschlichen Lebens.*" *In Diutscher Diute. Festschrift für Anthony van der Lee.* Eds. M.A. van den Broek and G.J. Jaspers. Amsterdam:

Rodopi, 1983. 155–172 (=*Amsterdamer Beiträge zur älteren Germanistik*, 20 [1983], 155–1720.

Studies the use and function of German proverbs and proverbial expressions in 21 sermons of the preacher Sigismund Suevus (also called S. Schwabe, 1527–1596) which were published under the title *Spiegel des menschlichen Lebens* (1587). Broek analyzes how the content of the proverbs and phrases reflects human relationships and behavior, law and justice, fortune and misfortune, superstition, trade, war, and parts of the human body. Many examples are cited, and the author also comments on the general importance of proverbs in Reformation literature.

3165. Broek, Marinus A. van den. "Sprichwort und Redensart in Veit Dietrichs *Etliche Schrifften für den gemeinen man.*" *Leuvense bijdragen*, 75, no. 3 (1986), 307–334.

Reviews the importance of proverbs, proverbial expressions and proverbial comparisons in the German writings of the 16th century and then presents a detailed analysis of the use and function of such proverbial language in the religious writings of the German preacher Veit Dietrich (1506–1549) from Nuremberg. It is argued that proverbial folk speech plays a major didactic and moralistic role in sermons, but it is also used in order to increase the level of communication with the general population. Broek includes a discussion of introductory formulas and presents numerous examples in context. A carefully annotated index of 123 texts is included, making this a major contribution to 16th century paremiography.

3166. Broek, Marinus A. van den. "Sprichwörtliche Redensart und sprichwörtlicher Vergleich in den Erbauungsschriften des Nürnberger Predigers Wenzeslaus Linck (1483–1547)." *Leuvense bijdragen*, 76, no.4 (1987), 475–499.

This is a third essay on the use and function of proverbial expressions and proverbial comparisons in the writings of a preacher during the age of the Reformation, this time the didactic essays and sermons of the preacher Wenzeslaus Linck (1483–1547) from Nuremberg. Broek discusses the content of many phrases and includes etymological, historical and cultural explanations. Most expressions refer to body parts (heart and hand), animals, war, and the devil. The essay concludes with an annotated index of 76 texts that is of much importance for historical paremiography.

3167. Broek, Marinus A. van den. "Sprichwort und Redensart in den Werken des Leipziger Volkspredigers Marcus von Weida." *Beiträge zur Erforschung der deutschen Sprache,* 7 (1987), 168–181.

A detailed analysis of the use and function of German proverbs, proverbial expressions and proverbial comparisons in the religious writings of the folk preacher Marcus von Weida (1450–1516) from Leipzig. Broek cites many examples out of sermons in context and argues that this proverbial folk speech adds to the didactic, moralistic and popular tone of this literature. He also includes a statistical table studying the frequency of the proverbial texts. An annotated index of 56 texts is attached, registering important variants for the historical study of German expressions.

3168. Broek, Marinus A. van den. "Sprichwörtliche Redensarten in Flugschriften der frühen Reformationsbewegung." *Zeitschrift für Germanistik,* 10, no. 2 (1989), 192–206.

In this long essay printed in double columns Broek presents a wealth of German proverbial expressions which he found in broadsheets from the years between 1518 and 1524. He is particularly interested in their language, content and meaning, and for most texts he adds detailed explanatory notes. The many texts are divided into groups like knights and war, law and government, peasants, hunting, customs, trade and occupation, housing, games and enjoyment, misfortune and need, Bible, and expressions referring to parts of the body. Broek includes a discussion of the importance of proverbial language during the age of the Reformation, arguing that it serves both a religious and a didactic purpose on these broadsheets. Due to space limitations there is unfortunately no proverb index that would have been of great benefit to the historically interested paremiographer.

3169. Broek, Marinus A. van den. "'lieb reden macht guot freund'. Zum Sprichwortgebrauch in der frühreformatorischen Flugschriftenliteratur." *Wirkendes Wort*, 40, no. 2 (1990), 164–178.

This article is an investigation of the *bona fide* proverbs that are included in the broadsheets from the years between 1518 and 1524 from which Broek had already culled the proverbial expressions for his previous article (no. 3168). The author once again includes some general statements of the use and function of proverbs during the age of the Reformation. Most proverbs that are used in the satirical and polemic broadsheets stem from the Bible, but there are also proverbs which comment on basic human behavior. It is certainly understandable that quite a few texts deal with God, priests and the devil in light of the religious struggles that were going on at the time. Broek includes an annotated index of the 57 proverbs at the end of the article.

3170. Broek, Marinus A. van den. "Sprachliche Vergleiche in der frühreformatorischen Flugschriftenliteratur." *Proverbium*, 8 (1991), 29–53.

This is the third article on the proverbial language of the German broadsheets from the years between 1518 and 1524 (see nos. 3168 and 3169). This time Broek reports on the proverbial comparisons, citing many texts with detailed linguistic, historical and cultural explanations. Most phrases deal with religion, God, Bible, devil, animals, pride, greed, money, etc. Broek also refers to variations which indicate that many of these proverbial comparisons were not as fixed as one would assume. At the end he once again includes an annotated index composed of 70 proverbial comparisons, a number that is increased to 92 if the variants are counted as well.

3171. Bronner, Simon J. "The Haptic Experience of Culture ['Seeing is Believing, but Feeling is the Truth']." *Anthropos*, 77 (1982), 351–362.

This paper discusses the sense of touch in cultural life in its relationship to the human processes of testing and expressing reality and meaning. Through a detailed analysis of the English proverb "Seeing is believing, but feeling is the truth" Bronner argues that humans are active, selective manipulators who use visual perception as a concomitant mechanism to haptic experience in order to judge reliability and clarity in palpable artifactual terms. Other proverbs and proverbial expressions referred are "To hear it from the horse's mouth," "The proof of the pudding is in the eating," "To be in good hands," "Adversity is the touchstone of friendship," "Touch my property, touch my life." With 7 illustrations. See also the next entry (no. 3172) and Alan Dundes (no. 2330).

3172. Bronner, Simon J. "['Seeing is Believing'] . . . but 'Feeling's the Truth'." *Tennessee Folklore Society Bulletin*, 48, no. 4 (1982), 117–124.

Somewhat shortened version of the previous paper (see no. 3171) arguing once again that humans use vision as a concomitant mechanism to haptic experience so as to evaluate standpoints and to judge reliability and clarity in palpable artifactual terms. The emphasis in this article lies on the interpretation of the English proverb "Seeing is believing, but feeling is the truth" in terms of American culture. See also Alan Dundes (no. 2330).

3173. Brooke, Pamela. "Picture Talk: Proverbs, Similes, and other Folk Speech." *Instructor*, no volume given (March 1987), 92–94.

A general magazine article discussing a number of English proverbs, proverbial expressions, and proverbial comparisons (similes) as "picture talk," i.e. metaphorical language. A few major collections of such phrases are mentioned as teaching materials, and a strong case is being made for including proverbial texts in the teaching of English. Possible classroom activities like changing proverbs, interpreting them, collecting them, writing a story about them, etc. are mentioned. Above all it is argued that students should be encouraged to translate the images of proverbs into humorous drawings. As part of cultural literacy proverbs certainly should be integrated into the language arts curriculum. With 5 illustrations.

3174. Brookman-Amissah, Joseph. "Akan Proverbs about Death." *Anthropos*, 81, nos. 1–3 (1986), 75–85.

Stresses the fact that the use of proverbs among the Akan peoples of Ghana in Africa is mainly an oral art which serves as a rhetorical device to add spice to speech and human discourse. Perhaps even more importantly, proverbs are used as a means of conserving and conveying the society's traditions, institutions, values, and culture. Brookman-Amissah analyzes a number of texts in English translation referring to death, studying their origin, meaning and function. The worldview concerning the universality and causes of death as well as the concepts of life after death and the role of God in proverbs commenting on death are analyzed. A bibliography (p. 85) and an English abstract (p. 85) are included.

3175. Brouzeng, Evelyne. "Stylistique comparée de la traduction de proverbes anglais et français." *Richesse du proverbe*. Eds. François Suard and Claude Buridant. Lille: Université de Lille, 1984. II, 51–60.

This is a careful analysis of the manifold problems of translating proverbs from one language to the other. Brouzeng cites English and French examples and comments on their translatability. If an identical proverb exists in the other language, then there is no problem. However, a translator often is faced with having to find an equivalent proverb with a different image but the same meaning in the target language. Sometimes there is no choice but to translate a given proverb literally, maintaining at least the proverbial structure, style and meaning. At the end Brouzeng argues that there is a definite need for bilingual proverb collections to aid translators with this vexing problem.

3176. Bruster, Douglas. "The Horn of Plenty—Cuckoldry and Capital in the Drama of the Age of Shakespeare." *Studies in English Literature 1500–1900*, 30, no. 2 (1990), 195–215.

The author starts with the description of a monument called "Cuckold's Haven" or "Cuckold's Point" which stood outside of London as a symbol of cuckoldry in the form of a makeshift arrangement of a wooden pole topped by animal horns. He then cites many examples out of Renaissance drama which refer to this sign of cuckoldry, including references from the plays of John Taylor (1578?–1653), Thomas Dekker (1570?–1632), William Shakespeare (1564–1616) and many others. But the essay also treats such proverbial expressions as "To wear the breeches" and above all "To be a cuckold." It is pointed out that merchants in particular were often shown as cuckolds. For more etymological essays on the proverbial figure of the cuckold and the proverbial expressions belonging to it see Johannes Bolte (no. 179 and 183), Paul Falk (no. 424), Hermann Dunger (no. 2333), (?) Lütcke (no. 2611), and Robert Graber and Gregory Richter (no. 3497).

3177. Buddruss, Georg. "Wakhi-Sprichwörter aus Hunza." *Studia Grammatica Iranica. Festschrift für Helmut Humbach.* Eds. Rüdiger Schmitt and Prods Oktor Skjaervo. München: R. Kitzinger, 1986. 27–44.

One of the very few linguistic and anthropological studies that deal with the proverbs of the Wakhi language from the Hunza area in northern Pakistan. The author had collected proverbs there during field research in 1982, and he now presents 24 transcribed texts with German translations. There are detailed etymological explanations, and Buddruss also provides very helpful semantic and cultural explanations. Altogether this is a fine example of studying proverbs from another culture about which is very little known. A useful bibliography (pp. 42–44) is attached.

3178. Buddruss, Georg. "Zur ältesten Sammlung von Sprichwörtern und Rätseln der Shina-Sprache." *Studien zur Indologie und Iranistik*, 13–14 (1987), 39–57.

Up to now nearly 800 proverbs have been recorded in the modern Indo-Aryan Shina dialect of Gilgit in Pakistan. The oldest corpus of Shina proverbs and riddles was collected by G.W. Leitner (1840–1899) in 1866 and published in *The Indian Antiquary*, 1 (1872), 91–92. Buddress now re-edits this valuable collection of 23 proverbs and 7 riddles on the basis of his own field research in the Gilgit region during 1980 to 1983. Leitner's phonologically underdifferentiated spellings are rewritten phonemically and his English translations and explanations have been corrected where necessary. An analytical glossary and etymological notes have been added as well. Parallels have been quoted from more recent collections of proverbs and riddles in Shina and some neighboring languages. With a helpful bibliography (pp. 55–56) and an English abstract (p. 57).

3179. Buhofer, Annelies Häcki. "Alltägliche Verstehens- und Erklärungsstrategien bei Phraseologismen." *Aktuelle Probleme der Phraseologie.* Eds. Harald Burger and Robert Zett. Bern: Peter Lang, 1987. 59–77.

This is an interesting study reporting on how adults on a Swiss radio program have dealt with explaining common Biblical proverbial expressions to children. Buhofer explains that their procedure falls into three categories: (1) explanations of the correct language and form of the phrases, (2) historical explanations of the metaphors, and (3) quite detailed explanations of the meaning. The author cites several transcriptions from the radio show in Swiss German and High German translations and argues that lay-people use definite metalinguistic strategies to explain phraseological units to young learners.

3180. Bülow, Ralf. "Stell dir vor, es gibt einen Spruch . . ." *Der Sprachdienst,* 27 (1983), 97–100.

An attempt to find the origin of the German expression "Stell dir vor, es gibt Krieg, und keiner geht hin" (Suppose they gave a war and nobody came). Bülow shows that this popular graffiti started in the United States during the Vietnam war. But its actual coining might go back to Thornton Wilder (1897–1975) or Carl Sandburg (1878–1967) who both lived in Chicago in the early thirties. Bülow mentions an early Wilder anecdote which might have been picked up by Sandburg in his epic poem *The People, Yes* (1936) as "Sometime they'll give a war and nobody will come." In the meantime this American statement has become proverbial in German as well and is found often as graffiti with appropriate variations. See also Reinhard Roche (no. 4247) and Beat Suter (no. 4450).

3181.   Bülow, Ralf. "Eine kleine Sponti-Bibliographie." *Der Sprachdienst,* 29 (1985), 79–80.

Bülow presents a 24–item German bibliography of collections of so-called "Sponti-Sprüche," i.e. modern graffiti and other one-liners collected from walls, newspapers, magazines, and posters. Many of them are in fact parodied proverbs, slogans, aphorisms, advertisements, etc. The author groups his titles according to publishers and adds short critical comments. He also lists the address of a German graffiti archive under the direction of Axel Thiel (H.-Pierson-Straße 6, 3500 Kassel, Germany). Many of the texts in these popular collections are varied "Antisprichwörter" (anti-proverbs).

3182.   Bünker, Michael. "'Gebt dem Kaiser, was des Kaisers ist!' -Aber was ist des Kaisers? Überlegungen zur Perikope von der Kaisersteuer." *Kairos. Zeitschrift für Religionswissenschaft und Theologie,* 29 (1987), 85–98.

A very detailed and scholarly study of the Biblical proverb "Gebt dem Kaiser, was des Kaisers ist" (Render onto Caesar the things which are Caesar's). Bünker starts with a discussion of how Martin Luther (1483–1546) and following him many theologians, historians and politicians have interpreted this imperial tax. There are many historical and legal references concerning the attitudes towards state taxes from Roman times to the modern age. Bünker includes, of course, also a discussion on the use of the proverb in various books of the Bible and in particular in the speech of Jesus (see Mark 12,13; Matt. 22,21; Luke 20,25). For other studies of this proverb see Ivar Benum (no. 142), Martin Rist (no. 1552), J. Denney (no. 2315), and Terence White (no. 3003).

3183.   Burger, Harald. "Neue Aspekte der Semantik und Pragmatik phraseologischer Wortverbindungen." *Phraseologie und ihre Aufgaben. Beiträge zum 1. Internationalen Phraseologie-Symposium vom*

12. bis 14. Oktober 1981 in Mannheim. Ed. Josip Matesic. Heidelberg: Julius Groos, 1983. 24–34.

Significant discussion concerning semantic and pragmatic aspects of phraseological units, especially German proverbial expressions. It is argued that such expressions are not at all as "fixed" in their structure and meaning as has usually been assumed. Burger also points out that the understanding of an expression does not necessarily depend on grasping the meaning of individual words, as can be seen in the comprehension of phrases with archaic words. A discussion of how literary quotations (geflügelte Worte) become proverbial follows, and finally there is a short statement on the different use of proverbial expressions depending on the stylistic level and mode of communication (television, news, everyday speech, etc.).

3184. Burger, Harald, "Phraseologie in den Wörterbüchern des heutigen Deutsch." *Studien zur neuhochdeutschen Lexikographie.* Ed. Herbert Ernst Wiegand. Hildesheim: Georg Olms, 1983. III, 13–66.

In this important study Burger investigates the chaotic lexicographical treatment of phraseology in modern German dictionaries, particularly in Günther Drosdowski, *Duden. Das große Wörterbuch der deutschen Sprache,* 6 vols. (1976–1981); Ruth Klappenbach and Wolfgang Steinitz, *Wörterbuch der deutschen Gegenwartssprache,* 6 vols. (1964–1977); Gerhard Wahrig, *Deutsches Wörterbuch* (1980); Lutz Mackensen, *Deutsches Wörterbuch* (1982); Gerhard Wahrig, *Deutsches Wörterbuch in sechs Bänden* (1980–1984), and others. Burger discusses the problems of defining and classifying various phraseological units and also mentions the confusing terminology to describe them. The second part of the article deals with various suggestions of how to treat idioms, proverbial expressions, proverbs, etc. in dictionaries. Burger argues that such fixed expressions should be listed under more than one of their key-words if at all possible, that semantic explanations should be added, and that they should be placed at the end of a given word entry. Above all, each dictionary should state clear guidelines at the beginning, and editors should be consistent in their treatment of phraseological materials.

3185. Burger, Harald. "Funktionen von Phraseologismen in den Massenmedien." *Aktuelle Probleme der Phraseologie.* Eds. H. Burger and Robert Zett. Bern: Peter Lang, 1987. 11–28.

Starting with a discussion of Werner Koller's work on the use and function of phraseological units in the mass media (see no. 894–896), Burger argues that such fixed phrases are not necessarily primarily manipulative as Koller had maintained. Citing examples of German proverbial expressions from the press, radio and television in context, the author is able to show that these phrases can also serve the purpose of political information, metaphorical argumentation, stating personal opinions, etc. At the end of his article Burger comments on the use of proverbial expressions in talk and quiz shows on television, stating that they are employed quite naturally in spontaneous verbal communication.

3186. Burger, Harald. "Normative Aspekte der Phraseologie." *Beiträge zur allgemeinen und germanistischen Phraseologieforschung.* Ed. Jarmo Korhonen. Oulu: Oulun Yliopisto, 1987. 65–89.

Interesting comments on normative aspects of phraseology, i.e. the "correct" use of a given proverbial expression. Burger starts by discussing synchronic aspects, pointing out that morphology, syntax and semantics all are decisive factors in deciding whether a phraseological unit is used "properly" or not. All of this is complicated by the fact that diachronic changes have taken place leading to variants that compete with each other. Next Burger mentions that dictionaries are of little use solving these problems since they are rather inconsistent in their treatment of proverbial texts. A detailed list of annotated German examples along these lines and a valuable bibliography (pp. 87–89) are included.

3187. Burger, Harald. "Die Semantik des Phraseologismus: ihre Darstellung im Wörterbuch." *Beiträge zur Phraseologie des Ungarischen und des Deutschen.* Ed. Regina Hessky. Budapest: Lorand-Eötvös-Universität, 1988. 69–97.

In this article Burger returns to the problem of how dictionaries should deal with the vexing problem of registering phraseological units (see no. 3184 above). A particular lexicographical concern is how to indicate the meaning of fixed phrases, and Burger makes the following suggestions: (1) there should be some comments relating to semantics, (2) some explanations dealing with pragmatics of actual use should be provided, and (3) dictionaries should indicate the difference between literal and figurative meaning. Burger cites many German and some English and French examples throughout the article. A helpful bibliography (pp. 95–97) is attached.

3188. Burger, Harald. "'Bildhaft übertragen, metaphorisch . . .' Zur Konfusion um die semantischen Merkmale von Phraseologismen." *Europhras 88. Phraséologie Contrastive. Actes du Colloque International Klingenthal-Strasbourg, 12–16 mai 1988.* Ed. Gertrud Gréciano. Strasbourg: Université des Sciences Humaines, 1989. 17–29.

This time Burger concentrates his discussion on the problem of how lexicographers of German and French dictionaries deal with the difficulty of labelling certain fixed phrases as being figurative or metaphorical. It is pointed out once again that there is a great deal of confusion in how to indicate semantic aspects of phraseological units in dictionaries. Burger cites many examples and comes to the conclusion that this chaotic situation needs definite attention from linguists, phraseologists, and lexicographers. As things stand now, dictionaries that use various symbols or verbal designations for the levels of metaphoricity of phrases are somewhat arbitrary at best and will confuse the actual user.

3189. Burger, Harald. "Phraseologie und Intertextualität." *Europhras 90. Akten der internationalen Tagung zur germanistischen Phraseologieforschung, Aske/Schweden 12.-15. Juni 1990.* Ed. Christine Palm. Uppsala: Acta Universitatis Upsaliensis, 1991. 13–27.

Burger reports on a study that investigated the use and function of phraseological units in 230 Austrian, German, and Swiss television advertisements. He found that 50% of these advertisements contain at least one fixed phrase, and he explains the use and function of these proverbs, proverbial expressions, and proverbial comparisons. They certainly add metaphorical language to advertising slogans, and they usually appear in the headline and with lesser frequency in the text itself. Burger cites numerous contextualized examples to prove that this proverbial language has become a major communicative element of television advertisements. He also explains that the fixed phrases are manipulated at times to create special effects so that the consumer will pay attention to the product being advertised. A short bibliography (pp. 26–27) is attached.

3190. Burger, Harald, Annelies Buhofer, and Ambros Sialm. *Handbuch der Phraseologie.* Berlin: Walter de Gruyter, 1982. 435 pp.

An extremely informative handbook of all aspects of phraseology based primarily on German textual materials. Section 1 (pp. 1–19) introduces phraseology and its relationship to other sciences (i.e. linguistics, philology, folklore, literature, etc.); section 2 (pp. 20–60) deals with questions of classification and terminology (ie. twin formulas, proverbs, literary quotations, etc.); section 3 (pp. 61–104) discusses formal and structural concepts (i.e. variability, variants, structure, and semantics); section 4 (pp. 105–167) analyzes pragmatic aspects (i.e. speech act, situation, context, stylistic level, rural and urban environment, social groups, etc.); section 5 (pp. 168–223) presents psycholinguistic aspects of using phraseological units (i.e. comprehension, modification, etc.); section 6 (pp. 224–273) studies the learning of fixed expressions (i.e. by children, students, foreigners, etc.); section 7 (pp. 274–314) contains problems of contrastive phraseology (i.e. dialect differences, foreign languages, wordplay, etc.); and section 8 (pp. 315–382) places phraseology in its historical perspective (i.e. etymology, translation, sources, dictionaries, etc.). Throughout the book many examples are cited from literature, speeches, advertisements, oral speech and other sources. Statistical tables, graphs, a Swiss German glossary (pp. 383–398), a very complete bibliography (pp. 399–408), and a detailed index of all expressions cited (with sections on German, Swiss German, Russian, French, English, and Swedish expressions) as well as a name index are included. This large handbook printed in double columns is without doubt a basic research tool for the entire field of synchronic and diachronic phraseology.

3191. Burger, Harald, and Angelika Linke. "Historische Phraseologie." *Sprachgeschichte. Ein Handbuch zur Geschichte der deutschen Sprache und ihrer Erforschung.* Eds. Werner Besch, Oskar Reichmann, and Stefan Sonderegger. Berlin: Walter de Gruyter, 1985. II, 2018–2026.

Significant handbook article describing the nature and purpose of historical phraseology. Burger and Linke start by discussing the definition, metaphor and semantics of phraseological units or fixed expressions. Next they analyze the lexicographical problems that arise from properly including proverbial expressions, clichés, and idioms in various types of dictionaries. A major section of this essay deals with the diachronic study of individual expressions, commenting on lexical, etymological, historical, and cultural matters. The authors also treat the structure, grammar and syntax of such fixed phrases. Special attention is paid to variants and twin formulas. Finally there are detailed comments on archaic as well as very modern expressions. Numerous German examples are cited throughout this highly informative article. A bibliography (pp. 2025–2026) is included.

3192. Burger, Harald, and Robert Zett (eds.). *Aktuelle Probleme der Phraseologie. Symposium 27.-29. September 1984 in Zürich.* Bern: Peter Lang, 1987. 321 pp.

This is a published collection of 18 major lectures delivered at an international symposium on phraseology from September 27–29, 1984, in Zürich, Switzerland. Included are: Harald Burger, "Funktionen von Phraseologismen in den Massenmedien" (pp. 11–28); Irina Cernyseva, "Strukturelle Mehrgliedrigkeit sprachlicher Zeichen als kognitives Problem" (pp. 29–40, not annotated); Gertrud Gréciano, "Das Idiom als Superzeichen. Pragmatische Erkenntnisse und ihre Konsequenzen" (pp. 41–57); Annelies Häcki Buhofer, "Alltägliche Verstehens- und Erklärungsstrategien bei Phraseologismen" (pp. 59–77); Jürg Häusermann, "Phraseologismen und Sprichwörter als

Formulierungshilfe in der argumentativen Rede" (pp. 79–95); Regina Hessky, "Ein kontrastives Arbeitsmodell—dargestellt an deutsch-ungarischem Material" (pp. 97–108); Werner Koller, "Überlegungen zu einem Phraseologie-Wörterbuch für Fremdsprachenunterricht und Übersetzungspraxis" (pp. 109–120); Peter Kühn, "Phraseologismen: Sprach-handlungstheoretische Einordnung und Beschreibung" (pp. 121–137); Károly Morvay, "Phraseology in Bilingual Dictionaries. Phraseological Aspects of the Compilation of a Concise Catalan-Hungarian Dictionary" (pp. 139–150); Hans-Peter Naumann, "Unikale Komponenten im Schwedischen" (pp. 151–168); Velta Ruke-Dravina, "Die lettische Phraseologie im Vergleich mit zwei germanischen Sprachen—dem Deutschen und dem Schwedischen" (pp. 169–186); Arno Ruoff, "Einschränkungsformeln in südwestdeutscher Alltagssprache" (pp. 187–200; not annotated); Rainer Eckert, "Zur literarischen Phraseologie (an slawischem Material)" (pp. 203–224); Wolfgang Eismann, "Zeichenbausteine als Zeichen. Das Alphabet in der Phraseologie" (pp. 225–243); Maria Leonidova, "Komparative Phraseologismen im Russischen, Bulgarischen und Deutschen" (pp. 245–257); Josip Matesic and Jürgen Petermann, "Zur Problematik der arealen Phraseologie am Beispiel des Kroatischen, Russischen und Deutschen" (pp. 259–267); Antica Menac, "Gemeinsame semantische Gruppen in der Phraseologie der europäischen Sprachen" (pp. 269–290); and Joze Toporisic. "Historisch bedingter geistiger Hintergrund slovenischer Sprichwörter und Redewendungen" (pp. 291–321). For annotations of these essays dealing with problems of function, phraseological units, mass media, idioms, comprehension, proverbs, orality, dictionaries, foreign languages, translation, speech acts, literature, semantics, semiotics, history, culture, etc. see nos. 3185, 3505, 3179, 3573, 3586, 3702, 3741, 3983, 3993, 4293, 3357, 3374, 3378, 3821, 3844, 4479.

3193. Burgos, Luis Antonio. *Inter-Rater Reliability and the Use of Proverb Interpretation in the Detection of Disordered Thinking.* Diss. United States International University, 1985. 89 pp.

This dissertation investigates the reliability among raters with similar training when using the interpretation of a proverbs test in the psychological assessment of disordered thinking. The results of the study of 45 individuals reacting to 10 proverbs showed a very low level of agreement among professional raters. This must be taken as a serious problem as far as the use of proverbs tests for the purpose of studying subjects' reasoning, thought disorder, cognitive focussing, and concept formation is concerned. A copy of the test (pp. 80–85) and a valubale bibliography (pp. 67–71) including references to the use of a proverbs test for analyzing schizophrenia are part of this study.

3194. Buridant, Claude. "Les proverbes et la prédication au Moyen Âge. De l'utilisation des proverbes vulgaires dans les sermons." *Richesse du proverbe*. Eds. François Suard and C. Buridant. Lille: Université de Lille, 1984. I, 23–54.

Starting with the premise that in the Middle Ages teaching and preaching is exegesis, this leading French paremiologist studies the use of popular proverbs in sermons. Buridant analyzes medieval proverb collections and many sermons from that period, proving that the proverbs function primarily as pedagogical, didactic and moralistic bits of wisdom in these religious contexts. Many Latin texts with French translations including introductory formulas and short contextual statements are cited. For the Biblical proverbs the author also provides the precise references to the Old and New Testament. The detailed notes (pp. 46–54) contain important bibliographical information.

3195. Buridant, Claude. "L'approche diachronique en phraséologie: quelques aspects de l'ancien et du moyen français." *Europhras 88. Phraséologie Contrastive. Actes du Colloque International Klingenthal-Strasbourg, 12–16 mai 1988.* Ed. Gertrud Gréciano. Strasbourg: Université des Sciences Humaines, 1989. 31–42.

Starting with the correct statement that phraseologists have hitherto been primarily concerned with synchronic studies of phraseological units, Buridant now advances the argument that much more attention needs to be paid to diachronic aspects of fixed phrases. He expresses the desire that all kinds of phrases from older periods of the French language should be looked at, i.e. twin formulas, proverbs, proverbial expressions, etc. They all are formulaic statements that express some kind of metaphorical authority within certain contexts. Cultural historians and linguists interested in phraseology of Old French and the medieval Middle French should work together to register and explain the meaning of this definite rich treasure of old expressions.

3196. Burkhart, Dagmar. "Bulgarische Rätsel und Sprichwörter (Ein Vergleich zweier Kurzformen der Volksdichtung)." *Bulgarien. Internationale Beziehungen in Geschichte, Kultur und Kunst.* Eds. Wolfgang Gesemann, Kyrill Haralampieff, and Helmut Schaller. Neuried: Hieronymus, 1984. 19–25.

This is a short but informative theoretical paper on the similarities and differences between riddles and proverbs. Burkhart starts by stating that both short forms of folk poetry have their rhythmic language, their use of metaphors and various rhetorical features (i.e. rhyme, alliteration, etc.) in common. These poetic textual matters increase the memorability of riddles and proverbs. But Burkhart also mentions that there are definite semiotic differences in these two genres which consist of one or more descriptive elements, notably the fact that riddles deal with specificity while proverbs concern themselves with generalizations. Three structural diagrams and many Bulgarian examples are included. It is, however, surprising that the Bulgarian texts are not cited with German translations.

3197. Burkhart, Dagmar. "Die semiotischen Dimensionen des russischen Sprichworts." *Beiträge zur russischen Volksdichtung.* Ed. Klaus-Dieter Seemann. Wiesbaden: Otto Harrassowitz, 1987. 13–37.

Starting with a discussion of definition problems regarding proverbs, Dagmar Burkhart presents an historical overview of Russian and Soviet paremiology and paremiography. Then she discusses proverbs as expressions of national character, their poetics, structure, content, etc. Of major importance is her linguistic analysis of numerous Russian examples without translations cited primarily out of *Poslovitsy russkogo naroda* (1862) by Vladimir Ivanovich Dal' (1801–1872). Proverbs are interpreted as signs, and it is argued that paremiology must consider the newest findings of semiotics. She refers especially to the previous work of Grigorii L'vovich Permiakov (nos. 1424, 1428, 1433), Peter Seitel (no. 1704), and Zoltán Kanyó (no. 829). Four diagrams and a useful bibliography (p. 37) are included in this major theoretical contribution.

3198. Burns, D.A. "A Potpourri of Parasites in Poetry and Proverbs." *British Medical Journal* 303 (December 21–28, 1991), 1611–1614.

This is a short essay on the appearance of such parasites as fleas, lice, mites, and bed bugs in English poetry and proverbs. Burns points out that these little insects play a major role in literary works and folk language, and he cites numerous examples from literary sources and proverb collections. Among the authors who have written poems about these parasites are John Donne (1573–1631), Robert Burns (1759–1796), and Gordon Bottomley (1874–1948). But these insects also are mentioned quite frequently in proverbs and proverbial expressions, where they usually refer to certain human character traits or to things of little value. The author also explains that the fixed phrases do contain basic medical wisdom. Three illustrations are included.

3199. Burrow, John Anthony. "'Young Saint, Old Devil'': Reflections on a Medieval Proverb." *Review of English Studies*, 30 (1979), 385–396; now rpt. in J. Burrow. *Essays on Medieval Literature*. Oxford: Oxford University Press, 1984. 177–191.

This is a philological and historical study of the medieval proverb "Young saint, old devil" and its variants. Burrow discusses its use and function in the context of the poem "The Merle and the Nychtingaill" by William Dunbar (1465?–1530?). He also quotes the proverb from two 15th century English proverb collections and cites two 13th century French texts as earliest occurrences of the proverb, for example from Vincent de Beauvais (1200–1264). In addition there are textual references from the works of Geoffrey Chaucer (1340?–1400) and Sir David Lindsay (1490–1555). The antithesis expressed in the proverb is also alluded to by William Shakespeare (1564–1616) and by Henry Fielding (1707–1754) in his novel *The History of Tom Jones*

(1749). Altogether a fine example of an historical and comparative study of an individual proverb from the Middle Ages (see also no. 241).

3200. Burton, John D. *An Information Processing Analysis of the Interaction of Proverbs by Grade Nine Students: An Exploratory Study*. Diss. University of Ottawa, 1989. 195 pp.

Burton used a proverbs test to study the ability of 80 ninth graders to understand proverbs. Students were given three proverb sets and each set contained one proverb, two abstract sentences, and six concrete sentences that were more or less related to the proverb's figurative meaning (for a sample see p. 81). Each student was asked to think aloud while ranking each sentence in a proverb set according to how well it illustrated the figurative meaning of the proverb. The author discusses various types of mental processing and concludes that many factors (analysis, analogy, cognition, etc.) make up the global process involved in the interpretation of proverbs. The second chapter (pp. 9–73) contains a detailed review of research on proverb comprehension, and 15 statistical tables, 6 graphs, a useful bibliography (pp. 155–170), and various appendices conclude this interesting dissertation.

3201. Burton, T.L. "Proverbs, Sentences and Proverbial Phrases from the English *Sidrak*." *Mediaeval Studies*, 51 (1989), 329–354.

This is an important paremiographical article registering the proverbs contained in the English *Sidrak* (14th century), a Middle English verse translation of an Old French prose encyclopedia cast in question and answer form. Burton registers all the proverbs, sentences and proverbial expressions from this early source with special reference to Bartlett Jere Whiting's (1904–) monumental collection *Proverbs, Sentences, and Proverbial Phrases from English Writings Mainly Before 1500* (Cambridge, Massachusetts: Harvard University Press, 1968). While his new texts provide many additional citations for Whiting's collection, Burton also has unearthed a total of 72 proverbial texts that were not listed in Whiting thus far. This is certainly a substantial addition to the corpus of Middle English proverbs.

3202. Bushui, Anatolii Mikhailovich et al. *Paremiologiia Uzbekistana.* Samarkand: Samarkandskii gosudarstvennyi pedagogicheskii institut, 1981, 1982, and 1983. III, 250 pp.; IV, 58 pp. V, 73 pp.

Having already published two bibliographical volumes previously (see no. 2255), Bushui and his colleagues T.A. Bushui, G.M. Gazarova, A.A. Iahshiev, S.D. Mastepanov, and R.H. Salimova now continue this extremely valuable work with three additional volumes registering the rich paremiological and paremiographical publications dealing with proverbs, proverbial expressions, clichés, idioms, and phraseology of the Uzbek Soviet Socialist Republic in central Asia of the Soviet Union. The third volume contains rich bibliographical information concerning the treatment of Uzbek proverbs in various languages (Russian, Bulgarian, English, etc.). The same attention is given to the Crimean proverbs of the Crimean Soviet Socialist Republic. The fourth volume covers proverbs in newspapers, proverbs of certain geographical regions in Uzbek, and the use of names in these texts. Finally, the authors continue the registration of proverbs in newspapers and magazines in the fifth volume of this meticulously prepared bibliography. It should also be mentioned that these volumes contain various indices, making them very user-friendly indeed and certainly a model for other such bibliographies.

3203. Bushui, Anatolii Mikhailovich. *Osnovnye voprosy teorii frazeologii.* Samarkand: Samarkandskii gosudarstvennyi pedagogicheskii institut, 1987. 236 pp.

This is a major bibliography of the impressive work that Soviet scholars have done in the field of phraseology. It is divided into many sections and does include publications from other Eastern European countries, including the German Democratic Republic. Bushui has registered dictionaries of phraseology and scholarship on classification problems, stylistics, structure, lexicography, content, variability, metaphor, etc. In the second part of the book he presents 22 examples of how scholars have dealt with various types of phraseological units in dictionaries, including such proverbial expressions as "To make a mountain out of a molehill" and "The other side of the coin." Altogether

the bibliography contains 1900 items and a good index, making it
an invaluable tool for the international study of phraseology.

3204. Bushui, Anatolii Mikhailovich, and A.A. Ivchenko. *Paremiologiia
Ukrainy.* Samarkand: Samarkandskii gosudarstvennyi
pedagogicheskii institut, 1982 and 1983. I, 150 pp.; II, 143 pp.

This is a two-volume bibliography of the paremiological and
paremiographical publications dealing with materials from the
Ukrainian Soviet Socialist Republic. The first volume includes
sections on the theory of paremiology, Ukrainian proverb
collections, the origin of proverbs, genre problems, language
(form, style, structure, etc.), geographical distribution, proverbs
from various historical periods, content, history and meaning of
individual proverbs, and the pedagogical methodology of the
teaching of proverbs. The second volume is basically an
addendum to the first and is structured in the same manner.
Both volumes contain very detailed indices, making them yet
another invaluable research tool that the untiring Anatolii
Mikhailovich Bushui has provided for internationally interested
paremiologists.

3205. Bushui, Anatolii Mikhailovich, and A.N. Lies. *Paremiologiia Kirgizii.*
Samarkand: Samarkandskii gosudarstvennyi pedagogicheskii
institut, 1987. 85 pp.

In this somewhat smaller bibliography the two authors have
assembled the paremiological and paremiographical publications
that concern themselves with the proverbial materials of the
Kirghiz Soviet Socialist Republic in Asia. The bibliography starts
with a list of the published and unpublished collections of
Kirghiz proverbs and proverbial collections. Collections of
Kirghiz proverbs translated into Russian and collections of
various peoples translated into Kirghiz are also included. A major
section of the bibliography is comprised of Kirghiz proverbial
materials appearing in newspapers and magazines. The last
section registers monographs as well as journal and newspaper
articles dealing with Kirghiz proverbs. A useful index is also
provided.

3206. Buttler, Danuta. "Przyslowia polskie z forma stopnia wyzszego lub najwyzszego." *Prace Filologiczne*, 33 (1986), 95–104.

The author investigates 100 Polish proverbs that contain adjectives, adverbs or participles used in the comparative or superlative. She pays particular attention to the sources, lexical stability, structure (ellipsis, parallelism, rhythm, rhyme, etc.), vocabulary, meaning, and stylistic features of these proverbs. Numerous examples are cited, of which many follow the structural pattern of "Im . . ., tym . . ." (The more . . ., the more . . .). It is pointed out that many proverbs go back to classical times and that there seems to be a lack of newer texts. The difficulty of understanding some of them is due to their archaic vocabulary and to their polysemanticity.

3207. Buttler, Danuta. "Dlaczego zanikaja przyslowia w dwudziestowiecznej polszczynie?" *Poradnik Jezykowy*, 5 (1989), 332–337.

Buttler attempts to explain why proverbs are slowly disappearing from the Polish language of the 20th century. She argues that proverbs are definitely used less, and if they are used at all, they are usually reduced to mere "Schwundstufen" (remnants). Literary authors and journalists often shorten the actual proverb texts in their book titles and newspaper headlines. People also merely allude to the old proverbs in oral speech rather than quoting the longer traditional proverb. The lesser use of proverbs in the modern Polish society might be explained by certain social and cultural changes, especially the change from a rural to an urban society. The archaic metaphors or older vocabulary of the proverbs are often no longer understood by the younger generation, and the result is that more and more proverbs seem to be disappearing.

3208. Bykova, A.A. "Semioticheskaia struktura velerizmov." *Paremiologicheskie issledovaniia.* Ed. Grigorii L'vovich Permiakov. Moskva: Nauka, 1984. 274–293; also in French translation as "La structure sémiotique des wellérismes" in *Tel grain tel pain. Poétique de la sagesse populaire.* Ed. G.L. Permiakov. Moscou: Éditions du Progrès, 1988. 332–356.

Solid study of the semiotic structure of wellerisms. Bykova offers a definition of this genre and then differentiates between the popular (folkloric) and literary wellerism. The latter goes back to the character Samuel Weller in Charles Dickens' (1811–1870) novel *The Pickwick Papers* (1837). While such "artificial" wellerisms usually serve entertaining or ironical functions, the traditional wellerisms function much more normatively. Three essential components belong to a *bona fide* wellerism: (1) a statement, (2) a speaker, and (3) a situation. But Bykova adds a fourth structural element, namely an introducer (words introducing the proverb). Many Russian examples and 2 diagrams are included.

3209. Bynum, Joyce. "Folk Speech—A Dying Art." *ETC. A Review of General Semantics*, 44 (1987), 308–311.

This is a short note suggesting that folk speech in a modern technological society like that of the United States is not necessarily decreasing in currency. Using cab drivers from San Francisco as her informants, Bynum presents a number of English clichés, idioms, and proverbial expressions in their conversational context. Many of the cited phrases would have to be classified as American slang, but there are also some variations of traditional proverbs that make use of standard proverbial structures.

3210. Bynum, Joyce. "More About Proverbs." *ETC. A Review of General Semantics*, 44 (1987), 192–195.

Basically an addendum to the previous general note (no. 3209) commenting on various types of proverb uses and functions. It is mentioned that orators and politicians make frequent use of proverbs in their speeches. Proverbs are often employed by people to console, advise, instruct, judge, etc. Bynum stresses in particular the fact that proverbs play a major role in modern American advertising. Numerous English examples are cited with short explanations. She closes her note by referring to some important Anglo-American proverb collections and bibliographies.

3211. Bynum, Joyce. "Proverbs." *ETC. A Review of General Semantics,* 44 (1987), 88–91.

In this third short article Bynum presents a general introduction to the study of proverbs by citing several English examples. She mentions the old *Proverbium* (1965–1975) journal and the new *Proverbium: Yearbook of International Proverb Scholarship* (1984ff.), points out the difficulty of defining proverbs and differentiating them form other genres (aphorisms, clichés, slogans, maxims, etc.), and mentions their importance in literature of all types. She also discusses the function, meaning, style, structure, and use of proverbs in the modern American society.

C

3212. Caluwé-Dor, Juliette de. "Les proverbes de Hendyng: Héroisme paien, charité chrétienne et réalisme bourgeois." *Richesse du proverbe.* Eds. François Suard and Claude Buridant. Lille: Université de Lille, 1984. I, 55–73.

The article starts with a review of the scholarship regarding the medieval English proverb collection entitled *Proverbs of Hendyng* (14th century). Caluwé-Dor compares this collection with others of that period, mentions the three manuscripts that exist of it, and speculates on who the author might have been. Next she presents a detailed content analysis of some of the proverbs, arguing that they comment on pagan heroism, Christian charity and medieval reality. In an appendix (pp. 65–73) the author translates a 39–stanza manuscript of Hendyng proverbs into French. See also Karl Kneuer (no. 877) and Samuel Singer (no. 1742).

3213. Calvez, Daniel Jean. *Le langage proverbial de Voltaire dans sa correspondance du 29 décembre 1704 au 31 décembre 1769.* Diss. University of Georgia, 1980. 343 pp.; now also published as *Le langage proverbial de Voltaire dans sa correspondance (1704–1769).* New York: Peter Lang, 1989. 312 pp.

The author states that proverbs were not held in high esteem in French literature and thought of the 18th century. However, an investigation of 35 volumes of letters by François-Marie Voltaire (1694–1778) proves that proverbs, proverbial expressions and sententious remarks continued to be used despite their condemnation by critics. Calvez studies Voltaire's use of French proverbial language, and he also includes remarks on his use of English, Spanish, Italian, and Latin proverbial materials. Voltaire prefers using sententious remarks and proverbial expressions, while he employs actual proverbs with circumspection, often

modifying them in one way or another. Calvez concludes that
Voltaire does not have a very positive attitude towards proverbs.
The major part of this book (pp. 33–285) is a richly annotated list
of all proverbial texts which is of highest value to French
paremiographers of the 18th century. A useful bibliography (pp.
287–296) and a key-word index (pp. 297–309) are included. See
also no. 246.

3214.   Camp, Claudia V. *Wisdom and the Feminine in the Book of Proverbs.*
Diss. Duke University, 1982. 359 pp.

A lucid treatment of the meaning and function of
personified wisdom in the Book of Proverbs, explaining its female
imagery. Camp analyzes the metaphorical quality of female
wisdom in this part of the Old Testament, she examines the
context and style in the presentation of this proverbial wisdom,
and she also interprets this personified wisdom as a religious
symbol. Some references to Biblical proverbs are included, and
the bibliography (pp. 322–344) contains important references to
wisdom literature.

3215.   Canavaggio, Jean. "Calderón entre refranero y comedia: De
refrán a enredo." *Aureum Saeculum Hispanum: Beiträge zu Texten des
Siglo de Oro. Festschrift für Hans Flasche.* Eds. Karl-Hermann Korner
and Dietrich Briesemeister. Wiesbaden: Steiner, 1983. 27–36.

Studies the use and function of Spanish proverbs in the plays
of Pedro Calderón de la Barca (1600–1681) of the Spanish
Golden Age. Canavaggio mentions that even some of the titles of
these plays are proverbial, but the proverbs obviously also play a
major role in the development of the dramatic plot. Numerous
Spanish examples are cited in their dramatic context, and it is
argued that Calderón uses them as expressions of popular
philosophy, worldview, wisdom, morality, and folk speech. No
proverb index is included, but a diagram (p. 36) illustrating the
use of proverbs in the speech acts of three plays is attached.

3216.   Canavaggio, Jean. "Calderón entre refranero y comedia: De
refrán a enredo." *Calderón: Actas del Congreso internacional sobre
Calderón y el teatro español del Siglo de Oro.* Ed. Luciano Garcia

Lorenzo. Madrid: Consejo Superior de Investigaciones Cientificas, 1983. I, 381–392.

This is a slightly expanded version of the previous paper (no. 3215) carrying the identical title. The major changes consist of the fact that Canavaggio was able to include a few more examples of Spanish proverbs in their dramatic context in the plays of Pedro Calderón de la Barca (1600–1681). Mention is once again made of proverbial titles, and it is argued that proverbs in the literary texts represent expressions of general philosophy, morality, wisdom, and folk speech. There is no proverb index, and the diagram of the previous study has also not been reproduced.

3217. Cantalapiedra, Fernando. "Los refranes en *Celestina* y el problema de su autoria." *Celestinesca: Boletin Informativo Internacional,* 8, no. 1 (1984), 49–53.

Detailed statistical analysis of the comical and tragicomical use of Spanish proverbs in the 21 acts of *La Celestina* (c. 1499). It is proven that in the first 12 acts the proverb frequency is much higher than in the second 9 acts. Cantalapiedra attempts to show by these findings that there is a definite break in the use of proverbial speech after the 12th act. Perhaps the first dozen acts are by an anonymous author while the last acts were in fact written by Fernando de Rojas (1465–1541). Six comparative tables of the proverb distribution in this major work of Spanish literature are included.

3218. Cantemir-Vlad, Elena. "Cîteva observatii asupra unor modalitati do construire a pseudo-proverbelor." *Proverbium Dacoromania,* 2 (1987), 41–46.

The author studies 16 Rumanian pseudo-proverbs from a linguistic and structural point of view. It is pointed out that such pseudo-proverbs follow the expected poetics of traditional proverbs, i.e. they exhibit parallelism, rhyme, metaphor, etc. In fact, some pseudo-proverbs are nothing more than intentional variations of existing proverbs. Cantemir-Vlad includes examples contrasting the real with the "false" proverb. Other pseudo-proverbs are based on established proverbial structures giving

them the appearance of having gained proverbiality. But what is
missing with these pseudo-proverbs or "anti-proverbs" is their
currency in the Rumanian language.

3219. Carnes, Pack. "The American Face of Aesop: Thurber's Fables
        and Tradition." *Moderna Språk*, 79 (1986), 3–17; rpt. in P. Carnes
        (ed.). *Proverbia in Fabula. Essays on the Relationship of the Fable and
        the Proverb*. Bern: Peter Lang, 1988. 311–331.

        An intriguing analysis of James Thurber's (1894–1961)
        adaptations of traditional Aesopian fables and fairy tales. Carnes
        explains that Thurber often closes his narratives with a proverbial
        epimythium, but the moralistic wisdom is usually expressed in the
        form of an "Antisprichwort" (anti-proverb). The author includes
        a splendid interpretation of Thurber's version of the fable of the
        "Tortoise and the Hare" and its new moral: "A new broom may
        sweep clean, but never trust an old saw." Other proverbial
        endings of Thurber's fables are for example "It is not as easy to
        get the lion's share nowadays as it used to be," "You can fool too
        many of the people too much of the time," "Early to bed and
        early to rise makes a male healthy and wealthy and dead," etc.
        Such proverb alienations and parodies are humorous or satirical
        statements indicating that established values and standards are no
        longer applicable in the modern American society. The notes
        (pp. 15–17) include valuable bibliographical references
        concerning the interrelationship of the fable (folk narrative) and
        proverb genres.

3220. Carnes, Pack. "Wayland Debs Hand as Folklorist." *Proverbium*, 3
        (1986), 1–4.

        A heartfelt introduction to the third volume of *Proverbium*
        which is a "Festschrift" for the American folklorist and
        paremiologist Wayland Debs Hand (1907–1986) who
        unfortunately died literally about ten hours before this yearbook
        could be presented to him at the annual meeting of the
        American Folklore Society in Baltimore, Maryland. Carnes
        reviews Hand's great influence on American and international
        folklore scholarship, especially in the areas of beliefs,
        superstitions, medical folklore, mythology, and proverbs. The

tribute praises Hand as one of the giants of folklore studies. For Wayland Hand's paremiological contributions see nos. 658–662 and nos. 2442–2443.

3221. Carnes, Pack (ed.). *Proverbia in Fabula. Essays on the Relationship of the Fable and the Proverb.* Bern: Peter Lang, 1988. 343 pp.

This is a highly significant essay volume of 13 previously published articles on proverbs and the fable put together by the leading American scholar on the fable. Among the essays are: Paul Franklin Baum, "The Fable of Belling the Cat" (pp. 37–46); Walter Wienert, "Das Wesen der Fabel" (pp. 47–64); Ben Edwin Perry, "Fable" (pp. 65–116); Karl August Ott, "Lessing und La Fontaine: Von dem Gebrauche der Tiere in der Fabel" (pp. 117–163); Walter Mettmann, "Spruchweisheit und Spruchdichtung in der spanischen und katalanischen Literatur des Mittelalters" (pp. 165–193); John-Theophanes Papademetriou, "The Mutations of an Ancient Greek Proverb" (pp. 195–208); Helmut van Thiel, "Sprichwörter in Fabeln" (pp. 209–232); Jan Fredrik Kindstrand, "The Greek Concept of Proverbs" (pp. 233–253); Roland Richter, "Sprichwort und Fabel als dialektischer Denkvorgang" (pp. 255–275); Burckhard Garbe, "Vogel und Schlange: Variation eines Motivs in Redensart, Fabel, Märchen und Mythos" (pp. 277–283); Anne-Marie Perrin-Naffakh, "Locutions et proverbes dans les fables de La Fontaine" (pp. 285–294); Sandra Dolby-Stahl, "Sour Grapes: Fable, Proverb, Unripe Fruit" (pp. 295–309); and Pack Carnes, "The American Face of Aesop: Thurber's Fables and Tradition" (pp. 311–331). The editor has included an informative general introduction (pp. 11–36) and a valuable bibliography (333–343) to this important essay volume that touches on a multitude of connections between fables and proverbs ranging from classical antiquity to the modern age. For annotations see nos. 112, 2079, 1435, 1395, 1202, 1406, 1916, 850, 1543, 501, 2738, 2901, 3219.

3222. Carnes, Pack. "The Fable and the Proverb: Intertexts and Reception." *Proverbium*, 8 (1991), 55–76.

This is a comprehensive study of the similarities and differences between the two related genres of the proverb and the fable. Carnes explains that many proverb/fable complexes share a common motif, such as can be seen in the proverbs and fables about "Sour grapes" or "Belling the cat," for example. The author also discusses aspects of metaphor, meaning, and function, drawing his examples from the fables of Aesop, Jean de La Fontaine (1621–1695), and James Thurber (1894–1961). He stresses in particular the intertexuality of these two genres, explaining that they appear in their full texts or in truncated form in songs, folk tales, epics, and literary works. The 61 notes (pp. 69–76) include important bibliographical information.

3223. Carpenter, Bruce N., and Loren J. Chapman. "Premorbid Status in Schizophrenia and Abstract, Literal or Autistic Proverb Interpretation." *Journal of Abnormal Psychology*, 91 (1982), 151–156.

The authors report on the results of using Donald R. Gorham's (see no. 557) proverbs test for testing correct abstraction, literalness and autism in schizophrenia. They conclude that process schizophrenics are not more literal than are reactives, but that the difference in correct abstracting ability is at least in part due to differences in autistic responding. Thus process schizophrenics tend to give more autistic responses to proverbs than do reactives. An informative bibliography (p. 156) and an English abstract (p. 151) are provided.

3224. Carracedo, Leonor. "Misoginia en textos proverbiales sefardies." *Revista de Dialectologia y Tradiciones Populares*, 43 (1988), 87–93.

Carracedo presents a general article on misogyny in Sephardic proverbs from Spain. She starts with a cultural and historical background of the Sephardic proverbial wisdom, and she then explains that there are many proverbs about women which are definitely misogynous and anti-feministic. The author also deals with proverbs that comment on the relationship between men and women. It is shown that men see women as being inferior, weak, and of lesser intelligence. Unfortunately these traditional proverbs are still cited today, even though they express a very negative value system and worldview. Numerous examples are cited together with short behavioral explanations.

3225. Carroll, Margaret D. "Peasant Festivity and Political Identity in the Sixteenth Century." *Art History*, 10, no. 3 (1987), 289–314.

This is primarily an article for art historians, but Carroll does include a short discussion of the treatment of peasant festivities in Johannes Agricola's (1494–1566) German proverb collection *Sybenhundert und fünfftzig Teütscher Sprichwörter* (1534). She also explains how the German artist Hans Sebald Beham (1500–1550) and the Dutch painter Pieter Brueghel (c. 1520–1569) used the proverbial theme of feasting and drunkenness in some of their paintings. Special mention is made of Brueghel's *Twelve Round Proverb Pictures* (1558) which depict these themes as well. With 1 illustration of a round proverb picture.

3226. Carter, Marjorie L. *The Assessment of Thought Disorder in Psychotic Unipolar Depression.* Diss. Catholic University of America, 1983. 197 pp.

Based among others on the John D. Benjamin proverbs test (see no. 141), the author compared 25 hospitalized psychotic depressives, 25 hospitalized chronic paranoid schizophrenics, and 25 normal control subjects. The results showed that psychotic depressives were significantly more thought disordered than normals. Chronic paranoid schizophrenics were also significantly different from normals, but not from depressives. Not only did depressives demonstrate thought pathology in areas more typically associated with schizophrenia, but on two depression-related measures, schizophrenics were not significantly different from depressives. Carter's results indicate that thought disorder is common and not specific to either schizophrenia or depression. Many statistical tables, a number of appendices, and a detailed psychological bibliography (pp. 142–151) are included, but there is little discussion concerning the difficulty with proverb meaning as such in standardized proverbs test that quote the proverbs without any context whatsoever.

3227. Case, Tammy Jean Smith. *The Role of Literal and Figurative Familiarity in Proverb Comprehension.* Diss. University of Cincinnati, 1991. 109 pp.

The author reports on two experiments based on a psychological proverbs test in which subjects were presented with proverbs that ranged in literal and figurative familiarity, preceded by either literal, figurative, or neutral biasing contexts, and time to read proverbs amd contexts was measured. Literal and figurative familiarity were separated by writing new proverbs high in figurative familiarity (subjects would be familiar with the figurative meaning) but low in literal familiarity (subjects would be unfamiliar with the literal form of the proverb). The results failed to support a multi-stage model of figurative comprehension in that there was no overall difference in reading time under the literal and figurative context conditions. However, an interaction between literal and figurative familiarity and type of biasing context is supportive of a multi-stage model. Proverbs higher in literal familiarity were read more quickly than more unfamiliar proverbs under all three biasing conditions. Case includes 14 statistical tables and 2 figures throughout the text of her dissertation, and she also provides a useful bibliography (pp. 82–85), a copy of the proverbs test (pp. 86–100), and 6 additional statistical tables (pp. 101–109) in an appendix.

3228. Catani, Maurizio. "Variations à propos du territoire, de l'espace symbolique et des systèmes de valeurs à travers un dicton espagnol et un proverbe italien qui ne paraissent pas avoir d'équivalent satisfaisant en français." *Revue de l'Institute de Sociologie*, nos. 3–4 (1984), 607–623.

Beginning with the Italian proverb "Moglie et buoi dei paesi tuoi" (Women and oxen should be chosen only from your villages) and the Spanish proverb "Màs vale lo malo conocido que lo bueno por conocer" (A possession [having] is worth more than two "you will have it"), Catani argues that they represent a particular worldview of these two countries. The article is divided into two lengthy comparative sections in which the author investigates the cultural and historical meaning of these two proverbs. In the conclusion it is stated that there does not appear to be any equivalent French proverb that expresses a similar metaphorical opinion. Sociological, anthropological, and geographical differences among national groups result in different value systems and proverbs.

3229. Cattermole-Tally, Francis. "From Proverb to Belief and Superstition: An Encyclopedic Vision or the Legend of Archer Taylor and Wayland D. Hand." *Western Folklore*, 48, no. 1 (1989), 3–14.

In this article Cattermole-Tally tells the story behind the foundation of the California Folklore Society in 1941 and the start of the *California Folklore Quarterly* in 1942 which by 1947 became the *Western Folklore* journal. Based on the correspondence between Archer Taylor (1890–1973) and his protégé and friend Wayland Debs Hand (1907–1986), the author explains how these two great American scholars of the proverb, belief, superstition and much more worked to get the society and the journal to become established as important folklore institutions. For the paremiological publications of Archer Taylor see nos. 1854–1908 and nos. 2933–2939, and for Wayland Hand's contributions to paremiology see nos. 658–662 and nos. 2442–2443.

3230. Cazier, Pierre. "Les 'sentences' d'Isidore de Séville, genre littéraire et procédés stylistiques." *Richesse du proverbe.* Eds. François Suard and Claude Buridant. Lille: Université de Lille, 1984. II, 61–72.

Investigation of the sententious remarks in the writings of the Spanish bishop Isidore of Seville (560?-636). Cazier starts with definition problems, contrasting the Latin term "sententia" with that of other gnomic expressions like the proverb. Next he analyzes Isidore's "sentences" which include much traditional wisdom and which follow stylistic and structural patterns of proverbs and maxims. A few examples in French translation are cited, and Cazier explains their aphoristic style, their proverbial structure, and their philosophical content which make these short sentences appear as early European wisdom literature.

3231. Céard, Jean, and Jean-Claude Margolin. "Rébus et proverbes." In J. Céard and J.-C. Margolin. *Rébus de la renaissance. Des images qui parlent*. Paris: Maisonneuve et Larose, 1986. I, 135–162.

This is a very important book chapter on the interrelationship of proverbs, art, and literature in the French Renaissance. The authors start with a discussion of medieval and later French proverb collections, and they then treat the use and function of proverbs in the works of Charles d'Orléans (1394–1465), François Villon (c. 1431–c. 1463), Eustache Deschamps (c. 1346–c. 1406) and others. But above all they analyze in great detail the proverb illustrations (182 woodcuts) and accompanying eight-line proverb stanzas of a 15th century French manuscript which was edited by Grace Frank and Dorothy Miner as *Proverbes en rimes. Text and Illustrations of the Fifteenth Century from a French Manuscript in the Walters Art Gallery, Baltimore* (Baltimore/Maryland: The Johns Hopkins University Press, 1937; see no. 470). The authors explain the symbolism, meaning, function and didacticism of these proverbial rebus, many of which refer to morals, fools and everyday wisdom. With 14 woodcuts and 108 notes that contain valuable bibliographical information.

3232.   Cheatham, G. "Shakespeare's *The Taming of the Shrew.*" *Explicator*, 42, no. 3 (1984), 12.

A concise note on William Shakespeare's (1564–1616) use of the English proverbial expression "To put [the] finger in the eye" in *The Taming of the Shrew* (1594). Cheatham refers to George Pettie's (1548?–1589) earlier use of the phrase in his *Petite Pallace* (1576) which makes clear that this proverbial gesture and expression has the sarcastic meaning of feigning a few tears.

3233.   Cherkasskii, Mark Abramovich. "Versuch der Konstruktion eines funktionalen Modells eines speziellen semiotischen Systems (Sprichwörter und Aphorismen)." *Semiotische Studien zum Sprichwort. Simple Forms Reconsidered I.* Eds. Peter Grzybek and Wolfgang Eismann. Tübingen: Gunter Narr, 1984. 363–377.

Very important theoretical essay continuing the work of Grigorii L'vovich Permiakov (see no. 1428) on a functional model concerning the semiotic system of proverbs and aphorisms. Cherkasskii discusses the cliché-like, aphoristic and sententious properties of phraseological units. Next he analyzes the semiotic structure of proverbs which is comprised of the explicitly expressed information of the text itself and its only implicitly contained information. This leads the author to a logical-linguistic consideration of proverbs which results in a model based on a logical structure. At the end Cherkasskii presents a two-page chart showing a functional paremiological model based on the German proverb "Besser man ist arm, aber gesund, als reich, aber krank" (It is better to be poor but healthy, than rich but sick). For the Russian original of this essay see nos. 274 and 1433.

3234. Cherkasskii, Mark Abramovich. "Zum Inhalt des Begriffs 'Subtext' unter dem Gesichtspunkt einer Theorie der kommunikativen Tätigkeit." *Semiotische Studien zum Sprichwort. Simple Forms Reconsidered I.* Eds. Peter Grzybek and Wolfgang Eismann. Tübingen: Gunter Narr, 1984. 359–361.

Analysis of the semiotic complexity of proverbs which arises due to semiotic "Inhomogenität" (inhomogeneity) and semiotic "Mehrstufigkeit" (multi-level). Cherkasskii explains various aspects that lead to this complex nature of proverbs, clichés and aphorisms once they are analyzed as signs made up of "subtexts." He comments on equivalent and hierarchical classes and on duplication, syncretism, allegory, and the aphoristic nature of such short texts as proverbs. If one were to consider all of these elements that make up proverbial signs, perhaps it would be possible to construct a generative model for a better and more detailed theoretical understanding of them. For the Russian original of this article see no. 4151.

3235. Chernelev, Vsevolod D. "Paremiia kak ob"ekt sravnitel'nogo issledovaniia." *Filologicheskie nauki*, no. 5 (1990), 21–29.

This is a comparative study of several variants of the Russian proverb "Slovo—ne vorobei" (A word is not a sparrow). Chernelev discusses the use of the noun "word" in various proverbs from classical antiquity to the modern age and then proceeds to analyze this specific Russian text, citing references from the 18th to the 20th centuries. He also includes careful comments on the structural, analogical and semantic aspects of this proverb, pointing out that a similar motif is expressed in Russian fairy tales. The use and function of the proverb and its variants in Russian literature are treated as well.

3236. Chernysheva, Irina I. "Strukturtypologische Phraseologieforschung in der Sowjetischen Germanistik (Überblick und Ausblick)." *Europhras 88. Phraséologie Contrastive. Actes du Colloque International Klingenthal-Strasbourg, 12–16 mai 1988.* Ed. Gertrud Gréciano. Strasbourg: Université des Sciences Humaines, 1989. 43–49.

This is a short review article of the major developments in the study of phraseology since about 1970 in the Soviet Union. Chernysheva stresses the fact that Soviet scholars have been particularly interested in the comparative analysis of phraseological units on a synchronic, diachronic and structural basis. Many studies have also dealt with thematic, semantic, semiotic, and morphological aspects of all sorts of fixed phrases. One of the major findings has been that phraseological units from one language to another are much more universal than was thought to be the case before. While national differences exist in metaphors, for example, the actual linguistic structure and the function of phraseological units as signs is rather similar throughout the world.

3237. Chevalier, Jean-Claude. "Proverbes et traduction (La traduction italienne de la *Célestine*, par Alphonso Hordoñez, Rome, 1506)." *Bulletin Hispanique,* 90. nos. 1–2 (1988), 59–89.

With reference to José Gella Iturriaga's list of 444 Spanish proverbs from the anonymous Spanish tragedy *La Celestina* (c. 1499), Chevalier investigates how Alphonso Hordoñes translated this work and its many proverbs into Italian. He refers to the grammatical problems that this early translator encountered trying to keep as close to the original text as possible. The translator had the most difficulty with the metaphors of the proverbs in those cases where the Italian language had no equivalent proverb. There were also problems with syntax, structure, and meaning, but on the whole the translation is quite satisfactory. Chevalier includes a comparative list of proverbs (pp. 77–89) to indicate Hordoñez' skill as a translator.

3238. Chiche, Michèle. "Proverbes . . . et mon enfance embaume ma mémoire." *Cahiers de littérature orale,* no. 13 (1983), 159–161.

This is a personal account concerning the frequent proverb use by the author's grandmother. Chiche explains how her grandmother talked essentially in proverbs with her grandchildren. Several French examples with short explanations are cited. The author also remembers how she and her sister memorized the proverbs, how they later used them for entertainment in proverb duels, and how they in turn are now teaching the same proverbs to their own grandchildren. A touching account of how traditional proverbs are handed on in a single family from generation to generation.

3239. Chitimia, I.C. "Filologie paremiologica si unitatea poporului român." *Revista de etnografie si folclor*, 36, nos. 3–4 (1991), 107–110.

In this article on paremiological philology Chitimia studies a number of proverbs from various regions of Rumania. The texts are in fact dialect proverbs that only appear to be quite distinct from each other due to some of the phonetic and morphological differences. By careful comparisons of his examples the author is able to show that these dialect proverbs actually go back to common origins, thus proving that indigenous Rumanian proverbs are folkloric proof of the national unity of the Rumanian people. With a French abstract (p. 110).

3240. Chitimia, I.C. "Necesitatea si prioritatea unui corpus paremiologic românesc." *Revista de etnografie si folclor*, 36, nos. 3–4 (1991), 200–204.

The author reviews various Rumanian proverb collections from previous centuries and also comments on regional collections of more recent publication dates. He then argues that it is high time that these impressive paremiographical accomplishments be combined into a major multi-volume national collection of Rumanian proverbs. He also discusses classification problems and makes a strong case for detailed historical annotations to be included for each proverb and its variants. The 16 notes include bibliographical information concerning numerous Rumanian proverb collections.

3241. Chong-ho, Ch'oe. "The Concept of Language in the Traditional Korean Thought." *Korea Journal,* 25, no. 10 (1985), 18–32.

Investigates traditional Korean thought concerning the value and importance of oral language as manifested in proverbs. Chong-ho collected 117 proverbs referring to language, words, speech, talk, etc. from a number of Korean proverb collections. His statistical research shows that 12 proverbs have positive contents, 52 negative contents, and 53 texts are neutral. What the Korean proverbs as a whole are saying is that one must speak when one must, but one must not speak carelessly or too often. Above all, speaking is never better than not speaking. It is concluded that the proverbial attitude towards language and speech is based on a repressionist, negativist, and passivist concept of language. Similar results are presented for this view based on examples in English translation from Korean poetry, novels, and textbooks. For similar studies on Japanese proverbs about speech see J.L. Fischer and Teigo Yoshida (no. 445) and for Indian proverbs see William K. McNeil (no. 1182).

3242. Choul, Jean-Claude. "Règle d'interprétation idiomatique." *Journal of the Atlantic Provinces Linguistic Association,* 4 (1982), 36–53.

Based on a comparative analysis of English and French idioms and proverbial expressions, Choul discusses the nature of their idiomaticity. Semantic and structural problems are analyzed, and there are references to the difficulty in interpreting expressions from a foreign language. Choul also deals in particular with the problem of recognizing what an idiom or a proverbial expression is in a foreign language. Former research on this matter is discussed, and a useful bibliography (pp. 51–53) is attached as well.

3243. Chu, Mike Shan Yuan. *An Approach to American Idioms.* Diss. University of Nebraska, 1985. 317 pp.

This dissertation proposes a method for the teaching of American idioms (including proverbs, proverbial expressions and proverbial comparisons) to non-native speakers of English. In the first part (pp. 1–56) the author discusses the typical language problems of non-native speakers, the problems of comprehending and using idiomatic speech of the target language, and how these problems can be met by classroom teaching and the preparation of textbooks. Chu also deals with the nature of English idiomaticity (figurative nature and grammatical use). In the second part (pp. 59–317) the author presents a teaching program based on 195 idioms and 30 proverbs. They are divided into 30 lessons, each including a dialogue, situation, model sentences, exercises, and a proverb. The short bibliography (pp. 57–58) does not do justice to the pedagogical literature on proverbs for bilingual education, but the textbook (with answers to the exercises) is indeed valuable.

3244. Cincotta, Mary Ann. "Reinventing Authority in *The Faerie Queene.*" *Studies in Philology*, 80, no. 1 (1983), 25–52.

Literary proverb investigation of Edmund Spenser's (1552?–1599) epic poem *The Faerie Queene* (1590–1596). Cincotta comments on the high frequency of proverbs in this work and points out the influence which Erasmus of Rotterdam's (1466–1536) *Adagia* (1500ff.) had on Spenser's interest in proverbs. She discusses the use and function of proverbs as authoritative statements, moral wisdom, practical knowledge, and human experience. Many English texts are cited in their literary context, but there is no proverb index.

3245. Claeys, Patricia Francisa. *Theoretical and Translational Aspects of Phraseology*. M.A. thesis University of New Brunswick, 1989. 175 pp.

This is indeed a valuable M.A. thesis containing superb theoretical and pragmatic information on English, French and German phraseology. In the first part (pp. 1–109) the author deals with a number of theoretical questions, including the problem of a confusing international terminology for phraseology, the distinction between metaphor, idiom and phraseologism, aspects of fixity, stability and variability, the nature of idiomaticity and lexicalization, and finally international findings on the syntactical, semantic and functional aspects of phraseology. The second part (pp. 110–146) is dedicated to translation theory and its application to phraseology. Here Claeys uses diagrams, tables and models to show how phraseological units can be translated from one language into the other, always citing impressive comparative examples from English, French and German. The appendix (pp. 147–166) includes questionnaires which the author used to test her own translation model. An impressive bibliography (pp. 167–175) completes this informative study.

3246. Clogan, Paul M. "Literary Genres in a Medieval Textbook." *Medievalia et Humanistica*, 11 (1982), 199–209.

Clogan analyzes 13 manuscripts of the 13th and 14th centuries of the medieval Latin textbook *Liber Catonianus* and discusses the following five literary genres treated in them: distich, eclogue, fable, elegy, and epic. Of particular interest are the distichs or couplets of Marcus Cato (234 B.C.-149 B.C.) which offered easy and practical wisdom in a collection of philosophical maxims. Included were also popular proverbs which helped to make them a major part in the educational training of the Middle Ages. The six authors included in this school book are Cato, Theodolus (10th cent.), Testus Rufius Avianus (4th cent.), Maximianus (5th cent.), Publius Papinius Statius (40?-96?), and Claudius Claudianus (375?-404?).

3247. Cohen, Gerald Leonard. *Studies in Slang*. 2 vols. Bern: Peter Lang, 1985 and 1989. I, 162 pp.; II, 198 pp.

Two important volumes on Anglo-American slang comprised of numerous essays of individual words, idioms, and proverbial expressions. The first volume is dedicated to Peter Tamony (1903–1985), one of the pioneering scholars of American slang. Quite appropriately this volume reprints several essays by Tamony, including "The real McCoy" (pp. 106–116) and "'Like Kelsey's Nuts' and Related Expressions" (pp. 120–123). Other essays by Cohen himself that are of interest to the paremiologist are "My name is Hanes" (pp. 66–67), "To be a shlemiel" (pp. 71–84), "To be a smart Aleck" (pp. 85–105), and "Hunky-dory" (pp. 125–133). The second volume is dedicated to Kathleen Tamony (1907–1987), sister and lifelong companion of Peter Tamony. Cohen includes his own notes on the following proverbs, proverbial expressions and phrases: "Close but no cigar" (pp. 100–102, with 1 illustration), "In a pig's eye" (pp. 112–113), "There's more than one way to skin a cat" (pp. 118–119), "No soap" (pp. 150–151), and "Semper Fi, Mac" (pp. 154–155). Of interest are also the reprint of Tamony's 1939 essay on "The Allusion in 'Cheese it'!" (pp. 109–111), Leonard Ashley's paper "British 'Get off at Gateshead' and Similar Expressions" (pp. 127–129), Virginia McDavid's "Cute as a button" (p. 135), Jane Robinson's "The goose hangs high" (p. 136), and H.P. Leighly's "He's burning corncobs" (p. 137). Ashley's essay on "Popular Music and the Origins of Some Popular Speech" (pp. 187–191) also includes comments on some phrases, notably "To have a banana with someone" and its sexual connotation. Both volumes contain detailed indices, making them extremely useful to phraseologists.

3248.   Cohen, Leonard Gerald. *Origin of New York City's Nickname "The Big Apple."* Bern: Peter Lang, 1991. 106 pp.

This is a truly fascinating monograph on the proverbial nickname of "The Big Apple" for New York City. In meticulous scholarly detective work Cohen establishes a four-stage development of this phrase: (1) Prior to the 1921 use of the phrase "big apple" in the language of horseracing, there was much proverbial talk about apples, especially about the big "Red Delicious" apples from Iowa that became a well-known trademark in the 1870s; thus the late 19th century expression "Bet you a big red apple . . ."; (2) At the New York horseracing tracks "the big apple" came to designate "the big time" for jockeys/trainers who made it to these races from far away. The journalist John J. Fitz Gerald (?) used the phrase in print the first time in 1921 in the horseracing newspaper *The Morning Telegraph*; (3) In the 1930s "the big apple" was picked up by African American jazz musicians to designate New York City in general as the place where the greatest jazz in the world was played; and (4) In 1971 Charles Gillett (19?-) popularized "The Big Apple" as part of a public-relations campaign on behalf of New York City. The monograph includes hundreds of references of this expression, numerous photographs, a comprehensive bibliography (pp. 83–97), and a detailed name and subject index (pp. 98–106).

3249. Cohen, Naomi G. "Al Taseg Gevul 'Olim' (Peah 5:6, 7:3)." *Hebrew Union College Annual,* 56 (1985), 145–166.

Careful philological and historical study of the Biblical Old Testament proverb "Remove not the landmark which your fathers set" (Prov. 22,28). Parallels from the Talmud, particularly the Mishnah, are cited in Hebrew. It is argued that this saying may well be a non-Biblical popular aphorism, possibly from a now lost part of Ben-Sira's sayings, and in any event of more or less the same vintage. A superb example of Form Criticism showing the history, variants, structure, form, and meaning of an ancient example of wisdom literature.

3250. Colahan, Clark, and Alfred Rodriguez. "Traditional Semitic Forms of Reversibility in Sem Tob's Proverbios morales." *Journal of Medieval and Renaissance Studies,* 13, no. 1 (1983), 33–50.

The two authors argue that the numerous examples of opposition and reversibility of values in Santob de Carrión's (Sem Tob, 14th cent.) medieval Spanish proverb collection *Proverbios morales* can be traced back to Semitic literary forms characterized by an oppositional focus. They discuss in particular three such literary forms: (1) Arabic books on both the good and bad aspects of things, (2) "Munazarat"—Arabic debates between personified abstractions or things (also assimilated into Hebrew literature), and (3) the "mikhtam"—a Hispano-Hebraic epigrammatic and often moralizing proverb featuring the rhyming of homonyms. Examples of this wisdom literature based on reversibility are cited in Spanish and discussed in much detail.

3251. Colless, Edward. "Jacky Redgate: Tradition." *Creative Camera,* 11 (1988), 18–22.

The article reports on a photographic series by the artist Jacky Redgate (19?-) entitled *Naar het Schilder-Boeck* (1985). In these photographs Redgate restages Pieter Brueghel's (c.1520–1569) illustrations of a number of Dutch proverbs in images derived from his famous painting variously known in English as *The Blue Cloak* or *The World Upside Down* or *The Netherlandic Proverbs* (1559). Colless explains that the camera artist has made considerable alterations in her modern pictures of Brueghel's depiction of traditional proverbs. It is argued that these differences are crucial not as demonstrations of photographic codification, nor as ironic commentaries on the source material, but rather for the change of meaning which causes the proverbial utterance to drift away from its didactic motivation. The photographs discussed in this article concern the following four proverbs and proverbial expressions: "Big fish eat little fish," "The world turns on someone's thumb," "To fill in the ditch after the calf has drowned," and "To swim against the stream." With 4 photographs.

3252. Colombi, Maria Cecilia. *Los refranes en "Don Quijote."* Diss. University of California at Santa Barbara, 1988. 236 pp.; now also published as *Los refranes en el Quijote: texto y contexto.* Potomac/Maryland: Scripta Humanistica, 1989. 142 pp.

An impressive literary study of the proverbs contained in Miguel de Cervantes Saavedra's (1547–1616) novel *Don Quijote* (1605–1615) that goes far beyond the traditional way of investigating proverbs in a literary work. Colombi starts with an introductory chapter (pp. 1–25) on definition problems emphasizing recent linguistic theories. In chapter two (pp. 26–46) she covers the structural and semantic aspects of proverbs, while chapter three (pp. 47–83) is dedicated to an analysis of proverbs in discourse. Here she deals with the integration of proverbs into conversation, the special syntax of proverbs, their function in context, and the use of introductory formulas by Cervantes. The fourth chapter (pp. 84–105) analyzes the use of proverbs in the novel by employing modern speech act theories. A short fifth chapter (pp. 106–110) summarizes the effective use that Cervantes has made of proverbs throughout his novel. An appendix (pp. 111–136) lists the 171 proverbs with rich annotations, and the detailed bibliography (pp. 137–142) is a clear indication of Colombi's awareness of modern paremiological research trends.

3253. Colombi, Maria Cecilia. "'Al buen callar llaman Sancho'." *Speculum historiographiae linguisticae.* Ed. Klaus D. Dutz. Münster: Modus Publikationen, 1989. 243–252.

This is an erudite study of the Spanish proverb "Al buen callar llaman Sancho" (A good silence is called Sancho) out of Miguel de Cervantes Saavedra's (1547–1616) novel *Don Quijote* (1605–1615). Colombi cites early 14th to 17th century variants and presents a detailed history of this popular proverb. While the article takes up only the first three pages, the following 17 notes contain significant diachronic materials in context with detailed references to many Spanish proverb collections. The attached bibliography (pp. 250–252) presents a useful list of these important proverb collections.

3254. Colombi, Maria Cecilia. "Los refranes en el Quijote: Discurso autoritario y des-autor-itario." *Proverbium*, 7 (1991), 37–55.

This is the slightly revised fourth chapter "Los refranes como actos de habla" (pp. 84–105) out of Colombi's book *Los refranes en el Quijote: texto y contexto* (see no. 3252 above). It starts with a discussion of proverbs as part of conversational discourse and speech act theory. Colombi then points out that proverbs express historically-derived authority and community-sanctioned wisdom, and she proceeds to show that the use and function of proverbs in Miguel de Cervantes Saavedra's (1547–1616) novel *Don Quijote* (1605–1615) reflect this concern with traditionality and authority. She also explains that proverbs use figurative language to communicate tradition and authority in an indirect fashion. A number of examples are cited in the literary context, showing clearly how Cervantes used proverbs for didactic purposes.

3255. Conca, Maria. "Sobre la semiòtica dels refranys." *Estudis de literatura catalana en honor de Josep Romeu i Fugueras*. Eds. Lola Badia and Josep Massot i Muntaner. Barcelona: Publicacions de l'Abadia de Montserrat, 1986. I, 345–355.

Literary proverb investigation of the *Lletra de batalla per Tirant lo Blanch* (1969) by the Peruvian novelist Mario Vargas Llosa (1936–), citing several proverbs in context and discussing their function. The second part of the article investigates the lyrical use and function of proverbs in the anonymous epic poem *Flor d'enamorats* (16th cent.), once again analyzing a few specific contextualized examples. Conca's particular interest lies in the semiotic aspects of proverbs in Spanish literature. There is no proverb index.

3256. Conca, Maria. *Paremiologia*. Valencia: Universitat de València, 1987. 112 pp.

This is a compact but highly informative monograph on the major theoretical aspects of the proverb based on Spanish materials. Conca starts with a chapter on proverbs as speech acts, emphasizing their descriptive and prescriptive nature (pp. 17–26). The second chapter (pp. 27–48) analyzes the form, structure, rhythm, rhyme, metaphor, and content of proverbs. In the third chapter (pp. 49–69) the author differentiates among such genres as proverb, proverbial expression, adage, sententious remark, apothegm, maxim, aphorism, and slogan, while chapter four (pp. 71–89) is dedicated to a detailed linguistic analysis of proverbs. The fifth chapter (pp. 91–100) covers modern semiotic approaches to the study of proverbs, and a short conclusion (pp. 100–103) gives a concise summary of this valuable study with many Spanish textual examples and structural diagrams. A useful bibliography (pp. 105–111) is attached as well.

3257. Conenna, Mirella. "Sur un lexique-grammaire comparé de proverbes." *Langages*, 23, no. 90 (1988), 99–116.

A very theoretical essay on French and Italian proverbs that begin with the pronoun "qui/chi" (who). Conenna presents a detailed structural analysis of the syntax of such proverbs, studying in particular the use of certain prepositions, adverbs, nouns, etc. Throughout the article the author cites examples in French and Italian, and she includes several comparative tables showing the differences and similarities of this type of proverb. The result is a clear lexical and structural comparison of a group of proverbs from two Romance languages. A useful bibliography (pp. 115–116) is provided.

3258. Constantinescu, Nicolae. "Structuri si expresii proverbiale în nuvela *Duios Anastasia trecea* de D.R. Popescu." *Limba si literatura*, 4 (1989), 567–573; a shorter version of this article with the same title appeared also in *Proverbium Dacoroamania*, 4 (1989), 2–5.

In this literary investigation Constantinescu studies the proverbs and proverbial expressions in the well-known Rumanian short story *Duios Anastasia trecea* (1967) by D.R. Popescu (1935–). Citing a number of examples in their literary context, the author analyzes the structure, meaning, and function of these proverbial texts. He points out that while Popescu quotes several of them in their traditional wording, he also quite often modifies them to suit his own style of writing. It is also pointed out that Popescu invents so-called pseudo-proverbs, i.e. texts which have a proverbial structure but which lack proverbial traditionality. The shorter version of this article in *Proverbium Dacoromania* contains an English summary (p. 5).

3259. Contossopoulos, Nicolas G. "Les proverbes crétois." *Richesse du proverbe.* Eds. François Suard and Claude Buridant. Lille: Université de Lille, 1984. II, 167–181.

General introduction to various aspects of modern Greek proverbs from the island of Crete. Contossopoulos starts by differentiating among proverbs, proverbial expressions and maxims, and then he discusses shortly the content and worldview expressed in them. The style and form (rhyme, rhythm, metaphor, etc.) are analyzed, and it is also pointed out that some texts can be traced back to folk narratives and folk songs. Numerous examples in Greek with French translations are cited together with valuable cultural and historical explanations.

3260. Cooper, Thomas C., and Liselotte Kuntz. "Jugendjargon im Vergleich: Amerika und Deutschland." *Schatzkammer der deutschen Sprache, Dichtung und Geschichte,* 13, no. 1 (1987), 88–110; rpt. in the same journal, 15, no. 2 (1989), 39–59.

Arguing that the youth culture has without doubt its own language that includes slang, idioms and proverbial expressions, the authors claim that attention should be paid to the phraseological units of this subculture by foreign language teachers at the High School level in particular. Based on field research in several schools in the South of the United States, Cooper and Kuntz have assembled a wealth of Anglo-American texts which they divided into 29 categories according to their theme (content), as for example "looks," "love," "homosexual," "agreement," etc. Where it is possible they also provide German equivalent expressions. The last section (no. 29, pp. 109–110) presents an intriguing list of graffiti based on proverbial structures from the German youth culture. The texts a very useful bilingual materials for teaching purposes.

3261. Coppens d'Eeckenbrugge, Monique. "Petits proverbes, grands effets . . . De l'usage des proverbes dans la publicité contemporaine." *Europhras 88. Phraséologie Contrastive. Actes du Colloque International Klingenthal-Strasbourg, 12–16 mai 1988.* Ed. Gertrud Gréciano. Strasbourg: Université des Sciences Humaines, 1989. 51–63.

Basing her remarks on 100 French and Belgian proverbs collected between 1964 and 1968 from television, radio and various journalistic writings, the author analyzes their use and function in the modern mass media. While many of the 38 French and 62 Belgian texts were registered only once, the proverb "Mieux vaut prévenir que guérir" (Prevention is better than cure) appeared 6 times and "Le temps c'est de l'argent" (Time is money) was noticed even 7 times. Three proverbs appeared in English or Latin, and quite a few texts were modified to fit the needs of the contemporary press. Coppens d'Eeckenbrugge also comments on the function, structure, meaning, and modification (changes in vocabulary and/or syntax) of the proverbs. Two statistical tables are included.

3262. Coulmas, Florian. "Ein Stein des Anstoßes. Ausgewählte Probleme der Idiomatik." *Studium Linguistik*, 13 (1982), 17–37.

A linguistically oriented study of the semantic, syntactical and pragmatic aspects of idiomaticity. Under discussion are such phraseological units as proverbial expressions, clichés, twin formulas, stereotypes, literary quotations (geflügelte Worte), proverbs, etc. The meaning, form and use of many German examples are explained in this theoretical paper. Coulmas also deals with definition problems of various proverbial genres. A detailed bibliography (pp. 35–37) is added which introduces the reader to the major scholarship on phraseology.

3263. Coulmas, Florian. "Diskursive Routine im Fremd-sprachenerwerb." *Sprache und Literatur in Wissenschaft und Unterricht*, 16, no. 56 (1985), 47–66.

   Convincingly argued article concerning the importance of including routine formulas in the teaching of foreign languages. Coulmas discusses grammatical, linguistic and contextual aspects of idioms. He explains their use and function in various types of speech acts, and he makes clear that communication in any language is based to a large degree on fixed phraseological units. Phraseology needs to play a much larger role in language instruction. A useful bibliography (pp. 65–66) is attached.

3264. Coy, José Luis. "Los *Dichos de sabios* del manuscrito escurialense b.II.7." *La Coronica: Spanish Medieval Language and Literature Journal and Newsletter*, 13, no. 2 (1985), 258–261.

   Publication of a small anonymous medieval Spanish proverb collection entitled *Dichos de sabios* (Proverbs of the Wise) whose manuscript is located in the library of El Escorial near Madrid. Coy provides a short introduction to the 40 Spanish proverbs which were clearly translated from the Latin. In fact, most texts start with the claim (in Latin) that Aristotle (384 B.C.-322 B.C.), Seneca (4.B.C.-65 A.D.) and others used to say these proverbs. The collection belongs to that group of small pseudo-Aristotelian proverb collections which were translated from the Latin into many vernacular languages during the Middle Ages.

3265. Cragie, Stella. "Translation Equivalence in English and Italian Proverbs." *The Incorporated Linguist*, 23, no. 2 (1984), 79–81.

   Discusses the difficulty of translating proverbs from one language into another, stating that often they are untranslatable. Even if there is an equivalent proverb in the target language, it does not necessarily have the same currency or popularity of the proverb of the source language. When translating proverbs their meaning, metaphor, structure, and style must be considered. The actual context of the proverb must also be understood in order to find a proper translation. All of this is illustrated by attempts of translating Italian proverbs into English and vice versa.

3266. Cram, David. "The Linguistic Status of the Proverb." *Cahiers de lexicologie*, 43 (1983), 53–71.

This is a clearly argued article stating from a linguistic point of view that the proverb should be viewed as a lexical element with a quotational status. The proverb is a lexical element in the sense that it is a syntactic string which is learned and reused as a single unit with frozen internal structure. Its quotational status derives from the fact that proverbs are typically "invoked" or "cited" rather than straightforwardly asserted. All of this is explained in detail in three sections of the paper: (1) proverbial competence: the proverb as a lexical item; (2) proverbial performance: the proverb as a speech act; and (3) proverbial logic: proverb systems and proverbial thinking. Cram proposes to view a proverb as a lexicalized syntactic string which serves as an illocutionary type of speech act. Two figures, numerous examples, and an informative bibliography (pp. 69–71) complement this significant linguistic study of proverbiality based on English materials.

3267. Cram, David. "A Note on the Logic of Proverbs." *Proverbium*, 2 (1985), 271–272.

A tongue-in-cheek yet at the same time only too true comment on the vexing problem of contradictory proverbs. In four stanzas of two rhymed couplets each Cram discusses the pragmatics, contradiction, logic, and lack of logic of proverbs. Despite its ironic intent, the poem does in fact address questions of proverbiality and the often (falsely!) claimed universality of proverbs. See also Nkeonye Otakpor (no. 4093).

3268. Cram, David. "Argumentum ad lunam: On the Folk Fallacy and the Nature of the Proverb." *Proverbium*, 3 (1986), 9–31.

This is a significant theoretical article on folk fallacies which Cram labels as "argumentum ad lunam" (i.e. If they can put a man on the moon, surely if they put their minds to it they could solve the problem of the common cold [or unemployment, foot odour, etc.]). Cram deals with the definition and taxonomy of folk fallacies, and he then shows how the existence of contradictory proverbs can be explained along these lines.

Whether a proverb is considered true very much depends on the particular interpretation of that text in the context of a given speech act. Two diagrams and an appendix of various types of folk fallacies are attached.

3269. Crane, Mary Thomas. *Proverbial and Aphoristic Sayings: Sources of Authority in the English Renaissance.* Diss. Harvard University, 1986. 464 pp.

A voluminous literary dissertation studying the authority of sayings—proverbs, aphorisms, maxims, gnomes, and adages—from classical times to the English Renaissance. The first chapter (pp. 24–98) investigates sayings in ancient logic and rhetoric, commenting in particular on the views of Aristotle (384 B.C.-322 B.C.), Marcus Tullius Cicero (106 B.C.-43 B.C.), Marcus Quintilian (c. 35 A.D.-c. 96 A.D.), and Seneca (4 B.C.-65 A.D.). In the second chapter (pp. 99–167) Crane discusses divine and human authority in the Bible and religious writers with special emphasis on Boethius (480?-524?), Saint Augustine (354–430), The Venerable Bede (673–735), and Saint Bonaventura (1221–1274). Chapter three (pp. 168–248) deals with Erasmus of Rotterdam's (1466–1536) view of traditional wisdom and the authority of sayings in 16th century England. The fourth chapter (pp. 249–324) covers gnomic epigrams and poems of 16th century England, especially by such authors as Robert Crowley (1518?-1588), John Heywood (1497?-1580), John Parkhurst (1512?-1575), and Sir Thomas Wyatt (1503–1542). The fifth chapter (pp. 325–377) is dedicated exclusively to Francis Bacon (1561–1626), and chapter six (pp. 378–442) investigates the sayings in the epigrams of Ben Jonson (1572–1637) and Robert Herrick (1591–1674). An invaluable bibliography (pp. 443–464) concludes this rich study.

3270. Csanda, Sándor. "Beniczky Péter magyar és szlovak verses példabeszédei." *Irodalomtörteneti kozlemények,* 89, no. 3 (1985), 259–270.

This is a detailed literary and textual study of *Les paraboles hongroises communes* (1664) by the Hungarian poet Péter Beniczky (1606–1664). The work is bssically a versified collection of

Hungarian and Slovakian proverbs and moral axioms, of which a manuscript containing the original Slovakian proverbs was found in 1984. Csanda now compares the Hungarian proverb texts with the Slovakian originals and is able to show that many of them are indeed identical while others show considerable differences. Many examples are cited, and the author argues that Beniczky probably wrote both language versions of the proverbs down in his poetic work. A French abstract (p. 270) is provided.

3271. Cunningham, Dellena M., Stanley E. Ridley, and Alfonso Campbell. "Relationship between Proverb Familiarity and Proverb Interpretation: Implications for Clinical Practice." *Psychological Reports*, 60 (1987), 895–898.

This psychological study examined whether performance on measures of proverb interpretation is influenced by the examinees' familiarity with the proverbs to be interpreted. Subjects used a seven-point scale to indicate the extent to which they were familiar with the 12 proverbs on a proverbs test. The 103 college students participating in this test definitely showed that familiarity with proverbs has a considerable influence on interpretation. Obviously this has important implications also for the clinical practice of using proverbs tests for schizophrenia and other mental testing. An English abstract (p. 895) and a 14–item bibliography (pp. 597–598) are included.

3272. Curat, Hervé. *La locution verbale en français moderne. Essai d'explication psycho-systématique.* Québec: Les Presses de l'Université Laval, 1982. 319 pp.

Superb linguistic study of French verbal phrases of which many are proverbial expressions. In 13 detailed chapters based on many examples and including numerous diagrams, charts and statistical tables, Curat deals with definition problems, language, form, meaning, structure, grammar, etc. of phraseological units. The author also investigates the use of nouns, verbs, infinitives, and adjectives in these expressions. While most of the examples concern themselves with modern texts, Curat does discuss the need for synchronic and diachronic approaches. A large appendix (pp. 215–298) presents a useful list of texts arranged alphabetically according to the verb of the phraseological units. Statistical tables of frequency studies are included as well, and a large bibliography (pp. 299–313) concludes this important book.

3273. Curat, Hervé. "La relation privilégiée entre l'agent et l'objet dans les locutions verbales." *La locution. Actes du colloque international Université McGill, Montréal, 15–16 octobre 1984.* Eds. Giuseppe Di Stefano and Russell G. McGillivray. Montréal: Editions CERES, 1984. 28–55.

Linguistic analysis of such French proverbial expressions as "Prendre racine" (To take root). Curat points out that in the pattern "prendre X" the definite article is missing, and he presents detailed structural and lexical comments based on many examples. Several diagrams and charts help to understand the special relationship between the agent and the objects in such phraseological units. A short bibliography (p. 55) dealing with such verb-noun phrases is attached.

3274. Curtius, Ernst Robert. "Verkehrte Welt." In E.R. Curtius. *Europäische Literatur und lateinisches Mittelalter.* Bern: Francke, 1948 (3rd ed. 1961). 104–108.

This is a short book chapter on the important proverbial motif "Die verkehrte Welt" (The World-upside-down) as it appears in Latin poetic works of the Middle Ages. Curtius states that these enumerations of proverbial impossibilities often employ animal metaphors, he cites a number of medieval examples, and he traces the motif back to the classical age of Aristophanes (445?-385 B.C.). He also refers to Pieter Brueghel's (c. 1520–1569) artistic depiction of this motif in his oil painting *Netherlandic Proverbs* (1559), and he cites a German literary example out of the works of Hans Jakob Christoffel von Grimmelshausen (c. 1622–1676).

3275. Cuxac, Ceselha. "Lo temps dels provèrbis." *Gai Saber: Revista de l'Escola Occitana*, 64 (1982), 360–364.

General article on weather proverbs in the Occitan language which is a dialect of Provençal. Cuxac cites examples dealing with the four seasons and particularly with saint days. Their value as weather prophecies is discussed, and there are also some comments concerning the validity of these proverbs for actual weather forecasting. Many of the texts are in fact superstitions, while others do contain rural weather wisdom that has been handed down from one generation to another.

3276. Czegle, Imre. "Szaraszi Ferenc, mint Erasmus Adagia-janak magyarra ültetöje." *A Raday Gyüjtemény Evkönyve,* 4–5 (1984–1985), 122–137.

This is a detailed philological study of how Latin proverbs out of Erasmus of Rotterdam's (1469–1536) *Adagia* (1500ff.) were translated into Hungarian. Czegle reports in particular on the handwritten notes by Ferenc Szaraszi (16th century) in a 1559 Basel edition of the *Adagia,* many of which are in fact Hungarian translations of these classical proverbs. The author compares these 16th century Hungarian texts with those that appeared in print in 1598 in a Hungarian translation of Erasmus' *Adagia.* About 70% of the texts agree with the renditions by Szaraszi, thus indicating that Erasmus of Rotterdam had a major influence on spreading classical proverbial wisdom in Hungary as is the case for all the other European national languages.

D

3277. Daalder, Joost. "Wyatt's Proverbial 'Though the Wound Be Healed, Yet a Scar Remains'." *Archiv für das Studium der neueren Sprachen und Literaturen*, 138 (1986), 354–356.

This is a study of the origin and history of the English proverb "Though the wound be healed, yet a scar remains" which is included in a poem by Sir Thomas Wyatt (1503–1542). Daalder also cites the use of the proverb in yet another poem by Henry Howard Surrey (1517?–1547) who probably was influenced by Wyatt's text. Ultimately the proverb goes back at least as far as the Greek philosopher Zeno (336? B.C.-264? B.C.), the founder of stoicism. The author includes a detailed analysis of the literary relationship between Wyatt and Surrey based on their treatment of this proverb.

3278. Dadson, Trevor J. "La Biblioteca de Alonso de Barros, autor de los *Proverbios morales* [1598]." *Bulletin Hispanique*, 89, nos. 1–4 (1987), 27–53.

Starting with a short discussion of Alonso de Barros' (1540?–1604) Spanish proverb collection *Proverbios morales* (1598), Dadson moves on to a detailed description of the life and works of this writer of the Golden Age of Spain. The major part of the article (pp. 35–53) is an annotated list of 151 books of Barros' personal library. The books concern such matters as politics, philosophy of moral instruction, and socio-cultural aspects of the 16th century. The learning that Alonso de Barros gained from these books is later reflected in his *Proverbios morales* that was issued in several editions. French and Spanish abstracts (p. 27) are included.

3279. Dalfovo, A.T. "Lugbara Proverbs and Ethics." *Anthropos*, 86 (1991), 45–58.

113

This is an informative anthropological study of 936 African proverbs which the author collected during field research among the Lugbara people from Uganda. Dalfovo analyzes the origin of these proverbs which express everyday experience and traditional wisdom of family life. Some proverbs also deal with magico-religious topics, and there are many texts which contain animal metaphors. In another section of his paper Dalfovo deals with the language of these proverbs, i.e. shortness, fixidity, metaphor, form, and pithiness. The second part of the article is concerned with the ethics (worldview and value system) expressed in these proverbs, showing that many of them are normative and didactic. It is stressed that proverbs need a context to be understood, but it is surprising that the author cites barely any examples to support his otherwise very interesting findings. Three statistical tables on the religious topics, the number of words in the texts, and the popularity of these proverbs are included, and so is an English abstract (p. 45).

3280. Daniel, Jack L., Geneva Smitherman-Donaldson, and Milford A. Jeremiah. "Makin' a Way outa no Way: The Proverb Tradition in the Black Experience." *Journal of Black Studies*, 17, no. 4 (1987), 482–508.

Stating that scholars of African American proverbs should have a global view of Africa and the African Diaspora, the three authors argue that proverbs are an essential dimension of communication because: (1) proverbs are an index of cultural continuity and interaction; (2) proverbs are significant in the socialization process; (3) proverbs are central to mental development and abstract thinking and reasoning; (4) proverbs are significant rhetorical devices in arguments, debates, verbal dueling, etc.; and (5) proverbs are indices of cultural assimilation. Various sections of this article deal with the use and function of proverbs in Africa, the Caribbean, and the African Diaspora (notably proverb use among African Americans in such cities as Pittsburgh and Detroit). Many examples are cited and explained as invaluable verbal art enabling African people everywhere to "make a way outa no way." An appendix lists 50 proverbs that were collected in the two American cites mentioned, and in a second appendix such well-known African

American proverbs like "What goes around comes around" are explained by citing comments from informants. A useful bibliography (pp. 506–508) concludes this important review article.

3281. Daniels, Karlheinz. "'Alles frisch'?" *Der Sprachdienst,* 26 (1982), 36–41.

A short study of the German advertising slogan "Alles frisch" (All fresh) which the Tschibo coffee manufacturer started to use in 1981 in the form of car window stickers. Even though this sticker did not even mention the name of the product, the slogan became very popular and effective. In the meantime there exist many variants of this slogan in the form of newspaper headlines, graffiti, posters, etc. In fact, the structural pattern "Alles X" is the basis for seemingly unending variations. But Daniels also shows that the pattern is considerably older than this particular advertising campaign.

3282. Daniels, Karlheinz. "Neue Aspekte zum Thema Phraseologie in der gegenwärtigen Sprachforschung." *Muttersprache,* 93 (1983), 142–170; 95 (1984–1985), 49–68 and 151–173.

These three review articles continue Karlheinz Daniels' two earlier reports on new studies of phraseology (for the first two see no. 339). In the third part he once once again presents detailed critical evaluations of primarily German publications dealing with proverbs, proverbial expressions, idioms, clichés, and stereotypes by such scholars as Annelies Buhofer (see no. 2248), Florian Coulmas (no. 2291), Heidemarie Gebhardt (no. 2397), Elisabeth Gülich (no. 2434), Wolfgang Mieder (no. 1268), Klaus Dieter Pilz (no. 1462), Harald Reger (no. 1526), Blanche-Marie Schweizer (no. 1684), Harald Thun (no. 1930), and others. At the end Daniels also includes bibliographical information (p. 170) about publications not discussed, including some that deal with the English, French, Spanish, Italian, Rumanian, and Russian languages. The reviews cover phraseological dictionaries, proverb collections, monographs, essay volumes, and collections of quotations. The fourth survey of recent phraseological studies includes a detailed review of the *Handbuch der Phraseologie* (Berlin:

Walter de Gruyter, 1982) by Harald Burger, Annelies Buhofer and Ambros Sialm (no. 3190). But Daniels also includes references to publications by Wolfgang Fleischer (no. 3405), Harald Jaksche (no. 2495), Josip Matesic (no. 3819), Irene Meichsner (no. 3838), etc. The emphasis lies on linguistic studies of phraseological units of the German and Russian languages. The fifth and unfortunately the final review article by Karlheinz Daniels contains numerous reviews of German proverb and graffiti collections as well as recent publications of "geflügelte Worte" (literary quotations). But there are also detailed comments on major paremiological works by Karl Friedrich Wilhelm Wander (a reprint of his scholarly book on proverbs from 1836; see no. 2028), Zoltán Kanyó (no. 829), Helmut A. Seidl (no. 4359), Wolfgang Mieder (no. 3856), and others. At the end (pp. 172–173) Daniels lists additional references of German publications on proverbs, idioms, graffiti, "Antisprichwörter" (anti-proverbs), wellerisms, etc. It is regrettable that Daniels decided to terminate his invaluable review articles with this fifth essay. The five surveys and Daniels' own insights are of major significance for modern linguistic advances in phraseology—a superb scholarly service for international phraseological research.

3283. Daniels, Karlheinz. "Geschlechtsspezifische Stereotypen im Sprichwort. Ein interdisziplinärer Problemaufriß." *Sprache und Literatur in Wissenschaft und Unterricht,* 16, no. 56 (1985), 18–25.

Based on numerous German proverbs, Daniels presents a discussion of the misogynous content of many texts that refer to women. Such sexual stereotypes have been handed down from one generation to another, but they are also still used today and new sterotypical slogans and graffiti continue to be created. At the same time one also finds so-called "Antisprichwörter" (anti-proverbs) that attempt to overcome this negative view of women. Daniels includes a valuable comparison between proverbs and stereotypes and argues that the emancipation movement has started to make some progress in overcoming the problems of sexual harassment through proverbial invectives. A useful bibliography (p. 25) is included.

3284. Daniels, Karlheinz. "'Idiomatische Kompetenz' in der Zielsprache Deutsch. Voraussetzungen, Möglichkeiten, Folgerungen." *Wirkendes Wort*, 35 (1985), 145–157.

Valuable paper on the problem of idioms in foreign language teaching. Daniels starts with a discussion of the idiomaticity of a language as a pedagogical problem for a teacher, and he then presents a typology of various phraseological units to be covered in the classroom: proverbs, maxims, proverbial expressions, twin formulas, proverbial comparisons, slogans, stereotypes, etc. He also discusses semantic, linguistic and contextual questions. The last section deals with practical suggestions for incorporating the many aspects of phraseology into foreign language instruction. A helpful bibliography (pp. 156–157) and many examples of German expressions are included.

3285. Daniels, Karlheinz. "Text- und autorenspezifische Phraseologismen, am Beispiel von Erich Kästners Roman *Fabian*." *Beiträge zur allgemeinen und germanistischen Phraseologieforschung*. Ed. Jarmo Korhonen. Oulu: Oulun Yliopisto, 1987. 207–219; a revised version of this article has appeared with the title "Erich Kästner als Sprach- und Gesellschaftskritiker dargestellt an seiner Verwendung sprachlicher Schematismen." *Wörter: Schätze, Fugen und Fächer des Wissens. Festgabe für Theodor Lewandowski*. Ed. Hugo Aust. Tübingen: Gunther Narr, 1987. 191–206.

This is a literary investigation of the use and function of various types of phraseological units in Erich Kästner's (1899–1974) novel *Fabian* (1931). By citing a number of German examples in their context, Daniels discusses how Kästner characterizes certain situations and characters through effective use of proverbial expressions, idioms, etc. He also shows how Kästner employs fixed phrases in order to attack and satirize the German political move towards National Socialism. The revised version of this article contains examples of how Kästner achieved similar goals in his epigrammatic poetry through the alienating use of proverbial expressions. A useful bibliography (pp. 217–219; or pp. 205–206) is attached.

3286. Daniels, Karlheinz. "Aktuelles Verstehen und historisches Verständnis von Redensarten. Ergebnisse einer Befragung." *Beiträge zur Phraseologie des Ungarischen und des Deutschen.* Ed. Regina Hessky. Budapest: Loran-Eötvös-Universität, 1988. 98–121.

In this article Daniels reports on a study from 1984 in which 60 informants (30 High School and 30 university students) were asked to answer two basic questions regarding 10 German proverbial expressions. For such old phrases as "Ins Gras beißen" (To bite the dust) the students were asked to explain their meaning and their possible origin. The expressions contained somewhat archaic nouns referring to medieval times, but most students did understand the meaning of these quite commonly used phraseological units. However, they definitely had difficulty explaining the realia and origin of these metaphorical phrases. Daniels cites some of the answers for all 10 expressions and shows how actual comprehension is possible without being able to give a proper historical explanation. The author concludes from this proverbs test that the actual teaching of the origin and meaning of traditional proverbial expressions would be quite appropriate for German natives but also for foreign language students of German. A useful bibliography (pp. 119–120) and a copy of the questionnaire (p. 122) are included.

3287. Daniels, Karlheinz. "Das Sprichwort als Erziehungsmittel - historische Aspekte." *Europhras 88. Phraséologie Contrastive. Actes du Colloque International Klingenthal-Strasbourg, 12–16 mai 1988.* Ed. Gertrud Gréciano. Strasbourg: Université des Sciences Humaines, 1989. 65–73.

The author starts this article on the use of proverbs for educational purposes by stressing the fact that they exhibit a polyfunctionality and polysemanticity which depend very much on the situation or context in which a particular proverb might appear. For this reason it would be wrong to continue to state that proverbs are always didactic in nature. Daniels then reviews how proverbs have been "misused" in German schools for centuries by having students compose essays explaining the didactic value of traditional proverbs. He argues that a more liberal pedagogical approach would be to have students also consider the so-called "Antisprichwörter" (anti-proverbs) as well as their manipulative use and function in the modern mass media. Proverbs should be taught, but care must be taken that students realize that proverbs are not universally true. A helpful bibliography (pp. 71–73) is included.

3288. David, Jean. "Tous les prédicats ne meurent pas idiomes. Mais nul n'est à l'abri." *Europhras 88. Phraséologie Contrastive. Actes du Colloque International Klingenthal-Strasbourg, 12–16 mai 1988.* Ed. Gertrud Gréciano. Strasbourg: Université des Sciences Humaines, 1989. 75–82.

The article starts with a discussion of the definition problem regarding idioms, stressing in particular aspects of meaning and structure. David then shows the difference between literal and figurative meanings of idioms and explains how new phrases can become idiomatic. A detailed analysis of the global proverbial expression "Donner le feu vert à quelqu'un" (To give someone the green light) is included. In addition to some other French examples the author also includes a few German idioms. He argues that idiomaticity is of major importance in foreign language teaching, and teachers must pay attention to both the old and new idioms if they want their students to be able to communicate effectively.

3289. Davies, M. "The Paremiographers on 'Ta tria ton Stesichorou'." *Journal of Hellenic Studies*, 102 (1982), 206–210.

This is a very detailed etymological study of the Greek proverb "Ta tria ton Stesichorou" (You don't even know three verses [or poems] of Stesichorus). Davies refers to some previous scholarship on this proverb, and he is able to add a number of new classical Greek references. In fact, the article contains a two-page comparative chart indicating the variants found in the works of various literary authors and paremiographers. The author concludes that the number "three" probably refers to Stesichorus' (640 B.C.-555? B.C.) own preference for triadic structures in his poetry.

3290. Davis, Natalie Zemon. "Spruchweisheiten und populäre Irrlehren." *Volkskultur. Zur Wiederentdeckung des vergessenen Alltags (16.-20. Jahrhundert).* Eds. Richard van Dülmen and Norbert Schindler. Frankfurt am Main: Fischer, 1984. 78–116 and 394–406 (notes).

This is a German translation of Natalie Davis' earlier English article "Proverbial Wisdom and Popular Errors" (1975; see no. 350) which has also been translated into French (no. 2310). It represents a fascinating study of primarily French proverb collections from the Middle Ages to the 17th century. Davis includes a particularly valuable analysis of the use and function of proverbs in the medieval dialogues entitled *Salomon and Marcolf* (12th century ff.), pointing out the wisdom and fallacies of traditional proverbs. Many literary and cultural references are given, and it is argued that the collections are usually very poor in their interpretation of popular culture. If collectors sometimes made comments concerning certain proverbs, they still disembedded them from their cultural context, not thinking about how a particular proverb was used or what it meant locally. The 104 detailed footnotes (pp. 394–406) contain invaluable bibliographical information on French paremiography in particular and European proverb scholarship in general.

3291. De Carli, Nicoletta. "'Sub rosa dicere' und 'avere il marchese'. Euphemismus und Symbolik in zwei Redensarten." *Schweizerisches Archiv für Volkskunde*, 86, nos. 1–2 (1990), 35–43.

An etymological, historical and cultural investigation of two proverbial expressions with fascinating explanations of their symbolic metaphors. The Latin phrase "Sub rosa dicere" (To say under the rose) goes back to medieval sources and has been loan translated into the European languages. De Carli cites various literary examples and explains that the "rose" is a symbolic euphemism for "virginity" (something to be silent about). The Italian phrase "Avere il marchese" (i.e. to menstruate) also serves as a euphemism and has been translated into other Romance languages. Again De Carli provides careful etymological proof for the fact that this phrase refers to a woman as being "marked" during menstruation.

3292. de Caro, Francis (Frank) A. "'A Mystery is a Muddle': Gnomic Expressions in *A Passage to India.*" *Midwestern Journal of Language and Folklore,* 12 (1986), 15–23.

Discusses the contextual use and function of a number of English proverbs in Edward Morgan Forster's (1879–1970) acclaimed novel *A Passage to India* (1924). De Caro is particularly interested in showing how proverbs are used by Forster to work out the idea that the English and Indian cultures operate with quite different conceptions of truth and language. Due to the culture-specific nature of many proverbs, Forster is employing them to indicate that their so-called absolute truth or universality is often no more than an inadequate cliché. The rigid worldview expressed in proverbs of the two cultures actually prevents the improvement of communication.

3293. de Caro, Francis (Frank) A. "Riddles and Proverbs." *Folk Groups and Folklore Genres. An Introduction.* Ed. Elliott Oring. Logan/Utah: Utah State University Press, 1986. 175–197.

General introductory essay on riddles (pp. 175–183) and proverbs (pp. 184–195). De Caro argues that riddles and proverbs are closely linked due to the key role that the metaphor plays in each genre. But while a riddle requires a question and an answer, a proverb is a fixed, traditional statement. The author differentiates among proverbs, proverbial expressions, proverbial comparisons, and wellerisms, and he then discusses such aspects as metaphor, structure, variation, content, context, function, worldview, frequency, etc. Special attention is paid to modern humorous or ironic parodies of proverbs that result in so-called "Antisprichwörter" (anti-proverbs). De Caro cites numerous Anglo-American proverbs and also some texts from other cultures and languages in English translation. A useful bibliography (pp. 195–197) concludes this readable and informative essay intended for folklore and proverb students.

3294. de Caro, Francis (Frank) A. "Talk is Cheap: The Nature of Speech According to American Proverbs." *Proverbium,* 4 (1987), 17–37.

The author argues that proverbs and their meaning can be used to gain certain insights into the worldview and ethos of a culture. Based on an analysis of 110 Anglo-American proverbs dealing with various aspects of speech, de Caro found that English proverbs current in America are decidedly "anti-speech." While there are some proverbs that comment positively on speech, most texts counsel against the spoken word and excessive talk. American proverbs in general oppose speech to action. The negative attitude of such proverbs in the American context can be seen to lie in American cultural norms and ideas which stress a life of getting things done. De Caro also refers to similar studies of attitudes towards speech expressed in Japanese and Indian proverbs (see nos. 445 and 1182), where negative views about speech were found to be due to high population density.

3295.   de Caro, Francis (Frank) A. "Proverbs in Graham Greene's *The Power and the Glory*: Framing Thematic Concerns in a Modern Novel." *Proverbium*, 6 (1989), 1–7.

This is a short literary investigation of a few proverbs that appear in Graham Greene's (1904–1991) novel *The Power and the Glory* (1940). De Caro states that proverbs play a role even in the works of the most sophisticated modern writers, and he then shows how Greene employs proverbs to frame his thematic concerns of love as well as good and evil. Citing several examples in their literary context, de Caro argues convincingly that the proverbs fit neatly into the basic idea of the novel. Just as proverbs used in actual speech acts can be said to "name" recurring human situations, Greene's proverbs and invented pseudo-proverbs "name" recurring themes and call attention to them through their metaphors, poetic structure, and proverbial wisdom.

3296.   Dedecius, Karl. "Letztes Geleit für den ersten Aphoristiker unserer Zeit: Lec." *Der Aphorismus. Zur Geschichte, zu den Formen und Möglichkeiten einer literarischen Gattung*. Ed. Gerhard Neumann. Darmstadt: Wissenschaftliche Buchgesellschaft, 1976. 452–477.

The author presents a biographical essay on the Polish aphoristic writer Stanislaw Jerzy Lec (1909–1966) whose several books of aphorisms he translated into German. The major part of the article (pp. 458–475) is dedicated to a careful analysis of the themes of Lec's many aphorisms, stressing that he attacked human and societal problems wherever he saw them in an ironic but understanding fashion. Dedecius includes important comments on the sources, structure and language of these aphorisms, illustrating by numerous examples that many of them are reactions to or parodies of traditional proverbs in the form of "Antisprichwörter" (anti-proverbs). For an even more specific analysis of these "sprichwörtliche Aphorismen" (proverbial aphorisms) see Iwona Frackiewicz (no. 3449).

3297. Delavigne, Raymond. "Sur les expressions angevines 'Aller à Brion bijer le cul de la vieille': Étude ethnomythique de littérature orale." *Langue et littérature orales dans l'Ouest de la France.* Eds. Michel Bonneau and Georges Cesbron. Angers: Publication de l'Université d'Angers, 1983. 111–143.

A detailed philological study of the French proverbial expression "Aller à Brion bijer le cul de la vieille" (To go to Brion to kiss the back of the old woman) which is in oral use in the province of Anjou in western France. Delavigne cites numerous variants and presents precise etymological and ethnomythical explanations. On pp. 127–132 the author also includes the transcript of a discussion that followed a lecture he had delivered on this expression and its variants. The notes and bibliography (pp. 133–143) are a convincing indication of the complexity of researching the origin, history, and meaning of a local proverbial expression.

3298. Demarolle, Pierre. "Autour de la 'Ballade des Proverbes': Aspects logiques de la poésie de François Villon." *Richesse du proverbe.* Eds. François Suard and Claude Buridant. Lille: Université de Lille, 1984. I, 75–85.

A careful literary and linguistic study of François Villon's (c. 1431–c. 1463) well-known "Ballade des proverbes." Demarolle identifies the medieval French proverbs in this ballad and shows that they all follow the proverbial pattern of "Tant . . . que" (So much . . . that). The author analyzes in particular the syntactical, lexical and semantic aspects of this four-stanza poem, Villon appears to express an antithetic worldview in this text, and his proverbial logic helps to create the impression of "des contre-vérités" (counter-truths). See also Pino Paioni (no. 1403), Barbara Schulz (no. 2842), Paul Sébillot (no. 2849), and Constantin Negreanu (no. 4010).

3299.   Deskis, Susan Elizabeth. *Proverbial Backgrounds to the 'Sententiae' of "Beowulf."* Diss. Harvard University, 1991. 176 pp.

The author shows that the sentential utterances of *Beowulf* (10th-12th century) are situated within a matrix of proverbs from Latin and vernacular sources. The cognate proverbs often clarify the meanings of these sentential verses in *Beowulf,* and the functions of the sententious remarks include summarization, characterization, transition, and thematic structuring. In some cases a "sententia" is found at the end of a short narrative segment, where it functions similarly to the moral of a fable. While some of the "sententiae" are based on folk proverbs, many of them stem from the Book of Psalms in the Old Testament of the Bible. Deskis has divided her contextualized examples into four main chapters based on thematic characteristics: (1) God and humankind (pp. 15–48), (2) joy and sorrow (pp. 49–73), (3) fate and death (pp. 74–120), and (4) warnings and advice (pp. 121–161). A helpful bibliography (pp. 166–176) is included, but there is no proverb index. See also Robert Burlin (no. 240) and Kemp Malone (no. 1141).

3300.   Dessons, Gérard. "Pour une rythmique du proverbe." *La Licorne,* 8 (1984), 9–30.

Actually an informative article on various aspects of French proverbs of which the rhythmic nature is only one part (pp. 19–22). The article starts with a discussion of the wisdom, truth, meaning, and reality of proverbs. Next Dessons analyzes the metaphorical nature of most proverbs, and this is followed by definitions of the proverb and proverbial expression. The author also comments on archaic words included in some proverbs and then presents a careful analysis of the form and style of proverbs: rhythm, alliteration, rhyme, phonetics, binary structure, etc. The 48 notes (pp. 24–30) contain useful bibliographical information on French proverb scholarship.

3301. Dessons, Gérard. "La parole du siècle dans les *Proverbes* de Musset." *Travaux de littérature*, 4 (1991), 197–207.

This is a literary proverb investigation of several so-called "proverbes dramatiques" (proverb plays) by Alfred de Musset (1810–1857). The author states that Musset wrote these plays based on French proverbs in order to make social and political statements. The proverbs also reflect the collective speech of the 19th century, and to a certain degree they represent the worldview of French society. Dessons cites and interprets contextualized examples from the plays *On ne badine pas avec l'amour* (1834), *Il ne faut jurer de rien* (1836), and *Il faut qu'une porte soit ouverte ou fermée* (1848). Not only do these plays have a proverb as their title, they also integrate numerous other proverbs throughout the dialogues. Many proverbs are taken seriously and express didactic and moral advice, but there are also those instances when proverbs add much humor to these short plays. See also Karl Holz (no. 747), Louise Luce (no. 1120), and Marjorie Shaw (no. 1722).

3302. De Vriendt-De Man, M.-J. "Des Sentences dorées ou la poussière de la sagesse populaire." *Communiquer et traduire. Hommages à Jean Dierickx.* Eds. G. Debusscher and J.P. van Noppen. Bruxelles: Editions de l'Université de Bruxelles, 1985. 47–54.

This article is primarily a description of an anonymous polyglot proverb collection with the title *Le Thresor de Sentences Dorées. Dicts Proverbes, Referains et dictions communs, réduicts selon l'ordre alphabeticq en quatre langues: à scavoir, Latin, Espagnol, Thiois et Français* (1650) located in the Bibliothèque Royale in Brussels, Belgium. The author points out how useful such proverb collections are for the translator, and he then discusses a number of Dutch/Flemish proverbs contained in this collection that refer to morality, work, animals, etc. He also cites comparative examples of Flemish and French proverbs, indicating their differences in metaphors, structure, and language.

3303. Diaféria, Michèle G. *Les Proverbes au conte de Bretaigne: A Critical Edition and Study.* Diss. Florida State University, 1988. 80 pp. Now also published as *Li Proverbes au conte de Bretaigne. Critical Edition and Study.* New York: Peter Lang, 1990. 166 pp.

The author starts her book with a general introduction about proverbs in the Middle Ages (pp. 1–14). This is followed by a survey of gnomic and didactic literature of that period in France, Germany and Spain (pp. 15–37). The second chapter (pp. 39–53) analyzes a manuscript of proverbs entitled *Li Proverbes au conte de Bretaigne* that was put together in 54 stanzas, each consisting of two tercets which introduce a medieval French proverb. Diaféria presents information concerning Conte Pierre de Bretaigne (13th century), she discusses the history of the manuscript, and she investigates its morphology and phonology. The third chapter (pp. 55–56) contains a short statement on the versification of the stanzas, while chapter four (pp. 57–83) contains the text of the 54 verses. In chapter five (pp. 85–96) the author cites rhyme patterns and other structural aspects, in chapter six (pp. 97–116) she quotes the entire manuscript in a modern French prose transcription, and in chapter seven (pp. 119–139) she provides an English prose translation. The short eighth chapter (pp. 141–144) treats the various themes (good, evil, wisdom, common sense, wealth, sin, etc.), and chapter nine (pp. 145–149) contains a photographic reproduction of the original manuscript. A selective glossary (pp. 151–153) makes up the tenth chapter. The author also includes a valuable bibliography (pp. 155–160), a genealogy table, and a comprehensive name and subject index. See also Johannes Martin (no. 1147).

3304. Dilcher, Gerhard. *Paarformeln in der Rechtssprache des frühen Mittelalters.* Darmstadt: C. Rinck, 1961. 76 pp.

This is a richly documented monograph on legal twin formulas from the early Middle Ages. Dilcher discusses the definition of these phraseological units, their sources, and the frequent use of alliteration in the first part of his book (pp. 11–33). The second part (pp. 35–66) is dedicated to the magical, religious, and legal content of curses and oaths that contain twin formulas. In the third part (pp. 67–76) the author deals with the function and meaning of these phrases, citing many Latin, Germanic, and early German examples. The numerous footnotes contain important historical and cultural information, and the bibliography (pp. 5–7) refers to important secondary literature concerning these formulas of which many are still in use today.

3305. Dingeldein, Heinrich J. "'Amerika' in der deutschen Sprache. Anmerkungen zu den sprachlichen Spuren eines kulturellen Kontakts." *Der Sprachdienst,* 27 (1983), 65–76.

A cultural and historical study of the words "Amerika," "Amerikaner" and "amerikanisch" in the German language with references to their appearances in proverbs, proverbial expressions, idioms, and literary quotations (geflügelte Worte). It is argued that such expressions are ample proof of the close linguistic and political relationship between the United States and Germany over the past 300 years. Dialect texts as well as examples of the very modern age are included. With 3 illustrations.

3306. Dion, Kenneth L. "Psychology and Proverbs: Folk Psychology Revisited." *Canadian Psychology/Psychologie Canadienne,* 31, no. 3 (1990), 209–211.

This is a short but important invited response to Tim B. Rogers' essay "Proverbs as Psychological Theories . . . Or Is It the Other Way Around?" that appeared in the same journal issue (see no. 4258). Dion argues that proverbs are not so much theories but rather hypotheses, and he also points out that psychologists have rarely studied the actual truth value of proverbs. However, he certainly agrees that proverbs express a certain folk psychology. Psychologists should definitely study them as expressions of wisdom, worldview and a society's value system. Proverbs play a major role in social life and in socialization processes, and as such they can tell a psychologist a great deal about people as social beings.

3307. Di Stefano, Giuseppe. "Locutions et datations." *La locution. Actes du colloque international Université McGill, Montréal, 15–16 octobre 1984.* Eds. G. Di Stefano and Russell G. McGillivray. Montréal: Editions CERES, 1984. 191–204.

Laments the fact that the scholarship on medieval French proverbial expressions is still limited. This is particularly true for the 14th and 15th centuries, and it is for this reason that Giuseppe Di Stefano has begun his work on a *Dictionnaire des locutions en moyen français.* He quotes and discusses a number of French expressions from that period with precise dates and shows how important they are for a more complete history of French proverbial texts. He also deals with classification problems of such phrases from a lexicographical point of view, and he comments shortly on the value of some of these texts for onomastics, popular culture, and folklore.

3308. Di Stefano, Giuseppe, and Russell G. McGillivray (eds.). *La locution. Actes du colloque international Université McGill, Montréal, 15–16 octobre 1984.* Montréal: Editions CERES, 1984 (=*Le Moyen Français*, 14–15 [1984], 1–497). 497 pp.

A major essay volume concerning French proverbial expressions by 21 scholars who participated at an international paremiological colloquium in October of 1984 at the Université McGill in Montréal, Canada. Included are Paul Bleton, "C'est juste une façon de parler: les locutions métalinguistiques" (pp. 3–18); Chantal Bouchard, "La locution: problème de traduction" (pp. 19–27); Hervé Curat, "La relation privilégiée entre l'agent et l'objet dans les locutions verbales" (pp. 28–55); André Dugas et Anne-Marie Di Sciullo, "Le rôle des déterminants dans les expressions figées de langues romanes" (pp. 56–69); David Gaatone, "La locution ou le poids de la diachronie dans la synchronie" (pp. 70–81); Ottavio Lurati, "La locution entre métaphore et histoire" (pp. 82–102); Jacqueline Picoche, "Un essai de lexicologie guillaumienne: la locution figée comme révélateur du signifié de puissance des polysèmes" (pp. 103–118); Alain Rey, "Les implications théoriques d'un dictionnaire phraséologique" (pp. 119–133); Elisabeth Schulze-Busacker, "Proverbe ou sentence: essai de définition" (pp. 134–167); Marc

Angenot, "La lutte pour la vie: migrations et usages d'un idéologème" (pp. 171–190); Giuseppe Di Stefano, "Locutions et datations" (pp. 191–204); Jane Everett, "Les locutions anciennes et les locutions québécoises" (pp. 205–228); Geneviève Hasenohr, "La locution verbale figurée dans l'oeuvre de Jean le Fèvre" (pp. 229–281); Madeleine Jeay, "'Les Evangiles des quenouilles': de la croyance populaire à la locution" (pp. 282–301); Ulla Jokinen, "Observations sur les locutions françaises dans les farces et dans les sotties" (pp. 302–322); Marie-Louise Ollier, "Spécificité discursive d'une locution: si m'aist Dex / se Dex m'ait" (pp. 323–367); Michèle Perret, "Ci a grant courtoisie: ci a + substantif abstrait" (pp. 368–383); Jean-Louis G. Picherit, "Formes et fonctions de la matière proverbiale dans le 'Songe du vieil pelerin' de Philippe de Mézières (pp. 384–399); François Rigolot, "Perspectives rhétorique et sémiotique sur la locution: locutio/locatio" (pp. 400–418); Gilles Roques, "'Sans rime et sans raison'" (pp. 419–436); and Terence R. Wooldridge, "La locution dans le métalangage dictionnairique français" (pp. 437–449). The essays deal with such varied matters as meta-proverbs, translatability, verbal expressions, classification, synchronic and diachronic approach, metaphor, lexicography, semantics, phraseology, definition, genre, ideology, worldview, dates, literature, Bible, speech act, function, Middle Ages, rhetorics, etc. Rose M. Bidler added three superb indices (pp. 453–497) which increase the value of this indispensable essay volume. For annotations see nos. 3141, 3154, 3273, 3333, 3460, 3798, 4171, 4229, 4346, 3060, 3307, 3390, 3570, 3643, 3646, 4073, 4156, 4170, 4238, 4272, 4572.

3309. Dittgen, Andrea Maria. *Regeln für Abweichungen. Funktionale sprachspielerische Abweichungen in Zeitungsüberschriften, Werbeschlagzeilen, Werbeslogans, Wandsprüchen und Titeln.* Frankfurt am Main: Peter Lang, 1989. 209 pp.

This study investigates the types of variations of fixed phrases in newspaper and advertising headlines, slogans, graffiti, and titles of films and books. The author starts with a short introductory chapter (pp. 9–12) in which she explains the popularity of linguistic puns as variations of fixed phrases. In chapter two (pp. 13–24) she defines "variation" and presents certain norms of classification. In the third chapter (pp. 25–44) Dittgen discusses the importance of linguistic competence and comprehension for the effective communication of such variations. The long fourth chapter (pp. 45–142) investigates the semantic, lexical and structural changes in such punning variations, including a special section on phraseological units (pp. 121–133). The following three chapters (pp. 143–166) present various types of variations with many German examples. Several indices, a useful bibliography (pp. 195–203), a list of sources (books on slogans, film and book titles, graffiti, etc.), and many illustrations are included.

3310. Djamo-Diaconita, L. "Contributions à la parémiologie balkanique." *Actes du premier congrès international des études balkaniques et sud-est européennes.* No editor given. Sofia: Association Internationale d'Études du Sud-Est Européen, 1968. VI, 277–309.

The author starts her comparative study of the proverbs of the Balkan countries by referring to previous scholarship (the 60 notes contain valuable bibliographical references). She points out that all Balkan countries have certain proverbs in common with the many other European countries. After citing numerous examples in their original languages, she presents a large list of those proverbs which the six Balkan countries Rumania, Albania, Bulgaria, Macedonia, Greece, and Turkey share. This is followed by other lists that include those proverbs which five or four national languages have in common. Here Djamo-Diaconita also includes Serbo-Croatian texts. The proverbs are organized according to certain ideas (content), including a few cultural and historical comments.

3311. Djap, Djam Dung. *Proverbial Understanding and the Development of Part-Whole Reasoning Skills.* Diss. University of Toronto, 1984. 238 pp.

A psychological study based on a 56–item proverbs test was conducted with 170 children (ages 8 to 15 years) to assess children's understanding of metaphorical proverbs. The children were given the task to find the correct meaning from four possible answers for each proverb. Djap found that there was a tendency for children with higher age to prefer the correct nonliteral interpretations of the proverbs. On the average for all children, the correct nonliteral paraphrase option was judged to be closest in meaning to the proverb followed in order by the incorrect nonliteral, the correct literal, and the incorrect literal options. It was established that the comprehension of proverbs definitely increases with age. A number of statistical tables are included.

3312. Dobre, Alexandru. "Proverbul în Dictionarul limbii române al lui Laurian si Massim." *Proverbium Dacoromania*, 4 (1989), 6–14.

This is a lexicographical study of the proverbs that are included in A.T. Laurian and J.C. Massim's *Dictionariulu limbei romane* (1871–1876). Dobre gives a short history of this Rumanian dictionary and points out that its 3474 pages contain rich proverbial materials. He argues that paremiographers should use this dictionary together with the standard Rumanian proverb collections. It should be noted that the same is true, of course, for all of the large multi-volume dictionaries of the national languages or dialects. With an English abstract (p. 14).

3313. Dobre, Alexandru, and Maria Rafaila. "O colectie de proverbe si ghicitori de la sfîrsitul secolului al XVIII-lea." *Revista de etnografie si folclor*, 36, nos. 3–4 (1991), 198–200.

This is a short descriptive article on a Rumanian manuscript from the end of the 18th century containing proverbs and riddles. The authors cite some of the texts and discuss their possible origin, history and meaning. They also present the history and the various owners of the manuscript, pointing out that such unpublished collections are of much importance for diachronic scholarship on these two genres. The proverbs are of great value for the scholarly paremiographical work that is taking place in Rumania with the hope of eventually editing a major historical dictionary of Rumanian proverbs.

3314. Dobrovol'skij, Dmitrij. "Zum Problem der phraseologisch gebundenen Bedeutung." *Beiträge zur Erforschung der deutschen Sprache*, 2 (1982), 52–67.

An important review of the research results concerning the phraseologically fixed meanings of the constituents of phraseological units. Dobrovol'skij discusses above all Soviet and German theoretical studies and concerns himself with lexical and semantic problems. Many German, Russian and English examples are quoted and compared. Of particular interest is the argument that proverbs can be divided into semantic parts which play different roles in the phraseological meaning of the individual proverb text.

3315. Dobrovol'skij, Dmitrij. *Phraseologie als Objekt der Universalienlinguistik*. Leipzig: VEB Verlag Enzyklopädie, 1988. 264 pp.

This is a major study of the field of phraseology from the point of view of universal linguistics. Dobrovol'skij starts his book with an analysis of phraseological universals, stressing lexical-semantic aspects and problems of classification (pp. 10–61). The second part of the book (pp. 62–209) is a detailed structural investigation of the phraseological systems of German, English, and Dutch. Here the author presents numerous comparative examples, and he emphasizes lexical, stylistic (formal), and semantic differences and similarities. Of special importance is also the section on variability of phraseological units (pp. 158–190). A comprehensive summary (pp. 210–217) in German, a large bibliography (pp. 228–253), a useful subject index (pp. 254–264), and numerous diagrams and structural formulas help to make this a most valuable theoretical monograph.

3316. Dobrovol'skij, Dmitrij. "Strukturtypologische Analyse der Phraseologie: Theoretische Prämissen und praktische Konsequenzen." *Europhras 90. Akten der internationalen Tagung zur germanistischen Phraseologieforschung, Aske/Schweden 12.-15. Juni 1990*. Ed. Christine Palm. Uppsala: Acta Universitatis Upsaliensis, 1991. 29–42.

In this theoretical and linguistic article Dobrovol'skij looks at phraseological units as signs that are based on a semiotic system. Citing German, English, and Dutch examples, he attempts a structural-typological analysis of fixed phrases. He is able to show that there are differences in the use of certain nouns, verbs, etc. in the phraseological units of these three languages. Problems of idiomaticity, structure, lexicography, and semantics are discussed, and the author argues that all of them have important implications for lexicographers working on bilingual phraseological dictionaries. In addition to linguistic differences there are also anthropological and social matters that enter into the meaning of fixed phrases. The different metaphors are yet another vexing problem for the translator who is confronted with finding an equivalent text in the target language. The 18 notes contain useful bibliographical references.

3317. Doctor, Raymond D. "Gujerati Proverbs: An Analytical Study." *Lore and Language*, 4, no. 1 (1985), 1–29.

An inclusive investigation based on about 5000 Gujerati proverbs collected in the State of Gujerati in the North-West region of India. Doctor starts by analyzing four levels of these proverbs: (1) the structural level (epiphonemic, prosodic, phonetic aspects); (2) the thematic level (mankind, social, material and physical environment, fate, heredity); (3) the semiological level (lexical and logical aspects); and (4) the argumentative level. In each section the author presents numerous Gujerati examples with English translations. Three charts and diagrams are also included to illustrate the application of symbolic logic, linguistic philosophy, and semantics in the study of proverbs.

3318. Doctor, Raymond D. "Predictive Sayings in Gujerati." *Folklore* (London), 97, no. 1 (1986), 41–55.

This is an interesting study of predictive sayings (i.e. weather proverbs) found in the State of Gujerati in the North-West of India. Doctor presents a clear description of the months and seasons according to the Hindu calendar and then analyzes 47 meteorological Gujerati proverbs with English translations and detailed cultural and linguistic annotations. It is argued that such sayings reflect people's conscious desire to impose logic and order on the phenomenon of nature. Two diagrams, an illustration, and a useful bibliography (pp. 54–55) are included as well.

3319. Dolgova, I.A. "Osobennosti leksiko-semanticheskikh protivopostavlenii v poslovichnykh izrecheniakh." *Vestnik Leningradskogo Universiteta,* serii 2, 1, no. 2 (1987), 100–102.

Dolgova presents a short discussion of the peculiarities of semantic oppositions of words in proverbial phrases. Many Russian examples are cited, and the author stresses situational and image-forming antonyms in these proverbs. Some comments regarding the source of the metaphorical expressiveness of proverbs are also included, showing clearly how these texts are based on linguistic and semantic contrasts. A short English summary (p. 102) is provided.

3320. Dor, Rémy. "'Metel' ou l'apprentissage du comportement. Le proverbe chez les Kirghiz du Pamir afghan." *Journal asiatique,* 270 (1982), 67–146.

This is an impressive example of an anthropological study of 116 proverbs and proverbial expressions that were collected during field research in the Afghan Pamir in 1972 and 1973. Dor begins by explaining that the Afghan Kirghiz have only the one word "metel" to signify both proverbs and proverbial expressions. These texts have two specific functions, namely as a means to teach children how to behave properly in society and to add prestige and authority to the speech of adults. The author presents his texts in the original language with French explanations, and he includes detailed linguistic and cultural explanations. A major bibliography (pp. 72–78), a subject index (pp. 142–146), and an English summary (p. 146) are provided as well.

3321. Dorn, Paméla J. "Gender and Personhood: Turkish Jewish Proverbs and the Politics of Reputation." *Women's Studies International Forum,* 9 (1986), 295–301.

Based on proverbs collected during field research in the Jewish community of Istanbul, Turkey, as well as in Turkish communities in Israel, the author studies the traditional separation between male and female domains in Middle Eastern societies and the critical gender role in defining personhood. A number of proverbs of Turkish Jews on men, women and wives are cited in the Turkish language with English translations and cultural as well as semantic annotations. The contrast of behavior between the sexes is clearly encoded in proverbs and is manifest in the manipulation of gossip and reputation. A small bibliography (p. 301) on Jewish and Middle Eastern proverbs and a short abstract (p. 295) are included.

3322. Doulaveras, Aristides N. *I emmetri ekfora tou neoellinikou paremiakou logou.* Athena: Panepistimio Ioanninon, 1989. 332 pp.

This is a major study of modern Greek proverbs based on 500 texts taken from various proverb collections from Greece. It is argued that 92.2% of the proverbs exhibit some kind of metrical form, making this poetic language the major characteristic of Greek proverbs. Citing many examples with 19 detailed statistical tables, Doulaveras draws the following conclusions: (1) the original form of the proverbs may have been in verse; (2) the main meters in the proverbial speech are iambic and trochaic; (3) the predominant verses in the iambic meter contain 15 syllables; (4) the predominant verses in the trochaic meter contain 8 syllables; (5) the dactylic, the mesotonic and the anapaestic meters exist only in very small percentages in Greek proverbial speech; (6) both iambic and trochaic proverbs have at times compound verses; (7) the alternations of iambus-trochee and trochee-iambus are quite frequent; (8) there are quite a few proverbs that do not have the correct metrical form; (9) mixed syllables exist in both iambic and trochaic proverbs; (10) those proverbs that are in prose probably derived from metrical originals; and (11) most proverbs continue to be quoted in metrical form since this is the speech pattern of the agricultural society where proverbs are used most often. A useful bibliography (pp. 319–323), an index (pp. 325–327), and an English summary (pp. 183–185) are included.

3323. Doulaveras, Aristides N. *O paroimiakos logos sto muthistorema tou N. Kazantzaki "Alexis Zormpas."* Athena: Bibliogonia, 1991. 134 pp.

In this literary proverb investigation Doulaveras deals with the proverbial speech in Nikos Kazantzaki's (1882–1957) novel *Alexis Zormpas* (1946; *Zorba the Greek*). The first part (pp. 19–42) contains a detailed discussion of various criteria of proverbiality, including the form, message, content, vocabulary, syntax, and poetics (rhyme, exaggeration, allegory, personification, metaphor, etc.) of the proverbs, proverbial expressions, and maxims. In the second part (pp. 43–51) the author analyzes the frequency of the proverbs in the novel, indicating that Zorba uses 142 of the 196 proverbial references (frequency tables are included). The third part (pp. 53–62) contains a list of the 196 proverbial texts arranged alphabetically according to key-words, while the fourth part (pp. 61–114) lists all the texts in the context of the novel with informative annotations. In the final sixth part (pp. 115–120) the author lists the major vocabulary of the proverbial speech of this well-known novel. An English summary (p. 123), a useful bibliography (pp. 127–130), and a general index (pp. 131–134) conclude this valuable study of the use and function of proverbs in a modern Greek novel.

3324. Dove, N.R. (pseud. Karl Friedrich Wilhelm Wander). *Politisches Sprichwörterbrevier. Tagebuch eines Patrioten der fünfziger Jahre, zur Charakteristik jener Zeit.* Leipzig: Wigand, 1872; rpt. ed. by Wolfgang Mieder. Bern: Peter Lang, 1990. 333 pp.

This is a fascinating book of 1206 satirical reactions to German proverbs which the well-known paremiographer Karl Friedrich Wilhelm Wander (1803–1879) wrote down during the years 1857 to 1862 and published under the pseudonym N.R. Dove in 1872. The entries are in the form of a diary, each starting with a proverb and then followed by Wander's aphoristic comments regarding the Philistinism of the German middle class and the reactionary policies of the German government during the middle of the 19th century. Wander questions the wisdom and universality of traditional proverbs, often parodying them in the form of "Antisprichwörter" (anti-proverbs). Altogether these texts (ranging in length from short aphorisms to prose satires of over one page) contain ample proof of the danger that proverbs can present when they are misused to manipulate people into political and social passivity. Wolfgang Mieder as editor has added a 37–page introduction, including a short biography of Wander, an interpretation of this unique proverbial "diary," and a bibliography concerning Wander's important paremiographical and paremiological work (pp. xxxi-xxxvii). For Wander see also nos. 2028–2029 and nos. 2988–2993.

3325. Doyle, Charles Clay. "Appendix D. Reports, Translations, and Adaptations of More's Latin Poems in the Sixteenth and Seventeenth Century." *Thomas More, Latin Poems.* Ed. Clarence H. Miller et al. New Haven/Connecticut: Yale University Press, 1984. 697–709.

A detailed analysis of the proverbial content of Sir Thomas More's (1478–1535) *Epigrammata* (1518ff.). Doyle discusses the parallels between epigrams and proverbs, calling the latter "oral epigrams." He quotes a number of examples and shows how they were cited by Erasmus of Rotterdam (1469–1536) and later collectors of proverbs, aphorisms and epigrams. It is possible that More's proverbial epigrams had some effect on the dissemination of proverbs in England. Such expressions as "Like lips, like lettuce," "There's many a slip 'twixt the cup and the lip" and "Happiness is like the good hours of an ague" were to become common in English, but not until 1518. Thomas More certainly is proof for the fact that epigrammatic writers from every literary period have versified, elaborated, or commented on proverbs.

3326. Doyle, Charles Clay. "The Homeless Ass in Jonson's *A Tale of a Tub.*" *Notes and Queries*, 229, new series 31 (1984), 241–242.

Short comments on the use of the proverb "An ass's ears are made of horns" in *A Tale of a Tub* (1633) by Ben Jonson (1572–1637). Doyle quotes the proverb in its dramatic context and cites a variant out of Sir Thomas More's (1478–1535) *History of Richard III* (1543). Other references are given, and Doyle points out the connection of this English proverb with an Aesopic fable.

3327. Doyle, Charles Clay. "Looking Behind Two Proverbs of More."
       Moreana, 23, nos. 91–92 (1986), 33–35.

         Comments on Sir Thomas More's (1478–1535) use of the
       proverbial expression "Out of the frying pan into the fire" and
       the proverb "All is good that helpeth" in his *Dialogue Concerning
       Heresies* (1528). For the first text Doyle is able to cite another
       reference in More's works, and he also quotes Greek and Latin
       variants, including two of them out of Erasmus of Rotterdam's
       (1469–1536) *Adagia* (1500ff.). For the second proverb he
       presents Italian variants based on a fable. It is not clear whether
       the tale itself had originally been told in Italian and More simply
       retained the Italian proverbial punch line, or whether the tale
       was a bilingual ethnic joke circulating in London at More's time.

3328. Doyle, Charles Clay. "Milton's Monolingual Woman and Her
       Forebears." *Proverbium*, 5 (1988), 15–21.

         Doyle sets out to prove that John Milton (1608–1674) most
       likely did not originate the misogynous English proverb "One
       tongue is enough for a woman." He comments on an anecdote
       repeated by various biographers of Milton claiming that Milton is
       supposed to have uttered this phrase to his daughter on various
       occasions. Doyle states that there is a tendency of certain
       proverbs being attached to famous persons even though their
       authorship cannot be proven. While he is not able to cite earlier
       precise references of this proverb, Doyle can show that its basic
       idea, i.e. women have no need for knowing any foreign
       languages, was expressed in epigrammatic writings in the 16th
       century by such authors as Sir John Davies (1565?–1618?) and Sir
       John Harington (1561?–1612). Doyle also speculates that this
       commonplace topos might actually have come about from Latin
       sources.

3329. Doyle, Charles Clay. "Folklore." *Spenser Encyclopedia.* Ed. A.C.
       Hamilton et al. Toronto: University of Toronto Press, 1990. 311–
       312.

         Even though this is but a concise encyclopedia article, Doyle
       succeeds in presenting a detailed review of Edmund Spenser's
       (1552–1599) frequent integration of folklore materials in his *The*

Faerie Queene (1590/96). He explains that Spenser made much use of Celtic, Irish, and British folk traditions. Many folk narratives found their way into his works, but he was particularly keen on using fables and proverbs. Doyle cites a number of examples for both genres and indicates that Spenser was well aware of the close relationship between them. He might use the actual fable, only the proverb associated with it, or for that matter both of them together. Examples would be "A dog in the manger," "Sour grapes," and "To blow hot and cold." A short bibliography (p. 312) is attached, but for all proverbs included in Spenser's works see Charles Smith (no. 1753).

3330. Doyle, Charles Clay. "More Paremiological Publications by Archer Taylor." *Proverbium*, 8 (1991), 191–197.

Following earlier bibliographies of Archer Taylor's (1890–1973) paremiological publications by C. Grant Loomis (see no. 1102), Wayland D. Hand (no. 662), and Wolfgang Mieder (no. 1243), Doyle is able to list 20 more reviews of books on proverb matters that the indefatigable Taylor has written. Even more importantly, Doyle unearthed a number of short notes on individual proverbs and proverbial expressions among the rich personal library and papers of Archer Taylor that are now located at the library of the University of Georgia in Athens, Georgia. Short comments on the following phrases were published by Taylor between 1923 and 1971: "As throng as Throp's wife," "Sold down the river," "Holy mackerel," "Sound as a dollar," "The beehive as a symbol of thrift," "Raw head and bloody bones," "The Shanghai gesture in England," "Chinese proverbs," "Names in folktales," and "A seamless web." For Taylor see nos. 1854–1908, nos. 2933–2938, and nos. 4468–4469.

3331. Dreismann, Hildegard. *"Die Stimme des Blutes." Sprichwortrezeption im Dritten Reich.* M.A. thesis University Freiburg, 1988. 95 pp.

This is a valuable M.A. thesis on the use and misuse of German proverbs during the Third Reich. Dreismann starts with a general introduction to proverbs (pp. 1–14) and then presents an overview of the manipulative value that National Socialists saw in traditional proverbs (pp. 15–23). The major part of the thesis is dedicated to an informative study of the use of proverbs under National Socialism (pp. 24–87), especially the interpretation of proverbs as expressions of racial ideology, the use of proverbs as guides towards Aryan population control, "German" ideals expressed in proverbs, and the terrible misuse of proverbs as "folk proof" for anti-Semitism. Dreismann presents many awful examples, showing how the Nazis perverted proverbial wisdom for their racial theories that resulted in the death of millions of Jews. An important bibliography (pp. 92–95) is attached that includes hateful and anti-Semitic proverb collections and publications. See also Wolfgang Mieder for this topic (nos. 3858 and 3863).

3332.   Dubno, Barbara Riss, and John K. Walsh. "Pero Diaz de Toledo's *Proverbios de Seneca* and the Composition of *Celestina*, Act IV." *Celestinesca*, 11, no. 1 (1987), 3–12.

Not so much a literary but rather a philological study of some proverbs that appear in the fourth act of the anonymous Spanish tragedy *La Celestina* (c. 1499). The authors are able to show that several proverbs from Pero Diaz de Toledo's (15th century) *Proverbios de Seneca* (c. 1442) found their way into this famous literary work. The book of *Proverbios de Seneca* is based on a collection of pseudo-Senecan proverbs by Publilius Syrus (1st century B.C.) which Diaz de Toledo translated from the Latin into Spanish. Several comparative textual references from *La Celestina* and the *Proverbios de Seneca* are cited to establish the definite influence that the proverb collection had on the tragedy. The authors also comment shortly on the appearance of many proverbs throughout the literary work with some reference to earlier scholarship in the 20 bibliographical notes.

3333.   Dugas, André, and Anne-Marie Di Sciullo. "Le rôle des déterminants dans les expressions figées de langues romanes." *La locution. Actes du colloque international Université McGill, Montréal, 15–16 octobre 1984.* Eds. Giuseppe Di Stefano and Russell G. McGillivray. Montréal: Editions CERES, 1984. 56–69.

This is a comparative analysis of various aspects of Italian, Spanish and French proverbial or fixed expressions. The authors review some of the linguistic research on such phrases and stress their grammatical peculiarities. They also deal with definition problems and point out the difficulty of a semantic interpretation of idiomatic expressions without a context. Many examples are cited to indicate lexical, syntactical and semantic characteristics of idiomaticity. A useful bibliography (pp. 67–69) is attached.

3334. Duhme, Michael. *Phraseologie der deutschen Wirtschaftssprache. Eine empirische Untersuchung zur Verwendung von Phraseologismen in journalistischen Fachtexten.* Essen: Die Blaue Eule, 1991. 222 pp.

Duhme presents a major study of the use and function of German phraseological units in newspaper and magazine articles dealing with economics and business. Following a short introductory first chapter (pp. 12–15), the author gives a solid review of recent phraseological scholarship in the second chapter (pp. 16–70). This is followed in chapter three (pp. 71–118) with an analysis of various aspects of these fixed phrases, among them classification, semantics, stability, structure, function, form, and metaphor. In the fourth chapter (pp. 119–157) Duhme continues this investigation by looking specifically at the idiomaticity, syntax, morphology, variants, and content of these fixed phrases. The fifth and last chapter (pp. 158–165) summarizes these findings and claims that there are numerous phraseological units which are clearly based on the language and concepts of economics, business, and trade. Many examples are cited, and an entire list (pp. 166–207) of them is provided at the end of this book together with a valuable bibliography (pp. 209–222).

3335. Duijvestijn, Bob W.Th. "Die erste deutsche Übersetzung der niederländischen Sprichwortsammlung *Proverbia Communia.*" *Rheinische Vierteljahrsblätter*, 53, no. 1 (1989), 52–91.

The author starts with a discussion of the 12 printed copies of the anonymous Dutch proverb collection *Proverbia communia sive seriosa* from the years 1480 to 1497. He mentions that the collection consists of 803 Dutch proverbs with Latin translations, he refers to Richard Jente's excellent scholarly edition of the collection (see no. 801), and he states that this work had much influence on the later collections of Heinrich Bebel (1472–1518),

Antonius Tunnicius (c.1470–c.1544), and Sebastian Franck (1499–1542). He then presents a comparative analysis of three German translations of this collection from 1485 and 1495, stressing in particular phonetic, lexical, morphological, and syntactical matters. Comparative charts and detailed discussions of linguistic matters like sound shifts, vowel changes, orthography, and vocabulary differences are included.

3336. Dumistracel, Stelian. "Valente cognitive ale contextelor paremiologice." *Proverbium Dacoromania*, 4 (1989), 15–18.

A short article on a number of Rumanian proverbs, proverbial expressions, and idioms that contain the word "tara" (lat. terra, i.e. land, country). Dumistracel explains that these phrases go back to the worldview of a rural and agricultural society where "tara" could also refer to the collective population of a state. He discusses the meaning of several examples and argues that proverbs can be important linguistic documents for etymological and diachronic studies of culture and history. A French summary (pp. 17–18) is attached.

3337. Dundes, Alan. *Life is Like a Chicken Coop Ladder. A Portrait of German Culture through Folklore.* New York: Columbia University Press, 1984. 174 pp.; now also in German translation as *Sie mich auch! Das Hinter-Gründige in der deutschen Psyche.* Weinheim: Beltz, 1985. 152 pp.

Based on numerous examples of German proverbs, proverbial expressions, graffiti, children's rhymes, songs, riddles, letters and literary sources Dundes presents a provocative picture of the "German national character." Following a brilliant discussion of various theories of national character and worldview, the author shows successfully that the Germans seem to have a more than ordinary interest in anal practices and products. His examples from oral and written folklore come from the Middle Ages and reach to the present day, including quotations from such cultural giants as Martin Luther (1483–1546), Wolfgang Amadeus Mozart (1756–1791), Günter Grass (1927–), and Heinrich Böll (1917–1985). Dundes offers Freudian interpretations of this preoccupation with feces on the one hand

and cleanliness on the other. He even attempts an explanation of German anti-Semitism from the early concept of the "Judensau" (Jew-sow) to the holocaust through this all-persuasive pattern. Proverbs clearly reflect the Germans' scatological preoccupation, and they are quoted liberally in this erudite yet controversial treatise. Nine illustrations, an excellent international bibliography (pp. 139–150), and a short index (pp. 151–152) add to the value of this courageous publication. For a similar annotation to the English edition of this book from 1984 see no. 2331.

3338. Dundes, Alan. "On Whether Weather 'Proverbs' are Proverbs." *Proverbium*, 1 (1984), 39–46; also published in A. Dundes. *Folklore Matters*. Knoxville/Tennessee: University of Tennessee Press, 1989. 92–97.

The author starts with a review of major collections and studies of so-called weather proverbs and then claims that they are not proverbs at all but rather nothing more than superstitions in rhymed fixed-phrase form. They are superstitions with textual features of proverbs, probably present for mnemonic purposes. Through such examples as "Red sky at night, sailor's delight" and "April showers bring May flowers" it is shown that superstitions are always interpreted literally while true proverbs are nearly always to be understood metaphorically. Dundes acknowledges, however, that the texts "Lightning never strikes twice in the same place" or "One swallow does not make a summer" could be understood both literally and metaphorically. Nevertheless, Dundes points out successfully that many weather proverbs are in fact superstitions, and he is correct in calling for a clearer generic differentiation on the part of folklorists. See Shirley L. Arora (no. 3076).

3339. Dunger, Rudolf. "Noch einmal: 'pucklige Verwandtschaft'." *Sprachpflege*, 37, no. 2 (1988), 24.

This is a very short note on the possible origin and meaning of the German proverbial expression "pucklige Verwandtschaft" (i.e. all distant relatives, the whole clan). Dunger speculates that the adjective "pucklig" comes from the gypsy word "puchlo" with the meaning of "far, distant, removed." For another attempt of solving this etymological question see Helmut Walther (no. 4525).

3340. Dunn, Robert D. "Corrections to the Oxford Dictionary of English Proverbs." *American Notes & Queries*, 24, no. 3 (1985), 52–54.

While working on his critical edition of William Camden's (1551–1623) *Remains Concerning Britain* (1614), Dunn noticed that Frank Percy Wilson (1889–1963) in his third edition of *The Oxford Dictionary of English Proverbs* (1970) had used a 1636 edition of this work. Dunn is thus able to provide earlier dates for a number of English proverbs from this source. He also presents a list of proverbs for which Wilson failed to provide a cross-reference to Morris Palmer Tilley's (1876–1947) *A Dictionary of the Proverbs in England in the 16th and 17th Centuries* (1950). A third list mentions proverbs for which Tilley antedates the *Oxford Dictionary*, and a fourth list includes proverbs that were not recorded in that standard historical proverb collection.

3341. Dunn, Robert D. "English Proverbs from William Camden's *Remains Concerning Britain*." *The Huntington Library Quarterly*, 49 (1986), 271–275.

The article contains the significant discovery that the German paremiographer Janus Gruterus (1560–1627) had obtained his list of English proverbs that he published in his *Florilegium Ethico-Politicum* (1610/12) from William Camden (1551–1623). In his edition of this list of "Proverbia Britannica" (*Washington University Studies, Humanistic Series*, 11 [1924], 409–423), Archer Taylor (1890–1973) had mistakenly supposed that Camden had copied from Gruterus. Hence, all citations of English proverbs credited to Gruterus in the standard historical proverb dictionaries should be credited to Camden. His list as published by Gruterus contained 335 proverbs. To this Camden added 54 more to form a separate chapter in his *Remains Concerning Britain* (1614). In 1623 he added 182 more proverbs for a total of 571 texts. Camden's main source was undoubtedly John Heywood's (1497?–1580?) *A Dialogue of Proverbs* (1546).

Dunn also includes a list of proverbs that appear in the *Remains* which are not part of the actual proverb chapter.

3342. Dzobo, N.K. "The Indigenous African Theory of Knowledge and Truth: Example of the Ewe and Akan of Ghana." *Phenomenology in Modern African Studies.* Ed. Sunday O. Anozie. Owerri: Conch Magazine, 1982. 85–102.

The author investigates what the indigenous African culture conceives to be knowledge and truth based on epistemological evidence as found in everyday speech and also in oral literature, i.e. proverbs and wise sayings of the Ewe and Akan people of Ghana. Dzobo deals with the concept of knowledge, the method of knowing, the passive way of knowing, categories of knowledge, attitudes towards knowledge, and the concept of truth and the various terms in the African languages for it. Throughout the essay the author quotes numerous African proverbs with English translations. He also contrasts this indigenous proverbial thought with Biblical concepts that the Christian missionaries brought to Africa.

E

3343. Eberhard, Wolfram. "Proverbs in Selected Chinese Novels." *Proverbium,* 2 (1985), 21–57.

A diligent investigation of six long and eight short Chinese novels from early times to the 20th century for their inclusion of proverbs. Eberhard lists all the titles of the novels and includes a short introduction to his statistical analysis. He establishes a list of 24 code numbers for such matters as proverbs with two lines, six words per line, rhyme, parallel structure, man speaks to woman, speaker gives advice, introduction (i.e. introductory formula), etc. The rest of the article presents a detailed statistical analysis in percentages along these lines based on 830 proverbs from the longer novels and 198 from the shorter works. At the end Eberhard cites the 20 most frequent proverbs in English translation. The various statistical tables provide much objective data as far as the use and function of proverbs in Chinese literature are concerned. It is to be hoped that other such studies based on research methods of the Social Sciences will be undertaken.

3344. Eckert, Rainer. "Neueste sowjetische Monographien zur russischen und slawischen Phraseologie. *Sprachwissenschaftliche Informationen,* 2 (1981), 85–102.

This is an important review article of recent Soviet monographs concerning Russian and Slavic phraseology. Eckert states that some scholars have spoken of a "phraseological explosion" in the Soviet Union, and he points out that many publications have dealt with the formation, semantics, and variants of phraseological units as well as comparative phraseology. The comments regarding Valerii M. Mokienko's *Slavianskaia frazeologiia* (1980, 2nd ed. 1989) are of particular interest (pp. 85–92), since this monograph deals with most theoretical questions of phraseology with many examples from various languages of the Soviet Union. These theoretical and primarily linguistic publications also concern questions of stability, structure, semiotics, metaphor, poetics, etc. The 20 notes (pp. 100–102) contain valuable bibliographical information. For Valerii Mokienko see no. 2651.

3345. Eckert, Rainer (ed.). *Untersuchungen zur slawischen Phraseologie I.* Berlin: Akademie der Wissenschaften der DDR, 1982. 152 pp. (=*Linguistische Studien*, series A, Arbeitsberichte, no. 95).

An important essay volume concerning Slavic phraseology edited by Rainer Eckert. The papers of interest to paremiologists are Rainer Eckert, "Zum Problem der Identität phraseologischer Wendungen" (pp. 1–33); Eugenie Rechtsiegel, "Zum Begriff der Stabilität in der Phraseologie" (pp. 62–76); Lutz-Rainer Howe, "Zur lexikalisch-quantitativen Varianz von Phrasemen am Beispiel des Slowakischen" (pp. 77–98); Helgunde Henschel, "Die morphologischen Formen phraseologischer Wendungen (am Material des Tschechischen)"; Marta Kostov, "Feste Vergleiche im Bulgarischen" (pp. 121–142); and Kurt Günther, "Über die Zeichenverwendung bei der Darstellung der Phraseologie" (pp. 143–152). These linguistic studies deal with such varied aspects as identity, stability, variability, and semiotics of phraseological units. The examples stem from such Slavic languages as Russian, Czech, Slovakian, Bulgarian, etc., but many German translations are provided. For annotations see nos. 3346, 4220, 3619, 3580, 3720, 3541.

3346. Eckert, Rainer. "Zum Problem der Identität phraseologischer Wendungen." *Linguistische Studien*, series A, Arbeitsberichte, no. 95 (1982), 1–33.

Eckert begins his intriguing article on the identity of phraseological units with a review of some of the subgenres that are part of the field of phraseology, namely proverbs, proverbial expressions, fixed phrases, idioms, etc. While discussing their stability and variability, the author concerns himself with the question of their textual identity from one contextualized use to another. He is able to show that these phrases are modified considerably in actual use as far as phonetic, lexical, grammatical, and syntactical matters are concerned. Such changes obviously also influence the meaning of fixed phrases and might lead to polysemantic and homonymous phrases. Eckert cites numerous Russian examples with German translations. The 79 notes (pp. 27–33) contain valuable bibliographical references to Soviet and German phraseological scholarship.

3347. Eckert, Rainer. "Diachronische slawische Phraseologie." *Phraseologie und ihre Aufgaben.* Ed. Josip Matesic. Heidelberg: Julius Groos, 1983. 35–58.

This is a very informative review article concerning the impressive historical research on Slavic phraseology by Soviet scholars. Eckert analyzes the work by major scholars, and he argues convincingly that linguists' have paid too much attention to synchronic studies. Diachronic investigations are also of much importance since they establish the origin and geographical dissemination of phraseological units. But the study of variants, archaic words, dialect terms, metaphors, equivalents in other languages, loan translations, etc. of proverbs definitely requires an historical approach. This is also true for the comparative analysis of international and national proverbs. A few Russian examples are included, and the 50 notes (pp. 54–58) contain valuable bibliographical information.

3348. Eckert, Rainer. "Phraseologie." *Die russische Sprache der Gegenwart: Lexikologie.* Ed. Kurt Gabka. Leipzig: VEB Verlag Enzyklopädie, 1984. IV, 203–228.

An impressive survey of the entire field of phraseology with special reference to the contemporary Russian language. Eckert includes a description of phraseology and then presents a definition of phraseological units. Next he considers the stability, idiomaticity, classification, structure, variability, synonymy, polysemy, homonymy, antonymy, function, style, origin, and derivation of fixed phrases. Eckert relies heavily on Soviet research results, and he cites many Russian examples with German translations. A precise and valuable introduction to the linguistic concerns of phraseology.

3349. Eckert, Rainer. "Russische Phraseme und Phraseotexteme mit 'khleb (-) sol''. Zur Definition des Objektbereiches und der Einheiten der Phraseologie." *Linguistische Studien*, series A, Arbeitsberichte, no. 120 (1984), 1–30.

Based on 300 Russian proverbial texts containing the words "khleb (-) sol'" (bread—salt), Eckert attempts to show the difference between normal sentences and phraseological units in which these words are present. He cites simple (short) and complex fixed phrases, and in one section he discusses such texts that refer specifically to the custom of greeting a guest with bread and salt. He also includes proverbial comparisons in his analysis of the various types of phraseological units that are based on these two words. Lexical, structural, and semantic identity and variability are analyzed by citing proverbs and their variants. Altogether Eckert quotes 100 Russian texts without translations. A useful bibliography (pp. 29–30) on Russian phraseology is attached.

3350. Eckert, Rainer. "Russische Phraseologismen mit der Komponente 'vologa'." *Slavia Orientalis*, nos. 3–4 (1984), 351–355.

Analyzes Russian phraseological units that contain the East Slavic dialect word "vologa" (a liquid fat food dish). The word comes from the Old Russian language of the 12th/13th century and is not in use anymore today. Eckert is able to cite a number of early Russian proverbs and proverbial expressions which include the word in the meaning of something that is eaten with bread or served with meat. He presents etymological, historical, and cultural explanations for these texts and argues that diachronic paremiology is important for an understanding of archaic words and older proverbial texts.

3351. Eckert, Rainer (ed.). *Untersuchungen zur slawischen Phraseologie II*. Berlin: Akademie der Wissenschaften der DDR, 1984. 254 pp. (=*Linguistische Studien*, series A, Arbeitsberichte, no. 120).

A second significant essay volume on Slavic phraseology edited by Rainer Eckert (see no. 3345 above). The articles touching on paremiological concerns are Rainer Eckert, "Russische Phraseme und Phraseotexteme mit 'khleb (-) sol''".

Zur Definition des Objektbereiches und der Einheiten der Phraseologie" (pp. 1–30); Kurt Günther, "Prädikativphraseme im Deutschen und Russischen" (pp. 31–66); Helgunde Henschel, "Die Minimalphraseme in konfrontativer Sicht (am Material des Tschechischen, Slowakischen, Russischen und Deutschen)" (pp. 67–95); Lutz-Rainer Howe, "Zur lexikalisch-quantitativen Varianz von Phrasemen im Tschechischen und Slowakischen (Versuch einer vergleichenden Beschreibung)" (pp. 96–120); Karina Rainsh, "K voprosu ob otrazhenii vo frazeologii kommunikativnogo mimikozhestovogo povedeniia" (pp. 121–137); Marta Kostov, "Vergleiche im Roman *Unter dem Joch* von Ivan Vazov in konfrontativer Betrachtung ihrer deutschen und russischen Wiedergabe" (pp. 138–174); Eugenie Rechtsiegel, "Phraseologismen im Text in konfrontativer Sicht (am Material des Polnischen und Deutschen)" (pp. 175–200); and Rainer Eckert, "Zur vergleichenden Phraseologie des Ostbaltischen" (pp. 201–216). The linguistic papers concern themselves with phraseological units, comparative phraseology, variability, gestures, literature, etc. Texts are cited from Russian, German, Czech, Slovakian, Polish, and Baltic languages. For annotations see nos. 3349, 3542, 3581, 3620, 4215, 3721, 4221, 3352.

3352. Eckert, Rainer. "Zur vergleichenden Phraseologie des Ostbaltischen." *Linguistische Studien*, series A, Arbeitsberichte, no. 120 (1984), 201–216.

A comparative analysis of phraseological units of the East Baltic languages, i.e. Lithuanian and Latvian. Eckert divides his 40 examples consisting of proverbs, proverbial expressions, idioms, etc. into sections which have complete, partial or semantic equivalents in the two languages. He broadens this investigation by also adding Russian and German fixed phrases to this comparison. The author cautions that his findings of parallel texts are only based on synchronic comparisons. Clearly diachronic considerations would have to be added if one wanted to research the origin of a particular expression and its translations from one language to another over time.

3353. Eckert, Rainer. "Satzwertige Phraseologismen im Russischen und Deutschen." *Linguistische Studien,* series A, Arbeitsberichte, no. 145 (1986), 35–42.

Eckert starts his article about fixed phrases that consist of complete sentences (i.e. proverbs, aphorisms, literary quotations, etc.) with a reference to the pioneering work of Grigorii L'vovich Permiakov (1919–1983; see no. 1428) who had stressed their realistic, semiotic, literal and semantic levels. He then cites a number of Russian and German examples explaining their levels of idiomaticity, function, polysemanticity, metaphor, stability, and variability. He also mentions introductory formulas and the fact that such complete sentences can also be changed to incomplete phraseological units (i.e. proverbial expressions, idioms, etc.).

3354. Eckert, Rainer. "Historische Phraseologie der slawischen Sprachen (unter Berücksichtigung des Baltischen). Prinzipien, Methoden und Resultate." *Zeitschrift für Slawistik,* 32 (1987), 801–807.

This is an important methodological article stressing the fact that it is high time that linguists interested in phraseology start to concentrate also on diachronic aspects of phraseological units rather than always stressing synchronic matters. For an historical approach to fixed phrases it will be necessary to investigate the special languages of occupations, social classes, folklore, and literature, and particular attention should be paid to written and oral dialect expressions. When discussing texts from older periods, it should be kept in mind that etymological, cultural, historical, and functional explanations be included. Obviously scholars should also investigate the various semantic levels, and in comparative historical research the problem of loan translations should be dealt with as well. Eckert includes a few Slavic and Baltic examples to illustrate these theoretical points.

3355. Eckert, Rainer. "Synchronische und diachronische Phraseologieforschung." *Beiträge zur allgemeinen und germanistischen Phraseologieforschung.* Ed. Jarmo Korhonen. Oulu: Oulun Yliopisto, 1987. 37–50.

Similar article to the previous one (no. 3354), stating once again that phraseologists have paid much attention to the linguistic and pragmatic aspects of phraseological units in contemporary languages. This synchronic approach must, however, be augmented by diachronic studies. Proverbs, proverbial expressions, and idioms which contain archaic words are of particular interest for an historical approach. Such texts also make reference to mythology, customs, beliefs, religion, etc. which are of significance for a better understanding of the worldview of people in earlier times. When studying a particular expression, it is wise to look at other texts that are related to it as well. The result would be diachronic and synchronic studies of fixed phrases that center around a certain motif, name, concept, word, etc. Such studies could, of course, be broadened to include texts from a number of different cultures and languages. Eckert includes a few Russian and German examples as well as a short bibliography (pp. 49–50).

3356. Eckert, Rainer. "Zur Bedeutung des *Wiener deutsch-russischen Lexikons* vom Ende des 17. Jhs. für die russische historische Lexikologie und Phraseologie." *Prekursorzy slowianskiego jezykoznawstwa porownawczego (do konca XVIII w.).* Eds. Hanny Orzechowskiej and Mieczyslawa Basaja. Wroclaw: Ossolineum, 1987. 151–157.

This is a short description of the high value of an old German-Russian dictionary for the historical study of Russian phraseological units. The dictionary *Teutscher, Und Reussischer, Dictionarium* was originally put together at the end of the 17th century, and it has been newly edited by the Austrian Slavist Gerhard Birkfellner with the title *Das Wiener deutsch-russische Wörterbuch* (1984). It contains close to one thousand pages, and on pp. 3–8 appears a list of Russian and German proverbs and literary quotations. Eckert explains that many proverbial expressions and idioms are listed throughout the dictionary, making it a valuable source for the historical and cultural study of older Russian phrases. He cites a few examples in both languages, also showing the difficulty that the early lexicographers had in finding German equivalents for the Russian expressions.

3357. Eckert, Rainer. "Zur historischen Phraseologie (an russischem Material)." *Aktuelle Probleme der Phraseologie.* Eds. Harald Burger and Robert Zett. Bern: Peter Lang, 1987. 203–224.

> This is yet another plea by Rainer Eckert for more emphasis by phraseologists on diachronic research. As an illustration he presents a detailed historical study of the Russian phrase "Valit' cherez pen' kholodu" (To do something as best one can, by hook or by crook). He cites 33 references from early written records to the 20th century, including many lexical variants as well as different types of expressions (proverbs, proverbial expressions, idioms, etc.). At the end of the article Eckert states that historical scholarship on fixed phrases must consider all expressions that contain a certain word, motif, concept, etc. over a long period of time and from different sources (folklore, religious writings, literature, mass media, etc.). Equivalents from related languages that might be loan translations should also be studied. In fact, serious diachronic studies of this type very quickly develop into philological, historical, and cultural monographs of considerable length.

3358. Eckert, Rainer. "Zur historischen Phraseologie der slawischen Sprachen." *Z problemow frazeologii polskiej i slowianskiej.* Eds. Mieczyslawa Basaja and D. Rytel. Wroclaw: Ossolineum, 1988. IV, 59–70.

> Once again Eckert stresses the importance of diachronic and comparative phraseological research, stating that phraseologists have been too preoccupied with synchronic questions about contemporary fixed phrases. This time he presents a detailed discussion of various types of phraseological units containing the Russian word "koza" (goat). He cites many examples from Slavic and Baltic languages, clearly showing the importance of dialect, occupational, social, and literary variants. He also argues that historical investigations must deal with such matters as idiomaticity, polysemanticity, and function. Comparative texts from other languages should be included, thus resulting in comprehensive studies of "phraseological nests" of all expressions concerning a particular noun, concept, motif, etc.

3359. Eckert, Rainer. "Die Bedeutung der Sprichwörter für die historische Erforschung und Etymologisierung der Phraseme (am Material des Russischen)." *Proverbium,* 6 (1989), 9–24.

In this article Eckart explains the importance of old or dialect proverbs for the diachronic study of all fixed phrases that contain the same major word, concept, motif, etc. He also presents a careful differentiation between proverbs and proverbial expressions, arguing that proverbs often are the origin of shorter phraseological units. Eckert then cites 28 historical variants of fixed phrases that contain the Russian word "vológa" (food, nourishment). Next he considers the Russian proverbial comparison "Kak v vodu gliadel" (Like looking into the water, i.e. to prophesy), this time citing 23 variants from various Russian and Baltic sources. For both sets of examples he is able to show that now extinct proverbs were the origin of this multitude of related phrases.

3360. Eckert, Rainer. "Phraseologische Untersuchungen zum Baltischen und Slawischen. Litauische Phraseologismen mit den variativen Komponenten 'kélmas', 'vélnias' und russische mit 'leshii' und 'chert'." *Zeitschrift für Slawistik,* 34, no. 2 (1989), 163–176.

This is a very detailed etymological and historical study of Baltic and Slavic fixed phrases that contain the Lithuanian words "kélmas" (tree stump) and "vélnias" (devil) or the Russian equivalent nouns "leshii" (forest spirit) and "chert" (devil). Eckert cites 11 Lithuanian and 23 Russian phraseological units, convincingly showing that one of the major characteristics of proverbial expressions is their variability over time and from language to language. The variants are especially pronounced in various dialect expressions. At the end of the article the author also states that some of these phrases play a considerable role in fairy tales.

3361. Eckert, Rainer. "Russ. 'Gol kak cokól'—'bettelarm': Versuch einer etymologischen Erklärung." *Zeitschrift für Slawistik,* 34, no. 5 (1989), 736–742.

In this interesting study Eckert investigates the many variants of the Russian proverbial comparison "Gol kak cokól" (very poor, i.e. as poor as a church mouse). He divides them into five major groups in which the comparative noun is replaced (1) by other nouns relating to parts of the hand, (2) by words for pole or stem of a tree, (3) by terms for beating tools, (4), by various words for weapon, and (5) by the noun "drum." As a sixth group Eckert refers to some variants that actually are identical to the quite widely distributed western European proverbial comparison that refers to a church mouse or rat.

3362. Eckert, Rainer. "Phraseologismen mit der Komponente 'Rettich' im Litauischen und Ostslawischen." *Lituanistica,* no. 1 (1990), 69–77.

This time Eckert studies numerous Lithuanian and East Slavic variants of fixed phrases that contain the word "radish." He includes etymological explanations and shows that these expressions usually have something to do with a dispute, quibble, quarrel, or argument. While there are many proverbial expressions based on this noun, there are also quite a few proverbial comparisons that make use of it. Eckert lists many examples and includes lexical, morphological, and semantic discussions. A Lithuanian abstract (p. 77) is provided.

3363. Eckert, Rainer. "Prinzipien und Methoden der historisch-vergleichenden Phraseologieforschung." *Proceedings of the Fourteenth International Congress of Linguistics, Berlin/GDR, August 10–15, 1987.* Eds. Werner Bahner, Joachim Schildt, and Dieter Viehweger. Berlin: Akademie-Verlag, 1990. III, 2461–2463.

In this short paper Eckert calls for a greater emphasis on historical and comparative studies of phraseology. He argues that phraseologists should be concerned with historical questions, especially since so many linguists have studied phraseological units from different countries only from a synchronic point of view. Citing a few Slavic examples, Eckert shows that the comparative analysis of fixed phrases has to ask questions concerning their origin and geographical dissemination. He also argues that scholars should not only look at literary texts from different centuries but also at professional and journalistic publications and their use of proverbs and proverbial expressions. Finally, the historical approach is of importance for the study of equivalent phraseological units in other languages.

3364. Eckert, Rainer. "Russkaia frazeologiia v nemetskoiazychnoi auditorii." *Zeitschrift für Slawistik,* 35, no. 3 (1990), 312–325.

Eckert starts with a statement that stresses the importance of teaching Russian phraseology in the German classroom. He argues that studying Russian as a foreign language must definitely include the instruction of the many proverbs, proverbial expressions, and other fixed phrases. He draws particular attention to the etymological, historical, and cultural value of learning phraseological units of the target language. The students will also learn to appreciate the use of archaic and dialect words in these traditional phrases. A useful bibliography (pp. 324–325) is provided.

3365. Eckert, Rainer. "Spezifisches bei der konfrontativen Untersuchung der Phraseologie zweier oder mehrerer Sprachen." *Zeitschrift für Slawistik,* 35, no. 4 (1990), 488–492.

In this theoretical article Eckert investigates some of the problems that arise from a comparative analysis of phraseological units of two or more languages. He mentions phonetic, lexical, and morphological similarities or differences, depending on how closely the compared languages are related to each other. There are also the difficult issues of metaphor, content, and semantics that need to be addressed. In any comparative study it becomes obvious very quickly that there exists a considerable difference or asymmetry in the form, structure, and meaning of fixed phrases. The 17 notes contain valuable bibliographical information.

3366. Eckert, Rainer. *Studien zur historischen Phraseologie der slawischen Sprachen (unter Berücksichtigung des Baltischen).* München: Otto Sagner, 1991. 262 pp.

With this book Rainer Eckert summarizes the important arguments and results of his individual historically oriented phraseological studies annotated above (see nos. 3344–3365).

The first part of the book (pp. 1–54) reviews the diachronic scholarship of Slavic and Baltic fixed phrases, and the author also includes valuable statements concerning the purpose, the sources, and the methodology of historical phraseology. In the second part (pp. 55–237) Eckert collects 12 exemplary studies that deal with certain groups of phraseological units. In each case he presents etymological, lexical, and semantic explanations while citing dozens of variants from dictionaries, different dialects, literature, special social and occupational groups, etc. The third part (pp. 237–246) summarizes the findings of these studies and states once again that diachronic phraseological research must consider so-called "phraseological nests," i.e. fixed phrases that all deal with a certain word, concept, motif, etc. Eckert also explains that variability and polysemanticity of the proverbial texts are of greatest importance in such investigations. A detailed international bibliography (pp. 247–262) concludes this invaluable book.

3367. Edwards, Gavin. "Repeating the Same Dull Round." *Unnam'd Forms. Blake and Textuality.* Eds. Nelson Hilton and Thomas A. Vogler. Berkeley/California: University of California Press, 1986. 26–48.

This is a valuable literary study of the proverbs and proverb-like statements that William Blake (1757–1827) used throughout his life. The first part of the article (pp. 26–40) deals with Blake's interest in formulaic language such as proverbs, aphorisms, clichés, etc., citing several examples from various poetic works. The second half (pp. 40–48) is dedicated specifically to Blake's interest in and use of proverbs and proverbial expressions. Several contextualized examples from the long poem "Proverbs of Hell" (1790) which is part of Blake's work *The Marriage of Heaven and Hell* (1790) are cited, but Edwards is able to show that Blake used proverbial speech in all of his writings. The main use and function of proverbs are to present analogies, add authority to a statement, and express poetic thoughts in everyday discourse. See also Randel Helms (no. 2457) and Michael Holstein (no. 2478).

3368. Ehegötz, Erika. "Die polnische Sprichwörtersammlung des C. Wurzbach." *Zeitschrift für Slawistik*, 31, no. 4 (1986), 565–570.

Interesting historical and biographical study of the paremiographer Constantin Wurzbach (1818–1893), a scholar and librarian from Vienna. Ehegötz presents a short sketch of his life and then gives a detailed description of Wurzbach's important Polish proverb collection published in German: *Die Sprichwörter der Polen historisch erläutert, mit Hinblick auf die eigenthümlichsten der Lithauer, Ruthenen, Serben und Slovenen und verglichen mit ähnlichen anderer Nationen, mit beigefügten Originalen. Ein Beitrag zur Kenntnis slawischer Culturzustände* (Lemberg 1846; 2nd ed. Wien 1852). This is an early comparative proverb collection of the Slavic languages meant to increase cultural awareness for Austrian and German readers. Wurzbach includes numerous explanatory notes, and he had much influence on later European paremiographers.

3369. Ehegötz, Erika. "Zur Entwicklung der polnischen idiomatischen Phraseologie in der zweiten Hälfte des 19. Jahrhunderts." *Zeitschrift für Slawistik*, 32, no. 6 (1987), 824–830.

In this article Erika Ehegötz attempts to show how Polish phraseology has changed towards the end of the 19th century. She cites major cultural and sociological changes of the Polish society that caused especially those fixed phrases to drop out of use that contain archaic words or refer to realia that have no more meaning in the modern age. She also claims that proverbial expressions with mythological or Biblical references are on a decline, while especially those phrases that refer to natural phenomena continue to be used with high frequency. The author mentions problems of idiomaticity, polysemanticity and semantics as contributory factors in the semantic innovations or eventual disappearance of phraseological units. Many Polish examples with German translations are cited to indicate that the phraseological corpus of modern languages does in fact undergo evolutionary developments.

3370. Ehegötz, Erika. "O znaczeniu niemieckojezycznych podrecznikow jezyka polskiego i rozmowek polsko-niemieckich XVIII i XIX w.

dla badan frazeologicznych." *Z problemow frazeologii polskiej i slowianskiej.* Eds. Mieczyslawa Basaja and D. Rytel. Wroclaw: Ossolineum, 1988. IV, 219–226.

This short article deals with German textbooks for the study of the Polish language and Polish-German dictionaries of the 18th and 19th centuries as valuable sources for the historical study of Polish phraseology. Citing numerous examples in both languages, Ehegötz shows that proverbs, proverbial expressions, and idioms were used quite often in these books for foreign language learning. Since many of them are quoted in sentences or dialogues, they are of much value to the diachronically interested phraseologist who needs contextualized texts to understand possible variations in meaning. These textbooks even contain proverbial texts that have not been listed in standard collections for such early dates.

3371. Ehegötz, Erika. "Über fremdsprachliche Einflüsse in der modernen polnischen Phraseologie (am Beispiel von 'jednym tchem')." *Wokol jezyka. Rozprawy i studia poswiecone,* no volume given (1988), 183–187.

The author starts with the statement that many archaic Polish proverbial expressions are dropping out of use while new fixed phrases become current that are based on the language and metaphors of technology, science, sports, economics, etc. There are also numerous examples of new phraseological units that are loan translated into Polish from other languages. The German phrase "In einem Atemzug" (In one breath, at the same time) has thus found its way into modern Polish as "Jednym tchem." Ehegötz cites references from various sources and shows that some variants exhibit definite semantic differences from the German original.

3372. Eismann, Wolfgang. "Psycholinguistische Voraussetzungen einer Definition der phraseologischen Einheit (phE)." *Phraseologie und ihre Aufgaben.* Ed. Josip Matesic. Heidelberg: Julius Groos, 1983. 59–95.

This is a valuable review article concerning the psycho- and neurolinguistic research on phraseology. Eismann points out that it is not enough to study only the texts themselves. It is also of great importance to ask the questions why people use phraseological units at all, how they remember and understand them, why certain mentally ill people do not comprehend them, etc. Eismann presents some explanations about the cognition of routine formulas, stereotypes, proverbs, proverbial expressions, etc. He points out that the comprehension and use of such fixed phrases is based on an understanding of their metaphors, the frequency of their use, their fixed structure, their familiarity, etc. It is also explained that schizophrenics have difficulty dealing with the abstract idea behind proverbs which they understand only literally. A helpful bibliography (pp. 91–95) is attached.

3373. Eismann, Wolfgang. "Bemerkungen zur Bedeutung von G.L. Permjakovs Theorie des Klischees für die Linguistik." *Semiotische Studien zum Sprichwort. Simple Forms Reconsidered I.* Eds. Peter Grzybek and W. Eismann. Tübingen: Gunter Narr, 1984. 277–293.

Important essay in German discussing Grigorii L'vovich Permiakov's (1919–1983) theoretical masterpiece *Ot pogovorki do skazki* (Moskva, 1970; in English translation: *From Proverb to Folk-Tale* [Moscow 1979]; see no. 1428) as it relates to modern linguistics. Eismann explains that Permiakov used a triadic model in his pioneering work on phraseological units or "clichés" as he called them: the linguistic level, the logico-semiotic level, and the level of realia. But while Permiakov worked primarily synchronically, Eismann argues that pragmatic and diachronic aspects of fixed phrases should be studied as well. He also discusses Permiakov's interest in homonymy, synonymy, polysemy, and structural analysis. A two-page (pp. 280–281) schematic chart of the relationship among types of language clichés, language levels, and disciplines studying them as well as another chart (p. 283) on types of clichés and their semiotic and structural nature are included.

3374. Eismann, Wolfgang. "Zeichenbausteine als Zeichen. Das Alphabet in der Phraseologie." *Aktuelle Probleme der Phraseologie.* Eds. Harald Burger and Robert Zett. Bern: Peter Lang, 1987. 225–243.

This is a fascinating comparative study of proverbs, proverbial expressions, and other fixed phrases that are based on various letters of the alphabet. Eismann cites English, French, German, Latin, and Russian examples, indicating clearly how international the use of letters as signs is throughout the world. Many expressions contain the three letters "ABC," others combine the two letters A and Z or X and Y, and there is of course also that almost universal American expression "Ok" or even "A-OK." Eismann indicates that some of the older phrases are hard to explain, but they certainly function as understandable signs with the individual letters contained in them being semiotic "building blocks." A useful bibliography (pp. 241–243) is attached.

3375. Eismann, Wolfgang. "Zum Problem der Äquivalenz von Phraseologismen." *Europhras 88. Phraséologie Contrastive. Actes du Colloque International Klingenthal-Strasbourg, 12–16 mai 1988.* Ed. Gertrud Gréciano. Strasbourg: Université des Sciences Humaines, 1989. 83–93.

A theoretical article dealing with the translation problem of phraseological units. Eismann starts with differentiating among several levels of equivalence and then discusses grammatical, structural, semantic, metaphorical and stylistic aspects that play a role in finding equivalent proverbial texts within the same language or among several languages. A few German examples are cited, but for the most part Eismann reviews major theoretical scholarship on linguistic equivalence that is also applicable to the comparative study of phraseology. His 21 notes contain important bibliographical references from the Soviet Umion.

3376. Eismann, Wolfgang. "Zur Frage der lexikographischen Berücksichtigung von nichtbinnendeutschen Phraseologismen in deutsch-slavischen phraseologischen Wörterbüchern." *Europhras 90. Akten der internationalen Tagung zur germanistischen Phraseologieforschung, Aske/Schweden 12.-15. Juni 1990.* Ed. Christine Palm. Uppsala: Acta Universitatis Upsaliensis, 1991. 43–61.

Eismann states that not much is known about those German phraseological units that are indigenous or at least linguistically unique to Austria and Switzerland. He points out that these fixed phrases are often quite different from their High German equivalents, especially in such areas as dialect, orthography, phonetics, pronunciation, morphology, vocabulary, and lexicology. Those expressions which refer to names, historical events, and special cultural facts are, of course, also different from basic German equivalents. All of this is of much importance for lexicographers who are working on bilingual phraseological dictionaries for the Slavic and German languages. Many examples are cited, and Eismann includes an index of Austrian phraseological units (pp. 56–61) with references to whether and how they are treated in German-Slavic dictionaries. A useful bibliography (pp. 55–56) is attached as well.

3377. Elchinova, Magdalena. "Poslovitsite i pogovorkite v plana na ezika i v plana na rechta." *Bulgarski folklor*, 14, no. 3 (1988), 8–16.

In her paper Elchinova studies a number of Bulgarian proverbs and proverbial expressions as part of language as such and as being used in actual speech acts. She stresses the fact that proverbial texts must be analyzed in context, their function and meaning clearly indicating cultural values. The author also considers aspects of semantic variation from the traditional fixed meaning, the style and structure of proverbs, the value system (worldview) expressed in them, and the competence of using proverbs effectively by native speakers. With an English summary (p. 16).

3378. Elizade, Zijnet E. "Atalar sfzi ve zerbi-mesellerin semantik inkishafyna dair." *Izvestiya Akademii Nauk Azerbaidzhanskoi SSR, Literatura, iazykai iskusstvo*, 2 (1984), 68–71.

In this short paper Elizade explains that proverbs and proverbial expressions reflect normal life, religious and legal concepts, and the worldview of a particular linguistic group of people. By analyzing a number of texts from the Azerbaijan Soviet Socialist Republic on the Caspian Sea, the author shows positive and negative values expressed in them. Equivalent proverbs in Russian, Latin, French, and German reveal many semantic similarities. A Russian abstract (p. 71) is provided.

3379. Emenanjo, E. Nolue. "Are Igbo Wellerisms Proverbs?" *Anu: Journal of Igbo Culture,* no. 5 (1989), 62–77.

> The author starts with a discussion of various verbal folklore genres such as riddles, proverbs, folk tales, etc. He then defines proverbs in particular and argues that Igbo wellerisms are a distinct genre with its own structure. These wellerisms consist of two parts, namely the matrix sentence and the noun phrase complement, as for example in "The monkey says that it remained a little for eyelids to spoil its face" (The monkey says that but for its eyelids, it would have been very handsome) or "(When) a woman cooks a bad meal she says that it is the one to her taste" (If a woman prepares a bad meal, she will say it is the one to her taste). Emenanjo cites numerous Igbo examples with English translations, analyzing especially their structure and meaning. It should be noted that this type of African wellerism is considerably different from the Euopean type which exhibits a definite triadic structure. A useful bibliography (pp. 76–77) is attached.

3380. Emeto-Agbasière, Julie. "Le proverbe dans le roman africain." *Présence francophone,* no. 29 (1986), 27–41.

> This is a literary proverb investigation dealing with the use and function of proverbial folk speech in the African novels of Amadou Hampaté Bâ (1899–) and Ahmadou Kourouma (1940–). The author starts with a discussion of proverbs as expressions of general truths and oral tradition, and she then presents numerous contextualized examples to illustrate how proverbs serve as metaphor, narrative device, and formulaic characterization. The form and content of the proverbs are also analyzed. A French abstract (p. 27) is included.

3381. Endstrasser, Vilko. "Poslovice u kontekstu." *Narodna umjetnost,* 28 (1991), 159–190.

> The author studies the use and function of Serbo-Croatian proverbs in Yugoslavian oral communication, literary texts, and

newspaper articles. Many contextualized examples are cited, and Endstrasser analyzes such aspects as structure, metaphor, form, variation, and meaning. It is argued that proverbs continue to be used in the modern age because they are part of folk speech, because they express the traditional worldview, and because they add expressiveness to oral speech acts as well as to literary and journalistic writings. The author also includes some ethnographical and linguistic comments regarding the high frequency of proverbs in modern discourse on various intellectual levels. A useful bibliography (pp. 188–189) and an English abstract (p. 190) are provided.

3382. Engelking, Anna. "'Klac na czym swiat stoi . . .' wedlug 'ksiegi przyslow' i slownikow jezyka polskiego." *Przeglad Humanistyczny,* 33, no. 7 (1989), 83–93.

The author explains that there are dozens of proverbs and proverbial expressions in the Polish language connected with "swearing" and "casting a spell." She cites numerous examples and explains their cultural background and meaning. For the proverbial expression "Klac na czym swiat stoi" (i.e. To swear up a storm) she includes a detailed analysis of its origin, history, and use to the present day. It is shown that historically and culturally interested paremiologists must also deal with beliefs, superstitions, and folklore in general to understand some of the archaic words and metaphors of phraseological units.

3383. England, Juliana Elizabeth. *Abstract Responding to a Proverbs Test by LCVA, RCVA, and Control Subjects.* Diss. State University of New York at Buffalo, 1986. 159 pp.

In order to examine the effects of cerebral hemisphere damage on verbal abstract reasoning, a "Proverbs Interpretation Test" was administered to adults with left (dominant) and right hemisphere brain damage and a control group. The psychological proverbs test consisted of 40 texts, of which half were presented auditorily and half visually on cards to the subjects. They responded verbally and their responses were examined as being abstract, literal, accurate, complete, and immediate. Results indicated that the groups do differ with respect to abstract reasoning ability. A copy of the proverbs test (pp. 118–130), many statistical tables, and a valuable bibliography (pp. 143–159) are included.

3384. Engler, Balz. "*Othello,* II,1,155: 'To Change the Cod's Head for the Salmon's Tail'." *Shakespeare Quarterly,* 35, no. 2 (1984), 202–203.

A short note attempting to explain the meaning of the proverbial expression "To change the cod's head for the salmon's tail" spoken by Iago in William Shakespeare's (1564–1616) tragedy *Othello* (1604). Basically the phrase expresses the idea of "to make a foolish exchange." Engler explains the food imagery and possible sexual meaning of cod's head (=penis), but above all he argues that the phrase most likely is a bawdy variation of the English proverb "Better be the head of yeomanry than the tail of the gentry."

3385. Ergis, G.U. "Poslovitsy i pogovorki." In G.U. Ergis. *Ocherki po iakutskomu fol'kloru.* Moskva: Nauka, 1974. 340–350.

In this book chapter the folklorist G.U. Ergis (1908–1968) presents a general overview of the proverbs and proverbial expressions from the Iakut (Yakut) Autonomous Soviet Socialist Republic. He starts with a definition of the two genres and includes detailed comments on their structure, style (brevity, rhythm. rhyme, etc.), metaphor, content, and meaning. Many examples from collections, literary works, and folk speech of the Iakutsk people from the northeastern part of the Soviet Union are included.

3386. Erichsen, Gerda Moter. "Wendungen in vier verschiedenen Sprachen—Versuch einer Klassifikation." *Moderna språk,* 82, no. 1 (1989), 29–34.

This is a clear discussion of the difficulty that arises when students or translators have to render phraseological units into another language. Erichsen mentions that the cultural differences have to be considered, and she explains in particular the semantic and metaphorical problems in the translation of proverbial expressions. Several comparative examples from

German, Norwegian, English, and French are cited, some being exactly the same in all four languages while others might only share a certain noun or verb in common. There are, of course, also texts with the same meaning whose metaphors and and/or lexical terms are completely different. The author includes some useful hints for teachers and translators of how to deal with such fixed phrases.

3387. Erler, Anette. "Zur Geschichte des Spruches 'Bis dat, qui cito dat'." *Philologus*, 130, no. 2 (1986), 210–220.

A detailed philological and historical investigation of the medieval Latin proverb "Bis dat, qui cito dat" (He gives twice who gives quickly). Erler explains that Erasmus of Rotterdam (1469–1536) was wrong when he pointed to Seneca (4 B.C.-65 A.D.) as the possible author of this proverb. He is able to show that longer variants of this text stem from the early Middle Ages, but it is not known who reduced them to the precise proverbial formulation in the 11th century. The author traces references of the proverb through the 15th century and concludes that this popular saying is not in current use anymore.

3388. Estill, Robert B., and Susan Kemper. "Interpreting Idioms." *Journal of Psycholinguistic Research*, 11 (1982), 559–568.

The authors designed a "proverbs test" in which each set of four sentences was designed around a common idiom or proverbial expression, including sentences in which (1) the contextualized idiom was used figuratively, (2) the idiom was used literally, and (3) the idiom's use was ambiguous between literal and figurative interpretations. A fourth sentence in each set contained the final word of the idiom used in a nonidiomatic expression. Using college students as subjects, it was found that idioms are automatically processed as discrete lexical entries, and that previously observed reaction time advantages for figurative expressions may reflect integrative processes rather than retrieval of meaning. An abstract (p. 559) and a short bibliography (p. 567–568) are provided.

3389. Ettinger, Stefan. "Einige Probleme der lexikographischen Darstellung idiomatischer Einheiten (Französisch—Deutsch)." *Europhras 88. Phraséologie Contrastive. Actes du Colloque International Klingenthal-Strasbourg, 12–16 mai 1988.* Ed. Gertrud Gréciano. Strasbourg: Université des Sciences Humaines, 1989. 95–115.

Basing his comments on the careful investigation of many French-German phraseological dictionaries, Ettinger reaches the conclusion that they are filled with inexact or even wrong information. He shows especially that they contain false diachronic statements, and quite often the stylistic levels are not indicated properly. There are also problems in explaining those fixed phrases that are based on gestures, and many dictionaries don't include information concerning the appropriateness of certain phrases for people of different age or social groups. Eight comparative tables illustrating these points and a very helpful bibliography are included in this lexicographical study.

3390. Everett, Jane. "Les locutions anciennes et les locutions québécoises." *La locution. Actes du colloque international Université McGill, Montréal, 15–16 octobre 1984.* Eds. Giuseppe Di Stefano and Russell G. McGillivray. Montréal: Editions CERES, 1984. 205–228.

Historical study of three medieval French proverbial expressions and their use and meaning in the modern French language spoken in the province of Québec in Canada. The phrases are "Avoir les piés (pieds) blancs envers quelqu'un" (To have the white feet against someone, i.e. to lack something or to fail), "Avoir son panier percé" (To have one's basket pierced, i.e. to make love), and "Faire le renard" (To make the fox, i.e. to flee). Everett shows how these expressions have undergone changes in their meaning, wording and use. Cultural and etymological explanations are included that help to understand the survival of these old phrases. A bibliography (pp. 226–228) is provided.

3391. Everman, Welch D. "Harry Mathews's *Selected Declarations of Dependence:* Proverbs and the Forms of Authority." *The Review of Contemporary Fiction,* 7, no. 3 (1987), 146–153.

The author begins his intriguing essay with a discussion of "Oulipo" (Ouvroir de Littérature Potentielle), a French school of experimental writers dedicated to a "workshop of potential literature." The American author Harry Matthews (1930–) attempts such "potential literature" in his *Selected Declarations of Dependence* (1977) by basing his poetic texts on "perverbs," a hybrid created by breaking traditional proverbs in half and joining different halves together. The result is a multitude of combinations and permutations of proverbs that take on the form of so-called "Antisprichwörter" (anti-proverbs). It is argued that Mathews liberates or undermines the collective authority and didacticism of traditional proverbs by these innovative linguistic "games."

F

3392. Fabian, Johannes. *Power and Performance. Ethnographic Explorations through Proverbial Wisdom and Theater in Shaba, Zaire.* Madison/Wisconsin: University of Wisconsin Press, 1990. 314 pp.

This is a superb study of performed theater in Zaire with special emphasis on performative ethnography, including important findings on the "anthropology of performance" and the "ethnography of speaking" (see chapter one, pp. 3–20). In the second chapter (pp. 21–39) the author discusses the proverb "Le pouvoir se mange entier" (Power is eaten whole) and cites many Luba texts that also refer to the use and abuse of power. Many ethnographic explanations are included, and Fabian explains the use of some proverbs in a careful analysis of an actually performed play trying to act out this proverb by the Troupe Théâtrale Mufwankolo in the next four chapters. The various scenes of the play are transcribed in different staging versions in their African original with English translations. On pp. 275–279 Fabian summarizes the use and function of proverbs in this new play, explaining that they express authoritative power. It must be stated, however, that this book is not so much concerned with paremiological questions but rather with traditional and experimental theater in Shaba, Zaire. The comprehensive bibliography (pp. 293–305) includes much relevant information concerning sociolinguistic aspects of African proverbs.

3393. Fadairo-Kédji, Dominique. "Proverbes fon du Bénin: une approche anthropologique." *Cahiers de littérature orale*, no. 13 (1983), 109–126.

An anthropological study of oral Fon proverbs from Benin in Africa. The author discusses their structure and language as well as their origin and function in everyday life. Many examples with

French translations are cited, but three proverbs are analyzed in greater detail, including their form, variation, use, meaning, and social significance. The Fon people are fond of using proverbs in their daily life to enrich their speech, to give it the authority of tradition and thus to convince listeners. Two illustrations, a short bibliography (pp. 123–124) and an appendix concerning the Fon language conclude this investigation. With an English summary (p. 179).

3394. Fallows, Noel. "A Note on the Treatment of Some Popular Maxims in the *Buscón.*" Romance Notes, 29, no. 3 (1989), 217–219.

This is a short note dealing with a few proverbial texts in Francisco Goméz de Quevedo y Villegas' biographical novel *La vida del buscón llamado Don Pablos* (1644). Fallows cites variants from Spanish proverb collections and argues that the inclusion of proverbs help the literal and symbolic nature of certain passages. The author also explains that certain proverbs about horses and pride are clear indications of the fact that Pablos is feigning nobility, always trying to be something that he is not.

3395. Fasani, Remo. "Un Manzoni milanese?" *Studi e problemi di critica testuale,* 41 (1990), 51–66.

Fasani starts with the claim that the Italian writer Alessandro Manzoni (1785–1873), who lived all of his life in Milan, exhibits plenty of Milanese words and phrases that tie him to that city and region. The author lists numerous proverbs, proverbial expressions, idioms, and dialect words from Manzoni's long novel *I Promessi Sposi* (1827). These enumerations include no literary context and serve only as paremiographical and lexical proof of Manzoni's Milanese beackground.

3396. Faucon, Jean-Claude. "La sagesse populaire au service du roi: De l'utilisation des proverbes par un chroniqueur du XIVe siècle." *Richesse du proverbe.* Eds. François Suard and Claude Buridant. Lille: Université de Lille, 1984. I, 87–111.

A detailed analysis of the popular proverbial wisdom in the French *Chronique de Bertrand du Guesclin* (14th century) by

Cuvelier (14th century). Based on about 150 proverbial texts, Faucon discusses their introductory formulas, their distribution, and their verse form (the chronicle was written in the form of a *chanson de geste*). He also points out that the content of the proverbs reflect the worldview of that time. Some texts refer to the feudal society, many comment on the terrible realities of war, and yet another group of texts deals in particular with the king and his duties. Many French texts are cited, and it becomes clear that old chronicles do contain important texts for diachronic proverb research. There is no proverb index that would have augmented the paremiographical value of this study.

3397. Feeny, Sarah Jane. *The Aesthetics of Orality and Textuality in Spenser's "Faerie Queene."* Diss. University of Missouri, 1991. 204 pp.

Feeny investigates various genres of oral folklore that have been integrated by Edmund Spenser (1552–1599) into his *The Faerie Queene* (1590/96). Following a detailed introduction (pp. 1–40) in which the author discusses orality and how it relates to literary texts, she analyzes various genres (folk narratives, fables, proverbs, proverbial expressions, etc.) that Spenser employed in her first chapter (pp. 41–66). Chapter two (pp. 67–95) treats genealogy and the creation of myth, and the third chapter (pp. 96–124) on the wisdom of "Faerieland" looks at the use and function of proverbs for didactic and moralistic purposes. The same is true for the fourth chapter (pp. 125–149) where Feeny treats certain lists of encyclopedic wisdom based on traditional knowledge and beliefs. The fifth chapter (pp. 150–188) is a summary discussion of how the various oral genres are adapted for the literary text. Many contextualized examples are cited, but there is no proverb index (for that see Charles Smith [no. 1753]). A valuable bibliography is attached (pp. 189–204).

3398. Feichtl, Nancy G. *Using Proverbs to Facilitate Metaphorical Language Comprehension: A Curriculum Study.* Diss. University of Maryland, 1988. 263 pp.

This dissertation consists of two major parts, a theoretical and experimental one and a pragmatic and instructional second part. In the first five chapters (pp. 2–73) Feichtl presents the results of a study of the effects that the teaching of proverbs to nine year olds had on their ability to comprehend novel (traditional and invented) proverbs and general figurative language. This is followed by a number of proverbs tests especially designed for this study (pp. 74–100). The four chapters of the second part (pp. 113–263) are an enrichment curriculum with the title "Proverbs to Facilitate Metaphorical Language Comprehension" that consists of a collection of novel, high interest proverbs to be used for instruction. Sample quizzes to test the recall and comprehension of those proverbs are included as well. The curriculum is constructed so that each week students are taught the meaning and implication of two proverbs. The 220 proverbs provided are enough texts for three years of instruction. Ten statistical tables and a valuable bibliography (pp. 101–112) are provided.

3399. Felitsyna, V.P. "Nazvaniia russkikh kushanii v poslovitsakh i pogovorkakh." *Slovari i lingvostranovedenie.* Ed. E.M. Vershchagina. Moskva: Russkii iazyk, 1982. 153–156.

A general article on the names of foods in Russian proverbs and proverbial expressions. Felitsyna cites texts that refer to bread, cabbage, potatoes, porridge, water, etc. It is shown that these proverbs contain much historical and cultural information concerning everyday life. Some etymological explanations of archaic language forms are included, and a special point is made that these traditional texts express Russian worldview towards various types of food.

3400. Fenster, Thelma S. "Proverbs and Sententious Remarks in the Octosyllabic *Lion de Bourges.*" *Neuphilologische Mitteilungen,* 86, no. 2 (1985), 272–279.

Lamenting the fact that many French proverbs and sententious remarks from the Middle Ages have still not been registered in proverb collections, Fenster presents 85 texts arranged alphabetically according to key-words out of the lengthy, unedited manuscript of the later version of *Lion de Bourges.* The manuscript probably stems from the end of the 15th century and its source is the alexandrine *Lion de Bourges* (14th century). In addition to the list the author also discusses the use, function, content, and metaphor of these proverbs, citing at least some texts are cited in context. An English abstract (p. 272) is provided. See also Jean-Louis Picherit (no. 1455).

3401. Fernandez, Roberto. "El refranero en *T.T.T.* [*Tres tristes tigres*]." *Revista iberoamericana*, 57, no. 154 (1991), 265–272.

This is a literary investigation of the use and function of Spanish proverbs and proverbial expressions in Guillermo Cabrera Infante's (1929–) novel *Tres tristes tigres* (1967). Fernandez points out that Cabrera Infante is so fond of proverbial wisdom that he presents actual clusters of proverbs in his prose. While some of these texts might go back to classical sententious remarks and Biblical wisdom, there are also those examples which show definite Cuban origins. The author shows that Cabrera Infante employs proverbs for the purpose of paradox, parody, and alienation. Quite often the traditional proverbs are expressed as variants or mere allusions, but the reader is usally able to recognize the original proverb that is being played with. Many contextualized examples are cited, but there is no proverb index. The 32 notes contain useful bibliographical references.

3402. Firment, Michael Joseph. *Interpretation Components as a Measure of Learning for Proverb-Based Conceptual Categories.* Diss. University of Cincinnati, 1990. 107 pp.

This short dissertation reports on a proverbs test that was devised to measure the relationship between subject-written interpretations of proverb-based categories and later performance in the recognition of new instances. Eighty-six college students participated in the study, and a positive relationship between completeness of interpretation and later transfer performance was found. A useful bibliography (pp. 54–50), two statistical tables and several graphs, the proverbs test (pp. 67–78), and the actual interpretations by the subjects (pp. 81–106) conclude this study. The latter texts are of significant value to the paremiologist since they reflect the modern Americn students' understanding of traditional proverbs.

3403. Fishler, Bracha. "Pitgam Alegori." *Jerusalem Studies in Jewish Folklore*, 7 (1984), 7–22.

The author discusses the use of allegorical proverbs in two stories, one from the Midrash and the other from the Babylonian Talmud. In the first tale the Hebrew proverb is introduced as part of a dialogue and it advances the plot, while in the second story the proverb is a comment made by the narrator. It is not necessary for the plot and its function is rather to summarize it. In each case, however, the metaphor of the proverb ties the story and the proverbial wisdom together. The functional analysis of the proverb also shows that they add much to the moral and didactic nature of the tales. An English abstract (p. vii) for this article in Hebrew is included.

3404. Fix, Ulla. "Der Wandel der Muster—Der Wandel im Umgang mit den Mustern. Kommunikationskultur im institutionellen Sprachgebrauch der DDR am Beispiel von Losungen." *Deutsche Sprache*, no. 4 (1990), 332–347.

This is a fascinating article on the linguistic change of political slogans that took place during the period of the German reunification. The author begins with the general observation that the change of phraseological units such as proverbs, quotations, and slogans is dependent on the extent of the freedom which individuals are allowed to exercise in society. She then discusses many political slogans which were used by the politicians of the German Democratic Republic prior to reunification. This is contrasted by the altered or new slogans that were created during the reunification process. Fix cites in particular the slogan "Wir sind das Volk!" (We are the people!) and its variant "Wir sind ein Volk!" (We are one folk, i.e. the people of both German countries belong together). The author also mentions numerous other political slogans that are based on the structures of proverbs, aphorisms, advertising slogans, nursery rhymes, quotations, sententious remarks, etc. The content of all of these innovative slogans indicates the movement to a free and reunited Germany. A helpful bibliography (pp. 344–345), an index of slogans (pp. 346–347), and German and English abstracts (p. 332) are included.

3405. Fleischer, Wolfgang. *Phraseologie der deutschen Gegenwartssprache.* Leipzig: VEB Bibliographisches Institut, 1982. 250 pp.

Very important study of phraseological aspects of the German language. Section one (pp. 7–33) presents the history and the main concerns of the field of phraseology, including a few pages on German collections of proverbs and proverbial expressions. In the second part (pp. 34–115) Fleischer discusses the nature of phraseological units as part of the language (i.e. idiomaticity, stability, lexicology, structure, etc.). The third section (pp. 116–165) deals with various classification systems of fixed phrases (i.e. content, syntax, semantics, etc.). In the fourth part (pp. 166–201) the author studies the word formation in phraseological units (i.e. polysemy, synonymy, antonymy, etc.), and the fifth section (pp. 202–232) interprets their stylistic and communicative-pragmatic aspects (i.e. variation, function, etc.). The pages 80–86 on proverbs, wellerisms, sententious remarks, maxims, aphorisms,, and literary quotations (geflügelte Worte) are of particular interest. Throughout the book many German examples are given and discussed. A the end a large bibliography (pp. 233–243) of German and Soviet scholarship is also included. This is a thoroughly researched book which belongs to the group of basic texts in phraseology.

3406. Fleischer, Wolfgang. "Phraseologie." *Kleine Enzyklopädie: Deutsche Sprache.* Eds. W. Fleischer, Wolfdietrich Gartung, Joachim Schildt, and Peter Suchsland. Leipzig: VEB Bibliographisches Institut, 1983. 307–322.

An important encyclopedic treatise on phraseology by a leading German linguist. Fleischer defines phraseology and then discusses the nature of phraseological units, including such aspects as idiomaticity, stability, lexicography, variability, structure, semantics, and classification. There is a special section on proverbs, proverbial expressions, wellerisms, sententious remarks, maxims, and aphorisms with the attempt of differentiating among these genres. Of particular interest are Fleischer's discussions of polysemy and synonymy in such fixed phrases as well as the various ways of classifying them: semantic-structural, syntactic-structural, functional, etc. Many German examples are cited with bibliographical references throughout the article.

3407. Fleischer, Wolfgang. "Zur funktionalen Differenzierung von Phraseologismen in der deutschen Gegenwartssprache." *Beiträge zur allgemeinen und germanistischen Phraseologieforschung.* Ed. Jarmo Korhonen. Oulu: Oulun Yliopisto, 1987. 51–63.

Starting his theoretical essay with a short discussion of idiomaticity and structural aspects concerning phraseological units, Fleischer moves on to show that their function has been studied from the point of view of textual linguistics, pragmatics, and speech act theories. The author argues that the situation or context in which a proverbial expression or idiom is being used is also of major importance for a functional study. In both written and oral communication scholars must also differentiate between levels of style, social class, and eduction. Numerous German examples and a useful bibliography (pp. 62–63) are included.

3408. Fleischer, Wolfgang. "Deutsche Phraseologismen mit unikaler Komponente. Struktur und Funktion." *Europhras 88. Phraséologie Contrastive. Actes du Colloque International Klingenthal-Strasbourg, 12–16 mai 1988.* Ed. Gertrud Gréciano. Strasbourg: Université des Sciences Humanines, 1989. 117–126.

In this theoretical paper Fleischer comments on the structure and function of those German phraseological units that have very unique and distinct lexical components. He shows that there are numerous fixed phrases that contain individual words which are otherwise not used in the language. There are also certain unique words, of course, that appear in several expressions. Fleischer talks of several levels of uniqueness, and he points out that such phrases obviously present particular difficulties for the translator. But there are also lexicographical, semantic, structural and functional issues of these unique expressions that need special attention by phraseologists.

3409. Fleischer, Wolfgang. "Zur phraseologischen Aktivität des Partizips II in der deutschen Gegenwartssprache." *Europhras 90. Akten der internationalen Tagung zur germanistischen Phraseologieforschung,*

Aske/Schweden 12.-15. Juni 1990. Ed. Christine Palm. Uppsala: Acta Universitatis Upsaliensis, 1991. 63–76.

Fleischer investigates the use of participles in German phraseological units and establishes the following structural types of such fixed phrases: (1) participle as perfective predicate, (2) participle in dependent clauses, (3) present and past perfect structures, (4) structures using third person singular, (5) infinitive form that can be used with different grammatical persons, (6) static passive, (7) phrases without specific persons, (8) not using "haben" (to have) or "sein" (to be), (9) certain verbs like "kommen" (to come) plus participle, (10) participles as part of proverbial comparisons, (11) participles with nouns as adjectives, and (12) participles as nouns. Fleischer includes numerous examples for each category, making his linguistic and grammatical analysis very useful for a better understanding of how participles function in German proverbs, proverbial expressions, and proverbial comparisons. A short bibliography (p. 76) is provided.

3410. Földes, Csaba. "Sind alle deutschen Redensarten wirklich deutsch?" *Sprachpflege*, 33, no. 9 (1984), 127–129.

By means of several examples it is shown that not all German proverbial expressions are necessarily of purely German origin. The author speaks first of all about migratory expressions, i.e. classical and Biblical phrases which were translated into German. A second group of fixed phrases refers to such basic human experiences that they have equivalents in many languages without any loan translation process (i.e. polygenesis does take place). And thirdly there are the modern loan translations from the French, Italian, etc. After this discussion Földes warns that one should be careful in looking for specific German characteristics in proverbial expressions current in the modern German language. A good example for these points are the various renderings of "Eulen nach Athen tragen" (To carry coals to Newcastle) in different languages.

3411. Földes, Csaba. "Eigennamen in deutschen phraseologischen Redewendungen. Eine etymologische und semantisch-stilistische Analyse." *Muttersprache*, 95 (1984–1985), 174–180.

The article starts by claiming that much more work needs to be done that combines the fields of onomastics and phraseology. It is shown that many German proverbs and proverbial expressions containing names need detailed etymological investigation. Of particular interest are phraseological units and idioms that have classical (mythological), Biblical, personal, geographical, and ethnic names. Földes also deals with the semantic and stylistic peculiarities of name phrases which in turn influence their function in oral and written communication.

3412. Földes, Csaba. "Russkie frazeologizmy v svete mezh'iazykovoi kommunikatsii." *Studia russica*, 8 (1985), 123–133.

Földes begins his article on comparative phraseology with some general comments regarding Russian phraseological units. He is quick to point out that many of these phrases are in fact internationally known, and he cites plenty of English, French, German, and Hungarian examples. The Russian language clearly also contains fixed phrases from the Bible that are current in other languages as well. It is also shown that some Russian expressions are in fact loan translations from other European languages, while yet another group of proverbs and proverbial expressions is truly indigenous to Russia. Földes supplies some comments on the structure, metaphor, and meaning of these proverbial texts, and the 17 notes include useful bibliographical references.

3413. Földes, Csaba. "Biblische Phraseologismen im Deutschen und Ungarischen." *Germanistisches Jahrbuch der DDR-UVR 1986*, 5 (1986), 176–191.

This is an informative and comparative study of Biblical phrases in the German and Hungarian languages. Földes explains that both languages started to accept many fixed phrases from the major Bible translations of the 16th century. He shows that some of the so-called Biblical expressions are actually much older than the Bible, that some of them are indeed recorded in the Bible for the first time, that quite a few are not precise translations of the Biblical original, and that there are also those phrases and proverbs which only appear to be Biblical. Many of these proverbial texts have undergone semantic, stylistic and pragmatic shifts over time. Földes cites numerous examples and explains in particular the lexical, metaphorical and stylistic similarities and differences between German and Hungarian equivalents of the same Biblical phrases.

3414. Földes, Csaba. "Konfrontative Aspekte der Phraseologieforschung (am Beispiel der deutschen und ungarischen Sprache)." *Kwartalnik Neofilologiczny*, 33, no. 3 (1986), 365–378.

In this article Földes analyzes the differences and similarities between German and Hungarian phraseological units in general. He explains that there exists quite a large number of equivalent phrases in both languages due to their historical and cultural contacts. Some of these expressions are internationally known, others are expressing such basic human experiences that they may have originated independently (polygenesis), and there are also plenty of loan translations. Földes also indicates that there are complete and partial equivalents with obvious lexical, stylistic, structural, and semantic variations. Many German and Hungarian examples are cited to show this close relationship between the phraseological corpus of two very different languages.

3415. Földes, Csaba. "O mezh'iazykovom sopostavlenii fra-zeologicheskikh edinits na materiale russkogo i vengerckogo iazykov." *Slavica*, 22 (1986), 5–13.

This time Földes investigates the differences and commonalities of Russian and Hungarian fixed phrases. He explains that some equivalent texts are rather international going back to classical or Biblical sources. Others are clearly loan translations from one language into the other. But there are many proverbs and proverbial expressions that are in fact quite different as far as lexical, structural and semantic aspects are concerned. Many Russian and Hungarian examples are provided to prove that the similarities between the proverbial phrases of these two unrelated languages are more pronounced than one might think.

3416. Földes, Csaba. "A frazeologiai univerzalék és az idegen nyelvek tanitasa." *Idegen nyelvek tanitasa*, no. 4 (1987), 109–116.

The article starts with a discussion of various types of phraseological units, including proverbs, proverbial expressions, idioms etc. Next Földes explains that such fixed phrases appear in oral and written communication. They are particularly noticeable in literary works and in the mass media. This being the case, it is of great importance that such proverbial texts be part of foreign language instruction. Földes includes many examples from several European languages to support his plea to cover the lexical, stylistic, metaphorical, and semantic aspects of phraseology in the teaching of foreign languages. There is clearly a great pedagogical benefit to exposing students to the proverbial expressions of foreign cultures.

3417. Földes, Csaba. "Anthroponyme als Strukturkomponenten deutscher Phraseologismen." *Zeitschrift für germanistische Linguistik*, 15, no. 1 (1987), 1–19.

This is a valuable study of the use of personal names (anthroponyms) in German phraseological units, especially first and last names, nicknames, and names of gods and animals. Földes cites many examples and discusses etymological, historical, cultural, structural, and functional aspects of these common proverbial texts. He explains in particular the Biblical, mythological, and historical names which often appear in phrases from other languages as well. But the author also treats the names that stem from German folk narratives, literature, and history. Some names like "Hans" and "Gretel" appear with much frequency, and some of these generic names are also used to create humorous puns. Földes concludes his informative essay with detailed comments on the semantic shift of some of these fixed phrases and their variants. A useful bibliography is attached, but one misses the seminal work on German names in proverbs and proverbial expressions by Otto Straubinger (see nos. 1820–1823).

3418. Földes, Csaba. "Voprosy obucheniia russkoi frazeologii v vengerskoi auditorii." *Lingvisticheskie i metodicheskie problemy prepodavaniia russkogo iazyka kak nerodnogo.* Eds. A.M. Shakhnarovich and N.V. Moshinskaia. Moskva: Nauka, 1987. 124–130.

Földes starts with the claim that it is of great importance for foreign language instructors of Russian to include the phraseology of that language in their teaching of Hungarian students. It is argued that fixed phrases appear in oral speech and written texts of all types, and any student who wishes to be fluent in a foreign language will have to be able to understand its proverbs and proverbial expressions. By studying phraseological units the students will also gain many etymological, historical, and cultural insights into the worldview of the speakers of the target language. Numerous Russian examples with Hungarian translations are included in this pedagogically oriented article.

3419. Földes, Csaba. "Phraseologie im Lernbereich Deutsch als Fremdsprache." *Acta Academiae Paedagogicae Szegediensis, Series Linguistica, Litteraria et Aestetica,* no volume given (1987–1988), 37–51.

Significant theoretical and pedagogical article on the necessity and purpose of teaching phraseology in foreign language classes. Földes states that students will gain much insight into the history and culture expressed in the foreign language, and they need to have an active and passive knowledge of fixed phrases in order to understand oral and written communication. Next the author discusses lexical, morphological, syntactical. stylistic, semantic, metaphorical, and functional aspects of phraseological units in general. He also deals especially with the problem of translatability and complete or partical equivalents. A helpful bibliography (pp. 48–50) as well as Hungarian (p. 50) and Russian (p. 51) abstracts are included.

3420. Földes, Csaba. "Eigennamen im Bestand ungarischer Phraseologismen." *Finnisch-Ugrische Forschungen,* 48 (1988), 199–224.

This time Földes treats the use of personal names (anthroponyms) in Hungarian fixed phrases. Once again he shows that the names refer to persons from mythology, history, the Bible, literature, folk narratives, etc. He explains that some names serve phraseological puns and euphemisms, that some common first names reach high phraseological frequencies, and that the new fashionable names have not found their way into proverbial expressions. Many Hungarian examples with German translations are cited, and the author shows how some of them have undergone significant semantic and functional shifts over time. The 75 notes include useful bibliographical information for the combined study of onomastics and phraseology. .

3421. Földes, Csaba. "Erscheinungsformen und Tendenzen der dephraseologischen Derivation in der deutschen und ungarischen Gegenwartssprache." *Deutsche Sprache*, 16, no. 1 (1988), 68–78.

Földes starts this article by lamenting the fact that scholars have dealt very little with the interesting phenomenon of reducing phraseological units to single words. He gives a definition of this dephraseological derivation of new phraseological word formations and cites numerous German and Hungarian examples. The paper comes to the conclusion that with German fixed phrases the lexico-semantic type of word formation (autonomization) and the morphological type (affixation and compounding) dominate, while in Hungarian the lexico-syntactic and the morphological types of word formation are more frequent. A useful bibliography (pp. 76–78) concludes this important essay on the relationship of lexicology and phraseology. German and English abstracts (p. 68) are included.

3422. Földes, Csaba. "Geographische Namen im phraseologischen deutschen Sprachgebrauch." *Germanistisches Jahrbuch DDR-UVR 1988*, 7 (1988), 240–255.

The author presents a detailed survey of the appearance of place names (toponyms) in German proverbs and proverbial expressions. He deals with names of continents, countries, regions, localities (cities, villages, etc.), streets, rivers, mountains, etc. Many examples are cited, explaining their interesting origins from mythology, the Bible, folk narratives, literature, history, etc. Földes also points out that quite a few fixed phrases contain humorous puns and euphemisms, and he outlines some of the semantic and functional shifts that phrases based on names have undergone. This is yet another article that proves the close ties that exist between onomastics and phraseology.

3423. Földes, Csaba. "Phraseologismen mit Anthroponymen in der deutschen und ungarischen Gegenwartssprache." *Beiträge zur Phraseologie des Ungarischen und des Deutschen.* Ed. Regina Hessky. Budapest: Lorand-Eötvös-Universität, 1988. 122–154.

Yet another interesting paper on the use of personal names (anthroponyms) in phraseological units, but this time Földes compares the appearance of first and last names in German and Hungarian expressions. He explains again that the names come from the Bible, mythology, history, folk narratives, literature, etc. Next the author treats such matters as the frequency, metaphor, meaning, style, function, variants, and equivalents of proverbs and proverbial expressions containing names. Many examples are cited from both languages, and a useful bibliography (pp. 150–154) for onomastic studies of phraseology is provided.

3424. Földes, Csaba. "Onymische Phraseologismen als Objekt des Sprachvergleichs." *Europhras 88. Phraséologie Contrastive. Actes du Colloque International Klingenthal-Strasbourg, 12–16 mai 1988.* Ed. Gertrud Gréciano. Strasbourg: Université des Sciences Humaines, 1989. 127–140.

In this article Földes takes his comparative analysis of names of all types in phraseological units one step further by comparing numerous equivalents from the Germanic, Romance, Slavic, Finnic-Ugrian, and Asian languages. He shows once again that the personal (anthroponyms) and place (toponyms) names of these fixed phrases come from the Bible, mythology, history, folk narratives, literature, etc. He discusses the frequency of certain names, and short statements concerning the metaphor, meaning, style, and function of onomastic phrases are included as well. On p. 136 Földes presents an impressive comparative list of equivalents to the classical proverbial expression "Eulen nach Athen tragen" (To carry coals to Newcastle). Similar polyglot lists are provided for phrases with the meaning of "to die," "to be intoxicated," and "to go to the toilet" (pp. 136–137), of which many use the names as humorous puns or euphemisms.

3425. Földes, Csaba. "Phraseodidaktische Lehrmittel für den Unterricht Deutsch als Fremdsprache." *Progressionsforschung. Beiträge zu Deutsch als Fremdsprache.* Ed. Helmut Hofmann. Potsdam: Pädagogische Hochschule "Karl Liebknecht," 1989. II, 96–115.

This is a review article of several German phraseological dictionaries which are especially suitable for teaching German as a foreign language. Földes starts with a statement that stresses the pedagogical importance of including the study of phraseology in foreign language instruction. Citing a few German examples he analyzes the structure, syntax, meaning, and function of phraseological units by also referring to the importance of the oral or written context in which the fixed phrases are being used. Comments concerning the lexicographical classification of proverbial expressions in language dictionaries are included as well. The 23 notes contain useful bibliographical information for German teachers.

3426. Földes, Csaba. "Die Bibel als Quelle phraseologischer Wendungen: Dargestellt am Deutschen, Russischen und Ungarischen." *Proverbium*, 7 (1990), 57–75.

Földes starts with some statistical figures showing that the German, Russian, and Hungarian languages have several hundred phraseological units that are based on the Bible. While some of them are clearly direct translations from the Bible, others were already current in classical times, and there are also those texts which only refer to the Bible or which have become proverbial only over time in the individual languages. The author has found that the three languages have many proverbial expressions from the Bible in common, but due to the difference in Bible translations and historical developments there exist also noticeable variations in lexical, syntactical and metaphorical aspects. Certain semantic shifts and modern innovative changes have also taken place. Many examples in the three languages are cited, and the 38 notes contain rich bibliographical sources for the phraseological study of the Bible.

3427. Földes, Csaba. "Phraseologie und Landeskunde—am Material des Deutschen und Ungarischen." *Zielsprache Deutsch*, 21, no. 2 (1990), 11–15.

This is another pedagogical article with an emphasis on the usefulness of phraseology in the teaching of culture and history in foreign language classes. Földes points out that proverbs, proverbial expressions, and other fixed phrases contain many references from folklore, history, literature, etc. Many of them include names and gestures, or they refer to money, measurements, food, etc. Such phrases express nationally specific cultural information and the worldview of the people speaking that particular language. Hungarian and German examples are cited to prove the point that students can learn a great deal about the foreign culture by being confronted with its phraseology.

3428. Földes, Csaba. "Zur Äquivalenz ungarischer und deutscher Phraseologismen." *Finnisch-Ugrische Forschungen*, 49, nos. 1–3 (1990), 169–187.

A slightly changed version of Földes' earlier comparative article (see no. 3414 above) on Hungarian and German phraseological units. The author states again that the two languages have a considerable number of fixed phrases in common due to their close historical relationship. There are, of course, also the classical and Biblical proverbs and proverbial expressions which have international currency, while other completely equivalent phrases might simply be due to the fact that they express basic human experiences (polygenesis). Nevertheless, Földes shows by means of several examples that some expressions are only partially equivalent due to lexical, stylistic, metaphorical, structural, and semantic changes over time.

3429. Földes, Csaba. "Farbbezeichnungen als phraseologische Strukturkomponenten im Deutschen, Russischen und

Ungarischen." *Europhras 90. Akten der internationalen Tagung zur germanistischen Phraseologieforschung, Aske/Schweden 12.-15. Juni 1990.* Ed. Christine Palm. Uppsala: Acta Universitatis Upsaliensis, 1991. 77–89.

Földes investigates 700 German, Russian, and Hungarian phraseological units that are based on colors. Three statistical tables indicate that the colors black, red, and white are the most popular, but such colors as green, blue, gray, and yellow are also mentioned quite frequently. The author cites numerous comparative examples, and he explains that there are mythological, cultural, historical, etymological, and literary reasons why colors play such a major role in proverbs, proverbial expressions, and proverbial comparisons. He includes special sections on the contrast of white and black as well as the important aspect of finding equivalent phrases in the three languages being discussed. For some of the older classical and Biblical expressions there exist identical equivalents, but this is not always the case for more indigenous phrases. The 24 notes (pp. 88–89) contain helpful bibliographical references.

3430. Földes, Csaba, and Zoltán Györke. "Ungarische Beiträge zur Erforschung der Phraseologie im Deutschen." *Deutsche Sprache,* 15, no. 1 (1987), 46–57.

This is an extremely important review article of the major Hungarian publications on German phraseology by such scholars as Csaba Földes himself, Regina Hessky (see nos. 2464 and 3585–3590), Zoltán Kanyó (nos. 827–829, 2510 and 3663–3664), and others. The authors discuss theoretical approaches, German-Hungarian bilingual phraseological dictionaries, comparative studies of equivalent fixed phrases, the importance of phraseology in foreign language instruction, specific paremiological studies by Hungarians based on German materials (especially Z. Kanyó), etc. A very useful bibliography (pp. 54–57) is included.

3431. Földes, Csaba, and Zoltán Györke. "Wortbildung auf der Grundlage von Phraseologismen in der deutschen, russischen und ungarischen Sprache." *Zeitschrift für Phonetik,*

Sprachwissenschaft und Kommunikationsforschung, 41, no. 1 (1988), 102–112.

A fascinating article on the phenomenon of reducing traditional fixed phrases to individual words based on a comparative study of German, Russian, and Hungarian examples. The authors start with some theoretical considerations concerning this dephraseological derivation of word formations from phraseological units, dividing their rich materials into lexico-semantic, morphological, and lexico-syntactic types of word formations. They even include a section showing how some of these reduced proverbs and proverbial expressions are borrowed as loan translations into other languages. A comprehensive linguistic bibliography (pp. 110–112) is attached.

3432. Földes, Csaba, and Helmut Kühnert. *Hand- und Übungsbuch zur deutschen Phraseologie.* Budapest: Tankönyvkiado, 1990. 146 pp.

An exemplary textbook based on serious scholarly research and sound pedagogical knowledge for instructors teaching and students learning German as a foreign language. In part one (pp. 1–56) the authors discuss in much detail and with many German-Hungarian examples the discipline of phraseology, the classification and definition of various types of phraseological units as well as the origin, history, structure, metaphor, style, content (names, animals, food, etc.), function, equivalents, etc. of German fixed phrases. The second part (pp. 57–145) consists of carefully designed exercises with humorous illustrations and suggestions for solutions to be used in the classroom and as homework assignments. A short bibliography (pp. 145–146) presents additional bilingual sources and phraseological dictionaries. This book is of such high instructional value that it should be made available as a textbook in other countries by simply translating the Hungarian equivalents into other languages.

3433. Folly, Dennis W. "'Getting the Butter from the Duck': Proverbs and Proverbial Expressions in an Afro-American Family." *A Celebration of American Family Folklore: Tales and Traditions from the Smithsonian Collection.* Eds. Steven J. Zeitlin, Amy J. Kotkin, and

Holly Cutting Baker. New York: Pantheon, 1982. 232–241 and 290–291 (notes).

Based on interviews that the author conducted with his own great-grandmother Clara Abrams (1898–) from Virginia, Folly presents eight proverbs and proverbial expressions in their spoken context. These textual transcriptions are followed by short comments that explain the function and meaning of the proverbs in the ethnic milieu of a traditional African-American family. It is argued that this type of proverbial language plays a major role in the family life of Black Americans, clearly expressing didactic and authoritative wisdom. With 1 illustration. For family proverbs see also Valerie Bornstein (no. 3152).

3434. Folly, Dennis W. *The Poetry of African-American Proverb Usage: A Speech Act Analysis.* Diss. University of California at Los Angeles, 1991. 246 pp.

Folly presents a detailed analysis of the form, aesthetics, function, and meaning of English and American proverbs in the speech acts of African-American informants. In the first chapter (pp. 1–43) he deals with such matters as previous African-American proverb scholarship, proverbial speech in Africa, the poetics of proverbs, and various proverb definitions. The second chapter (pp. 44–78) studies the proverbial speech in the context of ex-slave narratives, indicating in particular how traditional proverbs were varied to express personal needs. Chapter three (pp. 79–126) looks at the context, meaning, and function of proverbs among the contemporary African-American population of California and Virginia. Numerous contextualized examples based on Folly's important field research are cited and discussed from a sociolinguistic point of view. The fourth chapter (pp. 127–158) interprets these proverbs as an ethnic genre and interprets the aesthetics of proverb use. The final fifth chapter (pp. 159–175) summarizes the findings of this dissertation and argues that proverbs play a major symbolic, social, and didactic role in the speech acts that take place in African-American family life. A solid bibliography (pp. 176–197) and an invaluable appendix of proverbs (pp. 198–246) with much information concerning the informants, the context, and usage of the proverbs are provided as well.

3435. Fontaine, Carole R. *Traditional Sayings in the Old Testament. A Contextual Study.* Sheffield/United Kingdom: The Almond Press, 1982. 279 pp.

A major contribution to the study of proverbs in the Old Testament. Fontaine starts with a review of previous scholarship on traditional sayings in the Bible and also presents a survey of paremiology and folklore in their relationship to Biblical research. Next she analyzes proverb performance in five passages of the Old Testament, each time studying the interaction situation, the proverb situation, and the context situation. The final chapter deals with the contextual use of these proverbs. By explaining the form, style, image (metaphor), message, function, and use of these proverbs, Fontaine shows the wisdom of the proverbs at work and is able to present the reader with a structure of Old Testament proverb performance. Fourteen figures, notes, appendices, a large bibliography (pp. 253–268), and four indices are also part of this important book.

3436. Fontaine, Carole R. "Proverb Performance in the Hebrew Bible." *Journal for the Study of the Old Testament*, 32 (1985), 87–103.

This is a highly informative review article on the many studies that have dealt with the wisdom literature contained in the Hebrew Bible. Fontaine begins with a theoretical and historical consideration of the research on wisdom sayings, and she shows how Bible, proverb, and folklore scholars have analyzed this rich proverbial material. Her major interest is, however, to discuss the folk proverbs outside of wisdom literature that were incorporated into the Book of Proverbs. Citing numerous Biblical examples, the author discusses questions of definition, structure, semantics, context, function, and performance. She also mentions the practice of employing standard introductory formulas to signal that a folk proverb is being cited. Three diagrams and tables as well as 46 notes with rich bibliographical information are included.

3437. Fontaine, Carole R. "Queenly Proverb Performance: The Prayer of Puduhepa (KUB XXI,27)." *The Listening Heart.* Ed. Kenneth Hoglund et al. Sheffield/United Kingdom: Journal of the Study of the Old Testament Press, 1987. 95–126.

This is a very erudite study of the use and function of a few proverbs in the *Prayer of Puduhepa to the Sun-Goddess of Arinna and her Circle* from the 13th century B.C.E. Fontaine explains that this royal prayer from the ancient Hittite Empire (1450–1200 B.C.E.) is by its last known queen Peduhepa (13th century B.C.E.). She cites the entire prayer in English translation and then analyzes the interaction situation, the proverb situation, and the context situation of the proverbial statements. Stylistic, structural, and metaphorical features are discussed, and Fontaine also provides detailed comments on the historical, cultural, and socio-political background of this contextualized proverb performance. Two figures and a useful bibliography (pp. 120–126) are included.

3438. Forgas Berdet, Esther. "Una proposta d'ordenació paremiologica: La cultura material del pa en els refranys catalans." *Variation linguistique dans l'espace, dialectologie et onomastique. Actes du XVIIe Congrès International de linguistique et philologie romanes (Aix-en-Provence, 29 août-3 septembre 1983).* Ed. Jean-Claude Bouvier. Aix-en-Provence: Université de Provence, 1986. VI, 163–174.

The author presents a proposal for classifying rural Catalan proverbs according to cultural aspects. Citing many Spanish proverbs, Forgas Berdet uses the following classification system based on key-words for proverbs that deal with country life: work, sowing seeds, work in the field, reaping, harvest, grain, threshing, etc. For some of the texts additional information about the meaning and history is provided, but the major part of the essay is actually a list that exemplifies this particular classification system. While the texts are grouped according to certain themes like work, grain, etc., they are grouped alphabetically according to key-words in each thematic group.

3439. Förster, Uwe. "'Polnische Wirtschaft'." *Der Sprachdienst,* 27 (1983), 173–174.

An analysis of the origin and meaning of the German proverbial expression "Polnische Wirtschaft" (Polish household or state of affairs) which dates back to the year 1835. Förster quotes references out of literary works by Joseph von Eichendorff (1788–1857) and Gustav Freytag (1816–1895). He also refers to two operettas from 1889 and 1910 which used the phrase as titles. Actually the expression is a stereotypical statement which comments negatively on confusion or disorder by comparing it to a confused and disorganized Polish situation, making it in fact a national slur. See also Bernhard Stasiewski (no. 2906) and Peter Wörster (no. 4574).

3440. Förster, Uwe. "'So wahr mir Gott helfe'." *Der Sprachdienst*, 30 (1986), 173–174.

This is an informative note on the German formulaic oath "So wahr mir Gott helfe" (So help me God) which goes back to pre-Christian magical concepts. This pagan formula was later transferred to God, the meaning basically being that the person expressing this oath wants to declare that the oath is as true as it is obviously also true that he wishes for God's help. Förster also mentions a few other proverbial oaths that refer to God. It becomes clear that current proverbial expressions can be based on traditional legal customs and beliefs.

3441. Förster, Uwe, and Helmut Walther. "'Der sitzt da wie Bräsicke'." *Der Sprachdienst*, 26 (1982), 176–177.

A short etymological account of the origin and meaning of the German proverbial expression "Der sitzt da wie Bräsicke" (He sits there like Bräsicke). The authors show that the name "Bräsicke" comes from the Berlin dialect word "bräsig" with the meaning of "well nourished and corpulent." The German writer Fritz Reuter (1810–1874) used it in his novel *Ut mine Stromtid* (1862/64), and the expression is also found in dialect dictionaries and proverb collections of the Prussian area of Germany. With 1 illustration.

3442. Fort, Denise C. *Parent-Child Effects on Performance, Thinking, and Communication in Families of Normal and Schizophrenic Sons and the*

Role of Attention in Communication. Diss. The Catholic University of America, 1983. 351 pp.

An interesting psychological study regarding the question of whether the kinds of deviations in thinking and communication which have been observed in the parents of schizophrenics are effects of interacting with a schizophrenic child rather than factors contributing to their child's illness. Fort utilized a proverbs test that required listeners to identify and interpret proverbs similar in meaning to those described by speakers. Three dependent measures of speaker effects on listeners were obtained: (1) proverb identification, (2) proverb interpretation, and (3) attentional distractors representing, respectively, speaker effects on listener performance, thinking, and communication. It was found that schizophrenia as an illness and not as the outcome of defective parenting had a disruptive impact on the family. Numerous charts, statistical tables, the proverbs test (pp. 213–244), and an invaluable bibliography (pp. 336–351) are included.

3443.   Foulon, Jordanka Hristova. "Quand le proverbe se fait mémoire." *Cahiers de littérature orale,* no. 13 (1983), 67–90.

A general article on various aspects of Macedonian proverbs with comparisons to French and other European proverbs. The author deals first with those proverbs that contain universal human experiences and shows how such proverbs were disseminated throughout Europe. Greek, Latin, Macedonian, and Biblical proverbs are cited, and Foulon explains that certain concepts of these ancient proverbs were changed because of cultural differences, i.e. a cat might become a dog, etc., while the structure and idea of the proverbs remained the same. As proverbs get translated and accepted from one culture and language into another, certain philological, perceptive, and ethnic changes might occur. The second part of the article deals with local proverbs which contain particular places, customs, and historical events which are not universally understood. They are more specific in their content and less general in their ideas. A helpful bibliography (pp. 89–90) for Macedonian proverbs especially is attached. With an English summary (p. 178).

3444. Frackiewicz, Iwona. "Zastosowanie przyslow w nauczaniu jezyka niemieckiego." *Jezyki obce w szkole*, 29, no. 2 (1985), 137–141.

In this pedagogical article Frackiewicz argues that it is of much importance to include the study of proverbs in foreign language instruction. Citing numerous German examples with Polish translations, she examines their structure, style, form, stability, metaphor, and universality. She also states that especially rhymed and short proverbs are easy to learn by the language students. If the text of the target language is basically the same as that of the native language, students should not have any particular difficulty with them. Frackiwicz includes some sample exercises for Polish teachers and students to teach and learn German proverbs. At the end of the article she also refers to the popular "Antisprichwörter" (anti-proverbs) in modern German. They usually can only be understood if the original text is known, and students must be acquainted with them if they are to communicate orally with native speakers or read German literature and newspapers.

3445. Frackiewicz, Iwona. "Die niederländischen Phraseologismen im Bereich des Schiffbaus, der Schiffahrt und Fischerei, sowie ihre polnischen Äquivalente." *Neerlandica Wratislaviensia*, 3 (1986), 72–90 (=*Acta universitatis wratislaviensis*, no. 942).

In this comparative analysis of 123 Dutch phraseological units dealing with ship building, navigation, and fishing, Frackiewicz shows the similarities and differences between this specific corpus and its Polish equivalents. She presents six different levels of equivalence, basically ranging from identical phrases to those that are not at all translatable. The article includes a discussion of the historical and cultural content and worldview of the Dutch proverbial expressions, and the author also investigates their stylistic, structural, and metaphorical aspects.

3446. Frackiewicz, Iwona. *Analoge Sprichwörter im Deutschen, Niederländischen und Polnischen.* Diss. Uniwersytet Wroclawski, 1987. 925 pp.

This is a truly Gargantuan and Herculean dissertation of 925 (!) pages in which Iwona Frackiewicz presents an invaluable comparative study of analogous German, Dutch, and Polish proverbs. She starts with a general chapter (pp. 6–30) on the origin and dissemination of internationally disseminated proverbs. In the second chapter (pp. 31–62) she discusses the problem of equivalents, loan translations, sources (i.e. classical, Biblical, medieval, etc.), and such aspects as structure, style, and metaphor of proverbs that are analogous in these three languages. Chapter three (pp. 62–70) contains a short summary of previous comparative research and presents some of the polyglot collections. The important fourth chapter (pp. 71–123) contains a detailed analysis of the many criteria of analogous proverbs: structural, metaphorical, lexical, grammatical, rhetorical, stylistic, semantic, etc. As Frackiewicz explains these matters, she always includes several comparative examples. In the fifth chapter (pp. 124–137) she attempts a typology of analogous proverbs based primarily on structural similarities, and in chapter six (pp. 138–149) she deals with the problem of classifying her rich comparative materials according to key-words. Informative notes (pp. 154–190), a superb bibliography (pp. 191–227), a significant collection of 1215 parallel German, Dutch, and Polish proverbs (pp. 228–791) with variants and Latin originals (where possible), two indices of Dutch and Polish key-words (pp. 792–925), and a Polish summary (pp. 152–153) are all part of this masterful study.

3447. Frackiewicz, Iwona. "Zu allgemeinen Kriterien für eine konfrontative Sprichwörteranalyse: Am Beispiel der Sprichwörter im Deutschen, Niederländischen und Polnischen." *Proverbium,* 5 (1988), 23–37.

Referring especially to the theoretical work of the linguist and paremiologist Zoltán Kanyó (see no. 829), the author outlines various criteria that might be of help in determining analogous proverbs in general and those of the German, Dutch, and Polish languages in particular. Frackiewicz discusses especially contextual, metaphorical, syntactical, lexical, stylistic, phonetic, rhetorical, and semantic aspects, always citing examples of the three languages under discussion. This article sets up a model for paremiographers who wish to assemble a comparative collection of proverbs for two or more languages. A useful bibliography (pp. 35–37) is attached.

3448. Frackiewicz, Iwona. "Das Sprichwort im Deutschen und Polnischen. Glottodidaktische Implikationen." *Linguistik-Landeskunde-Linguolandeskunde.* Ed. M. Bobrels and S. Dudzirirki. Dzerzow: no publisher given, 1989. 129–145.

The author points out that many of the proverbs which the German and Polish languages have in common originate either from classical Greek or Roman literature, from the Bible, or from the medieval Latin proverbs current among educated circles throughout Europe. Most of these proverbs were loan translated into the vernacular languages which accounts for the fact that there are so many equivalent international proverbs in the modern European languages. Frackiewicz cites many examples from early sources with their German and Polish equivalents, drawing attention to the fact that there are at times small variations due to linguistic differences between German and Polish. The author discusses the metaphor, form, structure, and function of these internationally disseminated proverbs. The 14 notes include helpful bibliographical information. A Polish summary (pp. 145–146) is attached.

3449. Frackiewicz, Iwona. "Sprichwörtliche Aphorismen von Stanislaw Jerzy Lec." *Proverbium,* 7 (1990), 77–88.

This is a literary investigation of the aphorisms of the Polish writer Stanislaw Jerzy Lec (1909–1966). Frackiewicz explains that many of his texts are in fact proverbial aphorisms, i.e. short texts based on proverbs in the form of "Antisprichwörter" (anti-proverbs). A short biographical sketch of Lec and statements concerning his socio-political engagement as a writer are included. Above all Frackiewicz analyzes the use of parody and satire in these proverbial texts. Even though the traditional texts are manipulated or "perverted" by Lec, the reader can still recognize the structural and metaphorical aspects of the proverb. It is concluded that Lec's aphorisms have gained much popularity in Europe as the German translations upon which this article is based show so well. A bibliography (pp. 86–88) concerning the relationship of aphorisms and proverbs is provided. See also Karl Dedecius (no. 3296).

3450. Frackiewicz, Iwona. "Zum Einfluß der *Proverbia communia* auf die polnische Parömiographie." *Neerlandica Wratislaviensia,* 5 (1991), 301–311 (=*Acta universitatis wratislaviensis,* no. 1299).

Frackiewicz starts her article with a detailed introduction of the important proverb collection *Proverbia communia* (15th century) that contains 803 Dutch proverbs with Latin translations. It is a well-known fact this work had a great influence on western European paremiographers of the 16th century (see Richard Jente, no. 801). The author is able to show that the Latin book *Oratiuncule varie,* published in 1527 in Poland and based upon an earlier book from 1516 by the Dutch humanist Johannes Murmellius (1479–1517), contains the same list of 48 Latin proverbs. A careful analysis reveals that at least half of these texts are identical to those Latin texts in the *Proverbia communia,* thus establishing at least an indirect influence of this work on Polish paremiography. An annotated list of the proverbs (pp. 308–310) and a useful bibliography (pp. 310–311) are included.

3451. Fradejas Lebrero, José. "Evolucion de un refran." *Epos: Revista de Filologia,* 4 (1988), 393–397.

In this short article Fradejas Lebrero investigates the origin, history, and meaning of the Spanish proverbial question "Quién mató al Comendador?" (Who killed the commander?). It is pointed out that the proverbial expression is included in Lope Félix de Vega Carpio's (1562–1635) play *Fuenteovejuna* (c. 1614), but it also appears in many of the older Spanish proverb collections. The author traces the paremiographical history of this fixed phrase and shows that it is still in use today in a number of variants. It is also explained that the expression goes back to an actual historical incident that took place in 1476 in the city of Fuenteovejuna in Spain.

3452. Freidhof, Gerd. "Paronomasie und Sprichwort." *Gattungen in den slavischen Literaturen. Beiträge zu ihren Formen in der Geschichte.*

Festschrift für Alfred Rammelmeyer. Eds. Hans-Bernd Harder and Hans Rothe. Köln: Böhlau, 1988. 211–242.

This is an important theoretical study on the appearance of paronomasia (punning) in proverbs in general, but especially also in those of the German and Russian languages. Freidhof starts with a definition of "pun" and then presents detailed analyses of the importance of logical, semantic, rhetorical, semiotic, syntactical, lexical, and phonological structures in creating proverbial puns. Most of these wordplays in proverbs are based on changes of a certain letter or word, rhyme, antithesis, and parallelism. Many German and Russian examples are cited, and Freidhof is absolutely correct in concluding that this paronomastic feature of proverbs is actually quite widespread. The 54 notes contain valuable references.

3453. Freidhof, Gerd. "Russisches Sprichwort, Bibelzitat und semantische Distraktion. Zur Struktur und Semantik einer Einfachen Form." *Slavistische Beiträge,* 242 (1988), 35–64.

The author starts this fascinating article with a general discussion of how Biblical and classical proverbs entered many languages through loan translations. Many Bible quotations also became proverbial in the Russian language, as can be seen from older collections through the 19th century. More modern Soviet paremiographers appear to have excluded obvious Biblical proverbs from their collections. Next Freidhof presents very detailed theoretical explanations on how certain quotations from the Bible took on "proverbiality" in the Russian language. He discusses structural and semantic shifts over time and includes a model (p. 59) for various changes. His major finding is that a "semantic distraction" has taken place in the course of a Bible quotation becoming a proverb. A useful bibliography (pp. 62–64) is attached.

3454. Frenk Alatorre, Margit. "Refranes cantados y cantares proverbializados." *Nueva Revista de Filologia Hispanica,* 15 (1961), 155–168.

The author investigates anonymous songs of medieval Spain that contain proverbs. It is shown that proverbs played a considerable didactic role in the poetry of the Middle Ages. But there are also plenty of early folk songs whose refrains or certain other lines have become proverbial over time. Frenk Alatorre cites a number of examples in their lyrical context with cultural and historical explanations, and she points out that these rhymed proverbs are still in existence today. It is also shown that Lope Félix de Vega Carpio (1562–1635) and Miguel de Cervantes Saavedra (1547–1616) utilized the proverbial lines out of these songs in their dramatic and prose works. Obviously they are also included in the major Spanish collections.

3455. Fricke, Harald. *Aphorismus.* Stuttgart: Metzler, 1984. 168 pp.

An excellent book on German aphorisms with many bibliographical references throughout. Fricke emphasizes the history, form, and content of German aphorisms, and many of his examples contain proverbs and proverbial expressions which have been varied by such writers as Georg Christoph Lichtenberg (1742–1799), Friedrich Nietzsche (1844–1900), Karl Kraus (1874–1936), Elias Canetti (1905–) and others into "Antisprichwörter" (anti-proverbs). The section on genre differentiation (pp. 18–24) includes a discussion of proverbs and aphorisms, and so do the chapters on apothegma collections (pp. 29–33) and religious wisdom (pp. 33–40). Many examples of intellectual aphoristic reactions to proverbial wisdom are cited, and it becomes clear that there is such a subgenre as the "sprichwörtlicher Aphorismus" (proverbial aphorism).

3456. Friedländer, Max. *Pieter Bruegel.* Berlin: Propyläen Verlag, 1921 (see esp. pp. 62–64, pp. 80–84, and p. 98).

This book is to this day one of the standard studies of Pieter Brueghel (c. 1520–1569). Friedländer includes a discussion of three of Brueghel's well-known pictures illustrating proverbs and proverbial expressions: *Big Fish Eat Little Fish* (1557), *Netherlandic Proverbs* (1559), and *The Blind Leading the Blind* (1568). The author names the museums in which these pictures can be found, and he includes artistic and interpretative comments. With three plates (nos. 32, 44, and 49). See also Wilhem Fraenger (no. 460),

Jan Grauls (no. 586), Alan Dundes and Claudia Stibbe (no. 2332), etc.

3457. Friedländer, Max. *Pieter Bruegel.* Leyden: A.W. Sijthoff, 1976 (see esp. pp. 20–22).

This English translation of Friedländer's work on Pieter Brughel (c. 1520–1569) includes comments on two of his proverb pictures, this time *Twelve Round Proverb Pictures* (1558) and *Netherlandic Proverbs* (1559). Again Friedländer includes information on the museums as well as some short comments on the artistic value and meaning of these pictures. With four plates (nos. 8–9 and 14–15). For the round proverb pictures see especially Jozef de Coo (no. 299).

3458. Friese, Heinz-Gerhard. *Zeiterfahrung im Alltagsbewußtsein. Am Beispiel des deutschen Sprichworts der Neuzeit.* Frankfurt am Main: Materialis, 1984. 212 pp.

An illuminating investigation into the concept of "Zeit" (time) and its relationship to everyday life in German proverbs. By means of many examples the author shows how time is viewed in proverbial wisdom, how proverbs contain cause and effect ideas, and how they preach indifference since the golden age of the proverb during the Reformation. Friese explains this in interesting chapters on proverbs with such key-words as "heute" (today), "Tag" (day), and "Zeit" (time). He also includes special chapters on the proverbs "Zeit heilt Wunden" (Time heals wounds), "Andere Zeit, andere Freud" (Different time, different joy), and "Alles und jedes hat seine Zeit" (Each and every thing has its time) with their telling variations from different socio-cultural periods of Germany. The entire book makes clear the "danger" of proverbs when they are used blindly and as rigid didactic principles of the social status quo. Voluminous notes and a large bibliography (pp. 189–212) conclude this sociological study.

3459. Furnham, Adrian. "The Proverbial Truth: Contextually Reconciling and the Truthfulness of Antonymous Proverbs." *Journal of Language and Social Psychology,* 6 (1987), 49–55.

In this significant study Furnham investigates the reaction to the "truthfulness" of 203 English proverbs by British university students. The socio-psychological proverbs test that he devised showed clearly that students reacted quite similarly to the "truth" of individual proverbs and their antonyms. This leads the author to the following conclusions: (1) not all proverbs are seen as equally true in general, or in specific contexts, and are related to a person's social attitudes; (2) proverbs which are found in all cultures/languages are generally perceived as more true than those which are specific to a language or culture; (3) antonymous proverbs are frequently not seen as opposites, but rather they are interpreted to apply in different contexts; and (4) social interaction and social context are of greatest importance in deciding whether any particular proverb is true. A small bibliography (p. 55) is included.

G

3460. Gaatone, David. "La locution ou le poids de la diachronie dans la synchronie." *La locution. Actes du colloque international Université McGill, Montréal, 15–16 octobre 1984.* Eds. Giuseppe Di Stefano and Russell G. McGillivray. Montréal: Editions CERES, 1984. 70–81.

The article starts by defining the phraseological unit as a lexical and memorized phenomenon. Gaatone considers synchronic and diachronic aspects, arguing that scholars should deal with both of them in their studies of proverbial expressions. He also deals with syntactical characteristics of these fixed phrases. Special attention is paid to phrases that contain verbs, time adverbs, conjunctions, prepositions, etc. The semantic effects of such words is also discussed in this linguistic analysis of numerous French examples. A detailed bibliography (pp. 78–81) is attached.

3461. Gaborit, Lydia. "Proverbes et dictons dans l'île de Noirmoutier." *Cahiers de littérature orale*, no. 13 (1983), 145–150.

This small paper begins with definitions of the proverb and proverbial expression and then discusses their metaphorical, stylistic, and structural aspects. The author also treats proverbs as expressions of human experience, and she then investigates the content of about a dozen French proverbs from the island of Noirmoutier. The proverbs deal in particular with meteorological concerns and reflect the rural worldview of the inhabitants. It is argued that these traditional bits of wisdom continue to play a major role among the native residents of the island despite the increasing tourism industry.

3462. Gallego, André. "Pédagogie et parémiologie. L'utilisation des proverbes dans la formation des adolescents au XVIe siècle à l'Université de Valencia." *Richesse du proverbe.* Eds. François Suard and Claude Buridant. Lille: Université de Lille, 1984. II, 183–197.

Significant historical and pedagogical essay on the use of proverbs in the education of young students in the 16th century at the University of Valencia in Spain. Gallego starts by explaining the influence which Erasmus of Rotterdam's (1469–1536) *Adagia* (1500ff.) had on other European humanists, and he then deals in particular with the Spanish humanist Juan Lorenzo Palmireno (1514–1580) who published five Spanish-Latin proverb collections between 1560 and 1591 for instructional use. Palmireno stressed the importance of proverbs for the study of grammar and rhetorics, but he also was well aware of the didactic and moral value of proverbs. The 69 notes contain important bibliographical references. See also A. Gallego (no. 499).

3463. Gaman, Dumitru. "The Third National Romanian Symposium on Paremiology." *Proverbium,* 6 (1989), 177–179.

This is a short report on a proverb symposium that took place from June 11–12, 1988, in Baia de Arama in the county of Mehedinti in Rumania. Gaman states that most of the papers dealt with ethical, philosophical, and social aspects of Rumanian proverbs, but there were also more theoretical lectures on the structure, meaning, and worldview of the national corpus of Rumanian proverbs. The author states with legitimate pride that Rumanian paremiologists and paremiographers are also participating in the international scene of proverb scholarship, as can be seen from the work of such scholars as I.C. Chitimia (see nos. 277 and 3239–3240), Gabriel Gheorghe (nos. 3474–3475), Constantin Negreanu (nos. 2675–2686 and 3995–4013), Dumitru Stanciu (nos. 2903–2905 and 4410–4421), Cezar Tabarcea (nos. 1842–1843, 2929, and 4461–4462), and many others.

3464. Garbe, Joachim. "Das also war des Pudels Kern! 'Geflügelte Worte' und ihr Ursprung." *Praxis Deutsch,* 16 (July 1989), 30–32 and 37.

The author argues that it is of importance to teach German students at least the most commonly used "geflügelte Worte" (winged words, i.e. literary quotations) by such authors as Johann

Wolfgang von Goethe (1749–1832), Friedrich Schiller (1759–1805), Wilhelm Busch (1832–1908), etc. He states that they continue to appear in oral communication and also in modern literary works, newspaper headlines, and advertisements. Here they are usually parodied or "perverted," but in order to understand such wordplay it is necessary to know and understand the original text. Garbe includes instructional materials to help teachers incorporate the study of such fixed phrases in their German classes. With 1 illustration.

3465. Garcia, Constantino. "Creatividad en el habla popular (Refranes gallegos del mes de agosto)." *Verba: Anuario Galego de Filoloxia*, 10 (1983), 281–287.

The author disusses the creativity in popular speech by investigating a number of Galician proverbs that refer to the month of August. He explains that many of these texts exhibit considerable poetic form, and he also shows that the variants of particular proverbs are based on aesthetic considerations. The content of these proverbs is primarily meteorological, dealing with such matters as the length of days, weather signs, rain, sunshine, etc. The author also includes some Castilian examples and compares them with the Galician texts. Towards the end of the article Garcia indicates that these Spanish proverbs still have currency today as traditional expressions of weather rules and superstitions.

3466. Garcia-Page, Mario. "Propiedades linguisticas del refrán." *Epos: Revista de Filologia*, 6 (1990), 499–510.

This is a detailed investigation of the linguistic properties of Spanish proverbs. Basing his remarks on numerous examples, Garcia-Page begins his study with phonetic characteristics. He then presents a well-structured discussion of various types of rhymes and poetic devices in commonly used Spanish proverbs. A special section on the use of alliteration is included as well, and at the end the author deals with the problem of lexical variants. The 14 notes include useful bibliographical references.

3467. Garcia-Ruiz, Perla. "La vie des proverbes mexicains." *Cahiers de littérature orale*, no. 13 (1983), 91–108.

A survey of the form and content of Mexican proverbs, stressing especially proverbs referring to women and maize. Garcia-Ruiz cites 21 Mexican proverbs with French translations and provides cultural and contextual annotations. She also discusses such stylistic matters as comparison, opposition, and negation. Semantic problems, the transposition of Spanish proverbs to Mexico, the meaning, the worldview, and the use of these proverbs are analyzed as well, but special attention is paid to the socio-cultural content of proverbs about women. While such proverbs might still be considered valid in rural areas, they are being questioned by people living in the urban environment. With an English summary (p. 178).

3468. Garnett, James L. "Operationalizing the Constitution Via Administrative Reorganization: Oilcans, Trends, and Proverbs." *Public Administration Review*, 47, no. 1 (1987), 35–44.

The use of the word "proverb" in this article is somewhat misleading. Actually Garnett analyzes how Americans have used administrative reorganization to cope with the ambiguities in the Constitution. The four major trends lie in the areas of economy, management reform, politics, and ideology. They can be reduced to four principles (maxims): "Reorganizations fail to save governments money," "Governmental structure has little influence on performance," "Reorganization is nothing more than the continuation of politics by other means," and "The Franklin D. Roosevelt-Brownlow impact on governmental organization has been vastly inflated." Obviously these texts are not folk proverbs! An English abstract (p. 35) is provided.

3469. Gates, Charlene E. "'The Work Is Afraid of Its Master': Proverb as Metaphor for a Basketmaker's Art." *Western Folklore*, 50, no. 3 (1991), 255–276.

This article deals only tangentially with proverbs. The first part (pp. 255–265) includes some general comments regarding folk art and how folklorists should study artifacts. Gates also presents a biographical sketch of Mr. Paul Beechick (1922–), a

Russian immigrant who now lives as a basketmaker in Creswell, Oregon. This informant describes how he became interested in basketry, and he also relates the fact that his father taught him the proverb "Delo mastera boitsia" (The work is afraid of its master) which gave him the strength and courage to make a trade out of this work (see pp. 265–267). The proverb is seen as a guiding metaphor to do good work, and it has served this folk artist very well. The remainder of the article studies the craftsmanship of Mr. Beechick by including 6 illustrations of baskets in various stages of completion.

3470. Gautschi, Theres. *Bildhafte Phraseologismen in der National-ratswahlpropaganda. Untersuchungen zum Vorkommen und zum Gebrauch von bildhaften Phraseologismen in der National-ratswahlpropaganda der FDP, SVP und der SP des Kantons Bern von 1919–1979.* Bern: Peter Lang, 1982. 224 pp.

Important published dissertation concerning the use of German proverbs, proverbial expressions, sententious remarks, slogans, and Bible quotations for political election propaganda from 1919 to 1979 in the canton of Bern in Switzerland. The book contains a theoretical part (pp. 17–52) dealing with propaganda and politics as such, and this is followed by detailed analyses of a rich corpus of phraseological units. Gautschi deals with quantitative and qualitative issues, classification problems, strategy, function, frequency, manipulation, metaphor, dialect expressions, etc. The author also includes a diachronic study of the political use of such fixed phrases by three major parties over a time period of sixty years. Of particular interest are the frequency calculations (pp. 158–175) of certain expressions and their use by particular political parties. Many statistical tables, a useful index (pp. 197–215) of all phraseological units cited, and a helpful bibliography (pp. 217–224) make this one of the best studies of the political "power" of proverbial language.

3471. Gavrilova, T.S. "Poslovitsa i kontekst: Sobranie poslovits v samozapisi E.I. Kolesnikovoi." *Russkii Fol'klor,* 25 (1989), 144–152.

The author reports on an impressive collection of Russian proverbs which E.I. Kolesnikova assembled during field research among the Russian population of Salakas in Lithuania starting at the end of 1940. There are about 30,000 texts concerning various aspects of Russian life in this region, of which some have been recorded for the first time as a check in standard Russian proverb collections has shown. Gavrilova explains that Kolesnikova has provided some important annotations concerning the meaning, contextual use, and archaic vocabulary (dialect words) of these proverbs. Some texts definitely appear to have been created by the population of this Russian minority since they are not to be found in the normal repertory of Russian proverbs.

3472.   Gay-Para, Praline. "Le proverbe, parole de circonstance." *Cahiers de littérature orale*, no. 13 (1983), 151–157.

The author reports that she was able to collect more than 250 proverbs from her Lebanese mother in two interview sessions. About 20 of these Arabic texts are listed here in Lebanese with literal and more poetic French translations. For each proverb Gay-Para also provides linguistic and cultural annotations. Such stylistic and structural aspects as comparison, dialogue, prayer, etc. are treated, and at the end of this short sample the author includes a statement on the social function of proverbs in Lebanon.

3473.   Gergen, Kenneth J. "Proverbs, Pragmatics, and Prediction." *Canadian Psychology/Psychologie Canadienne*, 31, no. 3 (1990), 212–213.

This short note is an invited comment on Tim B. Rogers' paper "Proverbs as Psychological Theories . . . Or Is It the Other Way Around?" (see no. 4258) that was published in the same issue of *Canadian Psychology/Psychologie Canadienne.* Gergen agrees with Rogers that proverbs have no predictive value (meaning or empirical content) outside specific contexts. He then goes on to say that proverbs and propositions (for example scientific psychological theories) are discursive agents, i.e. they are employed by persons for social purposes, as means of warning, advising, teaching, or strengthening desired behaviors. Psychological theories do take on the status of proverbs as they enter the society more generally, but this is not so much as predictive statements but rather as pragmatic psychological wisdom.

3474. Gheorghe, Gabriel. "In legatura cu asa-zisa influenta orientala asupra limbiii (paremiologiei) si culturii române." *Proverbium Dacoromania*, 4 (1989), 19–21.

In this short summary of a longer lecture Gheorghe points out that there is at best very little Turkish influence on the Rumanian language and culture. As far as so-called Turkish proverbs as loan translations in the Rumanian language are concerned, he is able to show that they are actually ancient classical proverbs that entered the Rumanian proverbial corpus through Europe long before the Turks came in contact with European cultures. There appears to be no Turkish proverb influence on Rumania at all. A French summary (p. 21) is provided.

3475. Gheorghe, Gabriel. "Proverbele si istoria limbilor europene." *Revista de etnografie si folclor*, 36, nos. 3–4 (1991), 111–129.

Gheorghe begins with some general remarks concerning the value of proverbs for the study of European history and languages. He is able to show that certain French proverbs from the 12th to 14th centuries contain lexical relics that are either identical or very close in form and meaning to words currently in use in Rumania. Gheorghe cites 50 examples of such correspondences and adds important etymological, lexical, historical, cultural, and semantic explanations. Proverbs are thus seen as significant old texts to study the development of the Indo-European languages. The 61 notes include useful bibliographical information. With an English abstract (pp. 128–129).

3476. Gheorghe, Manuela. "PRO-VERB-ul: pentru vorbire?" *Proverbium Dacoromania*, 4 (1989), 22–25.

Gheorghe starts with a discussion of Frank de Caro's paper on "The Nature of Speech According to American Proverbs" (see no. 3294). Based on her own study of proverbs about "speech" from the Rumanian and Balto-Finnic languages and cultures, she concludes that there is such a great variety of meanings of proverbs about speech that one cannot possibly restrict them to the two poles of negative and positive statements. Even if there might be a certain concentration towards the negative side statistically speaking, this is not due primarily to geographical or demographic conditions but rather to the very function of the PRO-VERB as a concentrated folk phrase to give advice against the evil (speech included) in life and human communication. With an English summary (p. 25). See also J.L. Fischer and Teigo Yoshida (no. 445) as well as William McNeil (no. 1182) concerning similar studies on the interpretation of the value of speech in Japanese and Indian proverbs.

3477. Gibbs, Raymond W. "A Critical Examination of the Contribution of Literal Meaning to Understanding Nonliteral Discourse." *Text*, 2 (1982), 9–27.

Using a type of proverbs test this paper examines the role that literal meaning plays in the interpretation of nonliteral discourse which is based on proverbial expressions and idioms. Three types of psychological process models are discussed: (1) a "literal first model" where the literal interpretation of a nonliteral sentence is always computed before the conveyed meaning is derived; (2) a "multiple meaning model" where the literal and nonliteral meanings of a nonliteral sentence are simultaneously computed during understanding; and (3) a "conventional meaning model" where the conventional meaning of a nonliteral sentence is examined first during understanding before any possible literal interpretation is analyzed. It is suggested that literal or componental meaning plays a small role in understanding conventional, nonliteral (figurative, metaphorical) discourse. A helpful bibliography (pp. 26–27) and an English abstract (p. 9) are provided.

3478. Gibian, George. "How Russian Proverbs Present the Russian National Character." *Russianness: Studies on a Nation's Identity. In Honor of Rufus Mathewson, 1918–1978*. Ed. Robert L. Belknap. Ann Arbor/Michigan: Ardis, 1990. 38–43.

This is a short essay on how Russian proverbs contain comments regarding the Russian national character. Gibian takes his examples from Vladimir Ivanovich Dal's (1801–1872) famous proverb collection *Poslovitsy russkogo naroda* (1862), but he cites the proverbs in English only. It is stated that traditional proverbs still play a major role in oral and written communication in Russia and other Slavic countries. Many of them contain stereotypical attitudes if not slurs against Germans, Poles, and others. At the same time the proverbs praise the hospitality of Russians, the Russian motherland, God, and at times even the tsar. Proverbs also tell Russians to stay put and not move away, they preach conformity, stress love of country, and argue for a good life in Russia while expressing slurs against foreigners and their countries. Proverbs are also seen as expressions in praise of rural life, traditional wisdom, and the status quo.

3479. Gibson, Walter S. "Brueghel, *Dulle Griet,* and Sexist Politics in the Sixteenth Century." *Pieter Bruegel und seine Welt.* Eds. Otto von Simson and Matthias Winner. Berlin: Gebrüder Mann, 1979. 9–15.

An intriguing interpretation of Pieter Brueghel's (c. 1520–1569) picture *Dulle Griet* (1560/64) that includes detailed comments on earlier attempts by art historians and folklorists to understand its metaphorical message. Gibson agrees that it illustrates the Dutch proverbial expression "To plunder in front of Hell and return unscathed," but he also stresses the point that it is a rather aggressive and shrewish woman who is doing the looting. The author makes a good case for the fact that Brueghel might be commenting on sexual politics in this picture, wanting to show that there are women who are going far beyond their expected stereotypical roles as "emancipated" wives or even as rulers of certain European states. The 31 notes include valuable bibliographical information. With 10 illustrations.

3480. Gilly, Carlos. "Das Sprichwort 'Die Gelehrten, die Verkehrten' in der Toleranzliteratur des 16. Jahrhunderts." *Anabaptistes et dissidents au XVIe siècle. Actes du Colloque international d'histoire anabaptiste du XVIe siècle tenu à l'occasion de la XIe Conférence Mennonite mondiale à Strasbourg, juillet 1984.* Eds. Jean-Goerges Rott and Simon L. Verheus. Baden-Baden: Editions Körner, 1987. 159–172.

The author presents a detailed analysis of the use and function of the German proverb "Die Gelehrten, die Verkehrten" (The greatest scholars are not always the wisest) in the religious writings of the 16th century. He explains that the proverb was used as an invective against theologians and lawyers. Almost every writer of this time made use of it, among them Sebastian Brant (1458–1521), Thomas Murner (1475–1537), Martin Luther (1483–1546), and many others. Especially Sebastian Franck (1499–1542) helped to popularize the proverb through its inclusion in his major proverb collection *Sprichwörter / Schöne / Weise / Herrliche / Clugreden / vnnd Hoffsprüch* (1541). Many contextualized examples are cited throughout this informative article. For Gilly's longer monograph on this proverb see no. 3481 below. See also Heiko Oberman (no. 4059).

3481. Gilly, Carlos. "Das Sprichwort 'Die Gelehrten, die Verkehrten' oder der Verrat der Intellektuellen im Zeitalter der Glaubensspaltung." *Forme e destinazione del messaggio religioso. Aspetti della propaganda religiosa nel cinquecento.* Ed. Antonio Rotondo. Firenze: Leo S. Olschki, 1991. 229–375.

This is an exemplary monograph on the use and function of the German proverb "Die Gelehrten, die Verkehrten" (The greatest scholars are not always the wisest) during the 16th and 17th century. Gilly presents literally dozens of contextualized references from the end of the 15th century to the religious struggles during the following two centuries, citing texts from Thomas Murner (1475–1537), Erasmus of Rotterdam (1469–1536), Martin Luther (1483–1546), Ulrich von Hutten (1488–1523), Thomas Müntzer (1489–1525), Ulrich Zwingli (1484–1531), Johannes Agricola (1494–1566), Johann Fischart (1546–1590), etc. The paremiographer Sebastian Franck (1499–1542) included a lengthy section on this anti-intellectual proverb in his proverb collection *Sprichwörter / Schöne / Weise / Herrliche / Clugreden / vnnd Hoffsprüch* (1541) that shows just like the literary and religious use of the proverb how it became a propagandistic tool in the hands of various religious groups, including the Protestants, Anabaptists, etc. Gilly also presents a special section on a lengthy poem about this proverb (pp. 309–325) which once again indicates in what miscredit the scholars of the time had fallen. The 346 notes contain a wealth of sources and references to proverb collections. With 4 illustrations. See also Gilly's shorter article (no. 3480) and Heiko Oberman (no. 4059).

3482. Gilman, Sander L. "To Quote Primo Levi: 'Redest keyn jiddisch, bist nit kejn jid' ['If you don't speak Yiddish, you're not a Jew']." *Prooftexts: A Journal of Jewish Literary History*, 9, no. 2 (1989), 139–160.

This is an invaluable linguistic, cultural, and literary study of the use of Yiddish words, phrases, and proverbs in the works of the Italian Jewish writer and holocaust survivor Primo Levi (1919–1987). Gilman starts with an informative introduction to the traditional significance of the Yiddish language as a marker of "Jewishness." He explains in particular how Yiddish proverbs include the collective wisdom and mindset of the Jewish people. Gilman cites and interprets several contextualized examples from such prose works as *Se questo è un uomo?* (*What is a Man?*, 1947), *Se questo è un uomo, La tregua* (*The Reawakening*, 1963), and *Se non ora, quando?* (*If Not Now, When?*, 1982). The latter two novels also include the Yiddish proverb "Redest keyn jiddisch, bist nit kejn jid" (If you don't speak Yiddish, you're not a Jew), showing clearly what importance Levi saw in proverbial speech as an expression of a collective worldview and Jewish identity.

3483. Gils, J.B.F. van. *Een andere kijk op Pieter Bruegel den Ouden*. 2 vols. 's-Gravenhage: "Humanitas," 1940. I, 98 pp.; II, 203 pp.

This is indeed "een andere kijk" (another look) at the work of Pieter Brueghel the Elder (c. 1520–1569). In two splendid volumes Gils studies the folkloric elements in Brueghel's paintings, and there is a special section in volume one (pp. 1–52) on the oil painting *Netherlandic Proverbs* (1559) with 32 illustrations (details) of the picture and valuable explanations of the depicted Dutch proverbial expressions. The second volume (pp. 62–66) contains an analysis of Brueghel's *The Blind Leading the Blind* (1568) with 3 illustrations. But there are references to proverbs and fixed phrases on almost every page of these books. Luckily Gils has provided the reader with detailed indices of words, proverbs and proverbial expressions that are mentioned throughout the two volumes (I, pp. 83–97; II, pp. 187–201), thus making this a study of great value to the cultural paremiologist interested in the relationship of art, language, and proverbial wisdom. For a similar study of Brueghel see Jan Grauls (no. 586).

3484.   Glaap, Albert-Reiner. "Idiomatisches Englisch = Besseres Englisch? Zu einem vernachlässigten Bereich des fremdsprachlichen Unterrichts." *Sprache und Literatur in Wissenschaft und Unterricht*, 16, no. 56 (1985), 95–104.

A pedagogical essay arguing that the study of idioms should definitely be part of foreign language instruction. Glaap discusses definition problems and learning strategies, and it is clear that he has many types of phraseological units in mind, including proverbs, proverbial expressions, idioms, etc. To illustrate the importance of getting students to become aware of the phraseology in another language, Glaap quotes two lengthy passages out of the comedy *Absurd Person Singular* (1973) by the English dramatist Alan Ayckbourn (1939–). The rest of the article explains how a teacher can deal with such highly idiomatic texts, how students can acquire an active knowledge of fixed phrases, and what collections might be good resources for teachers and students.

3485.   Gläser, Rosemarie. "Idiomatik und Sprachvergleich." *Sprache und Literatur in Wissenschaft und Unterricht*, 16, no. 56 (1985), 67–73.

The author presents a convincing argument that comparative language studies should also deal with phraseological units and their idiomaticity. Gläser shows the importance of metaphors, metonymy, and names in proverbial expressions, twin formulas, and idioms. She explains the linguistic structure of them by analyzing certain patterns involving nouns, verbs, adjectives, and prepositions. Polysemy and function are also considered, and it is argued that especially foreign language instruction should deal with phraseological equivalence on a contrastive basis. Many English examples with German translations or equivalents are included.

3486. Gläser, Rosemarie. *Phraseologie der englischen Sprache.* Leipzig: VEB Verlag Enzyklopädie, 1986. 198 pp.

A very important book on English phraseology for German readers. The first chapter (pp. 13–53) deals with various theoretical aspects of phraseology such as definition, syntax, semantics, function, terminology, etc. The second chapter (pp. 54–62) considers the idiom as a prototype of phraseological units and also deals with grammatical criteria of idiomaticity and the classification of idioms according to word types. In the third chapter (pp. 63–121) the author presents numerous examples of proverbial expressions, twin formulas, and idioms and classifies them according to nouns, verbs, adjectives, prepositions, etc. Proverbial materials are dealt with especially on pp. 105–121. The fourth chapter (pp. 122–128) concerns itself with classical and Biblical quotations and allusions, English sententious remarks, and slogans. This is followed by a detailed analysis of 15 different types of routine formulas in chapter six (pp. 129–152), such as greeting formulas, condolence formulas, rhetorical formulas, etc. In the seventh chapter (pp. 153–164) Gläser investigates the use and function of fixed phrases in journalism (daily newspapers), English literature, and professional texts. Finally, the eighth chapter (pp. 165–178) covers translation problems and equivalents between English and German expressions. A glossary of German-English terminology (pp. 189–190), an invaluable bibliography (pp. 191–196), and an inclusive subject index conclude this seminal work.

3487. Glass, Arnold L. "The Comprehension of Idioms." *Journal of Psycholinguistic Research,* 12 (1983), 429–442.

This is a psychological study based on a proverbs test to examine how familiar idioms and proverbial expressions are interpreted. Subjects had to respond as rapidly as possible whether an idiom had the same or different meaning as a phrase which, on half of the tasks, was a paraphrase of either the figurative or literal meaning of the idiom. Other experiments based on the literal and figurative meaning of idioms were conducted with this test, and it is shown that whenever a familiar idiom is comprehended, both its literal and figurative interpretations are made. An appendix listing the 30 metaphors with literal and figurative paraphrases, a small bibliography (p. 442), and an English abstract (p. 429) are included.

3488. Goddard, R.N.B. "Marcabru, *Li Proverbes au Vilain,* and the Tradition of Rustic Proverbs." *Neuphilologische Mitteilungen,* 88, no. 1 (1987), 55–70.

An impressive literary proverb investigation of the poems of the medieval French troubadour Marcabru (flourished between 1130 and 1150). Goddard comments on these rustic proverbs in their verse context, and he then presents a detailed analysis of Marcabru's proverbs and their analogues in the proverb collection *Li Proverbes au Vilain* (13th century) and other medieval collections. Many parallels from Chrétien de Troyes' (1150?–1190?) epics are also cited. Two important tables showing the appearance of similar texts in these medieval French works are provided, and Goddard also includes remarks concerning the moral or satirical function of the proverbs.

3489. Goldberg, Harriet. "The Proverb in 'Cuaderna via' Poetry: A Procedure for Identification." *Hispanic Studies in Honor of Alan D. Deyermond. A North American Tribute.* Ed. John S. Miletich. Madison/Wisconsin: Hispanic Seminary of Medieval Studies, 1986. 119–133.

Literary investigation of medieval Spanish proverbs that appear in narrative poems written in "cuaderna via" (four-line stanzas with fourteen to sixteen-syllable lines rhyming aaaa, bbbb, etc.). Goldberg argues that most proverb definitions do not help the investigator to identify a certain text as a proverb. Of greatest importance for such an identification are the internal context (the proverb's meaning) and the social context. Certain introductory formulas are also of help and so are the formulaic structure, the repetition, and the imagery of most proverbs. Numerous proverbs from medieval Spanish literature are cited in an appendix with explanations of how they were identified as *bona fide* proverbs. The 31 notes contain significant bibliographical references to aspects of proverbiality.

3490. Golden, Bernard. "Originalaj proverboj en Esperanto." *Kontakto,* 5, no. 111 (1988), 3–4.

This is an interesting article on whether there is such a thing as Esperanto proverbs. Golden answers in the affirmative and refers to Ludwig Lazarus Zamenhof's (1859–1917) collection *Proverbaro Esperanta* (1910) which includes 1232 proverbs without any comments. He also analyzes Esperanto proverbs of contemporary life and their function, arguing that new proverbs can still be created by individuals that are unique to Esperanto. A few modern examples are cited, and Golden also includes a few bibliographical references (p. 4).

3491. Goldman, Deborah Sue. *Metaphorical Processes in Borderline, Schizophrenic and Normal Adults.* Diss. Adelphi University, 1984. 235 pp.

Making use of psychological metaphor and proverb interpretation tests, Goldman examined the abilities in symbolic capacity in borderline and schizophrenic persons. A generally lower metaphorical ability was found which reflected the overall effect of schizophrenia impairing subjects' performance across figurative tasks in ways not found among other diagnostic groups. Many statistical tables, graphs, appendices with tests, and a significant bibliography (pp. 160–173) are included. Of great value is also the second chapter (pp. 4–43) which reviews the previous use of proverbs and metaphors in psychological testing and particularly metaphor comprehension.

3492. Gómez, Isabel Mateo. "Los refranes en la silleria del coro de la catedral de León." *Revista de Dialectologia y Tradiciones Pupulares,* 43 (1988), 397–401.

A short discussion of a few proverbial scenes that appear in misericordes on the choir stalls of the cathedral of León in Spain. The author states that proverbs were of much importance in the 15th and 16th centuries in oral speech, in literary works, and in the numerous proverb collections. Little wonder that carvers also delighted in depicting secular proverbial scenes in churches in addition to the expected religious and Biblical motifs. With 4 illustrations.

3493.   Gontscharowa, Nelli. "Zur phraseologischen Antonymie in der deutschen Gegenwartssprache." *Beiträge zur Erforschung der deutschen Sprache*, 3 (1983), 120–143.

Detailed linguistic analysis of phraseological antonyms in the modern German language. Gontscharowa investigates especially such opposite proverbial expressions which differ by only one word, as for example "Ein weiches Herz haben" vs. "Ein hartes Herz haben" (To have a soft [or hard] heart). She differentiates among several basic structures of such phraseological pairs in which nothing but an adjective, a verb, a noun, or a preposition are in opposition. Structural and semantic aspects are discussed, and the author also analyzes the use and function of antonymous phraseological units in the novels of Dieter Noll (1927–). A useful bibliography (pp. 142–143) is attached.

3494.   Gosselin, Monique. "De la maxime au proverbe: Fragments du discours sentencieux dans les textes de fiction de G. Bernanos." *Richesse du proverbe*. Eds. François Suard and Claude Buridant. Lille: Université de Lille, 1984. II, 227–243.

Literary study of the maxims, sententious remarks, aphorisms, and proverbs in the novels of the French author Georges Bernanos (1888–1948). Gosselin attempts to show that the intellectual characters use more literary phraseology while members of the lower or middle classes utilize proverbs in their dialogues. Numerous examples are cited in their literary context, and it is argued that the proverbs and proverbial phrases express basic wisdom and colloquial language. The social tensions in the novels are also mirrored by the juxtaposition of maxims and proverbs in verbal communication.

3495.   Gonin, Hervé. "Cu ekzistas 'esperantaj proverboj'?" *Franca Esperantisto*, 50, no. 333 (January 1982), 16–17.

Short and general article on proverbs written in Esperanto discussing definition problems and differentiating among proverbs, maxims, sententious remarks, etc. Special reference is made to the importance of Erasmus of Rotterdam (1469–1536) for the dissemination of classical proverbs throughout Europe. Some of these texts are cited in Esperanto translation. Gonin also mentions Ludwig Lazarus Zamenhof's (1859–1917) proverb collection *Proverbaro Esperanta* (1910) with 1232 proverbs in Esperanto.

3496.   Goy, Eva-Maria S. *"Erst kommt das Fressen, dann kommt die Moral": A Proverbial Analysis of Bertolt Brecht's "Mutter Courage und ihre Kinder."* M.A. Thesis University of Vermont, 1990. 84 pp.

Taking Bertolt Brecht's (1898–1956) famous quotation "Erst kommt das Fressen, dann kommt die Moral" (First comes the grub, then come the morals) as a title, Goy presents an impressive literary analysis of the use and function of proverbs and proverbial expressions in Brecht's play *Mutter Courage und ihre Kinder* (1938/39). The first chapter (pp. 1–13) offers general comments on Brecht's innovative dramatic theory which includes the employment of proverbial materials to entertain, instruct and estrange. The second chapter (pp. 14–25) discusses Mother Courage's frequent use of proverbs in their dramatic context, and chapter three (pp. 26–42) analyzes the many proverbs that appear in her proverbial songs. The final chapter (pp. 43–54) studies the perversion of proverbial texts by some of the minor characters of the play, showing once again that Brecht employs proverbs both traditionally and in varied forms as expressions of alienation. A proverb index of 177 texts and a useful bibliography (pp. 79–84) are included.

3497.   Graber, Robert Bates, and Gregory C. Richter. "The Capon Theory of the Cuckold's Horns: Confirmation or Conjecture?" *Journal of American Folklore*, 100 (1987), 58–63.

An interesting article on how horns came to symbolize cuckoldry which in turn gave rise to the proverbial expression "To plant horns on, to bestow a pair of horns upon one's husband" and its variants to express adultery. The authors present etymological, cultural and historical evidence for the fact that there existed an old custom of cutting the spurs from cockerels when they were castrated and implanting them in the comb, where they would grow into hornlike members that made it easy to pick out the capons. The mark of the capon's literal castration was adopted to symbolize the figurative castration suffered by the cuckold. A bibliography (pp. 62–63) of other theories concerning the origin of this symbolism and the proverbial expression is provided. See also Paul Falk (no. 424) and Douglas Bruster (no. 3176).

3498. Grandpré, Chantal de. "La poésie comme parole." *Voix et images. Littérature québécoise,* 11, no. 2 (1986), 228–240.

This is a literary proverb study of the poetry of the French Canadian writer Michel van Schendel (1929–). The author investigates primarily the two Quebecois poem collections *Poèmes de l'Amérique étrangère* (1958) and *Autres, Autrement* (1983), indicating that Schendel is very interested in combining cultural and poetic traditions. Grandpré also shows that oral language forms play a major role in these poems which are based on the contrast of linguistic modernity and folkloric traditionality. Several contextualized examples are cited, and it becomes clear that these French proverbs add significantly to the poetic message of Schendel's works.

3499. Grassegger, Hans. "Redensarten in der Fernsehwerbung. Zur Struktur und Modifikation von Idiomen in multimedialer Kommunikation." *Europhras 88. Phraséologie Contrastive. Actes du Colloque International Klingenthal-Strasbourg, 12–16 mai 1988.* Ed. Gertrud Gréciano. Strasbourg: Université des Sciences Humaines, 1989. 141–154.

The author bases his comments regarding the use of proverbs, proverbial expressions, and idioms in Austrian television advertisements on a study of 400 ads that were aired between November 1987 and April 1988. He found that only 20 (a mere 5%) ads contained proverbial materials with the following functions: to direct certain modes of behavior, to prevent critical analysis, to encourage agreement with the ad's message, and to emotionalize the consumer. Grassegger also found that the product name is integrated quite often into the proverbial text. All of this adds up to effective advertisements, but Grassegger expresses surprise at this infrequent use of fixed phrases.

3500. Grauberg, Walter. "Proverbs and Idioms: Mirrors of National Experience?" *Lexicographers and Their Works.* Ed. Gregory James. Exeter/United Kingdom: University of Exeter Press, 1989. 94–99.

The article starts with some general comments regarding the fact that many proverbs and idioms are internationally disseminated due to their classical or Biblical origins. Grauberg also mentions the importance of Erasmus of Rotterdam's (1469–1536) *Adagia* (1500ff.) in spreading this traditional language throughout Europe. Next he investigates which semantic fields constitute the main sources of idioms and figurative expressions, basing his analysis on English, French and German texts. He found that in all three languages fixed phrases referring to the "body" are most frequent, followed by those expressions that deal with various types of movement, the military, nautical matters, food, and sports. This leads Grauberg to the conclusion that proverbs and proverbial expressions tend to mirror general human, rather than specific national, experiences.

3501. Gray, Nick. "Langland's Quotations from the Penitential Tradition." *Modern Philology,* 84 (1986), 53–60.

The author argues that a study of the sources of the Latin quotations in William Langland's (c. 1332–1400) epic poem *Piers Plowman* (A-text 1362, B-text 1378/79, C-text 1393) yields valuable indications of the breadth and detail of Langland's knowledge and reading. He discusses eight Latin quotations in detail and several others more briefly that may have derived from the Latin penitential tradition. Most of them are legal maxims of which texts like "Necessitas non habet legem" (Necessity knows no law) are also proverbial. Philological, cultural and legal explanations together with variants and references to other English literary sources are included.

3502. Gréciano, Gertrud. "Zur Semantik der deutschen Idiomatik." *Zeitschrift für Germanistische Linguistik,* 10, no. 3 (1982), 295–316.

Starting with definition problems of idiomaticity, Gréciano moves on to present linguistic and semantic analyses of German idioms and proverbial expressions. She deals in particular with the aspects of analogy that plays a major role in the comprehension and use of phraseological units. It is also pointed out that in the actual use of idioms there appears to be a tendency of amassing either synonymous or antonymous texts in one statement. Many examples are cited, and a valuable bibliography (pp. 315–316) is attached.

3503. Gréciano, Gertrud. "Forschungen zur Phraseologie." *Zeitschrift für Germanistische Linguistik*, 11, no. 2 (1983), 232–243.

Major review article concerning the linguistic research results in phraseology that were achieved in the time period from 1970 to 1982 by European, Soviet and American scholars. These studies have dealt with definition and classification problems of phraseological units, their polylexicality, stability, structure, metaphor, polysemanticity, polysituationality, multifunctionality, etc. Numerous German examples are cited, and Gréciano deals in particular with the work of Harald Burger (see no. 3190), Florian Coulmas (no. 2291), Wolfgang Fleischer (no. 3405), Werner Koller (no. 896), Klaus Dieter Pilz (nos. 1460 and 1462), Uta Quastoff (no. 2762), Harald Thun (no. 1930), etc. A useful bibliography (pp. 241–243) is attached.

3504. Gréciano, Gertrud. *Signification et dénotation en allemand. La sémantique des expressions idiomatiques.* Paris: Librairie Klincksieck, 1983. 469 pp.

Superb linguistic study on German idiomatic expressions which includes in the first chapter (pp. 17–38) a significant survey of definitions of proverbs, proverbial expressions, idioms, stereotypes, clichés, etc. In chapter two (pp. 38–113) Gréciano considers semantic, structural, lexical, functional, and pragmatic aspects of numerous German phraseological units (without French translations). The large third chapter (pp. 113–258) deals with theoretical questions of multifunctionality, polysemanticity, idiomaticity, context, synonymy, antonymy, polylexicality, etc. The fourth chapter (pp. 258–367) covers semantic matters with a special emphasis on the comprehension of idioms. It is here where Gréciano also refers to the importance of epistemology, signification, and denotation for the proper understanding of any phraseological unit in a written or oral speech act. The concluding fifth chapter (pp. 369–400) touches on the creativity of idiomatic language usage and summarizes the impressive materials put together in this voluminous study. Detailed notes (pp. 401–427), 33 diagrams, numerous structural models, a giant bibliography (pp. 433–455) as well as name and subject indices make this book a seminal contribution to phraseology by the leading French phraseologist.

3505. Gréciano, Gertrud. "Das Idiom als Superzeichen. Pragmatische Erkenntnisse und ihre Konsequenzen." *Aktuelle Probleme der Phraseologie.* Eds. Harald Burger and Robert Zett. Bern: Peter Lang, 1987. 41–57.

In this article Gréciano considers some pragmatic aspects of idioms as well as proverbial expressions with an emphasis on their use in actual speech acts. The main part of the essay deals with semiotic considerations, stressing interdisciplinary dimensions, functional levels, psycholinguistic realities, and the metaphorical language of these verbal signs. Many German examples are cited, and Gréciano also includes 2 diagrams and a helpful bibliography (pp. 55–57).

3506. Gréciano, Gertrud. "Idiom und sprachspielerische Textkonstitution." *Beiträge zur allgemeinen und germanistischen Phraseologieforschung.* Ed. Jarmo Korhonen. Oulu: Oulun Yliopisto, 1987. 193–206.

Based on German and French texts in contexts, Gréciano shows that idioms and proverbial expressions are often used in a humorous fashion. In fact, speech play is responsible for much of the intentional variation of phraseological units. The author points out that proverbial expressions don't appear to be as rigidly fixed as has often been claimed. Their lexical and structural stability is quite easily varied, and the humor results from placing the varied expression in juxtaposition with the original wording. A useful bibliography (pp. 203–206) concerning the modern wordplay with idiomatic expressions is included.

3507. Gréciano, Gertrud. "Europhras 88. Auf dem Weg zur vergleichenden Phraseologie: Deutsch-Französisch." *Europhras 88. Phraséologie Contrastive. Actes du Colloque International Klingenthal-Strasbourg, 12–16 mai 1988.* Ed. Gertrud Gréciano. Strasbourg: Université des Sciences Humaines, 1989. 155–163.

In this article Gréciano argues that much more work needs to be done in the field of comparative phraseology. While Soviet and German scholars have made considerable progress in this area, French phraseologists and linguists appear to lack behind in this important area. The author reviews some of the comparative work concerning German and French phraseological units, and she then states some of the desiderata for future research. On the one hand scholars should deal with diachronic and synchronic matters, including lexicographical, contextual, and functional questions. But there is also the need for structural, semantic, and semiotic studies on a comparative basis, including comprehension and cognition of fixed phrases. A helpful bibliography (pp. 161–163) is included.

3508. Gréciano, Gertrud (ed.). *Europhras 88. Phraséologie Contrastive. Actes du Colloque International Klingenthal-Strasbourg, 12–16 mai 1988.* Strasbourg: Université des Sciences Humaines, 1989. 496 pp.

This is an extremely important essay volume containing 42 articles by some of the leading European phraseologists. There is hardly a subject matter or language that is not mentioned in this book, as can be seen from the following list of authors and titles of their papers: Vilmos Bárdosi, "'Un ange passe': Contribution à l'étymologie d'une locution" (pp. 7–16); Harald Burger, "'Bildhaft, übertragen, metaphorisch . . .'. Zur Konfusion um die semantischen Merkmale von Phraseologismen" (pp. 17–29); Claude Buridant, "L'approche diachronique en phraséologie: quelques asepcts de l'ancien et du moyen français" (pp. 31–42); Irina Chernysheva, "Strukturtypologische Phraseologieforschung in der Sowjetischen Germanistik" (pp. 43–49); Monique Coppens d'Eeckenbrugge, "Petits proverbes, grands effets . . . De l'usage des proverbes dans la publicité contemporaine" (pp. 51–63); Karlheinz Daniels, "Das Sprichwort als Erziehungsmittel—

historische Aspekte" (pp. 65–73); Jean David, "Tous les prédicats ne meurent pas idiomes. Mais nul n'est à l'abri" (pp. 75–82); Wolfgang Eismann, "Zum Problem der Äquivalenz von Phraseologismen" (pp. 83–93); Stefan Ettinger, "Einige Probleme der lexikographischen Darstellung idiomatischer Einheiten (Französisch-Deutsch)" (pp. 95–115); Wolfgang Fleischer, "Deutsche Phraseologismen mit unikaler Komponente. Struktur und Funktion" (pp. 117–126); Csaba Földes, "Onymische Phraseologismen als Objekt des Sprachvergleichs" (pp. 127–140); Hans Grassegger, "Redensarten in der Fernsehwerbung. Zur Struktur und Modifikation von Idiomen in multimedialer Kommunikation" (pp. 141–154); Gertrud Gréciano, "Europhras 88. Auf dem Weg zur vergleichenden Phraseologie: Deutsch-Französisch" (pp. 155–163); Annelies Häcki-Buhofer, "Psycholingistische Aspekte in der Bildhaftigkeit von Phraseologismen" (pp. 165–175); Albert Hamm, "Remarques sur le fonctionnement de la négation dans les proverbes: L'example de l'anglais" (pp. 177–193); Regina Hessky, "Sprach- und kulturspezifische Züge phraseologischer Vergleiche" (pp. 195–204); Malcolm Jones, "The Depiction of Proverbs in Late Medieval Art" (pp. 205–223); Günther Kempcke, "Struktur und Gebrauch der somatischen Phraseme mit den Bedeutungskomponenten 'Kopf' und 'tête'" (pp. 225–232); Georges Kleiber, "Sur la définition du proverbe" (pp. 233–252); Jarmo Korhonen, "Zur syntaktischen Negationskomponente in deutschen und finnischen Verbidiomen" (pp. 253–264); Hans-Peder Kromann, "Zur funktionalen Beschreibung von Kollokationen und Phraseologismen in Über-setzungswörterbüchern" (pp. 265–271); Renaud Lallement, "Aspekt im Sprichwort" (pp. 273–279); Ricarda Liver, "Phraseologie, Wortbildung und freie Syntax im Bündnerromanischen" (pp. 281–290); Claire Marbot-Benedetti, "La famille à travers les proverbes" (pp. 291–300); Raymond Matzen, "Die elsässischen Wetter- und Bauernregeln als lebendiger Ausdruck von Land, Sprache und Kultur" (pp. 301–311); Christine Palm, "Die konnotative Potenz usueller und okkasioneller Phraseologismen und anderer festgeprägter Konstruktionen in Christa Wolfs Roman *Kindheitsmuster*" (pp. 313–326); Alain Raymond, "Essai d'étude des présuppositions pragmatiques des expressions idiomatiques allemandes" (pp. 327–335); Martin Riegel, "'Avoir' + Attribut de l'objet: construction syntaxique et paradigme idiomatique" (pp. 337–347); Francis Rodegem and P. Van Brussel, "Proverbes et pseudo-proverbes. La logique des parémies" (pp. 349–356); Lutz Röhrich, "Alemannische Sprichwörter. Form und Funktion" (pp. 357–370); Annely Rothkegel, "Phraseologien in Texten der internationalen Fachkommunikation" (pp. 371–378); Hans Ruef, "Zusatzsprichwörter und das Problem des Parömischen Minimums" (pp. 379–385); Barbara Sandig, "Stilistische Funktionen verbaler Idiome am Beispiel von Zeitungsglossen und anderen Verwendungen" (pp. 387–400); Ingrid Schellbach-Kopra, "Glück und Unglück in Sprichwort und Redensart am Beispiel Finnisch-Deutsch" (pp. 401–411); Annemarie Schmid, "Remarques sur le sémantisme de quelques lexies complexes à base de 'mettre'" (pp. 413–420); Elisabeth Schulze-Busacker, "Des *Disticha Catonis* en Espagne, Italie et France (pp. 421–430); Véra Simonin, "Histoire de la classification des phraséologismes dans les pays de l'actuelle Yougoslavie: motivations et réalisations" (pp. 431–440); Astrid Stedje, "Beherztes Eingreifen oder ungebetenes Sich-Einmischen. Kontrastive Studien zu einer ethnolinguistischen Phraseologieforschung" (pp. 441–452); Mario Wandruszka "Contraintes instrumentales et liberté créatrice" (pp. 453–458); Barbara Wotjak, "Ansatz eines modular-integrativen Beschreibungsmodells für verbale Phraseolexeme" (pp. 459–467); Gerd Wotjak, "Übereinzelsprachliches und Einzelsprachspezifisches bei Phraseolexemen" (pp. 469–483); and Jean-Marie Zemb, "Des atomes et des molécules" (pp. 485–493). For annotations of these important essays see nos. 3099, 3188, 3195, 3236, 3261, 3287, 3288, 3375, 3389, 3408, 3424, 3499, 3507, 3551, 3555, 3590, 3649, 3671, 3689, 3712, 3735, 3754, 3789, 3814, 3830, 4108, 4219, 4237, 4251, 4262, 4283, 4292, 4306, 4322, 4332, 4349, 4383, 4429, 4534, 4575, 4579, 4593.

3509. Gréciano, Gertrud. "Remotivierung ist textsortenspezifisch." *Europhras 90. Akten der internationalen Tagung zur germanistischen Phraseologieforschung, Aske/Schweden 12.-15. Juni 1990.* Ed. Christine Palm. Uppsala: Acta Universitatis Upsaliensis, 1991. 91–100.

This is a literary investigation of the use and function of proverbs and proverbial expressions in Ferdinand Raimund's (1790–1836) Austrian comedy *Der Bauer als Millionär* (1826). Gréciano shows that this humorous dramatist uses fixed phrases which he remotivates (changes) to fit the specific textual contexts of his dramatic dialogues. The phraseological units are used for characterization, humor, wordplay, and the depiction of ridiculous behavior. Many of the proverbial expressions are based on body parts, and it is this metaphorical language with its puns that makes this play such a telling comedy. Numerous contextualized examples are presented that show the effective use of traditional and varied fixed phrases. Gréciano argues that Austrian drama and literature in general include much metaphorical language, and she cites as an additional example the literary works of the modern Austrian writer Peter Handke (1942–). A useful bibliography (pp. 99–100) is provided.

3510. Gréciano, Gertrud. "Zur Aktivität der Phrasemkomponenten - Deutsch-französische Beobachtungen." *Sprichwörter und Redensarten im interkulturellen Vergleich.* Eds. Annette Sabban und Jan Wirrer. Opladen: Westdeutscher Verlag, 1991. 66–82.

With this article Gréciano continues her comparative studies of German and French phraseological units. She shows that structural typologies do exist and emphasizes fixed phrases with certain verbs and nouns. She then presents important frequency calculations for what nouns do in fact appear rather often in the fixed phrases of these two languages. A section on the distinction between variants and synonyms as well as remarks concerning the importance of the context in which proverbial expressions appear are included as well. A short bibliography (pp. 81–82) is attached.

3511. Green, Barbara L. "Solace, Self-Esteem, and Solidarity: The Role of Afro-American Folklore in the Education and Acculturation of Black Americans." *Texas Tech Journal of Education*, 11 (1984), 91–98.

In this paper Green argues that much more attention should be paid to African-American folklore and its significant, complex role as a tool of education and acculturation. In the presence of hostility and the absence of an opportunity for formal education, the black slave community carved out a meaningful social, cultural and intellectual life, including a rich body of oral literature in the form of songs, folk tales, proverbs, etc. Early proverbs of this enslaved American minority focus in particular on human relationships and attempt to answer daily ethical and social needs of individuals, as for example "Don't say more with your mouth than your back can stand" and "Tomorrow may be the carriage driver's day for plowing." Social historians and folklorists need to study the worldview of American slavery expressed in these proverbs. They certainly are strong expressions of solace, self-esteem, and solidarity.

3512.   Green, Thomas, and William Pepicello. "The Proverb and Riddle as Folk Enthymemes." *Proverbium*, 3 (1986), 33–45.

The authors argue that proverbs are ambiguous statements depending on context and on the analogic structure of the text itself. Thus one proverb may apply to multiple real-world situations, and conversely several proverbs may apply to a single situation. There also exists a multiple and sliding relationship between image and message in the proverb. In the rhetorical strategy of actual proverb use, the speaker relies on shared knowledge with the hearer and thus assumes the ability of the hearer to make "logical" connections. This informal type of reasoning (or persuasive logic) indicates that proverbs belong to the category of enthymemes, for enthymemic reasoning proceeds, according to Aristotle (384–322 B.C.), by signs and possibilities, as opposed to the formal logical progression of the syllogism. The authors also show that similar enthymemic patterns play a role in understanding the ambiguity of riddles.

3513.   Grésillon, Almuth, and Dominique Maingueneau. "Polyphonie, proverbe et détournement, ou un proverbe peut en cacher un autre." *Langages*, 19, no. 73 (1984), 112–125.

An interesting article on the polyphony of proverbs, arguing that the various ways of stating (expressing, enunicating) a proverb in a speech act will influence its meaning or message.

The major part of the paper deals, however, with the intentional variation of actual words in individual proverbs that result in so-called "Antisprichwörter" (anti-proverbs). The authors include modern German and French examples from the literary works of such writers as Kurt Tucholsky (1890–1935), Paul Éluard (1895–1952), Alfred Döblin (1878–1957), Karl Kraus (1874–1936), Richard Pietrass (1946–), etc. Many of these anti-proverbs are either humorous, parodistic, or satirical wordplays with traditional proverbial wisdom.

3514. Griffiths, Alan. "A Computational Study of Sardinian Based upon the Proverbs Published by Canon Giovanni Spano." *Literary and Linguistic Computing*, 1 (1986), 41–44.

This paper examines a collection of 2916 Sardinian proverbs and 88 variants by Canon Giovanni Spano (1803–1878) entitled *Proverbi Sardi* (1871). Using a computer program, Griffiths analyzed letter usage, the distribution of vowels and consonants, the 50 most common words, the lengths of words, and the fragments (groups of letters) found at various locations within the words. The author hopes that this statistical work (7 tables are included) will be the first stage towards a computerized trilingual dictionary dealing with Sardinian, Italian, and English. For the paremiologist it is of interest that the average word length is 6.56 letters, indicating the basic and short vocabulary that make up many proverb texts. An English abstract (p. 41) is included.

3515. Grigas, Kazys. "Tipo problema lyginamajame patarliu tyrinejime." *Lietuvos TSR Mokslu Akademijos darbai*, series A, 4, no. 97 (1986), 106–116.

In this theoretical article Grigas discusses the problem of so-called "proverb types" in the comparative study of proverbs. He reviews the previous work by Matti Kuusi (see no. 978) and Grigorii L'vovich Permiakov (no. 1428), and he then contrasts the national and international types of proverbs. He is able to show that the internationally disseminated proverb types might have some national variants. His major point is, however, to establish a classification system based on proverb types for Lithuanian national proverbs. He cites many examples and adds important comments concerning their content, form, and structure. A useful bibliography (p. 115) and a Russian summary (p. 116) are included.

3516. Grigas, Kazys. "Apie tarptautines patarlés [in Lithuanian], Ob internatsional'nykh poslovitsakh [in Russian], Das internationale Sprichwort [in German]." In K. Grigas. *Patarliu paralelés. Lietuviu patarlés su latviu, baltarusiu, rusu, lenku, vokieciu, anglu, lotynu, prancuzu, ispanu atitikmenimis.* Vilnius: Vaga, 1987. 8–33 (Lithuanian), 44–48 (Russian), and 81–108 (German).

This is a trilingual introduction to one of the very best polyglot proverb collections by the leading Lithuanian paremiologist and paremiographer Kazys Grigas. He starts with a review of major international proverb collections and then presents convincing arguments for the fact that there exist international structural models (types). Grigas also mentions polygenesis but is quick in pointing out that most internationally disseminated proverbs go back to classical and Biblical times. Many useful comments on the metaphors, equivalents, variants, semantics, age, and geographical distribution of these proverbs are included, citing numerous examples in their original languages together with annotations from national collections. The collection itself is arranged according to key-words with impressive equivalent texts and variants in many European languages for each proverb type. The bibliography (pp. 623–632) and various indices makes this indeed an exemplary international proverb collection.

3517. Grigas, Kazys. *Litovskie poslovitsy. Sravnitel'noe issledovanie.* Vil'nius: Vaga, 1987. 333 pp.

This is a Russian translation of Grigas' significant Lithuanian book *Lietuviu patarlés. Lyginamasis tyrinejimas* (Vilnius: Vaga, 1976). In this comparative study on Lithuanian proverbs the author attempts to discover the relationship between linguistic and extralinguistic factors which govern the origin, history, dissemination, longevity, and disappearance of proverbs. Grigas also deals with the question of what differentiates national from international proverbs. The former exhibit stylistic peculiarities, national vocabulary, and metaphorical motifs which point to typical events of national life, culture, and history. The latter are characterized by sameness of the message and the poetic image, recurrence of structural patterns, and origins that go back to classical and Biblical times. A large bibliography (pp. 297–312) is included. For an English summary see the Lithuanian original of this book (pp. 294–303) which has been annotated under no. 602.

3518. Grimm, Reinhold. "Ein Aphoristiker im Gehäus: Neues aus dem Nachlaß von Felix Pollak." *Modern Austrian Literature*, 24, nos. 3–4 (1991), 17–41.

Grimm begins his intriguing article on the aphorisms by Felix Pollak (1909–1987) with a short description of how this Jewish author had to flee his native Vienna to resettle in the exile of Madison/Wisconsin in the United States. While Pollak gained some recognition as a lyric poet, very little has been known about his aphorisms of which only a few were published in the American journal *Monatshefte*. Grimm now reports on a large manuscript (130 pages) of aphorisms which Pollak completed in 1953 and which is still awaiting publication. The author shows that Pollak was influenced by the aphorisms of the fellow Austrian writer Karl Kraus (1874–1936) who had criticized his age by careful analysis of its language. Pollak has written similar aphorisms in which he bases his social criticism on traditional proverbs and proverbial expressions which he manuipulates, parodies, and alienates to bring about new insights into human nature. Many of these proverbial aphorisms are in fact "Antisprichwörter" (anti-proverbs) which quite often include Americanisms in their German texts. For Karl Kraus' proverbial aphorisms see Wolfgang Mieder (no. 1271).

3519. Grote, Bernd. *Der deutsche Michel. Ein Beitrag zur publizistischen Bedeutung der Nationalfiguren*. Dortmund: Ruhfus, 1967. 89 pp.

This is a comprehensive monograph on the German national figure "Der deutsche Michel" (The German Michael). As a proverbial stereotype (blason populaire) it refers to Germans as being somewhat clumsy, sleepy, and stupid. In his first chapter (pp. 9–11) Grote talks in general about such national symbols as "John Bull," "Uncle Sam" and "Marianne," and he returns to this type of comparative analysis of the symbolism, mythology, and ambivalence of these figures in chapter four (pp. 78–82). The second chapter (pp. 12–18) treats the figure of Michael from Biblical times to the present day and theorizes about the origin of this particular German proverbial expression. The lengthy third chapter (pp. 38–77) presents many historical references to this national sterotype in literature and art, including modern political caricatures. A valuable bibliography (pp. 83–89) and 17 illustrations are included. See also Albert Muncke (no. 1335).

3520. Grzybek, Peter. "Bibliographie der Arbeiten G.L. Permjakovs." *Semiotische Studien zum Sprichwort. Simple Forms Reconsidered I.* Eds. P. Grzybek and Wolfgang Eismann. Tübingen: Gunter Narr, 1984. 203–214.

A complete and very important bibliography of all publications by Grigorii L'vovich Permiakov (1919–1983). The first part lists his translations of several books on myths, fairy tales, and legends from German into Russian. Next Grzybek presents Permiakov's publications on structural and semiotic paremiology in chronological order. He always lists the Russian titles with useful German translations, and he also refers to actual translations of these essays into English, German, etc. Book reviews written by Permiakov are included as well. The bibliography makes clear that Permiakov in addition to his paremiological concerns was also very interested in anthropology and folklore, especially in fairy tales, legends, and riddles. For annotations of the works of this great Russian scholar see nos. 1424–1433, 2737, and 4145–4155.

3521. Grzybek, Peter. "Grigorij L'vovich Permjakov (1919–1983)." *Semiotische Studien zum Sprichwort. Simple Forms Reconsidered I.* Eds. P. Grzybek and Wolfgang Eismann. Tübingen: Gunter Narr, 1984. 199–201.

This is a short statement on the life and scholarly work of the leading Soviet paremiologist Grigorii L'vovich Permiakov (1919–1983) who is to be regarded as one of the greatest theoreticians of the proverb. Grzybek points out that the theoretical writings of Permiakov amount to a "mere" 400 pages, but they are of utmost international importance for the linguistic, structural, semantic, and semiotic analysis of proverbs. The most important publications of Permiakov, including also major comparative proverb collections and a smaller collection of a 300–item proverbial minimum of the Russian language, are mentioned as a short introduction to this significant essay volume in German dedicated to the memory of G.L. Permiakov (see no. 3538 below).

3522. Grzybek, Peter. "Grigorij L'vovich Permjakov (1919–1983)." *Proverbium,* 1 (1984), 175–182.

An important necrology about Grigorii L'vovich Permiakov (1919–1983) who without doubt was the leading Soviet paremiologist and one of the truly outstanding theoreticians of the proverb in the world. Grzybek gives a short biographical sketch of Permiakov's life which was one of severe suffering due to a serious war injury in 1941. Despite his ailment Permiakov dedicated his life to the study of folklore, acting as a collector, translator, editor, and scholar. His major contributions, however, lie in the field of paremiology, where his semantic and semiotic theories gained him world recognition. Grzybek reviews Permiakov's paremiological publications and also includes a bibliography (pp. 181–182) with German translations of the Russian titles.

3523. Grzybek, Peter. "How to Do Things with Some Proverbs: Zur Frage eines parömischen Minimums." *Semiotische Studien zum Sprichwort. Simple Forms Reconsidered I.* Eds. P. Grzybek and Wolfgang Eismann. Tübingen: Gunter Narr, 1984. 351–358.

In this paper Grzybek reports on Grigorii L'vovich Permiakov's idea concerning the proverbial minimum of a given language (see no. 2737). Permiakov had conducted demoscopic research in Moscow in the 1970s in order to establish the most frequently used and best known Russian proverbs and proverbial expressions. The result was his proverb collection *300 obshcheupotrebitel'nykh russkikh poslovits i pogovorok* (1985) that lists and comments on the Russian proverbial minimum. The book has been translated into German and Bulgarian, and Grzybek is correct in arguing that similar books are needed for proper foreign language instruction and learning. The effective language teaching of phraseological units must be based on such empirical data concerning the frequency, currency, and knowledge of the texts.

3524. Grzybek, Peter. "Überlegungen zur semiotischen Sprichwortforschung." *Semiotische Studien zum Sprichwort. Simple Forms Reconsidered I.* Eds. P. Grzybek and Wolfgang Eismann. Tübingen: Gunter Narr, 1984. 215–249.

Major theoretical review article on semiotic paremiology. With special reference to André Jolles (see no, 811) and his concept of "einfache Formen" (simple forms), Grzybek discusses the text, context, and function of proverbs. By also reviewing the work of important paremiologists like Archer Taylor (no. 1858), Friedrich Seiler (no. 1701), Mathilde Hain (no. 640), Alan Dundes (no. 378), Arvo Krikmann (no. 923), Zoltán Kanyó (no. 829), Peter Seitel (no. 1704), and others, Grzybek explains the significance of heterosituativity, polyfunctionality, and polysemanticity of proverbs. Next he deals with paradigmatic, syntagmatic, logical, and structural questions, referring to scholars like Pierre Crépeau (no. 320), Algirdas-Julien Greimas (no. 595), V.P. Anikin (no. 45), George Milner (no. 1291), Matti Kuusi (no. 984), etc. Many pages are dedicated to analyzing Grigorii L'vovich Permiakov's (nos. 1428 and 1433) work, thereby making it more accessible to German readers. Eight structural diagrams are included, and an inclusive bibliography (pp. 447–455) is to be found at the end of this invaluable essay volume.

3525. Grzybek, Peter. "Zur lexikographischen Erfassung von Sprichwörtern." *Semiotische Studien zum Sprichwort. Simple Forms Reconsidered I.* Eds. P. Grzybek and Wolfgang Eismann. Tübingen: Gunter Narr, 1984. 345–350.

In this shorter paper Grzybek deals with the lexicographical problems of proverb collections. It is argued that they should be based on Grigorii L'vovich Permiakov's model which consists of two parts: the first classifies the proverb according to logical-semiotic criteria and the second presents the texts according to thematic groups. Grzybek is correct in adding that such a collection is in definite need of a key-word index. He also points out that such proverb dictionaries would be of particular use in foreign language teaching and learning, especially if the texts were to be based on the proverbial minimum of any given language.

3526. Grzybek, Peter. "Zur Psychosemiotik des Sprichworts." *Semiotiische Studien zum Sprichwort. Simple Forms Reconsidered I.* Eds. P. Grzybek and Wolfgang Eismann. Tübingen: Gunter Narr, 1984. 409–432.

Important study concerning the comprehension of metaphorical proverbs. Both folklorists and psychologists have studied this cognitive problem, and it is time that paremiologists also pay attention to the psycho-semiotic aspects of proverbs. Grzybek reviews the use of so-called proverbs tests in various types of psychological testing, especially for the detection of schizophrenia and for intelligence testing. The author also refers to the psychological and psychiatric work of John D. Benjamin (see no. 141), Donald R. Gorham (nos. 557–561), Richard P. Honeck (no. 752–754), etc. Bibliographical information is included in a major list at the end of this volume (pp. 447–455), but for additional references see Wolfgang Mieder (no. 1265).

3527. Grzybek, Peter. "G.L. Permyakov 1919–1983." *Scottish Slavonic Review*, no. 5 (1985), 170–171.

This is a shortened version of Peter Grzybek's earlier two obituaries (see nos. 3521 and 3522) concerning the great Soviet paremiologist Grigorii L'vovich Permiakov (1919–1983). Grzybek includes a short biographical sketch of this internationally acknowledged authority on structural folkloristics and semiotic paremiology. It is pointed out that Permiakov considered proverbs as signs and/or models of situations or relationships between objects. According to Permiakov, proverbs can be described on the basis of a set of logical rules on the one hand, and a limited number of complementary semantic binary oppositions on the other. Permiakov was without doubt the major scholar of the structural and semiotic approach to paremiology on an international basis.

3528. Grzybek, Peter. "Zur Entwicklung semiotischer Sprichwortforschung in der UdSSR." *Geschichte und Geschichtsschreibung der Semiotik—Fallstudien.* Eds. Klaus D. Dutz and Peter Schmitter. Münster: Münsteraner Arbeitskreis für Semiotik Publikationen, 1986. 383–409.

With this study Grzybek presents a valuable review of semiotic paremiology in the Soviet Union. He starts with a short historical survey of Russian and Soviet proverb research and then discusses the semantic indefiniteness of proverbs which arises from the texts themselves and also from their functional, pragmatic, and contextual indeterminacy. From this follows that heterosituativity, polyfunctionality, and polysemanticity must be considered as categories of the proverb. Grzybek also includes a section on Grigorii L'vovich Permiakov's (1919–1983) semiotic proverb studies which resulted in a logico-semiotic and a thematic classification system of proverbs. A useful bibliography (pp. 404–409) of Soviet scholarship is provided, leading scholars to a better understanding of the major paremiological research efforts that have gone on in the Soviet Union.

3529. Grzybek, Peter. "Foundations of Semiotic Proverb Study." *Proverbium*, 4 (1987), 39–85.

This is a somewhat shortened but also updated English version of Grzybek's original German paper "Überlegungen zur semiotischen Sprichwortforschung" (see no. 3524). He discusses in particular the work of such paremiologists as André Jolles (no. 811), Archer Taylor (no. 1858), Friedrich Seiler (no. 1701), Mathilde Hain (no. 640), Alan Dundes (no. 378), Arvo Krikmann (no. 923), Zoltán Kanyó (no. 829), Peter Seitel (no. 1704), etc. Proverbs as "einfache Formen" (simple forms) and their heterosituativity, polyfunctionality, and polysemanticity are analyzed, and the author also considers paradigmatic, syntagmatic, logical, and structural aspects. The paremiological work along these lines by Pierre Crépeau (no. 320), Algirdas-Julien Greimas (no. 595), V.P. Anikin (no. 45), George Milner (no. 1291), Matti Kuusi (no. 984), and many others is also mentioned. There is, of course, also a special section on Grigorii L'vovich Permiakov's (nos. 1428 and 1433) semiotic studies. Five structural diagrams and an important international bibliography (pp. 78–85) are included.

3530. Grzybek, Peter. "Sprichwort und Fabel: Überlegungen zur Beschreibung von Sinnstrukturen in Texten." *Proverbium,* 5 (1988), 39–67.

In this highly theoretical article on the relationship between proverbs and fables Grzybek goes far beyond the traditional way of looking at these two genres. Previous scholarship has concentrated on how proverbs might have become lengthened into fables and how fables were reduced to proverbs. Grzybek instead emphasizes the invariant semantic structure that is the basis for both these genres. Citing several examples, he shows that there are certain semantic potentials at work which in turn help to explain the heterosituativity, polyfunctionality, and polysemanticity of fables and proverbs. Throughout the article Grzybek quotes from structural and semiotic scholars, notably from Grigorii L'vovich Permiakov (no. 1428), Alan Dundes (no. 378), and Peter Seitel (no. 1704). Two diagrams and an invaluable bibliography (pp. 64–67) are provided. For a similar article by Grzybek in English see no. 3531 below.

3531. Grzybek, Peter. "Invariant Meaning Structures in Texts: Proverb and Fable." *Issues in Slavic Literary and Cultural Theory.* Eds. Karl Eimermacher, P. Grzybek, and Georg Witte. Bochum: Norbert Brockmeyer, 1989. 349–389.

This is a similar article on the proverb and the fable as the previous one written in German (see no. 3530), but this time Grzybek does not emphasize the folkloristic perspective but rather the linguistic aspects of invariant semantic structures in literary texts. Once again he includes a section on the traditional genre-oriented research on these two "einfache Formen" (simple forms), but then he considers in much detail the paradigmatics, syntagmatics, and the dual signification of the proverb and the fable. Next he deals with the proverb as a sign and model of situations, and he also investigates the situational specifics and the invariant thematic structures in fables. Many theoretically oriented structural and semiotic scholars are cited, several examples are presented, and 2 diagrams as well as a helpful bibliography (pp. 382–389) are included.

3532. Grzybek, Peter. "Two Recent Publications in Soviet Structural Paremiology." *Proverbium,* 6 (1989), 181–186.

This is a report on two major Soviet publications on structural and semiotic paremiology still under the editorship or authorship of Grigorii L'vovich Permiakov (1919–1983). The first is entitled *Tel grain tel pain. Poétique de la sagesse populaire* (Moscou: Éditions du Progrès, 1988) and is for the most part a French translation of the essay volume *Paremiologicheskie issledovaniia* which Permiakov had edited in 1983 and which was published only after his death in 1984 (see no. 4151). As Grzybek states, many of Permiakov's theoretical essays are now available in a second foreign language, but it would be desirable to have an English translation in addition to the German and French editions. The second book is edited as a posthumous collection of some of Permiakov's essays by his friend Georgii L. Kapchits under the title of *Osnovy strukturnoi paremiologii* (Moskva: Nauka, 1988). Many previously published articles are again included, but this volume does include important unpublished materials (see no. 4154). Grzybek includes a clear summary of Permiakov's structural and semiotic work, making this an informative essay rather than a typical book review.

3533. Grzybek, Peter. "Kulturelle Stereotype und stereotype Texte." *Natürlichkeit der Sprache und Kultur.* Ed. Walter A. Koch. Bochum: Norbert Brockmeyer, 1990. 300–327.

The author starts with a definition of stereotypes and presents some theoretical thoughts on stereotypical texts and their socio- and psycho-linguistic function. He also comments on Grigorii L'vovich Permiakov's (1919–1983) research on stereotypes and clichés, including a discussion of onto- and ethnogenetic aspects of stereotypes. Of particular interest is the section of the paper (pp. 313–321) that deals with proverbs, proverbial expressions, proverbial comparisons, wellerisms, riddles, and jokes that contain stereotypes. The essay concludes with an important bibliography (pp. 322–327) for the study of proverbial stereotypes (blasons populaires).

3534. Grzybek, Peter. "Das Sprichwort im literarischen Text." *Sprichwörter und Redensarten im interkulturellen Vergleich.* Eds. Annette Sabban and Jan Wirrer. Opladen: Westdeutscher Verlag, 1991. 187–205.

This is a theoretical paper concerning the study of proverbs in literary texts. Grzybek states that scholars must not stop at the identification of texts but rather present interpretations of the proverbial texts in the literary context. He also argues that proverbs in literature do not necessarily justify conclusions concerning a particular value system. The proverbs found in literature must undergo a careful semantic and semiotic analysis, especially in light of the fact that they are characterized by heterosituativity, polyfunctionality, and polysemanticity. The author concludes his comments with the statement that proverbs are "models" for situations, but he does not include examples from a literary text to illustrate his valuable points. A helpful bibliography (pp. 203–205) is attached.

3535. Grzybek, Peter. "Einfache Formen der Literatur als Paradigma der Kultursemiotik." *Cultural Semiotics: Facts and Facets / Fakten und Facetten der Kultursemiotik.* Ed. P. Grzybek. Bochum: Norbert Brockmeyer, 1991. 45–61.

Grzybek starts with some introductory comments regarding "einfache Formen" (simple forms) with special reference to the studies of André Jolles (see no. 811) and Grigorii L'vovich Permiakov (no. 1428). He also concerns himself with culture and cultural semiotics, arguing that there definitely exist certain semantic and semiotic structures and models. In the second half of his essay (pp. 52–58) he analyzes proverbs as signs (models) of situations and emphasizes their hetereosituativity, polyfunctionality, and polysemanticity. Proverbs are seen as "cultural texts" with different paradigmatic and syntagmatic levels of meaning. A useful bibliography (pp. 59–61) and two diagrams are included.

3536. Grzybek, Peter. "Sinkendes Kulturgut? Eine empirische Pilotstudie zur Bekanntheit deutscher Sprichwörter." *Wirkendes Wort*, 41, no. 2 (1991), 239–264.

This is indeed one of the most important studies ever undertaken to establish the actual familiarity of proverbs among speakers of a modern industrial society. Grzybek begins his article with a review of Grigorii L'vovich Permiakov's (1919–1983) significant demographic study to establish the Russian proverbial minimum (see no. 2737). Taking his cue from Permiakov, Grzybek asked 125 German citizens of various ages to complete a list of 275 German proverbs of which only the first half was cited. The result of this empirical study is summarized in 8 diagrams and statistical tables which establish the familiarity of certain German proverbs. Grzybek is able to show how proverb familiarity differs for various age groups, and he also discusses the somewhat surprising result that only 18 proverbs were known by all 125 participants in this experiment. By implication these might be considered the most popular German proverbs today, among them "Eine Hand wäscht die andere" (One hand washes the other), "Es ist nicht alles Gold, was glänzt" (All that glitters is not gold), "Viele Köche verderben den Brei" (Many cooks spoil the broth), etc. Obviously much more elaborate questionnaires and many more people from all areas of Germany are needed to establish a more precise proverbial minimum for the modern German language and culture, but Grzybek's study is definitely a solid start in the right direction. An interesting appendix of proverbs with various percentage figures (pp. 256–260) and a valuable bibliography (pp. 262–264) are attached.

3537. Grzybek, Peter. "Zur semantischen Funktion der sprichwörtlichen Wendungen in Bozena Nemcovas *Babichka*. *Zur Poetik und Rezeption von Bozena Nemcovas "Babichka."* Ed. Andreas Guski. Wiesbaden: Otto Harrassowitz, 1991. 81–126.

Grzybek presents a very detailed literary investigation of the use and function of proverbs and proverbial expressions in

Bozena Nemcova's (1820–1862) autobiographical Czech novel *Babichka* (1855) which appeared in German translation with the title *Großmutter* (1936). The first half of the article (pp. 83–100) deals with theoretical aspects of literary proverb use. Grzybek discusses the work of various literary and paremiological scholars, and he points out in particular that in addition to identifying the phraseological units within the novel their context and function must be analyzed. The second part (pp. 100–110) does exactly that for the proverbial language of this novel, citing many contextualized examples and adding valuable cultural and historical explanations. The proverbs are cited in German translation only, but in the actual proverb index (pp. 112–122) the fixed phrases are cited in the Czech original and in German translation. A useful bibliography (pp. 123–126) is also attached.

3538. Grzybek, Peter, and Wolfgang Eismann (eds.). *Semiotische Studien zum Sprichwort. Simple Forms Reconsidered I.* Tübingen: Gunter Narr, 1984. 259 pp. (=*Kodikas/Code, Ars Semeiotica: An International Journal of Semiotics*, 7, nos. 3–4 [1984], 197–456).

An extremely important essay volume acquainting German and to some extent English readers with the structural and semiotic approach to paremiology which had been pioneered by the Soviet scholar Grigorii L'vovich Permiakov (1919–1983). As one of the editors, Peter Grzybek has contributed the following articles: "Grigorij L'vovich Permjakov (1919–1983)" (pp. 199–201), "Bibliographie der Arbeiten G.L. Permjakovs" (pp. 203–214), "Überlegungen zur semiotischen Sprichwortforschung" (pp. 215–249), "Zur lexikographischen Erfassung von Sprichwörtern" (pp. 345–350), "How to Do Things with Some Proverbs. Zur Frage eines parömischen Minimums" (pp. 351–358), and "Zur Psychosemiotik des Sprichworts" (pp. 409–432). Some of Permiakov's own invaluable papers are presented in either German or English translation, and they include "Zur Frage einer parömiologischen Ebene der Sprache" (pp. 251–256), "Text Functions of Paremias" (pp. 257–262), "Structural Typology of Paremias" (pp. 263–268), "On Paremiological Homonymy and Synonymy" (pp. 269–271), "Kurze Überlegungen zur Struktur des parömiologischen Zeichens" (pp. 273–275), "Die Grammatik der Sprichwörterweisheit" (pp. 295–344),

"Universales Thematisches Verzeichnis" (pp. 433–443), and "The Relationship Between Structural and Comparative Paremiology" (pp. 445–446). Other scholars and essays included are Wolfgang Eismann (co-editor of the volume), "Bemerkungen zur Bedeutung von G.L. Permjakovs Theorie des Klischees für die Linguistik" (pp. 277–293); Mark Abramovich Cherkasskii, "Zum Inhalt des Begriffs 'Subtext' unter dem Gesichtspunkt einer Theorie der kommunikativen Tätigkeit" (pp. 359–361), and "Versuch der Konstruktion eines funktionalen Modells eines speziellen semiotischen Systems (Sprichwörter und Aphorismen)" (pp. 363–377); Iurii Iosifovich Levin, "Zu einigen Besonderheiten des semiotischen Status von Sprichwörtern" (pp. 379–385); and Arvo Krikmann, "1001 Frage zur logischen Struktur der Sprichwörter" (pp. 387–408). The 19 essays cover an extremely wide range of paremiological questions, in particular those dealing with linguistics, semiotics, lexicography, proverbial (paremiological) minimum, structure, function, typology (type), classification, homonymy, synonymy, semantics, logic, theme, cliché (phraseological unit), communication, metaphor, etc. An important international bibliography (pp. 447–455) concludes this superb theoretical volume. For annotations of the individual articles see nos. 3521, 3520, 3524, 3525, 3523, 3526 (Grzybek); 4145, 1428, 1429 (Permiakov); and 3373, 3234, 3233, 3780, 3730.

3539. Guillaume, Gabriel. "Locutions gallèses. Leçons d'une Bazougeaise: Adèle Denys." *Langue et littérature orales dans l'Ouest de la France.* Eds. Michel Bonneau and Goerges Cesbron. Angers: Publication de l'Université d'Angers, 1983. 330–340.

In this paper the author presents numerous French dialect expressions which he collected from the informant Adèle Denys. The language of these proverbial expressions is that of the town of Bazouges in the Bretagne (Brittany). Guillaume cites the phrases with etymological and at times cultural or historical explanations. For some of them he also explains how they might be used. Problems of orthography, phonetics, and style are discussed, and it is argued that much more field research like this needs to be done to record French expressions that are current in the various dialects.

3540. Guiraud, Charles. "Structure linguistique des proverbes latins." *Richesse du proverbe.* Eds. François Suard and Claude Buridant. Lille: Université de Lille, 1984. II, 73–82.

Based on August Otto's standard Latin proverb collection *Die Sprichwörter und sprichwörtlichen Redensarten der Römer* (Leipzig: Teubner, 1890; rpt. Hildesheim: Georg Olms, 1971), Guiraud investigates the linguistic structure of classical Latin proverbs. He shows that they usually consist of a subject and a predicate, that a binary structure is prevalent, that many texts have rhyme, alliteration, repetition of words, and assonance, and that some even include elements of wordplay. The numerous examples are cited with French translations, and the author has included some etymological and cultural explanations.

3541. Günther, Kurt. "Über die Zeichenverwendung bei der Darstellung der Phraseologie." *Linguistische Studien,* series A, Arbeitsberichte, no. 95 (1982), 143–152.

The author argues that bilingual dictionaries should follow a unified lexicographical method of registering phraseological units. Concerning the text itself, it is of importance that pronunciation, intonation, standard form, and variants are indicated. The particular expression also needs to be characterized according to such grammatical aspects as word types, inflection, verbal aspect, and morphology. Finally, the lexicographer must include semantic explanations which will insure proper usage of a certain fixed phrase. A comprehensive list of abbreviations of terms to be used to characterize phrases according to these desiderata is attached.

3542. Günther, Kurt. "Prädikativphraseme im Deutschen und Russischen." *Linguistische Studien,* series A, Arbeitsberichte, no. 120 (1984), 31–66.

Detailed linguistic analysis of German and Russian predicative phraseological units which have usually been called proverbial expressions or proverbial formulas. Günther starts with a review of the scholarship on these expressions, he states his definition and then presents four structural types with examples. Next he discusses such aspects as morphology, standard form,

244 International Proverb Scholarship, Supplement II (1982–1991)

stability, idiomaticity, polysemanticity, synonymy, antonymy, negation, and style. A helpful bibliography (pp. 64–66) is included.

3543. Günther, Kurt. *Wörterbuch phraseologischer Termini.* Berlin: Akademie der Wissenschaften der DDR, Zentralinstitut für Sprachwissenschaft, 1990. 164 pp. (=*Linguistische Studien,* series A, Arbeitsberichte, no. 205 [1990], 1–164).

This is a very useful dictionary of phraseological terms and concepts. Günther starts with a short introduction explaining the confused state of the international terminology in the field of phraseology, and he then presents a bibliography (p. 6) of other German and Russian studies that have dealt with this problem. The actual dictionary is comprised of 620 entries whose German key-words are usually also given in Russian. For each entry the author presents clear definitions and a few examples in German and Russian. At the end of the book (pp. 157–164) is a German alphabetical list of the terms treated in this valuable work. It might have been useful to indicate the equivalent English terms as well to add to the international importance of this dictionary.

3544. Günthner, Susanne. "Interkulturelle Aspekte von Schreibstilen. Zur Verwendung von Sprichwörtern und Routineformeln in Deutschaufsätzen chinesischer Deutschlerner/innen." *Texte schreiben im Germanistik-Studium.* Eds. Maria Lieber and Jürgen Posset. München: Iudicium Verlag, 1988. 145–159.

The author presents a socio- and psycho-linguistic study of the use and function of proverbs, proverbial expressions and routine formulas in 21 essays written by Chinese students studying German as a foreign language. From the 18 proverbial texts found in the context of these letters it becomes clear that the Chinese students place a high cultural value on the knowledge of proverbial wisdom. The proverbs are used to introduce an essay, to indicate cultural differences, to express social norms, and to state ritualistic feelings. There is no doubt that the Chinese students use proverbial materials as a stylistic and ethnographic device of communication, interpreting the proverbs very much in the traditional sense.

3545. Guthke, Karl S. *Letzte Worte. Variationen über ein Thema der Kulturgeschichte des Westens.* München: C.H. Beck, 1990. 225 pp.

This is a fascinating book on famous and not so well-known "letzte Worte" (last words) of the cultural history of the West. In chapter one (pp. 11–55) Guthke starts with a discussion of the meaning and form of this convention in life, literature, and biographies. The second chapter (pp. 55–74) analyzes last words as expressions of fulfillment, immortality, and a certain mystique about life. Chapter three (pp. 75–103) deals with the question of authenticity of those last words that are attached to certain persons. The long fourth chapter (pp. 104–157) contains a detailed description of collections of last words in various languages, and chapter five (pp. 158–181) presents a cultural history of last words, including a discussion of stereotypical last words, their modern secularized parody, and their popularization through the change from literary quotation or sententious remark to anonymous proverbs. One of the highlights of the book to a German reader is without doubt the section (pp. 88–94) on Johann Wolfgang von Goethe's (1749–1832) last words "Mehr Licht" (More light) which have long become proverbial. The detailed notes (pp. 182–204) include important bibliographical information on the cultural history of last words. Guthke also includes a list (pp. 205–214) of all foreign last words in German translation, and a useful name index (pp. 215–225) enables the reader to find the "last words" of numerous people of all walks of life.

3546. Guthke, Karl S. "'Gipsabgüsse von Leichenmasken'? Goethe und der Kult des letzten Worts." *Jahrbuch der deutschen Schillergesellschaft*, 35 (1991), 73–95.

This essay is a more detailed study of Johann Wolfgang von Goethe's (1749–1832) famous and proverbial last words "Mehr Licht" (More light) than Guthke was able to present in his comprehensive book on *Letzte Worte* (see no. 3545 above). He starts with some general remarks on last words and cites numerous examples from European and American sources. He then deals with Goethe in particular, explaining that there exists a literal "cult" about these two famous words. Guthke also shows that there are several variants of Goethe's supposed last words in circulation which are much more mundane than this more philosophical statement. Guthke's discussion of the authenticity of Goethe's last words is of particular interest, quoting many biographical details, later literary allusions, and modern parodies of this commonly known phrase.

3547. Gvozdev, V.V. "Paradigmaticheskie otnosheniia v poslovichnom fonde." *Filologicheskie naukie*, 4 (1982), 44–49.

This is a theoretical and linguistic article on the paradigmatic aspects of proverbs. Gvozdev discusses previous work by Arvo Krikmann (see nos. 923–924) and Grigorii L'vovich Permiakov (mo. 1428), and he then analyzes the structure, syntax, and meaning of proverbs. He also includes small sections on semiotic and lexicological questions, arguing that proverbs must be studied on a comparative basis. The author is particularly interested in the linguistic properties of proverbs which are of great importance in establishing certain proverb types. A few Russian examples are included, and the 12 notes contain useful bibliographical information concerning Soviet and East European scholarship.

3548. Györke, Zoltán, and Csaba Földes. "Issledovanie frazeologii inostrannykh iazykov v Vengrii (s prilozheniem izbrannoi bibliografii po frazeologii s 1950 po 1985 gg.)." *Acta Academiae Paedagogicae Szegediensis, series Linguistica, Literaria et Aestetica*, no volume given (1985), 29–43.

The two authors present an important review article of Hungarian phraseological scholarship dealing with fixed phrases of several foreign languages. In the first half of the paper (pp. 29–34) they discuss theoretical, pragmatic, lexical, structural, and semantic aspects of phraseological units and their importance in foreign language instruction. The second part (pp. 34–43) contains a detailed bibliography of the phraseological research that Hungarian scholars have accomplished between 1950 and 1985 on Russian, German, French, English, and some other European languages. Hungarian and German summaries (p. 43) are included.

3549. Györke, Zoltán, and Csaba Földes. "Osnovnye napravleniia i perspektivy issledovannia frazeologii russkogo iazyka v Vengrii (s prilozhenien izbrannoi bibliografii po izucheniiu frazeologii v Vengrii s 1950 po 1985 gg.)." *Zeitschrift für Slawistik,* 34, no. 3 (1989), 427–435.

In this review article Györke and Földes deal with those Hungarian publications that have dealt with phraseological aspects of the Russian language. In the first part of their article (pp. 427–431) they discuss theoretical, pragmatic, lexical, structural, and semantic aspects of phraseological units, and they also comment on the importance of fixed phrases for foreign language instruction. The second part (pp. 431–435) contains a detailed bibliography of the work that Hungarian scholars have done on Russian proverbs, proverbial expressions, idioms, etc. This bibliography is a superb compilation of the impressive phraseological scholarship in Hungary.

H

3550. Haase, Donald P. "Is Seeing Believing? Proverbs and the Film Adaptation of a Fairy Tale." *Proverbium,* 7 (1990), 89–104.

This is a fascinating study of the use of proverbs in Angela Carter's (1940–) and Neil Jordan's (1951–) film adaptation of the fairy tale *Little Red Riding Hood.* The 1984 movie is based on Carter's earlier literary rewriting of this well-known tale with the title *The Company of Wolves* (1979) in which the tale is interpreted as a dream of a contemporary adolescent girl. Haase explains that proverbs are used as a means of questioning the popular wisdom of the fairy tale. At the same time the apparent truth of proverbs is challenged through modern manipulation of their texts. The proverb "Seeing is believing" serves as a definite leitmotif in the film. Haase includes two annotated lists of proverbs in addition to interpreting them in the cinematic context: 25 texts that appear in the film version and 8 proverbs that are included in the earlier literary adaptation. A useful bibliography (pp. 102–104) is attached.

3551. Häcki-Buhofer, Annelies. "Psycholinguistische Aspekte in der Bildhaftigkeit von Phraseologismen." *Europhras 88. Phraséologie Contrastive. Actes du Colloque International Klingenthal-Strasbourg, 12–16 mai 1988.* Ed. Gertrud Gréciano. Strasbourg: Université des Sciences Humaines, 1989. 165–175.

The author studies various German proverbial expressions from a psycho-linguistic point of view, starting with a differentiation between the metaphorical and figurative nature of fixed phrases. She cites a number of earlier studies on the comprehension of metaphors and then explains how the meaning of verbal imagery is communicated and understood.

The images of two German expressions are studied in particular, namely "Da liegt der Hase im Pfeffer" (That's the fly in the ointment, That's the rub [snag]) and "Jdm. einen Bären aufbinden" (To pull someone's leg, To take someone for a ride). Häcki-Buhofer includes two interesting lists of associations that informants reported in decoding the meaning of the phrases. A short bibliography (pp. 174–175) is provided.

3552. Haines, Victor Y. "'Hony soyt qui mal pence': Can the Reader Sin?" *Revue de l'Université d'Ottowa/University of Ottawa Quarterly*, 53 (1983), 181–188.

Haines investigates why the letter "y" is missing in the proverb variation "Hony soyt qui mal pence" which is carefully inscribed at the end of a manuscript of *Sir Gawain and the Green Knight* (c. 1370). At the same time the author discusses the actual proverb "Honi soit qui mal y pense" (Evil to him who thinks evil) which is the motto of the Order of the Garter. It is pointed out that the "y" was left out on purpose in order to force the reader to think well ethically at the end of reading this medieval English romance.

3553. Hall, Ann C. "Educating Reader: Chaucer's Use of Proverbs in *Troilus and Criseyde*." *Proverbium*, 3 (1986), 47–58.

Literary investigation of the use and function of English proverbs in Geoffrey Chaucer's (1340?–1400) medieval epic *Troilus and Criseyde* (1385). The author studies in particular Pandarus' frequent and persuasive employment of didactic proverbs, but she also analyzes how the narrator neither embraces nor condemns conventional wisdom. Proverbs are often misapplied, and their wisdom appears to be no wisdom at all. By denying proverbs their absolute claim to universal truth in this epic, Chaucer attempts to educate the reader to look at proverbs with a more critical eye. Several proverbs are intepreted in their literary context, and the notes include bibliographical information on Chaucer's proverbial style and message. See also R.M. Lumiansky (no. 1121) and Donald MacDonald (no. 1131).

3554. Hallo, William W. "Proverbs Quoted in Epic." *Lingering over Words: Studies in Ancient Near Eastern Literature in Honor of W.L. Moran.* Eds. Tzvi Abusch, John Huehnergard, and Piotr Steinkeller. Atlanta/Georgia: Scholars Press, 1990. 203–217 (=*Harvard Semitic Studies,* 37 [1990], 203–217).

This very erudite article starts with a review of previous research on ancient Sumerian and Akkadian proverbs, showing that proverbs represent convincing examples of the phenomenon of intertexuality in cuneiform literature. The second part (pp. 211–217) deals in particular with the use and function of 10 ancient proverbs in the *Gilgamesh* (c. 2000 B.C.) and other epics. Hallo cites his examples in their original context and then indicates how these proverbs influenced later wisdom literature and literary works to the present day. The 10 proverbs are listed in transliterated Sumerian in an appendix (p. 217), and the 132 notes contain significant bibliographical references to individual studies of some of the world's oldest proverbs.

3555. Hamm, Albert. "Remarques sur le fonctionnement de la négation dans les proverbes: L'example de l'anglais." *Europhras 88. Phraséologie Contrastive. Actes du Colloque International Klingenthal-Strasbourg, 12–14 mai 1988.* Ed. Gertrud Gréciano. Strasbourg: Université des Sciences Humaines, 1989. 177–193.

The author reports on a study of 800 commonly used English proverbs of which close to a third employ negation of some type. It is argued that this is primarily due to the fact that proverbs represent an oral tradition in which didacticism, morality, ethics, and instruction were of major importance. Many examples are cited with detailed comments on such proverb structures as represented by "Waste not, want not." The author also includes a section on contradictory proverbs like "Clothes do not make the man" and "The tailor makes the man." Negation is seen as a stylistic device to teach people prudent behavior.

3556. Hannemann, Brigitte (ed.). *Erasmus von Rotterdam. "Süß scheint der Krieg den Unerfahrenen"—"Dulce bellum inexpertis."* München: Chr. Kaiser, 1987. 202 pp.

This is a meticulously edited reprint of a lengthy essay which Erasmus of Rotterdam (1469–1536) included in the 1515 edition of his *Adagia*. The essay concerns the classical proverb "Dulce bellum inexpertis" (War is sweet to the inexperienced) for which Erasmus gives detailed philological and historical explanations. Hannemann starts her book with a lengthy introduction (pp. 7–37) summarizing Erasmus of Rotterdam's interest in proverbs and tracing the editorial history of this particular proverb in the *Adagia*. The essay is printed in German translation (pp. 57–87), and then follow many pages of explanatory notes (pp. 89–202) on this proverb essay about war and peace. With 7 illustrations.

3557. Hansen, Aage. *Om Peder Laales danske ordsprog.* Eds. Merete K. Jørgensen and Iver Kjaer. Copenhagen: Munksgaard, 1991. 201 pp.

After the death of the Danish philologist and lexicographer Aage Hansen (1894–1983), the two editors prepared his important manuscript on the 1200 pairs of Latin and Danish proverbs collected by the legendary Peder Låle (14th century) as a posthumonous publication. Hansen starts with a comprehensive introduction (pp. 6–21) discussing the history of this important late medieval proverb collection of *Danske ordsprog* (oldest printing 1506) and explains that it had the pedagogical purpose of teaching wisdom and Latin. In the following chapters Hansen presents erudite analyses of the following aspects of the Danish proverbs: orthography (pp. 22–49), morphology (pp. 50–81), syntax (pp. 82–93), style (pp. 94–104), proverbial types (pp. 105–113), content (pp. 114–128), vocabulary (pp. 129–162), and origin of the proverbs (pp. 163–191). In this last part concerning the origin of the Danish proverbs, of which some are definitely indigenous to Denmark and not mere translations from the Latin, Hansen includes important comparative comments regarding other early European proverb collections, notably the *Proverbia communia sive seriosa* (pp. 185–189). A large bibliography (pp. 192–196), an essay by Iver Kjaer about Aage Hansen's life and work (pp. 197–201), and an English abstract (p. 2) help to make this a major philological and paremiological monograph.

3558. Haring, Lee. "'The Word of the Fathers': Proverbs in Madagascar." *Acta Ethnographica Academiae Scientiarum Hungaricae*, 33, nos. 1–4 (1984–1985), 123–164.

Harings's major study of Malagasy proverbs is divided into three parts that include many textual examples from Madagascar in the original language with English translations. The author starts with a detailed discussion of several proverb collections (pp. 123–130). This is followed by a review of the interpretative research on Malagasy proverbs (pp. 130–145), including comments on their origin, history, structure, meaning, metaphor, function, etc. The third part (pp. 145–164) analyzes particular structural patterns based on symmetry: symmetry with and without a conjunction, the symmetry doubled, and the symmetry concluded in a phrase growing out of the dialogue habit. Haring also refers to the importance of the context for a proper understanding of the meaning of these texts. A valuable bibliography (pp. 161–164) is attached to this inclusive study. See also Jan Wirrer (no. 4571).

3559. Harms, Wolfgang, John Roger Paas, Michael Schilling, and Andreas Wang (eds.). *Illustrierte Flugblätter des Barock. Eine Auswahl.* Tübingen: Max Niemeyer, 1983. 46–49, 56–57, and 84–85.

In this large book of illustrated German broadsheets of the 17th century, the editors have also included four examples that picture proverbs toegther with more or less didactic and versified texts. The illustrated proverbs are "Bei Hunden und Katzen ist Beißen und Kratzen" (Dogs and cats bite and scratch), "Aller guten Dinge sind drei" (All good things come in threes), "Wo Wein eingeht, da geht Witz aus" (When wine is in, wit is out), and "Große Fische fressen kleine Fische" (Big fish eat little fish). The editors provide precise bibliographical information for each broadsheet, they discuss the artists and printers, and they include detailed cultural and historical commentaries. All four broadsheets make clear that artistic proverb illustrations were popular in the Baroque age in Germany, and this interplay of art, didacticism, literature, and proverbs deserves much more attention by proverb scholars. With 4 illustrations.

3560. Harris, Amelia Johnston. *The Functions and Applications of the Proverb and Proverbial Expression in the German Poetry of Thomas Murner.* Diss. University of North Carolina at Chapel Hill, 1991. 368 pp.

This dissertation represents a detailed analysis of the German proverbs and proverbial expressions contained in the satirical works of Thomas Murner (1475–1537). Harris begins with an introductory chapter (pp. 1–32) dealing with the use of Early New High German proverbs in 16th century literature, and she also comments on the folk language that Murner used in his numerous writings. The second chapter (pp. 33–115) looks at the structural integration of fixed phrases, emphasizing their location at the beginning and end of chapters, their amassing, and their use for the purpose of alienation. The third chapter (pp. 116–148) studies the themes and variations of these phraseological units, while the fourth chapter (pp. 149–181) treats the metaphors as well as their applications and implications within the literary context. The fifth chapter (pp. 182–188) summarizes these findings which are based on numerous contextualized examples. Harris includes an invaluable annotated proverb index (pp. 189–364), and a useful bibliography (pp. 365–368) is also provided. See also Anna Risse (no. 1551).

3561. Harris, Joseph. "'Deor' and Its Refrain: Preliminaries to an Interpretation." *Traditio: Studies in Ancient and Medieval History, Thought, and Religion,* 43 (1987), 23–53.

Harris presents a scholarly study on the proverbial refrain of the Old English poem *Deor* (9th or 10th century) of 42 lines ending with "Thaes oferode, thisses swa maeg" (That passed, so can this). The author refers to previous research and notes in particular Archer Taylor's (1890–1973) and Bartlett Jere Whiting's (1904–) recognition of this proverbial line that today is usally cited as "All things (must/will/do) pass" or simply "This too will pass." Harris includes medieval Latin and later English variants, and he attempts an interpretation of the entire poem in light of this proverbial consolation. The 80 notes contain useful bibliographical information on this early proverb. See also Archer Taylor (no. 1898).

3562. Harrow, Martin, Linda S. Grossman, Marshall Silverstein, and Herbert Meltzer. "Thought Pathology in Manic and Schizophrenic Patients: Its Occurrence at Hospital Admission and Seven Weeks Later." *Archives of General Psychiatry*, 39 (1982), 665–671.

 By using the Donald R. Gorham proverbs test (see no. 557) and other thought disorder tests, the authors are able to show that most hospitalized manics are severely thought disordered, that hospital manics are as thought disordered as schizophrenics, that unmedicated manics are as severely thought disordered as unmedicated schizophrenics, that both manics' and schizophrenics' thought disorders improve after the acute phase, and that even after the acute phase some manics show severe thought pathology. The results indicate that thought disorder is certainly not unique to schizophrenia. A bibliography (p. 671) and an English abstract (p. 665) are included.

3563. Harrow, Martin, Ilene Lanin-Kettering, Mel Prosen, and Joan G. Miller. "Disordered Thinking in Schizophrenia: Intermingling and Loss of Set." *Schizophrenia Bulletin*, 9 (1983), 354–367.

 The authors analyzed the responses of 36 acute psychiatric patients to the Donald R. Gorham proverbs test (see no. 557) and other psychological tests. The patients suffered in particular from intermingling, frequently seen in the speech and thinking of schizophrenic patients. It involves the blending of personal material from one's experiences into one's thinking and communication, leading to bizarre and inappropriate speech. Results indicate that intermingling often leads to some loss of goal-directed thinking. Schizophrenics and other psychotic subjects showed significantly more intermingling in their proverb interpretations, not recognizing how inappropriate their personal material actually was. A useful bibliography (pp. 366–367) is attached.

3564. Harvilahti, Lauri. "'Zwei Fliegen mit einer Klappe'. Zum Parallelismus der Sprichwörter." *Finnisch-Ugrische Forschungen*, 48, no. 1 (1987), 27–38.

This paper deals with various elements of structural parallelism in Finnish proverbs. Harvilahti explains how phonological, morphological, and syntactical parallelism can be found in many Finnish proverbs. Such stylistic elements like alliteration and rhyme also add to this phenomenon, and so do synonymy and analogy. The author includes a section on such structural patterns in Mongolian proverbs, citing his numerous examples with German translations. A few comments on the difficulty of translating this type of proverb are added as well. A short bibliography (pp. 37–38) is provided.

3565.   Hasan-Rokem, Galit. "L'cheker hapitgam ha'amami ha'yehudi." *Tarbitz,* 51, no. 2 (1982), 281–292.

In this article written in Hebrew Hasan-Rokem summarizes a few of the findings of her larger study on Israeli folk narratives containing proverbs (see no. 3566 below). Looking in particular at the Hebrew proverb "Do not trust the gentiles even forty years in the grave," she presents a model for studying the meaning of proverbs which is based on the interaction of four levels: text, use, structure, and function. Many Middle Eastern variants of the proverb are cited, and the author discusses their appearance in folk narratives and oral speech. Hasan-Rokem also presents methods of paremiological field research and analyzes the proverbial texts in their various contexts. The 42 notes contain important bibliographical references to theoretical aspects of paremiology.

3566.   Hasan-Rokem, Galit. *Proverbs in Israeli Folk Narratives: A Structural Semantic Analysis.* Helsinki: Suomalainen Tiedeakatemia, 1982. 107 pp.

This is a seminal study of Israeli folk narratives containing proverbs. The author starts with definition problems and looks at a proverb as "a specifically structured poetical summary referring to collective experience" (p. 12) whose meaning depends on the context in which it is being used. According to Hasan-Rokem's model (pp. 16–17), proverb meaning is based on the interaction of four levels: text (quotation of proverb-texts), use (analysis of poetic strategy), structure (analysis of logico-semantic components), and function (relating of the proverb to semantic groups). This multilevel analysis of the proverb is exemplified by a fascinating study of the Hebrew proverb "Do not trust the gentiles even forty years in the grave" (pp. 23–53) and its variants, including numerous structural diagrams. Then follows a discussion of the proverb-tale tradition which includes an important section on the similarities and differences of quotations and proverbs (pp. 54–95). This is illustrated by a diachronic analysis of a Biblical verse (Ecclesiastes 10,20) which became proverbial in Hebrew as "A bird of the air shall carry the voice." An English summary (pp. 96–98), useful notes, and an important bibliography (pp. 103–107) conclude this exemplary diachronic and synchronic study of proverbs in folk narratives which is enhanced by detailed semantic and structural analyses.

3567. Hasan-Rokem, Galit. "The Pragmatics of Proverbs: How the Proverb Gets Its Meaning." *Exceptional Language and Linguistics.* Eds. Loraine K. Obler and Lise Menn. New York: Academic Press, 1982. 169–173.

Short but significant theoretical paper on the meaning of proverbs. It is argued that the specific meaning of a proverb, which itself is a poetic wording for a conceptual structure, is dependent on the context in which it is being used. Hasan-Rokem explains that lexical and syntactical analyses do not suffice to intepret the meaning of a proverb. Of great importance for an understanding of a proverb are its actual use in discourse and the pragmatic aspects of this proverb use. A number of Middle Eastern proverbs are discussed with references to their function in Jewish folk narratives.

3568. Hasan-Rokem, Galit. "And God Created the Proverb . . . Inter-Generic and Inter-Textual Aspects of Biblical Paremiology—or The Longest Way to the Shortest Text." *Text and Tradition: The Hebrew Bible and Folklore.* Ed. Susan Niditsch. Atlanta/Georgia: Scholars Press, 1990. 107–120.

Hasan-Rokem analyzes two Biblical passages from the Old Testament as instances of proverbs in narrative, namely "It is not good for man to be alone" (Genesis 2,18) and "That is why a man leaves his father and mother and is united to his wife, and the two become one flesh" (Genesis 2,24). The author explains that the meaning of these proverbs can only be understood from the narrative context in which they are being used. She investigates their structure and didactic function, arguing that they are indeed hermeneutic keys for this particular portion of the Genesis narrative. It is also pointed out that this wisdom literature reflects cultural and traditional insights that help readers of the Bible to understand and deal with necessary ethical decisions. A helpful bibliography (pp. 117–120) dealing with Hebrew and Biblical proverbs is attached, and an English abstract (p. 107) is provided as well. See also Roland Murphy (no. 3990).

3569. Hasan-Rokem, Galit. "The Aesthetics of the Proverb: Dialogue of Discourses from Genesis to Glasnost." *Proverbium,* 7 (1990), 105–116.

In this article Hasan-Rokem wants to go beyond the structural and semiotic preoccupation of theoretically minded paremiologists. She stresses the aesthetic characteristics of proverbs, arguing that proverbs constantly refer to discourses external of their own occurrence. In various short sections of her paper she investigates the dialogical use of proverbs in the Bible, in the speech of a Sephardic female informant in Israel, and in the traditional language of an informant who moved to Israel from Soviet Georgia. Hasan-Rokem explains that the context of interaction is of major importance in understanding the meaning and message of proverbs. She also sees proverbs as bridges between people in the sense that they are dialogues between discourses. The article closes with a few references to the meaning and function of Hebrew proverbs in the headlines of the Israeli daily newspaper *Haaretz,* where they were used to comment on the policy of "glasnost" in the Soviet Union under Mikhail Gorbachev.

3570. Hasenohr, Geneviève. "La locution verbale figurée dans l'oeuvre de Jean Le Fèvre." *La locution. Actes du colloque international Université McGill, Montréal, 15–16 octobre 1984.* Eds. Giuseppe Di Stefano and Russell G. McGillivray. Montréal: Editions CERES, 1984. 229–281.

Literary investigation of proverbial expressions in the medieval French works of Jean Le Fèvre (1326?–1380/87). Hasenohr deals particularly with the wealth of verbal phraseological units, and her major goal is to present an annotated collection of texts that are classified thematically. There are sections on life and death, destiny, fortune, knowledge, time, religion, marriage, sexuality, speech, etc. For each expression the author gives precise references and includes etymological, cultural and semantic explanations. Parallels from other medieval literary works and proverb collections are cited, and a subject index is also provided.

3571. Hassell, James Woodrow. *Middle French Proverbs, Sentences, and Proverbial Phrases.* Toronto: Pontifical Institute of Mediaeval Studies, 1982. 275 pp.

Even though this is a collection, it is included in this bibliography since the American paremiologist and paremiographer James Woodrow Hassell (1915–1987) addresses a number of important issues in his introduction (pp. 1–10), namely the scope (Middle French period, 1300–1515), choice of sources, definition and classification of the proverbial materials, and the composition of the dictionary. This discussion as well as the organization of the collection should be the basis for any historical dictionary of proverbs. Hassell followed the model (see no. 3007) which Bartlett Jere Whiting (1904–) established in his numerous English proverb collections. The bibliography (pp. 15–26) is of great importance to scholars interested in French paremiology and paremiography. This is most certainly an erudite historical proverb dictionary which is arranged alphabetically according to key-words, citing many texts and variants for each proverb and proverbial expression.

3572. Hattemer, K., and E.K. Scheuch. *Sprichwörter. Einstellung und Verwendung.* Düsseldorf: Intermarket. Gesellschaft für internationale Markt- und Meinungsforschung, 1983. 197 pp.

This is a very important demographic study concerning the perception and use of proverbs by 400 German residents who answered a questionnaire consisting of 27 questions. It is established that "Morgenstunde hat Gold im Munde" (The morning hour has gold in its mouth, i.e. The early bird catches the worm) is the most popular and commonly used German proverb. The frequency for many other proverbs is also established, and 186 statistical tables present the responses to various questions, among them: Do you use many proverbs? What kind of people use proverbs? When do you use proverbs? Do proverbs help to deal with certain situations or problems? Can one learn something from traditional proverbs? Do more men or more women use proverbs? Are more proverbs used during happy or sad situations? Can proverbs encourage people to deal with their problems? Do many of your friends use proverbs? What is the age of the people who use proverbs the most? What proverbs do you know? What varied proverbs (for advertisements) do you know? etc. The fascinating answers to these questions are of great significance for the understanding of how proverbs live on in a modern industrial society. Above all this survey shows that proverbs are still known, cited, and considered useful. Many more studies of this type are needed with the informed involvement of folklorists and paremiologists. The present questionnaire was commissioned by a German insurance company (Aachener und Münchener Versicherung AG, Aachen) and carried out by a marketing research company. Unfortunately the lengthy study has not been published, but a copy might be obtained from Intermarket, Gesellschaft für internationale Markt- und Meinungsforschung, Prinz-Georg-Straße 108, 4000 Düsseldorf 30, Germany. For a detailed review of this study see Wolfgang Mieder (no. 3884).

3573. Häusermann, Jürg. "Phraseologismen und Sprichwörter als Formulierungshilfe in der argumentativen Rede." *Aktuelle Probleme der Phraseologie.* Eds. Harald Burger and Robert Zett. Bern: Peter Lang, 1987. 79–95.

The author states that phraseological units play an important rhetorical role in spontaneous discussions broadcasted on the radio or television. Through the analysis of several transcribed speech acts in High German or Swiss German, Häusermann is able to show that proverbs and proverbial expressions are used primarily to underscore a particular argument or to add expressiveness to a speaker's opinion. Such metaphorical argumentation also helps to emotionalize the speaker's language, and it can even result in shrewd manipulation of the listeners who find themselves agreeing with this traditional wisdom and the vivid images without critically thinking about what is being said. A small bibliography (pp. 94–95) is attached.

3574. Hausmann, Franz Josef. "Phraseologische Wörterbücher des Deutschen." *Sprache und Literatur in Wissenschaft und Unterricht,* 16, no. 56 (1985), 105–109.

An enlightening review article of German phraseological dictionaries with the justified and deserved claim that Lutz Röhrich's *Lexikon der sprichwörtlichen Redensarten* (2 vols., 1973; 2nd ed. in 3 vols, 1991/92) is without doubt the best work available. Hausmann discusses the lexicographical problems of including phraseological units in normal dictionaries, and he argues that much more information on each proverbial expression, twin formula, proverbial comparison, etc. should be included. This is especially true for such aspects as use, style (colloquial, slang, literary, etc.), meaning, variants, linguistic explanations (etymology, structure, vocabulary, etc.), and contextualized texts. A few examples from the works of Theodor Fontane (1819–1898) and Thomas Mann (1875–1955) are cited, and the bibliography (pp. 108–109) contains major German idiomatic dictionaries.

3575. Hausmann, Franz Josef. "Das Zitatenwörterbuch." *Wörterbücher. Ein internationales Handbuch zur Lexikographie.* Eds. Franz Josef Hausmann, Oskar Reichmann, Herbert Ernst Wiegand and Ladislav Zgusta. Berlin: Walter de Gruyter, 1989. I, 1044–1050.

In this review article Hausmann presents a discussion of the various types of dictionaries of quotations and sententious remarks (geflügelte Worte), of which many include proverbs and proverbial expressions. Referring to standard collections from many languages, he analyzes their history, function, and classification systems. It is pointed out that they are usually set up either according to individual authors, key-words or themes. But there are also those dictionaries that are arranged alphabetically, chronologically, and by language groups. The author includes an impressive international bibliography (pp. 1047–1050) which reflects the fact that quotation dictionaries are extremely popular.

3576. Hecht, Peter. "The Debate on Symbol and Meaning in Dutch Seventeenth-Century Art: An Appeal to Common Sense." *Simiolus*, 16 (1986), 173–187.

This is actually an article dealing with various elements of symbol and meaning in Dutch art of the 17th century, but there are also a few references to realistic peasant scenes that depict proverbial expressions. Hecht refers in particular to the motif of two people pulling on the same pretzel (pp. 178–179) that can be found in Pieter Brueghel's (c. 1520–1569) *Netherlandic Proverbs* (1559) picture, in a 1624 emblem by Johan de Brune (1589–1658), and in other illustrations of folk life. The Dutch expressions that are being illustrated are most likely "Het achterste paar krijgt de krakelingen" (The last pair gets the pretzel) or "Twee die aan een krakeling trekken" (Two are pulling on the same pretzel). There is also a reference to Jacob Cats' (1577–1660) emblem from 1632 that illustrates the English proverb "A little pot is soon hot" (p. 184). With 4 illustrations.

3577. Hein, Jürgen. "Redensarten und Sprichwörter bei Johann Nestroy." *Sprache und Literatur in Wissenschaft und Unterricht*, 16, no. 56 (1985), 14–17.

A short literary study of the use and function of German proverbial expressions and proverbs in the plays of the Austrian dramatist Johann Nestroy (1801–1862). By quoting a number of examples in their literary context, Hein explains that they add to the humor of the plays. There is a lot of wordplay, juxtaposing the literal or real meaning of the proverbs with the figurative or metaphorical meaning. Nestroy also employs proverbial materials to indicate that there is no universal truth and that the relationship of language (communication) and reality is imperfect at best.

3578. Henne, Helmut. "Sprüchekultur." In H. Henne. *Jugend und ihre Sprache. Darstellung, Materialien, Kritik.* Berlin: Walter de Gruyter, 1986. 115–129.

Based on actual demoscopic research with questionnaires, the author collected 784 German phraseological units from teenagers. They include modern proverbial expressions, graffiti, clichés, idioms, slogans, etc. It is clear that some of them are based on proverbial structures, and such texts might be considered as "Antisprichwörter" (anti-proverbs). The young people also provided explanatory notes concerning the meaning of most of the expressions of which Henne includes a selected alphabetically arranged list. The author also discusses the use and function of such phrases in the youth culture. They certainly represent the language and worldview of a relatively free but frustrated group of people. The last page (p. 129) presents similar expressions from the German Democratic Republic. Altogether this is an important linguistic and cultural study of innovative phraseological units that are entering the modern German language.

3579. Henry-Rebours, Jacqueline. "Proverbes de Haute-Bretagne, Région de Jugon et Lamballe." *Cahiers de littérature orale*, no. 13 (1983), 163–169.

The author conducted field research in the Bretagne (Brittany) in France, and she presents a small collection of French dialect proverbs which she collected from elderly informants. Many of her texts deal with meteorology, agriculture, and nature, but there are also some texts that express basic popular wisdom of the region. The proverbs are cited in their dialect form with modern French versions of some of the archaic or incomprehensible words. It is pointed out that these traditional proverbs seem to disappear as the older rural population ceases to exist. But it is also noted that proverbs are surviving the modern forces of civilization better than some of the other oral folklore genres.

3580. Henschel, Helgunde. "Die morphologischen Formen phraseologischer Wendungen (am Material des Tschechischen)."

Linguistische Studien, series A, Arbeitsberichte, no. 95 (1982), 99–120.

Henschel presents a detailed analysis of morphological forms of phraseological units, stressing that morphological variants and grammatical changes of phrases in general have not been stressed enough in linguistic studies of fixed phrases. She discusses morphological categories of verbal and nominal phrases, mentioning in particular number (singular of plural), gender, and case restrictions. Numerous Czech examples are cited, but it is regrettable that the author does not provide German translations of them. A short bibliography (pp. 119–120) is attached.

3581.   Henschel, Helgunde. "Die Minimalphraseme in konfrontativer Sicht (am Material des Tschechischen, Slowakischen, Russischen und Deutschen)." *Linguistische Studien,* series A, Arbeitsberichte, no. 120 (1984), 67–95.

A linguistic and comparative investigation of so-called "minimal" phraseological units from the Czech, Slovakian, Russian, and German languages. Such fixed phrases usually contain a minimum of two words, and Henschel presents analyses of their meaning, metaphor, syntax, homonymy, structure, and grammatical function. Numerous examples from the four languages are cited, and it becomes clear that there are definite differences and similarities between the Slavic languages on the one hand and the Germanic language on the other. A bibliography (pp. 93–95) is included.

3582.   Heringer, Hans Jürgen. *Über die Mannigfaltigkeit der Lügenbeine.* Mannheim: Dudenverlag, 1990. 23 pp.

The author presents a general essay on the problem of lies in politics, and he uses the German proverb "Lügen haben kurze Beine" (Lies have short legs) as a leitmotif. He begins with some comments on the satirical use of this proverb by the German poet Joachim Ringelnatz (1883–1934), and he then comments on German political life and its many "lies." Heringer cites examples from political speeches and newspaper reports, arguing that politicians should pay much more attention to this traditional proverb. If they are not honest with people, they will eventually be caught in their many lies, or to state it proverbially, they will not get very far with their lies since they have, metaphorically speaking, only short legs. A small bibliography (p. 21) and 14 notes (pp. 22–23) are attached.

3583. Hernandez, José Luis Alonso. "Interprétation psychoanalytique de l'utilisation des parémies dans la littérature espagnole." *Richesse du proverbe.* Eds. François Suard and Claude Buridant. Lille: Université de Lille, 1984. II, 213–225.

Starting with a reference to Sigmund Freud's (1856–1939) assertion that folklore and thus also proverbs are of considerable importance for the interpretation of dreams, the author attempts to give a literary and above all psychological interpretation of some Spanish proverbs in Arcipreste de Hita's (c. 1283–c. 1350) *El Libro de Buen Amor* (1330), *La Celestina* (c. 1499), and Miguel de Cervantes Saavedra's (1547–1616) novel *Don Quijote* (1605/1615). Hernandez includes a detailed discussion of the polysemanticity of proverbs and shows how they express not necessarily the independent view of a character but rather the collective and subconscious worldview of an entire culture. He also argues that proverbs like dreams help to bring order to a perceived chaos, and he makes a good case for a psychoanalytical interpretation of literature on the basis of the contextualized proverbs.

3584. Hess, Peter. *Epigramm.* Stuttgart: Metzler, 1989. 178 pp. (proverbs esp. on pp. 20–21, 42–43, 79–82, and 162–163).

This is a compact yet major monograph on the epigram with rich bibliographical information at the end of various sections throughout the book. In chapter one (pp. 1–26) Hess deals with definition problems and includes a couple of pages (pp. 20–21) on the relationship of this genre with that of the proverb. Chapter two (pp. 27–70) presents a detailed history of the epigram and its form, structure, and meaning from classical times to the modern age. The major third chapter (pp. 71–164) is a comprehensive historical and critical analysis of the German epigram throughout the centuries. Hess cites many examples, of which texts by Friedrich Logau (1604–1655), Johann Wolfgang von Goethe (1749–1832), Ludwig Feuerbach (1804–1872), Karl Kraus (1874–1936), Bertolt Brecht (1898–1956), Erich Kästner (1899–1974), Arnfrid Astel (1933–), etc. contain proverbs and proverbial expressions. A valuable bibliography (pp. 165–170) of collections and studies on the epigram as well as a name index conclude this important book.

3585. Hessky, Regina. "Gleichartige idiomatische Wendungen im Ungarischen und Deutschen." *Sprache und Literatur in Wissenschaft und Unterricht*, 16, no. 56 (1985), 81–87.

In this article Hessky compares equivalent idiomatic expressions for the Hungarian and German languages. She argues that if equivalency is indeed present, then there might still be differences as far as literal meaning, structure, syntactical function, and connotation are concerned. For all these points she presents Hungarian examples with German translations, contrasting them with their German equivalents. It is pointed out that classical and Biblical phraseological units reach the highest level of equivalency between the two languages. These internationally disseminated texts are at times absolutely identical. But Hessky also cites several parallel texts where there are striking dissimilarities due to the difference in culture, history, language, and worldview. A small bibliography (p. 87) is provided.

3586. Hessky, Regina. "Ein kontrastives Arbeitsmodell—dargestellt an deutsch-ungarischem Material." *Aktuelle Probleme der Phraseologie.* Eds. Harald Burger and Robert Zett. Bern: Peter Lang, 1987. 97–108.

Somewhat similar paper as the previous one (see no. 3585) but with a definite emphasis on foreign language instruction of phraseological units. Hessky comments on the lexical, structural, and syntactical differences and similarities of Hungarian and German fixed phrases. She emphasizes the total equivalencies of internationally disseminated classical and Biblical phrases and then goes on to show that many proverbial expressions have only partial or apparent equivalencies in the two languages. Many German examples are cited with comparative statements concerning the parallel texts in Hungarian as the target language.

3587. Hessky, Regina. *Phraseologie. Linguistische Grundfragen und kontrastives Modell deutsch-ungarisch.* Tübingen: Max Niemeyer, 1987. 138 pp.

An important book on comparative phraseology between the German and Hungarian languages. In the first part of her study (pp. 13–40) the author deals with definition problems, reproducibility, idiomaticity, and synchronic and diachronic research aspects of phraseological units. The second part (pp. 43–126) investigates the various levels of equivalency between German and Hungarian fixed phrases: identity, meaning, structure, syntactical function, connotation, etc. In each case the author provides numerous contrastive examples, and many of them are cited in their literary or journalistic context. Hessky draws her texts in particular from such authors as Hermann Kant (1926–) and Christa Wolf (1929–) from the German Democratic Republic. The newspaper references come primarily out of the weekly newspaper *Die Zeit* from the Federal Republic of Germany. A large and useful bibliography (pp. 131–138) leads to further studies on bilingual problems of phraseology, including references to the importance of comparative phraseology for foreign language instruction.

3588. Hessky, Regina (ed.). *Beiträge zur Phraseologie des Ungarischen und des Deutschen.* Budapest: Loránd-Eötvös-Universität, 1988. 184 pp.

This is an essay volume on various aspects of Hungarian and German phraseology, including the origin and history of fixed phrases, innovative variants and wordplays with traditional proverbs, personal names in proverbial expressions, meaning, function and context of phraseological units, the subgenre of twin formulas, etc. The nine authors and their respective articles are: Regina Hessky, "Phraseologieforschung in Ungarn— Bibliographie der Veröffentlichungen zum Thema Phraseologie in Ungarn nach 1945" (pp. 6–25); Vilmos Agel, "Abgrenzung von Phraseologismen in einem historischen Text. Einige Indizien als Ergebnis einer historischen Valenzuntersuchung" (pp. 26–38);

Csilla Bernáth, "Phraseologische Neubildungen" (pp. 39–49); Mária Borbély, "Phraseologische Spiele mit Sprichwörtern" (pp. 50–68); Harald Burger, "Die Semantik des Phraseologismus: ihre Darstellung im Wörterbuch" (pp. 69–97); Karlheinz Daniels, "Aktuelles Verstehen und historisches Verständnis von Redensarten. Ergebnisse einer Befragung" (pp. 98–212); Csaba Földes, "Phraseologismen mit Anthroponymen in der deutschen und ungarischen Gegenwartssprache" (pp. 122–154); Peter Kühn, "Routine-Joker in politischen Fernsehdiskussionen. Plädoyer für eine textsortenabhängige Beschreibung von Phraseologismen" (pp. 155–176); and Csilla Majoros, "Zum Terminus 'Wortpaar' in der deutschen und in der ungarischen Fachliteratur" (pp. 177–184). For annotations of these significant papers see nos. 3589, 3037, 3134, 3151, 3187, 3286, 3423, 3742, 3805.

3589. Hessky, Regina. "Phraseologieforschung in Ungarn— Bibliographie der Veröffentlichungen zum Thema Phraseologie in Ungarn nach 1945." *Beiträge zur Phraseologie des Ungarischen und des Deutschen.* Ed. Regina Hessky. Budapest: Loránd-Eötvös-Universität, 1988. 6–25.

In the first part (pp. 6–13) of this survey article on the history of phraseological scholarship in Hungary Hessky reviews three major phases of interest in fixed phrases. There is the older research on proverbs and proverbial expressions dating back to the very beginning of philological studies, then there is the important work of the 19th and early 20th centuries, and now there is the linguistically oriented modern work on phraseological units of all types. Hessky stresses the importance of Gábor O. Nagy's (1915–1973) paremiological and phraseological research, and she also makes a special point regarding the importance of phraseology for the instruction of foreign languages. The second part (pp. 14–25) is a chronologically arranged bibliography of Hungarian phraseological scholarship from 1950 to 1986 without annotations.

3590. Hessky, Regina. "Sprach- und kulturspezifische Züge phraseologischer Vergleiche." *Europhras 88. Phraséologie*

Contrastive. Actes du Colloque International Klingenthal-Strasbourg, 12–16 mai 1988. Ed. Gertrud Gréciano. Strasbourg: Université des Sciences Humaines, 1989. 195–204.

The author starts with a definition of proverbial or phraseological comparisons, and she then analyzes their particular structures. She explains that some comparisons refer to objective experiences, while others are based on rather subjective judgments. She also states that the major function of metaphorical comparative phrases is to add expressiveness to an oral or written statement. In the final section of the paper Hessky attempts a differentiation between German and Hungarian comparisons, showing especially how they use unique adjectives, nouns, and symbols. Many examples are cited, and the Hungarian texts are quoted with German translations.

3591. Hess-Lüttich, Ernest W.B. "Kontrastive Phraseologie im DaF-Unterricht—anhand arabischer und niederländischer Brecht-Übersetzungen." *Textproduktion und Textrezeption.* Ed. Ernest Hess-Lüttich. Tübingen: Gunter Narr, 1983. 25–39; rpt. in *Sprichwörter und Redensarten im interkulturellen Vergleich.* Eds. Annette Sabban and Jan Wirrer. Opladen: Westdeutscher Verlag, 1991. 109–127.

This is a very intriguing article on contrastive phraseology based on contextual examples of Arabic and Dutch translations of Bertolt Brecht's (1898–1956) play *Mutter Courage und ihre Kinder* (1941). Hess-Lüttich starts by pointing out that cultural differences make the translation of proverbs particularly difficult. He also states that when Brecht integrated Arabic proverbs in his play *Der kaukasische Kreidekreis* (1949), he was able to make use of a proverb collection that included German translations whose texts he as a creative writer could change as he saw fit. A translator of literature on the other hand must try to translate proverbial passages as exactly as possible. In the case of Brecht this task is even more vexing since he so often alienates, manipulates, and perverts standard expressions. Hess-Lüttich also explains that the novels by Günter Grass (1927–) present similar problems for the translator. A number of examples are cited in their dramatic context to illustrate the problems of finding the best equivalent in the target language. A helpful bibliography (pp. 37–39 or pp. 125–127) dealing with the translatability of proverbial texts is provided. See also Eva-Maria Goy (no. 3496) and Aladin Hilmi (no. 3600).

3592. Hess-Lüttich, Ernest W.B. "Sprichwörter und Redensarten als Übersetzungsproblem. Am Beispiel deutscher Übersetzungen spanischer und türkischer Literatur." *Mehrsprachigkeit und Gesellschaft. Akten des 17. Linguistischen Kolloquiums Brüssel 1982.* Eds. René Jongen, Sabine De Knop, Peter H. Nelde, and Marie-Paule Quix. Tübingen: Max Niemeyer, 1983. II, 222–236.

A significant study on the difficulty of translating proverbs and proverbial expressions from Spanish and Turkish literature into German. Hess-Lüttich chose five translations of Miguel de Cervantes Saavedra's (1547–1616) novel *Don Quijote* (1605/15) and compares how the translators have dealt with a number of proverbial passages. In the second part he discusses how a German translator confronted the proverbial language of the Turkish novel *Ince Memed* (1955) by Yasar Kemal (1922–). Examples are cited in their literary context, and the author comments on aspects of textual equivalency in proverb translations. While there exist identical equivalents, more often than not the translator has to search for proverbs or proverbial expressions that contain different metaphors in the target language but which have at least the same basic meaning. A useful bibliography (pp. 234–236) is attached. For a longer study on translating proverbs from *Don Quijote* into German see Margarete Axnick (no. 3081).

3593. Heurck, Emile H. van, and G.J. Boekenoogen. *Histoire de l'imagerie populaire flamande et de ses rapports avec les imageries étrangères.* Burxelles: G. van Oest, 1910 (on proverbs esp. pp. 114–116, 153–155, 165–167, 178–180, 222–225, 383–385, and 399–400).

This is a major study with many illustrations and valuable explanations of popular Dutch and Flemish art in the form of broadsheets from the 16th to the 19th century. The authors also refer to many examples from other European countries containing folkloric materials, notably English, French, and German sources. The book includes 3 broadsheets on the proverbial theme of "De verkeerde wereld" (World-upside-down, monde renversé, de blauwe huyck, die verkehrte Welt), a fascinating illustration of the proverb "Crédit est mort, les mauvais payeurs l'ont tué" (Giving is dead), again 3 broadsheets of the famous proverbial motif of the "Grand combat à qui portera la culotte" (To wear the breeches), a picture of the German proverbial expression "Der blaue Montag" (Blue Monday), and many others. References to less important proverb pictures abound in this invaluable book on the relationship of art and proverbial language. With 10 illustrations of those expressions mentioned in this annotation.

3594. Hicks, Eric. "Proverbe et polémique dans le *Roman de la Rose* de Jean de Meun." *Richesse du proverbe.* Eds. François Suard and Claude Buridant. Lille: Université de Lille, 1984. I, 113–120.

This is a short literary investigation of the use and function of a few proverbs in Jean de Meun(g)'s (13th century) second part of the French medieval epic *Roman de la Rose* (1275/80). Hicks shows the effective rhetorical and polemical employment of proverbs by the narrator, who wishes to express traditional authority through this proverbial wisdom. This is also true for the various characters who state their arguments, convictions, and feelings through the help of metaphorical proverbs. A few examples out of context are cited. For a more detailed study see Judith Clark Larsen (no. 1003).

3595. Hidiroglu, Pavlos. *Ethnologikoi problematismoi apo ten tourkike kai ten Hellenike paroimiologia.* Athenai: Laographia, 1987. 164 pp.

The author presents an interesting study of 601 Turkish proverbs with Greek translations (pp. 45–110) for the purpose of understanding the worldview of the Turkish people. The proverbs deal with political and social attitudes, war, peace, friendship, law, etc. By explaining the value system and stereotypes expressed in them (pp. 15–43) Hidiroglu hopes to bring about a more objective understanding between the Greeks and Turks. The author also includes a list of 180 Greek proverbs about the Turks (pp. 111–132) of which many are proverbial slurs and invectives. A valuable bibliography (pp. 11–14), a large index

(pp. 145–162) and detailed English (pp. 133–137) and German
(pp. 138–145) summaries help to make this a significant
contribution to comparative paremiography.

3596. Higbee, Kenneth L., and Richard J. Millard. "Visual Imagery and
Familiarity Ratings for 203 Sayings." *American Journal of Psychology*,
96 (1983), 211–222.

The authors lament the fact that so much psychological
memory research has concentrated on single words rather than
on more complex verbal material. The purpose of their study is,
therefore, to provide a list of proverbs (sayings) that have been
scaled on visual imagery and familiarity to facilitate the extension
of memory research to longer sentences. In this study, 203
proverbs were rated on 7–point scales for visual imagery by 51
students and for familiarity by 50 students. The proverbs are
listed with their individual means and standard deviations for
imagery and familiarity. Also reported are the overall mean and
standard deviation, other ratings, and reliability data. These
ratings should help researchers to extend verbal-learning and
memory research beyond single words. The published lists of
ratings is of great importance to the paremiologist for an
understanding of the familiarity of students with traditional
proverbs. A small bibliography (p. 222) and an English abstract
(p. 211) are included.

3597. Higi-Wydler, Melanie. *Zur Übersetzung von Idiomen. Eine
Beschreibung und Klassifizierung deutscher Idiome und ihrer
französischen Übersetzungen.* Bern: Peter Lang, 1989. 335 pp.

This significant book on the problems of translating German
idioms into French is divided into three major parts. The first
part (pp. 3–134) presents a review of Soviet, American, German,
and French research on phraseology, it offers definitions for
various types of phraseological units (proverbs, proverbial
expressions and comparisons, twin formulas, etc.), it analyzes the
syntactical structures of fixed phrases, and it considers semantic
questions (metaphor, literal and figurative meaning,
expressiveness, etc.). In the second part (pp. 135–160) the author
deals with translation theories and explains different levels of

equivalencies in the translation of idioms, i.e. total, partial, and no equivalency at all. The third part (pp. 161–318) is a fascinating and detailed analysis of the translation of over 3000 German proverbial texts found in 20th century novels by such German authors as Alfred Andersch (1914–1980), Heinrich Böll (1917–1985), Elias Canetti (1905–), Max Frisch (1911–1991), Peter Handke (1942–), Peter Härtling (1933–), Ulrich Plenzdorf (1934–), and Luise Rinser (1911–). Many contextualized literary examples are cited in German with their French translations, and Higi-Wydler adds important stylistic, morphological, and syntactical explanations. She also discusses aspects of variability, wordplay, and various types of equivalencies. Four statistical tables and a superb bibliography (pp. 325–335) are included.

3598. Hill, Robert R., Jane E. Budnek, and Linda K. Wise. "An Empirical Validation of an English Proverb." *The Journal of Irreproducible Results*, 29, no. 4 (1984), 2–4.

An entertaining article on the English proverb "An apple a day keeps the doctor away." The authors start with a short historical survey of this common medical proverb and then try to prove by statistical calculations that a daily apple will in fact guarantee good health. They go on, tongue-in-cheek, to investigate the economic, medical, and nutritional implications of their empirical validation of this "medical" proverb of very high frequency in the Anglo-American language. With 1 illustration.

3599. Hills, Julian. "Proverbs as Sayings of Jesus in the *Epistula Apostolorum*." *Semeia*, 49 (1990), 7–34.

In this valuable article on Jesus' use of proverbs in the *Epistula Apostolorum* (2nd century A.D.), Hills starts with a review of various manuscripts of these apocryphal letters by the apostles. The major body of the paper presents four detailed analyses of the following proverbs, citing them in context, quoting them in their original Coptic and Ethiopian versions with English translations, discussing their origin in Biblical or non-Biblical sources, and analyzing their function within the individual contexts and the letters as a whole: "The foot of a ghost or a demon does not join to the ground," "What has fallen will [arise], and what is lost will be found and what is [weak] will recover," "Are the fingers of the hand alike or the ears of corn in the field?," and "A blind man who leads a blind man, [both] fall into [a] ditch." It is concluded that these sayings are inherently suited to the authoritative and didactic intent of the letters. A useful bibliography (pp. 30–34) is attached. With an English abstract (p. 7).

3600. Hilmi, Aladin. "Zum Problem der Übersetzung von Sprichwörtern und Redensarten." *Sprache im technischen Zeitalter*, no. 96 (1985), 283–285.

This is a very short article discussing the difficulty of translating German proverbs and proverbial expressions into Arabic and vice versa. Hilmi argues that the metaphors of equivalent expressions between these two languages are often very different due to the distinct cultures involved. A few examples are cited with special emphasis on Friedrich Rückert's (1788–1866) attempts to translate some Arabic proverbs. There is also a short section on Arabic translation difficulties of the proverbs in Bertolt Brecht's (1898–1956) play *Mutter Courage und ihre Kinder* (1941). For this latter point see Ernest Hess-Lüttich (no. 3591).

3601. Hockings, Paul. *Counsel from the Ancients. A Study of Badaga Proverbs, Prayers, Omens and Curses*. With an Outline of the Badaga Language by Christiane Pilot-Raichoor. Amsterdam: Mouton de Gruyter, 1988. 796 pp.

This is a superb linguistic and anthropological study of 1167 Badaga proverbs, prayers, omens, and curses from the indigenous community in the Nilgiri Hills of Tamilnadu State (formerly Madras) in Southern India. The author starts with a major section (pp. 1–50) discussing the Badaga people, their oral literature, their social values, and the importance of proverbial speech in their culture. This is followed by Christiane Pilot-Raichoor's outline of the phonology, morphology, grammar, and syntax of the Badaga language (pp. 51–84). The actual corpus of texts makes up the major part of the book (pp. 85–601), presenting each text in its original language with literal and figurative English translations. Hockings also provides invaluable historical and cultural annotations. This is followed by the publication of J.M. Bühler's earlier manuscript (c. 1850) of 540 Badaga proverbs (pp. 603–633). An informative bibliography (pp. 635–646), a comprehensive glossary and concordance (pp. 647–771), an index (pp. 773–796), 33 figures (diagrams) and 5 tables all help to make this one of the most significant proverb studies of a certain linguistic and ethnic group in recent years.

3602. Hoffman. Robert R. "Recent Psycholinguistic Research on Figurative Language." *Discourses in Reading and Linguistics.* Eds. Sheila J. White and Virginia Teller. New York: New York Academy of Sciences, 1984. 137–166.

The author begins by stating that psycholinguistic metaphor studies have become quite prevalent since about 1970. Relating his comments primarily to proverbs, proverbial expressions, and idioms, Hoffman surveys recent scholarship on the following topics: Persuasiveness of nonliteral communication, metaphor and inference-making, research methods and materials, anomaly and metaphor, imagery, memory for metaphors, metaphor and reaction time, metaphor in scientific problem-solving, and metaphor and meaning. He also includes a short section (pp. 139–140) dealing with a small proverb recognition test, showing that most people can come up with 20–30 proverbs in a period of 30 minutes, even though they most likely know (actively or passively) some 300 or more proverbs. An invaluable bibliography (pp. 161–166) of 119 references concludes this review article. With 2 diagrams and 4 tables illustrating psycholinguuistic research approaches.

3603. Hofmeister, Wernfried. *Sprichwortartige Mikrotexte. Analysen am Beispiel Oswalds von Wolkenstein.* Göppingen: Kümmerle, 1990. 307 pp.

This is the first complete study of the proverbial language in the entire lyric poetry of a medieval German poet. Hofmeister starts his valuable book on the proverbs in Oswald von Wolkenstein (1377?–1445?) with a theoretical introduction (pp.

3–54) in which he sets forth a careful model for an objective identification of the proverbiality of texts in medieval literature (see esp. pp. 46–47). He argues that any sentence must have at least some of the following characteristics in order to be labelled as a proverb: fixed form, anthropocentricity, based on experience, generalization, currency, structure of a complete sentence, brevity, metaphor, and several linguistic and poetic devices (rhyme, alliteration, indicative, imperative, present tense, etc.). He then presents 104 "micro-text" analyses (pp. 55–258), showing in great detail how he decided that these particular short sentences are in fact proverbs of the Middle Ages. These findings are summarized in an impressive table with generalizing comments (pp. 263–279). A carefully annotated proverb index (pp. 287–301) and a useful bibliography (pp. 303–307) help to make this exemplary study a model to follow for scholars interested in locating "new" proverbs in medieval literature.

3604. Hogan, Rebecca S.H. *The Wisdom of Many, the Wit of One: The Narrative Function of the Proverb in Tolstoy's "Anna Karenina" and Trollope's "Orley Farm."* Diss. University of Colorado, 1984. 275 pp.

This intriguing dissertation begins with an informative chapter (pp. 1–68) on the use of proverbs by the narrators and characters in the novels of such 19th century English and Russian authors as Charles Dickens (1811–1870), Anthony Trollope (1815–1882), Elizabeth Cleghorn Gaskell (1810–1865), George Eliot (1819–1880), Nikolai Vasil'evich Gogol' (1809–1852), and Lev Nikolaevich Tolstoy (1828–1910). In the second chapter (pp. 69–153) Hogan presents a detailed literary analysis of the narrative function of the Biblical proverb "Judge not that you may not be judged" (Matth. 7,1) in Trollope's *Orley Farm* (1862). The third chapter (pp. 154–235) treats the function of the same proverb in Tolstoy's *Anna Karenina* (1873/76). It is argued that the moralistic proverb operates as a stable reflecting device around which patterns of association about judgment are linked and from which the various points of view and judgments radiate out with varying degrees of refraction created by each individual angle of vision with its personal, emotional, psychological, and ideological colorations. The dialectical play of points of view and judgments centered around this proverb is intended to test, undercut, and question the reader's own judgments. A useful bibliography (pp. 268–275) is attached to this comparative and interpretative study.

3605. Holden, Marjorie H., and Mimi Warshaw. "A Bird in the Hand and a Bird in the Bush: Using Proverbs to Teach Skills and Comprehension." *English Journal,* 74, no. 2 (1985), 63–67.

The authors argue that English instructors might choose to incorporate proverbs into their lessons in order to teach such skills as (1) the use of specific grammatical forms in creative writing; (2) the grammatical analysis of unusual constructions; (3) the identification of themes in essays or other forms of expository writing; (4) recognizing main ideas through matching proverbs and the morals implied by fables or fictional works; (5) learning and practicing the techniques of ethnographic field research as related to language; (6) the creation of original proverbs according to specifications such as ellipsis, personification, etc.; (7) the expansion of vocabulary; (8) the recognition of rhetorical devices as preparation for understanding poetry; and (9) reading comprehension, writing ability, and cross-cultural sensitivity. Examples and suggestions for lesson plans are included in this pedagogical article.

3606. Holm-Hadulla, R.-M., and F. Haug. "Die Interpretation von Sprichwörtern als klinische Methode zur Erfassung schizophrener Denk-, Sprach- und Symbolisationsstörungen." *Nervenarzt,* 55, no. 9 (1984), 496–503.

Using a German psychological proverbs test, the authors asked schizophrenic patients for an interpretation of proverbs as a clinical method to exploring schizophrenic thought and speech disorders. Six proverbs are listed with a normal interpretation and one by a schizophrenic person. It becomes clear that schizophrenic patients lack the ability to abstract the meaning of the metaphor that is part of most proverbs. A bibliography with references to other proverbs tests for mental testing is attached, and a German abstract (p. 496) is included as well.

3607. Holtappels, Peter. *Die Entwicklungsgeschichte des Grundsatzes "in dubio pro reo."* Diss. University Hamburg, 1963. Hamburg: Cram, de Gruyter & Co., 1965. 104 pp.

The author traces the origin and history of the Latin legal maxim "In dubio pro reo" (In doubt for the accused) from Roman legal philosophy to its application in modern German law. In various small chapters he shows that the proverb became particularly accepted in medieval Italy. Its basic idea was picked up in German legal thought during the late Middle Ages and through the 17th century. The concept gained popularity during the Enlightenment of the 18th century, and the proverb was well established in German legal circles by the 19th century. Many Latin and German references are cited throughout this monograph, and a summary (pp. 96–97) as well as a bibliography (pp. 98–104) referring to legal proverb studies are provided. See also H. Holzhauer (no. 3609) and Konrad Moser (no. 3984).

3608. Holzapfel, Otto. "Stereotype Redensarten über 'den Deutschen' in der neueren dänischen Literatur." *Proverbium,* 4 (1987), 87–110.

An important study of proverbial stereotypes about Germans in modern Danish literature. Holzapfel discusses the nature of stereotypes and comments on the historical, social, cultural, and political aspects which led to these anti-German expressions. He quotes national characteristics of the Germans from such Danish authors as Klaus Rifbjerg (1931–), Jens Christian Hostrup (1818–1892), Leif Panduro (1923–), and others. Several sterotypes are cited in their literary context, and it is argued that they are used primarily for the purpose of differentiating the Danes from the Germans (especially due to the Nazi occupation of Denmark) even though both are Germanic people. The Germans are stereotyped as being too orderly and above all foreign (i.e. strange, a different nationality and worldview, etc.). The 45 notes include useful bibliographical references to the study of national stereotypes.

3609. Holzhauer, H. "'In dubio pro reo'." *Handwörterbuch zur deutschen Rechtsgeschichte.* Eds. Adalbert Erler and Ekkehard Kaufmann. Berlin: Erich Schmidt, 1978. II, cols. 349–358.

In many ways this is a summary of two previous monographs on the Latin legal maxim "In dubio pro reo" (In doubt for the accused) by Peter Holtappels (see no. 3607) and Konrad Moser (no. 3984). In his encyclopedia article Holzhauer again stresses the fact that the philosophical idea of this legal proverb goes back to Roman law. He then traces it to canonical law in medieval Italy, stating that it was also gaining recognition in legal circles in Germany. However, it took until the 18th and 19th centuries for it to become established as a principle of German law. Today it is considered to be one of the very basic legal proverbs of civilized societies.

3610. Honeck, Richard P., and Clare T. Kibler. "The Role of Imagery, Analogy, and Instantiation in Proverb Comprehension." *Journal of Psycholinguistic Research,* 13, no. 6 (1984), 393–414.

An important psychological study based on a proverbs test to establish the role that imagery, analogy, and instantiation play in proverb and metaphor comprehension. During acquisition, the subjects were presented proverbs and given rating tasks concerning these three aspects. During transfer, it was found that subjects who based their understanding of the proverbs on imagery performed less convincingly than those who attempted comprehension by means of analogy. Those subjects who based their comprehension on a combination of analogy and instantiation performed the best. A useful bibliography (pp. 413–414) and an English abstract (p. 393) are included.

3611. Honeck, Richard P., Judith Sugar, and Clare T. Kibler. "Stories, Categories and Figurative Meaning." *Poetics: International Review for the Theory of Literature,* 11, no. 2 (1982), 127–144.

Using a psychological proverbs test that was based on individual proverbs for which the authors had invented very short illustrative stories (5–6 lines), it was attempted to reach conclusions as to the understanding of figurative language and metaphorical proverbs in particular. In order to make a connection between the story and the proverb title, it is necessary to deal with an abstract, imagery-free, nonverbal, figurative level of meaning which is constructed in the reader's mind using complex reasoning and problem-solving processes. A valuable bibliography (pp. 143–144) and an English abstract (p. 127) are provided.

3612. Honeck, Richard P., Katherine Voegtle, Mark A. Dorfmueller, and Robert R. Hoffman. "Proverbs, Meaning, and Group Structure." *Cognition and Figurative Language.* Eds. Richard Honeck and Robert Hoffman. Hillsdale/New Jersey: Lawrence Erlbaum Associates, 1980. 127–161.

Excellent review article on the psychological study of proverbs with special emphasis on the light that proverbs shed on two interrelated problems—the nature of abstract mental entities and the generativity of behavioral acts. The authors present a summary of earlier psychological studies on proverbs and then discuss in particular the psycholinguistic properties of proverbs. The article contains detailed comments on the literal and figurative levels of proverbs, their use in intelligence testing, the way adults process the meaning of proverbs, and how and when children understand, remember and use proverbs. Sections on imagery, memory, synonymy, and the difference between metaphors and proverbs are also included. The authors conclude their valuable review by presenting their own conceptual theory for proverb understanding which they argue takes place in four phases: a preparatory or problem recognition phase, a literal transformation phase, a figurative or theory formation phase, and an instantiation phase. By this theory, complete understanding requires that a literal statement be recognized as incongruent in some context, that the statement and the context be transformed, such that a miniature theory arises that resolves the incongruity, and which can be used for recognizing and producing novel instances. A large bibliography (pp. 158–161) is attached.

3613. Höpel, Ingrid. "Sprichwort und 'Sinnbild' als moralisch verbindliche Zeichen bei Justus Georg Schottelius." In I. Höpel. *Emblem und Sinnbild. Vom Kunstbuch zum Erbauungsbuch.* Frankfurt am Main: Athenäum, 1987. 165–190.

Höpel begins her chapter on the relationship of proverbs and emblems in the 17th century with a general discussion of these two forms of expression as signs for moral values. She then points out that the German Baroque scholar Justus Georg Schottelius (1612–1676) dealt with both genres in his voluminous study of the German language entitled *Ausführliche Arbeit von der Teutschen Haubt-Sprache* (1663). In fact, he included a collection of 1230 proverbs and 560 proverbial expressions (pp. 1099–1146) with some important introductory remarks concerning the ethical, moral, and didactic value of proverbs. It is argued that emblems and proverbs are both significant means to educate people through imagery and language to a socially responsible life style. See also Ella Schafferus (no. 1639) and Wolfgang Mieder (no. 3853).

3614. Horn, Katalin. "Grimmsche Märchen als Quellen für Metaphern und Vergleiche in der Sprache der Werbung, des Journalismus und der Literatur." *Muttersprache*, 91 (1981), 106–115.

This article deals with the interesting reduction of fairy tales to metaphors and proverbial comparisons, usually containing the name of one of the heroes as Sleeping Beauty, Snow White, Cinderella, etc. Horn cites numerous German examples from the language of advertising and journalism. The last part of the essay deals with the use of numerous proverbial motifs based on Grimm fairy tales in modern German literature, citing prose and lyric examples from such well-known authors as Wilhelm Lehmann (1882–1968), Marie Luise Kaschnitz (1901–1974), Günter Grass (1927–), Hans Magnus Enzensberger (1929–), Rolf Hochhuth (1931–), Peter Handke (1942–), and a few others.

3615. Horodecka, Ewa, and Waclaw M. Osadnik. "Remarks on the Translation of Proverbs from English into Polish." *New Zealand Slavonic Journal*, no volume given (1991), 123–130.

The authors study various aspects of how to translate English proverbs into Polish. They point out that for classical and Biblical proverbs both the English and Polish languages have identical equivalents due to the fact that they have loan translated them from the same sources. Horodecka and Osadnik include several examples in which they cite the Latin original followed by English and Polish texts. However, for indigenous English proverbs there are often no exact equivalents in Polish. In that case a translator must try to find partial equivalents that have basically the same meaning but use a different metaphor. Again the authors cite a few examples, also showing that in some cases there are simply no equivalents in the target language. A few comments on recurrence, parallelism, and repetition in proverbs are included. Usually they are maintained in both the English and Polish translations from the Latin. A short bibliography (p. 130) is attached.

3616.   Horrall, Sarah M. "Latin and Middle English Proverbs in a Manuscript at St. George's Chapel, Windsor Castle." *Mediaeval Studies*, 45 (1983), 343–384.

A detailed historical and philological edition of an early 16th century English proverb collection of 136 texts from a manuscrupt that is kept at St. George's Chapel at Windsor Castle in Great Britain. It is a collection of miscellaneous Latin sayings, usually of two lines each, which are then translated into Middle English verse. As is the case with most early bilingual proverb collections, this one was most likely also intended for didactic and instructional purposes. Horrall includes comments on the history of the manuscript, the dialect of the proverbs, the nature of Middle English proverb collections, and an anlysis of the texts of this particular manuscript. The actual edition is annotated with references to standard historical proverb dictionaries.

3617.   Hose, Susanne. "Der Stand der Forschungen zum obersorbischen Sprichworterbe am Institut für sorbische Volksforschung Bautzen." *Wissenschaftliche Zeitschrift der Wilhelm-Pieck-Universität Rostock, Gesellschaftswissenschaftliche Reihe*, 36, no. 5 (1987), 105.

This is a short but informative state of research report on the proverb studies that have been in process for quite some time at the Institute of Sorbian Folklore in Bautzen, Germany. Hose refers to the work by Isolde Gardos (see nos. 507–510 and 2395) and reports on a Sorbian proverb archive of about 12,000 texts collected out of written sources from the 17th through 19th centuries. This material is being prepared for the publication of a Sorbian proverb dictionary that will list these important texts from this West Slavic language together with German translations. The author mentions classification problems and also states that most proverbs express social attitudes or moral and didactic values.

3618. Hose, Susanne. *Zur Überlieferung und Systematisierung der obersorbischen Sprichwörter.* Diss. Akademie der Wissenschaften der DDR, 1990. 167 pp.

This dissertation presents impressive results concerning the study of about 12,000 Sorbian proverbs which have been collected from literary sources from the 17th through 19th centuries and which will be edited as a Sorbian proverb collection by the Institute of Sorbian Folklore in Bautzen, Germany. In her introduction (pp. 5–12) Hose reviews previous research on the proverbs of this West Slavic language (see Isolde Gardos, nos. 507–510 and 2395). Chapter one (pp. 13–52) treats earlier collections of Sorbian proverbs and analyzes the problem of classifying proverbs, their variants, and subgenres. In chapter two (pp. 53–84) the author analyzes the international proverbs that have entered the Sorbian language through loan translations from classical sources and the Bible. The third chapter (pp. 85–100) is dedicated to such matters as content, values, worldview, and language. The next chapter (pp. 101–133) treats social aspects such as the family and folk life, and the final fifth chapter (pp. 134–147) discusses the classification problems that need to be overcome in order to publish a scholarly dictionary of these texts. Many examples are cited in their original language with German translations, and a very helpful bibliography (pp. 148–167) is provided as well. With 1 map.

3619. Howe, Lutz-Rainer. "Zur lexikalisch-quantitativen Varianz von Phrasemen am Beispiel des Slowakischen." *Linguistische Studien,* series A, Arbeitsberichte, no. 95 (1982), 77–98.

Howe starts with a review of a number of definition attempts of the term "phraseological unit." He then argues that these so-called "fixed phrases" have at best a relative stability since morphological, lexical, syntactical and semantic variations are quite possible. Such varied phrases might then become actual variants that take on a life of their own. Often phrases are simply shortened or lengthened, but there are also major lexical changes of nouns, adjectives, adverbs, etc. Howe includes many Slovakian examples and is able to present statistical calculations of these textual changes. A useful bibliography (pp. 97–98) is attached.

3620. Howe, Lutz-Rainer. "Zur lexikalisch-quantitativen Varianz von Phrasemen im Tschechischen und Slowakischen." *Linguistische Studien*, series A, Arbeitsberichte, no. 120 (1984), 96–120.

A similar paper to the previous one (no. 3619), but this time the author investigates the lexical variants of phraseological units of the Czech and Slovakian languages. This comparative study of two very closely related languages indicates once again that fixed phrases show less morphological, lexical, syntactical, and semantic stability than has usually been assumed. The variants in both languages are often identical or at least partially the same which is clearly due to their close cultural and linguistic ties. Many examples are cited in both languages with German translations. An informative bibliography (pp. 119–120) is included as well.

3621. Hu, Bingkun. *The Structure of Chinese Elliptical Proverbs.* M.A. Thesis University of California at Berkeley, 1985. 69 pp.

This is a structural analysis of Chinese elliptical proverbs, citing numerous Chinese examples together with transliterated texts and English translations. Hu reviews structural and linguistic proverb scholarship in the introduction (pp. 1–12), and in the first chapter (pp. 13–27) the author investigates the two-clause structure of elliptical proverbs. The second chapter (pp. 28–42) looks at the meaning of the metaphors in this type of proverb, and the third chapter (pp. 43–51) discusses the "bisociation" in elliptical proverbs. Chapter four (pp. 52–63) shows how these Chinese proverbs function in actual discourse, and chapter five (pp. 64–66) is a short summary of these findings. A useful bibliography (pp. 67–69) that refers to major Chinese paremiological research is attached.

3622. Huanyou, Huang. *The Proverb: Message, Image and Translation.* M.A. Thesis University of Sheffield, 1986. 185 pp.

This is a most welcome M.A. thesis that illustrates the difficulty of translating proverbs from such different cultures as those of the Chinese and English languages. Huanyou discusses some general questions of proverb equivalencies in his introductory chapter (pp. 1–9) and then deals with the question of defining proverbs, proverbial expressions and comparisons, wellerisms, etc. in the second chapter (pp. 10–27). The third chapter (pp. 28–46) deals with the message (advice, morality, didacticism) and certain national characteristics (worldview) expressed in proverbs, while the fourth chapter (pp. 47–61) treats the imagery and "cultural loading" of both Chinese and English proverbs. The fifth chapter (pp. 62–76) contains remarks on the translatability of proverbs in general, stressing such matters as literal and free translations, equivalents, etc. The largest sixth chapter (pp. 77–145) contains a detailed analysis of seven techniques of translating proverbs that range from identical eqivalents to the impossibility of finding a proverb in the target language. The author also includes a section (pp. 124–145) on the poetic style (structure, rhyme, alliteration, etc.) of proverbs and the difficulty it presents for the translator. Many examples are cited including the original Chinese characters and providing useful annotations for the translation attempts. A helpful bibliography (pp. 149–152) and a bilingual list of 350 proverbs (pp. 153–185) help make this a significant comparative study of Chinese and English proverbs.

3623. Huber, Herbert, and Armand Houillon. "Les pièges qui guettent le traducteur de citations." *Lebende Sprachen*, 33, no. 1 (1988), 26–29.

The authors start their short article with the observation that there are many traps for the translator of proverbs, maxims, literary quotations (geflügelte Worte), slogans, etc. Bilingual dictionaries often don't include these materials, except perhaps for some of the proverbial phrases. As far as quotations of various types are concerned, one can often translate them literally, but certain metaphors and structures do add considerable problems. The major part of this essay is a list of German literary or political quotations with attempted French translations. A list of book titles that have reached a certain "quotable" status is also included in this comparative analysis.

3624. Hudde, Hinrich. "'Conte à dormir debout': Eine Redensart als Bezeichnung für parodistische Märchen des 18. Jahrhunderts." *Romanische Forschungen*, 97, no. 1 (1985), 15–35.

Historical study of the French phrase "Conte à dormir debout" (A tale that bores one stiff, silly story) which was first recorded in 1611. Hudde traces its inclusion in French dictionaries and also cites references of it in the works of Jean Baptiste Molière (1622–1673), Charles Perrault (1628–1703), Jacques Cazotte (1719–1792), and others. The author is able to show that this formula was first primarily used in a positive sense to refer to bedtime stories such as fairy tales. Today the expression is also often cited to parody or satirize a boring situation. Many references in their literary context are included.

3625. Huisman, Claudia. "Dutch Proverbs: An Interdisciplinary Perspective." *Dutch Crossing: A Journal of Low Countries Studies*, 38 (1989), 110–121.

Taking her examples primarily from H.L. Cox's *Spreekwoordenboek in vier talen. Nederlands, Frans, Duits, Engels* (Utrecht: Van Dale Lexicografie, 1988), the author presents some general comparative remarks of the relationship of Dutch proverbs to those of the English, French, and German languages. She compares such aspects as structure, metaphor, style, and meaning, arguing that proverbs express structured moral codes. Many of the Dutch proverbs that have precise equivalents in other European languages clearly belong to the stock of internationally disseminated proverbs going back to classical times, the Bible or the Latin of the Middle Ages. But it is also emphasized that there are some indigenous Dutch proverbs that definitely reflect the Dutch national character and worldview.

Many examples are cited, and a useful bibliography (pp. 119–121) is included as well.

3626. Hülse, Horst. "Sprichwörter und Sinnsprüche im Werk Wilhelm Henzes." *Einbecker Jahrbuch*, 32 (1981), 27–34.

This is a short introduction to the use of proverbs, proverbial expressions, proverbial comparisons, and sententious remarks (geflügelte Worte) in the Low German works of Wilhelm Henze (1845–193?). The author starts with defining the various paremiological genres and then stresses the fact that Henze's literary works reflect the frequent use of proverbial language in the "Plattdeutsch" (Low German) of northern Germany. The major part of the article is a list of 144 texts (a selection of the 1500 that the author has found in Henze) arranged according to such subjects as farming, human behavior, social wisdom, education, wealth and poverty, fortune and misfortune, death, fatalism, speech (communication), etc.

3627. Hünert-Hofmann, Else. *Phraseologismen in Dialekt und Umgangssprache.* Marburg: N.G. Elwert, 1991. 302 pp. and 39 pp. (appendix).

Hünert-Hofmann presents a valuable and very detailed study of various types of phraseological units that she collected during field research in the small town of Allendorf in the state of Hesse in central Germany. Numerous examples in the Hessian dialect are cited throughout this book, and the author is able to quote them from her informants in actual speech acts. The first chapter (pp. 7–30) reviews previous research on idioms or fixed phrases, emphasizing such matters as dialect, lexicography, idiomaticity, etc. Chapter two (pp. 31–62) presents historical, cultural, social, and political aspects of Allendorf, chapter three (pp. 63–84) describes local informants and methods of interviewing them, and chapter four (pp. 85–107) discusses the dialect of that area. In the fifth chapter (pp. 108–169) the author looks at such genres as proverbial comparisons, twin formulas, proverbial expressions, proverbs, and routine formulas, analyzing their structure and function. Chapter six (pp. 170–255) investigates their use by various informants, and chapter seven (pp. 256–279) looks at their social differences (male and female, old and young, etc.) and how they influence the use of phraseological units. Following a short summary (pp. 280–286) is a useful bibliography (pp. 287–302), and the author has also included 9 diagrams and 2 statistical tables. A special appendix (39 pp.) includes the questionnaire used during field research, a list of the fixed phrases discussed, and sample interviews.

3628. Husar, Al. "[Ion] Creanga's Proverbs." *Cahiers roumains d'études littéraires,* 4 (1989), 82–91.

A literary investigation of the proverbs and proverbial expressions contained in the prose works of the 19th century Rumanian author Ion Creanga (1837–1889). It is pointed out that this regional writer with universal themes that gained him much recognition also outside of Rumania used a lot of traditional folk speech in his novels. Folklore and realism are combined with proverbial speech which adds humor and traditional wisdom to the literary message. Husar cites a number of lengthy passages in English translation that show the proverbs in context, explaining that they help to strengthen an argument, state a fact, explain a situation, etc. Creanga also often used introductory formulas to draw special attention to proverbial utterances by his characters.

3629. Hwang, Mei-shu. "Problems and Possibilities in Translating Proverbs and Allusions." *Tamkang Review: A Quarterly of Comparative Studies Between Chinese and Foreign Literatures,* 16, no. 2 (1985), 207–218.

The author starts with the observation that it is extremely difficult to translate proverbs and allusions between languages that have as different cultures as those of the Chinese and English people. The first task of any translator is always to look for equivalent texts. If none can be found, than the translator is forced to find expressions based on similar assumptions and implications. Hwang also comments on the literal vs. figurative translation attempts, always stressing the importance of maintaining the meaning and message of the original text in the target language. There will always be those texts that contain metaphors and images that simply don't exist in the other language. In that case translators must rely on their personal judgment and knowledge of the other culture to find suitable expressions. A number of Chinese texts and their English translations are presented and discussed.

I

3630. Ieraci-Bio, Anna Maria. "Le concept de 'paroimia': Proverbium dans la haute et la basse antiquité." *Richesse du proverbe*. Eds. François Suard and Claude Buridant. Lille: Université de Lille, 1984. II, 83–94.

An important survey of the concept of "paroimia" (proverbium) in Greek and Roman antiquity. The author traces definition attempts by Aristotle (384–322 B.C.), Diogenes (412?-323 B.C.), Theophrastus (372–287 B.C.), Marcus Tullius Cicero (106–43 B.C.), Marcus Quintilian (35?-96? A.D.), Saint Athanasius (293?-373? A.D.), Saint Cyril (315?-386 A.D.), Saint Basil (330?-379? A.D.), Synesios (370–412 A.D.), and others. It is shown that proverbs were considered as important rhetorical and metaphorical devices in oral and written communication. The definitions are cited in their Greek and Latin originals without French translations. The 67 notes include invaluable bibliographical information. For similar articles see Ludwig Bieler (no. 165), Jan Fredrik Kindstrand (no. 850), Bartlett Jere Whiting (no. 2060), and Joseph Russo (no. 4295).

3631. Iglesias Ovejero, Angel. "Figuración proverbial y nivelación en los nombres propios del refranero antiguo: Figuras vulgarizadas del registro culto." *Criticon*, 28 (1984), 5–95.

This is a significant study combining research interests of onomastics and paremiology. The author begins with general thoughts on the proverbialization and metaphorization of proper names in proverbs. This is followed by sections on Greek, Latin, and Biblical (Old and New Testament) names in Spanish proverbs. The largest part of the essay deals with names from literary and folkloric sources. Many examples are cited, and Iglesias Ovejero provides detailed historical and cultural explanations. The study concludes with a useful index of names, persons, and motifs.

3632. Iglesias Ovejero, Angel. "La Iconicidad de los nombres propios en el refranero medieval." *Les formes brèves. Actes du colloque international de la Baume-les-Aix, 26–28 novembre 1982.* Ed. Benito Pelegrin. Aix-en-Provence: Université de Provence, 1984. 122–140.

This article attempts to discuss the use of proper names in medieval Spanish proverbs. Iglesias Ovejero explains how the names became integrated into metaphorical proverbs and discusses their historical and cultural meanings. Numerous examples from proverb collections and literary works are cited, making it clear that many of the names go back to classical and Biblical times. The 71 notes include helpful bibliographical information on onomastics and paremiology. See the more detailed study by the same author (no. 3631 above).

3633. Inghult, Göran. "Lexikalische Innovationen in Wort-gruppenform. Zu einer Untersuchung über die Erweiterung des Lexembestandes im Deutschen und Schwedischen." *Europhras 90. Akten der internationalen Tagung zur germanistischen Phraseologieforschung, Aske/Schweden 12.-15. Juni 1990.* Ed. Christine Palm. Uppsala: Acta Universitatis Upsaliensis, 1991. 101–113.

Inghult investigates lexical innovations in modern German and Swedish phraseological units. It is shown that these changes take place on semantic, stylistic, morphological, syntactical, and metaphorical levels. Such adaptations also create difficulties for the translator who is confronted to find full or at least partial equivalents in the target language. The author shows all of this in much detail by an analysis of the German proverbial expression "Kalte Füße bekommen" (To get cold feet) which was current in Germany already during the 19th century. This fixed phrase now also exists in Swedish as "Få kalla fötter." It is a loan translation from the English language (not from German) and entered modern Swedish after 1945. A useful bibliography (pp. 112–113) is included.

3634. Iniobong Udoidem, Sylvanus. "The Epistemological Significance of Proverbs: An Africa[n] Perspective." *Présence africaine,* no. 132 (1984), 126–136.

Referring to Ibibio proverbs from Nigeria, the author explains the epistemological basis and significance of proverbs in African culture. It is argued that the actual use of proverbs in verbal communication involves memory, creativity, and knowledge, and that these three dimensions are constitutive in any epistemic process. The speaker and hearer of a proverb is involved in an intellectual analysis which results in a creative understanding or awareness of a given event or situation. This kind of awareness is philosophical knowledge or more precisely a certain communality of knowledge. A proverb thus places the perception of events and situations within a communal worldview.

3635. Iris Giovacchini, Teresa. "Sem Tob, posible fuente de la poesia aforistica de Antonio Machado." *Revista de Literatura,* 47, no. 93 (1985), 105–115.

The author presents a convincing literary argument that the early 20th century Spanish poet Antonio Machado y Ruiz (1875–1939) was influenced by Santob de Carrión's (14th century) medieval Spanish proverb collection *Proverbios morales* (1345). Iris Giovacchini starts with a discussion of Machado's interest in medieval literature and Biblical motifs, and she then moves on to a discussion of Santob's (or Sem Tob's) proverb collection. The major part of the essay is dedicated to a careful textual comparison between some of Machado's poems and texts from Santob's collection. It is clear from several contextualized examples that Machado's aphoristic poetry was definitely influenced by this important medieval work.

3636. Ishii, Mikiko. "Joseph's Proverbs in the Coventry Plays." *Folklore* (London), 93, no. 1 (1982), 47–60.

Ishii investigates the Middle English proverbs used by the Biblical Joseph in two religious Coventry plays. In the *Pageants of the Weavers* (1392) Joseph's use of proverbs help to characterize him as a weak husband, whereas in the *Shearmen and Taylors*

(1392) play he is shown to represent the traditional figure of the comic cuckolded husband. In both plays proverbs are used to achieve the fusion of the popular, secular figure of Joseph with that of Joseph as the servant of God. Many proverbs are cited in their dramatic context with references to standard historical proverb dictionaries. There is no proverb index to this otherwise significant study of proverbs in English medieval drama.

3637. Israelite, Neita, Patrick Schloss, and Maureen Smith. "Teaching Proverb Use through a Modified Table Game." *The Volta Review*, 88, no. 4 (1986), 195–207.

This study demonstrates that hearing-impaired students can be taught to discriminate correctly among selected proverbs and proverbial expressions. Using a modified version of the well-known table game *Monopoly*, the teachers succeeded in getting the students to acquire this structurally difficult idiomatic language. The results of various teaching sessions suggest that hearing-impaired students learn and comprehend proverbial idioms and their meaning as simple vocabulary items. A table that lists six standard English proverbs with their meaning and a sample textual passage are included and so is a small bibliography (p. 207). With an English abstract (p. 195).

J

3638. James, Barbara. "Frauenstrafen des 18. Jahrhunderts in Lied, Bild und Redensart." *Festschrift für Lutz Röhrich zum 60. Geburtstag.* Eds. Rolf Wilhelm Brednich and Jürgen Dittmar. Berlin: Erich Schmidt, 1982. 307–315 (=*Jahrbuch für Volksliedforschung*, 27–28 [1982–1983], 307–315.

Historical and cultural investigation of the origin and meaning of the German proverbial expression "Das isch e Feger" (That's a broom) which refers to women who have gone beyond the narrow ethical norms in their sexual behavior. James quotes two German folk songs dealing with various modes of punishments for women during the 18th century and is able to show that women who were accused of illicit sexual activities were forced to take up the broom and sweep the local streets. The misogynous and stereotypical dialect expression continues to be in use today, because the double moral standard for male and female sexuality still exists. The entire article is a good example for the importance of folk songs in diachronic proverb studies. With 1 illustration.

3639. Januschek, Franz. "Redensarten und Sprüche der 'Jugendsprache': Was bedeuten sie wirklich?" *Sprachwissenschaft und Volkskunde. Perspektiven einer kulturanalytischen Sprachbetrachtung.* Eds. Herbert E. Brekle and Utz Maas. Opladen: Westdeutscher Verlag, 1986. 90–102.

The author argues successfully that paremiologists and folklorists should pay closer attention to the origin, meaning, use, and function of truly modern proverbs and proverbial expressions. He shows that the youth culture of today transforms the metaphors of yesterday into modern expressions that befit a technological society. Several German phraseological neologisms are cited in their speech context based on actual interviews.

Januschek stresses the originality and creativity of young people in formulating their own phraseological units. Many of these fixed phrases are in fact innovative variants of traditional expressions maintaining the original proverbial structures. It remains to be seen which of these new "proverbs" will actually maintain a general currency in the future. A short bibliography (p. 102) concerning proverbial speech of young people is provided.

3640. Janz, Brigitte. *Rechtssprichwörter im "Sachsenspiegel." Eine Untersuchung zur Text-Bild-Relation in den Codices picturati.* Frankfurt am Main: Peter Lang, 1989. 586 pp.

This is an invaluable monograph studying 105 legal proverbs which Janz has found in the medieval German law book *Sachsenspiegel* (1221/24) by Eike von Repgow (1180/90–1233?). In the informative introduction (pp. 15–49) the author discusses the definition, origin, form, language, currency, value, and illustration of legal proverbs. The first chapter (pp. 51–147) presents short monographs on 23 legal proverbs that appear in the *Sachsenspiegel* without any commentaries, a particularly informative explanatory note (pp. 89–93) being for example Janz' observations on the proverb "Wer zuerst kommt, mahlt zuerst" (First come, first served). Chapter two (pp. 149–251) treats 23 proverbs whose content and meaning are explained by Eike, chapter three (pp. 253–282) covers 7 proverbs for which Eike provides justifications, chapter four (pp. 282–349) investigates 16 texts as legal rules, chapter five (pp. 351–391) analyzes 10 proverbs with contradictory explanations, chapter six (pp. 393–470) deals with 15 texts that are being questioned, chapter seven (pp. 471–495) comments on 6 proverbs that restrict earlier opinions in the law book, and chapter eight (pp. 497–521) concerns itself with 5 proverbs whose legal wisdom is negated. Throughout the discussions of the 105 texts Janz presents detailed historical, cultural, philological, and legal comments. She also includes 101 illustrations of these proverbs from the four illustrated manuscripts of the *Sachsenspiegel*. A useful index of the proverbs (pp. 579–586) and a valuable bibliography (pp. 535–577) conclude this important work. See also Ruth Schmidt-Wiegand (no. 2832).

3641. Jarosh, Jiri. "Zu der Funktion der Phrasen, Redensarten und Sprüche bei den Ortschronisten, Bibelleser[n] und Versemacher[n] in Mittelmähren." *Proverbium Paratum*, 3 (1982), 241–250.

An investigation of the function of proverbs, proverbial expressions, and other phraseological units in modern Czechoslovakian regional literature. Jarosh studies in particular regional newspapers that often include short literary texts by chroniclers, Bible interpreters, and poets. Much of this literature is didactic in nature and wishes to elucidate cultural and historical aspects of regional life. Many of the folkloric texts are stylized, and the authors portray a traditional worldview. The Czech texts are cited with German translations.

3642. Jarosinska, E. "Deutsche und niederländische Phraseologismen mit Tierbezeichnungen zur Charakterisierung von menschlichen Eigenschaften." *Neerlandica Wratislaviensia*, 5 (1991), 249–258 (=*Acta Universitatis Wratislaviensis*, no. 1299).

This is a comparative analysis of German and Dutch proverbial expressions, comparisons, and exaggerations based on animals and whose metaphors stand for indirect characteristics of human behavior. Jarosinska cites numerous examples referring to such common animals as the goat, lion, ass (donkey), goose, horse, chicken, dog, calf, sheep, bird, and cat. For many of these phraseological units there are precise equivalents because of the common origins in classical, Biblical, or medieval times. However, there are also those fixed phrases that use different animal metaphors to express the same meaning due to different cultural and historical developments.

3643. Jeay, Madeleine. "*Les évangiles des quenouilles*. De la croyance populaire à la locution." *La locution. Actes du colloque international Université McGill, Montréal, 15–16 octobre 1984.* Eds. Giuseppe Di Stefano and Russell G. McGillivray. Montréal: Editions CERES, 1984. 282–301.

Based on a 15th century collection of French superstitions entitled *Les évangiles des quenouilles*, Jeay investigates the interrelationship of traditional beliefs and proverbial expressions.

She shows how superstitions have become crystallized into fixed phrases that remain current today without the speaker's knowledge of their origin and precise meaning. Interesting comments are also included on how proverbial expressions are related to folk narratives. Several examples are cited in their folkloric context. A useful bibliography (pp. 300–301) is provided as well.

3644. Jeep, John M. *Stabreimende Wortpaare bei Notker Labeo.* Göttingen: Vandenhoeck & Ruprecht, 1987. 172 pp.

This is a superb diachronic study of 187 Old High German twin formulas (Zwillingsformel, Wortpaar) found in the works of the early monk and scholar Notker Labeo (950?–1022) from St. Gall, Switzerland. Jeep starts his monograph with a valuable bibliography (pp. 11–24) and an informative introductory chapter (pp. 25–30) on previous research of this proverbial subgenre. The lengthy second chapter (pp. 31–140) presents detailed philological explanations of the twin formulas which for the most part are characterized by alliteration. Chapters three to six (pp. 141–159) treat phonetic, phonological, morphological, and syntactical aspects of these texts, and chapter seven (pp. 160–164) offers some additional comments on semantic questions. The eighth chapter (pp. 165–166) comments on the distinct vocabulary of these fixed phrases, and this discussion is augmented by the detailed word index (pp. 169–172). Jeep's historical study is of much value to scholars interested in the origin and tradition of German twin formulas that are still in use today.

3645. Jerak, Zeljka Matulina, and Pavao Mikic. "O poimanju 'rada' u poslovicama u hrvatskom ili srpskom i njemackom jeziku." *Uporabno jezikoslovlje. Zbornik radova s V. kongresa Saveza drustava za primijenjenu lingvistiku Jugoslavije.* Ed. Inka Strukelj. Ljubljana: Zveza, 1989. 646–655.

This is a comparative study on the concept of "work" in German and Serbo-Croatian proverbs. The authors isolated seven main characteristics of these texts on various types of labor: work is good, work brings happiness, work is healthy, work leads to education, work means life, and work does not mix with emotions. Only 15% of these parallel texts are completely equivalent, 45% exhibit partially equivalent meanings and metaphors, 23% have no equivalency at all, and 17% are too culturally bound to be compared. A useful bibliography (pp. 653–654), one statistical table, and a German abstract (pp. 654–655) are included.

3646. Jokinen, Ulla. "Observations sur les locutions françaises dans les farces et dans les sotties." *La locution. Actes du colloque international Université McGill, Montréal, 15–16 octobre 1984.* Eds. Giuseppe Di Stefano and Russell G. McGillivray. Montréal: Editions CERES, 1984. 302–322.

Literary investigation of the use and function of proverbial expressions in French farces and short plays based on fools from the second half of the 15th century. Jokinen deals in particular with verbal phraseological units and cites numerous contextualized examples. She also points out that some of these fixed phrases are still current in the French language today while others have long become obsolete. Some cultural and historical explanations are provided, and at the end the author discusses a few medieval proverbial comparisons as well.

3647. Joly, Monique. "Le discours métaparémique dans *Don Quichotte.*" *Richesse du proverbe.* Eds. François Suard and Claude Buridant. Lille: Université de Lille, 1984. II, 245–260.

Interesting literary study of two meta-proverbial sections in Miguel de Cervantes Saavedra's (1547–1616) novel *Don Quijote* (1605/1615). Joly points out that Cervantes presents important considerations about the nature, origin, use, and function of proverbs while at the same time quoting 17 proverbs (3 in chapter 21 of part I; 14 in chapter 71 of part II). The speakers, the context, and the purpose of these texts are carefully analyzed. All 17 Spanish proverbs in French translation are listed in their literary context in an appendix, and a detailed diagram (p. 260) listing the situation, speaker, proverb, etc. is also included.

3648. Jones, Malcolm. "Folklore Motifs in Late Medieval Art I: Proverbial Follies and Impossibilities." *Folklore* (London), 100, no. 2 (1989), 201–217.

This is a very erudite and highly informative study on proverbial motifs in late medieval art in Europe, with a special emphasis on the secular motifs relating to stereotypes of human folly. While Jones comments on Pieter Brueghel's (c. 1520–1569) oil painting *Netherlandic Proverbs* (1559) as the artistic culmination of early proverb illustrations, he discusses primarily the representation of proverbial expressions on European misericords in such churches as Beverley Minster (Yorkshire), Manchester Cathedral, etc. It is pointed out that most of these choir stall carvings are based on the proverbial motif of "The World Turned Upside Down" in which a definite role reversal between man and animal is depicted. Jones cites numerous Dutch, English, French, and German examples that refer to such animals as the sparrow (also just birds), goose, hare, pig, snail, etc. Some proverbial expressions like "To shoe the goose" and "To put the cart before the horse" are analyzed in more detail, and the author includes many literary references in addition to his references to early misericords. Most of the examples stem from the 13th to the 16th century, and they often have their parallels not only in literary sources but also in the folk narratives of that time. The 120 notes (pp. 210–217) contain a wealth of bibliographical information on the fascinating interrelationship of art and paremiology.

3649. Jones, Malcolm. "The Depiction of Proverbs in Late Medieval Art." *Europhras 88. Phraséologie Contrastive. Actes du Colloque International Klingenthal-Strasbourg, 12–16 mai 1988.* Ed. Gertrud Gréciano. Strasbourg: Université des Sciences Humaines, 1989. 205–223.

Jones has divided this article on proverbs and proverbial expressions depicted in late medieval art into two major parts. The first section (pp. 205–209) treats the illustration of multiple proverbs on a silver-gilt pot, on painted glass adorning the Chambre des Comptes in Grenoble, on a German wooden painted plate from 1528, on a 15th century Flemish proverb tapestry, on various prints depicting the motif of "The World Turned Upside Down," and on Pieter Brueghel's (c. 1520–1569) famous painting *Netherlandic Proverbs* (1559). The second part (pp. 209–217) is somewhat similar to Jones' previous paper (see no. 3648) in that it deals primarily with individual proverb illustrations on misericords throughout Europe. It is mentioned again that many of them depict human follies through animal images such as the sparrow (or birds), goose, horse, etc. The 104 notes (pp. 217–223) once again include rich bibliographical materials for the study of art and proverbs. For the wooden plate depicting proverbial fools see Werner Mezger (no. 2636) and Friedrich Zarncke (no. 3026), and for the proverb tapestry see Ella Siple (no. 1745).

3650. Jones, Malcolm. "Folklore Motifs in Late Medieval Art II: Sexist Satire and Popular Punishment." *Folklore* (London), 101, no. 1 (1990), 69–87.

While this second article in a series of three (see nos. 3648 and 3651) does not specifically deal with proverbial illustrations, it nevertheless touches upon sexual stereotypes and proverbial forms of punishment in the late Middle Ages. Jones talks about the misogynous and anti-feminist attitudes in medieval European literature and art, and he explains in particular how they are depicted through the proverbial motif of "The World Turned Upside Down." Of special interest are the author's comments regarding the misericords that depict such proverbial expressions as "To wear the breeches" and "To be a cuckold." The 103 notes (pp. 78–87) once again contain a wealth of bibliographical references to proverbs in art.

3651. Jones, Malcolm. "Folklore Motifs in Late Medieval Art III: Erotic Animal Imagery." *Folklore* (London), 102, no. 2 (1991), 192–219.

This is the third of Jones' superb three-part series (see nos. 3648 and 3650) on folklore and especially proverbial motifs in late medieval European art. In this article the author investigates the much neglected erotic imagery of proverbs in literary works and misericords of that time. Special attention is paid to the cockerel and the cuckold's horns as well as the proverbial expression "To be a cuckold" and its sexual metaphor. Jones also treats the sexual and at times obscene meanings of the artistic illustrations of and literary allusions to such animals as the rabbit, the squirrel (and the nut), cockles and mussels, the foxtail, and the ass. There is no doubt that paremiologists, folklorists and art historians should be studying the sexual symbolism in these modes of expressions. Jones' 161 notes (pp. 209–219) certainly represent a rich reference tool to advance such studies.

3652. Jones, Malcolm. "Marcolf the Trickster in Late Mediaeval Art and Literature or: The Mystery of the Bum in the Oven." *Spoken in Jest.* Ed. Gillian Bennett. Sheffield/United Kingdom: Sheffield Academic Press, 1991. 139–173.

In this fascinating article combining his expertise in medieval art and literature, Jones studies the proverbial speech and tricks of the peasant and fool Marcolf as he is depicted in numerous anonymous dialogues with the wise King Solomon. The author deals especially with the anal symbolism expressed through such proverbial expressions as "Kiss my arse," "To show someone one's buttocks (bum, rump, ass)," and "To foul one's own nest." Many literary and artistic references from various European sources are included, and Jones even attaches three detailed appendices (pp. 171–173) that include a wealth of bibliographical information on these anal and scatological expressions in addition to the 79 notes. With 3 illustrations.

3653. Jones, Malcolm, and Charles Tracy. "A Medieval Choirstall Desk-End at Haddon Hall: The Fox-Bishop and the Geese-Hangmen." *Journal of the British Archeological Association,* 144 (1991), 107–115.

The two authors report on a fragment of wood sculpture from Haddon Hall near Bakewell, Derbyshire (England), which is shown to be a medieval desk-end of special iconographical and sculptural interest. Probably dating from around 1380, it incorporates one of the earliest known examples of the fox-as-bishop sequence of scenes in European woodwork, as well as the earliest extant English vernacular inscription in woodwork. This carving clearly shows a fox-bishop preaching to geese, and this scene is interpreted to be an illustration of the proverb "It is a blind goose that comes to the fox's sermon." There is, of course, also the other English proverb that states "When the fox preaches, then beware your geese." Jones and Tracy include detailed explanations about this secular and proverbial motif. The 63 notes (pp. 113–115) include important bibliographical references to proverbial misericords and the depiction of proverbs in art in general. With 13 illustrations and an English abstract (p. 107).

3654. Jordan, Rosan A. "Five [Mexican American] Proverbs in Context." *Midwestern Journal of Language and Folklore*, 8, no. 2 (1982), 109–115.

Based on actual field research, Jordan presents five Mexican American proverbs in their social context which she collected from an informant in Texas. The proverbs are cited in the Spanish original with English translations. For each text the author discusses the meaning, use, function, and context, and she also analyzes the strategies that went into the proverb reference in the particular speech acts. It is concluded that proverbs are used primarily in a directive or collaborative fashion, trying to influence or manipulate social behavior and collective opinion.

3655. Joyner, Charles. "Proverbs." *Encyclopedia of Southern Culture*. Eds. Charles Reagan Wilson and William Ferris. Chapel Hill/North Carolina: University of North Carolina Press, 1989. 516–517.

A short encyclopedia article on proverbs with special reference to the proverbial wisdom of the South of the United States. It is argued that southern proverbs express collective wisdom in metaphorical form, guiding southerners to appropriate social behavior and providing informal channels of general education. Most of the texts have their origin in Europe, either as English proverbs or loan translations from other languages. Joyner includes some general comments regarding the structure, form, language, style, metaphor, and meaning of proverbs. Even though he talks of "southern" proverbs, his examples are in fact current throughout North America. A small bibliography (p. 517) of basic paremiological and paremiographical tools is attached.

3656. Juillard, Alain. "Discours proverbial et écriture romanesque dans *La Comédie Humaine*: Le cas de *Un début dans la vie.*" *Richesse du proverbe.* Eds. François Suard and Claude Buridant. Lille: Université de Lille, 1984. II, 261–272.

Literary proverb investigation of Honoré de Balzac's (1799–1850) *La Comédie Humaine* (1829/54) with special emphasis on the novel *Un début dans la vie* (1842). Juillard points out that the primary use and function of proverbs in this work is to give a psychological and sociological characterization of people. Proverbs are also employed to reflect the deterministic worldview which is part of Balzac's literary realism. They appear in the narrative as well as the dialogues of the novel, and it is the rhetorical function of the proverbs that is especially noteworthy. The author quotes a number of contextualized examples, but there is no proverb index of all the texts that appear in this particular French novel.

3657. Jurika, D. "Internacionals sakamvardu tips un ta nacionalo versiju dinamika." *Latvijas PSR Zinatnu Akademijas Vestis,* no. 10 (1988), 41–51.

The author starts with some general remarks concerning the relationship between international proverb types and their national variants. Next Jurika chooses the proverb "All is not gold that glitters" and discusses English and Latvian variants. It is pointed out that there are definite syntactical, structural, phonetic, and semantic differences, even though all these texts are based on an internationally disseminated proverb. It is amazing to see how many variants there do exist for this popular proverb in the two languages under discussion. Such variants present difficult classification problems, and it is also problematic to decide which of them is the most frequently used national variant. A Russian summary (p. 51) is attached.

K

3658. Kahn, Charlotte. "Proverbs of Love and Marriage: A Psychological Perspective." *Psychoanalytic Review,* 70 (1983), 359–371.

Starting with a socio-cultural and psychological definition of proverbs, Kahn shows by an analysis of the proverb "Marry in haste, repent at leisure" that such rules and their meaning depend very much on each individual's experiences. She then quotes a number of German and English proverbs about love and marriage in which misogynous and stereotypical statements can be found. Whoever uses these texts obviously expresses his/her worldview, and it is for this reason that proverbs and their interpretation are of significance to the psychoanalyst. Proverbs are seen to fall somewhere between the fully unconscious, egocentric, affective experiences of a child and the fully conscious, logical, rule-governed, hypothetico-deductive behavior of a scientist. Proverbs, therefore, transmit connotations which may be idiosyncratic and important for psychoanalysis.

3659. Kammerer, Edmund. *Sprichwort und Politik. Sprachliche Schematismen in Politikerreden, politischem Journalismus und Graffiti.* M.A. Thesis University of Freiburg, 1983. 110 pp.

Kammerer investigates the use and function of proverbs and proverbial expressions in German politics. He deals in particular with proverbs in political speeches (pp. 20–36), political journalism (pp. 37–64), and in proverbial graffiti (pp. 65–94) which make political comments. For each of these major areas the author also studies the style, value, effectiveness, and intent of the proverb texts. While many expressions are cited in their traditional wording, a large number is varied to fit certain situations. Of special interest are Kammerer's interpretations of the structures and themes of graffiti, which are seen as intentional variations of proverbs (i.e. anti-proverbs or

"Antisprichwörter"), literary quotations, Bible quotations, advertising slogans, etc. He also comments on structural proverb patterns such as "Lieber (Besser) . . . als . . ." (Rather [Better] . . . than . . .) that are used repeatedly in these expressions of political protest. A useful bibliography (pp. 107–110) is included.

3660.   Kanfer, Stefan. "Proverbs or Aphorisms?" *Time* (July 11, 1983), p. 74.

A short popular magazine article dealing with the basic differences between proverbs and aphorisms. Several well-known definitions and a number of examples are cited for each genre. Kanfer points out that proverbs are still very much in the making, and he quotes the modern American texts "There is no such thing as a free lunch" and "Garbage in, garbage out," the latter stemming from the new computer age. The author basically concludes that proverbs and aphorisms have been and will continue to be significant expressions of the human condition. This essay was inspired by Hugh Kenner's earlier discussion along these lines (no. 3673).

3661.   Kann, Hans-Joachim. "Zu den Quellen von Spontisprüchen." *Der Sprachdienst*, 29 (1985), 75–79.

This is a concise survey of the possible sources of so-called German "Spontisprüche," by which are meant "spontaneous" slogans of the youth culture (primarily students) on all aspects of modern society and politics. Many of these slogans appear in the form of graffiti or on leaflets, in booklets and in humorous, parodistic or satirical book publications. Kann is able to show that the structures of these slogans are not really very original. Most of them are in fact based on such formulaic patterns as Biblical or literary quotations, verses from fairy tales or folk songs, proverbs (i.e. anti-proverbs or "Antisprichwörter"), advertising slogans, etc. Varied quotations from René Descartes (1596–1650), Karl Marx (1818–1883), Friedrich Nietzsche (1844–1900), etc. appear to be especially popular. Kann cites numerous examples to show that many "Spontisprüche" are innovative varations of traditional formulaic language.

3662. Kantola, Markhu. "Zum phraseologischen Wortpaar in der deutschen Gegenwartssprache." *Beiträge zur allgemeinen und germanistischen Phraseologieforschung.* Oulu: Oulun Yliopisto, 1987. 111–128.

The author presents a significant study of German "Zwillingsformeln" (twin formulas) that are current in today's language. The article starts with a definition of this type of phraseological unit and then studies the meaning, structure, synonymy, antonymy, identity, alliteration, rhyme, assonance, intensification, and lexicography (nouns, adjectives, verbs, and adverbs) of the word pairs. Kantola also includes diachronic considerations, stating that due to the considerable age of these fixed phrases they present etymological and cultural difficulties especially to those people who learn German as a foreign language. A statistical table of the frequency of such twin formulas in modern literature is included, for example in the works of Werner Steinberg (1913–), Max Frisch (1911–1991), Max Walter Schulz (1921–), etc. Many texts are cited, at times with Danish, Finnish, and Swedish equivalents. A valuable bibliography (pp. 126–128) is provided.

3663. Kanyó, Zoltán. "Myslitel'no-iazykovye usloviia otobrazheniia struktury poslovitsy." *Paremiologicheskie issledovaniia.* Ed. Grigorii L'vovich Permiakov. Moskva: Nauka, 1984. 179–199.

This is a Russian translation of Kanyó's earlier German paper "Sprachlich-gedankliche Bedingungen der Abbildung der Sprichwortstruktur" (1980; see no. 828). The article starts with a detailed review of proverb definitions by Algirdas Julien Greimas (no. 595), Alan Dundes (no. 378), Grigorii L'vovich Permiakov (no. 1428), and others. Kanyó also contrasts various structural, grammatical, and semantic theories and their applicability to modern paremiological research, arguing that paremiologists must continue to search for a solution to the concept of proverbiality by applying modern linguistic theories. He himself discusses in particular Noam Chomsky's and Richard Montague's linguistic theories and how they can be applied to proverb studies. A useful bibliography (pp. 198–199) for the cominatory study of linguistics and paremiology, many German and English examples (now in Russian translation), and a structural diagram add to the value of this review article.

3664. Kanyó, Zoltán. "O kommynikativnoi forme poslovits." *Paremiologicheskie issledovaniia.* Ed. Grigorii L'vovich Permiakov. Moskva: Nauka, 1984. 257–259.

A Russian translation of a short German lecture that Kanyó gave in Halle, Germany, in 1978. Starting with the basic sentence "Ich werde dich morgen besuchen" (I shall visit you tomorrow) and the proverb "Kalte Hände, heißes Herz" (Cold hands, warm heart), the author explains the use of a proverb as a special communicative speech act reproducing an impersonal, codified formula. A proverb is also different from a subjective sentence due to its surface and deep structure. For a more detailed investigation of Kanyó's semiotic approach to proverbs see his book *Sprichwörter—Analyse einer Einfachen Form* (1981; see no. 829).

3665. Kass, János, and András Lukácsy. *Id. Pieter Bruegel. "Flamand közmondások."* Budapest: Corvina Kiadó, 1985. 40 pp.

This is an introductory study of Pieter Brueghel's (c. 1520–1569) celebrated oil painting *Netherlandic Proverbs* (1559) for Hungarian readers. The two authors present a short introduction in which they talk about the general meaning of this picture based on over 100 Dutch proverbial expressions. They then publish the entire painting together with 18 full-page illustrations of certain scenes. For each of these details they include one page of philological, cultural, and historical explanations. The Dutch expressions are cited only in Hungarian translation, but the authors do include Hungarian equivalents wherever possible. With 19 colorful illustrations. For more detailed studies of this picture see Wilhelm Fraenger (no. 460), Jan Grauls (no. 586), and Alan Dundes and Claudia Stibbe (no. 2332).

3666. Katona, Imre. "A magyar népnyelv egyszerü és szolashasonlatai. Elömunkalatok szolasaink stilisztikajahoz." *Filologiai Közlöny,* 20 (1974), 129–154.

The author investigated a collection of 3000 Hungarian proverbs and proverbial expressions that include 516 proverbial comparisons. Such comparisons were not that frequent in 2000 folk songs, where the author only found 193 texts. Analyzing these texts it was found that most of them are based on verbs in the third person singular form. The nouns usually represent village and household items, whereas references to nature are almost completely absent. When such comparisons employ adjectives, they usually express negative characteristics. Many examples are cited in this lexical and grammatical study of traditional proverbial comparisons. Several statistical tables are included.

3667. Katona, Imre. "Alsonémedi és környékének szolasai." *Alsonémedi története és néprajza*. Ed. Ivan Balassa. Alsonémedi: Községi Tanacs VB, 1980. 404–423.

This is an anthropological study of numerous Hungarian proverbs from the village of Alsonémedi and its surroundings. Katona presents many detailed comments concerning the content and meaning of these traditional texts. But the author is also very interested in the language of these proverbs, showing in which way their vocabulary reflects the worldview and opinions of the village people. The regional flavor of these proverbs makes it clear that paremiologists should continue to study the proverbs in rural districts by using modern field research methods. Several statistical tables and some comments concerning structural aspects are also included.

3668. Kaufmann, Ekkehard. "'Wo kein Kläger, ist kein Richter'." *Juristische Schulung*, no. 6 (1961), 182–184.

The author presents a legal and historical analysis of the German proverb "Wo kein Kläger, ist kein Richter" (Where there is no accuser, there is no judge). He shows that this legal proverb goes back to the beginnings of German law, and he cites several historical references and legal cases exemplifying this legal maxim. Kaufmann also explains that the proverb basically argues that a clearly stated accusation is required in criminal and civil law in order for a judge to make any ruling at all. The 19 notes include some bibliographical references to proverbs relating to legal wisdom.

3669. Kaufmann, Ekkehard. "Rechtssprichwort." *Handwörterbuch zur deutschen Rechtsgeschichte.* Eds. Adalbert Erler and E. Kaufmann. Berlin: Erich Schmidt, 1986. IV, cols. 364–367.

This is a concise encyclopedia article on the so-called "Rechtsprichwort" (legal proverb). The author starts with a definition of this subgenre of proverbs and explains its poetic language, style, structure, currency, and meaning. He also refers to Jacob Grimm's (1785–1863) famous essay "Von der Poesie im Recht" (1815; see no. 2429) which was one of the early treatises on legal maxims. Several examples are cited, and Kaufmann includes legal explanations as well as references to major German collections of such proverbs referring to old German laws. A small bibliography (cols. 366–367) is attached.

3670. Kempcke, Günter. "Theoretische und praktische Probleme der Phraseologiedarstellung in einem synchronischen einsprachigen Bedeutungswörterbuch." *Beiträge zur allgemeinen und germanistischen Phraseologieforschung.* Ed. Jarmo Korhonen. Oulu: Oulun Yliopisto, 1987. 155–164.

The author presents a theoretical and practical discussion of how the German lexicographers of the six-volume dictionary *Duden. Das große Wörterbuch der deutschen Sprache* (1976–1981) and the two-volume *Handwörterbuch der deutschen Gegenwartssprache* (1984) have attempted to deal with various types of phraseological units. Kempcke argues that entries of such fixed phrases must include semantic, syntactical, and stylistic explanations. Most of them can be classified under the key-word (often the most significant noun). Many examples are included to illustrate how verbal and adverbial phraseological units could be classified lexicographically.

3671. Kempcke, Günther [sic]. "Struktur und Gebrauch der somatischen Phraseme mit den Bedeutungskomponenten 'Kopf' und 'tête'." *Europhras 88. Phraséologie Contrastive. Actes du Colloque International Klingenthal-Strasbourg, 12–16 mai 1988.* Ed. Gertrud

Gréciano. Strasbourg: Université des Sciences Humaines, 1989. 225–232.

In this article Kempcke investigates the differences and similarities of German and French phraseological units which include the somatic noun "Kopf" or "tête" (head). He mentions that some of them have complete equivalents in the other language, but there are also those which exhibit only partial or no equivalency at all in the target language. This clearly poses serious problems for the translation of such fixed phrases. Citing numerous examples from several dictionaries, Kempcke can show that semantic and structural equivalents exist that actually do not refer to the "head" but rather to other body parts. A few comments on the polysemanticity of these phrases are also included in this comparative and lexicographical study.

3672. Kemper, Susan. "Comprehension and the Interpretation of Proverbs." *Journal of Psycholinguistic Research,* 10, no. 2 (1981), 179–198.

Based on a psychological proverbs test of 16 paragraph sets of "unfamiliar" proverbs and their literal and figurative meaning expressed in short and long sentences, Kemper conducted four experiments with university students to establish the mechanism of proverb comprehension. It was found that when proverbs occur naturally in a linguistic context, figurative uses are understood more rapidly than literal uses. In contrast, figurative interpretations of isolated proverbs are more difficult to make than literal interpretations. Inferences from the literal meaning of the proverbs to their figurative meaning seem to be required only when subjects cannot use contextual information to generate expectations about what the speaker is likely to say. Six statistical tables, a short bibliography (p. 198), and an English abstract (p. 179) are included. See also Kemper's longer dissertation with the same title from 1978 (no. 839).

3673. Kenner, Hugh. "Wisdom of the Tribe. Why Proverbs are Better than Aphorisms." *Harper's,* 226, no. 1596 (May 6, 1983), 84–86.

Starting with a review of John A. Simpson's *The Concise Oxford Dictionary of Proverbs* (1982) and John Gross' *The Oxford Book of*

Aphorisms (1983), Kenner explains the difference between these two genres with the help of some examples. He then sides decisively with the traditional proverb over the "solitary ingenuity" of the aphorism. The aphorisms lack the ability to generalize whereas proverbs convey a substantial philosophy of life. Proverbs are seen as recipes for managing everyday affairs, and while traditional texts continue to be employed, new ones are also created to reflect modern mores. This is a strong endorsement of proverbial wisdom at a time when many people would argue against proverbial rigidity and the "ancient" truths expressed in proverbs. See also Stefan Kanfer (no. 3660).

3674.   Kepinski, Andrzej. "'Musi to na rusi . . .' W strone przyslow." *Ruch Literacki*, 29, nos. 1–2 (1988), 89–102.

The author begins with some general comments on the definition and collection of proverbs before looking in particular at the image of the Russians in Polish proverbs. The title refers to the stereotypical proverbial expression "Musi to na rusi" (He/she has to [must] only in Russian), expressing the fact that Poles blame the Russians for anything that someone must do. Many examples are cited showing how proverbs express national stereotypes and the worldview of the Polish people. The author also includes some proverbs from other cultures which comment in one way or another about the Russians. The 56 notes contain useful bibliographical information on the study of proverbial stereotypes.

3675.   Kerdilès, Yann. "Les acteurs langagiers dans les proverbes." *Richesse du proverbe*. Eds. François Suard and Claude Buridant. Lille: Université de Lille, 1984. II, 95–105.

By means of a rhetorical analysis of ten English proverbs, Kerdilès attempts to show that proverbs take on a function only in actual speech acts. The detailed study of the proverb "Give your dog a bad name and hang it" makes clear that each proverb use needs a speaker (protagonist) and a listener (deuteragonist). Only in a context (oral or written) does the proverb take on semantic significance as a metaphorical strategy in a discourse or narrative. The author discusses possible contexts for these proverbs but does not cite the texts in real communication. The English proverbs are cited without French translations.

3676. Khayyat, Shimon. "Relations between Muslims, Jews and Christians as Reflected in Arabic Proverbs." *Folklore* (London), 96, no. 2 (1985), 190–207.

Khayyat presents 100 Arabic proverbs in transliteration and with English translations. Each text is followed by references to standard proverb collections of the Middle East. Additional variants are cited, and the author also includes rich historical, cultural, and religious explanations. The proverbs all reflect the tensions that exist among the Moslems, Jews, and Christians. In addition they contain the stereotypical views of one group of believers against the other groups. A useful bibliography (pp. 206–207) is included. See also Khayyat's similar article from 1979 (no. 2519).

3677. Khorvat, Ivan. "Sravintel'nyi analiz poslovits i aforizmov." *Studia russica*, 7 (1984), 87–96.

This is a general comparative article on proverbs and aphorisms. The author starts with definition problems and then investigates aspects of structure and function of these two genres. His special interest lies in a comparative analysis of Russian and Hungarian examples to which some English equivalents are added as well. Khorvat shows that while there are some identical equivalents in the case of internationally disseminated proverbs, there are also those texts for which there are only partial or no equivalents at all. This leads to major translation problems and a definite challenge in foreign language instruction. Many examples are included, and there is a special section on comparing phrases with the key-word "head" in these three languages.

3678. Kibler, Clare T. *On the Structure of Conceptual Categories.* Diss. University of Cincinnati, 1984. 97 pp.

The author developed a psychological proverbs test in order to show that conceptual categories are organized around a tacit microtheory that allows one to comprehend events that are similar only on a figurative, i.e. non-perceptual and non-literal level. Subjects were confronted with 10 very short stories that illustrated, with various degrees of accuracy, the figurative meaning of a proverb. The microtheory was explicated as a set of abstract statements or components that together captured the figurative meaning of the proverb. A number of diagrams and statistical tables as well as a useful bibliography (pp. 89–93) concerning the comprehension of metaphorical proverbs are included.

3679. Kingsbury, Stewart A. "On Handling 250,000+ Citation Slips for American Dialect Society (ADS) Proverb Research." *Proverbium,* 1 (1984), 195–205.

   This is a detailed account describing the process of computerizing approximately 250,000 proverb citation slips that were collected by members of the American Dialect Society under the guidance of Margaret M. Bryant (see nos. 219–222) from 1945 through to 1980 and which have now been published as *A Dictionary of American Proverbs* (1992) by Wolfgang Mieder, Stewart A. Kingsbury, and Kelsie B. Harder. Kingsbury gives a short history of this project and reviews his own computer oriented work with the materials since 1975. Next he describes his computer program for classifying the proverbial materials which consist of proverbs as well as proverbial expressions, proverbial rhymes, proverbial comparisons, wellerisms, sententious remarks, etc. He also includes two sample pages of proverbs with the key-word "God" to indicate his classification and numbering system. The result is a significant paper on the use of the computer in proverb archiving.

3680. Kingsbury, Stewart A. "Names in Proverbs and Proverbial Sayings." *Festschrift in Honor of Allen Walker Read.* Ed. Laurence E. Seits. DeKalb/Illinois: North Central Name Society, 1988. 116–132.

   Referring to the large American collection of proverbs, proverbial expressions, proverbial rhymes, proverbial comparisons, wellerisms, sententious remarks, etc. described under the previous entry (see no. 3679), Kingsbury now offers some comments regarding the frequency and type of names in the 7640 key-words under which these texts have been organized. He found that only 366 of them are names (persons, places, Bible, etc.), such as Adam, America, Caesar, Fox River, Greek, January, Rome, etc. Most proverbial texts can be found under the names of "God," the devil (satan), heaven and hell, and a smaller group of assorted names (Christmas, Friday, Indian, Jack, and Monday). Many examples are cited, especially for these high frequency names (see pp. 120–131).

3681. Kinsman, Robert Starr. "Proverbs." *Spenser Encyclopedia*. Eds. A.C. Hamilton et al. Toronto: University of Toronto Press, 1990. 562–565.

Even though this is but a short encyclopedia article, Kinsman provides the Edmund Spenser (1552–1599) scholar with rich materials concerning this major English writer's use of proverbs. Kinsman explains that Spenser used proverbs very effectively to teach wisdom, to make didactic statements, and to add communal authority to his writings. Proverbs appear in all of his works, and he even wrote sonnets that are based on proverbs. His *The Faerie Queene* (1590/96) is filled with proverbs in their traditional wording but also in very interesting reversals that remind modern readers of so-called "Antisprichwörter" (anti-proverbs). A number of contextualized examples are cited, and Kinsman also includes a useful bibliography (pp. 564–565). See also Charles Smith (no. 1753).

3682. Kippar, Pille. "Rahvaluule lühivormidest loomamuinasjutus." *Emakeele seltsi aastaraamat,* 14–15 (1968–1969), 205–218.

Kippar investigates the relationship between Estonian animal tales and proverbs as well as proverbial expressions. The article starts with some general comments on Estonian folklore and folk narratives, and it is argued that proverbial speech plays a considerable role in traditional tales. The author explains that proverbs appear in the direct speech of the characters and also in the narrative portion of the tales. The major function is to add traditional expressiveness to the texts, but the use of proverbial language by the narrator is often highly didactic or moralistic.

Numerous examples are cited, and the author has also provided a Russian abstract (p. 218).

3683. Kirchner, Oswald Robert. *Parömiologische Studien (Zwei kritische Beiträge).* 2 vols. Zwickau: Realschule zu Zwickau, 1879 and 1880; rpt. ed. by Wolfgang Mieder. Bern: Peter Lang, 1984. 171 pp.

This is an early survey of German paremiology. Part one (22 large pages) treats the nature of paremiological research and gives detailed comments on such aspects as definition, origin, style, meaning, national and international dissemination, national character, collections, etc. Part two (37 pages) starts with a bibliographical review of proverb studies and then presents explanatory notes on the metaphors and meaning of several German proverbs and proverbial expressions. As the editor of this reprint Mieder has provided a short introduction (pp. i-v) about Oswald Robert Kirchner (1840–1882) and the importance of these two studies. He also added a bibliography of German proverb collections and studies of the 19th century (pp. 141–154), and this reprint now includes name, subject, and proverb indices as well. For an annotation of the original publication see no. 853.

3684. Kjaer, Anne Lise. "Zur Darbietung von Phraseologismen in einsprachigen Wörterbüchern des Deutschen aus der Sicht ausländischer Textproduzenten." *Beiträge zur allgemeinen und germanistischen Phraseologieforschung.* Ed. Jarmo Korhonen. Oulu: Oulun Yliopisto, 1987. 165–181.

In this enlightening article Kjaer explains that German dictionaries that are meant for native speakers do create considerable difficulties for people for whom German is a foreign language. This is especially the case in their lexicographical treatment of phraseological units. Kjaer argues that lexicographers should include more information concerning the syntactical, stylistic, and semantic aspects of proverbial expressions, idioms, etc. There should also be explanations of the grammatical variability or stability of such fixed phrases, and it should be indicated whether the expressions can be negated or modified in other respects. Numerous examples are discussed, and a useful bibliography (pp. 179–181) is attached as well.

3685. Kjaer, Anne Lise. "Phraseologische Wortverbindungen in der Rechtssprache." *Europhras 90. Akten der internationalen Tagung zur germanistischen Phraseologieforschung, Aske/Schweden 12.-15. Juni 1990.* Ed. Christine Palm. Uppsala: Acta Universitatis Upsaliensis, 1991. 115–122.

The author investigates legal terminology in German phraseological units. She explains that many of these fixed phrases are not particularly idiomatic or metaphorical. Some of them, even though they are fixed and repeated, barely seem to belong to phraseology as such. The author cites a few contextualized examples, and she shows that only a few of them have become current in colloquial speech. Most of them belong to the specialized legal vocabulary of the courts, but in that restricted domain they do act as phraseological units. Many consist of only two words (adjective plus noun), but they hardly belong in modern phraseological dictionaries that emphasize metaphorical and proverbial expressions.

3686. Kjaer, Iver. "Ordsprog og salmer og ordsprogssalmen." *Hvad Fatter gjör . . . Boghistoriske, litterare og musikalske essyas tilegnet Erik Dal.* Eds. Henrik Glahn et al. Herning: Kristensen, 1982. 221–252.

In this superb historical study Iver Kjaer investigates the relationship of proverbs and hymns. He discusses some examples of proverbs in the oldest Danish hymns and then presents a detailed philological analysis of the proverbs contained in an anonymous "proverb hymn" from around 1600. Kjaer prints the 20 strophes of the hymn and provides scholarly commentaries on the mixture of classical, Biblical, and Danish proverbs contained in them. The text is identified as a hymn sung by grammar school pupils when begging in front of the doors of the burghers. The literary function of the proverbs in this song is interpreted as a means to make the hymn more persuasive. The 53 notes contain valuable bibliographical references to major historical proverb collections.

3687. Kjaer, Iver. "En bog og dens skaebne. Om César Oudin: *Refranes o Proverbios Españoles*, Bruxelles: Rutger Velpius, 1608. Om bogens vej gennem tider, lande og haender ind i Universitetsbiblioteket i København—og ud i verden igen." *Bøger-Biblioteker-Mennesker. Et nordisk Festskrift tilegnet Torben Nielsen.* Eds. Erland Kolding Nielsen et al. København: Det Kongelige Bibliotek, 1988. 9–58.

This is a very erudite study of César Oudin's (died 1625) proverb collection *Refranes o Proverbios Españoles traduzidos en lengua Francesa. Proverbes Espagnols traduits en François* (1608). Kjaer presents a detailed description of this early collection, and he describes its various editions. He also points out that Oudin was influenced by Hernán Nuñez' (1472–1553) earlier collection *Refranes o proverbios en romance* (1555). The edition which Kjaer is describing is located in the library of the University of Copenhagen, and Kjaer includes a fascinating account of the history of this particular book in Denmark. It is shown that this is a valuable collection of alphabetically arranged Spanish proverbs with good French translations, making it one of the best bilingual proverb collections of the 17th century. With 9 illustrations.

3688. Klafkowski, Piotr. "Hand and Finger Measurements in Tibetan." *Lingua Posnaniensis*, 26 (1984), 85–97.

The author presents a careful etymological and linguistic analysis of Tibetan words that refer to ancient hand and finger measurements. He also cites 11 proverbs and proverbial expressions that contain "hand" or "finger" as key-words. The texts are cited from Yoseb Gergen's proverb collection *A Thousand Tibetan Proverbs and Wise Sayings* (1976). Each text is cited in Tibetan with English translations and cultural explanations. It becomes clear that somatic proverbs are as popular in this culture as they are in Europe, where proverbs also quite frequently refer to body parts. A small bibliography (pp. 96–97) is attached.

3689. Kleiber, Georges. "Sur la définition du proverbe." *Europhras 88. Phraséologie Contrastive. Actes du Colloque International Klingenthal-Strasbourg, 12–16 mai 1988.* Ed. Gertrud Gréciano. Strasbourg: Université des Sciences Humaines, 1989. 233–252.

This is yet another attempt to offer a useful definition of the proverb. Kleiber refers to some previous formulations and then claims that a proverb is above all a denomination, i.e. an act of naming (denominating) a situation. He then goes on to discuss proverbs as codified units of language that are used as signs. In addition to such a semiotic approach to proverbs the author also treats matters of function, structure, and semantics. Towards the end of the article he considers proverbs as general truths or "generic phrases" which are used to comment on particular situations in a figurative sense. A few French examples are cited, and a helpful bibliography (pp. 250–252) of the literature on various definition attempts is included.

3690. Klein, Arthur. *Graphic Worlds of Peter [sic] Bruegel the Elder.* New York: Dover Publications, 1963 (esp. pp. 137–143).

Klein includes and comments on two of Pieter Brueghel's (c. 1520–1569) pen drawings in gray and brownish ink from 1556 (engraved in 1557). The first illustrates the proverb "Big fish eat little fish" (see pp. 137–140), while the second drawing (pp. 141–143) with the title *The Ass at School* refers to the Dutch proverbial verse "Though a donkey go to school in order to learn, / He'll be donkey, not a horse, when he does return," i.e. in short "Once an ass, always an ass." The author includes comments regarding the didactic meaning of these drawings and also refers to some additional proverbial expressions that are depicted in them. With 4 illustrations.

3691. Klimaszewska, Z. "Versuch einer semantischen Charakterisierung verbaler Phraseologismen am Beispiel des Niederländischen." *Neerlandica Wratislaviensia*, 5 (1991), 259–271 (=*Acta Universitatis Wratislaviensis*, no. 1299).

The author starts this linguistic analysis with a definition of verbal phraseological units, arguing that such fixed phrases are characterized by their structural-lexical stability and their idiomaticity. Then follows the claim that the phenomenon of "phraseologization" could be defined as the destruction of the equivalency between semantic and structural categories. All of this is explained by numerous examples of Dutch proverbial expressions and idioms that contain the verb "geven" (to give). Klimaszewska shows that this verb can take on various meanings in these phrases, and there are also those expressions in which the verb itself may be replaced by an equivalent word. All of this leads to polysemanticity and to a definite problem for the person learning such phraseological units of a foreign language.

3692. Klosinski, Krzysztof. "Przyslowia." In K. Klosinski. *Mimezis w chlopskich powiesciach.* Orzeszkowej, Katowice: Uniwersytet Slaski, 1990. 86–90.

The author starts by explaining that Polish literature dealing with the peasant population is particularly rich in the use of proverbial language. He cites a few examples from some lesser-known regional authors before studying the use and function of Polish proverbs and proverbial expressions in the novels of Eliza Orzeszkowa (1841–1910). Klosinski points out that Orzeszkowa often uses the proverbs in a dialect form to add local color to the speech of her characters. Many of them express stereotypical views which indicate the worldview of the peasants. Many examples are cited in their literary context, and Klosinski also refers to some Belorussian proverbs which Orzeszkowa used in her novels.

3693. Knoblauch, Johann. "Wandel einer Redensart." *Der Sprachdienst*, 28 (1984), 132.

This is but a short yet interesting note on a modern Austrian variant of the Biblical proverbial expression "Mein Name ist Legion, denn wir sind viele" (My name is Legion, for we are many; Mark 5,9). In 1984 a journalist had exchanged the word "Legion" through "Legende" (legend), probably because people don't know the meaning of the Biblical (Roman) word signifying 3000 soldiers any more. Besides, the reference to legend makes the particular statement appear even more "magical." Knoblauch also cites an anonymous reference from the 14th century and two literary uses of it by Christoph Martin Wieland (1733–1813) and Heinrich Laube (1806–1884).

3694. Knoppers, Laura Lunger. "'Sung and Proverb'd for a Fool': *Samson Agonistes* and Solomon's Harlot." *Milton Studies*, 26 (1991), 239–251.

   The author builds a convincing argument that John Milton (1608–1674) must have made use of the seventh chapter of the Biblical Book of Proverbs in his description of Dalila as a harlot in his *Samson Agonistes* (1671). She refers to the recurrent references in this work to examples, proverbs, wisdom, and folly that are based on Solomon's characterization of a harlot. Samson himself even asks "Tell me, Friends, / Am I not sung and proverb'd for a Fool / In every street?" It appears that Milton wants to convince his readers through this "proverbial" language that it is female sexuality that has brought Samson to blindness and imprisonment, and that it is Dalila that represents a subversive threat to family, state, and religion—a threat that must be countered by male wisdom and authority. But Milton deconstructs the discourse of the Biblical harlot, arguing in fact that only divine wisdom provides the solution to the threat of foolishness and harlotry. See also D.M. Rosenberg (no. 4274).

3695. Knops, Mathieu. "*Das Sprichwort, Man musz entweder ein König, oder aber ein Narr geborn werden. Außgeleget vnd beschrieben von Herrn Erasmo Roterodamo, von den Tugenden einem Christlichen Fürsten vnd Herren zuständig, verdeutschet. Anno 1638.*" *Erasmus und Europa: Vorträge.* Ed. August Buck. Wiesbaden: Otto Harrassowitz, 1988. 149–161.

   This is a scholarly treatise on the editorial history of the classical proverb "Aut regem, aut fatuum nasci oportet" (Kings and fools are born, not made) in Erasmus of Rotterdam's (1469–1536) various expanded editions of the *Adagia* (1500ff.). The author makes clear how Erasmus used classical Greek and Latin sources, and how his philological comments are augmented by personal views concerning politics and government. But Knops also points out that Georg Spalatin (1482–1545) published a German translation of the explanatory essay on this proverb by Erasmus with the German title *Das Sprichwort, Man muß entwer ein konig oder aber ein narr geborn werden* (1520). This translation was printed anonymously again in 1638 with the title as it is stated in

Knops' own title to this study above. The author includes many
detailed comments on the two German editions, and he also
attaches a helpful bibliography (pp. 157–161).

3696. Koch, Ernst. "Agricola, Johann (Schneyder, Sneider, Schnitter)."
Die deutsche Literatur. Biographisches und bibliographisches Lexikon.
2nd series. *Die deutsche Literatur zwischen 1450 und 1620.* Ed. Hans-
Gert Roloff. Bern: Peter Lang, 1985. 453–480 (6th fascicle). Bern:
Peter Lang, 1990. 481–496 (7th fascicle).

This unique lexicon article on the religious and
paremiographical writings of Johann Agricola (1494–1566)
begins with an informative sketch of Agricola's life and works
(pp. 453–460), including an analysis of his relationship with
Martin Luther (1483–1546) and the Reformation movement as
well as comments on his proverb collections, notably the
Sybenhundert und fünfftzig Teütscher Sprichwörter (1534) and the
Fünfhundert Gemainer Newer Teütscher Sprüchwörter (1548). Koch
includes a complete bibliography (pp. 461–470) with exact titles
of the various editions of Agricola's proverb collections (pp. 463–
465). The rest of the article (pp. 470–496) presents
reproductions of every title page of Agricola's pamphlets and
books. There are alone 20 title illustrations (pp. 481–485) of the
editions of his proverb collections. Altogether these materials
represent a very reliable account of Agricola's religious, didactic,
and paremiographical publications. With 3 illustrations of
Agricola. See also Sander Gilman (no. 528), Heinz-Dieter Grau
(no. 577), and Mathilde Hain (no. 644).

3697. Koelb, Clayton. "*In der Strafkolonie*: Kafka and the Scene of
Reading." *German Quarterly,* 55 (1982), 511–525.

An interesting interpretation of Franz Kafka's (1883–1924)
story *In der Strafkolonie* (*In the Penal Colony* [1919]) by pointing out
that it reflects Kafka's common procedure to take a linguistic
commonplace, a piece of what has been called endoxal
knowledge, and develop a story out of a literal reading of the
topos. The German proverbial expression underlying this story is
"Etwas am eigenen Leibe erfahren" (To experience or feel
something for oneself), but the proverb "Wer nicht hören will,

muß fühlen" (He who refuses to hear, must feel) might also have been a possible starting point. The expressions become a text to be read, a scenario to be acted out in the fictional narrative.

3698. Kohn, Alfie. "You Know What They Say . . . Are Proverbs Nuggets of Truth or Fool's Gold?" *Psychology Today*, 22, no. 4 (1988), 36–41.

This is a somewhat popular magazine article on whether certain proverbs are in fact true. The author starts her observations with the statement that most proverbial "truisms" contain at best a hit-and-miss element of truth. She then quotes and discusses some of the most common English proverbs, notably "Spare the rod and spoil the child," "The squeaky wheel gets the grease," "Actions speak louder than words," "Beauty is only skin deep," "Marry in haste, repent at leisure," "Absence makes the heart grow fonder," "Birds of a feather flock together," etc. In each case Kohn presents a specific situation in which the proverb has no or only partial validity. What is wrong with this approach is, of course, that the author forgets that proverbs are never "universal" truths and that their wisdom and validity always depend on the context. With 5 illustrations.

3699. Kokare, Elza. "Latviesu sakamvardu un parunu publicesana un petisana (lidz 1940. g.)." *Krisjana Barona Pieminai*. Eds. H. Bendiks, V. Greble, and E. Kokare. Riga: Latvijas PSR Zinatnu Akademijas Izdevnieciba, 1962. 100–129 (=*Valodas un Literaturas Instituta Raksti, Latvian SSR*, 15 [1962], 100–129).

Kokare presents a detailed survey of the collections and studies of Latvian proverbs and proverbial expressions. She discusses the methodologies of collecting, archiving, classifying, and publishing proverbs. Next she describes various Latvian proverb collections from the 17th century to about 1940, commenting on their content and classification system. She also explains that early collections were assembled by German missionaries who used proverbs to be able to communicate through traditional language with the native population. It is shown that Latvian folklorists and linguists have done a great amount of ethnographical field research to establish solid proverb collections of the Latvian language. The 134 notes contain rich bibliographical information. With 1 illustration.

3700. Kokare, Elza. "Liviesu un latviesu sakamvardu paraleles." *Latvijas PSR Zinatnu Akademijas Vestis*, no. 10 (1988), 32–40.

This is a comparative study of Livonian and Latvian parallel proverbs. It is argued that if such equivalent proverbs exist at all between these two languages, they are usually internationally disseminated proverbs dating back to classical and Biblical times. However, some of the common proverbs found in Livonian and Latvian might also be based on more recent loan translations from the German. There are in addition very close contacts between the people speaking these languages, and some borrowing must also have gone on just from one language to another. Several examples are discussed in much detail, and a Russian abstract (p. 40) is provided as well.

3701. Koller, Werner. "Die einfachen Wahrheiten der Redensarten." *Sprache und Literatur in Wissenschaft und Unterricht*, 16, no. 56 (1985), 26–36.

Koller starts his article with 10 contextualized proverbs and proverbial expressions which he found in German newspapers, magazines, and advertisements. He then offers a definition for such phraseological units and discusses their style, language, form, classification, etc. The major part of the paper deals with the function of fixed phrases, with special emphasis on their use for the purpose of communicating projection, simplification, explanation, and authority. Koller also comments on the fact that these "einfache Wahrheiten" (simple truths) play a major role in oral and written communication, including literary works by modern German authors like Franz Xaver Kroetz (1946–) who amasses them in his play *Nicht Fisch Nicht Fleisch* (1985). A short bibliography (pp. 35–36) is attached.

3702. Koller, Werner. "Überlegungen zu einem Phraseologie-Wörterbuch für Fremdsprachenunterricht und Übersetzungspraxis." *Aktuelle Probleme der Phraseologie.* Eds. Harald Burger and Robert Zett. Bern: Peter Lang, 1987. 109–120.

The author laments the fact that there are not good enough phraseological dictionaries available for the purpose of teaching foreign languages and to help translators. He argues that such dictionaries of fixed phrases need to be based on frequency studies so that the most important texts will become part of the active vocabulary of the language learner. The entries in this type of dictionary should include contextualized examples, statements concerning the syntax and style of the expressions, as well as comparative notes and equivalent phrases from the target language. Koller exemplifies these points by a detailed presentation of the German proverbial expression "Die Hosen anhaben" (To wear the breeches) for Norwegian learners of the German language.

3703. Koltakov, S.A. "Poslovitsy i pogovorki v romane M.A. Sholokhova *Tikhii Don*." *Russkii iazyk v shkole*, no. 1 (1987), 50–55.

This is a short literary investigation of the use and function of proverbs and proverbial expressions in M.A. Sholokhov's (1905–1984) large novel *Tikhii Don* (1928/40). It is pointed out that Sholokhov is a frequent user of proverbial language both in the speech of his characters and in his narrative passages. The article discusses several contextualized examples, but Koltakov pays particular attention to various forms of introductory formulas which signal the quotation of a proverb. The article clearly illustrates the saturation of Russian prose fiction with proverbial speech, but Koltakov has not provided a proverb index as such.

3704. Kopperschmidt, Josef. "'Lieber theorielos als leblos': Anmerkungen zur Sprüchekultur." *Muttersprache*, 97 (1987), 129–144.

The author attempts to analyze the so-called "Sprüchekultur" (culture of slogans, graffiti, etc.) which has become extremely popular in Germany. He reviews previous scholarship on graffiti and discusses these slogans and drawings on walls as an aesthetic expression not only of the youth culture but of modern humankind in general. Kopperschmidt sees this mode of expression as a significant tool of communication, and it is certainly of importance that socio- and psycholinguists, folklorists, and even paremiologists study these texts. Many German examples are cited, and it can be seen that quite a large number is based on the structures of proverbs and literary quotations. Most of them express alienation or frustration with the status quo, but there are also those texts that appear to be nonsense or simply innovative wordplay with traditional patterns. Many of these graffiti are parodied proverbs or "Antisprichwörter" (anti-proverbs). A valuable bibliography (pp. 143–144) of graffiti collections and studies of this linguistic and artistic medium is attached.

3705.   Kordas, Bronislawa. "Quelques problèmes concernant la notion de proverbe en chinois moderne." *Richesse du proverbe.* Eds. François Suard and Claude Buridant. Lille: Université de Lille, 1984. II, 107–113.

In this short article Kordas states that the modern Chinese language also differentiates between proverbs and proverbial expressions. She explains that there is a distinct difference between written texts and those that are expressed orally. The former are actually more sententious remarks than proverbs, usually going back to classical Chinese literature. Proverbs often are introduced with so-called "introductory formulas," but they can also be recognized by their brevity, binary structure, metaphor, and figurative meaning. A few examples are cited in transliterated Chinese with French translations. For a more detailed study of the proverbs in modern Chinese see Bronislawa Kordas below (no. 3706).

3706.   Kordas, Bronislawa. *Le proverbe en chinois moderne.* Taipei/Taiwan: Editions Ouyu, 1987. 263 pp.

This is a significant study of modern Chinese proverbs. In the first part (pp. 13–110) Kordas reviews French, Polish and Russian scholarship on the proverb (pp. 13–43) before concentrating on a detailed analysis of Chinese paremiology (pp. 44–110). It is here where she also deals with such matters as translation difficulties, metaphor, structure, content, and origin of Chinese proverbs. In the second part (pp. 113–240) the author presents large sections on the rhyme, assonance, alliteration, and parallelism (metric, phonetic, syntactical, and semantic) of many Chinese proverbs. The examples are cited in the Chinese original with transliterations and French translations. An index of transliterated texts (pp. 245–251) and a valuable bibliography (pp. 252–260) are included, making this a welcome introductory study to the rich field of Chinese proverbs as used in the modern age.

3707. Kordas, Bronislawa. "The Poetic Function and the Oral Transmission of Chinese Proverbs." *Chinoperl Papers*, no. 15 (1990), 85–94.

The author investigates linguistic criteria that help Chinese speakers to remember the wisdom of proverbs. It is pointed out that many proverbs contain rhyme, assonance, and alliteration. In addition to these poetic elements they are also quite often based on the recurrence of certain sounds and on the repetition of particular words. Such aspects help with the memorization of the proverbs which enables native speakers to transmit these traditional bits of wisdom orally. Kordas cites ten Chinese examples together with transliterations and English translations. Diagrams are added to show such structural patterns as parallelism, and the author also provides a short bibliography (p. 94).

3708. Korhonen, Jarmo (ed.). *Beiträge zur allgemeinen und germanistischen Phraseologieforschung. Internationales Symposium in Oulu 13.-15. Juni 1986.* Oulu: Oulun Yliopisto, 1987. 255 pp.

This essay volume is a collection of 16 papers on general and German phraseology which were given at a symposium in 1986 in Oulu, Finland. The authors and their respective essay titles are as follows: Jarmo Korhonen, "Überlegungen zum Forschungsprojekt 'Kontrastive Verbidiomatik Deutsch-Finnisch'" (pp. 1–22); Hans Schemann, "Was heißt 'Fixiertheit' von phraseologischen oder idiomatischen Ausdrücken?" (pp. 23–36); Rainer Eckert, "Synchronische und diachronische Phraseologieforschung" (pp. 37–50); Wolfgang Fleischer, "Zur funktionalen Differenzierung von Phraseologismen in der deutschen Gegenwartssprache" (pp. 51–63); Harald Burger, "Normative Aspekte der Phraseologie" (pp. 65–89); Astrid Stedje, "Sprecherstrategien im Spiegel der Phraseologie" (pp. 91–109); Markhu Kantola, "Zum phraseologischen Wortpaar in der deutschen Gegenwartssprache" (pp. 111–128); Klaus Dieter Pilz, "Allgemeine und phraseologische Wörterbücher. Brauchen wir überhaupt phraseologische Wörterbücher?" (pp. 129–153); Günter Kempcke, "Theoretische und praktische Probleme der Phraseologiedarstellung in einem synchronischen einsprachigen Bedeutungswörterbuch" (pp. 155–164); Anne Lise Kjaer, "Zur Darbietung von Phraseologismen in einsprachigen Wörterbüchern des Deutschen aus der Sicht ausländischer Textproduzenten" (pp. 165–181); Hans-Peder Kromann, "Zur Typologie und Darbietung der Phraseologismen in Übersetzungswörterbüchern" (pp. 183–192); Gertrud Gréciano, "Idiom und sprachspielerische Textkonstitution" (pp. 193–206); Karlheinz Daniels, "Text- und autorenspezifische Phraseologismen, am Beispiel von Erich Kästners Roman *Fabian*" (pp. 207–219); Christine Palm, "Christian Morgensterns groteske Phraseologie—ein Beitrag zur Rolle der Phraseologismen im literarischen Text" (pp. 221–235); Christiane Pankow and Olli Salminen, "Routineformeln im finnisch-deutschen Spracherwerb—eine Forschungsaufgabe" (pp. 237–243); and Ingrid Schellbach-Kopra, "Parömisches Minimum und Phraseodidaktik im finnisch-deutschen Bereich" (pp. 245–255). These important essays deal with various aspects of phraseological units, especially idiomaticity, fixidity, synchronic and diachronic phraseology, function, speech act, twin formula, phraseological dictionaries, translation, wordplay, literature, routine formula, paremiological minimum, and foreign language instruction (the teaching of German phraseology in Finland). For specific annotations see nos. 3709, 4325, 3355, 3407, 3186, 4428, 3662, 4178, 3670, 3684, 3734, 3506, 3285, 4107, 4320.

3709. Korhonen, Jarmo. "Überlegungen zum Forschungsprojekt 'Kontrastive Verbidiomatik Deutsch-Finnisch'." *Beiträge zur allgemeinen und germanistischen Phraseologieforschung.* Ed. J. Korhonen. Oulu: Oulun Yliopisto, 1987. 1–22.

The author starts with a review of German-Finnish dictionaries and their treatment of phraseological units, concluding that much more comparative work needs to be done to improve such dictionaries for translators as well as teachers and learners of German as a foreign language. He also reports on the creation of a research project at the University of Oulu in Finland to improve this situation at least for verbal phraseological units. Korhonen presents a structural analysis of such fixed phrases, citing German examples with Finnish equivalents. A valuable bibliography (pp. 18–22) is attached.

3710. Korhonen, Jarmo. "Valenz und kontrastive Phraseologie. Am Beispiel deutscher und finnischer Verbidiome." *Valenzen im Kontrast. Ulrich Engel zum 60. Geburtstag.* Eds. Pavica Mrazovic and Wolfgang Teubert. Heidelberg: Julius Groos, 1988. 200–217.

This is a second report (see no. 3709 above) on the Finnish research project at the University of Oulu whose goal it is to establish a comparison between the verbal phraseological units of the German and Finnish languages. This time Korhonen shows in particular that the complex valences of such fixed phrases create great difficulties for the translator as well as the instructor and student of foreign languages. Korhonen analyzes the content, structure, and meaning of numerous examples, indicating the linguistic problem that arises when one particular idiom or proverbial expression has more than one equivalents in the target language. A short bibliography (p. 217) is provided.

3711. Korhonen, Jarmo. "Valenz und Verbidiomatik." *Linguistische Studien,* series A, Arbeitsberichte, no. 180 (1988), 105–118.

This is a third article (see nos. 3709–3710 above) on German and Finnish verbal phraseological units, but this time Korhonen investigates in particular the different valences that result due to certain prepositions and nouns. Some of these fixed phrases can take either the dative or the accusative case that result in different structural and syntactical forms. The author also touches on classification problems, and he once again deals with the difficulty of finding equivalent idioms in the target language.

Many Finnish and German examples are cited, and a useful bibliography (pp. 116–118) is included as well.

3712. Korhonen, Jarmo. "Zur syntaktischen Negationskomponente in deutschen und finnischen Verbidiomen." *Europhras 88. Phraséologie Contrastive. Actes du Colloque International Klingenthal-Strasbourg, 12–16 mai 1988.* Ed. Gertrud Gréciano. Strasbourg: Université des Sciences Humaines, 1989. 253–264.

Basing his remarks once again on a comparative analysis of Finnish and German verbal phraseological units, Korhonen investigates the various forms of negation in these fixed phrases. He points out that idioms are negated by means of prefixes, adverbs, pronouns, conjunctions, etc. He cites numerous German and Finnish examples and then compares equivalent expressions from both languages. The author reaches the conclusion that the German proverbial expressions exhibit a more varied way of negation which has important effects on the lexicographical and syntactical classification of these negative phrases in dictionaries. There are also important implications for the teacher and student of Finnish or German as a foreign language. A helpful bibliography (pp. 262–264) is attached.

3713. Korhonen, Jarmo. "Zur Negation in deutschen und finnischen Verbidiomen." *Zeitschrift für Phonetik, Sprachwissenschaft und Kommunikationsforschung,* 43 (1990), 3–17.

This is but a slightly expanded version of the previous article (see no. 3712), once again investigating German and Finnish verbal phraseological units which contain a negation element in the form of a prefix, adverb, pronoun, conjunction, etc. It is shown that German is much more varied and flexible than Finnish in such negated fixed phrases, and that creates difficulties for the translator as well as the teacher and learner of German or Finnish as a foreign language. Korhonen also explains that there are only very few exact equivalents of negative idioms in these two languages. Most of them have only partial equivalents in the other language, and the differences are morphological, syntactical, and lexical in nature. With a useful bibliography (pp. 16–17) and an English summary (p. 3).

3714. Korhonen, Jarmo. "Zur Syntax und Semantik von Satzidiomen im heutigen Deutsch." *Proceedings of the Fourteenth International Congress of Linguistics, Berlin (GDR), August 10–15, 1987.* Eds. Werner Bahner, Joachim Schildt, and Dieter Viehweger. Berlin: Akademie-Verlag, 1990. II, 980–982.

The author presents a few comments regarding the syntax and semantics of phrasal idioms in modern German. Citing numerous examples, he explains that such phraseological units are not at all treated with much uniformity in dictionaries. While one dictionary might list a certain fixed phrase in the infinitive form, another dictionary might cite it in the third person singular, and yet a third dictionary might register it in the imperative. In addition to such syntactical differences there are, of course, also the semantic variations which depend on the mode of communication, the function, and the context. Korhonen is quite correct in drawing attention to the fact that idioms and proverbial expressions are not as rigidly fixed as earlier research had claimed. In fact, there is plenty of variability which negates the overemphasis of the stability of fixed phrases.

3715. Korhonen, Jarmo. "Zu Verbphrasemen in Zeitungstexten des frühen 17. Jahrhunderts." *Neuere Forschungen zur historischen Syntax des Deutschen. Referate der Internationalen Fachkonferenz Eichstätt 1989.* Eds. Anne Betten and Claudia M. Riehl. Tübingen: Max Niemeyer, 1990. 253–268.

In this interesting article Korhonen investigates the use and function of 45 verbal phraseological units and their variants which he found in several issues of the two weekly German newspapers *Aviso* and *Relation* from the year 1609. The author discusses problems of identification and classification of these older fixed phrases, and he also analyzes their structure, syntax, and function in early journalistic contexts. This diachronic and linguistic study is of importance for an understanding of the continued and frequent use of proverbial expressions in the modern mass media. A useful bibliography (pp. 266–268) is attached.

3716.   Korhonen, Jarmo. "Kontrastive Verbidiomatik Deutsch-Finnisch. Ein Forschungsbericht." *Sprichwörter und Redensarten im interkulturellen Vergleich.* Eds. Annette Sabban and Jan Wirrer. Opladen: Westdeutscher Verlag, 1991. 37–65.

The author presents an impressive review of the work that has been accomplished by a team of phraseologists at the University of Oulu in Finland, of which Korhonen has been the director for a number of years. The special focus of this research is on the verbal phraseological units of the German and Finnish languages, and the team has compared more than 2000 German fixed phrases with their Finnish equivalents. In several sections of this paper Korhonen discusses problems of lexicography, syntax, lexicology, semantics, equivalency, occurrence, translatability, and history. Numerous German examples with at times more than one Finnish equivalent are analyzed, and Korhonen also states that a comparative dictionary of German-Finnish idioms will be published in due time. A valuable bibliography (pp. 62–65) is included.

3717.   Korhonen, Jarmo. "Konvergenz und Divergenz in deutscher und finnischer Phraseologie. Zugleich ein Beitrag zur Erläuterung der Verbreitung und Entlehnung von Idiomen." *Europhras 90. Akten der internationalen Tagung zur germanistischen Phraseologieforschung Aske/Schweden, 12.-15. Juni 1990.* Ed. Christine Palm. Uppsala: Acta Universitatis Upsaliensis, 1991. 123–137.

It is stated correctly that comparative phraseological studies of several languages have primarily been restricted to proverbs and not proverbial expressions. For this reason Korhonen investigates here the various equivalents of fixed phrases from nine European languages, namely Finnish, German, French, Italian, English, Swedish, Russian, Hungarian, and Estonian. He is able to show that the German proverbial expression "Mit dem Feuer spielen" (To play with fire) has precise parallels in the other eight languages. This he calls complete or total convergence, in which the metaphorical, semantic, lexical, and syntactical aspects are absolutely identical. As can be imagined, this type of agreement is rather rare, and a so-called partial convergence is much more common. However, as is indicated from additional examples, there is also a definite divergence among idioms of these languages. The most extreme case is when there are no equivalents for a particular expression at all in any language due to its cultural and linguistic uniqueness. A number of examples are discussed, and the author also provides a useful bibliography (pp. 134–137).

3718. Korhonen, Jarmo. "Zur (Un-)Verständlichkeit der lexikographischen Darstellung von Phraseologismen." *Budalex'88 Proceedings. Papers from the Eurolex Third International Congress Budapest, 4–9 September 1988.* No ed. given. Budapest: Akademiai Kiado, 1991. 197–206.

In this article Korhonen points out that most dictionaries do not at all present the reader, especially someone studying a foreign language, with clear explanations concerning the morphology, syntax, style, and meaning of the phraseological units. He cites several examples out of German dictionaries which indicate this confused state of affairs. Linguists and especially lexicographers need much more consistency in registering fixed phrases and their equivalents in the target language. If they do not include more precise information, then such dictionaries are of little use as far as metaphorical language is concerned. A bibliography (pp. 205–206) is attached.

3719. Korzyn, Waclawa Maria. "Religijnosc ludu rosyjskiego w swietle przyslow." *Dzielo chrystianizacji rusi kijowskiej.* Ed. Ryszard Luzny. Lublin: Redakcja Wydawnictw Katolickiego Uniwersytetu Lubelskiego, 1988. 159–173.

Korzyn investigates the religiousness of the Russian folk as expressed in its proverbs. It is argued that the Christian faith plays a major role in traditional proverbs that express a definite religious worldview. The author divides her many examples into three major groups: (1) proverbs dealing with God, (2) proverbs referring to elements of faith, and (3) proverbs that contain the word "church" in them. It is shown that such religious proverbs express the continued dependence and reliance on religion by the people of the Slavic cultures. With a Russian abstract (p. 419).

3720. Kostov, Marta. "Feste Vergleiche im Bulgarischen." *Linguistische Studien*, series A, Arbeitsberichte, no. 95 (1982), 121–142.

The author starts with a short discussion of the definition and different terminologies for proverbial comparisons. She then investigates the use of metaphors in Bulgarian examples, and she also points out that some proverbs include comparative statements. Her special interest is directed towards the structure of proverbial comparisons, and she discusses the use of certain conjunctions, adjectives, adverbs, verbs, and nouns in these fixed phrases. At the end of the article Kostov also includes some comments on stylistic peculiarities and the content of such phraseological units. A small bibliography (pp. 141–142) is attached.

3721. Kostov, Marta. "Vergleiche im Roman *Unter dem Joch* von Ivan Vazov in konfrontativer Betrachtung ihrer deutschen und russischen Wiedergabe." *Linguistische Studien*, series A, Arbeitsberichte, no. 120 (1984), 138–174.

Kostov presents a detailed analysis of the use and function of proverbial comparisons in Ivan Vazov's (1850–1921) Bulgarian novel *Pod igoto* ([1894]; German translation with the title *Unter dem Joch* [1918]). She states that Vazov was very interested in proverbial folk speech and that he amassed his writings with such colloquial language. The article shows in particular how German and Russian translators have dealt with the difficulty of translating the many proverbial comparisons. For most of them there exist complete or at least partial equivalents of the Bulgarian texts, but for others the translators had to find comparisons in the target languages that at least come close in image and meaning to the originals. A useful bibliography (pp. 171–174) is provided.

3722. Kostov, Marta, and Veselin Vapordzhiev. *Die Phraseologie der bulgarischen Sprache. Ein Handbuch.* Leipzig: VEB Verlag Enzyklopädie, 1990. 127 pp.

The two authors present a valuable study of the whole field of Bulgarian phraseology. Chapter one (pp. 7–27) treats the history of phraseological research not only in Bulgaria but in the

Balkan countries as well. The second chapter (pp. 28–44) deals with classification problems of fixed phrases, while chapter three (pp. 45–58) covers the structural differences among proverbs, proverbial expressions and comparisons, "geflügelte Worte (literary quotations), twin formulas, etc. The fourth chapter (pp. 59–74) is dedicated to a special treatise of twin formulas, and the fifth chapter (pp. 75–87) concerns itself with the difficulty of translating idioms and phrases. Chapter six (pp. 88–99) investigates the use and function of proverbial comparisons in Ivan Vazov's (1850–1921) Bulgarian novel *Pod igoto* ([1894], German translation with the title *Unter dem Joch* [1918]) and their translation into German (see Kostov's article above, no. 3721). The final seventh chapter (pp. 100–116) studies lexicographical problems of including phraseological units in Bulgarian and foreign language dictionaries. Throughout the book many Bulgarian examples are cited with German translations. There are two diagrams and tables, and an important bibliography (pp. 117–127) is included as well.

3723. Kramer, Günter. "Bildhafte Ausdrücke als lexikalische Einheiten mit ausgestalteter Konnotation." *Beiträge zur Erforschung der deutschen Sprache*, 6 (1986), 291–302.

A linguistic analysis of German phraseological units and their various connotations. Kramer discusses the stability of such fixed phrases and explains that many of them are either verbal or nominal expressions with certain images. He then discusses in particular structural and semantic aspects of many German examples, always explaining how each expression has taken on a definite metaphorical meaning. One of his best set of examples are numerous texts that revolve around the German noun "Ohr" (ear). Kramer also deals with the problems that such phrases present for lexicographers of language dictionaries, especially regarding those phrases whose metaphors are not understood any longer today. A small bibliography (pp. 301–302) is attached.

3724. Kramer, Samuel Noah. "Proverbs." *Sumerian Literary Texts in the Ashmolean Museum*. Eds. Oliver H. Gurney and S.N. Kramer. Oxford: Clarendon Press, 1976. 36–41.

Kramer presents 14 carefully transliterated Sumerian proverbs which are found on a cuneiform tablet in the Ashmolean Museum in Oxford/Great Britain. These are clearly some of the very earliest recorded proverbs, and they include some hitherto unknown sayings. The edition of this small proverb collection helps to restore and classify some of the published versions that have remained fragmentary and obscure until now. The author includes detailed philological, cultural, and historical comments, referring to the important previous scholarship on Sumerian proverbs. With 2 plates. See also Bendt Alster (nos. 27–28 and 3049–3055), Edmund Gordon (nos. 550–556), and S.N. Kramer (no. 911).

3725. Kramer, Wolfgang. "Über Phraseologismen in Artikeln des *Niedersächsischen Wörterbuchs.*" *Niedersächsisches Wörterbuch. Berichte und Mitteilungen aus der Arbeitsstelle.* Ed. Dieter Stellmacher. Göttingen: Vandenhoeck & Ruprecht, 1990. 33–51.

This article deals with the lexicographical problems of registering phraseological units in a multi-volume dialect dictionary of Low German. Kramer starts with a definition of phraseology and then makes a few short observations concerning such genres as routine formula, proverb, proverbial expression, proverbial comparison, wellerism, weather proverb, etc. Next he shows how the rich phraseological materials for the noun "Bur" (farmer) have been organized in the *Niedersächsisches Wörterbuch* (1953ff.) which lists a total of 520 texts chosen from 1350 items in the archive of this dictionary project. In a second part of the article (pp. 41–51) Kramer also concerns himself with the lexicographical difficulties that arise due to names for months, animals, and places. It is argued that lexicographers should establish a certain logical order of listing phraseological and onomastic texts that will enable readers to locate them without too much difficulty.

3726. Krawczyk-Tyrpa, Anna. *Frazeologia somatyczna w gwarach polskich. Związki frazeologiczne o znaczeniach motywowanych cechami cześci ciala.* Wroclaw: Zaklad Narodowy imenia Ossolinskich Wydawnictwo Polskiej Akademii Nauk, 1987. 270 pp.

This is a major study of Polish phraseological units that refer to various body parts. In chapter one (pp. 12–44) the author points out that somatic phraseology is an international phenomenon which should be studied historically and comparatively to understand this obvious preoccupation with the human body. The large second chapter (pp. 45–160) investigates the content, meaning, function, form, and structure of Polish somatic phrases, always citing numerous examples to underscore the high frequency of such expressions in oral and written communication. Chapter three (pp. 161–180) includes several statistical tables and graphs concerning the frequency of such nouns as "head," "hand," "foot," etc. A few summarizing comments (pp. 181–183), a large collection of somatic phrases (pp. 184–260), and a valuable bibliography (pp. 261–270) conclude this important investigation on how the human body is represented in the metaphors of Polish proverbial speech.

3727. Krikmann, Arvo. "Grigorii Permjakovi folkloristlikust pärandist." *Keel ja Kirjandus*, 27, no. 6 (1984), 364–366.

   In this short obituary Arvo Krikmann reviews the life and work of the Soviet scholar Grigorii L'vovich Permiakov (1919–1983). He explains that Permiakov had a very difficult existence due to a terrible war injury, but that he continued his important folkloristic, linguistic, structural, and semiotic work on proverbs in particular in Moscow. Krikmann includes short comments on the most important Russian publications by Permiakov, and he most certainly is correct in praising him for his lasting accomplishments in both paremiography and paremiology. For Permiakov's many books and articles see nos. 1424–1433, 2737, and 4145–4155).

3728. Krikmann, Arvo. "On Denotative Indefiniteness of Proverbs." *Proverbium*, 1 (1984), 47–91.

   This is a reprint of Krikmann's extremely important paper originally published in 1974 in Tallinn, Estonia, that was distributed in only small numbers as a pamphlet (see no. 923). Krikmann offers a theoretical discussion of three approaches to the semantics of proverbs, namely the "purely semantical" (virtual, context-free) mode, the "pragmatico-semantical" (actual, context-bound) mode, and the "syntactico-semantical" mode. It is argued that the semantic indeterminacy of proverbs springs first and foremost from the ambiguity of proverbial tropes (metaphors, images, allegories, etc.). The author also offers detailed linguistic analyses of two important phenomena in proverb meaning: the "absolute sum" of all possible meanings of a given text (i.e. its potentiality of interpretability) and the sum of its real meanings manifested in all of its actualizations up to the present moment. Many comprehensive notes and a bibliography (pp. 88–91) are also provided. The original publication contains a long Russian summary (pp. 41–48). See also no. 3731 below.

3729. Krikmann, Arvo. "Opyt ob'iasneniia nekotorykh semanticheskikh mekhanizmov poslovitsy." *Paremiologicheskie issledovaniia.* Ed. Grigorii L'vovich Permiakov. Moskva: Nauka, 1984. 149–178; also in French translation as "'Mécanismes sémantiques' de l'énoncé proverbiale" in *Tel grain tel pain. Poétique de la sagesse populaire.* Ed. G.L. Permioakov. Moscou: Éditions du Progrès, 1988. 82–113.

Final publication of a significant paper which Arvo Krikmann, the leading Eastonian paremiologist, wrote in the middle of the seventies. The article deals with certain peculiarities of the semantic mechanisms of the proverb, especially those that are derived from the principle of anthropocentricity typical of the proverb. The first part deals with some general characteristics which permit recognition of the proverb text in the speech act, namely (1) euphonic organization of the text, (2) generalizing nature of the statement, (3) syntactical-morphological symmetry, and (4) necessity to alter all or some of the literal "textual" meanings of the text elements into "actually meant" poetical meanings. Attention is also drawn to the necessity of taking into account both paradigmatic and syntagmatic aspects in the semantic analysis of proverbs. Many Estonian examples are included, but at the end Krikmann offers detailed semantic analyses of the two Estonian proverbs "Loodetuul on taeva luud" (North-westerly winds are the brooms of the sky) and "Haukuja koer ei hammusta" (A barking dog does not bite). Four diagrams and a short bibliography (pp. 177–178) are included.

3730. Krikmann, Arvo. "1001 Frage zur logischen Struktur der Sprichwörter." *Semiotische Studien zum Sprichwort. Simple Forms Reconsidered I.* Eds. Peter Grzybek and Wolfgang Eismann. Tübingen: Gunter Narr, 1984. 387–408.

A complex theoretical article on the logical structure of proverbs. Krikmann starts with a splendid review of previous structural analyses by such scholars as Alan Dundes (see no. 378), Zoltán Kanyó (no. 829), Grigorii L'vovich Permiakov (no. 1428), etc., and he then claims that paremiologists must employ the tools of symbolic (mathematical) logic to understand the logical structures of proverbs. Many examples are cited to indicate certain structural patterns, and Krikmann also includes comments on variability, form, content, metaphor, and context. All of these have to be part of an inclusive study of the structure of proverbs that is characterized to a large degree by binary oppositions.

3731. Krikmann, Arvo. "Some Additional Aspects of Semantic Indefiniteness of Proverbs." *Proverbium,* 2 (1985), 58–85.

This is yet another reprint (see no. 3728 above) of a pamphlet which Krikmann published in Tallinn, Estonia, in 1974, but which was disseminated in only very small numbers (see no. 924). Krikmann offers some additional remarks on the indefiniteness of proverbs with an emphasis on the modal (functional, pragmatical) indefiniteness, the indefiniteness of the information-bearing structure of the proverb, and the textual indefinitenss of the proverb as a type. Many examples are cited, and there are once again important notes and a bibliography (pp. 82–85). The original publication has a lengthy Russian summary (pp. 30–35).

3732. Krikmann, Arvo. *Some Statistics on Baltic-Finnic Proverbs.* Tallinn: Academy of Sciences of the Estonian SSR, Division of Social Sciences, 1985. 53 pp.

Part of this mathematical and statistical analysis of Balto-Finnic proverbs has also been published in Matti Kuusi's et al. comparative proverb collection *Proverbia septentrionalia. 900 Balto-Finnic Proverb Types with Russian, Baltic, German and Scandinavian*

Parallels (1985; see pp. 29–36). Taking this superb collection of Finnish, Karelian, Estonian, Vote, Vepsian, and Livonian proverbs as his basis, Krikmann analyzes the interrelationships among these 900 proverb types. He also includes statistical calculations concerning the Russian, Baltic, German, and Scandinavian parallels of the proverbs of these six Balto-Finnic peoples. The first part (pp. 3–30) includes methodological explanations of how to perform such comparative statistical work, and the second part (pp. 31–53) incorporates 16 statistical tables and 13 detailed graphs. The whole study is a model for the "mathematization" of comparative paremiography.

3733. Krohn, Dieter. "Zur emblematischen und idiomatischen Bedeutung von Verben bzw. Syntagmen im Feld der menschlichen Körperteilbewegung." In D. Krohn. *Die Verben der menschlichen Körperteilbewegung im heutigen Deutsch.* Göteborg: Acta Universitatis Gothoburgensis, 1984. 120–146.

In this book chapter on the emblematic and idiomatic meaning of verbs in phraseological units referring to such body parts as head, mouth, nose, hand, finger, etc., Krohn argues that these fixed phrases can only be understood properly if they are studied in the context of a speech act. He cites numerous German examples, indicating that some of them do have a literal and a figurative meaning. The author presents a discussion on the idiomaticity of verbal phrases with special reference to previous linguistic analyses by Harald Burger (see no. 232) and others. Comments on the actual use and significance of these proverbial expressions referring to the human body are also included.

3734. Kromann, Hans-Peder. "Zur Typologie und Darbietung der Phraseologismen in Übersetzungswörterbüchern." *Beiträge zur allgemeinen und germanistischen Phraseologieforschung.* Ed. Jarmo Korhonen. Oulu: Oulun Yliopisto, 1987. 183–192.

Kromann explains that translation or foreign language dictionaries are not at all satisfactory when it comes to the precise lexicographical recording of phraseological units and their equivalents in the target language. After a short discussion of the types of dictionaries available to the translator or the foreign language student, the author analyzes three major types of equivalents of fixed phrases in other languages: identical equivalents, partial equivalents, and those texts for which there are no equivalents in the target language at all. Numerous German examples with Danish equivalents are cited, and 3 diagrams as well as a useful bibliography (pp. 191–192) are included as well.

3735. Kromann, Hans-Peder. "Zur funktionalen Beschreibung von Kollokationen und Phraseologismen in Übersetzungswörterbüchern." *Europhras 88. Phraséologie Contrastive. Actes du Colloque International Klingenthal-Strasbourg, 12–16 mai 1988.* Ed. Gertrud Gréciano. Strasbourg: Université des Sciences Humaines, 1989. 265–271.

In this article Kromann deals primarily with the lexicographical difficulty of registering phraseological units in translation or foreign language dictionaries. He argues that a much more systematic approach is necessary in order for translators and foreign language students to be able to find the proper equivalents of such fixed phrases in the target language. The problem is not so great with simple collocations that have no idiomatic meaning, but in the case of metaphorical phrases some definite indications of their meaning, style, use, and function are needed. Kromann cites a few German examples with French equivalents and attaches a small bibliography (p. 271).

3736. Krüger, Sabine. "'Die Ratten verlassen das sinkende Schiff'." In S. Krüger. *Die Figur der Ratte in literarischen Texten: eine Motivstudie.* Frankfurt am Main: Peter Lang, 1989. 103–105.

This is but a short section on the internationally disseminated proverb "Die Ratten verlassen das sinkende Schiff" (The rats are leaving the sinking ship) in a fascinating book on the motif of the rat in literary texts. Krüger cites references from the works of Feodor Mikhailovich Dostoevsky (1821–1881), Albert Camus (1913–1960), Wolfgang Hildesheimer (1916–), Günter Grass (1927–), and Johannes Poethen (1928–). It is shown that this proverbial motif is used in prose fiction, dramatic speech, and in lyric poetry. Quite often the proverb is not cited entirely, but it is only alluded to as a piece of wisdom that is commonly known.

3737. Kucherova, Eleonora. "K otazke vidu v slovesnych frazemach (na ruskom a slovenskom materiali)." *Slavica slovaca*, 20 (1985), 121–131.

This is a linguistic investigation of the grammatical aspect in phraseological units of the Russian and Slovakian languages. Kucherova restricts her comments to verbal phraseological units which exhibit clear differences between perfective and imperfective aspect. She also differentiates among three major characteristics of these fixed phrases, namely the lexical meaning, the general meaning of the figurative expression, and the various grammatical categories used to integrate such expressions into speech acts. For the latter Kucherova presents examples that show changes in person, number, tense, gender, etc. Numerous comparative examples are cited, and a Russian abstract (pp. 130–131) is provided as well.

3738. Kucherova, Eleonora. "K voprosu ob 'ustoichivykh sravneniiakh'." *Recueil linguistique de Bratislava*, 8 (1985), 78–82.

This is a short study of Slovakian proverbial comparisons that starts with a precise definition of this subgenre. Kucherova is particularly interested in the lexicological and structural aspects of such fixed phrases, and she isolates three major aspects in comparisons: the object which is being compared, the object with which it is being compared, and the quality which is being compared. A discussion of the lexicographical problems that these proverbial comparisons present for language dictionaries is also included. Many Slovakian examples are cited, and the author provides some equivalent examples from other Slavic languages.

3739. Kühn, Peter. "Pragmatische und lexikographische Beschreibung phraseologischer Einheiten: Phraseologismen und Routineformeln." *Studien zur neuhochdeutschen Lexikographie*. Ed. Herbert Ernst Wiegand. Hildesheim: Georg Olms, 1984. IV, 175–235.

Significant treatise on lexicographical problems arising from the inclusion of phraseological units in German dictionaries. Kühn starts with a survey of recent theoretical publications on phraseology and then attempts a pragmatic description of various fixed phrases including routine formulas. Next he describes different ways in which phraseological units have been treated by lexicographers and attempts to give guidelines for what information should be included with individual expressions in dictionaries (i.e. meaning, style, etymology, origin, use, etc.). Of particular interest are the two detailed accounts of the chaotic lexicographical treatment of the proverbial expression "Die Hosen anhaben" (To wear the pants or breeches) and the routine formula "Hört! Hört! (Hear! Hear!) in various dictionaries. Useful notes and an important bibliography (pp. 228–235) conclude this study.

3740. Kühn, Peter. "Phraseologismen und ihr semantischer Mehrwert: 'jemandem auf die Finger gucken' in einer Bundestagsrede." *Sprache und Literatur in Wissenschaft und Unterricht,* 16, no. 56 (1985), 37–46.

Kühn argues that while the theoretical discussions concerning the definition and classification of phraseological units by linguists are indeed important, they must not forget to study the actual use, function, and meaning of fixed phrases. In order to present an example, the author examined a political speech by the German politician Willy Brandt (1913–) from the year 1984. In this speech Brandt used the proverbial expressions "Jemandem auf die Finger gucken" (To look on someone's fingers, i.e. To keep a sharp [close] watch [eye] on someone). Kühn gives a very detailed analysis of the multiple meanings of this phrase in this particular context, showing how Brandt used it very effectively to manipulate the opinions of his listeners. A useful bibliography (pp. 45–46) is attached.

3741. Kühn, Peter. "Phraseologismen: Sprachhandlungstheoretische Einordnung und Beschreibung." *Aktuelle Probleme der Phraseologie.* Eds. Harald Burger and Robert Zett. Bern: Peter Lang, 1987. 121–137.

The author argues once again that linguists have not paid enough attention to the actual use of phraseological units in speech acts. To illustrate the importance of such pragmatic aspects, Kühn investigates the use of the German proverbial expression "Sich etwas aus dem Kopf schlagen" (To get something out of one's head) in the dramatic context of Carl Zuckmayer's (1896–1977) celebrated play *Der Hauptmann von Köpenick* (1931). After this discussion (pp. 122–128) he also shows how lexicographers have dealt with this phrase in various German dictionaries, and on p. 134 he presents a model for how dictionaries should register such fixed phrases. A useful bibliography (pp. 136–137) is included.

3742. Kühn, Peter. "Routine-Joker in politischen Fernsehdiskussionen. Plädoyer für eine textsortenabhängige Beschreibung von Phraseologismen." *Beiträge zur Phraseologie des Ungarischen und des Deutschen.* Ed. Regina Hessky. Budapest: Loránd-Eötvös-Universität, 1988. 155–176.

This is a clear presentation of the fact that phraseological units need to be studied with particular attention being paid to the types of texts (literature, newspaper, magazine, television, advertising, etc.) in which they are being contextualized. It is argued that the use, function, and meaning of fixed phrases very much depend on the context. Kühn illustrates this by a detailed analysis of a transcribed political discussion (pp. 163–166) that was aired on German television in 1983. He isolates various routine formulas in this text and shows how they are being used as argumentative fixed phrases to state certain points more convincingly. A valuable bibliography (pp. 175–176) is provided as well.

3743. Kühn, Peter, and Ulrich Püschel. "Die deutsche Lexikographie vom 17. Jahrhundert bis zu den Brüdern Grimm." *Wörterbücher. Ein internationales Handbuch zur Lexikographie.* Eds. Franz Josef Hausmann, Oskar Reichmann, Herbert Ernst Wiegand, and Ladislav Zgusta. Berlin: Walter de Gruyter, 1990. II, 2049–2077.

This is a major encyclopedia article on German lexicography from the early 17th century to the middle of the 19th century.

Kühn includes a section on "phraseography" (pp. 2064–2066) in which he comments shortly on the German collections of proverbs and proverbial expressions of that period. He refers to Friedrich Petri (or: Peters, 1549–1617), Christoph Lehmann (1568–1638), Georg Philipp Harsdörffer (1607–1658), Justus Georg Schottelius (1612–1676), Johann Michael Sailer (1751–1832), Karl Friedrich Wilhelm Wander (1803–1879), and many others. A few remarks on the classification system of these collections and a reference to dialect proverb collections are included. An invaluable bibliography (pp. 2066–2077) contains dozens of dictionaries and lexicographical studies. See also Wolfgang Mieder (no. 3872).

3744. Kühnert, Helmut, and Anna Wróbel. "Die Rolle des Bildverständnisses bei Phraseologismen im Fremd-sprachenunterricht für Fortgeschrittene." *Jezyki obce w szkole*, 29, no. 2 (1985), 128–134.

The two authors discuss the importance of teaching phraseological units to advanced students in foreign language classes. The most difficult aspect for the students are the images contained in fixed phrases. If there are identical equivalents in the native and target languages, then the students can deal with the metaphors without any difficulty. But with expressions that only have partial or no equivalents the teacher has to provide explanatory comments and carefully planned exercises. The authors include several lists of German proverbial expressions with their Polish equivalents to illustrate the complexity and importance of phraseology in foreign language instruction.

3745. Kuiper, Gerdien C. "An Erasmian Adage as 'Fortune's Fool': Martial's 'Oleum in auricula ferre'." *Humanistica Lovaniensia*, 39 (1990), 67–84.

This is a philological and historical study of the Latin proverbial expression "Oleum in auricula ferre" (To have oil in the ear). It is pointed out that the Roman epigrammist Marcus Valerius Martialis (Martial, 38?–101?) used it in a distich in the 1st century A.D. Editors of Martial's works have usually referred to the fact that Erasmus of Rotterdam (1469–1536) has included this fixed phrase in his *Adagia* (1500ff.). Already the first edition had a short paragraph on this phraseological unit, and in the 1508 edition Erasmus lengthened his commentary considerably. Kuiper cites both passages from Erasmus and also includes other references from later proverb collections. It is argued that Erasmus was indeed very instrumental in spreading classical phrases all over Europe, first through his Latin *Adagia*, and then also through the translations of this important compilation with detailed commentaries.

3746. Kummer, Werner. "Die Sprüch-Wörter in Wolfgang Teuschls Bibelübersetzung *Da Jesus und seine Hawara*." *Sprichwörter und Redensarten im interkulturellen Vergleich*. Eds. Annette Sabban and Jan Wirrer. Opladen: Westdeutscher Verlag, 1991. 128–138.

Kummer discusses a few textual examples of Wolfgang Teuschl's (1943–) translation of the New Testament into the language of the Viennese middle and lower class. The controversial translation with the title of *Da Jesus und seine Hawara* appeared in 1971, and it is an interesting rendition of this part of the Bible into a city dialect with all of its proverbs, proverbial expressions, idioms, clichés, etc. Kummer argues that the translator has effectively used the "lingo" or "code" of these modern inhabitants of the largest Austrian city. He analyzes the metaphors, message, function, and meaning of this "new" Biblical language by contrasting a few original texts with much expanded dialect translations.

3747. Kunkel, Kathrin. "Untersuchungen zum Gebrauch von substantivischen Phraseologismen." *Beiträge zur Erforschung der deutschen Sprache*, 5 (1985), 225–237.

The author investigated three newspapers of the German Democratic Republic during 1981 for the use and function of nominal phraseological units. She located 322 texts in *Neues Deutschland, Leipziger Volkszeitung,* and *Weltbühne,* of which 64% were figurative and 36% literal phrases. Kunkel cites a number of examples in their journalistic context and discusses the way they were integrated (headline, text, etc.) by the journalists. She also shows that many of the phrases are twin formulas based on two nouns. Such expressions certainly play an important role in making the language of mass media more effective and expressive through metaphors. A useful bibliography is attached.

3748. Kunkel, Kathrin. "'Es springt ins Auge . . .' Phraseologismen und ihre Funktionen in einigen Textsorten fachgebundener Kommunikation der deutschen Gegenwartssprache." *Beiträge zur Erforschung der deutschen Sprache*, 10 (1991), 72–111.

Kunkel starts with the observation that linguists have usually studied the use and function of phraseological units only as they appear in literature and the mass media. She therefore investigated 117 texts with a total of 1590 pages from such "unusual" areas as dissertation abstracts, manuscripts of scholarly lectures, scientific essays, and legal documents. A total of 700 fixed phrases was isolated, of which Kunkel presents and discusses a large portion in their written context. It is found that such formulaic phrases do in fact find their use in these texts, albeit without the high frequency with which they appear in literary texts or the mass media. It might also be pointed out that many of them are rather literal and not particularly metaphorical. Actual proverbs and proverbial expressions play a relatively minor role in these scholarly texts. A helpful bibliography (pp. 108–111) concerning the sources and secondary literature is provided.

3749. Küntzel, Heinrich. "'Mich wundert, daß ich fröhlich bin'. Marginalien zu einem alten Spruch." *Deutsche Vierteljahrsschrift für Literaturwissenschaft und Geistesgeschichte*, 61 (1987), 399–418.

This is a painstaking diachronic study of the German proverbial verse "Ich lebe, weiß nicht wie lang / Ich sterbe, weiß nicht wann / Ich fahre, weiß nicht wohin / Mich wundert, daß ich noch fröhlich bin" (I live and don't know how long, I will die and don't know when, I travel and don't know where to, I am curious that I am still happy). Küntzel finds early stages of it in Greek and Latin antiquity, and he is able to show the same for the German Middle Ages. Precise references exist as early as the 15th century, and by the 17th century the "saying" appears in German proverb collections. In more recent times the two dramatists Ödön von Horvath (1901–1938) and Gerhart Hauptmann (1862–1946) have used it in their plays, and the philosopher Ernst Bloch (1885–1977) quoted it repeatedly as an expression of hope and optimism. Today the four lines are often reduced to the mere final statement of "Mich wundert, daß ich (noch, so) fröhlich bin" (I am curious that I am [still, so] happy). Very short German and English abstracts (p. 399) are provided, and the 40 notes include important bibliographical references.

3750. Kuraszkiewicz, Wladyslaw. "Rad bywa smard, gdzie rajtarka." In W. Kuraszkiewicz. *Polski jezyk literacki. Studia nad historia i struktura.* Warszawa: Panstwowe Wydawnictwo Naukowe, 1986. 662–670.

This is an etymological, historical, and cultural study of the Polish proverb "Rad bywa smard, gdzie rajtarka" (Glad is a rogue, wherever there is a robbery). Kuraszkiewicz explains that this proverb makes use of very archaic words which renders its meaning almost impossible to understand for modern Polish speakers. He cites numerous older references from literature, studying particularly the contextualized use and function of the proverb in the works of the Polish author Mikolaj Rej (1505–1569). Kuraszkiewicz also cites numerous variants from historical Polish proverb collections and succeeds in presenting a comprehensive history of this proverb, its variants, linguistic structure, and meaning.

3751. Kuusi, Matti. "Zur Einstellungsanalyse der Sprichwörter. Ein finnisch-südwestafrikanisches Experiment." *Proverbium*, 2 (1985), 87–95.

Matti Kuusi, the leading Finnish paremiographer and paremiologist, starts his comparative essay with some general remarks concerning proverbs as indicators of national character and worldview. It is his feeling that proverbs can be valid indicators of the attitudes of people that use these texts, but he warns that such scholarship must be undertaken with utmost care. In his article he compares 2087 Finnish proverbs with 166 Ovambo proverbs from South West Africa which all refer to the female members of these societies. He found that the Finnish proverbs express primarily negative (misogynous) attitudes towards women in general while the Ovambo proverbs contain positive statements. Regarding the figure of the mother, however, both the Finnish and Ovambo proverbs express positive feelings. Several statistical tables are included. See also Kuusi's other papers on Ovambo proverbs (nos. 974 and 977).

3752. Kuusi, Matti. "Kyllä-küll-gal-alkuisista sananlaskuista." *Virittaja*, 92 (1988), 143–154.

The author observes that there are many Finnish, Estonian, and Lappish proverbs beginning with the modal adverb Fin. "kyllä," Est. "küll," and Lap. "gal." This is a strengthening or emphatic particle belonging to the verb in a sentence (though the verb may be understood), sometimes in a concessive sense, with the meaning of "certainly, well enough, indeed, then." In distinction to the normal word order, proverbs beginning with this particle place their verb usually to the end of the statement. Using statistical methods Kuusi concludes that this proverb formula (pattern) is very frequent in West Finnish dialects and in the North of Estonia. Among the Lappish proverbs only 8% use this formula, which leads Kuusi to the justified conclusion that this proverb pattern was taken over from the Proto-Finnish neighbors of the Lapps. Several recurring semantic and structural variants are analyzed, and it is shown that they have to do with word-order rules of the Baltic-Finnic languages and with the varying stress (focus) given to different aspects of the proverbs. A small bibliography (pp. 153–154) and an English abstract (p. 154) are included.

L

3753. Lafond, Jean. "Des formes brèves de la littérature morale aux XVIe et XVIIe siècles." *Les formes brèves de la prose et le discours discontinu (XVIe-XVIIe siècles)*. Ed. J. Lafond. Paris: Librairie Philosophique J. Vrin, 1984. 101–122.

The author starts with the statement that writers did not differentiate between proverbs and maxims (sententiae, sententious remarks) in the Middle Ages. He then goes on to explain that beginning with the 16th century a definite distinction was drawn between the traditional and popular proverbs and the sententious remarks by known authors. This is, however, not to say that some of the following authors under discussion did not formulate their maxims on the structure of proverbs from time to time: Michel Eyquem Seigneur de Montaigne (1535–1592), François de Malherbe (1535–1628), Jean Louis Balzac (1597–1654), François La Rochefoucauld (1613–1680), Blaise Pascal (1623–1662), Jean de La Bruyère (1645–1696), etc. Lafond cites numerous examples from the 16th and 17th centuries that indicate how these authors used the "short form" of the maxim or sententious remark to express certain insights and wisdom. The 99 notes include useful bibliographical information.

3754. Lallement, Renaud. "Aspekt im Sprichwort." *Europhras 88. Phraséologie Contrastive. Actes du Colloque International Klingenthal-Strasbourg, 12–16 mai 1988.* Ed. Gertrud Gréciano. Strasbourg: Université des Sciences Humaines, 1989. 273–279.

A linguistic analysis of the grammatical nature of "aspect" in proverbs. Lallement states that proverbs are primarily characterized by the fact that they are complete sentences, that they exhibit a certain fixidity, and that they usually contain a metaphor. However, proverbs in their grammatical form also make use of aspect, i.e. they differentiate between the duration and the completion of an action. Using German, Hungarian, and French equivalent proverbs as his comparative examples, the author investigates the morphological, lexical, and syntactical ways in which grammatical aspect is being used in proverbs.

3755. Lamy, Yves. "'Tous les chemins mènent à Rome'. Avec des proverbes." *Le français dans le monde,* 26 (1986), 60–65.

This is a pedagogical essay trying to convince teachers of foreign languages that they should also teach proverbs. Lamy starts with a short definition statement and then presents various ways of teaching French proverbs to foreign language students. One task would be to find proverbial texts in French newspapers, magazines, and literature. Students could create small plays to illustrate certain proverbs in actual speech acts. Teachers could also utilize cartoons and comic strips to illustrate proverbs and their meaning. Proverbs could be tested through sentence completion exercises and puzzles. Finally, Lamy also suggests that the students would enjoy modifying traditional proverbs into "Antisprichwörter" (anti-proverbs) or even inventing "new" proverbs on old structures. With 10 illustrations.

3756. Landon, Sydney Ann. *"Sundry Pithie and Learned Inventions": "The Paradise of Dainty Devices" and Sixteenth Century Poetic Traditions.* Diss. University of Washington, 1986. 144 pp.

A literary investigation of the use and function of proverbs in a Tudor collection of poetry compiled by Richard Edwardes and published after his death under the title of *The Paradise of Dainty Devices* (1576). The collection contains proverb poetry by such authors as John Heywood (1497?–1580?), Lord Thomas Vaux (1509–1556), Francis Kinwelmersh (flourished 1570) William Hunnis (died 1597), Richard Edwardes (1523?–1566), and others. In chapter one (pp. 10–56) of her dissertation Landon discusses the moralistic and didactic use of English proverbs in this poetry. Chapter two (pp. 57–92) investigates the rhetorical structure of the poems, and in chapter three (pp. 93–130) the author shows that many of the poems deal with the generic convention of the "complaint" or meditation on worldly vanity. A valuable bibliography (pp. 135–140) and an index of the proverb poems (pp. 141–144) and their respective authors are included.

3757. Lang, George. "La Fontaine Transmogrified—Creole Proverbs and the *Cric? Crac!* of Georges Sylvain." *French Review*, 63, no. 4 (1990), 679–693.

This is a fascinating account of how the Haitian poet and diplomat Georges Sylvain (1866–1924) adapted the fables of Jean de La Fontaine (1621–1695) into his own Creole masterpiece *Cric? Crac! Fables de La Fontaine racontées par un montagnard haitien et transcrites en vers créoles* (1901). Lang gives a short background to the use of proverbs in the French texts of La Fontaine, explaining that they usually appear at the beginning or end of the texts for didactic and moralistic purposes. Sylvain's use of proverbs is quite similar, but he transmogrifies them into statements of wisdom that express the Creole culture and legacy. On occasion he substitutes the original proverbs with Creole texts, but often he simply changes the proverbs to fit the worldview and language of his own culture. Numerous contextualized examples are cited, and a useful bibliography (pp. 692–693) is attached.

3758. Lansverk, Marvin Duane. *The Wisdom of Many, the Vision of One: The Proverbs of William Blake.* Diss. University of Washington, 1988. 242 pp.

An important dissertation on William Blake's (1757–1827) use of proverbs in his poem "Proverbs of Hell" (1790) which is part of Blake's longer work *The Marriage of Heaven and Hell* (1790). The study is divided into two major parts of four chapters each. The first part deals with four important analogues of Blake: Chapter one (pp. 12–38) compares the themes, form, and function of Blake's "Proverbs of Hell" with the Book of Proverbs from the Bible. The second chapter (pp. 40–65) investigates the proverbs in John Bunyan's (1628–1688) work *The Pilgrim's Progress* (1678/84). Chapter three (pp. 66–89) looks at Emanuel Swedenborg's (1688–1772) use of proverbial materials in his writings, and chapter four (pp. 90–117) studies John Milton's (1608–1674) use of proverbs. The second part of this thesis occupies itself with Blake's proverbial speech in the literary context. His "proverbs" are certainly quite different from traditional texts. They seem to proclaim general truths and authority, but they actually work against such universal wisdom. In chapter five (pp. 119–149) Lansverk analyzes the proverbs in "Proverbs in Hell" as performative utterances, of which at least some are common proverbs or alterations of traditional texts. Chapters six through eight (pp. 150–235) look at the proverbial language in Blake's *Visions of the Daughters of Albion* (1793), *The Four Zoas* (1797/1804), and *Milton* (1804/08). This intriguing literary proverb study thus goes far beyond William Blake's manipulations of proverbial wisdom. A valuable bibliography (pp. 236–242) is attached. See also Randel Helms (no. 2457), Michael Holstein (no. 2478), and Barbara Meister (no. 3841).

3759. Lanzendörfer-Schmidt, Petra. "Sprachspiel mit Phraseologismen." In P. Lanzendörfer-Schmidt. *Die Sprache als Thema im Werk Ludwig Harigs. Eine sprachwissenschaftliche Analyse literarischer Schreibtechniken.* Tübingen: Max Niemeyer, 1990. 63–87.

The author investigates the experimental prose of Ludwig Harig (1927–) in his two novels *Sprechstunden für deutschfranzösische Verständigung und die Mitglieder des Gemeinsamen Marktes* (1971) and *Allseitige Beschreibung der Welt zur Heimkehr des Menschen in eine schönere Zukunft* (1974). It is pointed out that Harig literally amasses phraseological units in these works, sometimes stringing fixed phrases together for several paragraphs or pages. Such overuse of proverbs and proverbial expressions results in effective wordplay, since Harig often modifies or manipulates these phrases by means of lexical substitution, mixing of metaphors, and intentional play with the multisemanticity of idioms. Lanzendörfer-Schmidt cites many contextualized examples to show this linguistic play with proverbial language by a modern German author who is interested in letting his readers become aware of the world of clichés that surround them.

3760. Lapucci, Carlo. "I monti della pioggia: un proverbio meteorologico e la sua eccezione." *Studi Pienontesi,* 16, no. 2 (1987), 349–359.

Lapucci studies the origin, history, and dissemination of an Italian meteorological proverb and its variants, with special emphasis on the two texts "Quando la montagna ha il cappello / o valligiano prendi l'ombrello" (When the mountain has a hat, you have to take the umbrella) and "Quando il monte ha la cappa / presto aspettati la burrasca" (When the mountain has a cap, soon expect a storm [bad weather]). It is shown that this proverb goes back to classical antiquity, and there are quite a few dialect variants current still today in Italy. Lapucci cites about 100 weather proverbs of this type and explains that some of them have in fact opposite meanings. This is especially the case if one compares regional variants that include specific geographical names of the mountain. A useful bibliography (p. 359) of various Italian proverb collections is attached.

3761. Lassen, Regine. *Das katalanische Sprichwort. Literarische Tradition und umgangssprachlicher Gebrauch.* Tübingen: Gunter Narr, 1988. 164 pp.

This is a compact but informative study of Catalan proverbs in German, citing all textual examples in Spanish with German translations. After a short introductory chapter (pp. 11–12), Lassen presents a detailed survey of Spanish proverb collections from the Middle Ages to the present day in her second chapter (pp. 13–37). Chapter three (pp. 38–48) deals with definition problems of the proverb and its various subgenres. The fourth chapter (pp. 49–85) concerns itself with the use of proverbs in the context of speech acts, while chapter five (pp. 86–97) investigates the syntax, structure, style, and metaphor of Catalan proverbs. In chapter six (pp. 98–111) the author analyzes the variation of proverbs, indicating how one text can have several variants. Chapter seven (pp. 112–140) deals with the many functions of proverbs, and chapter eight (pp. 141–146) summarizes all these findings with special emphasis on Catalan proverbs. An invaluable bibliography (pp. 149–164) helps to make this book an excellent survey of Spanish paremiography and paremiology.

3762. Lassen, Regine. "'Wer der Gemeinschaft dient, der dient niemandem': Welche Funktionen haben Sprichwörter in

Eiximenis *Regiment de la cosa publica?" Zeitschrift für romanische Philologie*, 105, nos. 3–4 (1989), 313–321.

Lassen investigates the use and function of proverbs in the *Regiment de la cosa publica* (1383) by the Spanish cleric and scholar Eiximenis (1340–1409). She points out that he wrote this book in order to educate the citizens of Valencia, arguing throughout the book with the help of didactic proverbs that people should be interested in the common good for all members of society. Chapter 38 is a "proverb chapter" in which Eiximenis quotes several negative proverbs, notably "Qui serveix al comú no serveix a negú" (He who serves the community serves nobody). He then discusses them and explains the unchristian attitudes expressed in them. By giving such anti-lessons, Eiximenis hopes to change his contemporaries into more responsible citizens. Lassen concludes her article by discussing the structure, meaning, function, and metaphor of several additional texts from this medieval literary work.

3763.   Latané, Bibb, Kipling Williams, and Stephen Harkins. "Many Hands Make Light the Work: The Causes and Consequences of Social Loafing." *Journal of Personality and Social Psychology*, 37 (1979), 822–832.

The authors take their lead from the English proverb "Many hands make light (the) work" which captures one of the promises of social life, namely that with social organization people can fulfill their individual goals more easily through collective action. When many hands are available, people often do not have to work as hard as when only a few are present. But there is also a second, less hopeful interpretation: it seems that when many hands are available, people actually work less hard than they ought to. The authors devised a psychological test to check this decrease in performance which they term "social loafing." The article concludes with some statements on how this widespread occurrence of proverbial loafing can be minimized. With an English abstract (p. 822).

3764. Launay, Marie-Luce. "Les 'miettes' du sens: La folie dans les proverbes français au XVIIe siècle." *La folie et le corps.* Ed. Jean Céard. Paris: Presses de l'École Normale Supérieure, 1985. 31–48.

The author located about 350 French proverbs in various proverb collections that all somehow deal with aspects of folly, foolishness, and fools. She points out that these proverbs were particularly common in the 16th and 17th centuries, even though there appears to be an antithetical conflict between the wisdom of proverbs and the stupidity of fools. Citing numerous examples throughout her article, Launay discusses lexical matters (i.e. certain key-words like folly and fool) and the precise meaning of nouns and adjectives referring to foolishness. There is also a section on the pathological interest in the fool at that time, and in the final pages the author investigates those proverbs in which the fool as speaker exposes his folly, thus turning his proverbial anti-wisdom into a learning process through a negative example.

3765. Lawton, David. "Grammar of the English-Based Jamaican Proverb." *American Speech*, 59, no. 2 (1984), 123–130.

This is a linguistic analysis of English-based Jamaican proverbs which were published originally as *Jamaica Proverbs and Sayings* (1910) by Izett Anderson and Frank Cundall. Lawton is particularly interested in the peculiarities of Creole syntax, and he has found the following nine categories of syntactical interest in these proverbs: differentiated "be," undifferentiated "be," deleted "be" and "a" behavior, deleted and undeleted "do," negation and negative commands, passive and quasi-passive, possessive and nominal plural markers, "a" as preposition, infinitive, and "have" equivalent, and "se" as complementizer. Most of the proverb texts were recorded close to one hundred years ago, and this diachronic study clearly shows a continuity of syntactical arrangement to the present-day English-based Jamaican speech. There is thus no sign that points towards a merger of Creole with an ideal English syntax.

3766. Lawuyi, Olatunde Bayo. "The World of the Yoruba Taxi Driver: An Interpretative Approach to Vehicle Slogans." *Africa*, 58, no. 1 (1988), 1–13.

Lawuyi reports on the custom of African taxi drivers in Nigeria of writing slogans onto their vehicles as expressions of social attitudes, religious beliefs, and worldview in general. He gathered his texts during field research in the city of Ile-Ife with a population of about 380,000 inhabitants. He interviewed taxi drivers and owners, and he comes to the conclusion that these slogans have important implications for social interaction. A few of the texts are proverbs or are based on the structures of Yoruba proverbs. A bibliography (pp. 11–13) and a French abstract (p. 13) are included.

3767. Lazutin, S.G. "Poslovitsy." In S.G. Lazutin. *Russkie narodnye livicheskie pesni, chastushki i poslovitsy*. Moskva: Vysshaia shkola, 1990. 10–21 and 117–157.

This book on Russian folk songs, humorous folk verses, and proverbs also contains a short and general first chapter (pp. 10–21) on the nature of proverbs. Lazutin deals primarily with definition problems, differentiating among proverbs, proverbial expressions, and proverbial comparisons. He also discusses the content of proverbs, and the third part of the chapter is dedicated to an analysis of the structure, form, and language of proverbs. The seventh chapter (pp. 117–157) contains dozens of examples from the Soviet period (1917–1991), showing how proverbs were used and created during this time for political and social propaganda. A bibliography for Russian proverb collections and studies (pp. 231–232) is included in a general folklore bibliography at the end of the book.

3768. Leary, James P. "'The Land Won't Burn': An Esoteric American Proverb and Its Significance." *Folk Groups and Folklore Genres: A Reader*. Ed. Elliott Oring. Logan/Utah: Utah State University Press, 1989. 302–307.

This is a reprint of Leary's article that had previously been published in 1975 (see no. 1023). Leary explains that the proverb "The land won't burn" originated on a farm in Wisconsin around 1920. It is a "family proverb" that has not gained wide currency, but as Leary found out, it certainly is still being quoted in the family where it was coined originally. Referring to field research and oral interviews, the author presents the history and meaning of this esoteric proverb, citing it in a number of social contexts and adding explanatory comments.

3769. Lebedev, P.F. "Poslovitsy belorusskikh partizan." *Neman: Literaturno-khudozhestvennyi i obshchestvenno-politicheskii zhurnal,* 7 (1984), 171–172.

In this short article Lebedev reports on the proverbs used by the White Russian partisans during World War II in their fight against the German soldiers. The author explains that traditional and "invented" proverbs were used as propagandistic slogans on posters and in newspapers. The proverbs were usually deeply patriotic and expressed love for the Russian homeland and the native White Russian culture. Lebedev also points out that the partisans used these proverbs and proverbial expressions in their oral communication to create a patriotic spirit in the struggle against the enemy. A few examples from partisan fliers and newspapers are included. See also P.F. Lebedev's article below (no. 3771).

3770. Lebedev, P.F. "Poslovitsa vovek ne slomitsia." *Russkaia Rech'*, no. 1 (1987), 126–129.

Lebedev reports on the traditional proverbs current in the village of Mikhailovka in the Kursk region of the Soviet Union. He argues that these proverbs have survived many political and social changes and that they will continue to be relevant expressions of attitudes and worldview. Many Russian examples are cited that deal with thoughts on work ethics, workers, trade, tradesmen, and commerce. These proverbs are of clear historical and cultural value since they show what people have thought and continue to think about everyday life and work. With 1 illustration.

3771. Lebedev, P.F. "Poslovitsa ne klinok, a kolet v bok." *Russkaia Rech'*, no. 4 (1988), 123–126.

In this short essay Lebedev reports that he actually collected several thousand proverbs from the White Russian partisans during World War II in their fight against the German army. He explains that the partisans from the Kursk region of the Soviet Union used many proverbs in their oral communication, but traditional and "invented" proverbs were also employed as political slogans on fliers and in newspapers to encourage the partisans in their fight against the enemy. Proverbs thus became ideological and political weapons and played their part in the propagandistic fight against the foreign intruders. With one illustration. See also P.F. Lebedev's article above (no. 3769).

3772. Lebedev, V.V., and Madikha Makhmud Reda Akhmed. "Poslovitsy, pogovorki i aforismy v *Opisanii Rossii* egipetskogo uchenogo XIX v. Mukhammeda Aiiada at-Tantavi." *Vestnik Leningradskogo Universiteta. Seriia Istorii, Iazyka i Literatury*, 14 (1984), 47–52.

The authors comment on the work of Prof. Mukhammed Aiiad at-Tantavi (1810–1861), who was the first Arabic lecturer at the University of St. Petersburg. In his treatise *Opisanii Rossii* (1840; Arabic title: *Tuhfat al-adkiya*) he used over 20 Russian proverbs, proverbial expressions, and aphorisms to describe Russia to Arabic readers. These proverbs were taken partly from oral folklore tradition, partly from medieval Arabic literature. The proverbs and maxims help the author to express his attitudes about the Russian society. It was quite natural for him to include such proverbial language since the use of proverbs in literary works and scientific treatises has been a typical feature of Arabic literature throughout the ages. Various examples are cited in context in Russian translation. An English abstract (p. 51) is attached.

3773. Le Bourdellès, Hubert. "Les proverbes et leurs désignations dans les langues antiques." *Richesse du proverbe*. Eds. François Suard and Claude Buridant. Lille: Université de Lille, 1984. II, 115–120.

A short survey of various designations for "proverb" in ancient languages. The author starts with early Sumerian and Egyptian concepts of the proverb, explaining that proverbs were already in these early days recognized as effective rhetorical tools with important social functions. He also comments on Aristotles's (384–322 B.C.) definition of the proverb and then cites various definition attempts from Greek and Roman antiquity. The article closes with a few terms for "proverb" in the medieval languages of Europe. For more detailed studies see Jan Kindstrand (no. 850) and Bartlett Jere Whiting (no. 2060).

3774. Lech, Bogumila. "Uwagi o przyslowiu i przyslowioznawstwie rosyjskim." *Przeglad Humanistyczny,* 31, no. 4 (1987), 101–112.

This is an important review article in Polish regarding Russian paremiography and paremiology. Lech begins with a survey of the most important Russian proverb collections, and she also discusses various definition attempts of the proverb by Russian and Soviet scholars. It is argued that the Russians have always had a special fascination with proverbs and proverbial expressions, and it really should not be surprising that they have accomplished major lexicographical, structural, and semiotic breakthroughs. Lech presents a detailed analysis of major studies dealing with such matters as structure, semantics, form, context, function, etc. Many examples are cited, and the author includes useful bibliographical references throughout her article.

3775. Lemmer, Manfred. "Lutherdeutsch und Gegenwartssprache." *Sprachpflege,* 32, no. 11 (1983), 161–166.

The author presents a short analysis of Martin Luther's (1483–1546) influence on the German language with a special emphasis on what words, proverbs, and proverbial expressions are still in use today. Numerous examples are discussed, and Lemmer points out that some of the proverbs coined by Luther have undergone considerable lexical and structural changes over the years. A discussion of the relationship between Biblical quotations and proverbs is also included, and so are references to the use of Luther's proverbial language by such German authors as Friedrich Schiller (1759–1805), Thomas Mann (1875–1955), and Bertolt Brecht (1898–1956).

3776. Leonhardt, Rudolf Walter. "Vorsicht bei Bildern!" In R.W. Leonhardt. *Auf gut deutsch gesagt. Ein Sprachbrevier für Fortgeschrittene.* Berlin: Severin und Siedler, 1983. 149–151.

In this essayistic statement Leonhardt argues against the frequent use of proverbial expressions and idioms in both oral and written communication. As a journalist he opposes such phrases as "Die Spitze des Eisbergs" (The tip of the iceberg" and "Das Kind mit dem Bade ausschütten" (To throw the baby out with the bath water) which have become overused clichés. He also points out that many people use such fixed phrases incorrectly by mixing up metaphors and not really knowing what exactly the images mean. A few striking examples are cited to show how the frequent use of metaphorical expressions can in fact become a nuisance.

3777. Leonidova, Maria. "Poslovitsi i pogovorki s onomastichen komponent (v ruskiya, bulgarskiya i nemskiya ezik)." *Supstavitelno Ezikoznanie,* 7, no. 4 (1982), 13–20.

Leonidova discusses some theoretical and applied aspects of the functions of personal names (anthroponyms) in Russian, Bulgarian, and German proverbs and proverbial expressions. It is shown that such names in proverbs develop a more generalized meaning, that in most cases typical national names recur most often, and that anthroponyms do not have a concrete referent and thus lend themselves to be used as general statements. The author also claims that these names do not gradually lose their lexical meaning and that they do not become polysemantic as is the case with names in idioms. Many examples are cited to show the relationship of onomastics and paremiology. A useful bibliography (pp. 19–20) as well as Russian and German abstracts (p. 13) are provided.

3778. Leonidova, Maria. "Kontrastive Analyse einiger komparativer Phraseologismen im Bulgarischen, Russischen und Deutschen." *Aktuelle Probleme der Phraseologie.* Eds. Harald Burger and Robert Zett. Bern: Peter Lang, 1987. 245–257.

In this paper Leonidova compares numerous Bulgarian, Russian, and German proverbial comparisons. Obviously the two Slavic languages have many more exact equivalents in common, and German examples are only cited to show the difference between Slavic and Germanic images in these phrases. The examples are grouped according to such adjectives as "healthy," "strong," skinny," "fat," "beautiful," "stubborn," "angry," "smart," etc. Various metaphors are explained, especially if they are unique to one of the cultures. Leonidova also includes some comments concerning the lexicographical problems that these proverbial comparisons present for general and foreign language dictionaries.

3779. Lerer, Seth. "An Unrecorded Proverb from British Library MS Additional 35286." *Notes and Queries*, 230, new series 32 (1985), 305–306.

This is but a short note on an hitherto unrecorded English proverb found scribbled into the margin of a 15th century manuscript of Geoffrey Chaucer's (1340?–1400) *Canterbury Tales* (1387/1400) located in the British Library. The proverb is "Bewar I say of hadywyste / harde it is a man to trust," and it is the word "hadywyste" of this couplet that needs to be explained. Lerer found references to it in the *Oxford English Dictionary* with the meaning of "a vain regret, or the heedlessness or loss of opportunity which leads to it." The proverbial couplet does not appear to have any particular relevance to the actual text, and Lerer assumes that it is a mere reaction by a reader.

3780. Levin, Iu. I. "Proverbial'noe prostranstvo." *Paremiologicheskie issledovaniia*. Ed. Grigorii L'vovich Permiakov. Moskva: Nauka, 1984. 108–126; a shortened German translation of this essay appeared as "Zu einigen Besonderheiten des semiotischen Status von Sprichwörtern." *Semiotische Studien zum Sprichwort. Simple Forms Reconsidered I*. Eds. Peter Grzybek and Wolfgang Eismann. Tübingen: Gunter Narr, 1984. 379–385; also in French translation as "L'espace proverbial" in *Tel grain tel pain. Poétique de la sagesse populaire*. Ed. G.L. Permiakov. Moscou: Éditions du Progrès, 1988. 139–167.

A major article on the semiotic aspects of proverbs with special emphasis on their meaning. Levin states that several semantic levels are utilized simultaneously during any given proverb performance: (1) the direct or literal meaning of the text, (2) the basic meaning of the proverb, which is not

necessarily equivalent to the meaning which the text might have
in contextual use, (3) the meaning which is dependent upon
certain situations, and (4) the actual concrete meaning which
belongs to the "parole" and not the "langue" as do the first three
levels of meaning. Levin uses the term "heterogeneous
situationality" for the phenomenon that a proverb's meaning is in
fact dependent upon different contexts and that it can have
different meanings which lead to different interpretations. Based
on these findings the author argues successfully that proverbs of
any given culture should be considered as functioning in a
multidimensional space in which they interrelate to each other. It
is also maintained that this approach to proverb meaning could
be expanded to the proverb stock of other cultures. Many
Russian examples, detailed bibliographical notes, and two
schematic diagrams are part of this intriguing theoretical article.

3781. Levinton, G.A. "Dostoevsky i 'nizkie' zhanry fol'klora." *Wiener
Slawistischer Almanach*, 9 (1982), 63–82.

This is a rather general article on Feodor Mikhailovich
Dostoevsky's (1821–1881) use of verbal folklore in his novels. It is
pointed out that Dostoevsky was well versed in traditional folk
speech, including in particular Russian proverbs and proverbial
expressions. Levinton comments on the use and function of a few
proverbs in *The Brothers Karamazov* (1879/80) and some shorter
prose works, explaining that their metaphorical language gave
Dostoevsky the opportunity to create statements that have
intentional double meanings. The 41 notes include rich
proverbial materials from Dostoevsky's works which are not
necessarily quoted in the article itself. For a more detailed
analysis of proverbs in *The Brothers Karamazov* see Mark Workman
(no. 4573).

3782. Levy, Isaac Jack, and Rosemary Levy Zumwalt. "A Conversation in
Proverbs: Judeo-Spanish Refranes in Context." *Proverbium*, 7
(1990), 117–132.

This is a significant study of Sephardim or Judeo-Spanish
"refranes" (proverbs) as they were recorded by the two authors in
actual speech acts. The field research for this investigation was

carried out in Turkey, Israel, Greece, France, and the United States, always interviewing Judeo-Spanish informants in natural language use. The actual conversations are transcribed in the original language together with English translations, and most of the texts are recordings with the authors' mother Caden M. Israel, who stems originally from Milas, Turkey, but who now resides in Atlanta, Georgia. In addition to quoting numerous proverbs in the context of dialogues, the authors also study their linguistic features, structure, metaphor, meaning, and function. It is pointed out that they are often used to add humor to the conversation, but there are also times when proverbs express folk beliefs, religious thoughts, and above all worldview. Proverbs are seen as cultural knowledge and traditional wisdom, and they certainly continue to play a major role in modern Sephardim oral speech.

3783. Lewis, Nona L. *Ego Boundaries and Comprehension of Metaphor in Schizophrenia: A Study of Symbolic Processes.* Diss. Adelphi University, 1983. 244 pp.

This dissertation examines the relationship between schizophrenic disruption of ego boundaries and disturbances in verbal symbolic ability as measured by metaphor and proverb interpretation tasks. Lewis describes a psychological proverbs test in which patients had to interpret little-known proverbs or familiar ones where certain key-words were changed. It was found that the higher a schizophrenic person scored on a measure of disturbed ego boundaries, the more likely he/she was to have difficulty interpreting metaphors and proverbs. The study shows that schizophrenics have definite problems in abstract thinking which is manifested in perceptual and linguistic disturbances. The results support psychoanalytical theories linking the emergence of symbolic capacity to the development of self-other differentiation, as well as clinical observations that schizophrenics are deviant in both self-boundaries and in the ability to understand symbolic communication. Many statistical tables, appendices, and a bibliography (pp. 188–201) are supplied as well.

3784. Liapunov, Vadim, and Savelii Senderovich. "Ob odnoi poslovitse i triokh funktsiiakh plana vyrazheniia poslovits." *Russian Literature*, 19, no. 4 (1986), 393–404.

    The authors present a detailed study of the Russian proverb "Zhizn' prozhit'—ne pole pereiti" (To live a life is not as simple as walking across a field) which is part of the poem "Gamlet" that starts Boris Pasternak's (1890–1960) novel *Doktor Zhivago* (1957). After an analysis of the binary and poetical structure of the proverb the authors also investigate its rhythm, morphology, and use of the infinitive. Twelve variants are cited, and it is argued that this proverb expresses a certain aspect of Russian worldview. A short bibliography (p. 404) is included.

3785. Lieber, Michael D. "Analogic Ambiguity: A Paradox of Proverb Usage." *Journal of American Folklore*, 97 (1984), 423–441.

    It is argued that proverbs are used largely in situations which are reasonably complex, equivocal, and either adversarial or potentially so. Proverbs serve to interpret such situations, resolving their ambiguities by classifying them as being of a certain type. Proverbs thus are used to disambiguate complex situations and events. But while proverb usage functions to disambiguate, the structure of proverb usage is paradoxically inherently ambiguous, because it is one of analogy. Lieber gives clear examples of proverbs as devices for disambiguation, he shows the paradox of analogic ambiguity and proverb usage, he treats the socio-cultural use of proverbs, and he theorizes that a proverb text is potentially as ambiguous as the situation the proverb purports to gloss. This is so because most of the terms paired in any analogy have more than one relationship between them at more than one level of context. This multiplicity of relationships leads to Lieber's convincing statement that proverbs must have two or more categories of meaning, something that should be considered in particular during anthropological field research. A small bibliography (pp. 440–441) is attached.

3786. Lienert, Gustav A., and Hans Zur Oeveste. "Configural Frequency Analysis as a Statistical Tool for Development Research."

Educational and Psychological Measurement, 45, no. 2 (1985), 301–307.

Using the well-known psychological proverbs test by Donald R. Gorham (see no. 557–558) as a basis, the two authors suggest a configural frequency analysis as a technique for longitudinal research in developmental psychology. Stability and change in answers to multiple choice and yes-no item patterns obtained with repeated measurements are identified by such a configural frequency analysis. The authors discuss various statistical formulas and show how their methodology is applicable for a developmental analysis of an item from Gorham's proverbs test. An English abstract (p. 301), 2 statistical tables, and a small bibliography (pp. 306–307) are included.

3787. Liver, Ricarda. "Aspekte des Sprichworts: Zu einer neuen Sammlung von schweizerdeutschen Sprichwörtern." *Proverbium*, 1 (1984), 93–117.

Referring to Paul F. Portmann's recent collection of Swiss German proverbs *Di letschti Chue tuet's Törli zue* (1983), Liver investigates three aspects of proverbs: (1) grammatical and stylistic freedom (ellipsis, wordplay, unusual personification, nominalization, etc.), (2) functional significance of so-called proverbial commentaries, and (3) Swiss German proverbs and their European tradition. The author studies especially the origin, history, language, content, meaning, and geographical dissemination of seven common European proverbs which also exist in Swiss German. These diachronic analyses include among others such dialect proverbs as "Ohne Wii und Brot ist d Liebi tod" (Without wine and bread the love is dead), "D Liebi and de Hueschte sind bös z verbärge" (Love and the cough are hard to disguise), and "Wenn d Muus voll isch, de isch ds Mähl bitter" (When the mouse is full, the flour is bitter). These are interesting individual studies that show the complexity of proverb dissemination from one culture to another.

3788. Liver, Ricarda. "Sprichwortstrukturen im Surselvischen." *Das Romanische in den Ostalpen*. Ed. Dieter Messner. Wien: Verlag der Österreichischen Akademie der Wissenschaften, 1984. 391–402.

Liver studies the proverbs of a small dialect region in the Swiss Alps that belongs to the Rhaeto-Romanic language. Citing many examples without translations, she investigates the structure, syntax, and metaphors of these proverbs. Many of them are characterized by ellipsis, giving them a particularly noticeable brevity. Liver also explains that many texts have multiple variants, and as with proverbs in general, she is able to show that these texts exhibit a multisemanticity depending on the context in which they are cited. The author establishes certain proverb patterns or types, and she wonders at the end of her article whether these structural formulas might not be typical for other Romance languages or perhaps even for the Indo-European languages in general.

3789. Liver, Ricarda. "Phraseologie, Wortbildung und freie Syntax im Bündnerromanischen." *Europhras 88. Phraséologie Contrastive. Actes du Colloque International Klingenthal-Strasbourg, 12–16 mai 1988.* Ed. Gertrud Gréciano. Strasbourg: Université des Sciences Humaines, 1989. 281–290.

This is a somewhat similar article as the previous one (see no. 3788), but this time Liver investigates phraseological units of a different dialect region in the Swiss Alps that also belongs to the Rhaeto-Romanic language. She shows in particular that the proverbial comparisons and the proverbial exaggerations of this dialect use certain adjectives and adverbs to increase their expressive effect. In addition, the author analyzes certain morphological and syntactical chacteristics, including the use of suffixes. Numerous examples are cited with German translations, and a small bibliography is added (pp. 289–290) as well.

3790. Lobner, Corinna Del Greco. "James Joyce and the Italian Language." *Italica*, 60, no. 2 (1983), 140–153.

The author discusses James Joyce's (1882–1941) academic background in Italian and studies his use of the Italian language in his writings. It is pointed out that Joyce experimented with Italian vocabulary, at times even creating neologisms. Altered words, however, are only one aspect of Joyce's genuine empathy with the culture and language of Italy. Joyce also used Italian idioms and proverbs in his correspondence, and he sprinkled *Ulysses* (1922) and *Finnegans Wake* (1939) with proverbs, proverbial expressions, quotations, and other clever adaptations of Italian verbal folklore. A few examples are cited, and Lobner concludes that Joyce definitely used innovative techniques to integrate proverbial speech into his novels.

3791. Lockwood, W.B. "The Philology of 'auk', and Related Matters." *Neuphilologische Mitteilungen*, 79 (1978), 391–397.

This is primarily an etymological and philological study of the word "auk," citing numerous Old Norse, Gaelic, and English references with the general meaning of "razorbill" (a bird) or possibly also "hawk." On p. 395 the author also discusses the proverbial expression "As drunk as an auk," citing Scandinavian and English references. It is argued that the expression probably originated as a verbal comment on the swaying and stretching movement of the neck and head of the razorbill. This is definitely an example of a proverbial comparison whose meaning is not immediately clear but which can be explained through etymological and zoological study. With an English abstract (p. 391).

3792. Lopes, Ana Cristina M. "Texte proverbial et construction du sens." *Degrés: Revue de synthèse à orientation sémiologique*, 66 (1991), c1–c12 [sic].

In this theoretical and linguistic article Lopes investigates the "sense" of Portuguese proverbs. She begins with a review of recent proverb scholarship with special emphasis on the structural and semiotic work of the Soviet paremiologist Grigorii L'vovich Permiakov (1919–1983). Lopes then explains that it is certainly not enough to look only at the themes and language of proverbs. Scholars must also deal with semantic and pragmatic questions, realizing that proverbs are based on a logico-semiotic system. Numerous Portuguese examples are cited to illustrate how proverbs obtain their meaning in and out of context. A useful bibliography (pp. c11–c12) is included. See also Grigorii Permiakov (no. 1428).

3793. Loukatos, Démétrios. "Proverbes et commentaires politiques: Le public devant les télé-communications actuelles." *Proverbium*, 1 (1984), 119–126.

In this paper the leading Greek paremiologist Démétrios Loukatos (1908–) studies the use of proverbs as political commentaries, especially during the dictatorial regime in Greece from 1967 to 1974. He argues that fables, anecdotes, and proverbs were used to satirize the government and to express in figurative language critical feelings which could not be stated otherwise. In recent years the author has also collected proverbs from journalistic writings, and he states that traditional and varied proverbs play a considerable role in politically and economically oriented articles in newspapers. The same is true for political speeches and commentaries on the radio and television. Proverbs certainly continue to be popular in the modern Greek society and its mass media, and many examples in French translation are cited.

3794. Loukatos, Démétrios. "Paremiologika tis demosiographias mas." *Laographia*, 34 (1985–1986), 143–150.

This is a short study of the modern use of proverbs and proverbial expressions in Greek newspapers. Loukatos points out that proverbial language is used frequently in the headlines and journalistic prose of the mass media, and he explains that this is particularly the case for political aspects of the Greek society. Such proverbial motifs can also be observed in political cartoons and caricatures, where traditional proverbs or their variations are used as captions. The cartoonists create an effective interplay between the proverbial wisdom and the emblematic depiction of a particular political problem. It is argued that this type of iconographic communication on the basis of proverbs and proverbial expressions assures a general understanding of important political concerns. With 7 illustrations.

3795. Lühr, Rosemarie. "'Mit geru scal man geba infahan, ort widar orte' V.34, StD V.37 f." In R. Lühr. *Studien zur Sprache des Hildebrandliedes.* Bern: Peter Lang, 1982. I, 320; II, 588–596.

Lühr presents a detailed etymological and philological study of one of the oldest proverbs of the German language, namely "Mit geru scal man geba infahan, ort widar orte" (One shall [should] receive a gift with a spear, point [tip] against point). This Old High German proverb is included in the remnant of an older Germanic epic song called *Hildebrandslied* (c. 810). Lühr cites a few similar proverbs from that time, and she then analyzes every word with clear explanations of the meaning in the particular context of this proverb and the text. She also includes an important section on the formula "man scal" (one shall, should), for which Archer Taylor has written a study as well (see no. 1857). See also William McDonald (no. 3832).

3796. Lukasser, N. "Spruchweisheit des Volkes." In N. Lukasser. *Die Centurien des Johannes Nas, ihre Wurzeln und Formen, ein Beitrag zur Prosa des 16. Jhs.* Diss. University of Innsbruck, 1953. 279–295.

This dissertation about the writings of the mendicant friar, priest, and suffragan bishop Johannes Nas (1534–1590) includes a chapter on Nas' use of traditional German proverbs. Lukasser explains that Nas used proverbs frequently as expressions of experience and wisdom. His purpose in citing proverbs is not so much to give didactic sermons or educate his readers but instead the proverbs serve as a polemical and satirical tool to fight against Martin Luther (1483–1546) as well as the entire Reformation movement. On pp. 283–293 the author includes an annotated list of proverbs which he found in Nas' six *Centuriae* (1567–1569), and on p. 295 he presents an additional small list of Latin proverbs and sententious remarks. For an excellent study of Johannes Nas and the German proverb see Timothy C. Nelson (no. 4017).

3797. Luomala, Katharine. "A Bibliographical Survey of Collections of Hawaiian Sayings." *Proverbium*, 2 (1985), 279–306.

Taking Mary Kawena Pukui's collection '*Olelo No'eau: Hawaian Proverbs and Poetical Sayings* (1983) with its 2942 Hawaiian proverbs with English translations as a starting point, Luomala presents a detailed annotated survey of 35 publications on Hawaiian proverbs from the 19th and 20th centuries. She describes the classification, content, and value of the major collections, and she also explains that much more paremiographical work needs to be done on the indigenous Hawaiian proverbs. Luomala points out that many more texts could be located in traditional folk narratives and native chants. The attached bibliography (pp. 301–306) lists the 35 published collections, making this article a superb introduction to Hawaiian paremiography and paremiology.

3798.   Lurati, Ottavio. "La locution entre métaphore et histoire." *La locution. Actes du colloque international Université McGill, Montréal, 15–16 octobre 1984*. Eds. Giuseppe Di Stefano and Russell G. McGillivray. Montréal: Editions CERES, 1984. 82–102.

Lurati starts with the statement that linguists have paid much attention to certain lexical, grammatical, and metaphorical aspects of proverbial expressions, but he argues that their synchronic approach has prevented them from also investigating the cultural and historical importance of these fixed phrases. The author cites numerous examples from medieval French literature, at times also quoting German and Italian equivalents in his diachronic analysis. There is a large section on phrases which have the noun "chèvre" (goat) as their key-word and for which Lurati adds interesting explanatory comments. The 34 notes contain useful bibliographical information for proverbs of the Middle Ages.

3799.   Luxon, Thomas H. "'Sentence' and 'Solaas': Proverbs and Consolation in the *Knight's Tale.*" *The Chaucer Review*, 22, no. 2 (1987), 94–111.

This is a literary investigation of the use and function of proverbs in Geoffrey Chaucer's (1340?–1400) *Knight's Tale* (1387) which is part of the *Canterbury Tales* (1387–1400). Luxon starts with the quotation of the line "tales of best sentence and most solaas" and explains that the various tales do not necessarily indicate that proverbial wisdom (sentence) and consolation (solaas) go naturally together. Citing numerous proverbs in their literary context in the *Knight's Tale*, the author shows that there exists a definite tension between conventional folk wisdom and true consolation. Chaucer seems to want to show his readers that they must find consolation through a long, very difficult, and individual struggle, for which proverbs are mere collective expressions.

3800. Lyman, Thomas Amis. "Proverbs and Parables in Mong Njua (Green Miao)." *Zeitschrift der deutschen Morgenländischen Gesellschaft,* 140, no. 2 (1990), 326–342.

The author reports on his extended ethnological and linguistic research from 1962 to 1970 on the Mong Njua (Green Miao) people of Naan Province in northern Thailand. He starts his article with definitions of the proverb and parable, explaining the relationship between the two genres. The rest of the article consists of 33 texts which Lyman recorded during field research. Each text is cited in the original Mong language with English translations and detailed anthropological, cultural, and linguistic explanations. The Mong Njua are a non-literate people whose proverbs have survived for centuries in oral communication and which are of much interest to anthropologically oriented paremiologists.

M

3801. Macfie, A.L. and F. "A Proverb Poem by Levni." *Asian Folklore Studies*, 48, no. 2 (1989), 189–193.

This is a short note on a Turkish proverb poem by Ressam Levni (17th century-1732) for which the authors provide an English translation. They also include a short biographical sketch of Levni, and for the actual proverbs in the 15 four-line stanzas of this poem they also print the Turkish originals together with English translations. The poem is somewhat of a tour de force incorporating numerous traditional proverbs as a sign of wisdom. A short bibliography (p. 193) is attached, but unfortunately the two authors are not aware of two previous studies of this poem by Dimitri Theodoridis (no. 1915) and Helena Turková no. 1973). It should also be noted that they deal with a variant of this poem composed of 18 four-line stansas and one two-line stanza at the end.

3802. Maeterlinck, Louis. "Les miséricordes satiriques belges." *Revue de l'art chrétien*, 60 (1910), 173–182.

Maeterlinck studies numerous misericords on choir benches in Belgian churches, indicating that their secular motifs usually serve satirical functions. Quite a few of them are in fact illustrations of popular proverbs and proverbial expressions, as for example the carving that illustrates "La lutte pour la culotte" (The struggle over the breeches). Most of them illustrate the common motif of "De verkeerde wereld" or "Le monde renversé" (The World-upside-down), and it is clear that the tradesmen thoroughly enjoyed carving these worldly scenes as iconographic contrasts to religious motifs. See also Louis Maeterlinck's two books on 15th and 16th century proverb carvings and illustrations (nos. 1135–1136).

3803. Magaß, Walter. "'Alles palletti'." *Der Sprachdienst*, 28 (1984), 144–145.

   A short analysis of the possible origin of the modern German proverbial expression "Alles palletti" (All is saved, okay). Magaß argues that the word "palletti" goes back to the Hebrew of the Old Testament and that it has the meaning of "remains," especially as far as bankruptcy cases are concerned. Thus the expression states that everything is saved (okay) despite the financial or human ruin. The author then interprets the originally Yiddish expression as being a reflection on the history of the Jews all the way to the holocaust. He also states that it is a naive, ironic and prophetic statement which might account for its popularity in modern society. See also Hartmut Stegemann (no. 4432).

3804. Magaß, Walter. "Die Rezeptionsgeschichte der Proverbien." *Linguistica Biblica*, 57 (1985), 61–80.

   The author presents a short history and reception of Biblical wisdom literature that is a major part of the Old Testament. He explains that the proverbs express fundamental experiences of life, that they are used in the Bible for the purpose of argumentation and didacticism, and that they often function to provide direction in an existence filled with controversies. Magaß also points out that their vivid metaphors have remained effective rhetorical devices to the present day, but he does add that this type of traditional sapiential wisdom from the Bible appears to be declining in importance for people of the modern age. Numerous examples in German are cited to show that wisdom from the Old Testament is still "preached" today in the churches but also in everyday secular life.

3805. Majoros, Csilla. "Zum Terminus 'Wortpaar' in der deutschen und in der ungarischen Fachliteratur." *Beiträge zur Phraseologie des Ungarischen und des Deutschen*. Ed. Regina Hessky. Budapest: Loránd-Eötvös-Universität, 1988. 177–184.

   Majoros starts his article with definition problems of so-called "Paarformeln," "Zwillingsformeln," "Doppelformeln," and "Wortpaaren" (twin formulas, binary formulas, etc.) and also presents some of the studies on such phraseological units by German and Hungarian scholars. The author includes many examples from both languages and explains that twin formulas are particularly common in the German language. Basic structures, metaphors, alliteration, and other poetic and linguistic devices are analyzed, and it is shown that these fixed phrases are used with high frequency in everyday oral communication and in the language of the mass media.

3806. Malberg, Horst. *Bauernregeln: Ihre Deutung aus meteorologischer Sicht.* Berlin: Springer, 1989. 141 pp.

This is a collection and study of weather proverbs or weather superstitions by a leading German meteorologist. In his introductory chapter (pp. 1–5) Malberg states that while some of the proverbial statements are based on correctly interpreted weather signs, others are definitely mere superstitions without any scientific value. The second chapter (pp. 7–44) deals with weather rules concerning wind, fog, clouds, storms, etc. The third chapter (pp. 45–86) treats the popular weather rules that are attached to certain months of the year, and the fourth chapter (87–94) looks at the validity of weather proverbs which base their wisdom on the behavior of animals or plants. Chapter five (95–106) covers proverbial weather rules for harvests, and chapters seven and eight (pp. 107–120) deal with the predictive value of various almanacs. A short conclusion (pp. 121–126) arguing once again that not all weather proverbs are "nonsense," a small bibliography (pp. 127–128), and a useful glossary of meteorological terms (pp. 129–141) conclude this informative volume. With 22 maps and diagrams as well as 30 vignettes.

3807. Mampell, Klaus. "Schriftsteller bereichern die Sprache." *Sprachspiegel,* 43 (1987), 148.

A one-page note on how European literary authors have enriched the German language through their "geflügelte Worte" (sententious remarks), of which some have become proverbs and proverbial expressions. Mampell cites a few examples from Sir Thomas More (1478–1535), Martin Luther (1483–1546), Miguel de Cervantes Saavedra (1547–1616), Jean Baptiste Molière

(1622–1673), Jonathan Swift (1667–1745), Johann Wolfgang von Goethe (1749–1832), and Friedrich Schiller (1759–1805). He also includes some examples from folk narratives, but he fails to show that new literary quotations from 20th century authors have also become proverbial because of large editions, films, and the mass market in general.

3808. Manacorda, Giuliano. "Expressioni proverbiali romanesche in *Ragazzi di vita* e *Una vita violenta.*" *Galleria—Rassegna bimestrale di cultura*, 35, nos. 1–4 (1985), 31–37.

The author investigates Pier Paolo Pasolini's (1922–) two novels *Ragazzi di vita* (1955) and *Una vita violenta* (1959) for the use and function of proverbs and proverbial expressions. While Pasolini uses general Italian expressions, he also includes fixed phrases that belong to the Roman dialect. The proverbs appear in the dialogues of the novels, but Pasolini also integrates them into the narrative as such. Many examples are cited with references to a standard Italian proverb collection. It is shown that the proverbial texts in the literary context add a lot of colloquial speech and folk wisdom to these modern novels.

3809. Mandala, James Di Martini. *The Interpretation of Proverbs: A Cognitive Perspective.* Diss. California School of Professional Psychology at Berkeley, 1987. 235 pp.

Mandala starts with a short introductory chapter (pp. 1–8) on figurative language and the basic problems involved in understanding proverbs. The next three chapters review the theoretical literature on proverb interpretation in general (pp. 9–51), the scholarship on developmental literature concerning children and adolescents (pp. 52–79), and the studies on clinical uses of proverbs tests (pp. 80–111). Chapters five through seven (pp. 112–227) discuss the methods and results of using a proverbs test with a heterogeneous sample of 100 subjects consisting of (1) High School dropouts attending an adult education program, (2) teachers, teaching aides, and volunteers at the adult education program, (c) graduate students and postdoctoral fellows at a university medical school, and (4) library employees at a large university. Using various additional vocabulary and intelligence tests for comparative data, Mandala concludes that proverb response types are indicators of overall intelligence. He found that proverb interpretation requires the integrated functioning of both visual and verbal cognitive modalities, and the varying cognitive strengths lead to different response types when subjects of different intelligence interpreted proverbs. With 19 statistical tables and a valuable bibliography (pp. 228–235).

3810. Manley, Lawrence. "Proverbs, Epigrams, and Urbanity in Renaissance London." *English Literary Renaissance*, 15 (1985), 247–276.

This is a fascinating comparative study of the epigram and proverb as they are used in the poetry of English Renaissance authors like John Heywood (1497?–1580?), Sir John Davies (1569–1626), Henry Peacham (1576?–1643?), and others. The author starts with a definition of these two genres and then explains that the epigrams of that time borrowed heavily from names, places, allusions, proverbs, and proverbial expressions that were known to the inhabitants of London. In the second part of the article (pp. 249–256) Manley also mentions epigrams and proverbs from other European languages and cultures that refer to such cities as Rome, Paris, etc. But the major part of this paper deals with numerous textual examples indicating how various places of the city of London play a role in proverbs and epigrams.

3811. Mann, Jill. "Proverbial Wisdom in the *Ysengrimus.*" *New Literary History*, 16, no. 1 (1984), 93–109.

Mann begins her study of the proverbs in the *Ysengrimus* (1148/50) with a general introduction of their use and function in the Middle Ages, especially in *The Canterbury Tales* (1387/1400) of Geoffrey Chaucer (1340?–1400). She then explains that the *Ysengrimus* is a Latin beast epic of more than 6500 lines, recounting a series of episodes in the feud between the wolf Ysengrimus and the fox Reynard. It is pointed out that the proverbs are integrated throughout the epic in quite a different fashion than in animal fables where they function as moral lessons at the end of the didactic text. Citing several examples in the literary context, Mann is able to show that the proverbs in the epic are not at all to be understood as universally true pieces of wisdom. Often they are used ironically and exposed as lacking any connection with experiences of life that would give them moral value. But the author must admit at the end of her article that the proverbs are not entirely negated by the monk who wrote down the epic. He appears to have known that proverbs, even if mocked in certain contexts, seem to have the power to survive as folk wisdom.

3812. Manning, John. "Thomas Palmer and Proverbs: Antedatings and Additions to Tilley from *Two Hundred Poosees.*" *Notes and Queries,* 234, new series 36 (1989), 427–429.

The author reports that Thomas Palmer (1540–1626) based many of his emblems and accompanying epigrams on English proverbs that he most likely knew or collected from oral tradition. His emblem book *Two Hundred Poosees* (1565) contains numerous proverb allusions at an earlier date than the earliest references cited in Morris Palmer Tilley's *A Dictionary of the Proverbs in England in the Sixteenth and Seventeenth Centuries* (1950). Manning cites 37 texts antedating those registered in Tilley, and he is also able to list 4 additional proverbs which have not been included in Tilley's collection at all.

3813. Manuel, G.C. "La cultura del refran." *Cuadernos de Poética,* 4, no. 11 (1987), 57–62.

A general and somewhat essayistic discussion of Spanish proverbs. The author begins with a definition of the proverb and then explains its structure, form, style, metaphor, and content. Manuel also states that proverbs live above all in oral tradition and that a certain currency (popularity) is a basic characteristic. Proverbs are seen as didactic pieces of wisdom that contain practical intelligence based on everyday experiences. In the last section of this essay Manuel points out that proverbs express the social and philosophical attitudes of the people, and that the most common Spanish proverbs reflect the cultural worldview of Spain.

3814. Marbot-Benedetti, Claire. "La famille à travers les proverbes."
*Europhras 88. Phraséologie Contrastive. Actes du Colloque International
Klingenthal-Strasbourg, 12–16 mai 1988.* Ed. Gertrud Gréciano.
Strasbourg: Université des Sciences Humaines, 1989. 291–300.

The article starts with the description of a project
concerning proverbs in general which the author began in
Portugal as part of a pedagogically oriented study. But the major
subject matter of the paper concerns the use of proverbs in
foreign language instruction. The author has chosen several
French proverbs dealing with the family that will teach
Portuguese students certain cultural differences between family
life in France and Portugal. A detailed four-page lesson plan is
included explaining how the instructor can introduce the
proverbs to the students, how they can work with the texts in a
group, and how these newly learned proverbs can be practiced in
oral and written communication.

3815. Marian, Marin. "Adagiu folcloric la un concept psihanalitic."
Revista de etnografie si folclor, 36, nos. 5–6 (1991), 241–247.

Marian explains that there exist several Rumanian proverbial
expressions that follow the structure "Nunta fara . . ." (A wedding
[festivity] without . . .) to express the disappointment or
frustration about being unsuccessful or ineffectual. It is argued
that such phrases are a psychological reaction to absurd social
conditions in which the person feels utterly helpless. Especially
the phrase "Nunta fara lautari" (Wedding without musicians)
expresses this type of absurd and frustrating situation in a
metaphorical language which does not hide the psychoanalytical
problems created by the constant negation of dreams and
aspirations. A French summary (p. 247) is provided.

3816. Marton, Magda, and József Szirtes. "Saccade-Related Brain
Potentials During Reading Correct and Incorrect Versions of
Proverbs." *International Journal of Psychophysiology,* 6 (1988), 273–
280.

Using a reading task, the authors investigated saccade-
related brain potentials accompanying the perception of final
words of proverbs, i.e. of sentences where the context allows a

strong anticipation of the final word. The sentences were presented one at a time on a television monitor. The proverbs appeared either in their original form or with their final word changed to be incongruous with the sentence context. Complex brain wave measurements were taken which showed that a difference between saccade-related brain potentials to congruous versus incongruous final words of proverbs already appeared simultaneously with the saccade-related brain potential component indicating the analysis of the visual pattern of the word. This finding supports the authors' contention of an interactive model of word perception in the process of reading individual words in a normal context. The psychological proverbs test consisted of 156 well-known proverbs, but the authors unfortunately give no examples. Two graphs, a useful bibliography (pp. 279–280), and an English abstract (p. 273) are included.

3817.   Massing, Jean Michel. "Proverbial Wisdom and Social Criticism: 2 New Pages from the Walters Art Gallery's *Proverbes en Rimes.*" *Journal of the Warburg and Courtauld Institutes*, 46 (1983), 208–210.

The author reports that two leaves from the collection of medieval and Renaissance miniatures donated by Daniel Wildenstein to the Musée Marmottan in Paris were definitely originally part of the Baltimore manuscript of 182 eight-line French proverb stanzas with individual woodcuts from the 15th century which were published in 1937 by Grace Frank and Dorothy Miner as *Proverbes en Rimes* (see no. 470). The newly located leaves contain verses and illustrations of the proverbial expression "Faire de la terre le fossé" (To make a ditch of the ground, i.e. To make reasonable good shift with what one has) and the proverb "De bonne mere prent la fille" (Take the daughter of a good mother [in marriage]). Massing describes the two leaves and also comments on their social wisdom. While he cites the two eight-line stanzas in full, he unfortunately does not include the two woodcuts.

3818.   Masson, Alain. "Eric Rohmer: Le Capricorne souverain de l'onde occidentale sur les *Comédies et proverbes.*" *Positif*, no. 307 (1986), 43–45.

Masson gives a general survey of several films by the French director Eric Rohmer (1920–) which all belong to a series which Rohmer called *Comédies et proverbes* (1980/86). This generic title goes back to the preoccupation of French dramatists of the 18th and 19th centuries with so-called "proverbes dramatiques." Louis Carmontelle (1717–1806), Alfred Musset (1810–1857), and many other dramatists wrote these short plays centering around a proverb as their major theme to educate and entertain their audiences. Rohmer does not necessarily illustrate proverbs in such films as *Le Beau mariage* (1981), *Pauline à la plage* (1983), and *Le Rayon vert* (1986), but he lets a certain proverbial morality emerge from the behavior of the characters, who reveal themselves by their actions or passions, their impulses or illusions, by the vertigo born in the heart or the senses, and above all by the gap that appears between their words and their deeds. For the "proverbes dramatiques" see Clarence D. Brenner (nos. 205 and 2239).

3819. Matesic, Josip (ed.). *Phraseologie und ihre Aufgaben. Beiträge zum 1. Internationalen Phraseologie-Symposium vom 12. bis 14. Oktober 1981 in Mannheim.* Heidelberg: Julius Groos, 1983. 243 pp.

This is a collection of 15 papers on phraseology which were presented at the first International Phraseology Symposium on October 12–14, 1981, in Mannheim, Germany. The 8 articles that also deal with some proverbial questions are: Harald Burger, "Neue Aspekte der Semantik und Pragmatik phraseologischer Wortverbindungen" (pp. 24–33); Rainer Eckert, "Diachronische slawische Phraseologie" (pp. 35–58); Wolfgang Eismann, "Psycholinguistische Voraussetzungen einer Definition der phraseologischen Einheiten (phE)" (pp. 59–95); Josip Matesic, "Zum Terminus und zur Definition der 'phraseologischen Einheit'" (pp. 110–116); Jozef Mlacek, "Zur Frage des Verständnisses der Grenzen der Phraseologie" (pp. 133–146); Jürgen Petermann, "Zur Erstellung ein- und zweisprachiger phraseologischer Wörterbücher: Prinzipien der formalen Gestaltung und der Einordnung von Phrasemen" (pp. 172–193); Klaus Dieter Pilz, "Suche nach einem Oberbegriff der Phraseologie und Terminologie der Klassifikation" (pp. 194–213); and Stefan Rittgasser, "Zur Beschreibung von Phrasemen in ein- und zweisprachigen Wörterbüchern" (pp. 214–221). The articles deal with such matters as semantics, diachronic phraseology, definition of phraseological units, lexicography, dictionaries of fixed phrases, terminology, classification, etc. Most of the papers cite German or Russian examples and scholarship. For annotations of these linguistically oriented essays see nos. 3183, 3347, 3372, 3820, 3964, 4164, 4175, 4240.

3820. Matesic, Josip. "Zum Terminus und zur Definition der 'phraseologischen Einheit'." *Phraseologie und ihre Aufgaben.* Ed. J. Matesic. Heidelberg: Julius Groos, 1983. 110–116.

Matesic states that there has been much progress in the study of phraseology by linguists. Nevertheless, there appears to be quite a bit of confusion concerning the terminology and definition of various types of phraseological units. The author deals with this problem and lists four major characteristics of fixed phrases: (1) reproducibility of the entire phrase, (2) the phrase must have at least two words, (3) idiomaticity, and (4) the expression needs to be integrated into a sentence to take on any particular meaning. Matesic concludes that Soviet scholars have a definite lead in the study of phraseological units, and he hopes that German linguists will build their own work on this solid foundation.

3821. Matesic, Josip, and Jürgen Petermann. "Zur Problematik der arealen Phraseologie am Beispiel des Kroatischen, Russischen und Deutschen." *Aktuelle Probleme der Phraseologie.* Eds. Harald Burger and Robert Zett. Bern: Peter Lang, 1987. 259–267.

The authors present a short theoretical paper on the areal (geographical) study of phraseological units, drawing their examples from a comparison among Croatian, Russian, and German fixed phrases. They isolate four major characteristics of the comparative geographical study of phrases: (1) expressions belonging to one national language area only (dialects, standard language, regional variants, etc.), (2) distribution of phrases within the political boundaries of a state with more than one national language (i.e. Yugoslavia, Soviet Union, etc.), (3) related languages of different nations (i.e. Croatian and German, French and German, etc.), and (4) a large area of different national languages (i.e. Europe, Asia, Africa, etc.). In addition to such geographical analyses scholars must also pay attention to the historical, socio-political, and cultural aspects, and this type of contrastive research should also deal with lexical, structural, syntactical, and semantic matters.

3822. Mathumba, Isaac. *Some Aspects of the Tsonga Proverb.* M.A. Thesis University of South Africa (Pretoria), 1989. 210 pp.

This thesis contains an impressive study of Tsonga proverbs from the southern part of Africa. The first chapter (pp. 1–27) deals with definition problems, proverb research in general, and a review of earlier scholarship and collections of Tsonga proverbs. In the second chapter (pp. 28–95) Mathumba analyzes the form and structure of these proverbs with a special emphasis on such features as parallelism, elision, alliteration, metaphor, syntax, etc. Chapter three (pp. 96–134) is concerned with the meaning, use, and function of Tsonga proverbs, citing numerous examples in the context of speech acts and in African literature. In chapter four (pp. 135–163) the author investigates in which way the proverbs mirror the philosophy of life and worldview of the Tsonga people (marriage, sex, polygamy, women, children, hospitality, death, etc.). The final fifth chapter (pp. 164–170) is basically a summary of the thesis followed by a valuable bibliography (pp. 171–181). Mathumba also attaches a list (pp. 182–210) of the 233 proverbs with English translations which have been discussed in the thesis itself.

3823. Matta, Hilda. "Deutsche und ägyptische Sprichwörter. Ein Vergleich ihrer Strukturen, ihrer Bedeutungen sowie ihrer kulturellen, geschichtlichen und gesellschaftlichen Motivierung." *Kairoer Germanistische Studien*, 1 (1986), 100–106.

This paper represents a published summary of Hilda Matta's M.A. thesis with the identical title from the University of Cairo (see no. 2623). She starts with a discussion of definition problems and reviews some of the scholarship on German and Egyptian proverbs. The comparative thesis includes comments on linguistic differences and cultural peculiarities of the proverbs of these two very different languages. Matta pays particular attention to the problem of equivalency, citing 534 German proverbs with 436 more or less equivalent Egyptian proverbs and arranging her rich contrastive materials according to content. See also Matta's superb dissertation on German and Egyptian proverbs (no. 3824 below).

3824. Matta, Hilda. *Semasiologische und onomasiologische Untersuchung der Sprichwörter im Deutschen und Ägyptisch-Arabischen.* Diss. University of Cairo, 1986. 472 pp.

   Matta begins her invaluable comparative dissertation on German and Egyptian-Arabic proverbs with a general introductory chapter (pp. 1–7) in which she discusses the importance of such a contrastive investigation of equivalent proverbs of two very different languages and cultures. The second chapter (pp. 8–78) treats the definition, content, function, structure, style, and meaning of proverbs. The third chapter (pp. 79–419) is divided into 11 sections, each of which starts with a short list of German and Egyptian proverbs that belong together because of similar content, metaphors, and meaning. In each section (averaging about 30 pages each) Matta presents detailed discussions of the literal meaning, lexical peculiarities, and formal elements (rhyme, alliteration, synonymy, parallelism, repetition, personification, comparison, ellipsis, etc.). Aspects of homonymy and polysemy are also discussed, and each section includes a comparative table of semantic elements. An extremely important bibliography (pp. 437–461) and a useful index (pp. 462–472) of the 63 German and 48 Egyptian-Arabic proverbs discussed throughout the thesis are provided as well, citing the Arabic texts with transliterations and translations into German.

3825. Matta, Hilda. "Äquivalenzbeziehungen zwischen deutschen und ägyptisch-arabischen Wortpaaren." *Kairoer Germanistische Studien,* 2 (1987), 128–164.

   In this article Matta compares so-called "Wortpaare" or "Zwillingsformeln" (i.e. binary or twin formulas) of the German and Egyptian-Arabic languages. She begins with a definition of this proverbial subgenre and then divides her 80 German and 71

Egyptian texts into several groups of semantic equivalents. But it is pointed out that in addition to similar meanings there are also syntactical, stylistic, and lexical parallels between these twin formulas of two so different languages. The author provides very detailed linguistic analyses for each individual text, always attempting to show the differences and similarities between the metaphors and meanings. A short bibliography (p. 162) and a list (pp. 163–164) of the Egyptian-Arabic texts in the original script are included.

3826. Matta, Hilda. "Das Sprichwort: Versuch einer Definition." *Proverbium*, 5 (1988), 69–84.

Basing her comments on the corpus of 63 German and 48 Egyptian-Arabic proverbs which she studied in her comparative dissertation (see no. 3824 above), Matta now attempts to formulate a general definition of the proverb. She divides her list of criteria concerning proverbiality into four sections: (1) the content and function of proverbs serve as signs for relationships and situations, and it is this semiotic nature together with the expressed social value system, communication in speech acts, and traditionality that makes proverbs so effective, (2), linguistic and stylistic aspects (fixidity, syntax, tense, word choice, simplicity, brevity, etc.), (3) identification through introductory formulas and certain structural patterns, and (4) differentiation from such other genres as proverbial expressions, sententious remarks, advertising slogans, etc. A short bibliography (p. 84) is attached.

3827. Matta, Hilda. "Kommunikative Phraseologismen im Deutschen und Ägyptisch-Arabischen." *Kairoer Germanistische Studien*, 3 (1988), 193–232.

Matta states that the phraseological units which are used for certain standard communications have not been studied enough by folklorists and linguists. She is particularly interested in such routine formulas that are used at certain holidays, festivals, to wish a sick person well, to express condolences, to send someone off on a trip, and to start a meal. These fixed phrases are seldom varied and this rigid fixidity can be observed in the 47 Egyptian-Arabic and 29 German texts which the author compares in this study. For each text she provides detailed functional, semantic, structural, and lexical explanations, and a small bibliography (p. 232) is also attached. See, however, also Florian Coulmas (no. 2291).

3828. Matta, Hilda. "Deutsche und ägyptische Kommentarformeln in konfrontativer Sicht." *Kairoer Germanistische Studien*, 4 (1989), 33–58.

This is a similar article to the previous study (see no. 3827 above), but this time Matta investigates the routine formulas that express certain commentaries when something happens. She cites examples for fixed phrases which are uttered when a person sneezes, when someone has the hiccups, when it thunders, when a girl whistles, etc. Some of these proverbial commentaries are, of course, based on superstitions and other unfounded beliefs. Matta compares 26 Egyptian-Arabic and 27 German examples, presenting detailed statements concerning functional, semantic, structural, and lexical differences and similarities. See also Gerda Grober Glück (no. 607).

3829. Matulina-Jerak, Zeljka, and Pavao Mikic. "Biblijski izvori hrvatskih ili srpskih i njemackih poslovica." *Radovi*, 28, no. 18 (1988–1989), 105–111.

The article deals with the question of how Biblical proverbs from the New Testament have become proverbial in the Croatian, Serbian and German languages. Comparing 39 of these proverbs in the three languages, it is argued that the German equivalents are more "faithful" to the Biblical source than the Croatian and Serbian texts. In these languages the Biblical proverbs undergo considerable lexical changes and other modifications in content. This phenomenon can be explained by the fact that the Croatian and Serbian translators of the Bible "retold" many of the proverbial passages, while the German translators, notably Martin Luther (1483–1546), attempted to translate the Bible as closely as possible to the original. A small bibliography (p. 111) and an English summary (p. 111) are attached.

3830. Matzen, Raymond. "Die elsässischen Wetter- und Bauernregeln als lebendiger Ausdruck von Land, Sprache und Kultur." *Europhras 88. Phraséologie Contrastive. Actes du Colloque International Klingenthal-Strasbourg, 12–16 mai 1988.* Ed. Gertrud Gréciano. Strasbourg: Université des Sciences Humaines, 1989. 301–311.

The author investigates numerous so-called weather proverbs from the Alsatian dialect in France. He starts with a definition of this genre and explains that most of these texts refer to meteorological matters or to certain farm rules for planting and harvesting. It is shown that the more general phrases might go back to Latin sources and possess a general currency throughout Europe in numerous languages. However, the more specific the content the more localized the weather proverb or farm rule will be. Citing numerous examples from this German dialect Matzen explains the validity of these expressions, noting that many of them are based on superstitions, certain saint days, and the preference of general numbers without any particular scientific significance. He also comments in some detail on the language, style, metaphor, wordplay, humor, parallelism, alliteration, etc. of weather proverbs. A useful bibliography (p. 311) listing collections of weather signs is attached.

3831. Mayer, Reinhard. *Graffiti. Eine linguistische Untersuchung.* M.A. Thesis University of Heidelberg, 1985. 205 pp.

Mayer starts the first chapter (pp. 1–17) with a definition of the term "graffiti," he reviews previous research and bibliographies, and he argues that the study of graffiti should be based on interdisciplinary methodologies of such fields as linguistics, sociology, folklore, literature, art, and popular culture. The second chapter (pp. 18–174) deals primarily with the content and meaning of numerous German graffiti, including such matters as politics, war and peace, ethnic and social groups, feminism, alcohol and drugs, love, sexuality, etc. The section on "Maximen and Reflexionen" (pp. 137–150) deals with the fact that some graffiti are based on proverbial structures and that some of them have almost become proverbs in their own right. In the third chapter (pp. 175–196) Mayer considers some linguistic peculiarities of graffiti and describes their appearance on the streets and toilets in Germany. A useful bibliography (pp. 197–205) concludes this informative study.

3832. McDonald, William C. "'Too Softly a Gift of Treasure': A Rereading of the Old High German *Hildebrandslied*." *Euphorion*, 78 (1984), 1–16.

McDonald presents an intriguing literary interpretation of one of the oldest German proverbs which appears as "Mit geru scal man geba infahan, ort widar orte" (One shall [should] receive a gift with a spear, point [tip] against point) in the remnant of an older Germanic epic song called *Hildebrandslied* (c. 810). The author argues that the exchange of gifts in the form of a ring that is presented on the point of a spear might be understood as a metaphor and materialistic manifestation of human worth. McDonald cites numerous examples from early Germanic and English sources which show that the motif of exchanging golden treasures plays a major role as an ethical sign of respect and friendship. This leads the author to conclude that the use of this archaic Old High German proverb justifies the modern reader to look at the *Hildebrandslied* as an example of Germanic wisdom literature. The 60 notes contain important bibliographical references to earlier discussions of this proverb and its possible meaning. See also Rosemarie Lühr (no. 3795).

3833. McEnerney, John I. "Proverbs in Hrotsvitha." *Mittellateinisches Jahrbuch*, 21 (1986), 106–113.

This investigation of some of the proverbs in the early medieval Latin plays of the German nun Hrotsvitha von Gandersheim (935?-973?) serves two major purposes. First McEnerney is interested in showing how Hrotsvitha used proverbs in her didactic plays of Christian ethics, morality and sexual purity. Hrotsvitha is the first female German writer known, but in keeping with her own time she decided to write her six plays (between 960–970) in Latin. Since these small dramas have been translated into several languages, the author also investigates how English, German, and French translators have dealt with her proverbial languages. Citing numerous examples especially from the plays *Gallicanus*, *Dulcitius*, and *Abraham*,

McEnerney is able to show that they have not done a particularly good service. Many times they have failed to recognize the Latin proverb or they simply paraphrased it without looking for proverbial equivalents in the target language. The article concludes with a call for translators to be more cognizant of proverbial language and to attempt to give more precise translations.

3834. McKenna, Kevin J. "'Na poslovitsu ni suda ni raspravy': The Role of Proverbs in the Russian Language Curriculum." *Russian Language Journal,* 45 (1991), 17–37.

McKenna begins his valuable article with a review of Soviet scholarship (pp. 17–20) dealing with the converging interests of paremiologists and foreign language methodologists. He refers to Grigorii L'vovich Permiakov's (1819–1983) concept of a "paremiological minimum" (see nos. 2737 and 4147), and he argues that students who study Russian as a foreign language should also learn the most frequently used Russian proverbs. In the major part of the essay (pp. 20–35) McKenna explains how proverbs could be integrated into the teaching of Russian language and culture in the United States. Proverbs can be used to teach pronunciation and intonation, to explain grammar and syntax, to increase the students' vocabulary, to practice conversational drills, and to add to the students' social comprehension and level of "cultural literacy" in the target language. The author cites numerous Russian examples with English translations, and he also shows the frequent use of proverbs in Russian literature, the mass media, and in particular in the headlines of *Pravda* and other newspapers. The article is a convincing plea for the integration of proverbial wisdom into the Russian language curriculum, and the 24 notes (pp. 35–37) contain important bibliographical references for pedagogical, cultural, and literary studies of proverbs.

3835. McKenna, Steven R. *Orality, Literacy, and Chaucer: A Study of Performance, Textual Authority, and Proverbs in the Major Poetry.* Diss. University of Rhode Island, 1988. 272 pp.

This is a literary investigation of the use and function of proverbs in Geoffrey Chaucer's (1340?–1400) *Troilus and Criseyde* (1385) and *The Canterbury Tales* (1387/1400). However, McKenna is also especially interested in the interrelationship of orality and literacy in Chaucer's works. The first chapter (pp. 1–42) discusses orality, medieval literacy, and Chaucer's audience, stressing the fact that proverbs are collective and oral wisdom integrated into the literary text. The second chapter (pp. 43–133) treats the tension that exists between the oral and literate mind, especially as it relates to the contextualized proverbs as traditional expressions of authority. Many examples form *The Canterbury Tales* are cited and discussed, and the author also includes a special analysis of the proverbial wisdom in *Troilus and Criseyde* in his third chapter (pp. 134–196). A conclusion (pp. 197–207), an invaluable appendix (pp. 241–245) indicating the location of proverbs in Chaucer's works, and a large bibliography (pp. 253–272) conclude this important dissertation. See also R.M. Lumiansky (no. 1121) and Bartlett Jere Whiting (no. 2063).

3836. McLeod, M.D. "Asante Gold-Weights: Images and Words." *Word and Image: A Journal of Verbal/Visual Enquiry*, 3, no. 3 (1987), 289–295.

Following his previous article on Asante (Ashanti) gold-weights and their relationship to African proverbs (see no. 1179), McLeod presents another study on these decorative miniatures which illustrate various objects, creatures, and more abstract matters of life in general. But the author also explains that the meaning of these gold-weights is often governed by the way the subject matter is linked to a particular proverb. Thus a weight depicting a bird caught in a trap is linked to the proverb "Anoma niterfoo wode ba ha na eyi no" (The cunning bird is caught with plantain fibre). The relationship(s) embodied in the proverb provide(s) a pattern, a paradigm, by which the Asante attempt to order and manipulate their own experiences and their own perceptions. These proverbial gold-weights are an excellent illustration of how proverbial wisdom can become part of traditional art. Numerous examples are cited, and the author also includes 4 illustrations. See also R.S. Rattray (no. 1506).

3837. Mehlber, Leonhard. "'Einen Kater haben': Zur Entstehung der Redewendung." *Zeitschrift für deutsche Philologie,* 103 (1984), 430–437.

Interesting study of the very popular German proverbial expression "Einen Kater haben" (To have a hangover). The derivation of the word "Kater" (actually a male cat) in this expression referring to the after-effects of excessive alcohol consumption was believed to come from the Saxon dialect pronuncation of "Katarrh" and "Kater." However, Mehlber shows that there was no original connection with the symptoms of catarrh. It was rather the observation of animal behavior that gave rise to this expression as a document from 1574 indicates. It is believed that the phrase gained currency through university students but that it was quickly accepted throughout the German society. The article represents a good example for the historical, cultural, sociological, and philological study of an individual proverbial expression.

3838. Meichsner, Irene. *Die Logik von Gemeinplätzen. Vorgeführt an Steuermannstopos und Schiffsmetapher.* Bonn: Bouvier, 1983. 263 pp.

This is a very detailed analysis of various German "Gemeinplätze" (commonplaces) which are based on the topos or metaphor of the "Schiff" (ship, boat). Meichsner is particularly interested in the metaphor of the "Staatsschiff" (ship of state) and its "Steuermann" (helmsman, captain). Following a short introductory chapter (pp. 1–18) Meichsner talks about the political nature of many metaphors dealing with the ship and its captain in her second chapter (pp. 19–61). The important third chapter (pp. 62–152) contains an historical survey of how such philosophers and politicians as Plato (427–347 B.C.) Marcus Tullius Cicero (106–43 B.C.), Augustus (27 B.C.-14 A.D.), Saint Thomas Aquinas (1225?–1274), Thomas Hobbes (1588–1657), Franklin D. Roosevelt (1882–1945), Helmut Schmidt (1918–), and others have used ship metaphors to describe the social and political aspects of government and the state. The fourth chapter (pp. 153–170) summarizes the findings of this first part of the book, while the two remaining chapters of the second part deal with the logic of the metaphors (pp. 171–180) and their structure, meaning, and argumentative function (pp. 181–252). Many of the examples cited are in fact proverbial in nature, as for example the internationally disseminated proverbial expression "Wir sitzen alle in einem Boot" (We are all in the same boat). A large bibliography (pp. 253–263) is attached. For the phrase "Wir sitzen alle im selben Boot" see Wolfgang Mieder (no. 3933) and Dietmar Peil (no. 4136).

3839.   Meir, Ofra. "Proverbs Uttered by Characters in the Stories of the Talmud and the Midrash." *The 8th Congress for the International Society for Folk Narrative Research, Bergen, June 12–17, 1984.* Eds. Reimund Kvideland and Torunn Selberg. Bergen: Etno-Folkloristik Institutt, 1984. II, 57–66; also in *Proverbium,* 2 (1985), 97–108.

Meir offers an informative study of the interrelationship of narratives and proverbs in the Talmud and the Midrash. She starts with a short discussion of the difficulty of defining proverbs and then explains that it is difficult to decide whether the proverbs in the Talmudic-Midrashic stories were there to start with or whether they were added later when these oral narratives were written down. The author has found 40 proverbs in 700 stories, and she describes their function, meaning, and context by citing a few examples. Some of them use introductory formulas, but most of them are integrated into the dialogues of the characters. The proverbs represent ancient wisdom literature and are used to comment on everyday life while at the same time give authoritative and didactic rules for future conduct.

3840.   Meisser, Ulrich M. "Sebastian Franck." *Enzyklopädie des Märchens. Handwörterbuch zur historischen und vergleichenden Erzählforschung.* Eds. Kurt Ranke et al. Berlin: Walter de Gruyter, 1985. V, cols. 48–55.

This is an informative encyclopedia article on the life and works of the German paremiographer Sebastian Franck (1499–1542) whose collection of more than 7000 proverbs with the title *Sprichwörter / Schöne / Weise / Herrliche / Clugreden / vnnd Hoffsprüch* (1541) is one of the most important collections of the Reformation age. Meisser also comments on Franck's historical and religious writings, but he emphasizes the relationship of this proverb collection to folk narratives (legends, fables, etc.) and to earlier German and Latin proverb collections, especially those of Eberhard Tappe (16th century), Erasmus of Rotterdam (1469–1536), Heinrich Bebel (1472–1518), Johannes Agricola (1494–1566), and Antonius Tunnicius (1470?–1544?). A valuable bibliography (cols. 54–55) is included. For a more comprehensive study see Ulrich Meisser (no. 1191).

3841. Meister, Barbara. *The Interaction of Music and Poetry: A Study of the Poems of Paul Verlaine as Set to Music by Claude Debussy and of the Song Cycle "Songs and Proverbs of William Blake" by Benjamin Britten.* Diss. City University of New York, 1987. 273 pp.

This dissertation on the interrelationship of music and poetry deals only partially with proverb matters in two of its chapters where William Blake's (1757–1827) poem "Proverbs of Hell" (1790) is discussed which is part of Blake's longer work *The Marriage of Heaven and Hell* (1790). In chapter three Meister discusses the way in which Blake contradicts, parodies and perverts Biblical proverbs (see pp. 49–60) which has its expected effect on Benjamin Britten's (1913–1976) song cycle *Songs and Proverbs of William Blake* (1965). Chapter four (pp. 60–149) is then dedicated to a detailed analysis of this musical interpretation of Blake's proverb poem, showing that Britten understood Blake's anti-proverb statements very well by creating a musical work that is lacking in surface beauty and is rich instead in harsh, disturbing, and beguiling musical sounds. Meister includes many interpretative comments regarding both the poetry of Blake and the music of Britten. A useful bibliography (pp. 268–273) is provided. For literary studies of Blake's "Proverbs of Hell" see Randel Helms (no. 2457), Michael Holstein (no. 2478), and Marvin Lansverk (no. 3758).

3842. Meister, Gabi. "Russkie poslovitsy v sopostavlenii c nemetskimi (k probleme internatsional'nogo i natsional'nogo v fol'klore)." *Wissenschaftliche Zeitschrift der Wilhelm-Pieck-Universität Rostock, Gesellschaftswissenschaftliche Reihe,* 36, no. 5 (1987), 102.

A short note on Russian proverbs in comparison with German proverbs. The author points out that the two languages and cultures have quite a few proverbs in common. These are basically international proverbs going back to classical and Biblical times which were loan translated into many languages. However, there exist also indigenous or national proverbs that do not have precise equivalents in the other language. Meister explains that the content or theme of these proverbs is based on specific realia or metaphors which do not necessarily exist in both languages. A few examples are cited in Russian only, and the author concludes that proverbs illustrate certain similarities and differences between Russians and Germans that can also be seen from other folklore materials.

3843. Melissari, Renata. "I proverbi: testimonianza orale dell'Ethnos aspromontano (note introduttive)." *Historica*, 40 (1987), 34–39.

Melissari studies a number of Italian proverbs and proverbial expressions which she collected during field research in the small town of Santo Stefano d'Aspromonte in the Reggio Calabria area of southern Italy. She argues that the content of these fixed phrases reflect the local conditions, superstitions, popular culture, and worldview of the people from this region. Some examples also refer to human relations as well as the social and economic structure of this part of Italy. The examples are cited in dialect form, illustrating that regional proverbs are either variants of nationally known texts or in fact phrases current only in this specific area. At times considerable etymological and historical research has to be undertaken in order to understand archaic vocabulary and uncommon metaphors.

3844. Menac, Antica. "Gemeinsame semantische Gruppen in der Phraseologie der europäischen Sprachen." *Aktuelle Probleme der Phraseologie*. Eds. Harald Burger and Robert Zett. Bern: Peter Lang, 1987. 269–290.

The author differentiates between the phraseological units that are specific or indigenous to a national language and those fixed phrases which that language has absorbed through loan translations from other languages and cultures. The native phrases might refer to regional geographical names, they might contain dialect words, or they might refer to historical figures or events. Often these expressions are difficult to translate since there exist no real equivalents in other languages. The other group of phrases is rather internationally disseminated and often has its origin in Greek and Roman antiquity or the Bible. Menac compares many examples of this international group from two Slavic languages (Croatian and Russian), two Germanic languages (German and English), and two Romance languages (French and Italian). She is able to show that their form, structure, syntax, vocabulary, and metaphor are basically identical. The author also proposes a classification system of these phraseological units according to linguistic criteria (verbal phrases, nominal phrases, etc.).

3845. Mészaros, Istvan. "Magyar szolasok és közmondasok egy 1750–i frazeologia-tankönyvben." *Magyar Nyelvör,* 105 (1981), 292–302.

This is an investigation of a major polyglot dictionary for its contents of Hungarian proverbs and proverbial expressions that are listed as equivalents of Latin expressions. The dictionary under discussion is Franz Wagner's (1675–1738) *Universae Phraseologiae Latinae Corpus . . . linguis Hungarica et Slavica locupletatum* (1750, with later editions of 1775 and 1822). Mészaros begins with some general remarks concerning the author and the value of this early phraseological dictionary, but the major part of the article presents only a bilingual list of the phrases. There are no annotations, but obviously these materials are of much importance for the diachronic study of Hungarian proverbs.

3846. Mettmann, Walter. *"Proverbia Arabumkern:* eine altkatalanische Sprichwörter- und Sentenzensammlung." *Romanische Forschungen,* 101, nos. 2–3 (1989), 184–207.

Mettmann reports on a medieval manuscript from the beginning of the 14th century with the title *Ex proverbiis arabum.* He explains that the collection contains 392 proverbs, proverbial expressions, and sententious remarks. As the title indicates, the source of these proverbs must have been an earlier Arabic proverb collection. In the actual manuscript the first 56 texts are cited in Latin, while the other 336 texts are in medieval Catalan. Mettmann publishes the entire manuscript and provides very detailed philological and cultural annotations. It is pointed out that this collection is of much value for the diachronic study of Spanish proverbs in general.

3847. Meyer, Maurits de. *Volksprenten in de Nederlanden 1400–1900.* Amsterdam: Scheltema & Holkema, 1970 (esp. ills. 80, 88, 109, and 134).

The Belgian folklorist and art historian Maurits de Meyer (1895–1970) has located dozens of Flemish, Dutch, and French illustrations of proverbs and proverbial expressions (see nos. 1208–1214). In this book of popular broadsheets he includes proverb pictures of the sayings "De vos geeft zangles" (The fox is giving singing-lessons), "De wolf hoedt de schapen" (The wolf is watching over the sheep), and "De strijd om de broek" (The fight over the breeches). For the latter very popular proverbial motif Meyer presents three illustrations from the 17th and 19th centuries, all depicting the proverbial fight over who is to wear the breeches in the house. A few explanatory comments concerning the relationship of iconography and proverbs are included. With 5 illustrations.

3848. Mezger, Werner. "Steckenpferd-Hobbyhorse-Marotte. Von der Ikonographie zur Semantik." *Zeitschrift für Volkskunde,* 79 (1983), 245–250.

The author studies the iconographic history of the "Steckenpferd" (Hobbyhorse), including references to it starting in the 13th century. The hobbyhorse is identified as an attribute of children and the "Marotte" (Fool's staff) as an appropriate attribute of fools. These complementary symbols are part of two German proverbial expressions, namely "Sein Steckenpferd reiten" (To ride one's hobbyhorse) and "Eine Marotte haben" (To have a "Marotte," i.e. To have a whim). The article shows clearly the importance of the study of pictorial representations for a better understanding of proverbs and proverbial expressions. With 1 illustration.

3849. Mieder, Wolfgang. "Buchtitel als Schlagzeile." *Sprachspiegel*, 31 (1975), 36–43; rpt. in W. Mieder. *Sprichwort, Redensart, Zitat. Tradierte Formelsprache in der Moderne.* Bern: Peter Lang, 1985. 115–123.

The author investigates well-known titles of books that are being quoted as sententious remarks if not as proverbial wisdom. He shows that the title of John Le Carré's (1931–) novel *The Spy Who Came in From the Cold* (1963) has become extremely popular in German as *Der Spion, der aus der Kälte kam* (1964). It is usually quoted in a varied form as a newspaper headline, slogan, etc. The same is true for book titles by such authors as William Shakespeare (1564–1616), Jonathan Swift (1667–1745), Felix Dahn (1834–1912), Marcel Proust (1871–1922), Erich Maria Remarque (1898–1970), Carl Zuckmayer (1896–1977), Wolfgang Borchert (1921–1947), Edward Albee (1928–), Peter Handke (1942–), etc. More often than not the titles are parodied, and these manipulated "Antizitate" (anti-quotations) function as effective communicative devices in the mass media.

3850. Mieder, Wolfgang. "'Eine bibliographische Skizze zum Ursprung von 'O.K.' (Okay)." *Sprachspiegel,* 31 (1975), 132–135; rpt. in W. Mieder. *Sprichwort, Redensart, Zitat. Tradierte Formelsprache in der Moderne.* Bern: Peter Lang, 1985. 109–113.

This is a bibliographical essay reviewing major and minor scholarship on the internationally disseminated expression "okay." Mieder starts with some comments on Allen Walker Read's (1906–) five major studies on "o.k." from 1963 and 1964. Read discovered its first recorded citation in the *Boston Morning Globe* of March 23, 1839. The short article also lists other attempts regarding the origin and meaning of "okay" from 1904 to the present. Mieder concludes his survey by citing the "folklore" that has been created around the possible origin of this expression. While it is almost definitely of American coinage, there have also been scholars who have tried to prove German, Greek and other national origins.

3851. Mieder, Wolfgang. "'Sein oder Nichtsein'—und kein Ende. Zum Weiterleben des Hamlet-Zitats in unserer Zeit." *Der Sprachdienst,*

23 (1979), 81–85; rpt. in W. Mieder. *Sprichwort, Redensart, Zitat. Tradierte Formelsprache in der Moderne.* Bern: Peter Lang, 1985. 125–130.

The author investigates the modern survival of one of the most famous literary quotations by William Shakespeare (1564–1616), namely "Sein oder Nichtsein, das ist hier die Frage" (To be or not to be, that is the question) out of *Hamlet* (1600). He cites numerous examples from American and German newspapers and magazines, explaining that this "geflügelte Wort" (literary quotation) has basically taken on a proverbial status throughout the world. Even though the sententious remark is often quoted in its original wording, journalists and writers of advertisements or graffiti usually vary the statement for their specific needs. Due to its questioning structure it can be applied to almost any controversial context or situation, and its frequent use as a "Antizitat" (anti-quotation) in the mass media has basically reduced it to a cliché. The article concludes with the citation and interpretation of the poem "Sein oder Nichtsein" (c. 1968) by Kay Lorentz (1920–). The original journal article contains 4 illustrations of political cartoons and advertisements.

3852.   Mieder, Wolfgang. *Antisprichwörter.* 3 vols. Wiesbaden: Verlag der deutschen Sprache, 1982; Wiesbaden: Gesellschaft für deutsche Sprache, 1985; Wiesbaden: Quelle & Meyer, 1989. I, 235 pp.; II, 222 pp.; III, 195 pp.

These three books represent a new type of proverb collection each containing 1500 German proverbs and proverbial expressions which have been intentionally varied or parodied by literary authors, aphoristic writers, journalists, advertising agents, cartoonists, humorists, and originators of graffiti and slogans over the past 300 years. The introductions to the first and third volumes (pp. VII-XVI and pp. VII-XX) explain the term "Antisprichwort" (anti-proverb) and discuss the reasons for such proverb variations (wordplay, humor, satire, irony, etc.). The 4500 texts are numbered consecutively and arranged alphabetically according to the key-words of the underlying basic proverb. For each entry there is a precise bibliographical reference, and each volume also contains large bibliographies concerning modern proverb usage (I, pp. 220–235; II, pp. 207–222; and III, pp. 177–195). With over 100 illustrations of cartoons, advertisements, and newspaper or magazine headlines. The first volume also appeared as a paperback with the title *Honig klebt am längsten. Das Anti-Sprichwörter Buch* (München: Wilhelm Heyne, 1985).

3853. Mieder, Wolfgang. "Die Einstellung der Grammatiker Schottelius und Gottsched zum Sprichwort." *Sprachspiegel*, 38 (1982), 70–75.

This short article investigates the interest in proverbs and proverbial expressions by the two German grammarians Justus Georg Schottelius (1612–1676) and Johann Christoph Gottsched (1700–1766). Schottelius included a collection of 1790 texts in his voluminous work *Ausführliche Arbeit Von der Teutschen Haupt-Sprache* (1663) together with a treatise about the nature and importance of proverbial language for effective rhetoric and writing. Gottsched proceeded similarly in his book *Grundlegung einer deutschen Sprachkunst* (1748) which contains a collection of 971 texts. Just like Schottelius he argued that the German language is rich in proverbial expressions, that it is this folk language which differentiates German from French, and that fixed phrases should be used for meaningful oral and written communication. See also Ella Schafferus (no. 1639) and Ingrid Höpel (no. 3613).

3854. Mieder, Wolfgang. "'Eine aphoristische Schwalbe macht schon einen halben Gedankensommer'. Zu den Aphorismen von Felix Renner." *Sprachspiegel*, 38 (1982), 162–167; rpt. in W. Mieder. *Sprichwort, Redensart, Zitat. Tradierte Formelsprache in der Moderne.* Bern: Peter Lang, 1985. 65–71.

The author studies the aphorisms of the Swiss writer Felix Renner (1935–) and shows that many of his texts are in fact thought-provoking reactions to standard German proverbs and proverbial expressions. By putting the traditional wisdom of proverbs into question, Renner creates innovative aphoristic "Antisprichwörter" (anti-proverbs). He does this by switching letters, by substituting words, by coupling contradictory proverbs, by adding his own comments, etc. The result is that Renner shocks his readers into rethinking established rules of behavior. This wordplay with proverbs might be humorous, ironical or satirical, but everywhere one senses a sincere moral commitment on Renner's part. Many examples are cited throughout the paper by contrasting them with the folk proverbs. See also Mieder's second article on Renner's proverbial language (no. 3906 below).

3855.   Mieder, Wolfgang. "'Eine Frau ohne Mann ist wie ein Fisch ohne Velo'!" *Sprachspiegel,* 38 (1982), 141–142.

Short study of the misogynous nature of proverbs with special emphasis on the recent loan translation of the modern American proverb "A woman without a man is like a fish without a bicycle" into German as "Eine Frau ohne Mann ist wie ein Fisch ohne Velo (Fahrrad)." It is pointed out that there exists a long tradition in both the English and the German languages of the proverbial formula "Eine Frau ohne Mann ist (wie) ein(e) X ohne Y" and "A woman without a man is (like) an X without a Y." This is clearly the major reason why this new feminist proverb was able to gain currency so quickly in oral speech, in headlines, and on T-shirts.

3856.   Mieder, Wolfgang. *International Proverb Scholarship: An Annotated Bibliography.* New York: Garland Publishing, 1982. 613 pp.

Major bibliographical reference work for all aspects of regional, national, and international paremiology. The bibliography covers scholarly articles, dissertations, monographs, and books from as many languages as possible. Altogether 2142 studies published during the past 200 years have been critically annotated in English. The entries vary in length from four lines to a whole page for some of the major studies. They deal with research from such varied fields as anthropology, art, ethnology, folklore, history, law, linguistics, literature, mass communication (media), medicine, philology, psychology, religion, sociology, etc. Proverbs mentioned in the annotations are cited in their original language with an English translation, and for persons (literary authors, politicians, scholars, etc.) the dates are indicated as well. The entries also include references to whether a given study contains statistical tables, graphs, indices, bibliographies, abstracts (summaries), or illustrations. No abbreviations have been used in the book in order to maintain absolute clarity in the bibliographical entries and the annotations for an international readership. For every entry approximately a dozen key-words have been entered in the large name, subject, and proverb indices (pp. 531–613). The bibliography itself is organized alphabetically according to the authors' names and chronologically under each name. This study is the first attempt on an international basis to present proverb scholars with an inclusive bibliographical research tool of paremiology. For a supplement to this volume see Wolfgang Mieder (no. 3927).

3857. Mieder, Wolfgang. "'Nach Zitaten drängt, am Zitate hängt doch alles!' Zur modernen Verwendung von Goethe-Zitaten." *Muttersprache*, 92 (1982), 76–98; also in W. Mieder. *Deutsche Sprichwörter in Literatur, Politik, Presse und Werbung*. Hamburg: Helmut Buske, 1983. 158–180.

In this article Mieder analyzes the widespread modern use of intentionally varied literary quotations (geflügelte Worte) from Johann Wolfgang von Goethe (1749–1832) in German newspapers, magzines, literature, advertisements, cartoons, etc. There exists a long tradition of parodying quotations of classical authors, especially since many of them have in fact become proverbial. Many examples out of the play *Götz von Berlichingen* (1773), the novel *Die Leiden des jungen Werthers* (1774), *Faust* (1808/32), and poems, notably the ballad "Erlkönig" (1782), are discussed. The more known the quotations are (many of them are now proverbs), the more they are subjected to this type of wordplay, humor, punning, joking, and satire by their modern users. With 10 illustrations of cartoons, political caricatures, humorous photographs, etc.

3858. Mieder, Wolfgang. "Proverbs in Nazi Germany. The Promulgation of Anti-Semitism and Stereotypes through Folklore." *Journal of American Folklore*, 95 (1982), 435–464.

A detailed analysis of the perverted use of proverbs in Nazi Germany to spread anti-Semitism. The paper presents a short analysis of folklore studies under the Nazi regime and then discusses major Yiddish proverb collections of the 19th and early 20th centuries. This is followed by an investigation of the deliberate use of anti-Semitic proverbs and stereotypes by Adolf Hitler (1889–1945) and the National Socialists. This went as far as the publication of two major proverb collections against the innocent Jewish population by Karl Bergmann (see nos. 143–145) and Julius Schwab (no. 1680), who tried to show through proverbs that Jews are racially impure, dirty, criminal, subversive, etc. But Mieder also discovered a dissertation by Helene Heger (no. 697) and a number of "scholarly" articles along these lines (nos. 803, 1521, and 1647), indicating how proverbs were misused to influence, manipulate and poison people's feelings, thoughts and actions. An inclusive bibliography (pp. 461–464) concerning this racially discriminating and political use of proverbs by the Nazi propaganda machine concludes this essay. For a similar version of this article in German see Wolfgang Mieder (no. 3863).

3859. Mieder, Wolfgang. "Sexual Content of German Wellerisms." *Maledicta*, 6 (1982), 215–223.

Stating that sexually explicit or offensive proverbs and wellerisms have usually not been included in German proverb collections, Mieder lists and discusses the sexual content of a considerable number of German wellerisms with English translations. Some were found in older collections, others in the journal *Anthropophyteia*, and many in modern German literature and the mass media (magazines, graffiti, etc.) They deal with fornication, scatology, the penis, the vagina, sodomy, etc. Not all texts are necessarily obscene, but they still indicate the prevalence of sexual humor and a preoccupation with sexual mores. Many of the examples are based on wordplays and puns, but some are very direct in their sexual language and meaning.

3860. Mieder, Wolfgang. *Deutsche Sprichwörter in Literatur, Politik, Presse und Werbung.* Hamburg: Helmut Buske, 1983. 230 pp.

This is a collection of 11 articles on German proverbs in literature, politics, journalism, and advertising which Mieder published between 1973 and 1983 in the journal *Muttersprache.*

Included are "Verwendungsmöglichkeiten und Funktionswerte des Sprichwortes in der Wochenzeitung" (pp. 11–41); "Das Sprichwort als Ausdruck kollektiven Sprechens in Alfred Döblins *Berlin Alexanderplatz* (pp. 42–52); "Sprichwörter im modernen Sprachgebrauch" (pp. 53–76); "Der Krieg um den Krug: Ein Sprichwortgefecht. Zum 200. Geburtstag Heinrich von Kleists" (pp. 77–91); "Sprichwörtliche Schlagzeilen in der Wochenzeitung" (pp. 92–104); "Rund um das Sprichwort 'Morgenstunde hat Gold im Munde'" (pp. 105–112); "Karl Kraus und der sprichwörtliche Aphorismus" (pp. 113–131); "Die drei weisen Affen und das Sprichwort 'Nichts sehen, nichts hören, nichts sagen'" (pp. 132–143); "Bibliographische Skizze zur Überlieferung des Ausdrucks 'Iron Curtain'/'Eiserner Vorhang'" (pp. 144–157); "'Nach Zitaten drängt, am Zitate hängt doch alles!' Zur modernen Verwendung von Goethe-Zitaten" (pp. 158–180); and "Sprichwörter unterm Hakenkreuz" (pp. 181–210). Mieder also includes an introduction (pp. 7–9), a sizable bibliography on modern proverb scholarship (pp. 211–221), as well as a key-word index of the proverbs, proverbial expressions, aphorisms, and quotations cited. There are 27 illustrations and many statistical tables. For annotations of these essays dealing with mass media, literature, slogans, aphorisms, literary quotations (geflügelte Worte), politics, Nazi Germany, variation, tradition, innovation, structure, language, function, etc., see nos. 1233, 1223, 1244, 1251, 1264, 1263, 1271, 1274, 1278, 3857, 3863.

3861. Mieder, Wolfgang (ed.). *Friedrich Petri (Peters). Der Teutschen Weissheit.* Faksimiledruck der Auflage von 1604/05. Bern: Peter Lang, 1983. 1052 pp.

   A reprint of the first German mass proverb collection of 21,643 texts entitled *Der Teutschen Weissheit* (1604/05) by Friedrich Petri (or Peters, 1549–1617). In his introduction (pp. 9–54) Mieder discusses Petri's life and his activities as a protestant minister, he presents an historical account of German proverb collections of the 16th and 17th centuries, and he also analyzes the importance of Petri as a major paremiographer as well as the organization of his collection. This is followed by a first bibliography of Petri's own writings and the secondary literature concerning him as well as his proverb collection (pp. 55–69). To this is added a bibliography (pp. 69–74) of major proverb collections of the 17th century and of studies of the use and function of proverbs in the literary works of German authors of the Baroque era.

3862. Mieder, Wolfgang. "Martin Luther und die Geschichte des Sprichwortes 'Wes das Herz voll ist, des geht der Mund über'." *Sprachspiegel*, 39 (1983), 66–74.

Analyzes the origin and history of the Biblical proverb "Ex abundantia cordis os loquitur" (Matth. 12,34) which was translated into German by Martin Luther (1483–1546) as "Wes das Herz voll ist, des geht der Mund über" (Out of the abundance of the heart the mouth speaketh). Earlier translation attempts are discussed, but it is shown that of all variants Luther's version became the generally accepted proverb. Mieder ends his diachronic survey with modern parodies of this proverb in literature, aphoristic writings, and the mass media. See also John Kunstmann (no. 945), William Kurrelmeyer (no. 2567), and Timothy Nelson (no. 4015).

3863. Mieder, Wolfgang. "Sprichwörter unterm Hakenkreuz." *Muttersprache*, 93 (1983), 1–30; also in W. Mieder. *Deutsche Sprichwörter in Literatur, Politik, Presse und Werbung*. Hamburg: Helmut Buske, 1983. 181–210.

A somewhat different German version of Mieder's English paper on proverbs in Nazi Germany (see no. 3858 above). This study starts with a review of the publications on the nature of language abuse during the period of the National Socialists. It is pointed out that anti-Semitic proverbs and their use did not start with the Nazis, as can be seen from collections of the 19th and 20th centuries. But the Nazi propaganda machine and Adolf Hitler (1889–1945) himself were masters in the perverted use of anti-Semitic proverbs. Scholars of the German language participated in this, as evidenced by two large collections of such stereotypical proverbs by Karl Bergmann (see nos. 143–145) and Julius Schwab (no. 1860). There is also the misguided dissertation by Helene Heger (no. 697) and several smaller studies directed towards discrediting innocent Jews through hateful proverbs (see nos. 803, 1521, and 1647). Many examples are included to show how ill-conceived and misinterpreted proverbs became dangerous weapons against the Jewish population in the hands of inhuman leaders and people. Early reactions against this linguistic abuse by Karl Kraus (1874–1936), Bertolt Brecht (1898–1956), and others are quoted, and so are more modern prose texts and poems by Helmut Heißenbüttel (1921–) and Reinhard Döhl (1934–), who use proverbs and proverbial expressions to show the ills of that time and how the Germans are now trying to come to terms with their past ("Vergangenheitsbewältigung").

3864. Mieder, Wolfgang. "'Was Hänschen nicht lernt, lernt Hans nimmermehr'. Zur Überlieferung eines Luther-Sprichwortes." *Sprachspiegel,* 39 (1983), 131–138.

Mieder traces the German proverb "Was Hänschen nicht lernt, lernt Hans nimmermehr" (What little John does not learn, big John will not learn either) from its origin with Martin Luther (1483–1546) to modern aphorisms and parodies by Marie von Ebner-Eschenbach (1830–1916), Gerhard Uhlenbruck (1929–), and others. It is shown that this proverb has played a major role in German pedagogy and child rearing, but that its educational wisdom and value are being questioned today due to adult education programs, etc. Many variants and "Antisprichwörter" (anti-proverbs) of this well-known proverb are discussed.

3865. Mieder, Wolfgang. "'Wine, Women and Song': From Martin Luther to American T-Shirts." *Kentucky Folklore Record,* 29 (1983), 89–101; also rpt. in *Folk Groups and Folklore Genres: A Reader.* Ed. Elliott Oring. Logan/Utah: Utah State University Press, 1989. 279–290.

In this article Mieder traces the Anglo-American history of the German proverb "Wer nicht liebt Wein, Weib und Gesang, der bleibt ein Narr sein Leben lang" (Who loves not wine, woman [women], and song, remains a fool his whole life long) that is erroneously attributed to Martin Luther (1483–1546). It has been recorded in German for the first time in 1775 in a short poem by Johann Heinrich Voß (1751–1826), and it appears in English print in the middle of the 19th century in Henry Bohn's *A Polyglot of Foreign Proverbs* (1857). The poem "Doctor Luther" which William Makepeace Thackeray (1811–1863) included in his novel *The Adventures of Philip* (1861/62) helped to popularize the proverb, and it now has appeared in numerous English and American poems and drinking songs, as for example in poems by Ernest Christopher Dowson (1867–1900) and Eugene Field (1850–1895). In the meantime the proverb has been reduced to the triadic structure of "Wine, women, and song" or simply "Wine, women, and X," and it has become a popular formula for parodies, cartoons, and T-shirt slogans. With 4 illustrations. For a similar German version of this paper and a diachronic study of the German proverb see Wolfgang Mieder (nos. 3880 and 3866 below).

3866. Mieder, Wolfgang. "'Wer nicht liebt Wein, Weib und Gesang, der bleibt ein Narr sein Leben lang'. Zur Herkunft, Überlieferung und Verwendung eines angeblichen Luther-Spruches." *Muttersprache*, 94 (Sonderheft, 1983–1984), 68–103.

This is an historical and cultural investigation of the German proverb "Wer nicht liebt Wein, Weib und Gesang, der bleibt ein Narr sein Leben lang" (Who does not love wine, woman [women], and song, remains a fool his whole life long). Classical and medieval Latin variants are presented, and the possibility of Martin Luther's (1483–1546) authorship is discussed, even though the proverb in this form is only documented for the first time in 1775 in a short poem by Johann Heinrich Voß (1751–1826). Many German parallels and variants from the 13th century on are analyzed, and references to the proverb in German literature, in drinking songs, and poems are studied up to the present day, including such authors as Georg Christoph Lichtenberg (1742–1799), Johann Wolfgang von Goethe (1749–1832), Heinrich Heine (1797–1856), Heinrich August Hoffmann von Fallersleben (1798–1874), Arno Holz (1863–1929), Thomas Mann (1875–1955), and others. References are also made to musical treatments of this Epicurean piece of wisdom by Johann Strauß (1825–1899) and Oscar Straus (1870–1954), as well as to recent puns and parodies in aphorisms based on this popular proverb. With 3 illustrations. See also nos. 3865 and 3880 for the Anglo-American history of the proverb.

3867. Mieder, Wolfgang. "Christian Weises *Bäurischer Machiavellus* als sprichwortreiches Intrigenspiel." *Daphnis*, 13 (1984), 363–384.

A literary investigation of the use and function of proverbs in Christian Weise's (1642–1708) comedy *Bäurischer Machiavellus* (1681). Mieder starts with a discussion of the view of proverbs in the 17th century by such authors and grammarians as Georg Philipp Harsdörffer (1607–1658) and Justus Georg Schottelius (1612–1676). He shows that they as well as Weise considered proverbs to be of greatest importance as folk expressions and as welcome contrast to the stilted literary language of the Baroque era with its many French loan words. Weise's drama is then interpreted as a proverbial play of intrigue, in which proverbs are used effectively as manipulative and argumentative devices. An annotated index of 106 proverbs and an analysis of several proverbs in their dramatic context are included.

3868. Mieder, Wolfgang. "'Cogito, ergo sum'. Zum Weiterleben eines berühmten Zitats." *Der Sprachdienst*, 28 (1984), 161–167; rpt. in W. Mieder. *Sprichwort, Redensart, Zitat. Tradierte Formelsprache in der Moderne.* Bern: Peter Lang, 1985. 163–173.

Detailed analysis of the modern survival of René Descartes' (1596–1650) famous Latin quotation "Cogito, ergo sum" in the German society. Mieder cites humorous, ironical, and satirical poems, epigrams, and aphorisms by such authors as Karl Julius Weber (1767–1832), August Heinrich Hoffmann von Fallersleben (1798–1874), Peter Tille (1938–), Stanislaw Jerzy Lec (1909–1966), Albert Ehrismann (1908–), Kurt Leonhard (1910–), Heinrich Schröter (1917–), Nikolaus Cybinski (1936–), Eugen Roth (1895–1976), Werner Mitsch (1936–), Gerhard Uhlenbruck (1929–), and others who have all parodied this philosophical statement. In addition the author discusses advertisements, slogans, wordplays, and graffitis that are based on this quotation which has become so popular that it can be regarded as proverbial in intellectual circles. Many of the variations express political concerns, but some texts are also scatological, obscene or nonsensical. With 2 illustrations. See also Beat Suter (no. 4450).

3869. Mieder, Wolfgang (ed.). *Deutsche Sprichwörterforschung des 19. Jahrhunderts.* Bern: Peter Lang, 1984. 345 pp.

This essay volume reprints the following 9 important German essays on various aspects of proverbs and proverbial expressions which were published in the 19th century: Carl Prantl, "Die Philosophie in den Sprichwörtern" (pp. 15–44); Franz C. Honcamp, "Das Sprichwort, sein Werth und seine Bedeutung" (pp. 45–66); Carl Friedrich Schnitzer, "Begriff und Gebrauch der Redensart" (pp. 67–80); Wilhelm Urbas, "Die Sprichwörter und ihre Entstehung" (pp. 81–108); Moritz Callman Wahl, "Das Sprichwort innerhalb der Phraseologie der neueren Sprachen" (pp. 109–172); Josef Schiepek, "Bemerkungen zur psychologischen Grundlage des Sprichwortes " (pp. 173–199); Karl Maaß, "Über Metapher und Allegorie im deutschen Sprichwort" (pp. 201–260); Karl Spieß, "Das Sprichwort" (pp. 261–285); and Jakob Lautenbach, "Zur Parömiologie" (pp. 287–307). These paremiological essays treat such matters as definition, origin, meaning, function, use, context, form, style, language, metaphor, allegory, psychology, national character, internationality, variation, philosophy, etc. Although most examples are German texts, many proverbs are cited from other European languages so that the book actually also deals with comparative phraseology. Mieder has added an introduction (pp. 7–13), a bibliography of proverb collections and scholarship of the 19th century (pp. 309–321), and extensive name, subject, and proverb indices (pp. 323–345). See also Hans-Manfred Militz (no. 3954). For annotations of the individual essays see nos. 1481, 751, 2834, 1981, 2020, 1645, 1130, 1783, and 1017.

3870. Mieder, Wolfgang. "'Die Axt im Haus erspart den Zimmermann' (*Wilhelm Tell*, III,1). Vom Schiller-Zitat zum parodierten Sprichwort." *Sprachspiegel,* 40 (1984), 137–142; rpt. in W. Mieder. *Sprichwort, Redensart, Zitat. Tradierte Formelsprache in der Moderne.* Bern: Peter Lang, 1985. 155–161.

This article deals with the literary quotation "Die Axt im Haus erspart den Zimmermann" (The ax in the house saves the carpenter) which Friedrich Schiller (1759–1805) used in his drama *Wilhelm Tell* (1804). Mieder explains that Schiller might have been influenced by earlier German proverbs dealing with the "ax," but above all he shows that this quotation ("geflügeltes Wort") has long become a proverb in the German language. He also cites many modern aphorisms and parodies which have changed the quotation/proverb to a "Antisprichwort" (anti-proverb). The interrelationship of sententious remarks and proverbs is explained, and the author is able to illustrate the modern survival of this popular expression in literature as well as graffiti.

3871.   Mieder, Wolfgang. "'Eulen nach Athen tragen', 'To Carry Coals to Newcastle'." *Proverbium*, 1 (1984), 183–185.

A small note asking for the help from paremiologists in the search for international, national, and regional variants of the proverbial expression "Eulen nach Athen tragen" (To carry owls to Athens). A few texts of this proverb type referring to a superfluous deed (act) are listed in English translation: "To carry coals to Newcastle," "To carry straw to Egypt," "To carry fur trees to Norway," "To carry tea to China," "To carry indulgences to Rome," "To carry pepper to Hindustan," "To carry beer to Munich," etc. It is hoped that international cooperation will result in a global study of these expressions. See also Stanislaw Predota (no. 4195), Cesar Tabarcea (no. 4462), and Fionnuala Williams (no. 4561) for Polish, Rumanian, and Irish parallels.

3872.   Mieder, Wolfgang. "Geschichte und Probleme der neuhochdeutschen Sprichwörterlexikographie." *Studien zur neuhochdeutschen Lexikographie.* Ed. Herbert Ernst Wiegand. Hildesheim: Georg Olms, 1984. V, 307–358 (=*Germanistische Linguistik*, 3–6 [1984], 307–358).

This is a major review article of the chaotic situation of German proverb lexicography from the 16th century to the modern age. Mieder discusses the classification system as well as the purpose and importance of numerous proverb collections, including those by Johann Agricola (1492–1566), Martin Luther (1483–1546), Sebastian Franck (1499–1542), Christian Egenolff (1502–1555), Michael Neander (1525–1595), Friedrich Petri (Peters, 1549–1617), Christoph Lehmann (1568–1638), Justus Georg Schottelius (1616–1676), Ernst Mejsner (17th/18th century), Johann Jacob Heinrich Bücking (1749–18?), Andreas Schellhorn (1761–1819), Johann Michael Sailer (1751–1832), Wilhelm Körte (1776–1846), Josua Eiselein (19th century), Karl Simrock (1802–1876), Gotthard Oswald Marbach (1810–1890), Karl Friedrich Wilhelm Wander (1803–1879), Karl Rauch (1897–19?), Lutz Mackensen (1901–), and some others. After this survey (pp. 310–339) Mieder discusses lexicographical problems of proverb archives and collections, the interest in making international collections based on proverb types, the use of the computer by paremiographers, and the way a new diachronic German proverb collection could be modelled on the collections by the American paremiographer Bartlett Jere Whiting (1904–). An example of how variants of the German proverb "Morgenstunde hat Gold im Munde" (The early bird gets the worm) from 1582 to the present should be catalogued is included. The bibliography (pp. 349–358) contains a chronological list of major German proverb collections and studies on paremiographical lexicography.

3873. Mieder, Wolfgang. "G.L. Permiakov's Last Letter to Wolfgang Mieder." *Proverbium*, 1 (1984), 153.

Shortly before his untimely death on November 16, 1983, the leading Soviet paremiologist Grigorii L'vovich Permiakov (1919–1983) dictated a letter to his wife in which he expressed his delight about the newly planned *Proverbium: Yearbook of International Proverb Scholarship* under the editorship of Wolfgang Mieder. He also stated his views on the future direction of this publication in the following manner: "I should like to see in *Proverbium* a study not only of the proverbs, but also of all the other types of paremias, in particular, of wellerisms, omens, riddles, superstitions, and the others. The fact is that my research showed that all the types and kinds of paremias possess the set of the same text functions and differ only by the chief (dominating) functions. It is no mere chance that all of them often turn (or can turn) from one type to another. A proverb turns into a riddle (and vice versa), an omen into a proverb (and vice versa), and so on." Since 1984 the editors of *Proverbium* have tried to adhere to these criteria set forth by Permiakov.

3874. Mieder, Wolfgang. "International Bibliography of New and Reprinted Proverb Collections." *Proverbium*, 1 (1984), 251–271; 2 (1985), 373–378; 3 (1986), 421–430; 4 (1987), 361–368; 5 (1988), 213–218; 6 (1989), 273–279; 7 (1990), 299–303; and 8 (1991), 279–284.

As the title suggests, Mieder assembles an annual international bibliography of new and reprinted proverb collections for each *Proverbium* volume. Together the 8 volumes have registered 614 collections of proverbs, proverbial expressions, wellerisms, and idioms. These yearly bibliographies are intended to bring the newest paremiographical literature from around the world to the attention of scholars everywhere. While most of the items are scholarly diachronic or synchronic collections of regional, national or international texts, the bibliographies also include many popular collections. It is truly amazing to see how publishers flood the market with such small collections that are meant to serve the general reading public. They certainly show the great interest in proverbs that seems to exist in most cultures. Due to space restrictions in *Proverbium* there are no annotations to these bibliographical entries.

3875. Mieder, Wolfgang. "International Proverb Scholarship: An Updated Bibliography." *Proverbium*, 1 (1984), 273–309; 2 (1985), 379–396; 3 (1986), 431–480; 4 (1987), 369–405; 5 (1988), 219–243; 6 (1989), 281–307; 7 (1990), 305–323; and 8 (1991), 285–302.

These 8 annual bibliographies represent Mieder's attempt to keep international paremiologists up-to-date on the newest paremiological publications from around the world. They update the two volumes of Mieder's *International Proverb Scholarship: An Annotated Bibliography* (1982 and 1990), and all of the entries that have appeared between 1982 and 1991 are now included and annotated in the present third volume to this international bibliography. The 8 yearly bibliographies list a total of 2046 books, monographs, dissertations, and articles on proverbs published by scholars from everywhere. These bibliographical lists will be continued in *Proverbium*, but as usual it will not be possible to publish annotations due to space restrictions. The most important purpose of the yearly bibliographies is to inform scholars of the newest research results, and annotations will be provided in the next supplementary volume to Mieder's book-length bibliographies.

3876. Mieder, Wolfgang. *Investigations of Proverbs, Proverbial Expressions, Quotations and Clichés. A Bibliography of Explanatory Essays which Appeared in "Notes and Queries" (1849–1983)*. Bern: Peter Lang, 1984.

This bibliography includes approximately 10,000 notes explaining the origin, history, and meaning of individual proverbs, proverbial expressions, quotations, and clichés which have appeared in 228 volumes of the British journal *Notes and Queries* from 1849 to 1983. Most entries refer to English texts, but there are also explanatory notes on French, German, and Latin expressions. References to twin formulas, reduplicatives, wellerisms, and weather proverbs are also included, making this book a useful bibliography for the philological and historical study of proverbial materials. For additional references out of other journals see W. Mieder's *International Bibliography of Explanatory Essays on Individual Proverbs and Proverbial Expressions* (1977; see no. 1253). The present bibliography contains no annotations.

3877. Mieder, Wolfgang. "'Kredit ist tot'." *Proverbium*, 1 (1984), 187–189.

The author reviews the existing literature on the proverb "Kredit ist tot" (Credit is dead) and its variants in several European languages, but the major point of this note is the call for national and regional bibliographies registering the investigations of individual proverbs, proverbial expressions, wellerisms, etc. Many times such studies are mere notes, and they were published in obscure journals or newspapers. For the study of the origin, history, and dissemination of proverbs such bibliographies are absolutely essential. For the proverb "Credit is dead" see also Monique Coppens d'Eeckenbrugge (no. 301), Adolf Spamer (no. 1772), Walter Tobler (no. 1955), Kari Laukkanen (no. 2584), and René Saulnier and Henri van der Zée (no. 4311).

3878. Mieder, Wolfgang. "Mathilde Hain (1901–1983)." *Proverbium*, 1 (1984), 155–160.

A necrology of Mathilde Hain (1901–1983) who was one of the truly outstanding German folklorists and paremiologists of this century. Mieder gives a short biographical sketch and then reviews Hain's major paremiological contributions. Of special importance was Hain's seminal work *Sprichwort und Volkssprache. Eine volkskundlich-soziologische Dorfuntersuchung* (1951; see no. 640) in which she reported on the dialect proverb repertoire of the inhabitants of a small village in Germany. In addition to this study based on folkloric and sociological field research Hain also published comprehensive papers on the German proverb, the use of proverbs in literature, and the origin and history of individual expressions. For bibliographical information see M. Hain (nos. 640–645).

3879. Mieder, Wolfgang. "Recent International Proverb Scholarship: An Annotated Bibliography for 1982 and 1983." *Proverbium*, 1 (1984), 311–350.

Intended as an update to Mieder's *International Proverb Scholarship: An Annotated Bibliography* (1982), this bibliography of recent paremiological research from throughout the world lists 76 new publications from the years 1982 and 1983. The bibliography includes books, monographs, dissertations, and articles on all proverb genres and phraseology from various nationalities and languages. Mieder included a similar annotated bibliography in the second volume of *Proverbium* for the years 1983 and 1984 (see no. 3886 below), but this service of supplying annotations had to be dropped starting with the annual bibliography in volume three due to space limitations in

Proverbium. All of the entries and annotations are now included in the present volume.

3880. Mieder, Wolfgang. "'Wine, Women and Song': Zur anglo-amerikanischen Überlieferung eines angeblichen Lutherspruches." *Germanisch-Romanische Monatsschrift,* 65, new series 34 (1984), 385–403.

This is a similar German version of Mieder's English article (see no. 3865 above) on the Anglo-American history of the German proverb "Wer nicht liebt Wein, Weib und Gesang, der bleibt ein Narr sein Leben lang" (Who does not love wine, woman [women], and song, remains a fool his whole life long). The author points out that Martin Luther (1483–1546) did not originate the proverb, and that it appeared in print for the first time only in 1775 in a short poem by Johann Heinrich Voß (1751–1826). An English translation of the proverb appeared first in Henry Bohn's *A Polyglot of Foreign Proverbs* (1857), but Mieder shows that the triad of "Wine, women, and X" goes back to classical times and can be found in English proverb collections as well as in the poetry of Robert Burton (1577–1640), John Gay (1685–1732), George Byron (1788–1824), etc. The proverb might have gained more currency in the English language through the poem "Doctor Luther" which William Makepeace Thackeray (1811–1863) included in his novel *The Adventures of Philip* (1861/62). From more modern literature Mieder cites references by Eugene Field (1850–1895) and Ernest Christopher Dowson (1867–1900). An account of the lexicographical history of the proverb in English dictionaries and proverb collections is also included, and numerous modern parodies and jokes based on this popular proverb are analyzed as well. See also no. 3866 for a study of the German history of the proverb.

3881. Mieder, Wolfgang. "'Zitate sind des Bürgers Zierde'. Zum Weiterleben von Schiller-Zitaten." *Muttersprache,* 95 (1984–1985), 284–306.

This article investigates the justified claim that Friedrich Schiller (1759–1805) is a very sententious dramatist and poet whose "geflügelte Worte" (sententious remarks) have to a large extent become proverbial in the German language. Mieder cites many examples from such plays as *Die Verschwörung des Fiesco von Genua* (1784), *Jungfrau von Orleans* (1801), and *Wilhelm Tell* (1804), but he also analyzes the proverbial quotations from such poems and ballads as "An die Freude" (1786), "Die Bürgschaft" (1799), and "Lied von der Glocke" (1800). When these sententious remarks are quoted by literary authors like Theodor Fontane (1819–1898), Erich Fried (1921–1989), Heinrich Schröter (1917–), Hermann Kant (1926–), Gerhard Uhlenbruck (1929–), Christa Wolf (1929–), etc., they are usually parodied or quoted in a satirical context. Mieder also cites many modern aphorisms, graffiti, newspaper headlines, and advertising slogans to show how Schiiler's famous quotations are changed into "Antizitate" (anti-quotations). With 8 illustrations.

3882. Mieder, Wolfgang. "A Proverb a Day Keeps no Chauvinism away." *Proverbium*, 2 (1985), 273–277.

A short note to explain the misogynous nature of many proverbs whose stereotypical views of women are unfortunately still expressed today. Mieder points out that such traditional English proverbs as "A woman's tongue wags like a lamb's tail" and "Women are necessary evils" were obviously created by misogynists, and their anti-feminist attitudes can be found to this day in newspaper headlines, advertising slogans, etc. The author also explains that such common Biblical proverbs as "A man does not live by bread alone" (Deuteronomy 8,3; Matth. 4,4) might better be rephrased by changing "man" to "people." Fortunately there are now more modern anti-proverbs which change a traditional proverb like "A woman's place is in the home" to the liberated and politically desirable statement that "A woman's place is in the House—and in the Senate."

3883. Mieder, Wolfgang. "Einer fehlt beim Gruppenbild. 'Geflügelter' Abschied von Heinrich Böll." *Der Sprachdienst*, 29 (1985), 167–172.

In this short article Mieder explains how Heinrich Böll's (1917–1985) titles of short stories and novels have become sententious if not proverbial in the German language, notably

Wanderer, kommst du nach Spa . . . (1950), *Wo warst du, Adam?* (1951), *Und sagte kein einziges Wort* (1953), *Haus ohne Hüter* (1954), *Ende einer Dienstfahrt* (1966), *Gruppenbild mit Dame* (1971), and *Die verlorene Ehre der Katharina Blum* (1974). Mieder shows that these titles are quoted verbatim or in a varied form as parodistic and satirical comments in newspaper headlines, advertising slogans, graffiti, caricatures, etc. The modern adaptations of the titles are in the form of "Antizitate" (anti-quotations), and they are certainly indicative of the popularity of Böll's prose works in Germany. With 1 illustration.

3884. Mieder, Wolfgang. "Neues zur demoskopischen Sprich-wörterkunde." *Proverbium,* 2 (1985), 307–328.

Mieder starts this review of demographic paremiology with an analysis of the work by Gerda Grober-Glück (no. 607), Isidor Levin (no. 1049), and Grigorii L'vovich Permiakov (no. 2737) who all report on field research to establish which proverbs are particularly well known, used frequently, etc. But the major part of the article deals with an impressive study by the sociologists K. Hattemer and E.K. Scheuch entitled *Sprichwörter. Einstellung und Verwendung* (1983; see no. 3572). The two authors interviewed 400 German informants using a large questionnaire based on 27 questions to ascertain the importance of proverbs in the modern German society. It was established that "Morgenstunde hat Gold im Munde" (The early bird catches the worm) is the most popular and most frequently used German proverb. Questions of the questionnaire included the following: "Do you use proverbs a lot?," "When do you employ proverbs?," "Who uses proverbs (age groups and educational level)?," "What is the use and function of proverbs?," "Do men and women use proverbs with the same frequency?," "What is the communicative value of proverbs?," "How did you learn proverbs?," etc. The study includes dozens of statistical tables and extremely important results concerning proverbs as part of cultural literracy. Mieder argues that many more studies like this are needed to establish valid findings concerning the survival of proverbs in technological societies. The 13 notes include helpful bibliographical references.

3885. Mieder, Wolfgang. "Popular Views of the Proverb." *Proverbium*, 2 (1985), 109–143.

Realizing that there exist dozens of scholarly proverb definitions, Mieder asked 55 informants in Burlington, Vermont, the question "How would you define a proverb"? A word analysis of the most frequently used nouns, verbs, adjectives, and adverbs results in the following composite definition: "A proverb is a short, generally known sentence of the folk which contains wisdom, truth, morals, and traditional views in a metaphorical, fixed, and memorizable form and which is handed down from generation to generation." This definition could be reduced even more to a mere "A proverb is a short sentence of wisdom" by including only the words with the highest frequency counts. In the second part of the article (pp. 119–136) Mieder investigates how journalists and popular writers have defined a proverb in the mass media, and he concludes that they basically agree with the "folk" definition stated above. He concludes that people in general know quite well what a proverb is without knowing any of the erudite definition attempts by paremiologists. The 42 notes provide detailed bibliographical information.

3886. Mieder, Wolfgang. "Recent International Proverb Scholarship: An Annotated Bibliography for 1983 and 1984." *Proverbium*, 2 (1985), 397–467.

Intended as an update to Mieder's *International Proverb Scholarship: An Annotated Bibliography* (1982), this bibliography includes 106 annotations for books, monographs, dissertations, and articles published during the years 1983 and 1984 throughout the world. Mieder included a similar international bibliography in the first volume of *Proverbium* for 1982 and 1983 (see no. 3879 above), but this service was dropped with the third volume of *Proverbium* due to space limitations. Since that volume the author simply lists the publications in his annual bibliographies without any annotations which will be provided in later supplementary volumes to the book bibliography mentioned above. All of the entries and annotations of this bibliography are now included in the present volume.

3887. Mieder, Wolfgang. "Spiel mit Sprichwörtern. In memoriam Franz
       Fühmann (1922–1984)." *Sprachpflege,* 34 (1985), 1–3.

       This is a short literary investigation of Franz Fühmann's
       (1922–1984) use of proverbs in his prose work *Zweiundzwanzig
       Tage oder Die Hälfte des Lebens* (1974). Mieder shows that Fühmann
       usually changes the proverbs into so-called "Antisprichwörter"
       (anti-proverbs) in order to shock his modern readers into
       thinking more critically about the traditional wisdom of proverbs.
       He also discusses the game of mixing up individual halves of
       proverbs which Fühmann describes in this work. The result of
       such play with proverbs is often utter nonsense, but once in a
       while the innovative texts actually appear to make some sense.
       Mieder refers to this type of alteration of proverbs by the
       aphoristic writer Karl Kraus (1874–1936) and the poet Hansgeorg
       Stengel (1922–), explaining that Bertolt Brecht (1898–1956) was
       also very effective in the manipulative alienation of German
       proverbs in his plays.

3888. Mieder, Wolfgang. *Sprichwort, Redensart, Zitat. Tradierte
       Formelsprache in der Moderne.* Bern: Peter Lang, 1985. 203 pp.

       This essay volume is a collection of 19 previously published
       short articles by W. Mieder with the following titles: "Das
       Sprichwort als volkstümliches Zitat bei Thomas Mann" (pp. 11–
       14); "Carl Zuckmayer und die Volkssprache" (pp. 15–19);
       "Günter Grass und das Sprichwort" (pp. 21–25); "Kulinarische
       und emanzipatorische Redensartenverwendung in Günter Grass'
       Roman *Der Butt*" (pp. 27–35); "'Redensarten, Ausreden,
       Ansprüche'. Zu Helmut Heißenbüttels Prosatext *Rollenverteilung*
       (1965)" (pp. 37–44); "'Aus de windische Schprich de Wind
       rauslasse'. Zu Kurt Sigels redensartlicher Dialektdichtung" (pp.
       45–51); "'Ein Aphoristiker dreht of das Sprichwort im Munde
       herum'. Zu den Aphorismen von Gerhard Uhlenbruck" (pp. 53–
       63); "'Eine aphoristische Schwalbe macht schon einen halben
       Gedankensommer'. Zu den Aphorismen von Felix Renner" (pp.
       65–71); "Moderne deutsche Sprichwortgedichte" (pp. 73–90);
       "Sprichwörtliche Redensarten als Schlagzeile" (pp. 91–100);
       "'Der Apfel fällt weit von Deutschland." Zur amerikanischen
       Entlehnung eines deutschen Sprichwortes" (pp. 101–107); "Eine

bibliographische Skizze zum Ursprung von 'O.K.' (Okay)" (pp. 109–113); "Buchtitel als Schlagzeile" (pp. 115–123); "'Sein oder Nichtsein'—und kein Ende. Zum Weiterleben des Hamlet Zitats in unserer Zeit" (pp. 125–130); "Drillingsformeln: Texte, Titel und Tendenzen" (pp. 131–139); "Angloamerikanische und deutsche Überlieferung des Ausdrucks 'Last (but) not least'" (pp. 141–149); "'Zum Tango gehören zwei'" (pp. 151–154; with George B. Bryan); "'Die Axt im Haus erspart den Zimmermann' (*Wilhelm Tell*, III,1). Vom Schiller-Zitat zum parodierten Sprichwort" (pp. 155–161); and "'Cogito, ergo sum'. Zum modernen Weiterleben eines berühmten Zitats" (pp. 163–173). The essays deal with the use and function of proverbs and proverbial expressions in modern German literature, folk speech, aphorisms, proverb poems, mass media, headlines, graffiti, loan translations, "geflügelte Worte" (literary quotations), triadic formulas, "Antisprichwörter" (anti-proverbs), "Antizitate" (anti-quotations), etc. A large bibliography (pp. 175–186) and three indices of names, subjects, and key-words (pp. 187–203) are included. For individual annotations see nos. 1221, 1246, 1229, 1259, 1272, 1267, 1280, 3854, 1276, 1249, 1279, 3850, 3849, 3851, 1275, 1281, 3939, 3870, 3865.

3889. Mieder, Wolfgang. "'To Pay the Piper' and the Legend of 'The Pied Piper of Hamelin'." *Proverbium*, 2 (1985), 263–270.

The author starts by explaining the the English proverbial expression "To pay the piper" with its earliest citation from 1638 is most likely a shortened form of such proverbs as "He who pays the piper may order (can call) the tune" (1611), "Who pays the piper, calls the tune" (1611), or "Those that dance must pay the music" (1638). However, many lexicographers of phraseological dictionaries believe that the phrase originated from the famous German legend of "Der Rattenfänger von Hameln" (The Pied Piper of Hamelin) that dates back to 1284. Realizing how popular Robert Browning's (1812–1889) poem "The Pied Piper of Hamelin" (1842) continues to be in the Anglo-American world, one might well consider the legend and the poem as a "secondary" source of the proverbial expression. It certainly is true that the burghers of Hamelin had to pay the piper, losing their beloved children as it were.

3890.   Mieder, Wolfgang. "'alle redensarten und sprüchwörter sind aus den quellen zu belegen'. Sprichwörtliches im *Deutschen Wörterbuch* der Brüder Grimm." *Muttersprache*, 96 (1986), 33–52; rpt. with minor changes in W. Mieder. *"Findet, so werdet ihr suchen!" Die Brüder Grimm und das Sprichwort.* Bern: Peter Lang, 1986. 89–113.

The author explains that both Jacob Grimm (1785–1863) and Wilhelm Grimm (1786–1859) had very keen interests in German proverbs and proverbial expressions. While Jacob worked especially on legal proverbs, Wilhelm was particularly interested in Middle High German proverbs. Together they integrated hundreds of proverbs into the first few volumes of the *Deutsches Wörterbuch* (1854ff.). Already in a newspaper article in the *Leipziger Allgemeine Zeitung* from August 29, 1838, announcing the beginning of the work on this large German dictionary, the Brothers Grimm stated that proverbs and proverbial expressions would be included. Mieder shows how the Grimms engaged various friends and colleagues who excerpted German literature and proverb collections for texts, and he then illustrates how the Brothers worked lexicographically to integrate their rich materials at the end of individual entries, for example under "Apfel" (apple), "Armut" (poverty), "Arsch" (ass), "Bärenhaut" (bearskin), "Bart" (beard), "denken" (to think), "Dorn" (thorn), and "dünn" (thin). The author concludes that the 32 volumes of this major German dictionary represent also one of the largest German proverb collections.

3891.   Mieder, Wolfgang (ed.). *Christoph Lehmann. Florilegium Politicum. Politischer Blumengarten.* Faksimiledruck der Auflage von 1639. Bern: Peter Lang, 1986. 1038 pp.

This is a reprint of Christoph Lehmann's (1568–1638) massive German proverb collection *Florilegium Politicum* which appeared in 1630 with 12,605 texts until it reached 22,922 texts in the last edition of 1662. Mieder begins his long introduction with a discussion of the life and works of the scholar and historian Christoph Lehmann (pp. 7*-24*), and he then discusses in much detail the importance and nature of his Baroque proverb collection (pp. 25*-50*). This is followed by a precise bibliographical history of all editions (pp. 51*-68*) that includes information on where copies of them can be found in European and American libraries. The remainder of the introduction (pp. 69*-85*) is comprised of a bibliography concerning Lehmann's other publications, studies about Lehmann himself, critical comments on his proverb collection, other important proverb collections of his time, and studies of proverbs in 17th century German literature.

3892. Mieder, Wolfgang. *"Findet, so werdet ihr suchen!" Die Brüder Grimm und das Sprichwort.* Bern: Peter Lang, 1986. 181 pp.

The 12 chapters of this book treat the great interest in German proverbs which both Jacob Grimm (1785–1863) and Wilhelm Grimm (1786–1859) had throughout their scholarly life. Chapter one (pp. 15–20) shows how they used proverbs and proverbial expressions in their many letters, while chapter two (pp. 21–24) illustrates the use and function of proverbial language in their scholarly style. The third chapter (pp. 25–28) looks at comments that the Grimms made about proverbs in the three volumes of the *Altdeutsche Wälder* (1813/16). In the fourth (pp. 29–36) and fifth (pp. 37–42) chapters Mieder gives examples of how both Jacob and Wilhelm Grimm deal with etymological and semantic questions regarding proverbs in various volumes of their so-called *Kleinere Schriften*. The sixth chapter (pp. 43–47) points out how Jacob cites proverbs in his *Deutsche Grammatik* (1819/37) to explain certain grammatical points, and the seventh chapter (pp. 49–51) makes clear that Jacob refers quite often to legal proverbs in his *Deutsche Rechtsaltertümer* (1828). The eighth chapter (pp. 53–63) shows Wilhelm's great knowledge of Middle High German proverbs in his edition of *Vridankes Bescheidenheit* (1834), while the ninth (pp. 65–77) and tenth (pp. 79–88) treat Jacob's references to proverbs in his *Deutsche Mythologie* (1835) and *Geschichte der deutschen Sprache* (1848). This is followed by the longer eleventh chapter (pp. 89–113) which illustrates the frequent citation of proverbs by the Brothers Grimm in the *Deutsches Wörterbuch* (1856/63). Finally, the twelfth chapter studies the way Wilhelm added more and more proverbial language to the *Kinder- und Hausmärchen* during the seven editions between 1812/15 and 1857. Detailed notes (pp. 145–162), a comprehensive bibliography (pp. 163–168), and three name, subject and proverb indices (pp. 169–181) conclude this study on the Grimms' preoccupation with German proverbs.

3893. Mieder, Wolfgang. "'Spaß muß sein', sagte der Spaßmacher, aber ... Zu den Sagwörtern von Markus M. Ronner." *Sprachspiegel,* 42 (1986), 162–170.

This article investigates the modern "Sagwörter" (wellerisms) of the Swiss aphoristic writer Markus M. Ronner (1938–). In his collection of proverbial aphorisms entitled *Moment mal!* (1977) Ronner does not only parody German proverbs by changing them into "Antisprichwörter" (anti-proverbs), but he also creates his very own wellerisms. Mieder includes a definition of this subgenre and also cites traditional wellerisms that are based on the introductory statement "'Spaß muß sein', sagte ..." ("There has to be fun," said ...). He then shows how Ronner uses this pattern for his texts which are quite often critical comments on the value system and morality of modern society. As is the case with older wellerisms, Ronner's texts are also rather erotic and sexual in nature.

3894. Mieder, Wolfgang. "Sprichwörtliche Schwundstufen des Märchens. Zum 200. Geburtstag der Brüder Grimm." *Proverbium,* 3 (1986), 257–271.

Mieder explains that certain titles, characters, and motifs of such common German fairy tales as "Aschenputtel," "Dornröschen," "Rotkäppchen," "Hänsel und Gretel," "Schneewittchen," etc., play a considerable role in modern aphorisms, advertising slogans, newspaper headlines, graffiti, and literary works. These "Schwundstufen" (remnants, reminiscences) often are based on proverbial structures or are cited in the form of traditional wellerisms. Numerous examples are cited to show how these short texts are based on puns and wordplay, often resulting in sexual humor or in more serious social criticism. Many of the these modern texts could be classified as "Antisprichwörter" (anti-proverbs) using fairy tale allusions in a parodistic or satirical fashion. The 47 notes contain useful bibliographical information.

3895. Mieder, Wolfgang. "Wayland Debs Hand as Paremiologist." *Proverbium*, 3 (1986), 5–8.

This is a short tribute to the renowned American folklorist Wayland Debs Hand (1907–1986) to whom this third volume of *Proverbium* was offered as a much deserved "Festschrift." It had been my hope to present this volume to Wayland Hand at the annual meeting of the American Folklore Society in 1986, but unfortunately this great scholar and friend died on the way to this conference. In this note I praise him for his major contributions to the study of beliefs, superstitions, medical folklore, and folk narratives, stressing that he also made some major paremiological contributions as a student of Archer Taylor (1890–1973). Of particular value are his studies of "A Classical Proverb-Pattern in Germany" (1937; see no. 658) and "A Dictionary of Words and Idioms Associated with Judas Iscariot" (1942; see no. 659). For other publications and annotations see nos. 658–662 and nos. 2442–2443.

3896. Mieder, Wolfgang. "Wilhelm Grimm's Proverbial Additions in the Fairy Tales." *Proverbium*, 3 (1986), 59–83; a slightly changed version with the title "'Ever Eager to Incorporate Folk Proverbs': Wilhelm Grimm's Proverbial Additions in the Fairy Tales" appeared in *The Brothers Grimm and Folktale*. Eds. James McGlathery et al. Urbana/Illinois: University of Illinois Press, 1988. 112–132.

The author starts with the observation that both Jacob (1785–1863) and Wilhelm (1786–1859) Grimm had much interest in German proverbs and proverbial expressions. But it was Wilhelm Grimm who added a considerable amount of proverbial language to the seven editions of the *Kinder- und Hausmärchen* between 1812/15 and 1857. Mieder reviews previous scholarship on the proverbial style of the Grimm fairy tales, and then shows how Wilhelm was indeed a masterful "proverbial" stylist. Choosing the tales "Tischchen deck dich, Goldesel und Knüppel aus dem Sack," "Die goldene Gans," "Die Bremer Stadtmusikanten," "Vom klugen Schneiderlein," and "Hänsel und Gretel" as his major examples, Mieder shows how Wilhelm Grimm added more and more proverbs and proverbial expressions as he prepared later editions. There is no doubt that the "proverbial style" of these tales is to a large extent due to Wilhelm's efforts and not to traditional versions of these folk narratives. All textual references are cited in German in the first version and in English translation in the second slightly changed version of this article. The 35 notes contain useful bibliographical references. For a similar German chapter on this subject matter see Wolfgang Mieder (no. 3892 above).

3897. Mieder, Wolfgang. "Es 'kondomisiert' der Mensch, solang er strebt." *Der Sprachdienst,* 31 (1987), 165–167.

A short note which deals in part with the frequent use of the verb suffix "-ieren" to create new German verbs from foreign nouns, as for example the recent "kondomisieren" (to use a condom). The second part is concerned with Johann Wolfgang von Goethe's (1749–1832) proverbial quotation "Es irrt der Mensch, solang er strebt" (Man errs as long as he strives) out of his *Faust* (1808/32). Mieder shows that this "geflügelte Wort" (sententious remark) is often quoted as a parodied "Antizitat" (anti-quotation) in modern German literature, aphorisms, graffiti, advertising slogans, and newspaper headlines.

3898. Mieder, Wolfgang. "History and Interpretation of a Proverb about Human Nature: 'Big Fish Eat Little Fish'." In W. Mieder. *Tradition and Innovation in Folk Literature.* Hanover/New Hampshire: University Press of New England, 1987. 178–228 and 259–268 (notes).

This is a detailed study of the proverb "Big fish eat little fish" from its earliest recording in the works of Hesiod in the eighth century B.C. to the present day, stressing the Anglo-American history of this rather internationally disseminated proverb. Mieder starts with the observation that the proverb is known in many parts of the world and then traces its history from Hesiod to the Hebrew prophet Habakkuk (7th century B.C.), to the Greek historian Polybius (203?–120 B.C.), and to the Roman writer Marcus Varro (116–27 B.C.). Next he shows how such church fathers as St. Basil (330?–379?), St. Ambrose (340–397), and St. Augustine (354–430) made use of this wisdom about human nature, and he also explains the importance of the *Physiologus* bestiary from around 200 A.D. in the spread of the proverb throughout Europe, first in Latin and then in the second half of the eighth century also in Old English translation. After this the author cites contextualized references from numerous sources, including John Wycliffe (1320?–1384), William Shakespeare (1564–1616), Alexander Barclay (1582–1621), Randle Cotgrave (died 1634), Roger Williams (1603?–1683), William Penn (1644–1718), Jonathan Swift (1667–1745), John Adams (1735–1826), Abigail Adams (1744–1818), Theodore Parker (1810–1860), Bertolt Brecht (1898–1956), etc. The chapter also includes a section (pp. 198–206) on the iconographic history of the proverb, from early misericords to pictures by Hieronymus Bosch (1450?–1516) and Pieter Brueghel (1520?–1569) on to emblems by Jacob Cats (1577–1660), Joachim Camerarius (1534–1598), Peter Isselburg (1580?–1630?), and Giuseppe Maria Mitelli (1634–1718). The last part (pp. 217–228) treats the appearance of the proverb in modern advertisements, newspaper headlines, and political caricatures and cartoons. The 144 notes contain rich bibliographical references. With 6 illustrations. For the history of this proverb in the German language and culture see Wolfgang Mieder (no. 3904 below).

3899. Mieder, Wolfgang. "Lutz Röhrich: Master Folklorist and Paremiologist." *Proverbium*, 4 (1987), 1–16.

This paper represents the introduction to the 4th volume of *Proverbium* which was offered to the leading German folklorist Lutz Röhrich (1922–) on his sixty-fifth birthday as a much deserved "Festschrift." Mieder comments on Röhrich's life, his directorship of the "Institut für Volkskunde" at the University of Freiburg, and his many publications on German and international folklore. Mieder also points out that Röhrich's major paremiological achievement is doubtlessly his seminal *Lexikon der sprichwörtlichen Redensarten*, 2 vols. (1973) which has just been published in a completely revised and much enlarged second edition in three volumes (1991/92). Röhrich's 17 publications on proverbs are presented with annotations (pp. 7–16) in the second part of the article. For annotations see nos. 1570–1582, 2793–2794, and 4260–4262.

3900. Mieder, Wolfgang (ed.). *Proverbium, 1 (1965)—25 (1975)*. Eds.
Julian Krzyzanowski, Matti Kuusi, Démétrios Loukatos, and
Archer Taylor. 2 vols. Bern: Peter Lang, 1987. I, 552; II, 500.

This is a reprint of the international journal *Proverbium*
which was started by the American paremiologist Archer Taylor
(1890–1973) and his Finnish colleague Matti Kuusi (1914–) in
1965. Over the time of eleven years 25 issues were published in
Helsinki (Finland), and they were distributed free of charge to
about 500 institutes, libraries, and individual scholars by the
Society of Finnish Literature. The journal's goal was from the
outset to facilitate communication among the international and
interdisciplinary oriented proverb scholars. The 208 major papers
which appeared in *Proverbium* were written by some of the most
renowned proverb scholars from around the world, dealing with
all possible paremiological and paremiographical aspects. In
order to make all 25 issues more accessible, Kuusi had added a
name and subject index to the last issue (pp. 997–1008). He has
also provided an informative account of the genesis of *Proverbium*
for this two-volume reprint (pp. XIX-XXVIII). Wolfgang Mieder,
as the editor of this reprint, has added a preface (pp. XV-XVIII)
and a detailed annotated bibliography (pp. 1009–1052) in the
form of English abstracts for each of the major articles at the end
of the second volume. These informative and critical comments
should be of particular value to those scholars who might have
difficulties reading the many French, German, and Russian
articles. All 208 articles have, of course, also been annotated
under the individual scholars' names in the three volumes of
Mieder's *International Proverb Scholarship: An Annotated Bibliography*
(1982/90/92).

3901. Mieder, Wolfgang (ed.). *Sebastian Franck. Sprichwörter / Schöne /
Weise / Herrliche Clugreden / und Hoffsprüch.* Faksimiledruck der
Auflage von 1541. Hildesheim: Georg Olms, 1987. 774 pp.

This is a reprint of Sebastian Franck's (1499–1542) major
early proverb collection *Sprichwörter / Schöne / Weise / Herrliche
Clugreden / und Hoffsprüch* (1541). Next to the slightly earlier
collections by Johannes Agricola (1494–1566), this is the most
important and also the largest German proverb collection of the

Reformation era. In his introduction (pp. 5*-13*) Mieder gives a short survey of Franck's life and works, he discusses his sources for the about 7000 proverbs recorded in this collection, he explains the lexicographical classification system used by Franck, and he explains how the publisher Christian Egenolph (also Egenolff, 1502–1555) took 386 proverb "essays" from Agricola and 934 such treatises from Franck to create his own collection with the similar title *Sprichwörter / Schöne / Weise / Klugreden* that saw numerous editions from 1548 on, while Franck's superior work appeared in Egenolph's company only that one time. A bibliography (pp. 11*-13*) is included. For a detailed study of this proverb collection see Ulrich Meisser (no. 1191).

3902. Mieder, Wolfgang. "The Proverb in the Modern Age: Old Wisdom in New Clothing." In W. Mieder. *Tradition and Innovation in Folk Literature*. Hanover/New Hampshire: University Press of New England. 1987. 118–156 and 248–255 (notes).

In this book chapter Mieder investigates how traditional proverbial wisdom continues to live and function in modern society. He divides his comments on the traditional and innovative use of proverbs into four major sections: The first part (pp. 119–126) deals with proverb illustrations from early woodcuts and misericords to the proverb pictures of Pieter Brueghel (1520?–1569). Mieder also discusses the broadsheets depicting multiple proverb scenes on the motif of "The World-upside-down," and he shows how modern caricatures and cartoons continue an old iconographic tradition. The second part (pp. 126–135) treats misogynous proverbs from the Middle Ages to the present day, showing that the feminist movement has fought with some success against these proverbial invectives by changing traditional texts and creating new liberated slogans like "A woman without a man is like a fish without a bicycle." In the third section (pp. 135–144) the author analyzes proverb poetry from John Heywood (1497?–1580), John Gay (1685–1732), Samuel Taylor Coleridge (1772–1834), Eliza Cook (1818–1889), Alice Cary (1820–1871), Arthur Guiterman (1871–1943), W.H. Auden (1907–1973), Robert Colombo (1936–), etc. It is shown that literary authors have enjoyed for a long time to "play" with proverbs in innovative ways. The fourth section (pp. 144–154)

treats the history and Anglo-American survival of the German
proverb "Wer nicht liebt Wein, Weib und Gesang, der bleibt ein
Narr sein Leben lang" (Who does not love wine, woman
[women], and song, remains a fool his whole life long) from
Martin Luther's (1483–1546) alleged authorship to modern T-
shirt slogans (see no. 3865 above). With 5 illustrations and useful
bibliographical information in the 162 notes.

3903. Mieder, Wolfgang. *Tradition and Innovation in Folk Literature.*
Hanover/New Hampshire: University Press of New England,
1987. 313 pp.

The first half of this book on tradition and innovation in folk
literature contains three chapters on "Grim Variations: From
Fairy Tales to Modern Anti-Fairy Tales" (pp. 1–44), "'The Pied
Piper of Hamelin': Origin, History, and Survival of the Legend"
(pp. 45–83), and "Modern Variants of the Daisy Oracle: 'He
Loves Me, He Loves Me Not'" (pp. 84–117). The following three
chapters investigate the same phenomenon of "Dauer im
Wechsel" (constancy in change) in the way proverbs survive in
modern society. The fourth chapter treats "The Proverb in the
Modern Age: Old Wisdom in New Clothing" (pp. 118–156),
showing how traditional proverbs are changed to fit modern
attitudes and values. In the fifth chapter Mieder studies "The
Proverbial Three Monkeys: 'Hear No Evil, See No Evil, Speak No
Evil'" (pp. 157–177). This is a slightly changed reprint of an
earlier essay on this internationally disseminated proverb and
statue of three little monkeys from 1981 which includes 65
illustrations of Japanese Koshin stones, statues, posters, T-shirts,
caricatures, advertisements, and cartoons. The final sixth chapter
presents a "History and Interpretation of a Proverb about Human
Nature: 'Big Fish Eat Little Fish'" (pp. 178–228)., tracing it from
its earliest recorded variant in the eighth century B.C. to its use
and function in the Anglo-American world of the present day.
With 32 illustrations. Detailed notes (pp. 229–268), a large
bibliography (pp. 269–283), and an index conclude this book on
constancy and change in verbal folklore. For annotations of the
three proverb chapters see nos. 3902, 1283, and 3898.

3904. Mieder, Wolfgang. "'Die großen Fische fressen die kleinen'. Geschichte und Bedeutung eines Sprichwortes über die menschliche Natur." *Muttersprache*, 98 (1988), 1–37.

In this article Mieder gives a very detailed history of the German proverb "Große Fische fressen die kleinen" (Big fish eat little fish) from its first occurrence in the works of Hesiod (8th century B.C.) to the present day. Mieder cites references from the Hebrew prophet Habakkuk (7th century B.C.), the Greek historian Polybius (203?–120 B.C.), the Roman writer Marcus Varro (116–27 B.C.), and the three church fathers St. Basil (330?–379?), St. Ambrose (340–397), and St. Augustine (354–430). The earliest German reference appears to be an allusion from 1567 in the works of the theologian Johannes Nas (1534–1590). Friedrich Petri (1549–1617) included it in his *Der Teutschen Weißheit* (1604/05) for the first time in a German proverb collection. In the next section (pp. 13–20) the author surveys the iconographical history of the proverb as misericords, in paintings by Hieronymus Bosch (1450?–1516) and Pieter Brueghel (1520?–1569), and in the emblems of Jacob Cats (1577–1660), Joachim Camerarius (1534–1598), Peter Isselburg (1580?–1630?), and Giuseppi Maria Mitelli (1634–1718). This is followed by a contextualized analysis of the literay use of the proverb by such authors as Abraham a Santa Clara (1644–1709), Karl Friedrich Wilhelm Wander (1803–1879), Bertolt Brecht (1898–1956), Volker von Törne (1934–1980), Helmut Preißler (1925–), and others. The last section (pp. 25–37) investigates the appearance of this popular proverb in modern aphorisms, advertising slogans, newspaper headlines, and political caricatures and cartoons. With 12 illustrations. The 140 notes include useful bibliographical references. For a study of the Anglo-American history of this international proverb see Wolfgang Mieder (no. 3898 above).

3905. Mieder, Wolfgang. "'Die Hunde bellen, aber die Karawane zieht weiter'. Zum türkischen Ursprung eines neuen deutschen Sprichwortes." *Der Sprachdienst*, 32, no. 5 (19888), 129–134.

This article investigates when and how the German proverb "Die Hunde bellen, aber die Karawane zieht weiter" (The dogs

bark, but the caravan moves on) was loan translated from the
Turkish language. It appears in German translation for the first
time in 1870 in Karl Friedrich Wilhelm Wander's (1803–1879)
proverb collection *Deutsches Sprichwörter-Lexikon* (1867/80). But it
has become popular only since about 1966 due to the increased
Turkish population in Germany. Both German politicians
Helmut Schmidt (1918–) and Helmut Kohl (1930–) have used
the proverb, and it became particularly frequent on the political
scene and in the mass media in 1988. By now this originally
Turkish proverb is well established in the German language. With
2 illustrations.

3906. Mieder, Wolfgang. "'Ehrlich währt im Sprichwort am längsten'.
Zu Felix Renners sprichwörtlichen Aphorismen." *Sprachspiegel*, 44
(1988), 41–47.

In this literary study Mieder investigates Felix Renner's
(1935–) use of German proverbs and proverbial expressions in
his collection of aphorisms entitled *Vorwiegend Unversöhnliches an
kurzer Leine* (1987). Mieder shows that Renner formulates many
proverbial aphorisms which are based on satirical or parodistic
puns and wordplays. Most of these short texts express social
criticism and attempt to find new moral foundations for the
modern Swiss society. When Renner manipulates and perverts
the traditional wisdom of proverbs, he does in fact create so-
called innovative "Antisprichwörter" (anti-proverbs). See also
Mieder's previous article on Felix Renner's proverbial language
(no. 3854).

3907. Mieder, Wolfgang. "'Gedanken sind zollfrei': Zu K.F.W. Wanders
Politischem Sprichwörterbrevier." *Einheit in der Vielfalt. Festschrift für
Peter Lang zum 60. Geburtstag.* Ed. Gisela Quast. Bern: Peter Lang,
1988. 326–342.

Mieder reports on a fascinating proverbial diary which the
German paremiographer Karl Friedrich Wilhelm Wander (1803–
1879) kept from 1857 to 1862 and published ten years later
under the pseudonym N.R. Dove with the title *Politisches
Sprichwörterbrevier. Tagebuch eines Patrioten der fünfziger Jahre, zur
Charakteristik jener Zeit* (1872). This book contains 1208 satirical

short comments on traditional German proverbs which unfortunately express political defeatism, disinterest, and reactionary attitudes. The liberal Wander wrote these aphoristic comments in the form of "Antisprichwörter" (anti-proverbs) to awaken his contemporaries to act against reactionary oppression by the Prussian government. Many texts are analyzed by Mieder, and it is shown that Wander's favorite proverb was "Gedanken sind zollfrei" (Thoughts are free) which he reacted to ten times in this book. See also Günther Voigt (no. 2008) and Wolfgang Mieder's reprint of this significant political diary (no. 3324).

3908. Mieder, Wolfgang. "James Woodrow Hassell (1915–1987)." *Proverbium,* 5 (1988), 155–158.

A short obituary on the American paremiologist and paremiographer James Woodrow Hassell (1915–1987), who as Professor of French at the University of Georgia in Athens, Georgia, made important contributions to the use and function of proverbs and proverbial expressions in early French literature. He was particularly interested in the proverbial language of Bonaventure Despériers (des Périers, 1510?–1543/44), but his major publication is without doubt his invaluable and richly annotated collection *Middle French Proverbs, Sentences, and Proverbial Phrases* (1982). Mieder closes his remarks with an annotated list of six proverb publications by Hassell. For annotations see nos. 678–682 and 3571.

3909. Mieder, Wolfgang (ed.). *Karl Simrock. Die deutschen Sprichwörter.* Neudruck der Ausgabe von 1846. Stuttgart: Philipp Reclam, 1988. 631 pp.

This is a reprint of the extremely popular 19th century German proverb collection *Die deutschen Sprichwörter* (1846) by the prolific scholar of language, folklore, and literature Karl Simrock (1802–1876). The collection contains 12,396 texts without annotations which Simrock arranged alphabetically according to key-words. In his introduction (pp. 7–19) Mieder surveys Simrock's life and impressive achievements as a scholar and translator, he refers to Simrock's written and oral sources for this proverb collection, and he states that this work and its several editions were widely disseminated throughout the German-speaking countries. A small bibliography (pp. 17–18) is included. See also Hugo Moser (no. 2665).

3910. Mieder, Wolfgang. "Proverbs in American Popular Songs." *Proverbium,* 5 (1988), 85–101.

The author starts with a few comments on three 19th century proverb songs, namely "Root, Hog, or Die" (1856), "Paddle Your Own Canoe" (c. 1871), and "Never Miss the Water Till the Well Runs Dry" (1874). Next Mieder explains that the songs by W.S. Gilbert (1836–1911) and Sir Arthur Sullivan (1842–1900) abound with proverbs, notably "Faint Heart Never Won Fair Lady" from the musical *Iolanthe* (1882). Other songs cited are "Life Is Just a Bowl of Cherries" (1931) by Lew Brown (1893–1958), "It takes Two to Tango" (1952) by Al Hoffmann (1902–1960) and Dick Manning (1912–) and sung by Pearl Bailey (1918–1990), "Can't Buy Me Love" (1964) by the Beatles (John Lennon [1940–1980], Paul McCartney [1942–], George Harrison [1943–], and Ringo Starr [1940–]), "Like a Rolling Stone" (1965) by Bob Dylan (1941–), "Easy Come, Easy Go" (1967) by Elvis Presley (1935–1977), "Apples Don't Fall Far From the Tree" (1973) by Cher (Cherilyn Sakisian, 1946–), and others. When the proverb appears in the title it usually functions as a leitmotif throughout the song, but Mieder's contextualized analysis shows that there are also many songs from folk songs to country western tunes and even the latest hits of rock 'n' roll that incorporate proverbial wisdom throughout the lyrics.

3911. Mieder, Wolfgang. "Sprichwort." *Wörterbuch des Christentums.* Eds. Volker Drehsen et al. Gütersloh: Gerd Mohn, 1988. 1179–1180.

This is a short dictionary entry starting out with a definition of the proverb and its differentiation from other genres. Since this is a dictionary of Christianity, Mieder explains that about 300 Biblical proverbs have become generally known throughout the German speaking countries, and he cites the most frequently used texts from the Old and New Testaments. Martin Luther (1483–1546) used a lot of proverbs, but they have also been employed quite often by such preachers as Berthold von

Regensburg (1220–1272), Abraham a Santa Clara (1644–1709), and Jeremias Gotthelf (Albert Bitzius, 1797–1854). A few additional comments concerning the language, structure, meaning, content, and function of proverbs are included, and there is also a short bibliography (p. 1180).

3912. Mieder, Wolfgang. "'Wahrheiten: Phantasmen aus Logik und Alltag'. Zu den sprichwörtlichen Aphorismen von Werner Mitsch." *Muttersprache*, 98 (1988), 121–132.

In this literary investigation of about 12,600 aphorisms which the German writer Werner Mitsch (1936–) published in seven volumes from 1978 to 1984, Mieder is able to show that dozens of texts are in fact based on traditional German proverbs and proverbial expressions. In most cases Mitsch alters just one letter or one word, thereby changing the original meaning into a so-called "Antisprichwort" (anti-proverb). These proverbial aphorisms also use puns, wordplays, satire, parody, and irony as a means of questioning the wisdom of the underlying proverbs. Quite often Mitsch simply reduces a proverb to a certain structure and then subsitutes words at random which either create texts that make sense or that appear to be nonsense. Mieder also demonstrates that Mitsch invents wellerisms that ridicule standard proverbs. Numerous examples are cited that indicate Mitsch's effective way of playing with proverbial language.

3913. Mieder, Wolfgang. *American Proverbs: A Study of Texts and Contexts.* Bern: Peter Lang, 1989. 394 pp.

This book is the first comprehensive treatise of American proverbs, each chapter including an interpretative essay, a special bibliography, and numerous texts in contexts. The 15 chapters include the following: "The Proverb" (pp. 13–17), "American Proverbs" (pp. 29–45), "Proverbs of the Immigrants" (pp. 47–70), "Proverbs Current in the Various States" (pp. 71–97), "Proverbs of the Native Americans" (pp. 99–110), "Afro-American Proverbs" (pp. 111–128), "Benjamin Franklin's 'Proverbs'" (pp. 129–142), "Proverbs in Prose Literature" (pp. 143–169, especially Ralph Waldo Emerson [1803–1882]), "Proverb Poems" (pp. 171–193),

"Proverbs in Popular Songs" (pp. 195–221), "Wellerisms" (pp. 223–238), "Proverb Parodies" (pp. 239–275), "Proverbs in Comics and Cartoons" (pp. 277–292), "Proverbs in Advertisements" (pp. 293–315), and "'Different Strokes for Different Folks'" (pp. 317–332). The section on "Chapter References" (pp. 333–346) includes precise bibliographical information regarding the many texts, there is a large bibliography of paremiological and paremiographical works (pp. 347–359), and three indices of names, subjects and proverbs (pp. 361–394) are also provided. With 40 illustrations.

3914.   Mieder, Wolfgang. "'Ausnahmen können auch die Vorboten einer neuen Regel sein'. Zu den sprichwörtlichen Aphorismen von Marie von Ebner-Eschenbach." *Sprachspiegel,* 45 (1989), 66–73.

In this article Mieder treats about 500 aphorisms which the Austrian writer Marie von Ebner-Eschenbach (1830–1916) included in a small volume entitled *Aphorismen* (1890). Many of these short texts are based on German proverbs and proverbial expressions, and they can be considered as proverbial aphorisms and in part as "Antisprichwörter" (anti-proverbs). Mieder shows that these puns and wordplays with proverbial language are usually quite serious intellectual and didactic statements by one of the very few female aphoristic authors in the German language. Ebner-Eschenbach deals with moral and social issues, and it is noted in particular that quite a few of her anti-proverbs touch on ideas of modern feminism and emancipation.

3915.   Mieder, Wolfgang. "Das Sprichwörterbuch." *Wörterbücher. Ein internationales Handbuch zur Lexikographie.* Eds. Franz Josef Hausmann, Oskar Reichmann, Herbert Ernst Wiegand, and Ladislav Zgusta. Berlin: Walter de Gruyter, 1989. I, 1033–1044.

A survey article of the types and classification systems of German and international proverb collections. Mieder starts with an historical glance at paremiography and then discusses the lexicographical problems that arise in assembling proverb collections from popular books to serious diachronic and comparative volumes. This is followed by a review of major New

High German collections from the 16th century to the present day, and there is also a small section on specialized collections of weather, medical, and legal proverbs as well as wellerisms. The next two sections treat larger European and major comparative collections based on internationally disseminated texts. Some comments regarding phraseological dictionaries for foreign language instruction and the inclusion of fixed phrases in dictionaries of various types are included as well. The article concludes with a helpful bibliography (pp. 1039–1044) of paremiographical works and paremiological studies.

3916. Mieder, Wolfgang. "'Ein Bild sagt mehr als tausend Worte'. Ursprung und Überlieferung eines amerikanischen Lehnsprichworts." *Proverbium*, 6 (1989), 25–37.

The article begins with the proof that the very popular American proverb "A picture is worth a thousand words" originated as an advertising slogan by Fred R. Barnard in the advertising magazine *Printers' Ink* on December 8, 1921. This formulation caught on very quickly, and Mieder quotes over 30 references from advertising, newspaper headlines, greeting cards, and graffiti that all cite the proverb in its original form or in variants based on the formula or pattern "A (One) X is worth a thousand words." Next the author explains that due to the international scope of the mass media and the influence of the American language on modern German, the proverb was loan translated and became the German proverb "Ein Bild sagt mehr als tausend Worte" in the early 1970s. The first citation thus far is from 1975 to which Mieder adds several more modern references. The article concludes with the observation that this new proverb has not yet been included in German dictionaries and proverb collections. For a discussion of the Anglo-American history and use of this proverb see Wolfgang Mieder (no. 3924 below).

3917. Mieder, Wolfgang. "'Eulenspiegel macht seine Mitbürger durch Schaden klug'. Sprichwörtliches im *Dil Ulenspiegel* von 1515." *Eulenspiegel-Jahrbuch*, 29 (1989), 27–50.

This is a detailed investigation of the use and function of proverbs and proverbial expressions in Herman Bote's (1460?– 1520) chapbook *Dil Ulenspiegel* (1515). Mieder begins with some general comments regarding the didactic employment of proverbial wisdom in the 16th century and then explains that the prankster Eulenspiegel uses proverbs quite differently by interpreting them literally as "Antisprichwörter" (anti-proverbs). The article includes a section on German proverbs, proverbial expressions, and wellerisms that contain Eulenspiegel's name and of which at least some are in fact proverbial summaries of the longer tall tales of the chapbook. A statistical section shows the distribution of the proverbial texts as titles of certain tales, as repeated leitmotifs, as the beginning or conclusion of the tales, etc. The major part of the paper deals with a contextualized analysis of numerous texts, discussing such matters as introductory formulas, puns, wordplays, scatological humor, etc. An annotated list of the 111 proverbial texts is attached, and the 51 notes include useful bibliographical information. See also Hans-Jörg Uther (no. 4494).

3918. Mieder, Wolfgang. "'Gedankensplitter, die ins Auge gehen'. Zu den sprichwörtlichen Aphorismen von Gabriel Laub." *Kairoer Germanistische Studien*, 4 (1989), 141–158; also in *Wirkendes Wort*, 41 (1991), 228–239.

In this literary and stylistic investigation of Gabriel Laub's (1928–) collection of aphorisms entitled *Denken verdirbt den Charakter* (1984), Mieder is able to show that this author who has lived in Poland, the Soviet Union, Czechoslovakia, and Germany has indeed much insight into basic human nature. As an intellectual, moralist, and satirist Laub wants to encourage his readers to think more responsibly about the social and political ills of modern society. To achieve this goal he quite often creates so-called "Antisprichwörter" (anti-proverbs) from the partial truth of traditional proverbs through puns and wordplays. He also formulates his own wellerisms and repeatedly reacts to such proverbs that contain the word "Wahrheit" (truth) in them, notably "Im Wein ist Wahrheit" (In wine there is truth) which goes back to the Latin "In vino veritas." Many examples are cited indicating that the subgenre of the proverbial aphorism is very prevalent in Laub's texts.

3919. Mieder, Wolfgang. "'It's Five Minutes to Twelve': Folklore and Saving Life on Earth." *International Folklore Review*, 7 (1989), 10–21.

This article represents an ethical statement on how folklore is used and can be helpful in literature and the mass media to argue against war, to describe the nuclear threat, and to warn against the destruction of the environment. Mieder shows how certain fairy tale motifs, elements of the legend of "The Pied Piper of Hamelin" and well-known lines from folk and Christmas songs are being used for this purpose in modern poems, newspaper headlines, graffiti, slogans, and political caricatures and cartoons. Especially the proverb of the proverbial three wise monkeys "Hear no evil, see no evil, speak no evil" is repeatedly cited and illustrated to show the danger of this proverbial wisdom that advocates passivity and a laissez-faire attitude regarding the dangers that surround humankind. Mieder cites intriguing poetic interpretations of this proverb and many others by Erich Fried (1921–1989), Fritz Deppert (1932–), Wolf Biermann (1936–), and Otto Höschle (1952–). He also deals in particular with the internationally disseminated proverbial expression "It's five minutes to twelve" that refers to the immediacy of the danger of global destruction. With 16 illustrations.

3920. Mieder, Wolfgang. "Moderne Sprichwörterforschung zwischen Mündlichkeit und Schriftlichkeit." *Volksdichtung zwischen Mündlichkeit und Schriftlichkeit*. Eds. Lutz Röhrich and Erika Lindig. Tübingen: Gunter Narr, 1989. 187–208.

In this historical and theoretical article Mieder looks at the problem of orality and literacy regarding proverb collections. He explains that most proverb collections are not based on field research but have usually been assembled from published sources and written tradition. An exception are collections by anthropologists and by scholars who collected dialect proverbs. The author shows especially how today's users of Karl Friedrich Wilhelm Wander's (1803–1879) five-volume German collection

Deutsches Sprichwörter-Lexikon (1867/80) question the actual oral currency and frequency of its thousands of texts. Much more field research and frequency studies like those advocated and executed by Isidor Levin (see no. 1049), Grigorii L'vovich Permiakov (no. 2737), and K. Hattemer and E.K. Scheuch (no. 3572) are needed to establish at least the paremiological minima for various languages. In addition, it is high time that paremiologists with the help of folklorists, sociologists, and others prepare questionnaires to collect the proverbs that are in common use today, including such new proverbs like "Eine Frau ohne Mann ist wie ein Fisch ohne Fahrrad" (A woman without a man is like a fish without a bicycle) and many others. The article closes with the plea of establishing a special research team and archive at the "Institut für Volkskunde" at the University of Freiburg, Germany, to collect and study the proverbs of the 20th century.

3921. Mieder, Wolfgang. "Proverbs of the Native Americans: A Prize Competition." *Western Folklore*, 48 (1989), 256–260.

Mindful of the earlier German practice of scholarly competitions to encourage the study of certain important questions, Mieder announced a monetary prize and a promised publication in *Proverbium* for up to three papers that would investigate the proverbs of Native Americans. He argues that it is a criminal shame that scholars have neglected this American minority population as far as their proverbial speech is concerned. There have been arguments that American Indians have *no* proverbs at all, but Mieder questions this claim in view of the fact that some proverbs have been recorded. This scholarly plea concludes with a bibliography (pp. 259–260) of at least 15 short studies that have considered the proverbial speech of Native Americans. Three years later at the writing of this annotation I have yet to receive any reaction whatsoever to my plea. See especially the excellent studies by Keith Basso (no. 3114), Franz Boas (nos. 2217–2218), and Gary Gossen (no. 562).

3922. Mieder, Wolfgang. "Seven Overlooked Paremiological Publications by Archer Taylor." *Proverbium*, 6 (1989), 187–190.

Mieder announces with amazement that it was yet again possible to find 7 more publications by the prolific American folklorist and paremiologist Archer Taylor (1890–1973) that had escaped earlier bibliographers like Wayland Hand (see no. 662), C. Grant Loomis (no. 1102) and Mieder himself (no. 1243). This short note lists three additional book reviews and four very short notes on the following proverbial expressions: "Out of the horse's mouth" (1948), "One for the cutworm" (1958), "Spick and span" (1964), and "Raw head and bloody bones" (1964). Due to their shortness these notes have not been annotated in the present bibliography. In 1991 Charles Doyle found even more unnoticed publications by Taylor in his papers housed at the library of the University of Georgia at Athens, Georgia (see no. 3330).

3923. Mieder, Wolfgang. "'Zurück zur Natur'. Zum Weiterleben eines angeblichen Rousseau-Zitats." *Der Sprachdienst*, 33 (1989), 146–150.

In this article on the internationally disseminated imperative "Zurück zur Natur!" (Back to nature! or in French "Retour à la nature!") Mieder begins with the observation that this well-known quotation did not originate with Jean Jacques Rousseau (1712–1778). His name has become attached to the phrase only due to the fact that he advocates this return to a natural life style in his treatise *Du contrat social* (1762) and in his novel *Émile, ou de l'éducation* (1762). Mieder then cites modern examples of its use in the political speech of Petra Kelly (1948–1992) and the aphorisms of Erwin Chargaff (1905–), Gerhard Uhlenbruck (1929–), Werner Mitsch (1936–), and others. It is pointed out that these writers and also those authors of advertising slogans, newspaper headlines, and graffiti enjoy formulating so-called "Antizitate" (anti-quotations) with humorous, parodistic, or satirical intentions based on this famous quotation.

3924. Mieder, Wolfgang. "'A Picture is Worth a Thousand Words': From Advertising Slogan to American Proverb." *Southern Folklore*, 47 (1990), 207–225.

The article starts with a lexicographical history of the American proverb "A picture is worth a thousand words" in

Anglo-American proverb collections and shows that it originated in an advertisement by Fred R. Barnard which was published on December 8, 1921, in the magazine *Printers' Ink*. Mieder explains that Barnard might have gotten the idea for this slogan from literary sources by Christopher Marlowe (1564–1593), Ivan Turgenev (1818–1883), or George Bernard Shaw (1856–1950). He then cites many examples of the proverb being used in various advertisements, greeting cards, cartoons, etc. Often the proverb is varied following one of the following structures or patterns: "A (One) x is worth a thousand words," "A (One) picture is worth a thousand y's," A (One) x is worth a thousand pictures," and "A (One) x is worth a thousand y's." With 4 illustrations. For a study of the German loan translation of this proverb see Wolfgang Mieder (no. 3916 above).

3925. Mieder, Wolfgang. "Bartlett Jere Whiting: American Paremiologist and Paremiographer Par Excellence." *Proverbium*, 7 (1990), 1–6.

   With this essay Mieder introduces volume seven of *Proverbium* which is a "Festschrift" to honor the superb paremiological and paremiographical work of the American scholar Bartlett Jere Whiting (1904–). The first few pages describe Whiting's life as a Professor of Old English Literature at Harvard University from 1926 to 1975, where he was a renowned Geoffrey Chaucer (1340?–1400) scholar. Mieder reviews Whiting's many essays on the nature, origin, and literary use of English proverbs, and he also declares that Whiting is doubtlessly the greatest American paremiographer, having published several seminal historical proverb collections of the English and American languages. A bibliography (pp. 4–6) lists Whiting's 37 books and articles on proverbs. For annotations see nos. 2059–2075 and 3004–3007. Concerning Whiting's life and works see also Wolfgang Mieder (no. 1269), David Staines (no. 2902), and McKay Sundwall (no. 2913).

3926. Mieder, Wolfgang. "Consideraciones generales acerca de la naturaleza del proverbio." *Revista de Investigaciones Folklóricas*, 5 (1990), 7–16; also published in English as "General Thoughts on the Nature of the Proverb." *Revista de etnografie si folclor,* 36, nos. 3–4 (1991), 151–164.

This article is an attempt to review the major findings concerning the nature of proverbs by scholars writing in the English language. Mieder reviews the various definition attempts by scholars and the folk itself, and he then discusses the problems of traditionality, currency, and frequency that have to be established in order to consider a text to be a proverb. Obviously such markers as structure, brevity, and style (rhyme, parallelism, ellipsis, alliteration, personification, hyperbole, paradox, metaphor, etc.) help to recognize a proverb, but only a certain traditionality and currency will make texts like "Garbage in, garbage out," "It takes two to tango," or "Different strokes for different folks" qualify as modern proverbs. Mieder also analyzes aspects of origin, content, context, function, and meaning. Many examples are cited, and a major bibliography (pp. 15–16 or pp. 162–164) of Anglo-American scholarship on the proverb is provided.

3927. Mieder, Wolfgang. *International Proverb Scholarship: An Annotated Bibliography. Supplement I (1800–1981).* New York: Garland Publishing, 1990. 453 pp.

This is the first supplement to Wolfgang Mieder's *International Proverb Scholarship: An Annotated Bibliography* (1982; see no. 3856 above). It lists those international publications from about 1800 to 1981 that I had missed before, notably scholarship from the Soviet Union and other Eastern European countries. I also included many more references from the fields of phraseology and linguistics. But as in the original volume, there was once again a sincere attempt to be as inclusive as possible for the proverb scholarship originating from such varied fields as anthropology, art, ethnology, folklore, history, law, linguistics, literature, mass communication (media), medicine, philology, psychology, religion, sociology, etc. Proverbs mentioned in the annotations are cited in the original language with English translations. For persons (literary authors, politicians, scholars, etc.) mentioned in the annotations dates have been provided wherever possible. It is also indicated whether a certain article, dissertation, book, or monograph contains statistical tables, graphs, indices, bibliographies, abstracts (summaries), or illustrations. No abbreviations have been used to make this book as accessible as possible to international readers. Three large name, subject and proverb indices (361–436) are provided for these 892 new entries (nos. 2143–3034). They are once again arranged alphabetically by the authors' names and chronologically under each individual scholar.

3928. Mieder, Wolfgang (ed.). *Joachim Christian Blum. Deutsches Sprichwörterbuch.* Faksimiledruck der Ausgaben von 1780 und 1782. Hildesheim: Georg Olms, 1990. 503 pp.

This is a reprint of the most important German proverb collection of the 18th century by Joachim Christian Blum (1739–1790) with the title *Deutsches Sprichwörterbuch* (1780/82). In the first volume Blum presents 348 German proverbs with comments that range in length from a few lines to over eight pages. The second volume adds 418 further proverbs, thus totalling 766 texts that interpret proverbs in a moralistic, pedagogical, and didactic way as expressions of truth and wisdom. In his introduction (pp. 1*-32*) Mieder studies the role of proverbs in 18th century society, he discusses various proverb collections of that time, and he investigates the interest in and use of proverbs by such authors as Johann Christoph Gottsched (1700–1766), Gotthold Ephraim Lessing (1729–1781), Georg Christoph Lichtenberg (1742–1799), Johann Jakob Wilhelm Heinse (1746–1803), Johann Wolfgang von Goethe (1749–1832), and Friedrich Schiller (1759–1805). He also treats the life and works of Blum, stating that his proverb commentaries are filled with etymological, philological, cultural, and historical information. A useful bibliography (pp. 25*-32*) for proverbs in 18th century Germany is included.

3929. Mieder, Wolfgang (ed.). *"Kommt Zeit—kommt Rat!?" Moderne Sprichwortgedichte von Erich Fried bis Ulla Hahn.* Frankfurt am Main: Rita G. Fischer, 1990. 139 pp.

This book represents the first anthology of modern "Sprichwortgedichte" (proverb poems) which Mieder has assembled from 75 authors from Austria, Germany, Switzerland,

and the United States. Altogether there are 123 German poems by such authors as Ilse Aichinger (1921–), Rose Ausländer (1907–1988), Betrolt Brecht (1898–1956), Erich Fried (1921–1989), Ulla Hahn (1946–), Lisa Kahn (1927–), Erich Kästner (1899–1974), Karl Kraus (1874–1936), Günter Kunert (1929–), Christian Morgenstern (1871–1914), Kurt Schwitters (1887–1948), Kurt Sigel (1931–), Volker von Törne (1934–1980), Erich Weinert (1890–1953), and many others. In his introduction (pp. 11–18) Mieder explains that this proverbial subgenre of proverb poetry can be traced back to the Middle Ages. Especially poets of the 20th century use proverbs in their original or varied form as leitmotifs or "Antisprichwörter" (anti-proverbs) to express social and political criticism. Many poems are satirical or humorous reactions to modern existence, and the numerous puns and wordplays based on traditional proverb structures indicate an ambivalent feeling towards the wisdom of proverbs.

3930. Mieder, Wolfgang. "Paremiology and Psychology." *Canadian Psychology/Psychologie Canadienne*, 31, no. 3 (1990), 208 and 213–214.

In this invited reaction to Tim Rogers' article on "Proverbs as Psychological Theories" published in the same issue of this journal (see no. 4258), Mieder agrees with Rogers' criticism of psychologists who have interpreted proverbs to be universal truths. He refers to the semantic indefiniteness of proverbs which is due to their heterosituationality, polyfunctionality, and polysemanticity. It is for this reason that proverbs might not be as suitable for so-called proverbs tests that are being used for various types of mental testing (see Mieder no. 1265). The author concludes that psychologists using proverbs and folklore in their analytical work should be much more cognizant of the work of paremiologists and folklorists. A useful bibliography (pp. 213–214) is attached.

3931. Mieder, Wolfgang. "Prolegomena to Prospective Paremiography." *Proverbium*, 7 (1990), 133–144.

The author presents a survey of future desiderata for regional, national, and international paremiography. It is argued that there is a definite need for an annotated bibliography of proverb collections in addition to Mieder's annual "International Bibliography of New and Reprinted Proverb Collections" in *Proverbium* (1984ff.). Many historically important collections have been reprinted, and two major collections of medieval proverbs have been published. Historical proverb dictionaries continue to be produced primarily in England and the United States, but similar diachronic collections are needed for other languages. Very good paremiographical work is also going on in Africa, Estonia, Finland, and Germany which has resulted in superb national and comparative collections based on synchronic and diachronic methods. But Mieder also calls for more studies of the paremiological minima of modern European languages and for collections that are based on frequency studies of old and new proverbs current today. The 19 notes and the article itself contain much bibliographical information.

3932.　Mieder, Wolfgang. "'Wenige jedoch rudern gegen den Strom': Zu den sprichwörtlichen Aphorismen von Hans Leopold Davi." *Sprachspiegel*, 46 (1990), 97–104.

A literary investigation of two volumes of aphorisms entitled *Distel- und Mistelworte* (1976/84) by the Swiss writer Hans Leopold Davi (1928–). Mieder shows that this modern moralist and satirist bases many of his aphorisms on German proverbs and proverbial expressions, changing them through puns, wordplays and the addition of "aber . . ." (but . . .) statements into so-called "Antisprichwörter" (anti-proverbs). Davi's proverbial aphorisms contain much social and political criticism, but they also express some hope for humankind that is surrounded by cultural pessimism and defeatism. Some of his texts follow the structure of traditional wellerisms, and Davi also enjoys alienating well-known Biblical proverbs to shock his readers into a new type of analytical and responsible thinking.

3933.　Mieder, Wolfgang. "'Wir sitzen alle in einem Boot'. Herkunft, Geschichte und Verwendung einer neueren deutschen Redensart." *Muttersprache*, 100 (1990), 18–37.

The author traces the origin, history, use, and function of the internationally disseminated proverbial expression "In einem Boot sitzen" (To be in the same boat) from its first Latin citation "In eadem es navi" in a letter from the year 53 B.C. by Marcus Tullius Cicero (106–43 B.C.) to its inclusion in Erasmus of Rotterdam's (1469–1536) *Adagia* (1500ff.). Mieder points out that the phrase was then loan translated into English, and he presents a short survey (pp. 21–24) of its spread in England and the United States. Interestingly enough the expression was not translated from Erasmus into Dutch, German, or French. These languages adopted it as a loan translation only after 1945 through the influence of the Anglo-American language and culture. Mieder cites its lexicographical history in German phraseological and language dictionaries, and he cites contextualized references from such modern authors as Günther Anders (1902–), Günter Grass (1927–), Martin Walser (1927–), Arnfrid Astel (1933–), Werner Mitsch (1936–), Karin Struck (1947–), and others. Its appearance in political speeches, book titles, aphorisms, newspaper headlines, graffiti, and cartoons is also analyzed. With 4 illustrations and valuable bibliographical references in the 115 notes. See also Dietmar Peil (no. 4136).

3934. Mieder, Wolfgang. "'An Apple a Day Keeps the Doctor Away': Traditional and Modern Aspects of English Medical Proverbs." *Proverbium*, 8 (1991), 77–106.

The article starts with a general survey of English medical proverbs from the Middle Ages to their use and value as general rules for healthy living in the modern age. It is made clear that they seldom contain specific medical wisdom but rather common-sense statements on health. Mieder then investigates the origin, history, use, and meaning of four popular medical proverbs: "Prevention is better than cure" and its longer variant "An ounce of prevention is worth a pound of cure" (pp. 80–85), "Early to bed and early to rise, makes a man healthy, wealthy and wise" (pp. 85–92), "Stuff (Feed) a cold and starve a fever" (pp. 93–96), and "An apple a day keeps the doctor away" (pp. 96–103). Many examples are cited from literary works, newspaper headlines, advertisements, cartoons, greeting cards, graffiti, and comic strips. With 8 illustrations and a detailed bibliography (pp. 104–106) on medical proverbs.

3935. Mieder, Wolfgang. "'Des vielen Büchermachens ist kein Ende': Traditionelle und manipulierte Sprachformeln als Buchtitel." *Der Sprachdienst*, 35 (1991), 105–114.

Mieder analyzed 11,717 belletristic book titles of novels, plays, anthologies, etc. that were published in the German-speaking countries during the year 1989. He found that 243 (2.07%) titles are based on traditional formulas, namely on "Volkssprüche" (folk verses; 1 title), counting rhymes (2 titles), legends (3), folk songs (11), fairy tales (20), sententious remarks (44), proverbs (54) and proverbial expressions (108). Many examples are cited, and it is pointed out that most of the titles manipulate or parody the traditional formulas through linguistic puns, alienating wordplays, and other ironic innovations. The formulaic patterns and structures are obviously not sacrosanct when it becomes a matter of finding catchy book titles to lure the consumer into a purchasing choice.

3936. Mieder, Wolfgang. "'Eigener Unruheherd ist Goldes wert'. Zu den sprichwörtlichen Aphorismen von André Brie." *Sprachpflege und Sprachkultur*, 40 (1991), 8–11.

This literary study investigates two collections of aphorisms entitled *Die Wahrheit lügt in der Mitte* (1982) and *Am Anfang war das letzte Wort* (1985) by the writer and politician André Brie (1950–). Mieder shows that Brie bases his aphorisms quite often on German proverbs and proverbial expressions which he manipulates and alienates through clever changes of letters and words or through additions of contradictory statements. The resulting proverbial aphorisms contain much humor, irony, and satire without ever giving up on at least some hope for humankind in a world filled with societal and environmental problems. Many of his aphorisms are in fact "Antisprichwörter" (anti-proverbs) whose innovative message is directed to get people to think and to act with compassion, decency, and responsibility. With 1 illustration.

3937. Mieder, Wolfgang. "'Proletarier aller Länder, vereinigt euch!'— Wozu? Geflügelter Abschied vom Marxismus." *Sprachspiegel*, 47 (1991), 69–77.

At the collapse of Marxism in the Soviet Union and Eastern Europe Mieder analyzes the origin, history and possible survival of its three most famous quotations. It is shown that Karl Marx (1818–1883) merely popularized the idea that ¯"Religion ist Opium für das Volk" (Religion is the opium of the people) which he cites in an essay on *Zur Kritik der Hegelschen Rechtsphilosophie* (1844). German intellectuals and writers like Immanuel Kant (1724–1804), Novalis (1772–1801), Ludwig Feuerbach (1804–1872), and Heinrich Heine (1797–1856) had expressed the same idea before him. The other two quotations stem from the internationally known *Manifest der Kommunistischen Partei* (1848) which Marx wrote together with Friedrich Engels (1820–1895). They are "Ein Gespenst geht um in Europa" (A specter is haunting Europe) and "Proletarier aller Länder, vereinigt euch" (Proletarians of the world, unite). Mieder cites numerous references from German literature, newspapers, magazines, headlines, slogans, aphorisms, grafiiti, etc. Due to their proverbial status these quotations are easily parodied and manipulated to satirize the demise of communism and to attack various social problems.

3938. Mieder, Wolfgang. "'Veni, vidi, vici': Zum heutigen Leben eines klassischen Zitats." *Sprachpflege und Sprachkultur*, 40 (1991), 97–102.

The author begins with a discussion of the authenticity of Julius Caesar's (100–44 B.C.) thrasonical boast "Veni, vidi, vici" (I came, I saw, I conquered) after a victorious battle in 47 B.C. Mieder then proves its proverbial status by showing how it survives in modern advertisements, cartoons, comic strips, aphorisms, and graffiti. Even though the famous quotation is often quoted in its original Latin form or its precise German translation, it is today frequently parodied or perverted to make an equally boastful slogan out of it. Many examples from the mass media are cited, and Mieder also includes its use in poems and aphorisms by such German authors as Henryk Keisch (1913–),

Walter Löwen (1927–), Hans Leopold Davi (1928–), Gerhard Uhlenbruck (1929–), Werner Mitsch (1936–), etc. With 4 illustrations.

3939. Mieder, Wolfgang, and George B. Bryan. "'Zum Tango gehören zwei'." *Der Sprachdienst,* 27 (1983), 100–102 and 181.

The authors explain that President Ronald Reagan's (1911–) use of the American proverb "It takes two to tango" at a press conference on November 11, 1982, made it almost an instantaneous "hit" through the mass media in Europe. It appeared in German newspapers the next morning as "Zum Tango gehören zwei," and this loan translation has taken on a proverbial status in a very short time as can be seen from several more recent German references. Bryan and Mieder also point out that the proverb became very popular throughout the United States through the song "Takes two to tango" (1952) which was sung by Pearl Bailey (1918–1990) and written by Al Hoffmann (1902–1960) and composed by Dick Manning (1912–). Several American examples of the proverb being used in newspapers, in cartoons, and on greeting cards are cited, and it is also stated that this "new" proverb is most likely a variant of the much older proverb "It takes two to make a bargain (quarrel)" that dates back to the 16th century.

3940. Mikic, Pavao. "Zur Kontrastierung von Sprichwörtern." *Radovi,* 26 (1986–1987), 137–149.

Mikic presents a detailed comparative analysis of Serbo-Croatian and German proverbs, starting with the observation that there are quite a few proverbs which have total or at least partial equivalents in the two languages. Then he contrasts the structure, meaning, content (theme), use, and function of some of these texts. He pays particular attention to such matters as syntax, morphology, lexicology, parallelism, opposition, metaphor, and personification. A section on the Biblical, Latin and literary origin of proverbs is included as well, and Mikic concludes his article with a plea for integrating proverbs into foreign language instruction. It is argued that teachers should teach proverbs to their students so that they might learn about the cultural particularities and worldview of speakers of the target language. Yugoslavian and English abstracts (p. 149) are provided.

3941. Mikic, Pavao. "Zur Auffassung vom Tod in den Sprichwörtern der serbokroatischen und der deutschen Sprache." *Proverbium,* 6 (1989), 39–54.

In this article Mikic compares 65 Serbo-Croatian proverbs dealing with "death" with their German equivalents. Mikic points out that there are usually total or at least partial equivalents which is due to the relatively close cultural and European connection of the speakers. He groups his texts under such headings as "inescapable," "inexplainable," "powerful," "cunning," "frightening," "unpredictable," "evil," "omnipresent," etc. There is also a special section for those proverbs that comment on the contrast of life and death. A statistical table together with the list of equivalents helps to show that people of both cultures have similar concerns and fears about death.

3942. Mikic, Pavao, and Danica Skara. "Sprichwort im Kontrast: Zur Übertragbarkeit von Sprichwörtern." *Proverbium,* 5 (1988), 103– 115.

The two authors stress the fact that proverbs should definitely be included as part of foreign language instruction. Proverbial language belongs to oral and written communication, and if people want to speak or read another language fluently, they must have a good command of its phraseological units as well. To illustrate the importance of the teaching and learning of proverbs, the authors asked 22 students studying German and English in Yugoslavia to translate 20 proverbs from their native language into the target language and vice versa. The actual translations of the students are printed, and it becomes evident that the students had definite problems. It was slightly easier for them to translate the proverbs from the foreign language into their native language since they recalled the metaphorical equivalents of their own language. However, translating from Serbo-Croatian into English or German proved much more difficult due to the lack of knowledge of foreign metaphorical proverbs. Statistical tables are included, and the authors conclude that instructors need to teach their students in much more detail the metaphors and meanings of the proverbs of the target language.

3943. Mikic, Pavao, and Danica Skara. "Poslovice u kontrastu. Istovjetna pravila ponasanja i zivljenja izrazena u poslovicama hrvatskog ili srpskoga, njemackoga i engleskog jezika." *Zadarska Revija*, no. 3 (1989), 233–242.

In this article Mikic and Skara compare 55 common Serbo-Croatian, German, and English proverbs. It is shown that quite a few of them have exact equivalents in all three languages. This is the case when there is a classical or Biblical origin that resulted in identical loan translations more or less throughout Europe. There appears to be a closer relationship between the Serbo-Croatian and German proverbs due to their cultural and historical contacts. For some of the proverbs only partial or no equivalents at all exist for Serbo-Croatian and English. The authors also show that English and German proverbs exhibit a closer relationship than Serbo-Croatian and English proverbs. This again is due to much more prevalent cultural and historical ties between England and Germany.

3944. Militz, Hans-Manfred. "'Brüllen wie ein Stier—schweigen wie das Grab'. Der Vergleich als phraseologisch-stilistische Erscheinung." *Sprachpflege*, 31, no. 9 (1982), 134–136.

The author investigates German proverbial comparisons for which he establishes the following general structure: "Substantiv/Verb/Adjektiv + wie (+ Artikel) + Substantiv (+ qualifizierende Zusätze)/Adverb" (noun/verb/adjective + like [+ article] + noun [+ qualifying statements]/adverb). He analyzes the style, language, and meaning of numerous examples, also showing that many of these fixed comparisons deal with animals. Militz explains that the metaphors of such phrases are often quite drastic and that they are frequently based on puns and wordplays. At the end of the article the author includes a discussion of a few contextualized proverbial comparisons from the novels and short stories of such modern German authors as Erwin Strittmatter

(1912–), Günter de Bruyn (1926–), Klaus Möckel (1934–), and Armin Stolper (1934–).

3945. Militz, Hans-Manfred. "Zur Äquivalenz phraseologischer Wendungen in der Konfrontation Französisch-Deutsch." *Beiträge zur Romanischen Philologie*, 21, no. 2 (1982), 305–315.

This is a major comparative study of French and German phraseological units, especially proverbial expressions and proverbial comparisons. Militz argues that such contrasts of fixed phrases from two languages are particularly important for foreign language instruction. He then cites many French texts with their German equivalents. It is shown that some phrases are absolutely identical in both languages, and such expressions might well go back to Biblical or classical times. But there are also numerous French texts for which there are only partial or no equivalents at all in the German language. Militz discusses the partial semantic, metaphorical, and syntactical equivalents and explains the difficulty that this problem presents to the translator. He also stresses the importance of the context, function, and meaning of phraseological units in attempting to translate them. A small bibliography (p. 315) concerning the translatability of fixed phrases is attached. See also Hans-Manfred Militz (no. 3951 below).

3946. Militz, Hans-Manfred. "Kopfstand der Sprichwörter." *Sprachpflege*, 32, no. 6 (1983), 83–84.

A short paper stating that proverbs continue to be popular today even if their metaphors and wisdom appear to have become archaic and outdated in the modern German society. Militz explains that proverbs are either used in their traditional wording or that they are modified by changing certain letters or words, by additions or reductions, and by innovative negations. The resulting texts are so-called "Antisprichwörter" (anti-proverbs) which parody or satirize the original proverbs. For his examples of such modern manipulations of traditional proverbial wisdom Militz turns to a collection of poems and proverbial aphorisms by Klaus Möckel (1934–) entitled *Kopfstand der Farben* (1982).

3947.   Militz, Hans-Manfred. "'Sich einen Kopf machen'." *Sprachpflege*, 32, no. 11 (1983), 168–169.

In this short article the author records the new German proverbial expression "Sich einen Kopf machen" (To make a head for oneself, i.e., to be worried, to be concerned) which he located in two East German newspapers and a literary work by Helga Königsdorf (1938–). The expression is usually cited negatively and is reminiscent of similar phrases using the noun "Kopf" (head). Militz points out that such neologisms often build on existing phraseological units and only change one of the key-words while maintaining the basic syntactical structure. He also cites such examples as "Den Hut aufhaben" (To wear the hat, i.e., To wear the pants) and "Weg vom Fenster sein" (To be away from the window, i.e., Not to be in control any longer).

3948.   Militz, Hans-Manfred. "Der Apotheker und seine Heilmittel. Entwicklungsrichtungen eines phraseologischen Bereichs." *Sprachpflege*, 33, no. 5 (1984), 68–69.

Militz studies various German proverbs and proverbial expressions dealing with pharmacists and medicines. He cites in particular expressions with the key-words "Apotheke" (pharmacy), "Apotheker" (pharmacist), , "Medizin" (medicine), "Kräuter" (medicinal herbs), "Gift" (poison), "Pille" (pill), "Pflaster" (bandage), etc. It is argued that many of these proverbs are not current any longer since the occupation of the pharmacist has changed considerably. The same is true for some of the negative expressions about medicine and pills. But the proverbs containing ideas of folk medicine are also declining in frequency. Phrases with the key-word "Pille" on the other hand are increasing in number and currency. The article makes clear how proverbs fall out of use in a society as socio-economic changes occur.

3949.   Militz, Hans-Manfred. "Sprachspiele im phraseologischen Bereich." *Sprachpflege*, 33, no. 3 (1984), 32–33.

This short article studies the use and function of proverbs and proverbial expressions in East German newspapers. Militz points out that most proverbial headlines are characterized by intentional wordplays and puns, often negating positive expressions and vice versa. He also explains that normally only parts of phrases are being used and that this frequent reduction of fixed phrases leads to the autonomization of their component parts. Many times proverbial expressions are also employed as indirect questions in headlines which are supposed to gain the attention of the reader. The entire journalistic alienation of proverbial materials is thus intended to manipulate the reader to read and react to the actual text. Many German examples from the mass media are cited.

3950. Militz, Hans-Manfred. "An den Grenzen der Phraseologie." *Sprachpflege*, 35, no. 4 (1986), 52–53.

In this small note Militz explains that television reporters and journalists covering various types of sports have the annoying tendency of mixing up their proverbial metaphors. They might be reporting on a soccer game, but they use proverbial expressions and idioms that clearly come from a completely different realm. Often they also connect or intertwine two fixed phrases whose metaphors do not fit together at all. The result is that these neologisms are not understood or that they become so ridiculous as to bother the listeners or readers. The author includes a few examples from the German mass media, indicating clearly that the problem of mixed metaphors is indeed rather widespread.

3951. Militz, Hans-Manfred. "Phraseologie in Konfrontation: Deutsch-Französisch." *Fremdsprachenunterricht*, 30, nos. 8–9 (1986), 434–437.

Realizing that phraseology should be a major concern in foreign language instruction, Militz presents a clear comparative analysis of the difficulty connected with the translation of phraseological units. He cites numerous German proverbial expressions and proverbial comparisons with their French equivalents, indicating that there might be total, partial or no equivalent phrases in the target language. The author also explains that even in the case of fitting equivalents there might be small semantic, syntactical, stylistic, and functional differences.

The most serious challenge is the translation of the metaphor and the correct choice when there are several synonymous equivalents available in the target language. At times the translatability simply does not exist, and in those cases the proverbial text will have to be paraphrased. The 17 notes (pp. 436–437) include useful bibliographical information. See also Hans-Manfred Militz (no. above).

3952. Militz, Hans-Manfred. "Wertende Konnotation in der Phraseologie." *Sprachpflege*, 35, no. 8 (1986), 109–111.

This is an important essay on the various connotations that phraseological units might take on in different contexts. Militz explains that proverbs, proverbial expressions, idioms, etc. all belong to certain stylistic levels and their integration into an oral or written text brings with it a social and moral value judgment. Some phraseological dictionaries include information on style and value, but for the most part it isn't clear at all, especially for non-native speakers, how and when to use certain fixed phrases. In order to illustrate these points Militz cites a few contextualized examples from Wulf Kirsten's (1934–) prose work *Kleewunsch. Ein Kleinstadtbild* (1984). He shows clearly how phraseological units function as judgmental expressions in this literary work.

3953. Militz, Hans-Manfred. "Sprichwort, Aphorismus und Bedeutung." *Sprachpflege*, 36, no. 3 (1987), 29–32.

In this article Militz presents definitions for the proverb and aphorism, and he cites numerous German examples to illustrate his comparative comments. It is pointed out that most proverbs are based on a metaphor, but the author does refer to some proverbs which lack metaphorization. In those cases the proverbs have a literal meaning only, but there are, of course, also proverbs which exhibit a mixture of metaphorical and literal meaning. Militz also explains that there exists a widespread tendency of innovative variations of proverbs, and he refers in particular to the way modern aphoristic writers change traditional proverbs. Aphorisms are often based on puns and wordplays, and there appears to be a clear preoccupation to parody and alienate proverbs and proverbial expressions in modern aphorisms. This leads to proverbial aphorisms which basically take on the form and meaning of so-called "Antisprichwörter" (anti-proverbs). Many of these literary texts contrast two or more fixed phrases by interpreting them literally. The results are often satirical and moralistic texts which show how linguistic clichés reflect social attitudes and worldview.

3954. Militz, Hans-Manfred. "Wo hat das Sprichwörtliche seine Grenzen?" *Sprachpflege*, 36, no. 11 (1987), 159–163.

Militz starts with a clear differentiation between proverbs and proverbial expressions, stressing the fact that proverbs are characterized by stability and independence in form. He also shows clearly that the definitions of these two genres were quite different in the 19th century in comparison to those that have been proposed by modern linguists who are interested in so-called phraseological units. To illustrate this point the author reviews the findings of 9 German scholars whose articles Wolfgang Mieder has collected in the essay volume *Deutsche Sprichwörterforschung des 19. Jahrhunderts* (1984; see no. 3869 above). While these scholars definitely stressed only proverbs and proverbial expressions from a literary or folkloric point of view, scholars from the 20th century, primarily linguists, have moved to a structural and semiotic analysis of phraseological units in general. Militz concludes that a shift from paremiology to phraseology has taken place, where folklorists and literary or cultural historians continue to be interested primarily in proverbs and proverbial expressions while linguists look at a much broader range of fixed phrases.

3955. Militz, Hans-Manfred. "Phraseologische Wendungen in der Klassifikation und im Text." *Sprachpflege*, 37, no. 6 (1988), 77–79.

The author begins with a discussion of the problems that scholars face regarding the classification of the many different types of phraseological units. He refers in particular to the work which the lexicographer and literary author Erhard Agricola (1921–) has achieved in his dictionary *Wörter und Wendungen* (1962). Agricola differentiates among such subgenres as verbal phrases, idioms, twin formulas, proverbs, proverbial expressions, sententious remarks, etc. Some of the criteria include free, loose, or stable form (stability, fixidity) and certain stylistic levels. Next Militz analyzes what types of phraseological units the scholar Agricola has used in his novel *Im Bann der zaubermächtigen Kirke* (1987). Citing numerous examples, Militz shows that Agricola has a definite preference for twin formulas and that he has a tendency of changing "stable" phraseological units to fit particular contexts. There is clearly a difference in the lexicographical classification of fixed phrases and their actual use and function in oral and written communication.

3956. Militz, Hans-Manfred. "Sprichwörtliches aus Québec." *Fremdsprachen*, no. 3 (1989), 184–185.

This is a short paper on the French proverbs of the Province of Québec in Canada. Militz bases his examples on Pierre DesRuisseaux's *Le livre des proverbes québécois* (1974, 2nd ed. 1978) and explains that many proverbs were brought to the New World by French immigrants in previous centuries. While it is easy to prove their French origin, it must be noted that some texts have undergone some phonetical, lexical, and morphological changes. In addition to such variants there are also proverbs which are definitely indigenous to the Québécois people. Lately there has also been a considerable influence of Anglo-American proverbs due to the importance of the English language in other Canadian provinces. For a more detailed analysis of Québécois proverbs see Hans-Manfred Militz (no. 3958 below).

3957. Militz, Hans-Manfred. "Eigennamen im Sprichwort." *Sprachpflege und Sprachkultur*, 39, no. 2 (1990), 33–35.

A short but informative onomastic article on the use, function, and meaning of names in German proverbs. Militz explains that there are three sources for these names: those that go back to classical mythology (Bacchus, Mars, Venus, etc.), those that refer to Biblical persons (Adam, Eve, Noah, etc.), and those that are very popular first names in Germany (Hans, Grete, etc.). The author cites numerous examples of the use of such generic names, and he includes a section on twin formulas based on two names. He also discusses the phenomenon of personification in proverbs where such adjectives as "ehrlich" (honest) or "ungeschickt" (clumsy) become names used as subjects of proverbs. All names are basically used to add to the degree of generalization and metaphorization of the proverbs.

3958. Militz, Hans-Manfred. "Les proverbes québécois." *Proverbium*, 7 (1990), 145–151.

This is a much expanded French version of Hans-Manfred Militz' previous German article on the French proverbs of the Province of Québec in Canada (see no. 3956 above). The author gives detailed background information concerning the immigrants from France who began to settle in Québec in the early 17th century. Obviously they brought their language and proverbs with them, and many of these old French proverbs are still in use today. However, citing many examples from Pierre DesRuisseaux's collection *Le livre des proverbes québécois* (1974, 2nd ed. 1978), Militz is able to show that quite a few of them have undergone phonetical, lexical, and morphological changes over time. In addition to such variants there are, of course, also those proverbs which are truly indigenous to the Québécois people. This is particularly the case with local weather proverbs and those texts that refer to animals and social attitudes about marriage. Today it is noticeable that more and more Anglo-American proverbs are being used in Québec as well due to the major role that the English language plays throughout Canada. The 21 notes contain useful bibliographical information.

3959. Militz, Hans-Manfred. "Das Antisprichwort als semantische Variante eines sprichwörtlichen Textes." *Proverbium*, 8 (1991), 107–111.

This intriguing article presents an analysis of some of the slogans which became popular among the population of the former German Democratic Republic during the Fall of 1989. Militz, as one of the leading paremiologists and phraseologists of that state, had the opportunity to observe how some traditional German proverbs were changed into so-called "Antisprichwörter" (anti-proverbs) to serve as socio-political slogans in the move towards democracy. Numerous examples are cited, but of special interest is the change of the noun "Krieg" (war) to "Sozialismus" (socialism) in the expression "Stell' dir vor, es ist Krieg, und keiner geht hin" (Imagine it is war and nobody shows up) by the well-known author Christa Wolf (1929–) during a big demonstration on November 4, 1989, in Berlin. Militz also refers to the slogan "Wir sind *das* Volk" (We are the folk) which was at first used by the East German population to express the fact of a new empowerment. It was, however, appropriately changed to "Wir sind *ein* Volk" (We are one folk) when it became clear that a move towards German reunification was desired as well. Such examples show that anti-proverbs are based on lexical changes that bring about semantic variants.

3960. Miller, Anthony. "A Reminiscence of Erasmus in *Hamlet*, III,ii,92–95." *English Language Notes*, 24 (1986), 19–22.

In this short etymological note Miller explains that Hamlet's statement "I eat the air, promise-cramm'd—you cannot feed capons so" does include an allusion to the proverbial expression "To feed (live) on air." He is able to cite a reference from Erasmus of Rotterdam's (1469–1536) *Colloquia familiaria* (1518ff.) which proves that feeding on hope is indeed a proverbial common place. Miller includes detailed explanatory comments showing that Erasmus might well have influenced William Shakespeare (1564–1616) in formulating Hamlet's unusually vivid use of the phrase. He also shows that Shakespeare used references from the *Colloquia* in other plays, thus strenthening his argument that Shakespeare was also influenced by Erasmus in this particular case. Miller includes a detailed contextualized analysis of the proverbial phrase, discussing its function and meaning in *Hamlet* (1600).

3961. Milne, Louise Shona. *Dreams and Popular Beliefs in the Imagery of Pieter Bruegel the Elder, c. 1528–1569.* Diss. Boston University, 1990. 635 pp.

This is a fascinating dissertation on the iconographic representation of dreams and popular beliefs in many pictures by Pieter Brueghel (c.1520–1569). Various large chapters deal with the imagery of the body, hell, misogyny, ships, carnival, death, etc., always explaining how Brueghel uses dreams and beliefs to parody or satirize social conditions and human nature. Of special interest to the paremiologist is chapter three (pp. 246–282, notes pp. 459–472) which deals with Brueghel's proverbial illustrations. Milne discusses the motif of "The world-upside-down," and she includes a special section on the famous proverb picture *Netherlandic Proverbs* (1559). She analyzes how Brueghel has perverted proverbial wisdom in this oil picture by referring to various proverb collections of the 16th century. It becomes clear how Brueghel contrasts proverbial wisdom and human folly in many of his pictures. This ambivalence is part of his age and can be found in literature (including proverb collections) and art. Of the 88 illustrations included at the back of the dissertation, nos. 22, 23, 23a, 58a–b, and 59 deal with proverbial matters. The bibliography (pp. 502–526) is of much value to folklorists and paremiologists.

3962. Mine, Hisayo, Hiroshi Mine, and Haruyo Hama. "Affectional Expressions in Japanese Proverbs." *The Japanese Journal of Psychology*, 54 (1984), 382–385.

Based on a collection of 7096 Japanese proverbs the authors selected 412 texts because of their frequent use in everyday life. Fifty-five students rated the relevance of these proverbs regarding 13 categories of affectional words. The categories were pessimism, optimism, cold-hearted, warm-hearted, tension, relaxation, hesitation, daring, anger, fear, surprise, dislike, and like. Three to four affectional words were assigned to each category to define it more clearly. As a result of this psychological experiment four bipolar factors (cruelness-kindness, hesitation-daringness, fortunateness-unfortunateness, and laziness-perseverance) and two monopolar factors (surprise and hostility) were extracted. The article is written in Japanese, but it contains an English summary (p. 382).

3963. Mitschri, Elena. "Zur semantischen Klassifizierung der idiomatischen attributiven Wortverbindungen mit substantivischem Kern in der deutschen Gegenwartssprache." *Beiträge zur Erforschung der deutschen Sprache*, 2 (1982), 68–81.

A linguistic and theoretical article on the semantic classification of phraseological units based on a noun and an attribute (usually an adjective). The author begins with a discussion of structural, semantic, and stylistic classification attempts by phraseologists, and she then proceeds to show that fixed phrases or idioms might best be classified according to semantic criteria. She points out that the idiomaticity of phrases composed of a noun and an attribute may depend on all components, on the noun only, or only on the attribute. In any case, this idiomatic nature adds stability and reproducibility to such fixed phrases. Mitschiri cites numerous examples, especially groups of idioms that make use of the adjectives "bunt" (colored) or "dick" (thin). In addition to presenting structural paradigms she analyzes semantic aspects of these German texts.

3964. Mlacek, Jozef. "Zur Frage des Verständnisses der Grenzen der Phraseologie." *Phraseologie und ihre Aufgaben. Beiträge zum 1. Internationalen Phraseologie-Symposium vom 12. bis zum 14. Oktober 1981 in Mannheim.* Ed. Josip Matesic. Heidelberg: Julius Groos, 1983. 132–146.

This is a theoretical paper concerning the question of what kind of phrases belong to an inclusive study of phraseology. While basing his remarks primarily on Soviet scholarship, Mlacek discusses minimal phraseological units and argues that proverbs, literary quotations ("geflügelte Worte"), and weather proverbs should be part of the wider concerns of phraseology. He points out that the difference between proverbs and quotations is still not clearly defined and that folklorists and paremiologists should pay more attention to the research results by linguists. It is also argued that stability is a basic characteristic of all phraseological units. Of importance is that scholars of such disciplines as folklore, phraseology, and paremiology should work together on the analysis of proverbs, proverbial expressions, quotations, twin formulas, etc. A short bibliography (p. 146) is attached.

3965. Mlacek, Jozef. "O vystavbe jedneho typu suvetnych prislovi." *Kultura slova*, 19, no. 2 (1985), 37–43.

This is a linguistic study concerning Slovakian proverbs that consist of complex and compound sentences. Mlacek shows that many proverbs have relative pronouns, and such texts are considerably longer than proverbs that consist of just one sentence. Mlacek includes some statistical information, stating that 90% of such complex proverbs have two sentence elements and only 10% have three to six sentence elements. Such texts usually follow a parallel structure which reflects their enumerative nature. It is also pointed out that the subordinate clause usually precedes the independent clause. Numerous examples are cited to illustrate that the syntax of proverbs can actually be quite involved.

3966. Mlacek, Jozef. "Zanrova charakteristika jedneho druhu prislovi." *Kultura slova*, 19, no. 1 (1985), 10–15.

In this linguistic and structural analysis of Slovakian proverbs Mlacek examines one particular proverbial pattern that is very popular, namely "Kto . . ., ten . . ." (He who . . ., he . . .). The author cites numerous examples, one of them being "Kto liha medzi otruby, prichodi svini pod zuby" (He who lies down in the pig's food, he comes right underneath the teeth of the pig). By presenting many variants the author is able to show that this proverbial structure can yield quite short but also rather long proverbs. Much depends on what realia are mentioned and how metaphorically they are expressed. This particular pattern is certainly not unique to this language and culture. In fact, it is a proverbial structure which appears to be in use in almost all national proverb stocks.

3967. Moeran, Brian. "When the Poetics of Advertising Becomes the Advertising of Poetics: Syntactical and Semantic Parallelism in English and Japanese Advertising." *Language and Communication*, 5, no. 1 (1985), 29–44.

It is argued that there is a tendency for English advertising slogans to take on forms of syntactical and semantic parallelism similar to those found in many traditional proverbs. Not only do slogans frequently fall into two matching halves, but also into matching quarters, so that there is a quadripartite balance based on both syntactical and semantic factors. Indeed, the value and popularity of such slogans would appear to be a direct function of the extent to which the symmetry of semantic content matches that of the syntactical form. This argument is then illustrated by comparing Japanese advertising slogans cited in transliteration with English translations. The quadripartite structure is not a preferred form in Japanese slogans since it is not part of the poetic function of that language. But it is argued that Japan's wholesale adoption of Western culture may also start to affect the way in which the Japanese will structure certain advertising slogans on English proverbial structures. The article includes a large section (pp. 36–44) in which the quadripartite structure of these proverbial slogans is illustrated through diagrams. For discussions of the quadripartite structure of English proverbs see George Milner (nos. 1291–1295).

3968.   Mohapatra, Kulamoni. "Social Context of Oriya Proverbs." *Folk Culture V: Folk Culture and the Great Tradition.* Ed. K. Mohapatra. Cuttack/Orissa: Institute of Oriental and Orissan Studies, 1984. 151–154.

The author reports on his field research during 1967/68 and again in 1976/77 in Bantalla, a multi caste village in Cuttack district, Orissa (India). He collected numerous proverbs through informal interviews from members of the seven castes. The proverbs belong to two major sources, namely the long literary tradition of Sanskrit proverbs and also the genuine folk proverbs from oral tradition. Without citing any examples whatsoever, Mohapatra explains that the folk proverbs usually characterize an individual or a group of people, they condemn certain actions, they give moral advice, they comment on agricultural matters, etc. There are also those proverbs which are cited in the form of a riddle or as part of a nursery rhyme for small children. The short article concludes with the statement that Oriya proverbs are not equally well known by members of the different castes.

3969.   Mokienko, Valerii M. "Printsipy leksikograficheskogo opisaniia cheshskoi i russkoi frazeologii." *Bulletin russkeho jazyka a literatury,* 26 (1985), 79–95.

Mokienko presents theoretical considerations regarding the lexicographical description of Czech and Russian phraseological units. The author discusses classification possibilities which range from alphabetizing phraseological units according to the first word to ordering them on the basis of key-words and on to thematic groupings. There are, however, also grammatical and structural problems to consider when preparing a bilingual phraseological dictionary. Additional questions deal with how the meaning should be explained, whether stylistic levels should be indicated, and how many variants should be registered. Mokienko argues correctly that phraseological lexicography is a very complex area, yet bilingual phraseological dictionaries are very much needed to improve oral and written communication among people from different languages. Several comparative Czech and Russian examples are cited, and the 18 notes include useful bibliographical information. A Czech abstract (p. 95) is attached.

3970. Mokienko, Valerii M. *Bibliograficheskii ukazatel' "Voprosy terminologii po frazeologii, obshchemu i prikladnomu iazykoznaniiu."* Samarkand: Samarkandskii Gosudarstvennyi Universitet, 1986. 156 pp.

This is a valuable bibliographical study concerning the confused terminology of phraseology. Mokienko refers to dozens of publications that deal with such matters as phraseological units (i.e., proverbs, proverbial expressions, proverbial comparisons, etc.), structure, semantics, metaphor, function, and style. Usually the author adds helpful annotations, making this book extremely important for Soviet and international scholars alike. The book is also a superb indication for the fact that phraseology has attained a very important position in Soviet linguistic studies. Three detailed indices of terms (pp. 124–141), authors (pp. 141–146), and subjects (pp. 147–156) are included, making this study of utmost importance for anybody wanting to understand and appreciate the vast amount of Soviet phraseological research.

3971. Molho, Mauricio. "Del poema como significante: refrán." *Homenaje al Professor Antonio Vilanova.* Ed. Marta Cristina Carbonell. Barcelona: Departamento de Filologia Española, Universidad de Barcelona, 1989. II, 427–432.

This is one of the few examples where a scholar has dealt with a proverb poem by a relatively modern author. In this case Molho analyzes the short poem "Refrán" by the Spanish poet Frederico Garcia Lorca (1898–1936) which appeared in *Canciones* (1927). After citing the poem, the author makes some general comments regarding the interrelationship of poetry and proverbs. This is followed by a detailed analysis of every line of the poem, including comments on the structure, rhyme, meter, language, and style of the poem. Molho shows in particular how Garcia Lorca uses proverbial language in this poem to comment on traditional proverbial wisdom. For the subgenre of proverb poetry see Wolfgang Mieder (nos. 1273, 1276, and 3929).

3972. Monitto, Gary V. "Shakespeare and Culmann's *Sententiae pueriles.*" *Notes and Queries*, 230, new series 32 (1985), 30–31.

A short note lamenting the fact that Robert Dent did not utilize Leon(h)ard Culman(n)'s (1497?–1562) *Sententiae pueriles* (1540) as one of the sources for his collection of *Shakespeare's Proverbial Language* (1981). Monitto explains that William Shakespeare (1564–1616) definitely knew this compendium of Renaissance maxims and proverbs, and he points out that Michael Drayton (1563–1631) refers specifically to his own use of the book. Monitto also comments on Charles G. Smith's study of *Shakespeare's Proverb Lore: His Use of the "Sententiae" of Leonard Culman and Publilius Syrus* (1963; see no. 1752) that lists 209 Shakespeare parallels to the *Sententiae pueriles.*

3973. Monye, Ambrose A. "Kinds of Relationships in Igbo Proverbs Usage." *Africana Marburgensia*, 18 (1985), 72–79.

The author argues that in Igbo as in other communities certain relationships exist between proverbs and their referents in the context of usage, that an understanding of these relationships will help the listener to understand what is going on in the two worlds, and that this will enable him/her to understand and appreciate proverb usage in general. Citing four Igbo proverbs with English translations from the Aniocha area of Nigeria, Monye explains that their metaphorical language permits a transfer of association which renders them meaningful

in any particular communicative context. Detailed explanations
of the metaphorical relationships and the relationships based on
transfer of association are included for the four African proverbs
and their contextualized use. For a more detailed study of these
relationships see no. 3974 below.

3974. Monye, Ambrose A. "Proverb Usage: Kinds of Relationships."
Proverbium, 3 (1986), 85–99.

This is a similar but much expanded version of the previous
article (see no. 3973), once again explaining that in a certain
proverb usage various kinds of relationships in metaphor, social
life, action, meaning, and transfer of association could be used by
a speaker to describe and qualify the idea he/she wants to relay
to his/her listener. Monye shows that the social context is of
much importance for the proper understanding of proverbs, and
it is exactly the strategic social use of metaphor which makes
proverbs such important communicative tools. The author cites
three Igbo proverbs with English translations from the Aniocha
area in Nigeria, and he places these African proverbs into actual
contexts. He then gives detailed analyses of the metaphorical
relationships and shows how a transfer of association takes place
in the use of proverbs. It is argued in particular that the meaning
of proverbs can only be understood on the basis of a solid
knowledge of the social life and attitudes of the people using the
proverbs.

3975. Monye, Ambrose A. "Devices of Indirection in Aniocha Proverb
Usage." *Proverbium*, 4 (1987), 111–126.

In this article Monye studies the importance of indirection as
a strategic use of language in general and of proverbs in
particular. As far as the proverbial speech of the Igbo people
from the Aniocha area in Nigeria is concerned, three devices of
indirection are used, namely metaphor, simile, and wellerism.
Monye cites four examples each with English translations, and he
provides intriguing social contexts for all of them. Some of the
reasons for verbal indirection are the ability to make a point
pithily and precisely, the ability to cloak or characterize an idea
so as to avoid monotony, the ability to be coherent in order to be

understood properly, the ability to convince, win sympathy, and justify one's cause, the ability to situate one's argument, etc. Often the device of proverbial indirection is used for the purpose of observation, sizing-up, comparison, and transfer of reference. Monye also includes a fascinating interview (pp. 120–123) with an elderly African man discussing the social importance of indirection through the use of proverbs. The 10 notes contain useful bibliographical information.

3976. Monye, Ambrose A. *Proverbial Lore in Aniocha Oral Literature.* Diss. University of Nigeria at Nsukka, 1988. 726 pp.

Monye presents a voluminous and highly informative dissertation on the oral proverb tradition of the Igbo people of the Aniocha area in Nigeria, Africa. He starts his study with a first chapter (pp. 1–53) on the culture and society of the people of Aniocha. The second chapter (pp. 54–89) treats various genres of oral literature from Aniocha, namely folk tales, myths, legends, folk drama, oral poetry, and riddles. In the third chapter (pp. 90–124) the author reviews previous scholarship on African proverbs by native and foreign scholars, and this chapter is of much importance for an understanding of African paremiology. The fourth chapter (pp. 125–251) is a contextual study of Aniocha proverbs based on Monye's collection of 1649 proverbs. The texts are all cited in the African original with English translations, and the author provides invaluable ethnographic annotations regarding the use and function of proverbs in oral communication. Chapter five (pp. 252–335) presents a number of transcribed interviews with native speakers commenting on the value and meaning of proverbs in their social context, thereby answering the question of how the folk itself views its proverbial wisdom. The sixth chapter (pp. 336–397) investigates the form, style, and structure of Aniocha proverbs, and chapter seven (pp. 398–406) is a summary of this thesis. An invaluable bibliography (pp. 407–424), two lists of government reports and interviews (pp. 425–427), and a large appendix (pp. 428–726) of the 1649 African proverbs with English translations conclude this significant work.

3977. Monye, Ambrose A. "The Use of the Ideophone as a Taxonomic Element in the Oral Literary Criticism of Aniocha Proverbs." *Proverbium,* 5 (1988), 117–127.

In this article Monye investigates how the Igbo people of the Aniocha area in Nigeria react to their own folklore. He states that scholars should pay much more attention to such oral literary criticism by eliciting the meaning of certain folklore items from African native speakers. He reviews the literature on "meta-folklore" and then defines an "ideophone" as a descriptive word or phrase which emotively and graphically presents the concrete image of an object or idea discussed in a given communicative event. Citing numerous examples, the author shows that preliterate societies have some taxonomies which they employ in the oral literary criticism of their folklore and that ideophones in particular are used to comment on traditional proverbs. Most Aniocha ideophones evoke the images of sound, color, size, sense, taste, smell, etc., to capture the ideas which are observed or stated. They often are the spontaneous responses given to witty, humorous, and sex-related proverbs.

3978. Monye, Ambrose A. "The Paucity of God-Based Proverbs in Aniocha." *Proverbium,* 6 (1989), 55–65.

Monye demonstrates convincingly that there is a definite paucity of God-based proverbs in the proverbial language of the Igbo people of the Aniocha area in Nigeria, Africa. He starts with a distinction between those proverbs which contain God-based personal names and the true proverbs which refer to God. Using a statistical table, Monye proves that the word "God" appears with very little frequency in Aniocha proverbs in comparison to such words as "Child," "head," "animal," etc. In fact, Monye only cites 11 examples with English translations of God-based proverbs. Some of the reasons for this paucity of proverbs referring to God might be that it is impossible to have a concrete image of God, that people don't have any concrete knowledge of God, that they don't feel the need to involve God in trivial everyday matters, and that people don't feel comfortable in attributing a speaking role for God in proverbs.

3979. Monye, Ambrose A. "On Why People Use Proverbs." *Africana Marburgensia,* 23 (1990), 3–11.

A rather general article on some of the reasons why people use proverbs at all. Monye cites numerous African examples with English translations from the Igbo people of the Aniocha area in Nigeria, arguing that folklorists and paremiologists should pay more attention to what native speakers themselves say about proverb usage. Some of the reasons are to comment obliquely on experiences, to evaluate social situations, to express matters through indirection, to state ideas in images (metaphors), to educate people through didactic and traditional wisdom, to identify with the past, to argue convincingly, etc. Proverbs definitely are used as effective verbal strategies in social relationships, and the fact that they express matters metaphorically and indirectly makes them applicable to many different contexts.

3980. Moran, William L. "Puppies in Proverbs—From Samsi-Adad I to Archilochus?" *Eretz-Israel,* 14 (1978), 32–37.

This is a very erudite etymological study of an ancient Sumerian proverb which in English translation is "The hasty bitch produces blind puppies." Moran refers to the considerable previous scholarship regarding this text, and he cites modern parallels from Italian, German, English, and Greek. Above all he is able to cite a new reference form the early Greek lyrical poet Archilochus (700?-645? B.C.). Other references to early variants are included, and Moran presents detailed philological comments on lexical and morphological matters. The 35 notes include valuable bibliographical information concering this old proverb that is still in use today.

3981. Morton, Gerald W. "An Addendum to Apperson." *Notes and Queries,* 228, new series 30 (1983), 437.

The author reports on the fact that he has located an additional early variant of the proverb "Time and tide wait for no man" which has not been referenced in G.L. Apperson's *English Proverbs and Proverbial Phrases* (1929). Morton found the text ""Tyme & tide will stay for no man" in *De Pugna Animi,* an unpublished and privately performed play written by the minor Cavalier poet Mildmay Fane (1602?–1666), Earl of Westmorland, in 1650 to be performed at his estate at Apethorpe. Morton also shows that this proverbial line is very close to that used by Richard Brathwait (1588–1673) in *English Gentleman* (1641), and he conjectures that Fane most likely got this variant from Brathwait.

3982. Morvay, Károly. "Apuntes sobre la investigación de la fraseologia mexicana." *Proverbium Paratum*, 3 (1982), 274–281.

This is a review article on recent paremiographical and phraseological dictionaries of the Mexican language. The author starts with some general comments regarding various types of phraseological units, and he then presents a number of Mexican collections of proverbs, proverbial expressions, proverbial comparisons, and idioms. This is followed by a short comparative section on Spanish and Mexican fixed phrases, indicating that many traditional expressions from Spain continue to be in use in Mexico. But there are, of course, also those phrases which are indigenous to this country in South America. In an appendix (pp. 279–281) Morvay also shows in which way the Mexican phraseological units might differ from those in common use in Argentina.

3983. Morvay, Károly. "Phraseology in Bilingual Dictionaries. Phraseological Aspects of the Compilation of a Concise Catalan-Hungarian Dictionary." *Aktuelle Probleme der Phraseologie.* Eds. Harald Burger and Robert Zett. Bern: Peter Lang, 1987. 139–150.

In this article Morvay discusses the important question of how to include phraseological units in a bilingual dictionary. He refers particularly to the complexity of such work in the case of a planned Catalan-Hungarian dictionary which deals with two very different languages. The author analyzes classification problems and argues that nominal phrases should be listed under the main noun, wheras verbal phrases should be registered both under the verb and noun. He also argues that this dictionary should include some illustrative sentences. Above all it is of importance that the lexicographers indicate at least to some degree when a particular expression might be used, to what stylistic level it belongs, and what its particular historical background might be.

3984. Moser, Konrad. *"In dubio pro reo." Die geschichtliche Entwicklung dieses Satzes und seine Bedeutung im heutigen deutschen Strafrecht.* Diss. University of München, 1933. München: A. Huber, 1933. 116 pp.

Moser starts his detailed historical study on the Latin legal maxim "In dubio pro reo" (In doubt for the accused) with a section (pp. 16–30) on its Roman origin, its use in medieval Italy, and its spread throughout Germany until 1879. The second section (pp. 31–111) shows the importance of this proverb in modern German criminal law. Moser explains in particular how judges and lawyers need to interpret this expression in regard to the possible guilt of an accused person. Many legal examples are cited throughout these pages, and it is shown that this legal proverb is of greatest importance in protecting the rights of the accused. The third section (pp. 112–115) comments shortly on the application of this proverb to political issues. A useful bibliography (pp. 7–12) on legal proverbs is included. See also the two studies on "In dubio pro reo" by Peter Holtappels (no. 3607) and H. Holzhauer (no. 3609).

3985. Mrazovic, Pavica. "Gleichartige Phraseologismen im Deutschen und Serbokroatischen." *Sprache und Literatur in Wissenschaft und Unterricht,* 16, no. 56 (1985), 88–94.

This is a comparative treatise on German and Serbo-Croatian phraseological units. The author begins with a definition of fixed phrases and discusses in particular elements of idiomaticity, stability, and reproducibility. She then analyzes various degrees of equivalency. In the case of total equivalency, the phrases usually have a classical, Biblical, or literary origin and have been loan translated into most of the European languages. But many phraseological units have only partial equivalents in German and Serbo-Croatian. The differences are morphological, syntactical, lexical, and metaphorical, and there are also those expressions for which no equivalents exist at all. Mrazovic cites numerous examples including proverbs, proverbial expressions, idioms, and literary quotations.

3986. Mulinacci, Anna Paola. "'Cercar Maria per Ravenna': Da un proverbio, a un cantare, alla 'Fantesca' di G.B. Della Porta." *Italianistica: Revista di letteratura italiane,* 19, no. 1 (1990), 69–77.

Mulinacci presents a detailed study concerning the origin and meaning of the Italian proverbial expression "Cercar Maria per Ravenna" (To look for Maria in Ravenna) which appears in Giovanbattista Della Porta's (1535–1615) comedy *La Fantesca* (1592). The fixed phrase goes back to a folk narrative and has three basic meanings: (1) to look uselessly for something that is right in front of someone, (2) to look for things where they are not to be found, and (3) to look for something for one's own harm and shame. The author cites many contextualized references from Italian literary sources and also includes variants that refer to other cities (Rome, for example). The 36 notes contain helpful bibliographical information.

3987. Müller, Gernot. "'Die Gelegenheit beim Schopf ergreifen'.— 'Geschwätz, gehauen nicht und nicht gestochen'. Zur Verankerung zweier Phraseologismen im Werk Heinrich von Kleists." *Europhras 90. Akten der internationalen Tagung zur germanistischen Phraseologieforschung, Aske/Schweden 12.-15. Juni 1990.* Ed. Christine Palm. Uppsala: Acta Universitatis Upsaliensis, 1991. 139–153.

The author investigates the use and function of the two German proverbial expressions "Die Gelegenheit beim Schopf ergreifen" (To take time by the forelock) and "Das ist weder gehauen noch gestochen" (That is neither cut nor thrust, i.e., That is neither fish nor fowl) which appear in Heinrich von Kleist's (1777–1811) comedy *Der zerbrochene Krug* (1811). Müller interprets them in their literary context and explains that Kleist uses them for the purpose of wordplay. Additional references from two other plays by Kleist are cited, and the author states that Kleist has a skeptical attitude regarding the communicative value of metaphorical language. For the use of other proverbs and proverbial expressions in Kleist's *Der zerbrochene Krug* see also Wolfgang Mieder (no. 1251) and Ria Stambaugh (no. 1797).

3988. Müller-Salget, Klaus. "Volkslied, Sprichwort, Bibel, Gesangbuch: Geistliches und Weltliches im Dienste der Bekräftigung und Vergewisserung." In K. Müller-Salget. *Erzählungen für das Volk. Evangelische Pfarrer als Volksschriftsteller im Deutschland des 19. Jahrhunderts.* Berlin: Erich Schmidt, 1984. 314–326.

In this chapter the author investigates the use and function of folk songs, proverbs, Biblical quotations, and religious songs in the prose writings of such 19th century German Protestant ministers as Otto Glaubrecht (1807–1859), W.O. von Horn (1798–1867), etc. It is shown that these authors used oral folklore genres in order to make their narratives more accessible to the common folk. They were also very interested in didactic, moral, and religious messages to their readers, and it should not be surprising that folk proverbs and Biblical quotations play a major role in their short novels. Müller-Salget cites numerous examples in their literary context and explains that the proverbs function primarily as elements of folk speech and as expressions of traditional wisdom.

3989. Müller-Thurau, Claus Peter. *Laß uns mal 'ne Schnecke angraben. Sprache und Sprüche der Jugendszene.* Düsseldorf: Econ, 1983. 176 pp.

A fascinating study of the language and slogans of the German youth subculture. Throughout the chapters many new phrases and idioms are cited which have proverbial currency among the young people. The chapters on linguistic ridicule (pp. 11–14) and youth slogans (pp. 61–71) show that many of the new slogans and expressions are based on traditional proverb structures (patterns), while their content and meaning reflect the concerns of modern society. For example, the old proverb "Was lange währt, wird endlich gut" (What lasts long will finally turn out well) is changed to "Was lange gärt, wird endlich Wut" (What ferments long will finally become anger). Even more of such "Antisprichwörter" (anti-proverbs) are included in a small collection (pp. 90–97) which is organized according to content: nuclear power, armament, political protest, attitudes toward life, irony, and nonsense. A word index with many new expressions (pp. 98–172) comprises the second half of the book.

3990. Murphy, Roland. "Proverbs in Genesis 2?" *Text and Tradition. The Hebrew Bible and Folklore.* Ed. Susan Niditsch. Atlanta/Georgia: Scholars Press, 1990. 121–125.

This is a short note commenting on Galit Hasan-Rokem's article (see no. 3568) about two proverbs in the second chapter of Genesis in the Old Testament of the Bible. The two texts are "It is not good for a man to be alone" (Genesis 2,18) and "That is why a man leaves his father and mother and clings to his wife and they become one flesh" (Genesis 2,24). Murphy agrees with Hasan-Rokem that these two pieces of wisdom are important statements, but he disagrees with her about their significance to the actual narrative in Genesis. He cites a number of other passages from this second chapter and concludes that the two proverbs and their paradox of "being alone" and "two becoming one flesh" (thus once again being alone as one being) have little to do with the narrative flow itself.

3991. Muthmann, Hans-Otto. "'Bei mir . . .'—Eine Sondergruppe der Berliner Redensarten." *Proverbium*, 3 (1986), 273–276.

The author starts with a short discussion of the special sense of humor that is characteristic of the native inhabitants of Berlin. He then explains that especially during the 1920s people started using expressions that began with the two words "Bei mir . . ." (In my case . . .). He points out that this formulaic pattern is a loan translation from the Russian "U menia . . ." which many of the Russian immigrants brought to Berlin at that time. Muthmann cites a few German examples which make clear that most of these proverbial sayings express certain identifications or imperatives. Quite a few of them are also sexually oriented and rather obscene. This particular type of proverbial phrase appears to be no longer in use today, but Muthmann argues that it would be worthwhile to make a collection of them as an example of how a particular formulaic pattern became popular for some time in Germany's capital.

N

3992. Nail, Norbert. "'Dich haben sie wohl mit dem Klammerbeutel gepudert!' Nicht ganz 750 Jahre Berlinisches in unserer Umgangssprache." *Der Sprachdienst*, 31, no. 4 (1987), 109–110.

A short note on some German proverbial expressions and proverbial comparisons that originated in Berlin. The inhabitants of this city have always been known for their special type of humor which often includes a solid dose of irony or satire. Nail mentions a few phrases like "Frech wie Oskar" (To be very insolent), "Treulose Tomate" (Not to be very faithful), etc. Many expressions refer to names, persons, or buildings, and there are also quite a few fixed phrases that comment on culinary matters. The author includes some etymological and lexical explanations, and he certainly is correct to look at Germany's capital as a center for innovative proverbial expressions of which many have been disseminated throughout that country. For a more detailed study of this phenomenon see Gerda Grober-Glück (no. 608).

3993. Naumann, Hans-Peter. "Unikale Komponenten im Schwedischen." *Aktuelle Probleme der Phraseologie.* Eds. Harald Burger and Robert Zett. Bern: Peter Lang, 1987. 151–168.

Naumann starts with a short survey of Swedish phraseology and then presents a linguistic study of those Swedish phraseological units which contain words whose meaning or form are unique to the particular phraseological environment. His examples are proverbial expressions, proverbial comparisons, twin formulas, and routine formulas which are cited in Swedish with German translations. The author explains the semantic, morphological, grammatical, and syntactical particularities of such fixed phrases. Towards the end of the article he also deals with problems of equivalency, indicating that for some Swedish expressions there are identical German equivalents. However, there are also those expressions for which a translator could only find partial equivalents in which lexical and semantic differences occur.

3994. Nedo, Paul. "Sprichwort, sprichwörtliche Redensart und Spruch." In P. Nedo. *Grundriss der sorbischen Volksdichtung.* Bautzen: VEB Domowina-Verlag, 1966. 93–105 and 262–263 (notes).

In this book chapter Nedo gives a survey of Sorbian proverb scholarship, emphasizing the collections that have been assembled to this point. He also deals with definition problems and then states that Sorbian proverbs and proverbial expressions serve many social functions. This is made clear by a content analysis of many examples which are cited in the original language with German translations. Many proverbs express views on class conflicts, injustice, and other social concerns. They certainly contain the everyday attitudes and the worldview of the Sorbian people. The notes (pp. 262–263) contain useful bibliographical information. For detailed studies on Sorbian proverbs see especially Isolde Gardos (nos. 507–510 and 2395) and Susanne Hose (nos. 3617–3618).

3995. Negreanu, Constantin. "Cîteva observatii asupra propozitiilor subiective din proverbe." *Scoala Mehedintiului,* 8–9 (1982), 148–153.

Constantin Negreanu (1942–1991) had established himself as one of the leading Rumanian paremiologists at the time of his unexpected death. His contributions during his short life were primarily in the area of linguistic paremiology (see nos. 2675–2686 and nos. 3996–4013 below). This is also the case with this particular article on the structural analysis of Rumanian proverbs which are composed of a main clause followed by a subordinate clause. Negreanu develops a structural formula (pattern) for such texts and analyzes the grammatical, syntactical, and semantic relationship between the two clauses. Various structural models are established, and the author also includes a diagram to explain the way the two halves of the proverbs are linked. The 28 notes include useful bibliographical information on Rumanian paremiological scholarship.

3996. Negreanu, Constantin. "Convergenta procedeelor stilistice în proverbe." *Mehedinti. Cultura si civilizatie,* 4 (1982), 519–526; also in French translation as "La convergence des procédés stylistiques dans les proverbes roumains." *Proverbium,* 5 (1988), 129–136.

In this paper Negreanu investigates various stylistic aspects of Rumanian proverbs. He argues that proverbs exhibit a definite poetic style that differentiates them from ordinary speech or prose. Citing numerous examples he shows how the form of proverbs is characterized by such poetic devices as rhyme, meter, symmetry, repetition, parallelism, alliteration, etc. The poetic language of the proverbs helps the reproducibility and memorability of the proverbial wisdom contained in them. Negreanu includes two structural diagrams to indicate how several of these poetic markers make up part of the so-called proverbiality of a particular statement.

3997. Negreanu, Constantin. "Termeni concreti în proverbe." *Mehedintiul literar-artistic,* no volume given (1982), 105–108.

A linguistic study of about 6000 Rumanian proverbs to establish the relationship between abstract and concrete (realistic) concepts contained in them. Negreanu points out that the actual nouns of the proverbs are usually very concrete, referring to various professions, aspects of the weather, certain measurements, etc. The same is true for the verbs which belong to those that are frequently employed in everyday speech. But out of these concrete lexical units arises a metaphorical meaning for the entire proverb as an expression of traditional wisdom. This metaphorical nature of the proverb makes it possible to apply it to different situations and contexts. Many examples are cited to show how concrete individual words take on a general meaning that is quite different from its realistic meaning.

3998. Negreanu, Constantin. "Forme verbale în proverbe." *Caiet metodico-stiintific. Limba româna. Limbi moderne,* 2 (1983), 41–44.

In this linguistic analysis Negreanu studies the various grammatical uses of verbs in Rumanian proverbs. He explains that most proverbs are expressed in the indicative, but there are also those texts that use the imperative or the subjunctive. Some proverbs also cite the verb in the infinitive. The third person singular and plural are common in proverbs, but in the proverbs that use the imperative the second person singular or plural are found as well. In the second part of the article Negreanu also investigates the various ways of expressing negation in proverbs. Many examples are cited, and it becomes clear that the verb tense is almost always the present.

3999. Negreanu, Constantin. "Primul simpozion de paremiologie româneasca." *Buletinul Socetatii pe anul 1983*, no volume given (1983), 130.

A short report on the first Rumanian paremiological symposium that took place on June 18, 1983, in Drobeta-Turnu-Severin, Rumania. Negreanu is correct in pointing out that there is a high level of scholarly activity among Rumanian paremiologists, and the symposium certainly attracted internationally known scholars from that country. In addition to Constantin Negreanu himself the following proverb scholars participated: I.C. Chitimia, Cezar Tabarcea, Pavel Ruxandoiu, Nicolae Constantinescu, Dumitru Stanciu, Alexandru Stanciulescu-Bîrda, etc. The symposium dealt with linguistic, structural, ethnological, didactic, semantic, and historical topics. See also Constantin Negreanu's English reports on this and a second paremiological symposium (no. 4006 below).

4000. Negreanu, Constantin. *Structura Proverbelor Românesti.* Bucuresti: Editura Stiintifica si Enciclopedica, 1983. 259 pp.

This is a superb study concerning the structure of Rumanian proverbs based on the close conceptual, linguistic, and stylistic examination of 5994 texts. Constantin Negreanu (1942–1991) starts his book with a review of the heterogeneous methods of paremiology, a short history of the study of proverbs, a discussion of proverb definitions, and an analysis of the terminological problems confronting paremiologists (pp. 9–43). In the section dealing with the conceptual structure (pp. 44–57) the author discusses the worldview (funadamental concepts) of the Rumanian people as expressed in their proverbs. Even though proverbs might not reflect national character, they do mirror specific Rumanian thoughts and feelings on wisdom, work, justice, education, dignity, truth, humanity, beauty, etc. In the long section (pp. 58–152) on linguistic structure Negreanu investigates the binary structure of proverbs as it is reflected in the lexical and morphological aspects of the texts (nouns, verbs, adjectives, pronouns, numbers, and negations are treated). The final part of the book (pp. 153–214) studies the stylistic (aesthetic) aspects of proverbs, especially metaphor, comparison, repetition, symmetry, rhyme, and alliteration. Many structural diagrams, charts, statistical tables, and examples are included. A comprehensive bibliography (pp. 215–223), a large proverb index (pp. 224–245), a name index (pp. 246–249), and a long French summary (pp. 250–257) are all part of this fascinating and exemplary study based on rigorous textual and statistical analyses.

4001. Negreanu, Constantin. "Die Lebensauffasssung in Sprichwörtern." *Rumänische Rundschau*, 38, no. 10 (1984), 32–34; also in Russian translation as "Paremiologiia i mirosozertsanie." *Rumynskaia Literatura*, 38, no. 10 (1984), 31–33.

A short and general article dealing with the content of Rumanian proverbs. Negreanu points out that while the Rumanian language has plenty of international proverbs which were translated from classical, Biblical, and European sources, it also includes many texts which are truly indigenous to the Rumanian people and their cultural history. Basing his comments on a statistical analysis of many proverbs, the author concludes that most of them deal with wisdom, irony, work, prudence, intelligence, justice, education, dignity, and goodness. They express, at least to some extent, the "national" character and the moral and spiritual worldview of the Rumanian people.

4002. Negreanu, Constantin. "Aspecte ale cercetarii paremiologice comparate." *Memoriile sectiei de stiinte filologice, literatura si arte*, series IV, 8 (1986), 215–220; also in English translation as "Some Aspects of Comparative Paremiological Research." *Proverbium*, 5 (1988), 159–165.

This is an important review article on recent international proverb scholarship for Rumanian readers. Negreanu starts with a short discussion of the *Proverbium* (1965–1975) journal, its successor *Proverbium Paratum* (1981–1989), and the new *Proverbium: Yearbook of International Proverb Scholarship* (1984ff.). He then comments briefly on the work of such international scholars as Matti Kuusi, Démétrios Loukatos, Grigorii L'vovich Permiakov, Peter Grzybek, Arvo Krikmann, Algirdas Julien Greimas, Zoltán Kanyó, Alan Dundes, Kwesi Yankah, and Wolfgang Mieder. In the second part of the article he points out that the Rumanian paremiologists Cezar Tabarcea, Dumitru Stanciu, and Gabriel Gheorghe have joined this international team through their significant work. The 27 notes contain significant bibliographical information. The English version is slightly shortened, but its 23 notes also include valuable bibliographical references.

4003. Negreanu, Constantin. "Contributia colectiei COGITO la cunoasterea tezaurului paremiologic si aforistic românesc." *Proverbium Dacoromania*, 2 (1987), 36–40; and 3 (1988), 23–27.

These are two reports summarizing the content of the many collections of Rumanian proverbs, aphorisms and literary quotations which have been published between 1972 and 1986 in a book series called COGITO. Negreanu gives precise bibliographical information for each book and then cites a few examples. In the case of the proverb collections he explains the classification system, describes the content, and indicates their value for serious paremiographical work. Some of the collections are popular in nature, basically listing proverbs dealing with various subject matters as collections to be enjoyed by the general population. The books of aphorisms are of importance for proverb scholars since many of these literary texts are in fact based on traditional proverbs, changing them into so-called "Antisprichwörter" (anti-proverbs).

4004. Negreanu, Constantin. "Functiile proverbului in opera lui Nicolae Filimon." *Memoriile sectiei de stiinte filologice, literatura si arte*, series IV, 9 (1987), 73–81.

In this article Negreanu studies the use and function of proverbs, proverbial expressions, and literary quotations in the works of the Rumanian author Nicolae Filimon (1819–1865). He starts with some general remarks concerning the identification and interpretation of proverbial language in literary works, and he then shows that Filimon integrated much proverbial speech into his writings as a music critic and as an author of travel literature and novels. Negreanu investigates in particular the prose works *Escursiuni în Germania meridonala* (1860), *Nenorocirile unui slujnicar* (1861), and *Ciocoii vechi si noi* (1863). Many examples are cited in their literary context, and Negreanu explains that they are used to express social criticism as well as didactic and moral intentions by the author. For Filimon's proverbial aphorisms see Constantin Negreanu (no. 4007).

4005. Negreanu, Constantin. "Quelques observations sur les termes concrets qui réfèrent à la flore et la faune des proverbes." *Proverbium*, 4 (1987), 127–141.

Stating that proverbs of a particular region will contain those concrete (realistic) nouns that are part of that culture, Negreanu investigated about 6000 Rumanian proverbs for words that refer to the fauna and flora of that country. Regarding the former, Negreanu found many proverbs commenting on such domestic animals as the dog, sheep, ox, horse, cow, donkey (ass), cat, goat, etc. Other texts refer to wild animals like the wolf, fox, lion, monkey, etc. Three other groups of proverbs include nouns for birds, insects, and fish. Regarding the flora, Negreanu found many proverbs dealing with edible plants (grapes, cabbage, wheat, grain, mushroom, etc.). But there are, of course, also proverbs which refer to trees in general, fruit trees, flowers, etc. Many examples are cited with French translations, and it is argued that these concrete references are clear indicators of the life and culture of the Rumanian people. Many statistical tables are included to indicate the frequency of these various aspects of the fauna and flora.

4006. Negreanu, Constantin. "Two Romanian Paremiology-Symposia (1983 and 1986)." *Proverbium*, 4 (1987), 243–248.

Realizing that most international paremiologists did not know that two important paremiological symposia took place in

Rumania on June 18, 1983 and on June 16–17, 1986, Negreanu put together a list of the speakers and the titles of their lectures in English so that scholars not knowing the Rumanian language would have an idea of the significance of these symposia. Many of the internationally known Rumanian paremiologists participated at these two meetings, including I.C. Chitimia, Cezar Tabarcea, Pavel Ruxandoiu, Nicolae Constantinescu, Dumitru Stanciu, Alexandru Stanciulescu-Bîrda, Constantin Negreanu, etc. The topics dealt with linguistic, semantic, ethnological, pedagogical, historical, syntactical, social, and semiotic aspects of proverbs. See also Constantin Negreanu's Rumanian report on the first symposium (no. 3999 above), and Anca Pegulescu (no. 4134).

4007. Negreanu, Constantin. "Aforistica lui Nicolae Filimon." *Limba si literatura româna*, 18, no. 1 (1989), 40–42.

A short note concerning the aphorisms of the Rumanian author Nicolae Filimon (1819–1865), who used numerous proverbs and proverbial expressions in his novels. Negreanu points out that Filimon's aphorisms comment on social problems, trying to give moral guidance and being quite didactic in nature. Some of them are based on proverbial structures, and they could be looked at as "Antisprichwörter" (anti-proverbs). Negreanu cites a few examples and comments on their language, structure, content, and meaning. For an article on Filimon's use of proverbs see Constantin Negreanu (no. 4004 above).

4008. Negreanu, Constantin. "Cîteva observatii asupra elementelor paremiologice din limba povestirilor lui Petre Ispirescu." *Proverbium Dacoromania*, 4 (1989), 26–30.

This is a short literary investigation of the use and function of proverbs in the works of the Rumanian author Petre Ispirescu (1838–1887). This writer is known for his reworkings of Rumanian fairy tales which he had collected and for other prose works. Negreanu cites numerous contextualized examples and explains that Ispirescu used proverbs in order to teach virtue and to indicate social attitudes like virtue, wisdom, prudence, etc. It is shown that the proverbs function as characterization, reasoning through traditional wisdom, resignation, advice, didacticism, etc.

A very short English summary (p. 30) is attached. See also Constantin Negreanu's more detailed study on Petre Ispirescu (no. 4013 below).

4009. Negreanu, Constantin. "Observatii asupra elementelor paremiologice din opera lui Ion Creanga." *Revista de etnografie si folclor*, 34, no. 6 (1989), 525–541.

In this literary study Negreanu investigates the use and function of proverbs and proverbial expressions in the works of the Rumanian author Ion Creanga (1837–1889). Negreanu starts with a review of previous comments on Creanga's proverbial language, and he also comments on the need of interpreting the proverbial texts in their actual literary context. Citing numerous examples from various prose works, especially the autobiographical narrative *Amintiri din copilarie* (1880), Negreanu is able to show that Creanga used proverbs frequently for characterization, explanation, conclusion, argument, justification, warning, consolation, resignation, etc. Proverbial speech is definitely part of the regional color and humor which makes Creanga's stories and novels so charming to the present day. An English abstract (p. 541) is included.

4010. Negreanu, Constantin. "O schita paremiologica: *Scrisoarea XII (Picala si Tindala)* de C. Negruzzi." *Limba si literatura*, 4 (1989), 527–537; also in French translation as "Littérature et parémiologie chez François Villon et Constantin Negruzzi." *Proverbium*, 8 (1991), 113–119.

The title of the somewhat shortened French translation of this article is a more precise description of the content of this important article dealing with the interrelationship of literature and paremiology. The first half of the article does in fact concern itself with the proverb poetry of the late medieval French poet François Villon (1431?–1463?), notably his "Ballade des proverbes" and some other ballads containing numerous proverbs. In the second part of his article Negreanu shows that the Rumanian author Constantin Negruzzi (1808–1868) also amassed proverbs in this fashion in his work *Scrisoarea XII (Picala si Tindala)* (1842). For both authors Negreanu cites numerous proverbs in their literary context, and he discusses their structure, language, style, meaning, and function. It is concluded that both authors present small proverb collections in their literary works, and it is clear that proverbial language was of great aesthetic importance for them.

4011. Negreanu, Constantin. "Romanian Contributions to the Structuralist Research of Proverbs." *Proverbium*, 6 (1989), 191–205.

   Negreanu presents a detailed and much needed critical survey of the significant accomplishments by Rumanian paremiologists. It is indeed amazing to see how much proverb scholarship has gone on in this small country during the past few decades. There is no doubt that the Rumanian scholars have made major contributions to structural paremiology in particular, and it is to be hoped that some of their books and articles might be translated into some more accessible languages. Negreanu mentions especially the work by I.C. Chitimia, Pavel Ruxandoiu, Cezar Tabarcea, Nicolae Constantinescu, Constantin Negreanu, Ovidiu Bîrlea, Dumitru Stanciu, Gabriel Gheorghe, and some others. Their studies have been listed and annotated in my two previous bibliographies as well as the present volume, and they make clear that Rumanian paremiologists are some of the most active proverb scholars in the world, especially in the area of linguistic, structural, and semiotic studies of proverbs. The 77 notes that Negreanu includes in this article contain important bibliographical information.

4012. Negreanu, Constantin. "The Early Days of Romanian Paremiology and a Manuscript Dating from the Nineteenth Century." *Proverbium*, 7 (1990), 153–162.

   The author surveys the earlier periods of Rumanian proverb scholarship, starting with the interest in proverbs by certain chroniclers of the 15th and 16th centuries. He also comments on the increased paremiographical work that went on during the 17th and 18th centuries, and he then gives a detailed historical report on a large manuscript of 854 pages from the 1840s which the Rumanian Minister of Justice Iordache Golescu (1768–1848) assembled. It contains 18,306 proverbs and maxims which eventually were published in I.A Zanne's (1855–19?) ten-volume collection of *Proverbele Românilor* (1895–1903). Negreanu cites numerous examples and explains that Golescu's collection comprises the entire eighth volume and part of the ninth volume of Zanne's huge proverb collection.

4013. Negreanu, Constantin. "Petre Ispirescu si limba popularia (Lucutiuni, expresii, proverbe)." *Revista de etnografie si folclor*, 36, nos. 3–4 (1991), 179–191.

This is a much more detailed literary investigation of Petre Ispirescu's (1838–1887) proverbial language than Negreanu's previous shorter paper (see no. 4008 above). Negreanu starts with some comments regarding Ispirescu's life and works in general, commenting on the fact that he is of considerable importance to Rumanian folklore due to the fact that he collected fairy tales. It is pointed out that this author also was very interested in proverbs, proverbial expressions, and idioms, and they certainly play a major stylistic role in his prose works. Since Ispirescu was interested in commenting on social matters and also willing to write with moral and didactic intentions, proverbs became quite naturally part of his metaphorical style. Negreanu cites numerous examples in their literary context, and he concludes that these prose works employ proverbs and proverbial expressions for the purpose of characterization and local color. Altogether Ispirescu is an excellent example of a 19th century writer using popular folk speech to reflect the language and worldview of his characters.

4014. Nel, Philip Johannes. *The Structure and Ethos of the Wisdom Admonitions in "Proverbs."* Berlin: Walter de Gruyter, 1982. 142 pp.

The author begins his study of the Book of Proverbs with a chapter on the wisdom literature of Israel (pp. 1–6). In the second chapter (pp. 7–17) he treats the formal structure of the wisdom contained in this book of the Bible, notably as expressed in such genres as the parable, allegory, fable, riddle, proverb, etc. In the third chapter (pp. 18–82) Nel investigates the structure of the wisdom admonitions in subordinate, descriptive, interrogative, conditional, and imperative clauses. He also shows that some of the proverbs serve as expressions of prediction, promise, wisdom, etc. The fourth chapter (pp. 83–115) analyzes the ethos of the wisdom, while at the same time commenting on the function of this wisdom literature in the Book of Proverbs. In the fifth chapter (pp. 116–127) the author shows that the ethos might be interpreted as a recognition of the evil in humankind and the world. Numerous contextualized examples are cited, and Nel also includes a valuable bibliography (pp. 128–135) and a list of textual references from the Bible (pp. 136–142).

4015. Nelson, Timothy C. "'Ex abundantia cordis os loquitur': Ein Beitrag zur Rezeptionsgeschichte eines umstrittenen Sprichworts." *Proverbium*, 3 (1986), 101–123.

Nelson begins his exemplary diachronic study of the New Testament proverb "Ex abundantia cordis os loquitur" (Matth. 12,30) and its German translation "Wes das Herz voll ist, des gehet der Mund über" (Out of the abundance of the heart the mouth speaketh) with a review of the previous scholarship on this proverb. He explains that Geiler von Kaisersberg (1445–1510) certainly used it in German before Martin Luther (1483–1546) rendered it into German in 1522. He then claims that not only theologians and preachers of the Reformation employed this proverb in their polemics against their opponents of the old faith. On the contrary, the Catholic priest and scholar Johannes Nas (1534–1590) used the proverb and its variants 22 times between 1565–1571 in his polemical writings against Luther's followers. Nelson cites all these texts in their literary context and adds significant interpretative comments. See also John G. Kunstmann (no. 945), William Kurrelmeyer (no. 2567), and Wolfgang Mieder (no. 3862).

4016. Nelson, Timothy C. "'Ordhskvidhir' in der *Gisla saga Súrssonar.* Form und Funktion." *Proverbium*, 4 (1987), 143–172.

This is an erudite study of the 17 Old Norse or Icelandic proverbs and proverbial expressions contained in the *Gisla saga Súrssonar* (13th century). Nelson starts with a short review of previous research concerning the proverbial language of this saga, and he then analyzes the form, above all rhythm and alliteration, of these old Germanic proverbs. Next he cites every text in its Old Norse wording together with a German translation. This is followed by annotations from Icelandic proverb collections and, where possible, by variants of the proverb. Nelson also comments in great detail on the actual use and function of each text in the saga. It is concluded that most of the proverbs are used for characterization, but they also function as argumentation, warning, and traditional wisdom. The 42 notes contain important bibliographical information.

4017. Nelson, Timothy C. *"O du armer Luther . . ." Sprichwörtliches in der antilutherischen Polemik des Johannes Nas (1534–1590)*. Diss. Uppsala Universitet, 1990. 305 pp.

There is no doubt that this exemplary dissertation on the use and function of German proverbs and proverbial expressions in the works of the Catholic scholar and priest Johannes Nas (1534–1590) belongs to the very best studies of this type. In the first chapter (pp. 1–52) Nelson discusses the life and works of Nas, explaining in particular his polemics against Martin Luther's (1483–1546) Reformation movement. The second chapter (pp. 53–67) shows how Nas used proverbs and proverbial expressions to add metaphorical expressiveness through folk speech to his polemics. The third chapter (pp. 68–113) investigates the form and use of this proverbial language in Nas' six *Centuriae* (1565/70) with special emphasis on variations, allusions, amassments, introductory formulas, etc. The important fourth chapter (pp. 114–149) deals with the interrelationship of fables and proverbs and also includes a section on wellerisms. The fifth chapter (pp. 150–165) shows how Nas used traditional proverbs to argue against the doctrines of Martin Luther. In an appendix Nelson offers an enlightening section (pp. 166–187) that proves that Nas used some of the major proverb collections of the 16th century, especially that of Johannes Agricola (1492?–1566). This is followed by a superb and richly annotated proverb index (pp. 188–292) of 1213 texts which is invaluable for the historical research on German proverbs. A large bibliography (pp. 296–305), 6 illustrations, and a German summary (pp. 293a–b) help to make this a truly outstanding study. See also N. Lukasser (no. 3796).

4018. Nelson, Timothy C. "Sprichwörtliche Polemik in der Gegenreformation: Zu Johannes Nas' *GAsinus Nasi BattimontAnus* (1571)." *Proverbium,* 7 (1990), 163–183.

In this article Nelson studies the polemical use and function of German proverbs and proverbial expression in the satirical work *GAsinus Nasi BattimontAnus* (1571) by the Catholic scholar and priest Johannes Nas (1534–1590). After a short discussion of this important document of the Counter Reformation, the author explains that it contains 260 proverbial texts on 240 pages. Next he analyzes four proverbial woodcuts in great detail, showing that one of them depicts at least seven proverbial expressions (most of them with the key-word "Esel" [donkey]). In the last section of the article Nelson cites a few contextualized proverbs, among them "Gleich und gleich gesellt sich gern" (Birds of a feather flock together), and he indicates how the frequent use of proverbial language by Nas adds to his polemics against the Lutherans. With 4 illustrations.

4019. Nelson, Timothy C. "Die verkehrte Welt." *Europhras 90. Akten der internationalen Tagung zur germanistischen Phraseologieforschung, Aske/Schweden 12.-15. Juni 1990.* Ed. Christine Palm. Uppsala: Acta Universitatis Upsaliensis, 1991. 155–161.

Nelson comments shortly on the proverbial motif of "Die verkehrte Welt" (World-upside-down) in such paintings as Pieter Brueghel's (1520?–1569) *Netherlandic Proverbs* (1559), and he then argues convincingly that this motif can also be found in literary texts of the 16th century. He cites several contextualized examples out of the six polemical *Centuriae* (1565–1570) of the Catholic scholar and priest Johannes Nas (1534–1590). Nelson explains that Nas amassed proverbial expressions to show the "nonsense" of Martin Luther's (1483–1546) Reformation ideas. Nas attacks his followers bitterly and makes the motif of the "World-upside-down" an effective proverbial weapon of the Counter Reformation movement.

4020. Neumann, Renate. *Das wilde Schreiben: Graffiti, Sprüche und Zeichen am Rand der Straßen.* Essen: Die Blaue Eule, 1986. 341 pp.

This is one of the most complete studies of German graffiti collected in major cities between 1979 and 1984. The author begins with an historical introduction (pp. 9–22) and then starts with a chapter on graffiti stories from the Bible and literary sources (pp. 23–32). The second chapter (pp. 33–50) deals with names as part of graffiti, while chapter three (pp. 51–76) investigates the special graffiti of hitchhikers. In the fourth chapter (pp. 77–126) Neumann analyzes graffiti drawings, and in the fifth chapter (pp. 127–166) she deals with graffiti that alter various types of traffic signs and advertisements. The sixth chapter (pp. 167–194) treats the negative imperatives of many graffiti, and the seventh chapter (pp. 195–234) points out the references to concrete and cement in these texts found in big cities. While the author cites numerous examples throughout her book that might be considered variations of German proverbs, this intentional alteration and manipulation of proverbs can be seen in particular in the eighth chapter (pp. 235–264) where Neumann analyzes the slogan character of graffiti. The short ninth chapter (pp. 265–271) serves as a conclusion and presents a convincing argument that graffiti are important documents of the worldview of modern city dwellers. The index of texts (pp. 272–333) includes many graffiti based on proverbial structures, a valuable bibliography (pp. 334–341) is attached, and the book contains 136 illustrations.

4021. Neumann, Siegfried. "'Dat seggt man, wenn . . .' Sagwörter im Munde eines alten mecklenburgischen Maurers." *Kikut. Plattdütsch gistern un hüt,* no. 12 (1987), 55–61.

In this article Neumann presents a collection of 44 German wellerisms which he collected from one local informant. The author interviewed the mason Heinrich Tiedemann (1902–) on various occasions, and he established the fact that this man had an impressive repertory of wellerisms. Since Tiedemann also mentioned the use and function of most of his texts in certain contexts, the author is able to supply the reader with important materials showing the communicative value of wellerisms in the northern German state of Mecklenburg. The texts are cited in the Low German dialect, and Neumann also includes comments on the style, form, humor, and content of these traditional texts that continue to be in oral use in modern Germany. A short bibliography (p. 61) is attached.

4022. Neuss, Paula. "Proverbial Skelton." *Studia Neophilologica*, 54 (1982), 237–246.

Neuss begins her article with the statement that John Skelton (1460?–1529) does indeed use a lot of proverbs in his moral play *Magnyfycence* (c. 1516). She lists 119 proverbs and proverbial expressions found in this drama, and she also provides historical annotations from Morris Palmer Tilley's *A Dictionary of the Proverbs in England in the Sixteenth and Seventeenth Centuries* (1950) and Bartlett Jere Whiting's *Proverbs, Sentences, and Proverbial Phrases from English Writings mainly before 1500* (1968). In the second part of the essay Neuss discusses some contextualized examples showing how Skelton uses proverbs for didactic and moralistic purposes in this "proverbial" play. See also Robert Kinsman (no. 2524) and Andrew Welsh (no. 2998).

4023. Neuss, Paula. "The Sixteenth-Century English 'Proverb' Play." *Comparative Drama*, 18, no. 1 (1984), 1–18.

The author presents a solid argument that there were definitely English authors who wrote so-called "proverb plays" during the 16th century. In the first part of this literary investigation Neuss analyzes William Wager's (fl. 1550–1575) plays *Enough is as Good as a Feast* (c. 1571) and *The Longer Thou Livest the More Fool Thou Art* (1559). She explains that the proverbial titles are used as leitmotifs in the plays, and it is also shown that proverbs function for clarification, amplification, and personification. In the second part (pp. 13–17) Neuss analyzes William Shakespeare's (1564–1616) plays *All's Well that Ends Well* (1593) and *Measure for Measure* (1604), once again illustrating that these two plays could be considered as "proverbial" plays. Neuss also refers shortly to similar plays by Ulpian Fulwell (1546?–1578) and John Skelton (1460?–1529). Many contextualized examples are cited, and the article concludes with the claim that

English literature had its "proverbe dramatique" perhaps even before they became such a fashion in French literature.

4024. Nguyén, Nguyén, Edward F. Foules, and Kathleen Carlin. "Proverbs as Psychological Interpretations Among Vietnamese." *Asian Folklore Studies*, 50, no. 2 (1991), 311–318.

The authors state that proverbs play a major role in Vietnam in everyday conversation, in written communication, and in pedagogy. But proverbs also provide the opportunity to offer psychologically sensitive insights to a person manifesting problems. For this reason psychotherapists often use proverbs to describe succinctly to patients observations about their behavior or inner conflicts. Citing 10 Vietnamese proverbs in transliteration and with English translations, the authors explain how they might be used for therapeutic purposes. They comment on their meaning in the Vietnamese culture, and they also add explications of the metaphors based on mental mechanisms from Western psychoanalytical psychology required to understand the individual proverbs. A short bibliography (p. 318) and an English abstract (p. 311) are provided.

4025. Nierenberg, Jess. "Proverbs in Graffiti: Taunting Traditional Wisdom." *Maledicta*, 7 (1983), 41–58.

In this interesting article Nierenberg studies the modern use of English, American and German proverbs in graffiti. He starts with a discussion of proverb parodies and the content and importance of graffiti, and he then presents numerous examples which he found in printed collections of graffiti, in the Folklore Archive of the University of California at Berkeley, and during his own fascinating field research in the United States and Germany. To each graffiti text which varies a standard proverb the traditional proverb is added for comparison, and Nierenberg also includes interpretative comments on their aggressive, scatological, obscene, sexual, and defiant messages. Proverbial graffiti are seen as revolting against rationality, conformity, and moral standards of the traditional proverbial rules and the societal mores that they represent. Freudian psychological interpretations of the humor in these parodied proverbs are added to a number of the texts. The German examples are cited with English translations. A useful bibliography (pp. 57–58) is provided as well. See also Klaus Dieter Pilz (no. 4179).

4026. Nikolaieva, I. "Publications parémiologiques soviétiques (fin 1982–début 1985)." *Tel grain tel pain. Poétique de la sagesse populaire.* Ed. Grigorii L'vovich Permiakov. Moscou: Éditions du Progrès, 1988. 378–387.

This bibliography of recent Soviet paremiological scholarship from 1982 to 1985 was prepared specially for the French translation of Grigorii L'vovich Permiakov's (1919–1983) Russian essay volume *Paremiologicheskie issledovania* (1984; see no. 4151). It contains 70 articles and monographs from scholars throughout the Soviet Union. The publications deal with proverbs as well as proverbial expressions and phraseological units in general. Nikolaieva also includes a section (p. 385) on various dissertations and theses, a list of collections (p. 386), and a few references to useful bibliographies (pp. 386–387). Even though this bibliography spans only the short period of three to four years, it is nevertheless a valuable source and indicates the high level of paremiological and paremiographical work that is going on in the various Socialist Republics of the Soviet Union.

4027. Nippold, Marilyn A. "Comprehension of Figurative Language in Youth." *Topics in Language Disorders*, 5, no. 3 (1985), 1–20.

An important review article of the psychological scholarship addressing comprehension of metaphors, similes, idioms, and proverbs by normal and learning-impaired children and adolescents. Assessment tasks that might be tried with language-impaired young people include perceptual tasks in which figurative meanings are expressed visually or through other sensory modalities and linguistically more complex tasks where figurative expressions occur within sentences or paragraphs. Factors to consider when designing intervention programs with the language-impaired clients are also discussed. Studies consistently indicate that literal meanings of figurative expressions are comprehended before nonliteral meanings, that detection of figurative meanings precedes explanation, and that figurative understanding becomes increasingly refined throughout childhood, adolescence, and into the adult years. The developmental scholarship also indicates in particular that children as young as seven years of age can comprehend some proverbs and that comprehension steadily improves in later years. A valuable bibliography (pp. 19–20) of the publications under discussion is attached.

4028. Nippold, Marilyn A., Stephanie A. Martin, and Barbara J. Erskine. "Proverb Comprehension in Context: A Developmental Study with Children and Adolescents." *Journal of Speech and Hearing Research*, 31 (1988), 19–28.

Although previous studies have reported that proverb comprehension remains quite literal before adolescence, the results of the present study using a psychological proverbs test indicated that fourth graders performed well on a proverb comprehension task involving contextual information and a written multiple-choice format. It was also found that performance on the proverb task steadily improved at least through the eighth grade and was significantly correlated to performance on a perceptual analogical reasoning task. The study contributes to the growing body of information concerning language development during preadolescent and adolescent years and may have some important implications for the assessment of youngsters of this age range who have comprehension deficits that are troublesome, yet difficult to document. 3 statistical tables, a bibliography (pp. 25–26), the proverbs test consisting of 30 texts (pp. 26–28), and an English abstract (p. 19) are included.

4029. Norrick, Neal R. "Proverbial Perlocutions: How to Do Things with Proverbs." *Grazer Linguistische Studien*, 17–18 (1982), 169–183.

This linguistic study starts with a theoretical consideration of perlocutionary acts that speakers perform with proverbs. Perlocutionary acts such as convincing, affronting, and consoling someone are performed *by* performing locutionary acts (uttering words) and illocutionary acts such as asserting, questioning, and promising, whereas these latter acts are performed *in* performing locutionary acts. It is argued that some perlocutionary effects are associated with all proverbial utterances (intentionally or unintentionally), because proverbs are performed, inventorized linguistic units and they are traditional items of folklore. Norrick discusses a number of English examples and closes his paper with an analysis of particular proverbial perlocutions, in which the perlocutionary acts associated with the proverbs are always intentional. The article illustrates that intentional perlocutionary acts are not only associated with individual proverbs, but that perlocutionary acts are unintentionally associated with all proverbs. A useful bibliography (pp. 182–183) is included.

4030.   Norrick, Neal R. "Zur Semantik des englischen Sprichworts." *Arbeiten aus Anglistik und Amerikanistik*, 8, no. 2 (1983), 183–196.

Norrick begins with a detailed analysis of Friedrich Seiler's (1851–1927) German proverb definition (see no. 1701), and he then presents his own linguistically oriented definition. He emphasizes that many proverbs are used with an introductory formula, that they exhibit a fixed form, that they are often metaphorical, and that they might be didactic. Next he deals with the semantics of proverbs as texts and within certain contexts. Norrick also states that proverbs are often varied or reduced to mere "kernels," as for example "Rolling stone" for "The rolling stone gathers no moss." This linguistic and theoretical paper also includes a discussion of synonymous and metaphorical proverbs, and the author deals with structural proverb types as well. Many English examples, 5 diagrams, statistical analyses, and a valuable bibliography (pp. 195–196) are included in this important study. An English abstract (p. 183) is provided.

4031.   Norrick, Neal R. "Stock Conversational Witticisms." *Journal of Pragmatics*, 8 (1984), 195–209.

This is a fascinating article on so-called "stock conversational witticisms" which might be defined as humorous utterances that are recalled and re-used in recurring performances. Norrick is not concerned with the origin or history of such fixed phrases but rather emphasizes their textual syntax and semantics. He deals in particular with proverbial comparisons, retorts, and quips, showing that their humor is often based on puns, wordplays, and humorous images. Typical examples for these three proverbial subgenres are "As little chance as a snowball in hell," "Do you have the time?—If you have the place," and "(for belches): Bring that up again and we'll vote on it." The author also discusses the pragmatic function of such phraseological units in actual speech acts by citing numerous English examples. Two diagrams, a helpful bibliography (pp. 207–209), and a short English abstract (p. 195) are included.

4032. Norrick, Neal R. *How Proverbs Mean. Semantic Studies in English Proverbs.* Amsterdam: Mouton, 1985. 213 pp.

With this extremely important book Neal Norrick has provided paremiologists with a superb survey of major theoretical aspects of proverb research. In chapter one (pp. 1–10) he explains why it is worthwhile to study the language, meaning, and function of proverbs. The second chapter (pp. 11–30) deals with proverbs in contexts and interactions, stressing their use and meaning in oral speech as well as literary and journalistic writings. Chapter three (pp. 31–78) is dedicated to an important attempt at defining the proverb, including such matters as traditionality, brevity, syntax, structure, didacticism, form, metaphor, etc. In the fourth chapter (pp. 81–100) Norrick analyzes literal proverb meaning, and the fifth chapter (pp. 101–143) concerns itself with the more prevalent figurative meaning of proverbs, emphasizing metaphorical, metonymical, hyperbolical, and paradoxical proverbs. The sixth chapter (pp. 145–167) investigates the proverb inventory, discussing in particular the problem of synonymous, oppositional, and ambiguous proverbs. Finally, the short seventh chapter (pp. 169–173) contains a conclusion and a comment on the directions for future research. Appendix A (pp. 175–195) is an annotated list of 172 English proverbs (whose key-words all start with the letter "F") that have been cited thoughout this book as examples, and Appendix B (pp. 197–202) contains a second annotated list of proverbs in four plays by William Shakespeare (1564–1616) which were discussed in chapter two. An invaluable bibliography (pp. 203–210) and an index (pp. 211–213) conclude this significant study.

4033. Norrick, Neal R. "Stock Similes." *Journal of Literary Semantics*, 15 (1986), 39–52.

The author begins with a definition of stock similes which have usually been called proverbial comparisons. He discusses their basic structure and points out that many of them refer to animals. Colors are also mentioned quite frequently. Citing numerous examples out of F.P. Wilson's *Oxford Dictionary of English Proverbs* (1970), Norrick explains the use of metaphors, irony, humor, and punning in many of these fixed phrases. There is also a small section which treats the use and function of proverbial comparisons in William Shakespeare's (1564–1616) tragedy *Romeo und Juliet* (1595). A small bibliography (pp. 51–52) is attached. See also Norrick's paper on "Comparative Noun-Adjective Compounds" (no. 4036 below).

4034. Norrick, Neal R. "Der Vergleich im Mittelenglischen unter besonderer Berücksichtigung der *Towneley Plays*." *Neuphilologische Mitteilungen*, 88 (1987), 256–267.

This article describes the syntax, structure, and literary function of proverbial comparisons in the Middle English *Towneley Plays* (15th century). Norrick classifies and compares constructions with "as," "like," "so" and "sich" in these six plays with special emphasis on the two *Shepherds' Plays* of this play cycle. It is shown that the textual functions of these stock similes go beyond mere exemplifications of properties to their subtle insinuation of value judgments, the characterization of dramatic figures, and the injection of both pathos and humor. The humor in these fixed phrases results from either exaggeration or incongruency between the tertium and the vehicle of the comparison. Recurrent similes apparently reveal cognitive prototypes and associated common places valid in the linguistic community of their origin. Especially the metaphorical similes recurring in diverse dramatic contexts provide a key to the concepts and ultimately to the thought patterns of the social culture in 15th century England. Many contextualized examples are cited, and an English summary (p. 256) is provided.

4035. Norrick, Neal R. "Humorous Proverbial Comparisons." *Proverbium*, 4 (1987), 173–186.

In this article Norrick analyzes the humor in such English proverbial comparisons as "Like a fish out of water," "As high as a kite," and "Nutty as a fruitcake." He explains the structural types of such stock similes and then provides some theoretical background for an understanding of humor and laughter in verbal communication. This is followed by a discussion of numerous examples of whimsical, ironic and punning comparisons. In each case the author shows how the humor is created through contrast, overstatement, imagery, etc. Norrick also includes a few comments on the function of such fixed phrases in oral and written communication. A short bibliography (pp. 186–186) is attached.

4036. Norrick, Neal R. "Semantic Aspects of Comparative Noun-Adjective Compounds." *Neuere Forschungen zur Wortbildung und Historiographie der Linguistik. Festgabe für Herbert E. Brekle.* Eds. Brigitte Asbach-Schnitker and Johannes Roggenhofer. Tübingen: Gunter Narr, 1987. 145–154.

This article is at least partially identical to Norrick's previous paper on "Stock Similes" (see no. 4033 above). The author begins with a definition of such comparative noun-adjective compounds as "Razor sharp" and "Sky blue" and explains their relationship to the longer proverbial comparisons "Sharp as a razor" and "Blue as the sky." He then analyzes many examples found in F.P. Wilson's *Oxford Dictionary of English Proverbs* (1970) by discussing structural and lexical aspects of the tertium and vehicle of the similes. Towards the end Norrick shows once again how William Shakespeare (1564–1616) made use of proverbial comparisons in his tragedy *Romeo und Juliet* (1595). A small bibliography (pp. 153–154) is included.

4037. Norrick, Neal R. "Binomial Meaning in Texts." *Journal of English Linguistics*, 21, no. 1 (1988), 72–87.

The author presents an important linguistic analysis of English binomials such as "Odds and ends," "Sooner or later," "Head over heels," etc. These fixed phrases have traditionally also been referred to as twin formulas or binary formulas. Norrick wants to show in particular how the literal meaning of binomials relates to their often figurative meaning in actual speech acts. He spends a considerable amount of space on the definition and structure of these phraseological units, showing that they are usually based on incongruity and repetition. A special discussion of the idiomaticity of binomials is included as well, and there are certainly many examples cited to illustrate Norrick's theoretical points. A small bibliography (p. 87) is attached.

4038. Norrick, Neal R. "How Paradox Means." *Poetics Today*, 10, no. 3 (1989), 551–562.

Norrick starts with a clear definition of "paradox" as a figure of speech, and he then explains the use of metaphor and contradiction in paradoxical speech. It is pointed out that there are many English proverbs and proverbial expressions that are based on paradox, as for example in "A friend to everyone is a friend to no one" or "Someone's fingers are all thumbs." The author shows that folk speech abounds in such paradoxical statements, and he illustrates that they are usually characterized by wordplay or humor. It must, however, be remembered that the hidden implications of some metaphorical proverbs based on paradoxical contradictions might be hard to comprehend. In fact, some older proverbs are so paradoxical that they almost escape comprehension. A useful bibliography (pp. 561–562) is included.

4039. Norrick, Neal R. "Proverbial Paradox." *Proverbium*, 6 (1989), 67–73.

This is an informative article on the use of paradox in various proverbial subgenres, such as proverbial comparisons, proverbial exaggerations, proverbial expressions, and proverbs. Some English examples discussed are "Clear as mud," "Slow as molasses running uphill in January," "To build castles in the air," and "Every couple is not a pair." It is shown that many of these metaphorical paradoxes are based on exaggeration, contradiction, inconsistency, impossibility, conflict, punning, wordplay, irony, etc. Such paradoxical statements are usually full of humor, and Norrick argues correctly that this humorous content of proverbial speech has not been studied enough by proverb scholars. He also feels that much could be learned from applying theories of the joke to paradoxical proverbs.

4040. Norrick, Neal R. "'One is None': Remarks on Repetition in Proverbs." *Proverbium*, 8 (1991), 121–128.

This article describes the structure and function of some types of repetition in proverbs, particularly repetition of a word or phrase with little or no change as in "Fight fire with fire," "Enough is enough," and "A place for everything and everything in its place." Clearly repetition produces parallelism and it also facilitates memorization. But repetition in wording does more than make a proverb noticeable and memorable: it suggests conviction and it enhances persuasive power. Citing many English examples, Norrick analyzes repetition as a rhetorical strategy, as an expression of paradox, and as a means of creating the surprisingly frequent tautological proverbs. The author also includes a small section on the use of repetition in proverbial punning and wordplay. A short bibliography (p. 128) is provided.

4041. Noueshi, Mona. "Zum Problem der Translierbarkeit von Phraseologismen im Text." *Kairoer Germanistische Studien*, 1 (1986), 138–145.

The author reports on the problem of translating literally hundreds of Egyptian phraseological units from literary sources into the German language. Realizing that the Arabic and German cultures are very different, it is explained that there are only very few internationally disseminated proverbs and proverbial expressions which are totally equivalent in both languages. In most cases translators have to try to find partially equivalent fixed phrases in German for the Arabic originals. This means that the structures and metaphors can often not be maintained. There are even cases where it might be best to translate an Egyptian proverb by a single word rather than citing a German proverb that is close in meaning but has connotations that do not fit the literary context. Noueshi cites numerous examples in Arabic script with German translations.

4042. Noueshi, Mona. "Die Figur Gohas in den arabischen Anekdoten und arabischen Sprichwörtern." *Kairoer Germanistische Studien*, 3 (1988), 233–256.

    This is an interesting article about the Arabic prankster figure "Goha" and his appearance in folk narratives and proverbs. Noueshi discusses Goha as a possible historical person and compares him with the German prankster Till Eulenspiegel. This is followed by several tall tales about Goha which illustrate his role as a "wise fool" who employs proverbs to pull off some of his pranks. The second part of the article is dedicated to an analysis of Egyptian proverbs and proverbial expressions that contain Goha's name. It is explained that some of these texts are in fact "Schwundstufen" (remnants) of the longer tall tales or anecdotes. Additional proverbial texts have been created due to the popularity of this prankster in the Arabic culture. Several texts in Arabic script with German translations and explanations are cited. A useful bibliography (pp. 255–256) is provided.

4043. Nuessel, Frank H. "Incorporating Proverbial Language into the Spanish Curriculum." *Canadian Modern Language Review*, 39 (1982), 83–90.

    Nuessel argues that proverbs should play a role in the teaching of foreign languages. They should be considered as supplementary aids to effective teaching and not as mere substitutes. Using Spanish proverb examples, the author explains that they are useful for teaching and testing various aspects of phonetics, syntax, and vocabulary. Nuessel also shows that proverbs are of particular value in the instruction of cultural patterns. The incorporation of proverbs into the Spanish school curriculum can enrich the classroom experience of the students, as can be seen from Nuessel's specific suggestions of how to integrate proverbs into foreign language instruction.

4044. Nuessel, Frank H., and Caterina Cicogna. "Proverbial Language in the Italian Curriculum." *American Association of Teachers of Italian Newsletter*, no volume given (Fall 1991), 9–13.

    The two authors present a similar argument for the inclusion of proverbs in foreign language instruction as was done in the previous paper (see no. 4043). But this time they concern themselves with the teaching of Italian proverbs. They point out that proverbs are a great pedagogical tool because of their cultural significance alone. However, teachers of Italian can also make use of proverbs to teach grammar, pronuncation, orthography, vocabulary, and comprehension. Several examples are included to illustrate various methodologies of using proverbs as an effective teaching tool. A small bibliography (p. 13) listing proverb collections is attached.

4045. Nuessel, Frank H., and Caterina Cicogna. "The Integration of Proverbial Language into the Italian Curriculum." *Il Forneri*, 5, no. 2 (1991), 90–103.

This is a much expanded version of the previous paper (see no. 4044 above) dealing with various aspects of integrating proverbs into the study of Italian as a foreign language. The authors point out that proverbs are of great importance lingustically, historically, and culturally, and they certainly should play a larger role in the instruction of foreign languages. They present six subsections that indicate how proverbs can be used for the teaching of phonetics, grammar, vocabulary, reading comprehension, writing, and culture. Numerous Italian examples are cited, and the authors outline several sample exercises that teachers could use in their classes. The article concludes with a list (pp. 100–101) of recommendations for the successful integration of proverbial language into the Italian curriculum. A helpful bibliography (pp. 101–103) listing phraseological collections and critical scholarship is attached.

4046. Nwachukwu-Agbada, J.O.J. "Bèkeè' in Igbo Proverbial Lore." *Proverbium*, 5 (1988), 137–144.

In this paper Nwachukwu-Agbada investigates several Igbo proverbs from Nigeria which include references to "bèkeè" (the white man). He starts with an historical account of the British colonization of this African country, and he points out that the Igbo proverbs are not very positive about the white rulers. The white man is seen as being powerful and intelligent, whose military superiority is not in question. But there are also those texts which show clearly that the white man, in spite of his brain and brawn, is equally human as the native population. The foreigners are definitely seen as a threat to the indigenous culture, and these proverbs contain some very understandable stereotypes. The Igbo proverbs are cited with English translations, and a small bibliography (pp. 143–144) is included.

4047. Nwachukwu-Agbada, J.O.J. "Igbo 'Obscene' Proverbs: Context, Function and Annotation." *International Folklore Review*, 6 (1988), 42–52.

This is an important study of so-called obscene proverbs from the Igbo people in Nigeria. Nwachukwu-Agbada begins with the observation that these proverbs are not necessarily vulgar in actual oral communication. They are usually used to express valuable ethical precepts, to resolve social and personal conflicts, and to create some humor in an otherwise tense situation. The major part of the article is a richly annotated list of 105 obscene proverbs which has been divided into sections on proverbs referring to lover, pubic hair, penis, vagina, sexual act, pregnancy, scrotum and testicles, buttocks, anus, fart, excrement, and urine. Each text is cited in the original Igbo language with an English translation. The author also provides detailed anthropological comments concerning the meaning and function of each proverb in a speech act.

4048. Nwachukwu-Agbada, J.O.J. "The Old Woman in Igbo Proverbial Lore." *Proverbium*, 6 (1989), 75–89; also in *Southern Folklore*, 46 (1989), 241–254.

Nwachukwu-Agbada begins his paper with the general observation that old men in the Igbo society and its proverbs are held in high esteem because of their knowledge, wisdom, and experience. However, the attitude towards old women is quite different. Citing 35 Igbo proverbs with English translations, the author shows that the old woman is depicted as having some of the following characteristics: boastfulness, vulgarity, dishonesty, trickery, selfishness, ingratitude, ugliness, dirtiness, impatience, and unscrupulousness. One reason for this negative opinion of old women is that women in general have a poor image in the

Igbo culture. There are also the reasons of misogyny and the worldview among the Igbo that old women are of lesser importance to society. See also J. Olowo Ojoade (no. 4067).

4049. Nwachukwu-Agbada, J.O.J. "Nigerian Pidgin Proverbs." *Lore and Language*, 9, no. 1 (1990), 37–43.

In this article Nwachukwu-Agbada explains that in the complex linguistic situation of Nigeria it was basically inevitable that a certain Nigerian Pidgin English had to develop over time. This "language" also exhibits many proverbs of which the author cites 30 examples with detailed cultural and semantic explanations. He also states that pidgin proverbs are very popular in oral communication and in the mass media. People hear them in everyday conversation as well as on the radio and television. The proverbs refer to common cultural and social aspects of Nigeria, and they often combine proverbial patterns of both Igbo and English proverbs. Since many native people use Pidgin English as a common language, these proverbs are of great importance as expressions of generally held attitudes and worldview.

4050. Nwachukwu-Agbada, J.O.J. "Origin, Meaning and Value of Igbo Historical Proverbs." *Proverbium*, 7 (1990), 185–206.

This is a major article on the origin and importance of Igbo historical proverbs for a better understanding of the cultural history of Nigeria. Nwachukwu-Agbada begins with a theoretical discussion of the value of proverbs for historical studies and concludes that they are of considerable importance in the assessment of the past. He then cites numerous Igbo examples with English translations that refer primarily to the colonial period. The proverbs refer to previous wars, certain places and events, and the military might of the white people. Even though the texts might not be precise history, they nevertheless contain valuable information concerning the folk interpretation of historical events. In the last section of the paper the author also discusses such aesthetic aspects as repetition, metaphor, parallelism, brevity, etc. as linguistic means to bring about the memorability of these historical facts in proverbial form. A useful bibliography (pp. 205–206) is attached.

4051.   Nwachukwu-Agbada, J.O.J. "Aliases Among the Anambra-Igbo: The Proverbial Dimension." *Names*, 39, no. 2 (1991), 81–94.

In this fascinating article on proverb-aliases one of the leading African paremiologists draws attention to the fact that using parts of proverbs as aliases is particularly prevalent among the Igbo people in Anambra State of Nigeria. He explains that these aliases are by no means nicknames in the usual sense of that word. Instead they are often chosen by the individual himself/herself to express a personal motto, a philosophy of life, a personality trait, an attitude toward God, a thought on human existence, etc. While whole proverbs might serve as aliases, it is usually only the first half that is uttered with the second part acting as a response. Nwachukwu-Agbada includes a table of 32 proverb-aliases (pp. 89–91) that is divided into four columns: (1) the content or allusion of the alias (i.e., God, truth, money, patience, work, etc.), (2) the proverb-aliases (first half of the proverb), (3) the response (second half of the proverb), and (4) the contextual meaning. Many social and cultural explanations are added, and the author also comments on the aesthetics of this onomastic use of African proverbs. A geographical map of Anambra State (p. 83), a short English abstract (p. 81) and a helpful bibliography (pp. 93–94) are included.

4052.   Nwachukwu-Agbada, J.O.J. "Wisdom in a Melting-Pot: Nigerian Urban Folk and Pidgin English Proverbs." *International Folklore Review*, 8 (1991), 124–129.

In this article Nwachukwu-Agbada explains the origin and nature of Nigerian Pidgin English proverbs. Linguistically speaking they are based on the English language but contain many elements of the local Nigerian languages and elements of Portuguese, French, and Spanish. As more and more Nigerians move to the cities and become urbanites, their ethnic languages are replaced by this Pidgin English as a common form of communication. The author lists 34 annotated examples, citing in each case first the Nigerian Pidgin English text, then a standard English translation, and including also comments concerning the meaning and context of the proverbs. These Pidgin English proverbs certainly represent a rich field for African paremiographers since they include so many languages and cultures. A useful bibliograpohy (p. 129) is attached.

4053. Nyéki, Lajos. "Proverbes et opérations logiques (Enseignements tirés d'une étude contrastive franco-hongroise)." *Cahiers de littérature orale*, no. 13 (1983), 19–32.

Based on numerous Hungarian and French examples the author investigates the logical processes in proverbs. He divides his article into five sections which analyze identification, negation, antithetical and non-antithetical parallelism, succession, and generalization. The question is also raised as to how far proverbs are based on modalities, such as the verbs "valoir" (to be worth), "falloir" (to be necessary), "pouvoir" (to be able to), "devoir" (to have to), and "vouloir" (to want to), the imperative, and the subjunctive. The author tries to reach some comparative socio-psychological conclusions from these considerations, but he warns himself that such interpretations of worldview must be carried out with much prudence. A small bibliography (pp. 31–32) and an English summary (p. 175) are included.

4054. Nyéki, Lajos. "Le statut linguistique des proverbes: Considérations générales à la lumière d'une enquête contrastive franco-hongroise." *Contrastes*, 8 (1984), 27–49.

This is a linguistic and comparative analysis of French and Hungarian proverbs. The author studies a series of features or markers generally held to characterize proverbs, among them brevity, structure, form, metaphor, meaning, style, etc. Nyéki also deals with older proverbs that contain dialect words, regionalisms, and archaic words. Many examples from both languages are cited, and the author is able to show that the proverbs of these two languages are quite similar, even though some of their metaphors might be different. It is also pointed out that proverbs continue to play a significant role in both French

and Hungarian literary texts and oral communication. A useful
bibliography (pp. 46–49) is attached.

4055. Nze, Chukwuemeka. "The Concept of Contrariety in Igbo
Proverbs." *The Nigerian Journal of Social Studies*, 2, no. 1 (1985),
12–17.

The author studies a number of Igbo proverbs with English
translations that contain in themselves some sense of opposition.
The opposition arises because things both naturally and normally
exist relationally. Nze analyzes in particular contrary and
contradictory opposition in proverbs. The former is an
opposition between a universal affirmative proposition and a
universal negative one, while the latter exists between a universal
negative proposition and a particular affirmative proposition. In
addition to citing his examples the author develops certain
logical patterns of contrariety in Igbo proverbs, illustrating that
these "simple" pieces of wisdom are actually rather complex
logical utterances. See also Damian Opata (no. 4077).

4056. Nze, Chukwuemeka. "The Ethicality of Igbo Contrary Proverbs."
Africana Marburgensia, 23, no. 1 (1990), 12–22.

Nze once again deals with the aspects of contrary and
contradictory opposition in Igbo proverbs from Nigeria (see no.
4055 above), but this time he is concerned with the ethical
message contained in them. Citing a number of Igbo examples
with English translations, the author explains that these proverbs
express moral values. The ethicality of these texts encourages
inward-looking, it preaches self-discovery and self-reliance, it
offers adjustment, and it recommends reconciliation. The Igbo
people use these proverbs to point out an imbalance or injustice
in a human action and to question the motive, norm or rationale
of one's action. The proverbs are cautionary and guiding
principles for the healthy existence of humane and communal
life in this African country. They are both advisory and
admonitory ideas in proverbial language aimed at self-control
and participation in the work towards the common good.

O

4057. Obelkevich, James. "Proverbs and Social History." *The Social History of Language*. Eds. Peter Burke and Roy Porter. Cambridge: Cambridge University Press, 1987. 43–72.

Obelkevich starts his fascinating article with the observation that historians have dealt very little with proverbs while literary scholars, folklorists, and anthropologists can point to a long tradition of studying proverbs. In the first section (pp. 45–48) of his essay the author discusses users and uses of proverbs in Europe during different historical periods. The second section (pp. 48–55) deals with various meanings of proverbs in their historical and social context, and the third section (pp. 55–66) is dedicated to an analysis of how proverbs were used by the educated class in England. Obelkevich mentions several English proverb collections and explains how such authors as Geoffrey Chaucer (1340?–1400), William Shakespeare (1564–1616), William Blake (1757–1827), George Eliot (1819–1880), Oscar Wilde (1854–1900), and others made use of proverbs. Many English examples are cited in their literary context with special emphasis on their meanings as expressions of "mentalities." The 81 notes (pp. 67–72) contain important bibliographical references.

4058. Oberhuber, Karl. "Nochmals 'Kamel' und Nadelöhr." *Sprachwissenschaftliche Forschungen. Festschrift für Johann Knobloch.* Eds. Hermann M. Ölberg, Gernot Schmidt, and Heinz Bothien. Innsbruck: Institut für Sprachwissenschaft der Universität Innsbruck, 1985. 271–275.

Yet another short article on the perplexing Biblical proverb "It is easier for a camel to go through the eye of a needle, than for a rich man to enter into the kingdom of God" (Matth. 19,24). Oberhuber explains that "camel" is the mistranslation of an ancient Greek word that actually means "rope." He cites numerous etymological and philological explanations and succeeds in giving a more plausible interpretation of the actual meaning of the paradoxical proverb. The 45 footnotes contain rich bibliographical information, and footnote no. 1 (pp. 273–274) alone contains twenty-five references to various attempts by scholars to explain the wording of this proverb. See also Georg Aicher (no. 19) and Paul S. Minear (no. 1296).

4059. Oberman, Heiko A. "'Die Gelehrten, die Verkehrten': Popular Response to Learned Culture in the Renaissance and Reformation." *Religion and Culture in the Renaissance and Reformation.* Ed. Steven Ozment. Kirksville/Missouri: Sixteenth Century Journal Publishers, 1989. 43–63 (=*Sixteenth Century Essays & Studies,* 11 [1989], 43–63).

Only a short section (pp. 43–48) of this study deals with the German proverb "Die Gelehrten, die Verkehrten" (The greatest scholars are not always the wisest." Oberman points out that this proverb was a popular slogan during the Renaissance and Reformation, especially in the decade from 1515 to 1525. It was cited as a powerful weapon against scholars on broadsheets, usually arguing that the common population also had a solid understanding of religious and worldly life. The proverb thus was used as a verbal expression to point out the sharp conflict between the learned culture and the little educated members of 16th century society in Germany. In its manipulative use and function the proverb became an effective propagandistic tool. For longer discussions of this proverb see Carlos Gilly (nos. 3480–3481).

4060. Ochs, Franz. "'Wo Unrecht Gesetz ist, wird Widerstand Pflicht'." *Der Sprachdienst,* 31, no. 6 (1987), 178.

This is a short note on a German graffito found on a bathroom wall in Heidelberg. Ochs explains that the text "Wo Unrecht Gesetz ist, wird Widerstand Pflicht" (Where injustice is the law, resistance becomes a duty) might have its origin in Franz Grillparzer's (1791–1872) tragedy *Ein Bruderzwist im Hause Habsburg* (1872). The author cites a similar literary passage and also explains how literary scholars have commented on this quotation that has a proverbial ring to it. However, Ochs has to admit that the precise origin of this particular modern variant commenting on the modern German society is not known.

4061. O Corrain, Ailbhe. *A Concordance of Idiomatic Expressions in the Writings of Seamus O Grianna.* Belfast: Institute of Irish Studies, The Queen's University, 1989. 419 pp.

The author has put together a comprehensive and quite unique concordance of all the proverbial expressions, proverbial comparisons, fixed phrases, and idioms that appear in the works of the Irish writer Seamus O Grianna (pseud. Maire, 1889–1969). Following a general introduction (pp. viii-xvii), O Corrain presents 419 pages of Irish phraseological units which are catalogued alphabetically according to key-words. For each entry the author cites first the Irish phrase followed by an English translation. Next he quotes the particular expression in its literary context, always including precise references to O Grianna's works. Altogether this is a most impressive lexicographical study of the wealth of proverbial speech included in the literary works of a 20th century author.

4062. Odlin, Terence. "Language Universals and Constraints on Proverbial Form." *Proverbium*, 3 (1986), 125–151.

Odlin begins his study by stating that proverbs have usually been seen as being based on certain structural, formal, and metaphorical "signals" or markers. But he argues that there are four constraints in particular which influence proverbial form in the English language: (1) parallelism, (2) affirmative comparison, (3) singularity, and (4) ordering of causes before effects. By using a proverbs test and citing numerous contrastive examples of normal sentences and actual proverbs, the author is able to show that informants agree that these constraints help the comprehension and learnability of proverbs. A useful bibliography (pp. 144–148) and a copy of the test (pp. 148–151) are included.

4063.   O'Donnell, Paul E. "'Entre chien et loup': A Study of French Animal Metaphors." *French Review*, 63, no. 3 (1990), 514–523.

Following s short introduction concerning French proverbial expressions and proverbial comparisons based on animal metaphors, O'Donnell presents a list of major phrases organized alphabetically according to the animals mentioned. In addition to the French texts he also provides English equivalents or translations. It is argued that French speakers might use such animal expressions more frequently than speakers of the English language. Such key-words as "chat" (cat), "cheval" (horse), "chien" (dog), "loup" (wolf), and "vache" (cow) appear in many fixed phrases. Footnote 5 (pp. 520–522) includes a second list of such phraseological units which exhibit a more regional flavor and a lower frequency.

4064.   Ohaeto, Ezenwa. "Poetic Eloquence: The Concept of Madness in Igbo Proverbs." *Proverbium*, 7 (1990), 207–215.

Ohaeto begins with some general comments regarding the fact that proverbs play a major role in the socialization process in the Igbo culture of Nigeria. He then explains that there are many proverbs which express certain ideas and beliefs about madness, citing examples from the novels of Chinua Achebe (1931–) and from informants. It is concluded that these proverbs show that the madman is characterized by continuous movement, incessant speeches, abnormal physical appearance, and deviant behavior. However, madness is also portrayed as an aid to those who are desirous in presenting the truth on any issue. The implication is that the Igbo perceive madness as a state in which the individual could condemn evil without fear of punishment. Madness thus can become a mask or an indirect way of expressing criticism in this African society.

4065.   Oinas, Felix. "'To Bite the Dust'." *Proverbium*, 1 (1984), 191–194.

Referring to J.D.M. Ford's earlier discussion of the proverbial expression "To bite the dust" (see no. 452) in English, German, French, Italian, and Spanish sources, Oinas argues that it is questionable whether it was derived from ancient Greek or Latin sources. The appearance of this phrase in an early Danish historical legend and in Estonian legends would rather suggest independent origins (polygenesis) based on the frequent observation of the convulsive opening and shutting of the mouth at the time of a violent death on the battlefield. Oinas argues for a similar independent origin of the German fixed phrase "Ins Gras beißen" (To bite into the grass) and the Estonian expression "To chew a reed" with the same meaning as "To bite the dust" (i.e., to die).

4066. Ojoade, J. Olowo. "African Sexual Proverbs: Some Yoruba Examples." *Folklore* (London), 94, no. 2 (1983), 201–213.

Ojoade states that it is important that folklorists also collect and study obscene proverbs. He explains that Yoruba proverbs from Nigeria contain plenty of obscenities and erotica, but when seen in the actual context of oral communication, it becomes clear that they nevertheless contain valuable ethical precepts. While individual words might be obscene, the message of the proverb is of considerable social value. The major portion of this article is a collection of 104 sexual proverbs from the Yoruba people. Each text is cited in its original African form with English translations. Ojoade also adds many explanatory comments, including references to folk narratives which exemplify the proverb. Most of the proverbs make references to the penis, the vagina, sexual intercourse, and sex in general.

4067. Ojoade, J. Olowo. "The Old Woman as Seen through African Proverbs: Fragmentary Remarks about African Society through Sayings." *Folklore* (Calcutta), 26, no. 6 (1985), 110–114.

Ojoade assembles numerous African proverbs that comment on the role of the old woman in traditional society. Citing his examples from the Yoruba, Ewe, Ovambo, Hausa, and Edo people in English translation only, the author deals in particular with the rather negative image of the older woman as a mother-in-law. The major part of the essay concerns itself with the sexual life of old women, explaining how proverbs comment on their attitude towards marriage as well as sexual intercourse. The exemples center on the hymen, the vagina, and the penis, all of them basically arguing that the old woman is sexually and above

all socially of limited value. Ojoade argues that this negative view
is of importance as traditional African societies are changing and
new ways of dealing with the elderly in a socially responsible way
have to be found. See also J.O.J. Nwachukwu-Agbada (no. 4048).

4068. Ojoade, J. Olowo. "Proverbial Evidences of African Legal
      Customs." *International Folklore Review*, 6 (1988), 26–38.

In this important article Ojoade comments on the
importance of proverbs in customary law throughout Africa. He
explains that proverbs express rules of conduct especially in a
non-literate society where legal precepts are transmitted orally
(*lex non scripta*). Citing numerous examples in English translation
only from many ethnic African groups, the author shows how
these legal proverbs comment on the power and conduct of the
king or chief, crimes and penalties, trial by ordeal, witnesses, the
guilty, evidence, inheritance, bribery, marriage and divorce, the
poor, strangers, liability, justice, and other aspects of African life.
Many explanatory notes are added that stress the importance of
these legal maxims expressed as common proverbs. A valuable
bibliography (pp. 37–38) is attached. See also John Messenger
(no. 1200).

4069. Okamoto, Yoshito. "The Attitude and Behavior toward
      Superstitions and Proverbs [in Japanese]." *Japanese Journal of
      Psychology*, 59, no. 2 (1988), 106–112.

Two hypotheses were developed: (1) people who have
experienced many misfortunes and calamities believe in
superstitions and proverbs and often practice them as compared
to those with few such experiences, and (2) university students'
attitude and use regarding superstitions and proverbs are related
to those of their parents. 103 students and their parents were
asked to indicate their attitude and practice regarding 42
superstitions and proverbs, visits to fortune tellers and exorcism
rites, and experiences of misfortunes and calamities. People with
such experiences had a higher ratio than those without them
only in visits to fortune tellers and exorcism rites. There was no
such trend in the 42 superstitions and proverbs. There was a close
parent-child relationship in the attitude towards superstitions and

superstitious practice in family life. However, no parent-child relationship was found for the proverb-related attitude and behavior. An English abstract (p. 106) is provided.

4070. Okanlawon, O.L. "Principal Images and Figures in 100 Igbo Proverbs: A Folkloristic Study." *Proverbium Paratum,* 3 (1982), 259–273.

This is a content analysis of 266 Igbo proverbs from Nigeria. Okanlawon begins with a review of published Igbo proverb collections and then shows by the first 100 texts of his own collection that their principal images and figures relate to animals (chicken, fox, tiger, ant, toad, goat, sheep, etc.), humans (nobility, adult-child, women, etc.), objects (knife, pot, pitcher, rice, palm-tree, etc.), public affairs (all aspects of social life), and gods and spirits. Each example is cited with an English translation, and the author also provides anthropological explanations. A short bibliography (pp. 272–273) is attached.

4071. Olinick, Stanley L. "On Proverbs: Creativity, Communication, and Community." *Contemporary Psychoanalysis,* 23 (1987), 463–468.

The author starts by quoting a few American "proverbs" by Nelson Algren (1909–1981), Satchel Paige (1906?–1982), and W.C. Fields (1880–1946), as for example "Never go to bed with a woman who has more problems than you," "Don't get out in front; they'll throw rocks at you," and "Never give a sucker an even break." He contrasts these new proverbs with traditional texts and points out that proverbs are clearly still created in modern societies. It is argued that individuals who create such new proverbial texts must have had intense experiences which they wanted to share and master in a communal setting. An individual's creativity may transform such experience into a cautionary adage, partly through the mechanism of condensation of a longer narrative just as the reduction of a fable to a proverb. Olinick sees proverbs as expressions of individual creativity, arising out of traumatic experience, transmuted through as yet incompletely understood manipulations of fantasy and imagination akin to dreamwork (condensation and displacement, elaboration and transformation, and considerations of representability), and impelled to this work through the phatic communication that represents common needs and feelings and the transference imago whose presence relies upon compulsive repetition and calls for mastery.

4072. Oliver, Venita Sue. *Ideational Fluency and Proverb Comprehension: Comparisons Among and Between Bilingual and Monolingual College Students.* Diss. Northern Arizona University, 1991. 286 pp.

Oliver reports on a study using a psychological proverbs test to find out whether bilinguals understand metaphorical language better than monolinguals. She designed a questionnaire and tested 330 American college students. The data indicated that no significant difference existed between monolingual and bilingual subjects regarding the number of correct responses to cues to proverb comprehension or on ideational fluency subtest scores. However, significant differences were found within one language group: bilinguals who were fluent in two languages and scored high on ideational fluency subtests performed better on transfer tasks than bilinguals who scored low on the ideational fluency subtests. No support was found for increased performance on measures of cognitive ability as a function of increased bilingual facility. The author presents 3 diagrams and 24 statistical tables throughout the text of her dissertation. A number of sample questionnaires (pp. 120–169), the proverbs test with illustrations (pp. 170–244), tabulated results (pp. 245–286), and a helpful bibliography (pp. 114–119) are attached at the end.

4073. Ollier, Marie-Louise. "Specificité discursive d'une locution: 'Si m'aist dex' vs. 'Se dex m'ait'." *La locution. Actes du colloque international Université McGill, Montréal, 15–16 octobre 1984.* Eds. Giuseppe Di Stefano and Russell G. McGillivray. Montréal: Éditions CERES, 1984. 323–367.

A very detailed and richly documented study of the use and function of the medieval French routine formula "Si m'aist dex" and its variant "Se dex m'ait" (i.e., with God's help) in the works of Chrétien de Troyes (1150?–1190?), numerous *chansons de geste,* medieval poetry, and religious sermons. Citing many contextualized examples from French literature, Ollier investigates the frequency, lexicography, distribution, and function of this popular phraseological unit. She includes careful interpretations of the meaning of this fixed phrase in the literary contexts, and she also registers many variants from the 12th to the 14th century. This long philological essay is an exemplary study of the origin, etymology, meaning, and use of one medieval phrase that shows the complexity of diachronic proverb research.

4074. Olmo Lete, Gregorio del. "Nota sobre Prov 30,19." *Biblica*, 67 (1986), 68–74.

This is a short study of the Biblical proverb "Three things are too wonderful for me; four I do not understand; the way of an eagle in the sky, the way of a serpent on a rock, the way of a ship on the high seas, and the way of a man with a maiden" (Prov. 30,19). Olmo Lete discusses similar enumerative proverbs in the Old Testament, and he presents detailed philological explanations for all four parts of this "number" proverb. The 22 notes contain useful bibliographical information on the meaning and function of proverbs in the Bible. See also Louise Keyes (no. 2517) and Edmund Sutcliffe (no. 2924).

4075. Olteanu, A.Gh. "Proverbele în manualele de limba si literatura româna." *Proverbium Dacoromania*, 2 (1987), 30–35.

The author presents a pedagogical study of the appearance of proverbs in books on the Rumanian language and literature used by students. The article starts with a short introduction concerning the importance of proverbs in general, and Olteanu then explains how proverbs are used to teach the Rumanian language. Proverbs obviously also play a major role in the literature of Rumania. Numerous examples are cited to indicate the educational value of traditional proverbs at various levels of the students' linguistic and intellectual development.

4076. Olteanu, Pandele. "Contributii la o istorie a paremiologiei românesti în context comparat." *Revista de etnografie si folclor*, 36, nos. 3–4 (1991), 165–178.

Olteanu attempts to show how the history of paremiology in Rumania is very much linked up with traditions that are similar for most of the European languages. The author begins by stating that many Rumanian proverbs stem from the ancient wisdom literature tradition, the Bible, Greek and Latin literature, and the medieval Latin proverbs that were loan translated into many vernacular languages. Various examples are cited, and Oltenau explains in particular how the proverbs from the popular pseudo-scientific work commonly called *Physiologus* (Greek original c. 200 A.D. with many later Latin versions through the Middle Ages) also became part of the national stock of Rumanian proverbs. References to various Rumanian proverb collections and the comparative work of the Rumanian scholar Gabriel Gheorghe (see nos. 3474–3475) are included.

4077. Opata, Damian U. "The Concept of Contrariety in Igbo Proverbs: A Rejoinder." *The Nigerian Journal of Social Studies*, 3, no. 1 (1986), 12–18.

This article is a critical response to Chukwuemeka Nze's earlier article on "The Concept of Contrariety in Igbo Proverbs" (1985; see no. 4055). The position adopted in this paper is that the author failed to establish the principle of opposition in any of the proverbs cited as examples. Opata feels that Nze supposes erroneously that the proverbs cited for illustration are statements, and not merely sentences. Given this, adjudicative statements about truth and falsity cannot be applied to the examples cited. Secondly, the principle of logical opposition obtains in the area of paired propositions or in single propositions that contain mutually exclusive terms. All the proverbs cited are single sentences that contain no mutually exclusive terms. Opata then demonstrates that the principle of opposition cannot obtain in the examples in which Nze has alleged it exists. Pages 17–18 contain a short reply from Nze to Opata's rejoinder. With an English abstract (p. 12).

4078. Opata, Damian U. "Adynation Symbols in Igbo Proverbial Usage." *Lore & Language*, 6, no. 1 (1987), 51–57.

Opata explains that Igbo proverbs from Nigeria use adynation symbols (i.e., symbols of impossibility) very much in the same way as European proverbs. He points out that adynation symbols in proverbial usage are employed for a variety of purposes, for example: (1) as rhetorical devices in traditional verbal art, (20) as a stylistic device for making definitive assertions, (3) as titular names, and (4) as a vehicle for expressing the unbridgeable gulf between appearance and reality. The author cites many examples with English translations, illustrating that the symbols usually touch on parts of the human body, animals, or on natural objects and phenomena. Interestingly enough, there is no evidence that some of these symbols cut across cultures; for example there are no proverbial expressions like "To bring water in a basket" or "To pour water in a sieve" which are quite common in European languages.

4079. Opata, Damian U. "Personal Attribution in Wellerisms." *International Folklore Review*, 6 (1988), 39–41.

The article discusses the use of personal names in Igbo wellerisms from Nigeria. Opata explains that in these texts the speaker is announced before the proverbial statement according to the structural pattern of "[any personal name] said that . . ." Citing numerous examples with English translations, the author points out that usually the dates of origin of these texts can be established, that they are fairly restricted in their geographical distribution, and that they are of relatively recent origin. If the names of the originators are dropped, these so-called wellerisms become in fact normal proverbs. It should be pointed out that these African wellerisms do not follow the triadic structure of European wellerisms which are based on a proverbial statement, the identification of a speaker, and a comment. See also Olowo Ojoade (no. 1377).

4080. Opata, Damian U. "Characterization in Animal-Derived Wellerisms: Some Selected Igbo Examples." *Proverbium*, 7 (1990), 217–231.

In this article on Igbo wellerisms from Nigeria Opata reviews some of the African and European scholarship on this genre, pointing out that the African texts are composed of only the speaker followed by a proverbial statement. European wellerisms, however, follow the triadic structure of a proverbial statement, the identification of the speaker, and a comment. Opata explains that many African wellerisms have as their speakers domestic and wild animals, such as the fowl, dog, tortoise, snake, toad, monkey, mosquito, leopard, sheep, lizard, etc. These texts follow the pattern of "[any animal] says that . . ." and they depict essential behavioral features of such animals, they express attitudes of humans towards animals, and they describe the physical appearance of the animals. However, their figurative meaning usually refers to the behavior and attitudes of humans. Many examples are cited, and an appendix (pp. 226–230) contains additional African texts with English translations. A short bibliography (pp. 230–231) is also included.

4081. Orbán, A.P. "Het spreekwoordelijk beeld van de rusticus, de boer, in de middeleeuwen." *Gewone mensen in de middeleeuwen.* Eds. R.E.V. Stuip and C. Vellekoop. Utrecht: HES Uitgevers, 1987. 69–87.

A detailed study of many medieval Latin proverbs referring to the "rusticus" or peasant. Orbán cites his examples from the *Disticha Catonis* (11th century), the *Carmina Burana* (c. 1230), and major Latin proverb collections that contain texts from the European Middle Ages. Giving his examples in Latin with Dutch translations, the author shows that many of them express an antithesis between the clerics and the peasants. He also explains that quite a few of the proverbs contain stereotypical views of the peasants. Altogether the proverbs give a rather negative picture of the lower members of medieval society. A useful bibliography (pp. 86–87) is attached.

4082. Orkin, Martin R. "A Proverb Allusion and a Proverbial Association in *1 Henry IV.*" *Notes and Queries,* 228, new series 30 (1983), 120–121.

Orkin argues convincingly that William Shakespeare (1564–1616) is alluding to two English proverbs in the third act of *1 King Henry IV* (1597) which have escaped earlier commentators on the play. The proverbs in question are "Children are to be deceived by comfits and men with oaths" and "The tailor must cut three sleeves for every woman's gown." Citing the particular proverb allusion in its dramatic context, Orkin points out that proverbs in literature are treated much more freely than their rigid form and structure would suggest.

4083. Orkin, Martin R. "A Cluster of Proverb Allusions in *Julius Caesar*." *Notes and Queries*, 229, new series 31 (1984), 195–196.

In this short note Orkin proves that William Shakespeare (1564–1616) is alluding to an English proverb and a proverbial expression in the first act of *Julius Caesar* (1599) which have not been noticed by scholars before. It is shown that Brutus in his speech actually refers to the proverb "There is a time to speak and a time to hold one's peace" and the phrase "To chew the cud upon a thing." For the latter expression Orkin cites additional references from 16th century English literature and Shakespeare's comedy *As You Like It* (1599). In all cases the texts are quoted in their dramatic context.

4084. Orkin, Martin R. "'After a Collar Comes a Halter' in *1 Henry IV*." *Notes and Queries*, 229, new series 31 (1984), 188–189.

Another note explaining that a proverbial allusion in the second act of William Shakespeare's (1564–1616) play *1 King Henry IV* (1597) is based on the English proverb "After a collar comes a halter." Orkin discusses its meaning in the dramatic context and also cites the variant "After a collar comes a rope." He then traces the paremiographical history of the proverb in standard English proverb collections. There are also references to other appearances of the proverb in 16th century English literature, including a second allusion to the proverb in Shakespeare's *Romeo and Juliet* (1595).

4085. Orkin, Martin R. "Shakespeare's *As You Like It*." *Explicator*, 42, no. 2 (1984), 5–7.

In this article Orkin shows that Rosalind alludes to at least two English proverbs in her witty dialogue in the fourth act of William Shakespeare's (1564–1616) comedy *As You Like It* (1599). She is in fact punning with the proverbs "Help hands for I have no lands" and "Trouble brings experience and experience brings wisdom." The author cites both texts in their dramatic context, he includes annotations from major English proverb collections, and he explains their meaning and function. It is shown in particular that Shakespeare has a definite gift for creating effective wordplays with proverb allusions.

4086. Orkin, Martin R. "Shakespeare's *Henry IV, I.*" *Explicator*, 42, no. 4 (1984), 11–12.

This short note reports on yet another identification of a proverbial allusion in William Shakespeare's (1564–1616) play *1 King Henry IV* (1597). Here it is Prince Hal who in the second act alludes to the English proverbial expression "To roar like a bull." Orkin cites it in its dramatic context, he quotes a number of variants from 16th century English literature, and he refers to citations of this phrase in standard English proverb collections. Again it is argued that Shakespeare is a true master of using proverbial speech in innovative and truncated ways, always knowing that his contemporaries would understand these mere proverbial allusions.

4087. Orkin, Martin R. "Sir John Falstaff's Taste for Proverbs in *Henry IV, Part 1.*" *English Studies*, 65, no. 5 (1984), 392–404.

This is a much longer literary investigation of the use and function of proverbs in William Shakespeare's (1564–1616) play *1 King Henry IV* (1597). Orkin studies in particular the witty way in which Falstaff employs English proverbs and proverbial expressions, as for example the texts "Discretion is the better part of valor," "He is a gentleman that has gentle conditions," "Live within compass," "Some complain to prevent complaint," "Neither fish nor flesh nor good red herring," "The tree is known by the fruit," etc. Citing numerous examples in their dramatic context, the author shows that Shakespeare creates fascinating puns and wordplays from the traditional proverbial language. Orkin also refers to the appearance of some of these proverbs in other works of 16th century English literature, proving in fact that they were so popular and commonly known that Shakespeare's audience would have had no difficulty in understanding these proverbial allusions.

4088. Orkin, Martin R. "'He Shows a Fair Pair of Heels' in *1 Henry IV* and Elsewhere." *English Language Notes*, 23, no. 1 (1985), 19–23.

Orkin returns one more time to William Shakespeare's (1564–1616) play *1 King Henry IV* (1597), explaining that Prince Hal in the second act alludes to the English proverbial expression "To show a fair pair of heels" with the meaning of "To run away." He cites the phrase in its dramatic context, he refers to its inclusion in standard English proverb collections, and he quotes variants from other 16th century literary works. Special consideration is given to the use and function of this fixed phrase in Thomas Heywood's (1497?–1580?) play *The Four Prentices of London* (c. 1545, published 1615).

4089. Orkin, Martin R. "Touchstone's Swiftness and Sententiousness." *English Language Notes*, 27, no. 1 (1989), 42–47.

In this article Orkin explains that Touchstone in William Shakespeare's (1564–1616) comedy *As You Like It* (1599) is indeed yet another dramatic character that uses many proverbial allusions throughout the play. His witty mind creates puns and wordplays with such English proverbs and proverbial expressions as "Every man likes his own thing best," "To swear and forswear," "Rich pearls are found in homely shells," etc. The texts are cited in their dramatic context, they are annotated by referring to standard English proverb collections, and their innovative use is shown to add a great deal to the humor of this play.

4090. Orlando, Sandro. "Relitti francesi nei proverbi (e negli aforismi medici) in lingua d'oc del Palatino 586." *Medioevo Romanzo*, 15, no. 2 (1990), 277–298.

The author reports on the French language of the proverbs and medical aphorisms contained in a 17th century manuscript of the National Library of Florence. The manuscript is written in the langue d'oc dialect, reflecting linguistic forms of the 13th century. Orlando gives a detailed description of the manuscript itself, he compares it with parallel manuscripts of the Middle Ages, and he presents valuable etymological and philological explanations of the aphorisms (pp. 285–289) and the proverbs (pp. 290–298). A few comparative remarks concerning 13th century French proverb collections are also included, showing the possible sources of this particular manuscript. See also J. Morawski (no. 1313).

4091. Oroz Reta, José. "El genio paremiológico de san Agustín." *Augustinus*, 33 (1988), 93–125.

The article starts with a general introduction to proverbs in classical Greek and Latin writings as well as the Bible. Oroz Reta discusses the rhetorical value, the form, and the content of these ancient proverbs. In the second part of the essay (pp. 109–125) he cites numerous Latin examples from the works of St. Augustine (354–430), citing the texts primarily from the *Confessiones* (397). It is shown that St. Augustine uses proverbs quite frequently. Many of the proverbs come from the Bible, and they are usually employed to make religious, moralistic, or didactic statements. Proverbs referring to God are especially prevalent in the rhetorical writings of this religious writer.

4092. Orzechowski, Kazimierz. "Aphorismus: Fisch oder Fleisch?" *Neuere Studien zur Aphoristik und Essayistik. Mit einer Handvoll zeitgenössischer Aphorismen.* Eds. Giulia Cantarutti and Hans Schumacher. Bern: Peter Lang, 1986. 163–183.

Orzechowski begins his article with a definition of aphorisms, and he then presents a detailed history of this term and genre in Polish publications from the 19th and 20th centuries. In addition to reviewing various definition attempts, he also describes some of the major Polish collections of aphorisms. It is pointed out that there exists a considerable state of confusion among Polish scholars about the differences and similarities of such related genres as those of the maxim, sententious remark, epigram, and proverb. The author does include important comments regarding the close relationship between aphorisms and folk proverbs. The 45 notes (pp. 180–183) include helpful bibliographical references to theoretical works on the aphorism and major collections of this literary genre.

4093. Otakpor, Nkeonye. "A Note on the Logic of Proverbs: A Reply." *Proverbium*, 4 (1987), 263–269.

This article represents a short response to David Cram's earlier paper entitled "A Note on the Logic of Proverbs" from 1985 (see no. 3267). Otakpor points out that proverbs represent points of view, that they are not logical absolutes, and that they are not universally true. They may and often do contradict each other in actual speech acts. Proverbs are thus classifiable but cannot be systematized. They are never deductively valid; neither correct nor incorrect, neither sound nor unsound, but suitable or unsuitable, reasonable or unreasonable, within specific speech contexts. Proverbial usage is thus based on analogical arguments. Arguments from analogy in turn are based on similarity and resemblance of things, situations, circumstances, etc. No logical necessity is implied in analogical arguments and *a priori* demonstrations are not even required. Arguments from analogy are never demonstratively valid but are inductively valid. The same is true for proverbs and their wisdom.

4094. Overballe, Inge-Lise. "Bjerregaards ordsprogssamling." *Folk og kultur*, no volume given (1985), 58–68.

The author reports on an unpublished Danish proverb collection of 652 proverbs, proverbial expressions, and clichés by Niels Peter Bjerregaard (1880–1955). Most of the texts were collected during field research by Bjerregaard in the early decades of the 20th century. He has included many contextual comments which illustrate the function of the proverbs in Denmark at that time. Thus most of the examples reflect the daily life of a self-sustaining agricultural society and a rather static social pattern where rigid sex roles and sharp class barriers exist. Other examples show the generation gap, the depreciation of certain occupations, or religious and political discrepancies. The article concludes with the call for modern field research to establish how proverbs function in the talk of ordinary people in such mass media as the radio and television. With an English abstract (p. 68).

4095. Owomoyela, Oyekan. "Proverbs: Exploration of an African Philosophy of Social Communication." *Ba Shiru: A Journal of African Languages and Literature,* 12, no. 1 (1984), 3–16.

This article deals with African proverbs as a tool for social communication and an expression of social attitudes. Owomoyela points out that proverbs play a particularly important role in the oral communication of the Yoruba people. In this traditional and for the most part non-literate society proverbs are used for the purpose of rendering advice through indirect speech. The metaphors of the proverbs enable the speaker to direct his/her didactic or critical comments in an indirect fashion. The popularity of proverbs among most African people is due to their effectiveness in conveying even the most delicate and potentially exceptionable message in the most unobtrusive, innocuous, and economic (because of the proverb's brevity) manner. Proverbs are thus seen as a code for a message or as a "minimum message." Many Yoruba examples with English translations are cited throughout the article to illustrate this important communicative and social role of the proverb.

P

4096. Paczolay, Gyula. "Schlandt Henrik brassoi közmondaslexikonjainak helye a magyar szolaskutatas történetében." *Ethnographia*, 90, no. 3 (1979), 395–406.

The leading Hungarian paremiographer Gyula Paczolay begins this article with a short biographical sketch of Henrik (Heinrich) Schlandt (1858–1935) and then presents a detailed analysis of Schlandt's comparative German and Hungarian proverb collections. 4198 German and 6836 Hungarian proverbs are included in *Deutsch-magyarisches Sprichwörter-Lexikon* (1913), and 4143 Hungarian and 6737 German proverbs are presented in *Magyar-Német Közmondasok Lexikona* (1913). Paczolay refers to earlier comparative proverb collections from the 18th and 19th centuries and then cites a number of examples from Schlandt's books. A valuable bibliography (pp. 404–405) of major collections and a German abstract (p. 406) are included.

4097. Paczolay, Gyula. "Lengyel és magyar proverbiumok összehasonlitasa." *A lengyel nyelvoktatas Magyarorszagon*. Ed. Janusz Banczerowski. Budapest: Lengyel Tajékoztato és Kulturalis Központ, 1982. III, 61–113.

This is a comparative study of Polish and Hungarian proverbs. Paczolay cites 20 Hungarian proverbs and their Polish equivalents, and he then lists four Hungarian proverbs and their parallels from up to thirty European languages and their Chinese and Japanese equivalents. The proverbs treated in this polyglot fashion are "Don't look a gift horse in the mouth" (pp. 68–73), "You can see a mote in another's eye but cannot see a beam in your own" (pp. 74–77), "Time is money" (pp. 78–79), and "Walls have ears" (pp. 80–83). The rest of the article (pp. 84–109) illustrates how proverbs from classical Greek and Latin authors, from the Bible, and from the Middle Ages were loan translated into many European languages. Paczolay cites numerous examples in Hungarian, Polish, and English, often adding also French and German equivalents. A bibliography of proverb collections (pp. 110–111) and a Polish summary (pp. 112–113) are part of this significant paremiographical study.

4098. Paczolay, Gyula. "Készulöben van egy összehasonlito szolas-és közmondastar (nyelvtörténeti adatokkal)." *Magyar Nyelvör*, 109, no. 2 (1985), 129–139.

In this article Paczolay outlines his project for a comparative dictionary of Hungarian proverbs with English translations and their English, German, Italian, Polish, Estonian, Latin, and Greek equivalents. The dictionary subsequently appeared with the title *Magyar-észt közmondasok és szolasok német, angol és latin megfelelöikkel* (1985), and it is one of the major accomplishments of comparative paremiography. The article presents comparative texts for the following five proverbs: "One swallow does not make a summer" (with parallels from 30 languages!), "You can see a mote in another's eye but cannot see a beam in your own," "A leopard does not change his spots," "He who cannot speak Arabic, should not speak Arabic," and "Out of a dog there will be no lard." A bibliography (pp. 137–139) listing major proverb collections is attached.

4099. Paczolay, Gyula. "Some Common Proverbs in Komi, Estonian and Hungarian and Their European Relationships." *Congressus Internationalis Fenno-Ugristarum 6, Studia Hungarica Syktyvkar 1985*. Eds. Istvan Dienes, Péter Domokos, Janos Kodolanyi, and Vilmos Voigt. Budapest: Nemzetközi Magyar Filologiai Tarsasag, 1985. 223–230.

Paczolay begins this comparative study of Komi, Estonian, and Hungarian proverbs with a discussion of three characteristic degrees of equivalency: (1) absolute identity (metaphor, structure, vocabulary, meaning, etc.), (2) metaphorical similarities but same structure, and (3) same idea but different images and structures. He then presents seven European proverbs and their equivalents in the three languages already mentioned as well as in English, German, Polish, Italian, Spanish, and some others. The proverbs are: "He who digs a pit for others, falls in himself," "Don't look a gift horse in the mouth," "If you run after two hares, you will catch none," "Crows will not pick out crows' eyes," "When the cat's away, the mice will play," "Empty vessels make the most sound," and "Do as you would be done by." The article concludes with three proverbs for which Paczolay provides primarily East European parallels, namely "Every Gypsy praises his own horse," "You may repeatedly throw dry peas to the wall, they will not stick," and "The child of seven nurses is always blind."

4100. Paczolay, Gyula. "Lengyel, magyar és észt közmondasok és szolasok összehasonlitasa." *A lengyel nyelv és irodalom magyarorszagi kutatasairol. 1985 marcius 19–20. között tartott tudomanyos konferencia anyaga.* Ed. Janusz Banczerowski. Budapest: Lengyel Tajékoztato és Kulturalis Központ, 1986. 88–107.

This is another comparative study of Polish, Hungarian, and Estonian proverbs. In the first part (pp. 88–98) Paczolay presents forty texts in English with Polish, Hungarian, and Estonian equivalents, and he also provides historical annotations giving dates of origin and references to standard proverb collections. The second part (pp. 98–105) lists additional texts for which the author includes equivalents from some additional European languages. A small discussion of various levels of equivalency is part of this section. A bibliography of major proverb collections (pp. 106–107) and a Polish abstract (p. 107) are attached to this paremiographical study of East European proverbs.

4101. Paczolay, Gyula. "Magyar proverbiumok europai rokonsaga. A 'Nem minden arany, ami fénylik' példajan." *Ethnographia,* 97, nos. 2–4 (1986), 334–360.

The article starts with a discussion of the scholarship on common European proverbs which have their origin in classical Greek and Latin times, in the Bible, or in the Latin language of the Middle Ages. This is followed by a detailed analysis (pp. 340–352) of the proverb "Nem minden arany, ami fénylik" (All that glitters is not gold) for which Paczolay is able to cite parallels from 33 European languages. Variants are also included, and the author is able to show by means of some African, Chinese, and Japanese examples that these cultures have proverbs which express the same idea but in considerably different form. The proverb originated in the Middle Ages in Western Europe and appears as a Hungarian loan translation for the first time in 1613. A map (p. 351) indicating the geographical dissemination of the proverb throughout Europe including historical dates, a superb bibliography of major national and international proverb collections (pp. 352–359), and an English abstract (p. 360) are provided.

4102. Paczolay, Gyula. "Proverbs in Hungarian Literature: A Bibliography." *Proverbium*, 5 (1988), 207–211.

With this bibliography citing 29 publications concerning the use and function of proverbs and proverbial expressions in Hungarian literature, Paczolay presents an important addendum to Wolfgang Mieder's earlier book on *Proverbs in Literature: An International Bibliography* (1978; see no. 1262). Some of the authors that have been investigated for the integration of proverbial folk speech in their works are Janos Arany (1817–1882), Peter Beniczky (17th century), Gabor Bethlen (1580–1629), Mihaly Csokonai Vitez (1773–1805), Janos Kemeny (1607–1662), Peter Pazmany (1570–1637), Sandor Petofi (1823–1849), and others. Paczolay merely lists the publications and does not include any annotations.

4103. Paczolay, Gyula. "Közmondasaink és rokonsaguk." *Uj Horizont*, 18, no. 2 (1990), 47–50.

This is a general article on comparative paremiography, explaining how many Hungarian proverbs do in fact have precise equivalents in most of the other European languages. It is explained that this is due to their common origin in classical Greek and Latin times, the Bible, or the Latin of the Middle Ages. Erasmus of Rotterdam's (1469–1536) *Adagia* (1500ff.) also played a major role in spreading proverbs all over Europe. Paczolay cites a few comparative examples from Western and Eastern Europe, but since this is a popular article, he quotes all of his texts only in Hungarian translation. With 1 illustration.

4104. Paczolay, Gyula. "Some External Relationships of Proverbs in Some of the Finno-Ugric Languages." *Congressus Septimus Internationalis Fenno-Ugristarum, Sessiones Sectionum Dissertationes, Linguistica.* Ed. Jakab Laszlo et al. Debrecen: CIFU, 1990. 120–125.

In this short article Paczolay presents some fascinating statistics concerning the origin of the proverbs in major Hungarian and Estonian proverb collections. It is shown that 30.6% of the texts in the Hungarian collection exist in only that language, 64.7% are proverbs also current in other European languages, 4% are Slavic only, and 0.6% are Turkish. In the case of the Estonian collection, 11.7% are regional Estonian proverbs, 58.7% are common European proverbs, 17.8% are loan translations from the Swedish and Finnish languages, 9.9% are Russian, and 2% are Latvian or Baltic. Paczolay also includes a few statements on Cheremis, Mari, Maltese, and Japanese proverbs, arguing that no statistical figures are available as yet. The article contains 3 statistical tables, 2 diagrams, and a short bibliography (p. 125).

4105. Paducheva, E.V. "O semanticheskikh sviaziakh mezhdu basnei i ee moral'iu (na materiale basen ezopa)." *Paremiologicheskie issledovaniia.* Ed. Grigorii L'vovich Permiakov. Moskva: Nauka, 1984. 223–251; also in French translation as "Liens sémantiques entre la fable et sa morale" in *Tel grain tel pain. Poétique de la sagesse populaire.* Ed. G.L. Permiakov. Moscou: Éditions du Progrès, 1988. 168–206.

The main concern of this article is that the relationship between a fable and its moral resembles the relationship between a proverb and the situations in which it appears. In the first part of her study Paducheva shows that Aesop's fables often lead to morals which might not be congruous with the actual fable text because of the "point of view" of the interpreter. The second part deals with an analogous deviation in another domain, i.e. with relationships between a proverb and its corresponding situations. Here Paducheva stresses in particular wellerisms since this genre often contains a deviating morality to its quoted proverb text. These findings are of much value for the study of folk narratives and proverbs, and they are based on numerous Russian examples that illustrate the relationships between these genres.

4106. Page, Mary H., and Nancy D. Washington. "Family Proverbs and Value Transmission of Single Black Mothers." *The Journal of Social Psychology*, 127, no. 1 (1987), 49–58.

Defining the "family proverb" as a text by which the collective experiences of a people are coded and transmitted from one generation to another, the two authors argue that the frequent use of certain proverbs indicates behavioral and motivational values and attitudes of the speakers. They devised a psychological proverbs test of 15 common proverbs and asked single African-American mothers to rate them according to their value and whether they would transmit their didactic message to their children. It was found that the American proverb "What goes around comes around" was valued very highly because it expresses social wisdom that definitely should be transmitted. Some other proverbs of high ratings are "Blood is thicker than water" and "Don't count your chickens before they are hatched." The two social scientists found that proverbs that express independence and security were judged to be meaningful enough to be handed on to children. Two statistical tables and an English abstract (p. 49) are included.

4107. Palm, Christine. "Christian Morgensterns groteske Phraseologie—ein Beitrag zur Rolle der Phraseologismen im literarischen Text." *Beiträge zur allgemeinen und germanistischen Phraseologieforschung*. Ed. Jarmo Korhonen. Oulu: Oulun Yliopisto, 1987. 221–235.

In this literary proverb investigation Palm studies the use and function of various types of German phraseological units in the poetic works of Christian Morgenstern (1870–1914), especially in his collections of poems entitled *Galgenlieder* (1905) and *Palmström* (1910). It is shown that his grotesque poems are often based on puns and wordplays with proverbs and proverbial expressions. This is accomplished by antonymous and homonymous substitutions of individual words, by contaminating phraseological units with word additions, and by remotivating proverbial expressions in realistic contexts. Many examples are cited in their literary context, and a short bibliography (pp. 234–235) is attached as well.

4108. Palm, Christine. "Die konnotative Potenz usueller und okkasioneller Phraseologismen und anderer festgeprägter Konstruktionen in Christa Wolfs Roman *Kindheitsmuster.*" *Europhras 88. Phraséologie Contrastive. Actes du Colloque International Klingenthal-Strasbourg, 12–16 mai 1988.* Ed. Gertrud Gréciano. Strasbourg: Université des Sciences Humaines, 1989. 313–326.

This is a detailed literary analysis of the use and function of German phraseological units in Christa Wolf's (1929–) novel *Kindheitsmuster* (1976). Palm explains that many of the fixed phrases contained in this novel dealing with the problem of "Vergangenheitsbewältigung" (coming to terms with the past) illustrate how conventional idioms and proverbial expressions played their role during the time of National Socialism in Germany. Many contextualized examples are cited, including proverbs, proverbial expressions, "geflügelte Worte" (sententious remarks), slogans, idioms, etc. Palm studies their function, repetition, variation, and meaning, and she shows that they are used primarily for characterization and emotionalization purposes. A short bibliography is attached. See also Palm's second essay on Christa Wolf (no. 4110 below).

4109. Palm, Christine (ed.). *Europhras 90. Akten der internationalen Tagung zur germanistischen Phraseologieforschung, Aske/Schweden 12.-15. Juni 1990.* Uppsala: Acta Universitatis Upsaliensis, 1991. 264 pp.

This is a valuable volume of 16 linguistic essays that were delivered as lectures at a phraseological conference that took place from June 12–15, 1990, in Aske, Sweden. The European scholars and their individual contributions are as follows: Harald Burger, "Phraseologie und Intertextualität" (pp. 13–27); Dmitrij Dobrovol'skij, "Strukturtypologische Analyse der Phraseologie" (pp. 20–42); Wolfgang Eismann, "Zur Frage der lexikographischen Berücksichtigung von nichtbinnendeutschen Phraseologismen in deutsch-slavischen phraseologischen

Wörterbüchern" (pp. 43–61); Wolfgang Fleischer, "Zur phraseologischen Aktivität des Partizips II in der deutschen Gegenwartssprache" (pp. 63–76); Csaba Földes, "Farbbezeichnungen als phraseologische Strukturkomponenten im Deutschen, Russischen und Ungarischen" (pp. 77–89); Gertrud Gréciano, "Remotivierung ist textsortenspezifisch" (pp. 91–100); Göran Inghult, "Lexikalische Innovationen in Wortgruppenform" (pp. 101–113); Anne Lise Kjaer, "Phraseologische Wortverbindungen in der Rechtssprache" (pp. 115–122); Jarmo Korhonen, "Konvergenz und Divergenz in deutscher und finnischer Phraseologie" (pp. 123–137); Gernot Müller, "Zur Verankerung zweier Phraseologismen im Werk Heinrich von Kleists" (pp. 139–153); Timothy Nelson, "Die verkehrte Welt" (pp. 155–161); Christine Palm, "Fundgrube *Kindheitsmuster* und kein Ende. Zur semantischen Analyse einiger Phraseologismen im Text" (pp. 163–179); Klaus Dieter Pilz, "Phraseologie in der (regionalen) Tageszeitung" (pp. 181–209); Ingrid Schellbach-Kopra, "Zur Höflichkeitsphraseologie im Finnischen und Deutschen" (pp. 211–223); Barbara Sandig, "Formeln des Bewertens" (pp. 225–252); and Astrid Stedje, "Zur Semiotik der Blumen in deutscher Phraseologie" (pp. 253–264). The articles written in German deal with such matters as structure, lexicography, expressions referring to colors or flowers, innovation, law, literature, mass media, dissemination, semantics, etc. Many of them contain comparative examples from the German, Finnish, and Swedish languages. For annotations see nos. 3189, 3316, 3376, 3409, 3429, 3509, 3633, 3685, 3717, 3987, 4019, 4110, 4180, 4324, 4307, 4430.

4110. Palm, Christine. "Fundgrube *Kindheitsmuster* und kein Ende. Zur semantischen Analyse einiger Phraseologismen im Text." *Europhras 90. Akten der internationalen Tagung zur germanistischen Phraseologieforschung, Aske/Schweden 12.-15. Juni 1990.* Ed. Christine Palm. Uppsala: Acta Universitatis Upsaliensis, 1991. 163–179.

This is Palm's second paper on the use and function of phraseological units in Christa Wolf's (1929–) novel *Kindheitsmuster* (1976). She includes a statistical table that shows that Wolf employs 848 fixed phrases on 530 pages of text, of which 56 are "geflügelte Worte" (sententious remarks), 9 proverbs, 25 lines from poems and songs, 8 advertising slogans, and 9 nursery rhymes. The majority are idioms and proverbial expressions which serve various functions, primarily to illustrate the mentality of the German people under National Socialism. Palm analyzes 24 contextualized examples in some detail, discussing the way several speakers or the narrator use phraseological units to express certain social or historical observations. See also Palm's earlier article on this novel (no. 4108 above).

4111. Panajoti, Jorgo. "Le caractère national des proverbes populaires albanaises." *Culture populaire albanaise,* 8 (1988), 3–41.

Panajoti begins his article with a general discussion of the differences between international and national (regional) proverbs, and he also discusses in which way proverbs can reflect national character. In the second part (pp. 12–20) he compares Albanian proverbs and their European equivalents and shows that the truly indigenous Albanian proverbs often refer to specific historical events and cultural matters. The third part (pp. 20–40) explains more specifically how national customs and stereotypes are expressed in Albanian proverbs. The author refers to onomastics (names of rivers, towns, etc.), certain structural and linguistic peculiarities, historical persons and events, and ethnic groups. Many examples are cited in Albanian with French translations, and a useful bibliography (pp. 40–41) is included as well.

4112. Pape, Walter. "Der ästhetische Erzieher: Christian Felix Weiße oder die bürgerliche Utopie. 6d: Die moralische Anstalt für Kinder." In W. Pape. *Das literarische Kinderbuch. Studien zur Entstehung und Typologie.* Berlin: Walter de Gruyter, 1981. 211–235.

Pape discusses the tradition of the so-called "proverbes dramatiques" in 17th and 18th century France and then shows how the German author Christian Felix Weiße (1726–1804) was influenced by them to write short plays based on well-known German proverbs. Most of his plays were intended for children, and they definitely served pedagogical, didactic, and moralistic purposes. They are usually only one act long and either carry the proverb in the title or have a proverb as the message of the play. Pape mentions several of the plays and includes more detailed analyses of *Der ungezogene Knabe* (1777) and *Friedensfeyer* (1779). He also refers to the fact that Weiße used proverbs in his German textbook *Neues ABC Buch* (1772), indicating that this literary author had clear pedagogical goals in mind when citing proverbs.

4113.   Pape, Walter. "Zwischen Sprachspiel und Sprachkritik. Zum literarischen Spiel mit der wörtlichen Bedeutung von Idiomen." *Sprache und Literatur in Wissenschaft und Unterricht,* 16, no. 56 (1985), 2–13.

In this article Pape analyzes the critical view of proverbs by German literary authors and philological scholars from the 17th to the 20th century. He mentions Justus Georg Schottelius (1612–1676), Johann Christoph Adelung (1732–1806), Johann Gottfried Herder (1744–1803), Gotthold Ephraim Lessing (1729–1781), Jean Paul (1763–1825), Clemens Brentano (1778–1842), Friedrich Nietzsche (1844–1900), Christian Morgenstern (1871–1914), and some others. There are also two important sections on Pieter Brueghel (1520?–1569) and Lewis Carroll (1832–1898). It is shown that while philologists might attack proverbs because of their stylistic overuse as clichés in oral and written communication, literary authors tend to parody proverbs by innovative puns and wordplays. Numerous examples are cited that indicate how the wisdom of proverbs is being questioned in German literature from various historical periods. A useful bibliography (pp. 12–13) is attached.

4114.   Papp, György. "A proverbiumok jelentéstani, kom-munikacioelméleti vizsgalata." *Tanulmanyok. A Magyar Nyelv, Irodalom és Hungarologiai Kutatasok Intézetének Kiadvanya,* 21 (1988), 103–129.

Papp presents a semantic study of Hungarian proverbs with an emphasis on their use and function in oral and written communication. Citing some contextualized examples, he shows that the meaning of any given proverb very much depends on the situation in which it is being used and on the intention of the speaker. Proverbs exhibit a wide range of meanings which are dependent on the context and the motivation for their use. It is thus of great importance in the analysis of proverb use in actual speech acts that all aspects of the proverb utterance are being considered. Papp includes 2 illustrations of a cartoon and playing cards, and he also provides 3 diagrams to illustrate the multisemanticity of proverbs.

4115. Papp, György. "A proverbiumok nyelvtipologiai és kontrasztiv nyelvészeti vizsgalata." *Hungarologiai Közlemenyek*, 21, nos. 1–2 (1989), 205–223.

This is a theoretical article on the comparative study of Serbo-Croatian and Hungarian proverbs. Papp touches on problems of translation and lexicography, but his major emphasis is on gradation of comparability (equivalency). He explains that for some proverbs of these two cultures there exists a total identity in form, structure, vocabulary, metaphor, and meaning. But there are also those texts for which the target language has no equivalent proverbs at all. Numerous examples are cited to illustrate the difficulty of comparative paremiography. Four diagrams, a small bibliography (p. 222), as well as Serbo-Croatian (p. 222) and English (p. 223) abstracts are included.

4116. Paredes, Américo. "Folklore, Lo Mexicano, and Proverbs." *Aztlan*, 13 (1982), 1–11.

Paredes begins his general article with a short discussion of folklore and what folklorists and social scientists understand under the concept of "lo mexicano" which describes the stereotypical Mexican-American. He then defines the proverb, proverbial expression, and proverbial comparison and attempts to explain in which way this folk speech characterizes the ethnic minority and identity of Mexican-Americans. Numerous examples are cited in Spanish with English translations, and Paredes explains how their content, use, meaning, and function express the value system of this population in the Southwest of the United States.

4117. Parker, Carolyn A. "Techniques and Problems in Swahili Proverb Stories: The Case of Baalawy." *Design and Intent in African Literature.* Eds. David F. Dorsey, Phanuel A. Egejuru, and Stephen H. Arnold. Washington/D.C.: Three Continents, 1982. 71–80.

This is a literary proverb investigation of Suleiman Oman Said Baalawy's (1945–) two collections of short stories entitled *Hadithi za Bibi Maahira* (1969) and *Bibi Maahira Tena* (1968). Many of these texts are based on or illustrations of traditional Swahili proverbs. Citing her examples with English translations, Parker shows how 29 proverbs function in these narratives by citing them in their literary context. She includes a statistical table that illustrates how many proverbs are quoted by the various characters or the narrator, and she also explains how many proverbs are merely paraphrased or which are repeated several times. A complete proverb index (pp. 78–80) in both Swahili and English is attached.

4118. Parsons, Elsie Clews. "Riddles and Metaphors among Indian Peoples." *Journal of American Folklore,* 49 (1936), 171–174.

This is one of the few short articles that deals at least slightly with the existence of proverbial metaphors among the Native Americans. Parsons explains that the Pueblo Indians from New Mexico have barely any riddles, and the same appears to be true of proverbs as well. A few riddles have been recorded, but they seem to be of European origin for the most part. Parsons is able to quote a very few metaphors as "The beam is broken" (stated as a warning against the presence of a stranger) and "Sweat in your hands" (refers to the war ceremonial of the ritual posture of folded arms and closed hands whereby the hands sweat). It is not clear how proverbial such metaphors are, but in the absence of recorded proverbial speech among the Native American population they are at least an indication of the existence of phraseological units. See also Wolfgang Mieder (no. 3921).

4119. Pasamanick, Judith R. *The Proverb Moves the Mind: Abstraction and Metaphor in Children Six-Nine.* Diss. Yeshiva University, 1982. 395 pp.

This dissertation explores the development of abstract and metaphorical reasoning among 48 children of the age between six and nine. It was found that (1) children of this age group can reason abstractly and analogically comprehend and generate metaphors by interpreting proverbs and using them appropriately to rehearse their ideas in stimulating interactional settings; (2) these settings encourage a dialectical exchange among concrete and abstract thinkers to the benefit of both, and a sociolinguistic usage of a rich body of social knowledge; and (3) peer generated thought is a powerful stimulant to abstraction. Pasamanick also discusses the implications of her findings for teaching, diagnosis, and evaluation of this age group, whose abstracting competence has been underestimated by previous psychological research. Many statistical tables, figures, and a fascinating appendix (pp. 365–395) listing contextualized responses to the proverbs by the children are included, and so is a helpful bibliography (pp. 356–363) for the study of metaphors and their comprehension.

4120. Pasamanick, Judith R. "Talk 'Does' Cook Rice: Proverb Abstraction through Social Interaction." *International Journal of the Sociology of Language*, 44 (1983), 5–25.

Pasamanick once again explores the abstract and metaphorical reasoning ability of children aged six through nine by engaging them in informal discussions about proverbs. She employs a discursive form of social interaction which enables children to apply events in their own lives to the proverbs' base meanings and thus to abstract them more effectively than traditional psychological proverbs tests allow. The interesting responses by children to the four proverbs "One does not have to learn how to fall into a pit. All it takes is the first step," "Break one link and the whole chain falls apart," "Don't bite off more than you can chew," and "Talk does not cook rice" clearly show that working-class and middle-class children of this age group can reason abstractly and metaphorically. They used three major processes to interpret proverbs: (1) a dialectical exchange of concrete and abstract thought, (2) a complex set of abstraction strategies, and (3) the sociolinguistic use of a body of social knowledge. The reproduced group discussions among the children are of particular value for an understanding of how children comprehend proverbs. A useful bibliography (pp. 24–25) is attached.

4121. Pasamanick, Judith R. "Watched Pots Do Boil: Proverb Interpretation through Contextual Illustration." *Proverbium*, 2 (1985), 145–183.

> This second study on the comprehension of proverbs by children of the age between six and nine is once again based on Pasamanick's important dissertation on this subject matter (see no. 4119 above). This time the author presents the transcripts of 22 situations in which children interpret such standard proverbs as "You can't have your cake and eat it too," "A bird in the hand is worth two in the bush," "Don't count your chickens before they are hatched," "Every dog has his day," "You can't unscramble eggs," "You can't teach an old dog new tricks," "The early bird catches the worm," and "Don't bite off more than you can chew." It is shown that these children definitely have the ability to reason abstractly and metaphorically. In fact, they even cited additional proverbs while discussing the meaning of the proverbs under discussion. Their sociolinguistic knowledge of the social wisdom of proverbs is quite impressive. A small bibliography (pp. 182–183) is provided.

4122. Patnaik, Eira. "Proverbs as Cosmic Truths and Chinua Achebe's *No Longer at Ease.*" *Africana Journal,* 13, nos. 1–4 (1982), 98–103.

> Patnaik offers a literary investigation of the use and function of African proverbs in Chinua Achebe's (1931–) novel *No Longer at Ease* (1978). Several examples are cited in their literary context, and it is shown that the proverbs function as effective tools of verbal communication, as means of characterization, and as expressions of worldview. Patnaik also explains that proverbs transmute the literal into the symbolic, and that they metamorphose the common person into a poet because of their artistic form and metaphors. The entire novel is seen as a reservoir of rich proverbial images reflecting the close-knit social kinship of traditional African culture.

4123. Pavlik, Jaroslav. "Dänische Sprichwörter und bildersprachliche Wortverbindungen in *Mudroslovi*: Frantisek Ladislav Celakovskys Vermächtnis und Appell." *Slavica Othiniensia*, 6 (1983), 55–81.

This is a detailed analysis of the important proverb collection *Mudroslovi narodu slovanskeho ve prislovich* (1852) by the Czech poet and scholar Frantisek Ladislav Celakovsky (1799–1852). In the first part of his essay (pp. 55–61) Pavlik discusses the content of this collection which includes proverbs, proverbial expressions, and so-called weather proverbs. He also presents a statistical table to show which foreign proverbs from the Greek, Latin, Romance, Germanic, Baltic, Finno-Ugric, and Arabic languages have been included. Of greatest interest to Pavlik is the fact that Celakovsky cites 41 Danish proverbs and proverbial expressions which are reprinted in this article. The second part (pp. 62–67) calls for more comparative work concerning Czech and Danish proverbs, and Pavlik presents a small bilingual collection of weather proverbs referring to the months of the year, the seasons, and Christmas. Extensive notes (pp. 67–77) and a valuable bibliography (pp. 77–81) listing 55 Czech and Danish proverb collections are part of this study.

4124. Pavlova, E.G. "Opyt klassifikatsii narodnykh primet." *Paremiologicheskie issledovaniia. Sbornik statei.* Ed. Grigorii L'vovich Permiakov. Moskva: Nauka, 1984. 294–299; also in French translation as "Essai de classification des présages populaires" in *Tel grain tel pain. Poétique de la sagesse populaire.* Ed. G.L. Permiakov. Moscou: Éditions du Progrès, 1988. 357–363.

Pavlova begins her article with a definition of folk superstitions and omens, pointing out that many of them are based on proverbial structures. She classifies this rich material into two major groups, namely those that express rules and those that contain predictions. It is shown that many so-called weather proverbs belong into this genre of sayings. The author cites a number of examples, explaining that they refer to natural phenomena, human experiences and beliefs, taboos, magic, etc. A classification diagram based on functional grounds is included, and so is a useful bibliography (pp. 362–363). This is an important article concerning the argument whether such proverbial superstitions should be considered as proverbs or not. See also Alan Dundes (no. 3338) and Shirley Arora (no. 3076).

4125. Paziak, Mikhail Mikhailovich. "Dosiagnennia suchasnoi bilorus'koi paremiografii ta paremiologii." *Narodna Tvorchist' ta Etnografiia*, no. 4 (1982), 74–78.

This is an informative review article on B(y)elorussian paremiography and paremiology. Paziak cites and discusses the major proverb collections, both from an historical and classificational point of view. It is shown that B(y)elorussian scholars have a definite interest in proverbs and proverbial expressions. This is also indicated by Paziak's review of linguistic, cultural, and folkloric studies of B(y)elorussian phraseological units. The article contains many examples and references, but the author has not added a special bibliography at the end. Anybody interested in the proverbs of the B(y)elorussian Soviet Socialist Republic in the western part of the Soviet Union will find this survey very useful. See also K. Gutschmidt (no. 2436) for a similar article in German.

4126. Paziak, Mikhail Mikhailovich. "Prisliv'ia ta prikazki pro khliborobs'ku diial'nist' liudei." *Narodna Tvorchist' ta Etnografiia*, no. 5 (1982), 43–49.

In this short article Paziak investigates Ukrainian proverbs that deal with agricultural matters. He explains that proverbs contain much wisdom about planting and harvesting, giving farmers an idea for planning various activities throughout the year. He cites proverbs dealing with certain crops, foods, and other farm products, and he also refers to so-called weather proverbs which continue to be of importance to traditional farmers. Numerous examples are cited to illustrate how proverbial wisdom continues to guide the work and worldview of farmers in the Ukrainian Soviet Socialist Republic which is considered to be the breadbasket of the Soviet Union.

4127. Paziak, Mikhail Mikhailovich. "Evoliutsiia formi ta semantichnikh znachen' u skhidnoslov'ian'kikh prisliv'iakh i prikazkakh." *Narodna Tvorchist' ta Etnografiia*, no. 4 (1983), 28–37.

Paziak presents a general comparative study of Slavic proverbs and proverbial expressions with a special emphasis on their form and meaning. Citing many examples in Russian he shows that many phraseological units follow definite structural patterns which also are of significance concerning their semantic aspects. This is particularly the case for those proverbs which are based on certain contrasting pairs of words like "small—large," "short—long," "one—many," etc. It is shown that these patterns exist in various Slavic languages. Even though the realia and metaphors of the texts may be different, the resulting proverbs have the same meanings.

4128. Paziak, Mikhail Mikhailovich. "Rukopisni paremiografichni zbirki u fondakh institutu im. M.T. Ril's'kogo." *Narodna Tvorchist' ta Etnografiia*, no. 1 (1983), 53–57.

This is a short report concerning a number of paremiographical manuscripts kept in the M.T. Ril's'kii Institute in Kiev. Paziak lists the manuscripts and provides detailed descriptions of their history and content. He argues that these early proverb collections from the 18th and 19th centuries are a clear indication that there exists a long tradition of interest in the proverbs of the Ukrainian Soviet Socialist Republic. While some newer Ukrainian proverb collections have been assembled and published, some of the materials described here are still awaiting scholarly attention. The proverbs contained in these manuscripts are clearly of importance for the historical study of Ukrainian proverbs.

4129. Paziak, Mikhail Mikhailovich. *Ukrains'ki prisliv'ia ta prikazki. Problemi paremiologii ta paremiografii.* Kiev: Kiev Naukova Dumka, 1984. 203 pp.

Paziak presents an important and inclusive study of Ukrainian proverbs which is divided into three major parts. In the first part (pp. 13–85) he covers the origin, history, and dissemination of proverbs. He also includes a major section on collections of proverbs and proverbial expressions, discussing the various classification systems used by the paremiographers. This is followed by a discussion of major contributions to paremiology by

Ukrainian, Soviet, and international scholars. The second part (pp. 86–172) contains a valuable review of the various paremiological genres and a detailed content analysis of dozens of proverbial texts. Paziak shows how proverbs comment on people in general, nature, agriculture, food, religion, etc. The third part (pp. 173–197) includes a discussion of the style, form, language, poetics, and structure of Ukrainian proverbs, making this book an extremely useful introduction to proverbs in general and Ukrainian proverbs and proverbial expressions in particular. The 227 notes contain rich international and national bibliographical materials.

4130. Paziak, Mikhail Mikhailovich. "Zbirka prisliv'iv M. Nomisa (do 120–richchia vixodu v svit knigi ~Ukrains'ki prikazki, prisliv'ia i take inshe. Zbirniki O.V. Markovicha i drugix.—SPB., 1864'). *Narodna Tvorchist' ta Etnografiia*, no. 1 (1984), 15–23.

In this article Paziak comments on M. Nomis' (1823–1901) very important Ukrainian proverb collection *Ukrains'ki prikazki, prisliv'ia i take inshe* (1864) which was published 120 years ago in St. Petersburg. Paziak points out that its 14,339 proverbs and proverbial expressions were collected together with Opanas Vasil'ovich Markovich (1822–1867) and some other field researchers. He compares this collection with earlier and later paremiographical works, arguing that this book still represents one of the most important sources for Ukrainian proverbs. Citing numerous examples Paziak explains the classification system of this collection and also provides some linguistic and cultural explanations. The 28 notes contain important bibliographical information concerning Ukrainian paremiography, and 4 illustrations are included as well.

4131. Paziak, Mikhail Mikhailovich. "Transformatsiia narodnikh prisliv'iv i porivnian' u tvorchosti Iuriia Fed'kovicha." *Narodna Tvorchist' ta Etnografiia*, no. 4 (1985), 12–22.

This is a literary investigation of the use and function of proverbs in the works of the Ukrainian author Iurii Fed'kovich (1834–1888). Paziak begins with a discussion of Fed'kovich's interest in folklore in general and in folk songs and proverbs in particular. He then cites numerous passages from his poems, plays, and prose works to illustrate how this author made use of Ukrainian proverbs and proverbial expressions. It is argued that this proverbial language gave his literary works a more regional and authentic flavor, especially when Fed'kovich employed dialect expressions as well. While Fed'kovich often cited proverbs in their traditional wording, he also was willing to transform them in order to add humor or satire to the speech of his characters. With 3 illustrations.

4132. Paziak, Mikhail Mikhailovich. "Tvorennia skhidnoslov'ians'kykh prisliv'iv ta prikazok za strukturnimi modeliami." *Narodna Tvorchist' ta Etnografiia*, no. 4 (1985), 10–18.

In this article Paziak shows how Slavic proverbs and proverbial expressions follow certain structural models. He explains in particular how the structural work of such scholars as Grigorii L'vovich Permiakov, Matti Kuusi, Elza Kokare, and others is applicable to Ukrainian proverbs as well. Paziak cites numerous examples for equational and contrastive proverbs, pointing out that the structure of these texts also is of much importance for their meaning. While the realia and metaphors of various Slavic proverbs might be quite different, their similar structure actually can result in semantic identity. These findings are clearly of much importance for the comparative study of proverbs of the Slavic languages and those of other nationalities.

4133. Paziak, Mikhail Mikhailovich. "Kontrastnist' u prisliv'iak ta prikazkakh." *Narodna Tvorchist' ta Etnografiia*, no. 3 (1986), 25–32.

Paziak continues his structural and semiotic analysis of proverbs from the previous article (see no. 4132) and shows how most proverbial texts can be reduced to certain contrastive elements like "friend—enemy," "small—large," "short—long," "one—many," etc. He bases his discussion on the universal structural patterns developed by Grigorii L'vovich Permiakov (see esp. no. 4153), indicating that Permiakov's system definitely has value for national and international paremiography. The classification system according to such contrastive pairs will enable paremiographers to group many proverbs with different realia and metaphors together under the same structural and semantic heading.

4134. Pegulescu, Anca Vladut. "Al II-lea simpozion de paremiologie româneasca." *Proverbium Dacoromania*, 2 (1987), 57–60. Also in English translation as "The Second Romanian Paremiology Symposium." *Proverbium*, 4 (1987), 249–254.

This is a report concerning a paremiological symposium that was held from June 16–17, 1986, at Drobeta-Turnu-Severin in Rumania. Pegulescu gives the titles and short summaries of the major talks that dealt with various aspects of national and international paremiography and paremiology. Some of the areas covered by the impressive work of Rumanian paremiologists deal with the following aspects: bibliography, origin, age, history, dissemination, structure, form, language, meaning, ethical value, worldview, literature, culture, pedagogy, etc. There was even a report on the history and importance of the journal and yearbook *Proverbium*. What this report clearly shows is that Rumanian scholars like I.C. Chitimia, Dumitru Stanciu, Pavel Ruxandoiu, Constantin Negreanu, and many others have established a solid base for serious regional and comparative work on proverbs. See also Constantin Negreanu (nos. 3999 and 4006).

4135. Pegulescu, Anca Vladut. "Determinarea referentiala în proverbe." *Proverbium Dacoromania*, 4 (1989), 47–51.

In this short article Pegulescu touches on a number of theoretical concerns. It is explained that proverbs are based on selective restrictions of the referential world, i.e., proverbs contain those realia that are part of the culture in which they are being used. While their content, especially in the case of regional or purely national proverbs, might not be universally applicable, it is the meaning of the proverbs which gives them a certain universality. The author also adds some comments regarding the structure and translatability of proverbs, showing by means of Rumanian examples how difficult it is to find equivalent texts in the target language. With an English abstract (p. 51).

4136. Peil, Dietmar. "'Im selben Boot'. Variationen über ein metaphorisches Argument." *Archiv für Kulturgeschichte*, 68, no. 2 (1986), 269–293.

Peil presents a detailed study of the origin, history, and dissemination of the Latin proverbial expression "In eadem es navi" (To be in the same boat). He traces it back to Marcus Tullius Cicero (106–43 B.C.) and shows that it was an established metaphor for the political "ship of state" as well as the feeling of solidarity in the political arena. Erasmus of Rotterdam (1469–1536) was instrumental in getting the phrase translated into many European languages through the popularity of his *Adagia* (1500ff.) which contains it with a reference to Cicero. While Peil refers to English and French versions of the expression, his main interest is to show how the phrase "Wir sitzen alle in einem Boot" functions in the political sphere in modern Germany. He cites numerous contextualized examples from the mass media and includes 2 caricatures from German newspapers. The 55 notes contain important historical references. See also Wolfgang Mieder's study of this proverbial expression (no. 3933).

4137. Peil, Dietmar. "Beziehungen zwischen Fabel und Sprichwort." *Germanica Wratislaviensia*, 85 (1989), 74–87.

In this theoretical article on the relationship between the fable and the proverb Peil is interested in showing that these two genres have a number of similarities which make them so well suited for each other. He begins his study with a definition of both genres and then presents the convincing argument that they are both characterized by a dual nature in that they have a meaning not only as a text but also as a didactic statement. In addition, they express their message indirectly, and they also exhibit a polyfunctionality depending on the context in which they are cited. To illustrate these points and to show how a fable and its appended proverb or proverbs interrelate, the author includes an extensive discussion of Martin Luther's (1483–1546) fable *Vom Wolff vnd Lemlein* (c. 1530).

4138. Peil, Dietmar. "Karl Friedrich Wilhelm Wander und sein *Deutsches Sprichwörter-Lexikon*." *Proverbium*, 8 (1991), 129–145.

The author gives yet another analysis of Karl Friedrich Wilhelm Wander's (1803–1879) monumental achievement of putting together the large German proverb collection in five volumes entitled *Deutsches Sprichwörter-Lexikon* (1867–1880). He starts with a biographical sketch of Wander, showing that this paremiographer was also a liberally minded teacher who wrote political and pedagogical pamphlets, articles, and books. He then gives a short history of Wander's fifty years of work on this major proverb collection. Taking the key-word "Aal" (eal) as one of his examples, Peil discusses lexicographical matters, pointing out that the lexicon contains dialect expressions, foreign equivalents, and historical annotations in addition to the thousands of High German texts. He also comments on Wander's personal statements in these volumes which were usually political commentaries against reactionary and repressive thoughts expressed in the proverbs that reminded Wander of his own time. Peil concludes his article with a reference to Wander's proverbial diary *Politisches Sprichwörterbrevier* (1872) in which he reacts quite negatively to the conservative wisdom of proverbs. The 38 notes (pp. 142–145) contain useful bibliographical information. See also Annelies Herzog (no. 725), Wolfgang Mieder (nos. 3324 and 4533), and Klaus Dieter Pilz (no. 1461).

4139.   Penavin, Olga. "A proverbiumokrol. A jugoszlaviai magyarok szolas- és közmondaskinese alapjan." *Hungarologiai Közlemények,* 11, nos. 39–40 (1979), 155–180.

Penavin starts her article with a detailed review of scholarship on Hungarian proverbs, and she then moves on to a discussion of how Hungarian proverbs survive in Yugoslavia among native speakers of Hungarian. The article also treats such basic paremiological aspects as the grammatical, stylistic, and structural characteristics of proverbs. Penavin interprets proverbs as a linguistic and poetic code which have important communicative functions in oral and written speech. Citing numerous examples it is shown that the meaning of proverbs is very much dependent on the function in particular contexts. The intent of the speaker is also of importance in rendering meaning to a proverb text. The article concludes with a discussion of classification problems of proverbs based on structural and semantic aspects. A useful bibliography of Hungarian paremiological publications (pp. 177–179), one diagram, as well as Serbo-Croatian (p. 179) and English (pp. 179–180) abstracts are included.

4140. Penavin, Olga. "Sprichwörter und Redensarten in der ungarischen Sprache von Jugoslawien." *Finnisch-ugrische Forschungen*, 44, nos. 1–3 (1982), 43–59.

This is a considerably shortened and somewhat different German version of the previous article (see no. 4139) without any of the bibliographical details. Penavin shows once again that Hungarian proverbs continue to be very much in use among Hungarian speakers in Yugoslavia. She explains the historical and cultural background of the Hungarians as an ethnic minority, and she then shows how proverbs need to be studied in the situations of actual speech acts and in the mass meida. She discusses the use of informants and points out that the older generation uses and knows proverbs and proverbial expressions much more than the younger people. A few comments regarding the age, structure, variants, meaning, and function of proverbs are included, citing numerous Hungarian examples with German translations.

4141. Penfield, Joyce. *Communicating with Quotes: The Igbo Case.* Westport/Connecticut: Greenwood Press, 1983. 138 pp.

This is a slightly revised version of Penfield's (formerly Joyce Ann Okezie) doctoral dissertation with the more telling title of *The Role of Quoting Behavior as Manifested in the Use of Proverbs in Igbo Society* (1977; see no. 1383). Based on Jan Mukarovsky's theoretical work Penfield presents a clear analysis of the use of 72 Igbo proverbs in conflict situations, studying them as quoting behavior in their interactional settings (i.e., contexts). Five functional properties in proverb use were isolated: (1) depersonalization (desubjectivization), (2) foregrounding (deautomization), (3) authoritativeness, (4) reference to societal norms and values, and (5) prestige (through knowledge and proper use of proverbs). The third chapter on the ethnography of quoting behavior (pp. 31–75) is particularly valuable and shows how proverbs are used primarily for conflict reduction. Penfield discusses 16 contextual cases which indicate that proverbs are quoted in interactional events to advise, insult, intimidate, point out a mistake, exchange words, mediate, and to make a general statement. This ethnographic study shows how a traditional society communicates with proverbs in a most effective way. It includes a proverb index with English translations of the Igbo texts, several tables and charts, a map, and a valuable bibliography (pp. 121–133).

4142. Penfield, Joyce, and Mary Dura. "Proverbs: Metaphors that Teach." *Anthropological Quarterly*, 61, no. 3 (1988), 119–128.

The authors report on field research that was carried out among children of the Igbo society in Nigeria to understand the sociolinguistic role which proverbs play in the development of these young people. Citing 25 contextualized examples with English translations from a total of 100 folk accounts of proverbs being used for pedagogical purposes, the authors succeed in showing that the understanding and knowledge of proverbs as well as the ability to use them in social discourse is of great communicative value in this traditional society. Children must be able to deal with proverbial wisdom if they want to succeed in a culture in which proverbs are judged to be of high moral and informational value. A diagram concerning the meaning of proverbs in their ethnographic context, a useful bibliography, and an English abstract (p. 119) are included.

4143. Penn, Nolan E., Teresa C. Jacob, and Malrie Brown. "Comparison Between Gorham's Proverbs Test and the Revised Shipley Institute of Living Scale for a Black Population." *Perceptual and Motor Skills*, 66 (1988), 839–845.

A total of 278 African American women (183) and men (95) were administered the Gorham's Proverbs Test and the Shipley Institute of Living Scale. The authors then compared the abstract scores on the psychological proverbs test with the vocabulary and abstract scores on the Shipley Institute of Living Scale. The two tests were remarkably similar in terms of score distributiuons and susceptibility to the effects of age, perceived socio-economic level during childhood, education, and perceived quality of education. Analysis also showed that abstract reasoning, as measured by these tests, is not free from the effects of vocabulary skills. The authors include 2 statistical tables, a short bibliography (pp. 844–845), and an English abstract (p. 839). See also Donald R. Gorham (nos. 557–558).

4144. Penn, Nolan E., Teresa C. Jacob, and Malrie Brown. "Familiarity with Proverbs and Performance of a Black Population on Gorham's Proverbs Test." *Perceptual and Motor Skills*, 66 (1988), 847–854.

As in the previous study (see no. 4143 above) the Gorham's Proverbs Test was administered to 278 African American participants residing in a large metropolitan area in Southern California. Respondents were also asked to indicate whether they were familar with each of the 40 proverbs in the test. Scores were significantly affected by respondents' ages, education, and perceived childhood socio-economic status. Familiarity with a proverb increased the probability of its correct interpretation. Familiarity of proverbs and attempts to interpret them were definitely associated, i.e., respondents tended not to attempt interpretation of unfamiliar proverbs. The number of familiar proverbs per test was not significantly associated with respondents' test scores. The mean abstract score obtained in this study was comparable to mean scores previously reported in the psychological literature, suggesting that ethnic differences do not affect performance on this proverbs test very much. Of the 3 statistical tables included in this study the one giving the percentages of familiarity is of particular value to paremiologists. A short bibliography (pp. 853–854) and an English abstract (p. 839) are provided. See also Donald R. Gorham (nos. 557–558).

4145. Permiakov, Grigorii L'vovich. "K voprosu o paremiologicheskom urovne izayka." *Sbornik statei po vtorichnym modeliruiushchim sistemam.* Tartu: no publisher given, 1973. 26–33; also in German translation by Peter Grzybek as "Zur Frage einer parömiologischen Ebene der Sprache." *Semiotische Studien zum Sprichwort. Simple Forms Reconsidered I.* Eds. Peter Grzybek and Wolfgang Eismann. Tübingen: Gunter Narr, 1984. 251–256.

This is a significant article in which the renowned Soviet paremiologist Grigorii L'vovich Permiakov (1819–1983) talks about a certain paremiological level of language. He mentions the fact that some proverbs and proverbial expressions in common use refer to anecdotes, fables, and other folk narratives, making them dependent on the knowledge of the "story" for proper understanding. He also states that fixed phrases can be reduced to mere remnants or changed grammatically to fit into the flow of oral and written communication and their specific contexts. No matter how proverbs are used, they always function as traditional signs and models for commenting on typical situations.

4146. Permiakov, Grigorii L'vovich. "On the Paremiological Level of Language and the Russian Paremiological Minimum." *Proverbium*, no. 22 (1973), 862–863; also in Russian as "O paremiologicheskom urovne iazyka i russkom paremiologicheskom minimume." *Paremiologicheskie issledovaniia.* Ed. G.L. Permiakov. Moskva: Nauka, 1984. 262–263.

This is a short note which G.L. Permiakov had suggested for discussion at the "International Symposium of Paremiology" (Helsinki, June 19–21, 1974; see nos. 953, 967, 981, 985, and 1241 concerning this meeting). The following six points were raised by Permiakov with explanatory comments: (1) the paremiological level of language (all types of paremia), (2) building the case for the paremiological level of language (knowledge of a certain number of the most widely used paremia is essential), (3) a large paremiological experiment (demographic study in Moscow to find the most widely used Russian folk sayings), (4) revealing a passive paremiological minimum (high frequency studies), (5) identifying the active paremiological minimum (drawing up a list of sayings for active assimilation in the process of teaching Russian as a foreign language), and (6) thoughts on paremiological minima of other people (comparison of Russian proverbs to basic paremiological stocks of other European, Asian, and African languages).

4147. Permiakov, Grigorii L'vovich. "K voprosu o russkom paremiologicheskom minimume." *Slovari i lingvostranovedenie.* Ed.

E.M. Vereshchagina. Moskva: Russkii iazyk, 1982. 131–137; also in shortened form in *Paremiologicheskie issledovaniia.* Ed. G.L. Permiakov. Moskva: Nauka, 1984. 265–268. The original publication appeared in English translation by Kevin J. McKenna as "On the Question of a Russian Paremiological Minimum." *Proverbium,* 6 (1989), 91–102.

In this extremely important article Permiakov argues for the definite inclusion of proverbs, proverbial expressions, and clichés in foreign language dictionaries. He explains that foreigners who study the Russian language need to know fixed phrases in order to understand conversational speech and written texts. Such expressions should be included as independent lexical items under key-words in such dictionaries. In the case of specialized idiomatic dictionaries, each text should be accompanied by a word-for-word translation, a contextualized example, an equivalent proverb text from the native language, and other philological and cultural information. This lexicographical method is illustrated by numerous examples, including "U semi nianek ditia bez glazu—Viele Köche verderben den Brei" (Many cooks spoil the broth; literal translation from Russian: Seven nannies have a child without an eye). Dictionaries of this type are very much needed if students want to gain a knowledge of at least the most common (the minimum) Russian expressions or those of any other foreign language.

4148. Permiakov, Grigorii L'vovich. "Grammatica poslovichnoi mudrosti." In G.L. Permiakov. *Poslovitsi i pogovorki narodov vostoka. Sistematizirovannoe sobranie izrechenii dvukhsot narodov.* Moskva: Nauka, 1979. 7–57; also in German translation by Peter Grzybek as "Die Grammatik der Sprichwörterweisheit" in *Semiotische Studien zum Sprichwort. Simple Forms Reconsidered I.* Eds. Peter Grzybek and Wolfgang Eismann. Tübingen: Gunter Narr, 1984. 295–344; and in French translation by Victor Rosenzweig as "La grammaire de la sagesse proverbiale" in *Tel grain tel pain. Poétique de la sagesse populaire.* Ed. G.L. Permiakov. Moscou: Éditions du Progrès, 1988. 11–81.

This is one of the most important essays of modern theoretical paremiology in which G.L. Permiakov advances his ideas of the logico-semiotic aspects and semantic structures of proverbs and proverbial expressions. He begins his study with an analysis of various classification systems of proverbs, i.e., alphabetical, according to key-words, thematic, etc. All of them have certain advantages and disadvantages, but they really don't address the commonality of proverbs which becomes clear from the comparative study of proverbs from around the world. Permiakov argues that all proverbs are, in fact, linguistic signs for certain situations and relationships based on the logic of common sense. This logico-semiotic aspect is reflected in the semantic structures of proverbs, and the author includes a number of lists that illustrate some of the logical thought patterns on which proverbs are based, among them such thematic contrasting pairs as "large-small," "long-short," "high-low," "much-little," etc. While the realia of proverbs vary largely from one language and culture to another, the logically and semantically based proverbial types are indeed invariant. Permiakov even succeeds in isolating a mere 28 types of relationships into which all of the thematic pairs can be grouped. Many examples, 5 schematic tables, and various lists of invariant pairs of logico-semiotic terms are included, making this a pioneering analysis of semiotic and structural paremiology.

4149.   Permiakov, Grigorii L'vovich. "In Lieu of a Conclusion: The Relationship between Structural and Comparative Paremiology." *Semiotische Studien zum Sprichwort. Simple Forms Reconsidered I.* Eds. Peter Grzybek and Wolfgang Eismann. Tübingen: Gunter Narr, 1984. 445–446.

This is but a two-page German translation of G.L. Permiakov's previous and much longer essay on "K voprosu o strukture paremiologicheskogo fonda" (On the Structure of Paremiological Stock; see no. 1430 for the Russian original, and no. 1428 for its complete English translation). The editors P. Grzybek and W. Eismann chose these pages as a fitting summary to their essay volume on semiotic and structural paremiology in which Permiakov's work is featured in German translation. Permiakov here makes a strong argument for his theoretical approach, pointing out that structural and comparative-historical approaches do not contradict but rather complement each other.

But the more synchronous linguistic and semiotic method of classifying and studying proverbs on an international basis will lead to more practical results as far as comparative paremiographical research goals are concerned.

4150. Permiakov, Grigorii L'vovich. "Kurze Überlegungen zur Struktur des parömiologischen Zeichens." *Semiotische Studien zum Sprichwort. Simple Forms Reconsidered I.* Eds. Peter Grzybek and Wolfgang Eismann. Tübingen: Gunter Narr, 1984. 273–275.

This short essay is published here for the first time from Permiakov's remaining manuscripts. The author presents a diagram of a tetrahedron to illustrate the structure of the paremiological sign. Corner (angle) A represents the real situation (context), B refers to the proverb (as sign), C is the literal meaning of B, and D encompasses the meaning of the proverb performance. Permiakov explains how these four points of reference interrelate to enable the proverb to function as a logico-semiotic element of verbal communication. This semiotic model is a clear summary of Permiakov's involved theoretical deliberations in his longer papers.

4151. Permiakov, Grigorii L'vovich (ed.). *Paremiologicheskie issledovannia. Sbornik statei.* Moskva: Nauka, 1984. 320 pp. The book has apperaed in French translation as *Tel grain tel pain. Poétique de la sagesse populaire.* Ed. G.L. Permiakov. Moscou: Éditions du Progrès, 1988. 391 pp. (see no. 4155 below).

An extremely important and valuable essay volume of recent Soviet paremiological research edited by the late G.L. Permiakov. While this publication also includes articles on riddles and superstitions, it deals primarily with theoretical proverb studies. The following titles alone clearly indicate that paremiology has some of the finest scholars in Eastern Europe and the Soviet Union: Iu.I. Levin, "Proverbial'noe prostranstvo" (pp. 108–126); Nigel Barley, "Strukturnyi podkhod k poslovitse i maksime" (pp. 127–148; translated from the English, see no. 86); Arvo Krikmann, "Opyt ob'iasneniia nekotorykh semanticheskikh mekhanizmov poslovitsy" (pp. 149–178); Zoltán Kanyó, "Myslitel'no iazykovye usloviia otobrazheniia struktury poslovitsy" (pp. 179–199); E.N. Savvina, "O transformatsiiakh klishirovannykh vyrazhenii v rechi" (pp. 200–222); E.V. Paducheva, "O semanticheskikh sviaziakh mezhdu basnei i ee moral'iu" (pp. 223–251); Zoltán Kanyó, "O kommynikativnoi forme poslovits" (pp. 257–259); G.L. Permiakov, "O paremiologicheskom urovne iazyka i russkom paremiologicheskom minimume" (pp. 262–263); A. Barulin, "Russkii paremiologicheskii minimum i ego rol' prepodavanii russkogo iazyka" (pp. 264–265); G.L. Permiakov, "Iz stat'i 'K voprosu o russkom paremiologicheskom minimume'" (pp. 265–268); Dumitru Stanciu, "Rumynski poslovitsy na balkanakh" (pp. 269–270); Bozor Tilavov, "Svode poslovits Tadzhikskogo naroda" (pp. 270–273); A. Bykova, "Semioticheskaia struktura velerizmov" (pp. 274–293); E.G. Pavlova, "Opyt klassifikatsii narodnykh primet" (pp. 294–299); G.L. Permiakov, "Prilozhenie paremiologicheskie publikatsii 1975—nachala 1982" (pp. 300–318). For annotations of these papers on proverbs, proverbial expressions, clichés, and wellerisms regarding meaning, structure, semantics, semiotics, proverbiality, folk narrative (esp. proverb and fable), frequency, paremiological minimum, instruction (teaching of foreign languages), lexicography, aesthetics, field research, archiving, and bibliography see nos. 3780, 3100, 3729, 3663, 4313, 4105, 3664, 4146, 3110, 4147, 4414, 4476, 3208, 4124, 4152.

4152. Permiakov, Grigorii L'vovich. "Prilozhenie paremiologicheskie publikatsii 1975—nachala 1982." *Paremiologicheskie issledovaniia.* Ed. G.L. Permiakov. Moskva: Nauka, 1984. 300–318; also in French translation as "Publications parémiologiques soviétiques (1975—début 1982)" in *Tel grain tel pain. Poétique de la sagesse populaire.* Ed. G.L. Permiakov. Moscou: Éditions du Progrès, 1988. 364–378.

An extremely important bibliography of primarily East European paremiographical and paremiological publications which appeared between 1975 and 1982. Permiakov was aided in this compilation by A.M. Bushui, Arvo Krikmann, L.R. Kontsevich, B.L. Riftin, Matti Kuusi, Agnes Szemerkényi, Dumitru Stanciu, Iordanka Kotseva, and Boguslav Benesh. The bibliography is of special value for semiotic, structural, and linguistic analyses of proverbs, proverbial expressions, wellerisms, clichés, and phraseology in general. Many references also deal with folk narratives and their relationship to paremiology. It is of importance that Western scholars acquaint themselves with the superb Soviet and East European scholarship. This bibliography and the essay volume in which it is included (see no. 4151 above) should definitely add to the international scope of proverb research.

4153. Permiakov, Grigorii L'vovich. "Universales thematisches Verzeichnis." *Semiotische Studien zum Sprichwort. Simple Forms Reconsidered I*. Eds. Peter Grzybek and Wolfgang Eismann. Tübingen: Gunter Narr, 1984. 433–443.

This is a slightly adapted German translation of Permiakov's list of universal thematic pairs based on the logico-semiotic aspects of the structure of proverbs which he originally had published in his seminal study on "Grammatica poslovichnoi mudrosti" (1979; see no. 4148 above). A short introductory note stresses that this classification system is suitable for any national or international proverb collection. Altogether 181 thematic pairs such as "alt-jung" (old-young), "dünn-dick" (thin-thick), and "Freund-Feind" (friend-enemy) are listed. This classification system is of particular value for finding proverbial types that can accommodate the many proverbs of the world with their different realia.

4154. Permiakov, Grigorii L'vovich. *Osnovy strukturnoi paremiologii*. Ed. G.L. Kapchits. Moskva: Nauka, 1988. 236 pp.

In this posthumous collection of various essays by Grigorii L'vovich Permiakov (1919–1983), the editor G.L. Kapchits has assembled the structural, semantic, and semiotic research results of this extremely important paremiological theoretician from the Soviet Union. The first part of the book (pp. 11–142) consists of essays that deal with classification problems, paremiological homonymy and synonymy, logical structures of proverbs, the semantics of proverbs, and proverbs as a semiotic system (for annotations see esp. nos. 1424–1432). The second part (pp. 143–169) reprints Permiakov's publications that deal with the important questions surrounding a "paremiological minimum" (see nos. 1431, 2737, and 4146–4147). A lengthy appendix (pp. 170–221) includes Permiakov's universal thematic index of proverbs (see nos. 4148 and 4153) and various incomplete notes and observations from Permiakov's archive. Kapchits also includes a bibliography (pp. 222–231) of Permiakov's impressive private library as well as a list (pp. 232–235) of all the publications by this great scholar. This essay volume certainly belongs to the foundations of theoretical and international paremiology, and it should be translated into other languages to make Permiakov's significant work more known among scholars not being able to read Russian. For English, French, and German translations already available see above all nos. 1428, 4155, and 3538.

4155.   Permiakov, Grigorii L'vovich (ed.). *Tel grain tel pain. Poétique de la sagesse populaire.* Translated by Victor Rosenzweig and Annette Taraillon. Moscou: Éditions du Progrès, 1988. 391 pp. For the 1984 Russian edition of this book see no. 4151 above.

This essay volume is basically a French translation of the important Russian essay volume *Paremiologicheskie issledovaniia* (1984; see no. 4151 above) edited by G.L. Permiakov. While pages 207–331 deal with the riddle, the remainder of the book contains major theoretical essays by leading paremiologists of Eastern Europe and the Soviet Union. Included are: G.L. Permiakov, "La grammaire de la sagesse proverbiale" (pp. 11–81); Arvo Krikmann, "'Mécanismes sémantiques' de l'énoncé proverbial" (pp. 82–113); Eléna Savvina, "Transformations discursives des locutions figées" (pp. 114–138); Youri Lévine, "L'espace proverbial" (pp. 139–167); Eléna Padoutchéva, "Liens sémantiques entre la fable et sa morale" (pp. 168–206); Alvica Bykova, "La structure sémiotique des wellérismes" (pp. 332–356); Evguénia Pavlova, "Essai de classification des présages populaires" (pp. 357–363); G.L. Permiakov, "Publications parémiologiques soviétiques (1975—début 1982)" (pp. 364–378); and I. Nikolaieva, "Publications parémiologiques soviétiques (fin 1982—début 1985)" (pp. 378–387). For annotations of these helpful French translations of major essays on proverbs, proverbial expressions, clichés, and wellerisms regarding meaning, structure, semantics, semiotics, proverbiality, folk narrative (esp.

fable and proverb), and bibliography see nos. 4148, 3729, 4313, 3780, 4105, 3208, 4124, 4152, 4026.

4156. Perret, Michèle. "Ci a grant courtoisie: ci a + substantif abstrait." *La locution. Actes du colloque international Université McGill, Montréal, 15–16 octobre 1984.* Eds. Giuseppe Di Stefano and Russell G. McGillivray. Montréal: Éditions CERES, 1984. 368–383.

The author presents a philological investigation of French phraseological units that follow the structural pattern "Ci avoir + (adjectif évaluatif) + substantif abstrait." Most examples cited from medieval French literary sources indicate that the somewhat unusual grammatical form of "Ci a . . ." (That is . . ., or: What a . . .!) is used primarily for exclamatory remarks such as "Ci a grant courtoisie" (That is a great courtesy, or: What a great courtesy!). The contextualized examples show that this fixed phrase was used quite often in medieval epics and lyric poetry to express surprise, astonishment, and excitement.

4157. Perry, Theodore A. (ed.). *Santob de Carrión. "Proverbios Morales."* Madison/Wisconsin: The Hispanic Seminary of Medieval Studies, 1986. 233 pp.

This is a masterful edition of Santob de Carrión's (14th century) medieval Spanish proverb collection entitled *Proverbios morales* (1345). In his introduction (pp. I-VI) Perry discusses the text, the manuscripts, the ideology, the Jewish elements, and the purpose of the present edition. This is followed by a valuable bibliography (pp. VII-XIII). A small subject index (pp. 1–4) proceeds the actual new Spanish edition of the *Proverbios morales* (pp. 5–93). To this Perry has added an invaluable philological, historical, and cultural commentary (pp. 95–203) which makes this important work much more accessible to modern readers. A Spanish glossary (pp. 205–233) concludes this superb edition of one of the most important paremiographical sources of the Spanish language. For Perry's English translation and more detailed interpretation of the *Proverbios morales* see no. 4160 below. See also John Zemke (no. 4594).

4158. Perry, Theodore A. "Judeo-Christian Forces and Artistic Tension in Medieval Letters: The Case of the *Libro de los buenos proverbios*." *La Chispa '87: Selected Proceedings. The Eighth Louisiana Conference on Hispanic Languages and Literatures.* Ed. Gilbert Paolini. New Orleans: Tulane University, 1987. 251–256.

Perry explains that the Coptic Christian physician Honein Ibn Isaac (809–873), the celebrated translator of Greek scientific treaties into Arabic, also assembled a collection of the wisdom and sayings of the sages of Greek antiquity, of which two medieval translations are known: the anonymous Spanish version known as *Libro de los buenos proverbios* (13th century), and the *Musrei ha-Filosofim* (13th century), which is a Hebrew translation by the Jewish poet Al-Harizi (1170–1235). Perry discusses the artistic, religious, and cultural similarities and differences of these two translations, noting that the main divergencies occur by way of deletion. He concludes his short essay by arguing that a more detailed comparison of these two works would render valuable information concerning Christian and Jewish cultural values in medieval Spain. See also Harlan Sturm's edition of the *Libro de los buenos proverbios* (no. 2921).

4159. Perry, Theodore A. "Quadripartite Wisdom Sayings and the Structure of Proverbs." *Proverbium,* 4 (1987), 187–210.

The author begins with the observation that the structural feature of parallelism is particularly prevalent in proverbs. Choosing his examples from medieval Spanish sources and the Book of Proverbs of the Bible, Perry investigates especially those texts that include four propositions. He groups them according to equational/contrastive, conjunctive, and partial quadripartite structures, arguing that such complex and long sayings are derived logically rather than from experience. These proverbs are drawn from wisdom's own structures, but they always refer to experience, either directly or by implication. They are figures of thought rather than of speech, less literary structures than logical ones, less forms of expression than structures of thinking. In fact, these wisdom sayings require solution by analogy with concrete contexts. The 40 notes (pp. 204–210) contain valuable bibliographical information.

4160. Perry, Theodore A. *The "Moral Proverbs" of Santob de Carrión. Jewish Wisdom in Christian Spain.* Princeton/New Jersey: Princeton University Press, 1987. 198 pp.

   An exemplary English translation and interpretation of Santob de Carrión's (14th century) medieval Spanish proverb collection entitled *Proverbios morales* (1345). Perry includes an introduction (pp. 3–9) explaining the importance of this early paremiographical and philosophical work, and he then prints his translation of the *Moral Proverbs* (pp. 11–62). This is followed by eight chapters investigating the deeper meaning of this work (pp. 63–165), dealing with such matters as Jewish-Christian polemics, metaphors of oppression and triumph, the deadly sins, the physical world, the ways of the human world (esp. ethics and behavior), Santob's understanding of Ecclesiastes (esp. vanity), and the role of God and repentance. An appended chapter (pp. 167–181) interprets the ideology of the *Proverbios morales* as expressed by an anonymous commentator. An invaluable bibliography (pp. 183–191), an index (pp. 193–194) of passages of the *Proverbios morales* cited in Spanish and English translation in the interpretative chapters, and a general index (pp. 195–195) conclude this important study. See also Perry's Spanish edition of this work (no. 4157 above), and John Zemke (no. 4594).

4161. Perumal. V. "A Comparative Study of Tamil and Kannada Proverbs." *Folk Culture I: Folk Culture and Literature.* Ed. Chittaranjan Das. Cuttack/Orissa: Institute of Oriental and Orissan Studies, 1984. 175–181.

   The author begins his short essay with a general introduction to proverbs and includes a section on various definition attempts of the genre. This is followed by the observation that there exists a rich tradition of Tamil and Kannada proverbs in India, especially expressing wisdom about society, education, and economics. Perumal cites a number of examples in English translation, and he also attaches a list of 10 Tamil and Kannada proverbs in their original languages with English translations. The comparative list shows clearly that there exist basic intellectual, linguistic, and cultural similarities between the people of the two groups.

4162. Perumal, V. "Principles of Classification of Tamil Proverbs." *Folk Culture I: Folk Culture and Literature.* Ed. Chittaranjan Das. Cuttack/Orissa: Institute of Oriental and Orissan Studies, 1984. 165–174.

> Perumal presents various ways of classifying a rich corpus of proverbs, basing his examples on Tamil proverbs from India which he cites together with English translations. It is pointed out that there are two types of classification bases: the full basis (including all texts, as for example in the classification according to themes) and the partial basis (including only part of the texts of a given corpus, for example only the religious proverbs). The author then presents the following possibilities of ordering all proverbs (full basis): size basis, morphological basis, tier basis, subject (theme) basis, chronological basis, geographical basis, standard basis, acoustic basis, word basis, and alphabetical (word order) basis. Due to space restrictions only the first four bases are discussed with some examples.

4163. Perumal, V. "A Comparative Study of Proverbs: Examples from Tamil and English Literatures." *Folklore* (Calcutta), 27, no. 4 (1986), 61–70.

> The author begins his comparative analysis of Tamil and English proverbs with a discussion of their definition, origin, geographical distribution, and context in oral and written communication. Citing numerous Tamil proverbs in English translation and adding English proverbs for comparison, Perumal shows that there exist quite a few proverbs from these two different cultures which are very similar in their metaphor, content, structure, and meaning. The same is true for proverbial expressions, proverbial comparisons, and twin formulas from both languages and cultures. Nevertheless, obviously there are also those texts which have no real equivalents due to the cultural, social, and historical differences. A small section (p. 69) on the worldview expressed in Tamil proverbs about the English people is included.

4164. Petermann, Jürgen. "Zur Erstellung ein- und zweisprachiger phraseologischer Wörterbücher: Prinzipien der formalen

Gestaltung und der Einordnung von Phrasemen." *Phraseologie und ihre Aufgaben.* Ed. Josip Matesic. Heidelberg: Julius Groos, 1983. 172–193.

The author presents a clear discussion of the many problems which the lexicographer faces in putting together various types of phraseological dictionaries. He argues that scholars must first of all differentiate among nominal, verbal, adjectival, pronomial, and adverbial phraseological units. Then there is the vexing problem of variants which becomes even more complex in the case of bilingual dictionaries. Petermann also includes a detailed discussion of how to arrange fixed phrases that contain the same key-word under one heading. He touches on stylistic levels of these fixed phrases and also deals with the problem of citing contextualized examples. A useful bibliography (pp. 190–191) concerning these linguistic and lexicographical questions is attached.

4165. Peters, Issa. "The Attitude Toward the Elderly as Reflected in Egyptian and Lebanese Proverbs." *The Muslim World,* 76, no. 2 (1986), 80–85.

Peters states that it appears to be a given fact that there exists a high regard and concern for the elderly in the Arabic and Islamic cultures. By analyzing many proverbs about the elderly from Ahmad Taymur's Arabic proverb collection *Al-Amthal al-Ammiyya* (3rd ed. 1970) and Anis Freya's *Dictionary of Modern Lebanese Proverbs* (1974), Peters is able to show that while many of them comment positively on old people, there are also those texts that are neutral or definitely negative. Citing some examples in transliterated Arabic with English translations, it is concluded that although both collections contain proverbs which view the elderly as honorable, wise, or experienced, there are those that project a negative attitude. Such proverbs portray the older population as acting immaturely and inappropriately, or being ungrateful, fussy, useless, or burdensome. It is argued that some of these negative opinions may be a reflection of the economic necessities of the culture. As long as the elderly are able to function well within the social system, they are viewed positively, but when their physical and mental abilities begin to wane, they become a social and economic burden and begin to lose their honorable place.

4166. Pfeffer, Wendy. "The Riddle of the Proverb." *The Spirit of the Court: Selected Proceedings of the Fourth Congress of the International Courtly Literature Society (Toronto 1983)*. Eds. Glyn S. Burgess, Robert A. Taylor, Alan Deyermond, Dennis Green, and Beryl Rowland. Dover/New Hampshire: Brewer, 1985. 254–263.

In this article Pfeffer continues the work that was begun by Claude Buridant (see no. 236) on the use and function of proverbs in the medieval French *Jeux-Partis* (c. 1240–1310) of the troubadours. The author explains that even though it might seem strange that folk proverbs would appear in the love poetry of the upper classes, they actually are very much an integral part of the play-element of these courtly lyrics. Citing several examples in their literary context and showing that most proverbial texts are used at the end of the stanzas, Pfeffer convincingly argues that the proverbs give traditional answers to the riddles of love expressed in many of these poems. The essay includes some very informative comments on the importance and interrelationship of riddles and proverbs in this French poetry of the Middle Ages, and the 38 notes contain useful bibliographical information concerning the use of proverbs in medieval literature.

4167. Pfeffer, Wendy. "'Eu l'auzi dir en un ver reprovier'. Aimeric de Peguilhan's Use of the Proverb." *Neophilologus*, 70 (1986), 520–527.

In this essay Pfeffer investigates the use and function of proverbs in the poetry of the medieval French troubadour Aimeric de Peguilhan (1175?–1220?). Even though he is by no means the most proverbial poet of love songs, Aimeric does employ 20 proverbs in the 52 poems attributed to him. Citing several examples in their literary context, Pfeffer shows how the poet uses introductory formulas to add authenticity and authority to his proverbial statements. She is also able to illustrate that Aimeric uses folk proverbs and a text from the Bible to add traditional values to his argumentation. Altogether Aimeric's effective integration of proverbs in his poems is a clear indication that he was well aware of their utility as a rhetorical tool.

4168. Pfeffer, Wendy. "'Ben conosc e sai que merces vol so que razos dechai': L'emploi du proverbe chez Folquet de Marselha." *Actes du premier congrès international de l'association internationale d'études occitanes.* Ed. Peter T. Ricketts. London: Association Internationale d'Études Occitanes, Westfiled College, 1987. 401–408.

The author continues her literary investigations of medieval French troubadours and their use of proverbs to add traditional language and wisdom to their love poetry. This time she studies Folquet de Marselha (1178?–1231) who used the impressive number of 25 proverbs in the 19 poems attributed to him. Pfeffer explains that Folquet was a well-educated person who included sententious materials throughout his poetry. However, he also recognized the value of the folk wisdom expressed in proverbs. To add special weight to these proverbs he quotes them at times with introductory formulas. Citing several examples in their literary context, Pfeffer presents a convincing argument that Folquet was well aware of the fact that proverbs would be an effective rhetorical device to be used in his poetry.

4169. Pfeffer, Wendy. "Rotten Apples and Other Proverbs in *The Song of the Albigensian Crusade.*" *Proverbium*, 8 (1991), 147–158.

This is an intriguing interpretative analysis of the proverbial language in the *Canso de la Crosada* (*The Song of the Albigensian Crusade*) that was written down by Guilhem de Tudela (12th/13th century) and a subsequent anonymous author between the years of 1210 to 1228. The first half of the article deals with how especially Guilhem uses proverbial expressions of worthlessness to state his negative attitudes. Many of these expressions refer to small coins, clothing, the kitchen, and rotten apples. The anonymous writer of the second half of the work does not use such fixed phrases due to his more positive feeling towards the crusade. The second part (pp. 153–156) of the article treats the use and function of proverbs in this account, explaining that the anonymous author used them more frequently. Numerous contextualized examples are cited, and a useful bibliography (pp. 157–158) is attached.

4170. Picherit, Jean-Louis G. "Formes et fonctions de la matière proverbiale dans le *Songe di vieil pèlerin* de Philippe de Mézières." *La locution. Actes du colloque international Université McGill, Montréal, 15–16 octobre 1984.* Eds. Giuseppe Di Stefano and Russell G. McGillivray. Montréal: Éditions CERES, 1984. 384–399.

Following a general introduction to proverbial speech in medieval French literature, Picherit investigates the use and function of proverbs and proverbial expressions in Philippe de Mézières' (1327?–1405) allegorical work *Songe du vieil pèlerin* (14th century). He discusses the problem that many of the seemingly proverbial texts might in fact be pseudo-proverbs without any particular currency in folk speech. He also cites various introductory formulas used by the author, and he then analyzes numerous examples in their literary context. Most of the proverbs are very metaphorical, adding much traditional wisdom to this moralistic work of the French Middle Ages.

4171. Picoche, Jacqueline. "Un essai de lexicologie guillaumienne: La locution figée comme révélateur du signifié de puissance des polysèmes." *La locution. Actes du colloque international Université McGill, Montréal, 15–16 octobre 1984.* Eds. Giuseppe Di Stefano and Russell G. McGillivray. Montréal: Éditions CERES, 1984. 103–118.

Picoche begins her linguistic study with a short discussion (pp. 103–105) of the various meanings of the French proverbial expression "N'être pas sorti de l'auberge" (Not yet having left the inn, i.e., still having a lot to do before one's goals are achieved). Referring to the semantic theories of G. Guillaume in his *Langage et science du langage* (1964), she then investigates the polysemanticity of individual words of fixed phrases which gives them their different meanings. This is shown especially by an analysis of several phraseological units that include the words "créneau" (fort), "doigt" (finger), "savoir" (to know), and "connaître" (to be acquainted with). The author includes interesting comments concerning the popular expression "Mon petit doigt m'a dit que . . ." (My little finger has told me that . . .), and there are also 2 diagrams to illustrate the semantic influence of individual words on the meaning of fixed phrases.

4172. Pierce, Dann L. "Stylistic Devices in Graphic Rhetoric: Nast's Tools." In D.L. Pierce. *An Investigation of Thomas Nast's Graphic Satire of the Tweed Ring.* Diss. University of Iowa, 1985. 175–229.

This informative dissertation (443 pp.) on the famous American illustrator and caricaturist Thomas Nast (1840–1902) deals in particular with his satirical caricatures against the five members of the so-called Tweed Ring, a group of politicians who misappropriated millions of dollars in New York City between 1868 and 1871. In the chapter on his stylistic devices Pierce includes a small section (pp. 201–205) that analyzes Nast's use of proverbs and proverbial expressions as part of his visual and verbal art. It is pointed out that his favorite fixed phrase as a caption of his cartoons was "What are you going to do about it?" which he used for the first time on June 10, 1871. Pierce also explains how Nast used hyperboles, symbols, and metaphors to add spice to his political satire. There is no doubt that political cartoons and proverbial language as captions work together very well to bring across effective political satire, as can still be seen in modern cartoons and caricatures.

4173. Pilichkova, Sevim. "Prilog kon prouchuvanjeto na narodnite poslovitsi kaj turtsite od SR Makedonija." *Makedonski folklore,* 39–40 (1987), 257–303.

The author begins her study of Turkish proverbs current among the Turkish population of Macedonia with a general discussion of their content. Following ten years of field research in Macedonia, Pilichkova concludes that the proverbs are valuable indicators of the social life, experiences, aspirations and historical as well as socio-economic conditions of the Turks living in Macedonia. A few variants from Turkish proverbs used in Turkey, Bulgaria, Rumania, and Iraq are included, illustrating that there is a strong oral tradition of proverbial wisdom in this area of Europe. The second part of the article (pp. 275–300) presents a collection of 546 Turkish texts with Russian translations, and the 31 notes include useful bibliographical information. An English abstract (p. 303) is attached.

4174. Pilipp, Frank. "Volksgut versus Volkswirtschaft: Zur Funktion von Sprichwort und Redensart in Franz Xaver Kroetz' Milieudrama *Mensch Meier.*" *Proverbium,* 5 (1988), 145–154.

Pilipp investigates the use and function of German proverbs and proverbial expressions in Franz Xaver Kroetz' (1946–) play *Mensch Meier* (1979) which depicts the everyday life and problems of Martha and Otto Meier and their son Ludwig. It is shown that the language in general and the proverbial speech in particular reflect the social problems in this family, where traditional values are confronted by a capitalistic system. Citing numerous examples in their dramatic context, Pilipp explains how the proverbs are expressions of the worldview of the lower social classes, their milieu, and their problems in struggling to deal with a changing world. It is argued sucessfully that Kroetz uses proverbial language in order to show the conflict between traditional wisdom and modern capitalism. The 27 notes (pp. 152–154) include useful bibliographical references for the use of proverbial speech in modern German drama.

4175. Pilz, Klaus Dieter. "Suche nach einem Oberbegriff der Phraseologie und Terminologie der Klassifikation." *Phraseologie und ihre Aufgaben.* Ed. Josip Matesic. Heidelberg: Julius Groos, 1983. 194–213.

This is a significant linguistic and theoretical article concerning the chaotic situation regarding the terminological aspects of the growing field of phraseology. Pilz refers to approximately 80 general concepts in German alone which more or less compete with each other, most of them being composed of an adjective and a noun, as for example "sprichwörtliche Redensart" (proverbial expression), "metaphorische Redensart" (metaphorical expression), "feste Wendung" (fixed phrase), etc. Next he analyzes the terminology of the different genres (classes) that make up the broad study of phraseology, such as proverb, proverbial expression, stereotype, slogan, formula, cliché, topos, literary quotation (geflügeltes Wort), etc. Many tables and examples are presented, and a helpful bibliography (pp. 212–213) refers to major studies dealing with questions of terminology and classification.

4176. Pilz, Klaus Dieter. "Zur Terminologie der Phraseologie." *Muttersprache*, 93 (1983), 336–350.

This is a revised version of the previous article (see no. 4175) in which Pilz also incorporates the findings of the *Handbuch der Phraseologie* (1982), edited by Harald Burger et al. (see no. 3190). Once again Pilz shows the terminological chaos of the international field of phraseology and argues strongly for the publication of a precise international dictionary of phraseological terminology. He presents a detailed comparison of various classification systems, for example semantic, structural, syntactical, stylistic, pragmatic, functional, communicative, and contrastive. He also discusses special genres such as common place, proverb, cliché, twin formula, etc. Many German examples are cited, and the notes contain important bibliographical references. The same chaotic situation that Pilz describes for the German language exists in other languages as well, making a phraseological dictionary of commonly accepted terms and definitions a most urgent matter.

4177. Pilz, Klaus Dieter. "Herzlichen Glückwunsch—nachträglich! Verspätetes Grußwort—statt einer Rezension [von *Proverbium*, Bd. 1]." *Proverbium*, 2 (1985), 257–258.

This is a generous congratulatory note to the editors Daniel Barnes, Galit Hasan-Rokem, and Wolfgang Mieder for having established the new publication *Proverbium: Yearbook of International Proverb Scholarship* in 1984 (from 1984–1987 published in Columbus, Ohio; from 1988 on in Burlington, Vermont). Pilz recalls the important journal *Proverbium* whose 25 issues were edited by Matti Kuusi et al. from 1965 to 1975 in Helsinki. He also mentions Vilmos Voigt's attempt to continue its publication under the title of *Proverbium Paratum* in Budapest (4 issues between 1980–1989). Recalling the fact that the German paremiographer and paremiologist Karl Friedrich Wilhelm Wander (1803–1879) had already tried to start a journal and a society for proverb scholars in 1836, Pilz now expresses his best wishes for this new international yearbook which serves scholars from around the world.

4178. Pilz, Klaus Dieter. "Allgemeine und phraseologische Wörterbücher. Brauchen wir überhaupt phraseologische Wörterbücher?" *Beiträge zur allgemeinen und germanistischen Phraseologieforschung.* Ed. Jarmo Korhonen. Oulu: Oulun Yliopisto, 1987. 129–153.

In this detailed analysis of 25 German dictionaries of various types Pilz investigates the difficult lexicographical problems of integrating phraseological units into such books. He touches upon the difficulty of classification and argues that especially phraseological dictionaries should include examples of how the fixed phrases work in actual contexts. He also points out that illustrations in the form of pictures, caricatures, and cartoon would be of much help, especially to persons for whom the particular language might be a foreign language. Questions concerning the layout of various expressions under one key-word are also addressed. But the most impressive part of this article is its appendix (pp. 145–153) where Pilz presents three detailed statistical tables dealing with how the 25 German dictionaries have integrated up to 261 phraseological units based on the noun "Wort" (word). The third table (p. 153) shows this in particular for the proverbial expression "Das große Wort führen" (To do all the talking, to monopolize the conversation). A useful bibliography (pp. 141–144) is also included.

4179. Pilz, Klaus Dieter. "Graffiti-Dialoge. Kommunikation im Intimbereich einer Universität." *Dialog. Festschrift für Siegfried Grosse.* Eds. Gert Rickheit and Sigurd Wichter, Tübingen: Max Niemeyer, 1990. 439–452.

Basing his many interesting texts on field research in male bathrooms at the University of Bochum in Germany, Pilz analyzes the content, linguistic features, and messages of this graffiti by the German intelligentsia. He explains that they may be grouped according to monologues, wordplays, and dialogues (whole rows of comments). The texts clearly indicate that scatological and sexual themes are very popular, but there are also graffiti which comment more seriously on political and social concerns. Pilz also includes a group of texts that is based on linguistic and literary wordplays, and it is here where proverbs and literary quotations are quite often parodied. Many of the texts are, in fact, so-called "Antisprichwörter" (anti-proverbs) in which traditional proverbs are manipulated into revealing puns. The 67 notes include useful bibliographical information. See also Jess Nierenberg (no. 4025).

4180. Pilz, Klaus Dieter. "Phraseologie in der (regionalen) Tageszeitung am Beispiel einer Ausgabe der *Westdeutschen Allgemeinen Zeitung* (=WAZ) vom Samstag/Montag, 30. Dez. 1989/1. Jan. 1990." *Europhras 90. Akten der internationalen Tagung zur germanistischen Phraseologieforschung, Aske/Schweden 12.-15. Juni 1990.* Ed. Christine Palm. Uppsala: Acta Universitatis Upsaliensis, 1991. 181–209.

In this article Pilz has investigated the phraseological units contained in just one issue of the regional German newspaper *Westdeutsche Allgemeine Zeitung* covering the end of the year 1989 and the beginning of 1990. He shows how fixed phrases are used in headlines, in letters to the editor, and in the sections on sports, politics, economics, etc. Proverbs and proverbial expressions also play a role as captions of pictures and cartoons, and it is interesting to note that of 131 headlines in this newspaper issue an impressive 40 (30.5%) are based on phraseological units. Pilz cites many examples in context, and he includes several statistical tables comparing the proverbial language of this newspaper with other German mass media publications. An informative appendix (pp. 195–209) presents copies of several pages of the newspaper to show some of the fixed phrases in their journalistic context. A list of all the expressions that Pilz found in this one newspaper issue is also part of this appendix.

4181. Pinheiro Torres, Alexandre. "*O Malhadinhas*, visto através do seu adagiário." *Colóquio-Letras*, 85 (1985), 50–56.

The author presents a literary investigation of the use and function of Portuguese proverbs and proverbial expressions in

Aquilino Ribeiro's (1885–1963) novel *O Malhadinhas* (1922). The article begins with a biographical sketch of Ribeiro, explaining that he is one of the most important modern writers of Portugal. Pinheiro Torres then shows how Ribeiro employs proverbs in order to depict rural life through its authentic folk language. Citing many examples in their literary context it is pointed out that proverbs add a lot of peasant wisdom and regional flavor to this picaresque novel about António Malhadas. While some proverbs are cited in their traditional wording, there are also those texts which are varied in order to achieve certain ironical effects.

4182. Pinkernell, Gert. "Une réplique haineuse à la *Ballade des proverbes*, de François Villon, émanant du cercle de Charles d'Orléans." *Archiv für das Studium der neueren Sprachen und Literaturen*, 224 (1987), 110–116.

Pinkernell presents an interesting study concerning François Villon's (1431?–1463?) personal and literary relationship with Charles d'Orléans (1394–1465). It is pointed out that Villon's ballads *Ballade des proverbes* and *Ballade des menus propres* have elements in them that help to explain the strained friendship between these two medieval writers and Villon's attempts at reconciliation. Pinkernell also reports in much detail on a very hateful rejoinder which Pierre Chevalier (15th century) wrote as a parody of Villon's *Ballade des proverbes* which helps to shed some light on why Villon and Charles d'Orléans had these personal problems. This parody of one of the best-known proverb poems of French literature is printed in its complete text together with a very detailed interpretation.

4183. Piper, Klaus. "Zum Sprachgebrauch in den Sprichwörtern und in der Trommelsprache der Ewondo und der Bulu." *Afrika und Übersee*, 72, no. 1 (1989), 1–16.

This is an anthropological study of linguistic features of the proverbs and the drum language of the Ewondo and Bulu people of the Cameroons in Western Africa. Piper bases his analysis on previously collected texts and on his own field research in this area. Citing several examples with the African original and then in German translation, Piper adds significant linguistic and cultural explanations. He also provides detailed comments on certain verbal structures and explains that there are some relationships between the language of proverbs and that of communicating by drums. Both modes of expression certainly communicate collective wisdom of an oral society that very much depends on formulaically expressed bits of social information.

4184. Piret, Michael. "Canon Hutchinson and the *Outlandish Proverbs* [of George Herbert]." *Notes and Queries*, 232, new series 24 (1987), 312–313.

Piret presents but a short note concerning the manuscript history of George Herbert's (1593–1633) early proverb collection entitled *Outlandish Proverbs* (1640) which contains 1032 foreign proverbs which Herbert had selected and translated into English from various sources, mainly from Italian, French, and Spanish. In his edition of *The Works of George Herbert* (1941), F.E. Hutchinson made an error concerning the erasure of the initials "G.H." on the title-page of one of the manuscripts. This error has been repeated in Hutchinson's reprint of 1945 and in subsequent reprints, and it is the purpose of this note to correct this mistake.

4185. Piret, Michael. "Herbert and Proverbs." *The Cambridge Quarterly*, 17, no. 3 (1988), 222–243.

In this article Piret discusses the authorship of the English proverb collection *Outlandish Proverbs* (1640) and concludes that George Herbert (1593–1633) was in fact its compiler, having translated the 1032 foreign proverbs from primarily Italian, French, and Spanish sources into English. The major portion of the article is a literary investigation of Herbert's use of proverbial language in his various prose works, including *The Country Parson* (written 1632, published 1652) and others. Piret also analyzes Herbert's innovative use of proverbs and proverbial expressions in his poems, showing that he quite often alters traditional proverbs for satirical effects. Many examples are cited in their literary context, and it is argued that Herbert is definitely part of the rich tradition of using proverbs in 17th century English literature. See also James Thorpe's similar essay (no. 2948) which Piret does not cite.

4186.   Pittaluga, Stefano. "Proverbi e facezie di Antonio Cornazzano." *Res Publica Litterarum*, 9 (1986), 231–239.

This is a literary investigation of a collection of nine short Italian novellas in verse by Antonio Cornazzano (1429–1484) entitled *De proverbiorum origine* (1503). Each of these short prose works carries a proverb as its title, and the story itself is a sensual if not erotic exemplification of the proverbial wisdom. Pittaluga cites several proverbs in context and shows how Cornazzano interprets them rather sexually to entertain his readers by this novel look at traditional wisdom. Many of the proverbs go back to classical sources, and they were also employed in Giovanni Boccaccio's (1313–1375) *Decamerone* (1348/53). These works from the 15th century based on proverbs are a clear indication that proverbs were not always interpreted as moralistic and didactic rules.

4187.   Planatscher, Franz. "'Da brat' mir doch einer einen Storch'!" *Der Sprachdienst*, 27 (1983), 52.

In this short note Planatscher explains the meaning of the German proverbial expression "Da brat' mir doch einer einen Storch!" (Go fry me a stork, i.e., that is very surprising, incredible, unbelievable, impossible, etc.). Already in the Bible (Leviticus [3. Mos.] 11,19) the meat of the stork was not to be eaten, and in the Middle Ages many superstitions became attached to this large bird, again making it impossible as a food source. Realizing that today also nobody would think of actually frying a stork, this expression has come to refer to something that is basically impossible. It is used in modern German quite frequently to express utter disbelief or suprise.

4188.   Planatscher, Franz, and Helmut Walther. "Kopf und Kragen." *Der Sprachdienst*, 29 (1985), 47–48.

The two authors analyze a number of German proverbial expressions which are based on the twin formula of "Kopf und Kragen" (head and collar). They explain that most of them have the meaning of losing one's life by having one's head cut off at the collar (neck), as was the practice in the Middle Ages. Some expressions are "Kopf und Kragen riskieren" (To risk one's life), "Es geht um Kopf und Kragen" (It is a matter of life and death), "Es kostet Kopf und Kragen" (It will cost one's life), "Sich um Kopf und Kragen bringen" (To bring an end to one's own life), etc. In the modern German mas media there now has appeared a new variant, namely "Um eigenen Kopf und Kragen reden" (To talk for one's own survival) which appears to be gaining some currency, even though it has a definite positive meaning in opposition to the traditional negative connotation of this twin formula.

4189. Pollio, Howard, Michael Fabrizi, Abigail Sills, and Michael Smith. "Need Metaphoric Comprehension Take Longer than Literal Comprehension?" *Journal of Psycholinguistic Research*, 13 (1984), 195–214.

To determine whether the comprehension of metaphors necessarily depends on a more complex process than literal comprehension, 120 subjects in six different experiments were asked to code a series of sentences into one of the following logical sentence categories: analytic, synthetic, contradictory, anomalous, and metaphoric. Prior to this task, all subjects were given practice in learning to code examples of each of the various categories. Results of the experiments revealed few systematic differences among the various categories in reaction time and a high degree of consistency in coding patterns across both the learning and reaction time phases of the psychological experiments. The authors conclude that metaphoric recognition (including proverbs, proverbial expressions, idioms, etc.) need not be conceptualized as depending on a more inferential level of semantic processing than literal recognition and that future theories of metaphor comprehension must be more context-sensitive. Numerous statistical tables, a useful bibliography (pp. 213–214), and an English abstract (p. 195) are included.

4190. Pottier Navarro, Huguette. "Paraphrase et parasynonymie dans les proverbes espagnols et français." *Contrastes*, 3 (1982), 17–31.

The author presents a comparative analysis of a number of Spanish and French proverbs, starting her remarks with a definition of proverbs from a linguistic point of view. She then explains that even though the two languages often have equivalent proverbs, they might take on different meanings in the two cultures and in specific contexts. As far as equivalent proverbs are concerned, it is shown that they might in fact be identical or differ to certain degrees as far as vocabulary, structure, metaphor, etc. are concerned. All of this creates great difficulties for translators who wish to find close equivalents in the target language. For proverbs with origins in classical antiquity or the Bible this is relatively easy, since most of them have been translated word-for-word into the European languages. But the problem becomes quite vexing when a translator deals with regional proverbs that have no precise equivalents in the other languages.

4191. Prager, Carolyn. "'If I be Devil': English Renaissance Response to the Proverbial and Ecumenial Ethiopian." *Journal of Medieval and Renaissance Studies*, 17, no. 2 (1987), 257–279.

This is a fascinating literary study of the use of the proverbs "Can the Ethiopian change his skin?" (see Jeremiah 13,23) and "To wash an Ethiopian/blackamoor is to labor in vain" in 17 English Renaissance dramas by such authors as Thomas Kyd (1558–1594), Robert Greene (1558–1592), Thomas Dekker (1570?–1632), John Marston (1575?–1634), John Fletcher (1579?–1625), Ben Jonson (1572–1637), Philip Massinger (1583–1640), and others. Prager cites numerous examples in their dramatic context, showing how this old and unfortunate stereotype is used to express racial prejudices based on color of skin. There is no doubt that these proverbs as well as their variants and mere allusions played a significant role in perpetuating the derogatory meaning of blackness in this period. The author successfully explains that the proverbial metaphor was used for venting social, political, and moral frustrations without paying attention to its dangerous racial implications. A short discussion of the early references to this proverb by Aesop and in the Old Testament of the Bible is included, and the 22 notes include useful bibliographical information.

4192. Pratelli, Rufin. "La représentation du corps dans les dictons, locutions et proverbes en usage dans la région florentine." *La représentation du corps dans la culture italienne.* Ed. Maryse Jeuland-Meynaud. Aix-en-Provence: Université de Provence, 1982. 29–41.

Pratelli gives a detailed account of Italian proverbs, proverbial expressions, and proverbial comparisons current in the Tuscany region of Florence in Italy. All of the examples have to do with the human body, i.e., with the head, hand, finger, foot, etc. The author explains that many of these fixed phrases do in fact refer to gestures, and it is this interrelationship of gestures and proverbial language which indicates a kind of a "body language" with which people communicate their feelings, emotions, desires, etc. Some of the expressions are rather humorous and also somewhat suggestive, but altogether they are metaphors to express human behavior in traditional folk speech.

4193. Predota, Stanislaw. "Proba porownania przyslow niderlandzkich i polskich." *Sprawozdania Wroclawskiego Towarzystwa Naukowego,* 39 (1984), 7–9.

This is a short report by the leading Polish paremiologist Stanislaw Predota concerning a research project about Dutch and Polish proverbs. It is explained that the two languages and cultures have a considerable number of proverbs in common. Most of these identical equivalents are, in fact, loan translations from classical Greek and Latin or from Biblical proverbs. Some other texts have only partial equivalents, i.e., they have at least some words, the structure, or the metaphor in common. Finally there are also those texts which are so indigenous to one or the other national language that there are no equivalents at all. Predota cites several examples in this comparative study, and he includes precise statistical information about the level of similarity between Dutch and Polish proverbs.

4194. Predota, Stanislaw. "Parallelen tussen Nederlandse en Poolse spreekwoorden." *Jaarboek van de Stichting Instituut voor Nederlandse Lexicologie,* no volume given (1986), 47–54.

This is a slightly expanded Dutch version of the previous paper (see no. 4193), once again comparing 1500 proverbs of the

Dutch and Polish languages. It is shown that 70% of the Dutch proverbs have complete semantic equivalents in Polish, and 37% have the same metaphor. Predota explains that the complete identity between some Dutch and Polish proverbs is due to their common classical or Biblical sources. It is a well established fact that many of these older texts were loan translated into the European languages. But there are, of course, also those examples that have only partial or no equivalents at all in the two compared languages and cultures. Many examples are cited, and the author also includes statistical information.

4195. Predota, Stanislaw. "Polnische Entsprechungen der Redensart 'Eulen nach Athen tragen'." *Proverbium*, 3 (1986), 233–241.

Predota presents an interesting list of Polish proverbs and proverbial expressions with the meaning of doing something superfluous or unnecessary. The classical example is, of course, "Nosic sowy do Aten" (To carry owls to Athens; or in German: Eulen nach Athen tragen). However, this phrase is not in current use in Poland any longer. Instead there are about two dozen fixed phrases which are based on forest, water, and fire metaphors that have taken the place of the classical expression. Predota cites these examples with historical dates and paremiographical sources, and he also checked with native speakers which of these phrases are in common use in Poland today. See also Wolfgang Mieder (no. 3871), Cesar Tabarcea (no. 4462), and Fionnuala Williams (no. 4561) for German, Rumanian, and Irish parallels.

4196. Predota, Stanislaw. "Zur niederländischen Sprichwörterlexikographie im 20. Jahrhundert." *Acta Universitatis Wratislaviensis*, no. 942, *Neerlandica Wratislaviensis*, 3 (1986), 103–119.

This is a major review article concerning Dutch paremiographical dictionaries of the 20th century. Predota begins his survey with a short statement that the tradition of proverb collections in the Netherlands goes back to the 15th century. He then cites 10 major collections of the present century, including such standard works as F.A. Stoett,

Nederlandsche spreekwoorden, spreekwijzen, uitdrukkingen en gezegden (1901), K. ter Laan, *Nederlandse spreekwoorden, spreuken en zegswijzen* (1950) and C. Kryskamp, *Apologische spreekwoorden* (1947). The latter collection is a major work on wellerisms which is of much importance for the historical and comparative study of this proverbial genre. Predota includes short descriptions of each collection and analyzes their lexicographical set-up, their content, and their scholarly value.

4197. Predota, Stanislaw. "Ergänzungen zur Bibliographie der polnischen Parömiologie des 19. und 20. Jahrhunderts." *Proverbium*, 4 (1987), 345–360.

Anybody interested in Polish paremiography and paremiology must definitely consult this extremely important bibliography covering major Polish research results from the 19th and 20th centuries. Altogether Predota includes 116 references, among them some significant publications by renowned scholars like Samuel Adalberg, Stanislaw Baba, Jan Stanislaw Bystron, Iwona Frackiewicz, Stanislaw Predota, Leon Sternbach, and Stanislaw Swirko. For Julian Krzyzanowski (1892–1976) Predota includes 24 references alone, a clear indication that Krzyzanowski was Poland's greatest proverb scholar in the 20th century. There are no annotations, but the author of this bibliography has selected extremely important contributions by Polish scholars to Polish, Slavic and international proverb studies.

4198. Predota, Stanislaw. "Zalozenia *Niderlandzko-polskiego slownika frazeologicznego.*" *Sprawozdania Wroclawskiego Towarzystwa Naukowego*, 42 A (1987), 39–45.

Predota reports on a large research project concerning 5000 Dutch and Polish phraseological units, including proverbs, proverbial expressions, proverbial comparisons, idioms, etc. He discusses the different types of fixed phrases and explains the lexicographical problems involved in organizing such a comparative corpus of texts. A particularly vexing problem is the question of how to deal with lexical, structural, and semantic variants. Predota cites numerous examples to illustrate his classification method for so many phraseological units from two quite different languages and cultures. The result of this major task will be a comprehensive dictionary entitled *Niderlandzko– polskiego slownika frazeologicznego* that will be of special use for foreign language instruction and translators.

4199. Predota, Stanislaw. "Zur konfrontativen Analyse deutscher und niederländischer Sprichwörter." *Zur jüngeren Geschichte der deutschen Sprache.* Ed. Rudolf Große. Leipzig: Karl-Marx-Universität, 1987. 96–104.

The author compares many German and Dutch proverbs and discusses the different levels of equivalencies in the proverbial speech of these two closely related languages and cultures. Predota explains that there are semantic, metaphorical, stylistic, and structural similarities, and he also points out that many of the texts have identical versions in both languages. These parallel proverbs often go back to classical or Biblical sources and were loan translated into Dutch and German. But there are also those identical proverbs which were translated from one of the two modern languages into the other. It is also shown that there are those texts which have at least partial equivalents in the other language. Of course there exist also some proverbs that simply are so indigenous to one of the two cultures that there are no equivalent texts.

4200. Predota, Stanislaw. "Over de lexicografische grondbeginselen van het *Klein Nederlands-Pools spreekwoordenboek.*" *Acta Universitatis Wratislaviensis*, no. 1130, *Neerlandica Wratislaviensia*, 4 (1989), 171–181; also in German translation as "Zu den lexikographischen Grundprinzipien des *Kleinen deutsch-polnischen Sprichwörterbuches.*" *Sprichwörter und Redensarten im interkulturellen Vergleich.* Eds. Annette Sabban and Jan Wirrer. Opladen: Westdeutscher Verlag, 1991. 28–36.

This is a report concerning the lexicographical problems that arose during Predota's work on his *Maly niemiecko-polski slownik przyslow/Kleines deutsch-polnisches Sprichwörterbuch* (1992). In this dictionary of German-Polish proverbs the author has assembled 2000 well-known German proverbs with their Polish equivalents or translations. Only those proverbs were registered for which Predota could establish a high frequency in today's German language. The texts are arranged alphabetically according to key-words, and an additional index of other major nouns and verbs is attached as well. In addition to the basic proverbs the author lists major variants, and a few dialect proverbs, wellerisms, and modern "Antisprichwörter" (antiproverbs) are also registered in this useful proverb dictionary.

4201. Predota, Stanislaw. "Zum modernen parömiologischen Handapparat." *Acta Universitatis Wratislaviensis*, no. 1061, *Anglica Wratislaviensia*, 17 (1991), 105–114.

In this survey article Predota presents some important paremiological publications of the 20th century, arguing that they belong to the basic research tools in the field of international proverb scholarship. He starts with some descriptive and evaluative remarks concerning the following three comprehensive studies: Friedrich Seiler, *Deutsche Sprichwörterkunde* (1922; see no. 1701); Archer Taylor, *The Proverb* (1931; no. 1858); and Lutz Röhrich and Wolfgang Mieder, *Sprichwort* (1977; no. 1582). Next the author discusses six major bibliographies: Ignace Bernstein, *Catalogue des livres parémiologiques* (1900; no. 150); Wilfrid Bonser, *Proverb Literature* (1930; no. 190); Otto Moll, *Sprichwörterbibliographie* (1958; no. 1302); and Wolfgang Mieder's *International Bibliography of Explanatory Essays on Individual Proverbs and Proverbial Expressions* (1977; no. 1253); *Proverbs in Literature* (1978; no. 1262); and *International Proverb Scholarship: An Annotated Bibliography* (1982; no. 3856). This is followed by a short analysis of seven essay volumes: Archer Taylor, *Selected Writings on Proverbs*, ed. by W. Mieder (1975; no. 1243); W. Mieder's *Das Sprichwort in unserer Zeit* (1975; no. 1242); *Deutsche Sprichwörter in Literatur, Politik, Presse und Werbung* (1983; no. 3860); *Ergebnisse der Sprichwörterforschung* (1978; no. 1258); *D e u t s c h e Sprichwörterforschung des 19. Jahrhunderts* (1984; no. 3869); W. Mieder and Alan Dundes, *The Wisdom of Many* (1981; no. 1284); and Peter Grzybek and Wolfgang Eismann, *Semiotische Studien zum Sprichwort* (1984; no. 3538). Finally Predota also includes valuable comments concerning the journal *Proverbium*, 25 issues (1965–1975); its successor *Proverbium Paratum*, 4 vols. (1980–1989); and the new *Proverbium: Yearbook of International Proverb Scholarship*, 1ff. (1984ff.).

4202. Predota, Stanislaw. "Zur niederländisch-polnischen Parömiographie und Phraseographie." *Acta Universitatis Wratislaviensis*, no. 1299, *Neerlandica Wratislaviensia*, 5 (1991), 235–247.

In this article Predota describes the lexicographical problems that he encountered in putting together his *Slownik przyslow niderlandzko-polski maly/Klein Nederlands-Pools spreekwoordenboek* (1986). He points out that he chose 1500 truly well-known and frequently used Dutch proverbs for this comparative dictionary of Dutch and Polish proverbial speech. The texts are arranged alphabetically according to key-words, and an index of additional nouns and verbs is attached as well. For some Dutch texts Predota is able to include variants before citing Polish equivalents or translations. For those proverbs that go back to classical or Biblical sources the two languages have identical proverbs due to the fact that they are precise loan translations. But for many texts there are only partial equivalents in which the metaphors and vocabulary are quite different from each other. Finally, there exist also those texts for which the Polish language has no eqivalents at all.

4203. Priest, John F. "'The Dog in the Manger'. In Quest of a Fable." *Classical Journal*, 81, no. 1 (1985), 49–58.

Priest gives a detailed philological history of the fable and the proverb of "The dog in the manger." showing that it is most likely older than its account in Aesop (late 7th/early 6th cent. B.C.). The author cites Near Eastern variants, and he also traces the history of the fable in classical Greek and Latin sources. References are made to allusions to this fable or its shortened proverb in the Bible, and Priest shows how this text was picked up by medieval compilers of fables. Many variants are discussed, and it is argued that the fable probably goes back to Aramaic wisdom literature. The article is a splendid example concerning the interrelationship of fables and proverbs. But see also Gyula

Moravcsik's earlier study (no. 1312) of this fable and proverb which Priest does not refer to in his article.

4204. Profantová, Zuzana. "K poetike pranostik." *Slovensky národopis,* 29, no. 4 (1981), 530–536; also in German translation as "Zur Poesie der Bauernregeln und Wettersegen in der Slowakei," *Proverbium Paratum,* 3 (1982), 251–258.

The author analyzes numerous Slovakian weather proverbs of which most are in fact superstitions and prophecies based on proverbial structures. Profantová studies in particular the poetic form of these so-called proverbs, indicating that they employ such stylistic features as metaphor, metonymy, personification, synecdoche, hyperbole, rhyme, etc. She also indicates that almost all of the texts have a rhyme, thus making the sayings more memorable. As far as the function of these old expressions is concerned, the author believes that they used to be mythological or magical ways of interpreting the world. Many of the examples are quite old, as can be seen from their archaic vocabulary. Russian (pp. 535–536) and German (p. 536) abstracts are attached.

4205. Profantová, Zuzana. "Antiteza: Funkcny prostriedok vyjadrenia patriarchalno-rodinnych vzt'ahov v slovenskych prisloviach." *Slovensky národopis,* 31, nos. 3–4 (1983), 575–581.

In this article Profantová examines the antithetical nature of many Slovakian proverbs that deal with patriarchal family relationships. It is argued that the use of antithesis in these proverbs is a way to express the problems that exist in the real world. In addition these proverbs employ such stylistic features as metaphor, metonymy, parallelism, etc. Citing numerous examples the author explains that they contain rich cultural information concerning traditional values. These proverbs are normative statements of social behavior and worldview, and they certainly have played an important role in maintaining a solid patriarchal family structure in Czechoslovakia. Detailed German (pp. 579–580) and Russian (pp. 580–581) summaries are provided.

4206. Profantová, Zuzana. "Pavol Dobsinsky a slovenská paremiológia." *Slovensky národopis,* 34, no. 3 (1986), 391–397.

The author presents a detailed description of Pavol Dobsinsky's (1828–1885) work as a 19th century Slovakian folklorist who in 1863 called for the serious collection of folk narratives, folk songs, proverbs, proverbial expressions, etc. Profantová explains that this scholar was interested in folk speech from an ethnographical and lexicographical point of view. Having collected many Slovakian proverbs for his archive, Dobsinsky had to deal with the problem of classifying his materials. He also was interested in the content, context, and function of proverbs, emphasizing throughout his scholarly career that traditional phraseology is of great importance for historical lexicographers and folklorists. Russian (p. 396) and German (p. 397) summaries are included.

4207. Profantová, Zuzana. *Kulturno-historicke a sucasné spolocenské kontexty pranostik. Analyza a interpretácia zánru (Autoreferát dizertácie.* Bratislava: Slovenská Akadémia Vied, 1987. 22 pp.

This is a published summary of the contents of Zuzana Profantová's dissertation on the cultural and historical aspects of Slovakian weather signs or proverbs. Most of these texts are actually weather superstitions or prophecies, but they have usually been considered as sayings based on proverbial structures. The author gives a short discussion of the scholarship regarding this particular genre of folk speech, and she then investigates the form, language, meaning, style, and structure of many Slovakian examples. She also treats these so-called weather proverbs from a functional and semiotic point of view. It is argued that while these old weather and planting rules might be based on mythological and magical interpretations of the environment, they nevertheless contain certain amounts of realistic wisdom. A short bibliography (pp. 3–4) and a Russian abstract (pp. 21–22) are included.

4208. Profantová, Zuzana. "Zbojnicka tematika v prislovnej tradicii na slovensku." *Slovensky národopis,* 36, nos. 3–4 (1988), 519–525.

Profantová investigates numerous Slovakian proverbs which contain the word "zbojnik" (rogue) or the name "Janosik" of a Slovakian folk hero. She begins her article with an etymological and historical analysis of these two terms and then cites a number of examples. She explains that many of them are linked to traditional folk narratives, and she provides detailed cultural explanations to clarify the meaning of these old proverbs and proverbial expressions. Some of them are analyzed in the context of oral narratives and literary works, enabling the author to discuss their function as "liberating" wisdom along the lines of English sayings around the figure of Robin Hood. A useful bibliography (pp. 524–525) is attached.

4209. Profantová, Zuzana. "Socialna tvorivost a prislovia." *Slovensky národopis*, 37, no. 4 (1989), 505–510.

In this article Profantová analyzes the social values and attitudes expressed in Slovakian proverbs. She argues that proverbs play a major role in the socialization of the individual members of any given society. Proverbs contain much traditional and cultural wisdom, and they are based on the collective experiences and observations of generations of people. On the one hand proverbs express the social ideal, but on the other hand they also indicate clearly the imperfect social reality. Proverbs are primarily normative and function in a didactic way to maintain traditional social values or to improve the individual's life in the society as a whole. They continue to regulate and direct social behavior, but their wisdom is also being questioned in certain situations and contexts in the modern Czechoslovakian society. Russian (pp. 508–509) and German (pp. 509–510) summaries are provided.

4210. Prokhorov, Iu. E. "Iz istorii opisaniia natsional'no-kul'turnogo komponenta semantiki russkikh poslovits, pogovorok i krylatykh vyrazhenii." *Slovari i lingvostranovedenie.* Ed. E.M. Vereshchagina. Moskva: Russkii iazyk, 1982. 137–142.

This is a short article investigating the national and cultural components that give Russian proverbs their specific meaning. The author realizes that international proverbs that were translated from classical and Biblical sources into Russian do not indicate any particularly Russian attitudes or beliefs. However, those proverbs which are indigenous to the Russian people can be regarded as expressions of a typically Russian worldview. Prokhorov cites numerous examples and includes linguistic, historical, and cultural explanations that show how these proverbs reflect Russian attitudes concerning social and human matters. A bibliography (pp. 141–142) referring primarily to major Russian proverb collections is attached.

4211.   Puhvel, Martin. "Chaucer's *Troilus and Criseyde* III.890; V.505; V.1174–5." *Explicator*, 42, no. 4 (1984), 7–9.

The author attempts an explanation of the proverbial phrase "haselwodes shaken" in Geoffrey Chaucer's (1340?–1400) *Troilus and Criseyde* (1385). He argues that other references to the hazel or hazelwood in Chaucer's works appear to have the meaning of incredulity or derision. It is also shown that the hazel in early folklore sources has miraculous virtues. Thus the phrase "haselwodes shaken" could mean "what a miracle you're coming up with." Puhvel concludes his short study by stating that there might have been a longer proverb current in medieval England that was the basis for this short phrase, but this particular text has not been recorded thus far.

4212.   Purohit, V.P., R.A. Silas, and R.D. Gaur. "Plants in the Folk Songs, Proverbs and Folk Tales of Raath Zone (Pauri Garhwal)." *Eastern Anthropologist*, 38, no. 1 (1985), 33–44.

In this study the three authors investigate the references to various types of plants in the folk songs, proverbs, and folk tales of the Raath district, a remote part of Garhwal Himalaya in India. While the majority of the texts illustrates plants in folk songs, the authors have included a few proverbs which contain the names of indigenous plants (see pp. 42–43). It is interesting to note that these texts are cited in the form of questions or riddles to see whether someone knows the plants being referred to by a speaker. The authors explain that the vegetational surroundings are of great importance for the livelihood of the people of this area, and it is for this reason that the flora plays such a major role in the folklore of these people. The proverbs are cited in their original dialect together with English translations and ethnographical explanations.

R

4213. Racy, Jihad. "Music and Dance in Lebanese Proverbs." *Asian Music,* 17 (1985), 83–97.

Racy begins with some general remarks concerning Lebanese proverbs and then considers particularly those texts that relate to music and dance. He divides his many examples into four groups: (1) proverbs on singers and singing, (2) proverbs dealing with instruments and instrumentalists, (3) proverbs relating to wedding festivities, and (4) proverbs referring to dances and dancing. Each text is cited in transliterated Lebanese with English translations. The author also provides historical and cultural explanations which help to understand the metaphorical meaning of these Arabic texts. Many of the proverbs are quite old and are starting to drop out of use due to social changes. A small bibliography (pp. 96–97) is attached.

4214. Radwan, Kamal. "Phraseologismen. Ein Forschungsbericht." *Sprache im technischen Zeitalter,* no. 96 (1985), 278–279.

This is a short review article concerning the work on phraseology that has been going on in the Department of German at the University of Cairo in Egypt. Radwan mentions in particular the dissertations of Hilda Matta (see no. 3824) and Mona Noueshi (no. 4041) who have dealt with the problem of translating German and Arabic proverbs and proverbial expressions. It is shown that while there are some equivalent expressions in these two languages, there are also many for which a translator has to find phrases which have different metaphors but at least similar meanings. The author also mentions that the function, style, and syntax cause additional translation problems. This situation will improve when more comparative studies have been conducted that might eventually result in a much-needed German-Arabic phraseological dictionary.

4215. Rainsh, Karina. "K voprosu ob otrazhenii vo frazeologii kommunikativnogo mimikozhestovogo povedeniia." *Linguistische Studien*, series A, Arbeitsberichte, no. 120 (1984), 121–137.

The author presents an important analysis of phraseological units that are based on gestures. She explains that such expressions go back to old gestures which over time have taken on metaphorical meaning. Citing numerous Russian examples, she is able to show that diachronic research based on linguistics, folklore, and cultural history is necessary to explain the image and meaning of such phrases. It is amazing to see how many proverbs, proverbial expressions, and other phrases contain gestures. Some of this mimicry is rather international, but there are also those proverbial gestures which are known only in the Slavic world or specifically in Russia itself. Much more work needs to be done on this fascinating aspect of phraseology, and Rainsh includes at least a short bibliography (p. 137) concerning Soviet scholarship.

4216. Rath, Banamali. "Folk Culture as Reflected in Oriya Proverbs." *Folk Culture I: Folk Culture and Literature*. Ed. Chittaranjan Das. Cuttack/Orissa: Institute of Oriental and Orissan Studies, 1984. 20–23.

This is an anthropological study of the proverbs from Oriya in India. The author begins with a general discussion of proverbs, explaining that the worldview and culture of the Oriya people is expressed in them. This is followed by some historical and cultural explanations concerning these inhabitants from India. The point is made that most of the proverbs contain references to religion and philosophy. Numerous examples are cited in the Oriya language with English translations. Rath has divided these texts into such categories as faith in God, jurisprudence, reason, envy, greediness, pretension, opportunism, etc. For some of the proverbs the author has provided short comments explaining their meaning, use, and function in oral communication.

4217. Ray, Robert H. "John Dunton and the Origin of 'A Penny Saved Is a Penny Earned'." *Notes and Queries*, 229, new series 31 (1984), 372–373.

>   A short note explaining that Edward Ravenscroft's (1650?– 1697) *Canterbury Guests* (1695) does not contain the first printed version of the proverb "A penny saved is a penny got." Ray points out that variants were recorded already earlier in the 17th century, notably by the paremiographer George Herbert (1593– 1633). The proverb in this precise wording was cited four years before Ravenscroft by John Dunton (1659–1733) in his *A Voyage Round the World* (1691). Ray feels that until an earlier reference is found it is John Dunton who should be credited as the first author to have cited this common variant of a very popular English proverb.

4218. Raylor, Tim. "The Source of 'He that Fights and Runs away, [May Live to Fight another Day']." *Notes and Queries*, 231, new series 33 (1986), 465–466.

>   Raylor points out that F.P. Wilson's *Oxford Dictionary of English Proverbs* (1970) is incorrect in citing the *Musarum Deliciae* (1656) as a source for the English proverb "He that runs away, may live to fight another day." The proverb is not to be found in the first (1655) or second edition (1656) of this work. In fact, Raylor argues that the proverb did not exist in this wording in the 17th century at all. He explains how this mistake might have come about through a series of false assumptions. Be that as it may, the mistake should be corrected in the next edition of the standard English proverb collection mentioned above.

4219. Raymond, Alain. "Essai d'étude des présuppositions pragmatiques des expressions idiomatiques allemandes." *Europhras 88. Phraséologie Contrastive. Actes du Colloque International Klingenthal-Strasbourg, 12–16 mai 1988*. Ed. Gertrud Gréciano. Strasbourg: Université des Sciences Humaines, 1989. 327–335.

>   The author investigates numerous German phraseological units which express a reprimand. Citing a number of examples he shows the importance of the linguistic, social, and cultural context for a proper understanding of such proverbial

expressions. This is particularly evident when a translator has to deal with such phrases. Only if he/she has a sound understanding of the meaning of the phrase in its particular context will a proper translation be possible. The problem is increased in the case of phrases that reflect certain historical events or allusions. For many German expressions the French language has identical equivalents, usually when the texts go back to classical sources or the Bible. However, it is often quite difficult to find French equivalents for German idiomatic expressions which are only current in the German society.

4220. Rechtsiegel, Eugenie. "Zum Begriff der Stabilität in der Phraseologie." *Linguistische Studien*, series A, Arbeitsberichte, no. 95 (1982), 62–76.

    This is an important theoretical discussion of the concept of "stability" in the study of phraseology. Rechtsiegel begins her article with a review of previous scholarship on the fixed form of phraseological units. It is shown that stability can refer to form, structure, language, meaning, etc. In the second half of the article she cites a number of Slavic examples with German translations to explain the stability of fixed phrases while at the same time showing that they might be changed under certain circumstances. It would certainly be a mistake to argue that phraseological units are never changed. People alter them quite often during speech acts in order to express innovative ideas, to add satire, irony or humor to a statement, or to play with such fixed language for various reasons. A useful bibliography (pp. 73–76) is provided.

4221. Rechtsiegel, Eugenie. "Phraseologismen im Text in konfrontativer Sicht (am Material des Polnischen und Deutschen)." *Linguistische Studien*, series A, Arbeitsberichte, no. 120 (1984), 175–200.

    In this article Rechtsiegel deals with the difficulty of translating phraseological units from Polish into German. She begins with some general remarks concerning the fact that fixed phrases are often varied in literary or journalistic texts. Such innovative use of traditional phrases adds to the difficulty of providing accurate translations. In the second half of the article Rechtsiegel cites numerous examples and shows that only for some of them can precise equivalents be found in the target language. At times only partial equivalents exist, and there are also those instances where the translator has to find a similar expression or be satisfied with a word for word translation of the original. Translating texts which are based on joining two or more proverbial expressions into puns are particularly hard if not impossible to translate. A valuable bibliography (pp. 198–200) about translation problems of fixed phrases is included.

4222. Reiman, Jeffrey, and Ernest Van den Haag. "On the Common Saying that 'It is Better that Ten Guilty Persons Escape than that One Innocent Suffer'—Pro and Con." *Social Philosophy and Policy,* 7, no. 2 (1990), 226–248.

This is a philosophical and ethical discussion of the legal proverb "It is better that ten guilty persons escape than that one innocent suffer." The authors begin their study with an historical analysis of this moral maxim, and they then present several arguments for punishment constraint, primarily from the point of view of retributivism, utility, and social contract. This is followed by arguments against punishment constraint, stressing the importance of punishing the guilty and upholding penal justice. It is concluded that neither retributivist, utilitarian, nor contractarian theory justifies the punishment constraint. Innocent people are more protected without the punishment constraint than with it—less protected from punishment, but much more protected from crime. A net gain in protection is likely if standards of proof are lowered somewhat but remain reasonable. Since the punishment constraint is unjustifiable, so is the current requirement of proof of guilt "beyond a reasonable doubt." Clear and convincing evidence should suffice for a guilty verdict, which should require only a two-thirds majority of jurors. The 32 notes include useful references to legal proverbs and their social value.

4223. Resnick, David A. "A Developmental Study of Proverb Comprehension." *Journal of Psycholinguistic Research,* 11 (1982), 521–538.

This study investigates the development of proverb comprehension in children (grades three to seven) and attempts to account for that development by examining the sequential emergence of specific underlying abilities, especially story matching, transfer of relations, desymbolization, proverb matching, and paraphrase. A rich variety of cognitive and linguistic phenomena are involved: the transition from the concrete to the abstract mode, from concrete to formal thought, and from concrete to metaphorical symbolism. Ten English proverbs were used to test the developmental basis of proverb comprehension. It was found that the structure of the proverbs did not constitute a major source of proverb difficulty, while intelligence is an important factor. Resnick closes his report on this psychological proverbs test by wondering to which extent the amount and quality of social experience or social perception might affect proverb comprehension. Five statistical tables, a small bibliograpohy (pp. 537–538) and an English abstract (p. 521) are included.

4224. Ressel, Gerhard and Svetlana. "Zum Wortschatz einiger Sprichwörter und Redensarten aus Istrien und von den Kvarner Inseln." *Festschrift für Herbert Bräuer*. Eds. Reinhold Olesch and Hans Rothe. Köln: Böhlau, 1986. 389–406.

This is a detailed analysis of the vocabulary of 726 Istrian proverbs which were collected at the end of the 19th century on the peninsula of Istria and several islands in the Adriatic Sea. The texts are basically Serbo-Croatian, but they certainly exhibit distinct linguistic peculiarities. The authors comment on the syntax, structure, and poetic form of these proverbs, but they are particularly interested in the use of certain nouns. They are able to divide all of the texts into 21 groups according to the themes suggested by these nouns, i.e. man, woman, nutrition, medicine, nature, plants, animals, sea, occupation, clothing, money, measurements, family, language, belief, etc. While many examples are cited, it is regrettable that the authors have provided no translations. A short bibliography (p. 406) is attached.

4225. Ressel, Svetlana and Gerhard. "Zur inhaltlichen und sprachlichen Struktur bulgarischer Sprichwörter." *Einundzwanzig Beiträge zum II. internationalen Bulgaristik-Kongreß in Sofia 1986.* Eds. Wolfgang Gesemann, Kyrill Haralampieff and Helmut Schaller. Neuried: Hieromymus, 1986. 223–252.

This article contains a solid introduction to Bulgarian proverbs. The authors begin with some general comments regarding the origin, use, and function of proverbs, and they also discuss the difference between indigenous and foreign proverbs, the latter having entered the Bulgarian language as loan translations from proverbs of classical antiquity, the Bible, or neighboring cultures. This is followed by a content analysis with special emphasis on proverbial comparisons. The second half of the article deals with such matters as semantics, metaphor, personification, irony, brevity, antithesis, tautology, form, style, etc. Many examples are cited in transliterated Bulgarian, but the authors unfortunately do not provide any translations. A useful bibliography for Bulgarian proverb collections and studies (pp. 251–152) is attached.

4226. Reulos, Michel. "Un humaniste s'intéresse aux dits et façon de parler français: Les deux recueils de proverbes de Charles de Bovelles." *Actes du Colloque International tenu à Noyon les 14–16 septembre 1979. Charles de Bovelles en son cinquième centenaire 1479–1979.* Ed. Guy Trédaniel. Paris: Éditions de la Maisnie, 1981. 231–236.

A short article drawing attention to two 16th century proverb collections by the French mystic and humanist scholar Charles de Bovelles (1470?–1553?). His *Vulgarium proverbiorum libri tres* (1531) contains early French proverbs with Latin translations to which Bovelles has added valuable commentaries concerning the interrelationship of philosophical and popular wisdom. The collection *Proverbes français* (1557) presents only French proverbs and again is a valuable document of early proverb interpretations by a leading humanist. Reulos cites a number of examples and points out that the proverbs deal with various aspects of social life, philosophy, nature, law, etc. For a more detailed analysis of the Latin collection see Pierre Quillet (no. 1488) which Reulos does not cite.

4227. Reuter, O.R. *Proverbs, Proverbial Sentences and Phrases in Thomas Deloney's Works.* Helsinki: The Finnish Society of Sciences and Letters, 1986. 146 pp.

Reuter's book represents a significant study of the proverbial language contained in the works of Thomas Deloney (1543?–1600), a silk weaver by profession whose prose narratives are characterized by the vivid and idiomatic style of everyday language among the Elizabethan working classes. Reuter includes an introduction (pp. 4–33) that presents a short biographical sketch on Deloney and discusses the frequency, use, function, content, and themes of the proverbs in four major prose stories. While the author keeps his literary interpretation of the proverbs to a minimum, he presents the paremiographer with an extremely important annotated list of 486 proverbial statements from Deloney's works. For about 130 texts Reuter was unable to find parallels in other writers or proverb collections, and these texts will be of help in updating major English proverb collections. The valuable proverb index (pp. 34–129) is arranged alphabetically according to key-words, and a word index (pp. 132–146) catalogues additional key-words for each text. A short bibliography (pp. 130–131) is included as well.

4228. Reuter, O.R. "Some Notes on Thomas Deloney's Indebtedness to Shakespeare." *Neuphilologische Mitteilungen,* 87 (1986), 255–261.

In this article Reuter proves that Thomas Deloney (1543?–1600) was a close reader and a great admirer and imitator of William Shakespeare (1564–1616). By careful textual comparisons Reuter is able to show that Deloney cites numerous passages out of Shakespeare's plays *Venus and Adonis* (1593) and *The Rape of Lucrece* (1594). Contrasting the texts by these two authors it becomes clear that Deloney also borrowed proverbial passages from Shakespeare for his prose narratives. Some of these proverbs and proverbial expressions he obviously knew from oral speech as well, but the similarity between Shakespeare's use of this proverbial language and Deloney's texts leaves hardly any doubt that he made liberal use of Shakespeare's dramatic dialogues.

4229. Rey, Alain. "Les implications théoriques d'un dictionnaire phraséologique." *La locution. Actes du colloque international Université McGill, Montréal, 15–16 octobre 1984.* Eds. Giuseppe Di Stefano and Russell G. McGillivray. Montréal: Éditions CERES, 1984. 119–133.

This is a rather general article concerning the theoretical implications of a phraseological dictionary. Rey begins with a short survey of some earlier French proverb dictionaries and then adds some thoughts on the purpose and structure of phraseological dictionaries without any reference to the considerable theoretical scholarship on this matter. He points out that there are morphological, lexical, metaphorical, and semantic problems that need to be overcome when cataloguing phraseological units in a dictionary. Lexicographers and phraseologists also need to ask themselves for whom and for what purpose they assemble such dictionaries. This will lead to such important questions as whether contextualized examples should be added, whether stylistic levels should be indicated, whether parallels from other languages should be included, etc. The truly valuable phraseological dictionaries should address as many of these aspects as possible.

4230. Reye, Hans. "'La belle cage ne nourrit pas l'oiseau'. Frankreichs Tiersprichwörter—ein belebendes Sprachelement." *Französisch heute*, 18, no. 4 (1987), 317–322.

This is a general linguistic and cultural survey of French proverbs, proverbial expressions, and proverbial comparisons based on various animals. Many of the texts refer to such common animals as cats, dogs, wolves, cows, fish, insects, etc. Reye explains how this proverbial language expresses general folk wisdom, peasant life, social attitudes, stereotypes, humor, etc. For some expressions the author includes English, German, and Spanish equivalents, clearly illustrating that some phrases are internationally disseminated. This is the case particularly for those texts which have been translated from early Greek and

Latin sources or from the Bible. But there are also those examples which appear to be indigenous to the French language and which have only a limited geographical distribution.

4231. Rezus, Petru. "Consideratii despre geneza si culegerea proverbelor." *Proverbium Dacoromania*, 2 (1987), 3–6.

In this short and general article Rezus considers the origin and collection of proverbs citing Rumanian examples. He states that proverbs are often elliptical and metaphorical statements that express moral ideas based on common experience. They contain ethical and social wisdom in popular language, and the fact that many of them are short and rhymed makes them memorable and repeatable. While it is easy to recognize proverbs as such in actual proverb collections, it is much more difficult to spot them in contextualized oral speech or printed books, magazines, etc. When introductory formulas are used, this task is somewhat easier, but it usually takes someone interested in proverbial language to recognize those texts that might be cited only in a truncated form. A French summary (p. 6) is attached.

4232. Rezus, Petru. "Arhetipuri paremiologice." *Proverbium Dacoromania*, 4 (1989), 31–34.

Rezus argues that especially the very ancient proverbs might be looked at as paremiological archetypes. Many of these Greek, Latin, or Biblical proverbs have been translated into numerous languages and have remained current in the different languages and cultures for many centuries. They are archetypical statements concerning human nature, animals, behavior, belief, etc. Rezus cites a number of Rumanian examples of such "basic" proverbs, and he points out that some of the newer proverbs might also take on such universal character. There appears to be no doubt that some very popular proverbs express basic human character traits. A French summary (p. 34) is provided.

4233. Richards, David. "Owe l'esin òrò: Proverbs Like Horses: Wole Soyinka's *Death and the King's Horseman.*" *The Journal of Commonwealth Literature*, 19 (1984), 86–97.

This is a literary proverb investigation of the play *Death and the King's Horseman* (1975) by the Nigerian writer Wole Soyinka (1934–). Richards analyzes in particular the proverbial speech of the protagonist Elesin Oba and shows through many contextualized examples how he manipulates this traditional language for his own benefit. The dramatic use and function of the proverbs in this play express the Yoruba worldview, thus enabling readers of other cultures to gain a better understanding of the African philosophy of life. Richards provides no proverb index, but see Greta Avery-Coger's catalogue of the proverbs in Soyinka's earlier plays (no. 2173).

4234. Richman, Karen E. "'With Many Hands, the Burden Isn't Heavy': Creole Proverbs and Political Rhetoric in Haiti's Presidential Elections." *Folklore Forum*, 23, nos. 1–2 (1990), 115–123.

Richman explains that the ability to use proverbs as an interpersonal weapon is a valued skill in Haitian communities. Where social norms emphasize the avoidance of direct confrontation, expressing a proverb under the transparent veil of non-directed, objectified discourse serves as a vehicle for persuasive maneuvering, venting hostilities, and exercising personal power. The speaker can deny any specific aggressive or partisan intent because responsibility for assigning meaning to the message belongs to the unnamed target hearer rather than the sender. Citing a number of contextualized examples, the author shows how Creole proverbs were employed in this fashion during one of Haiti's presidential elections. It becomes clear that proverbs are most effective rhetorical tools in political communication.

4235. Richmond, Edmun B. "Utilizing Proverbs as a Focal Point to Cultural Awareness and the Communicative Competence: Illustrations from Africa." *Foreign Language Annals*, 20 (1987), 213–216.

The author observes correctly that foreign language teachers often insert proverbs into courses in order to impart cultural awareness to their students. However, these proverbs are usually randomly selected and learned without little attention being paid to their use in communicative contexts. While this pedagogical approach might work somewhat with the more commonly taught European languages, it certainly is insufficient for the teaching of African languages that belong to cultures where proverbs are major elements of normal discourse. In order to help foreign language instructors, Richmond presents a model of cross-cultural proverb relationships which explains the problem of total, partial, or no equivalent proverbs in the native and target languages. He admits, however, that while equivalent texts might help the students to understand the metaphor and meaning of a proverb in the foreign language, the teacher must still instruct the students to employ the proverb properly in oral and written communication. A diagram and an abstract (p. 213) are included.

4236. Riegel, Martin. "'Qui dort dîne' ou le pivot implicatif dans les énoncés parémiques." *Travaux de linguistique et de littérature*, 24, no. 1 (1986), 85–99.

In this important theoretical article Riegel investigates the logical structure of proverbs and its implication for the meaning of those proverbs which are based on the same structural model. He reviews the work which Zoltán Kanyó has done concerning such structural analysis (see no. 829), and he then presents a detailed study of numerous French proverbs based on the pattern "Qui dort dîne" (He who sleeps forgets his hunger). It is shown that this formulaic pattern can be expanded into proverbs of different lengths by adding various descriptive elements. Riegel investigates the meaning of these texts and concludes that the semiotic and structural approach to the study of proverbs is of great importance for a better understanding of logical thought processes expressed in proverbial language. A short bibliography (p. 99) of major theoretical proverb scholarship is attached.

4237. Riegel, Martin. "'Avoir' + Attribut de l'objet: construction syntaxique et paradigme idiomatique." *Europhras 88. Phraséologie Contrastive. Actes du Colloque International Klingenthal-Strasbourg, 12–16 mai 1988.* Ed. Gertrud Gréciano. Strasbourg: Université des Sciences Humaines, 1989. 337–347.

In this linguistic article Riegel investigates fixed phrases that are based on the structure "avoir" + attribut de l'objet" (i.e.. "to have" + attributive object). He explains that many French idiomatic expressions follow this pattern. These idioms might use a personal pronoun or a noun as the subject. This is followed by a form of "avoir" and a direct object which usually is modified by an adjective. A number of French examples are cited, and Riegel explains that they differ in syntactical and stylistic complexity. The pattern certainly belongs to one of the most common French idiomatic structures, and Riegel argues that similar formulaic constructions make up the basis of large numbers of phraseological units.

4238. Rigolot, François. "Perspectives rhétorique et sémiotique sur la locution: 'locutio/locatio'." *La locution. Actes du colloque international Université McGill, Montréal, 15–16 octobre 1984.* Eds. Giuseppe Di Stefano and Russell G. McGillivray. Montréal: Éditions CERES, 1984. 400–418.

The first part of this article investigates the meaning of the French word "locution" (expression), tracing it back to rhetorical theories of classical antiquity. Rigolot cites early references of this concept, arguing that it is based on the Latin "locutio" (expression) and "locatio" (i.e., "lieu commun" or commonplace). The second half of the study investigates the use and function of this word in the novel *Gargantua et Pantagruel* (1532/34) by François Rabelais (1494–1553). Several examples are cited to indicate how Rabelais uses this term, but Rigolot also includes some comments concerning the use of French proverbial expressions in this significant novel of the 16th century.

4239. Ritchie, Ian. "Hausa Sensory Symbolism." *Anthropologica*, 32 (1990), 113–119.

The author investigates Hausa folk tales and proverbs from Nigeria and points out that this African culture has traditionally placed a high value on non-visual modes of experiencing the world. Many proverbs refer particularly to taste and smell, while sight is de-emphasized in comparison to western cultures. Ritchie cites a number of Hausa examples with English translations, grouping his materials according to taste (food, tasting, eating, and swallowing), hearing, smell, and sight. There are even entire folk tales constructed in the idiom of taste, and there exists a rich and developed system of proverbial metaphors related to eating. Based on these narrative and proverbial texts it is concluded that the gustatory and auditory senses exercise a wider and more developed role than they enjoy in European cultures. A useful bibliography (pp. 118–119) is attached.

4240. Rittgasser, Stefan. "Zur Beschreibung von Phrasemen in ein- und zweisprachigen Wörterbüchern." *Phraseologie und ihre Aufgaben.* Ed. Josip Matesic. Heidelberg: Julius Groos, 1983. 214–221.

This is a theoretical study concerning the organization and classification of a bilingual phraseological dictionary. Rittgasser begins with the definition of phraseological unit and then argues that the lexicographer or phraseographer must consider lexicographical, semantic, semiotic, and structural aspects of the fixed phrases. He also explains how to deal with nouns, verbs, adjectives, and adverbs in deciding how to classify a large number of expressions. A particular problem is also the lack of precise equivalents for the proverbial expressions of two given languages. Many Serbo-Croatian examples are cited to illustrate these points, but the author has provided no translations. The article indicates the many difficulties which have to be dealt with in the preparation of comparative phraseological dictionaries.

4241. Rivière, Daniel. "Le thème alimentaire dans le discours proverbial de la Renaissance française." *Pratiques et discours alimentaires à la Renaissance.* Eds. Jean-Claude Margolin and Robert Sauzet. Paris: Maisonneuve et Larose, 1982. 201–217.

Rivière presents a detailed analysis of 607 French proverbs from the 16th century that refer to various types of food. He cites examples of proverbs commenting on fish, wine, bread, meat, eggs, apples, salad, etc., and he provides valuable historical, cultural, and social explanations. It is argued that these proverbs do not only contain rich information about vegetables, fruit, and meat, but they are also of much importance to understand certain dietary rules and beliefs. The author analyzes such health rules or medical proverbs dealing with the consumption of certain food, and he shows that this proverbial wisdom was still very much accepted during the 19th century. In fact, many of these proverbs continue to be in use today, and they appear to be valid for the modern age just as they provided people during the French Renaissance with solid nutritional advice.

4242. Robea, Mihail M. "Creatiile paremiologice în monografiile satesti ale cadrelor didactice în deceniile 4 si din secolul nostru." *Proverbium Dacoromania*, 4 (1989), 35–38.

This is a short report on a number of pedagogical manuscripts from the 1940s and 1950s which contain valuable paremiological information. The authors of these unpublished theses deal with the questions of how proverbs can and should be utilized in Rumanian language instruction. They argue that proverbs provide valuable social, historical, and cultural information for young students. In addition, students can also learn stylistic and poetic aspects of the Rumanian language from traditional proverbs. The theses also include small proverb collections that were assembled through field research, thus presenting scholars with lists of those proverbs which were current in oral communication among the rural population of Rumania. The theses are located in the archive of the Rumanian Ministry of Education, and they certainly should be studied by both paremiographers and paremiologists in their attempt to gain even more insights into the use and function of proverbs as educational material. A French summary (p. 38) is provided.

4243. Roberts, John M., and Jeffrey C. Hayes. "Young Adult Male Categorizations of Fifty Arabic Proverbs." *Anthropological Linguistics*, 29, no. 1 (1987), 35–48.

This article is based on an interesting experiment which the two authors conducted with 20 Palestinians in Lebanon. They provided each informant with fifty cards that contained one commonly known Arabic proverb each. The informants were then asked to categorize the proverbs according to some general themes. Three figures and statistical tables indicate that these native speakers did agree in general with the ethnographic meaning of these proverbs. The authors argue that outside anthropologists would have definite difficulties in assigning semantic values to proverbs of a foreign culture. This is obviously even more difficult if the proverbs are cited in a collection without any communicative context. Roberts and Hayes conclude that anthropologists interested in proverbs should definitely base their research on the invaluable insights of native informants. An English abstract (p. 35) and a useful bibliography (pp. 47–48) are included.

4244. Roberts, Warren. "The Proverb." *Studies in Cheremis Folklore.* Ed. Thomas A. Sebeok. Bloomington/Indiana: Indiana University Press, 1952. I, 118–169.

Roberts begins his classification scheme for a large corpus of Cheremis proverbs with a short introduction (pp. 118–122) in which he discusses various methods of classifying proverbs. He rejects the alphabetical arrangement according to individual letters or key-words and instead proposes a system that is based on the subject (i.e., theme. idea, or content) of the text. Some of the major categories are cleverness and foolisness, planning and acting, property, man and wife, the individual and society, youth and old age, etc. These categories are then once again subdivided: under the heading of "man and wife" Roberts includes such sub-headings as good qualities of a woman, bad qualities of a woman, handsome and ugly women, love, married life, young (unmarried) girls, widows and widowers, spinsters and bachelors, and marriage. The proverbs themselves are grouped into these sections by a system of four numbers for each text: the first number refers to the large subject-matter class, the second to the sub-group to which it belongs, the third gives the position of the proverb in that sub-group, and the fourth indicates a variant. The actual classified collection of Cheremis proverbs in English or German translation is presented on pp. 122–163, and Roberts has also included a valuable index of key-words (pp. 163–169).

4245. Robinson, Herbert. "Family Sayings from Family Stories: Some Louisiana Examples." *Louisiana Folklore Miscellany*, 6, no. 4 (1991), 17–24.

The author reports on three American family sayings which go back at least fifty years to the 1920s and 1930s. His informants stem from the rural area of Lee's Creek in Washington Parish, Louisiana, and they recall certain stories about some relatives which subsequently have been reduced to family expressions. They are not proverbs as such, but they may be considered as proverbial expressions even though they are only current and known to family members. Robinson cites three stories which have been reduced to the expressions "We're on that Rio Road now," "You sure that wasn't Uncle Pompey calling his hogs you heard," and "You got to hold her, Knute." Only the stories themselves explain the meaning of these phrases to the outsider, but actual family members know exactly to which situation these expressions refer to. It is argued that they are humorous comments for the insiders of this particular family, and they are proverbial for this small group of people. Robinson is correct in calling for more studies of such family sayings and the obvious relationship between folk narratives and proverbial expressions.

4246. Roche, Reinhard. "Demosprüche und Wandgesprühtes. Versuch einer linguistischen Beschreibung und didaktischen Auswertung." *Muttersprache*, 93 (1983), 181–196.

Roche presents an interesting linguistic and cultural analysis of modern German slogans, posters, bumper stickers, and graffiti. He discusses the political and socio-economical content of numerous examples. He also comments on their language, structure, style, and satirical content. Several examples are based on traditional proverbs whose wisdom is put into question by word changes and additions. The results are what Wolfgang Mieder (see no. 3852) has called "Antisprichwörter" (anti-proverbs). They are effective expressions of the concerns of the youth subculture of the German society. Roche argues that the satire, irony, humor, wordplay, and nonsense expressed in them make such expressions also interesting from a pedagogical point of view in the sociolinguistic study of the modern German language in schools and universities. With 1 illustration.

4247. Roche, Reinhard. "'Stell dir vor . . .'." *Der Sprachdienst*, 27 (1983), 158–160.

This is a short statement that Bertolt Brecht (1898–1956) did not originate the popular slogan or graffiti "Stell dir vor, es gibt einen Krieg, und keiner geht hin" (Suppose they gave a war and nobody came). This proverbial text of the peace movement has no connection with Brecht's poem "Wer zu Hause bleibt, wenn der Kampf beginnt" (c. 1935). Roche shows how journalists and others have credited Brecht with this phrase, and he argues that much more philological caution is needed before assigning certain popular expressions to literary figures. For a possible source of the "proverb" see Ralf Bülow (no. 3180), who traces it back to the American writers Thornton Wilder (1897–1975) and Carl Sandburg (1878–1967). See also Beat Suter (no. 4450).

4248.   Rodegem, Francis M. "La parole proverbiale." *Richesse du proverbe.* Eds. François Suard and Claude Buridant. Lille: Université de Lille, 1984. II, 121–135.

Rodegem begins his significant article with the observation that there exists a definite confusion regarding paremiological terminology. Paremiographers and paremiologists often use different genre designations for the same texts, and this fact makes it terribly difficult for international scholars to communicate effectively with each other. The first part of the article deals with the definition of proverbs and analyzes in particular their analogical and normative function. The second half is an attempt to differentiate among such subgenres as maxim, aphorism, proverbial expression, slogan, maxim, apothegm, wellerism, etc. Rodegem includes African and French examples, and he also attaches three comparative tables (pp. 133–135) to illustrate the stylistic and semantic differences among these proverbial forms. See also the similar article by Francis Rodegem and P. Van Brussel (no. 4251 below).

4249.   Rodegem, Francis M. "'Est bon, tout ce qui fait petiller le feu'." *Afrika Focus*, 1 (1985), 31–48.

In this article Rodegem deals with the vexing problem of proverb classification. He explains that most proverb collections are organized according to the letters of the alphabet or by means of key-words. He argues that this method separates proverbs which actually have the same basic idea but different metaphors or structures. A more useful way of putting together proverb collections might be to group the proverbs according to a semantic content system. This approach would also permit paremiographers to register similar proverbs from different languages together in one group. The author proceeds to show how this could be done for African and French proverbs dealing with human beings. These texts are grouped under such thematic concepts as people in general, young girls, old people, women, love, adultery, etc. The last page (p. 48) also includes a schematic plan of how to set up a proverb collection of this type.

4250. Rodegem, Francis M. "Proverbes et pseudo-proverbes." *Annales Aequatoria*, 6 (1985), 67–83.

Rodegem argues that there is a definite state of confusion among paremiologists in regard to the various proverbial subgenres. He points out that scholars should investigate the orality, memorability, analogy, function, structure, and content of the various types of sayings. In the second part of the article the author presents a paremiological typology, discussing such subgenres as aphorism, maxim, proverb, proverbial expression, slogan, apothegm, etc. He also discusses the content and themes of proverbs, cites numerous French examples, and includes 3 statistical tables. The point is also made that paremiologists must pay more attention to so-called pseudo-proverbs. While they are also short statements containing some insight or wisdom, they certainly lack the common currency in oral and written language which true proverbs exhibit.

4251. Rodegem, Francis M., and P. Van Brussel. "Proverbes et pseudo-proverbes. La logique des parémies." *Europhras 88. Phraséologie Contrastive. Actes du Colloque International Klingenthal-Strasbourg, 12–16 mai 1988.* Ed. Gertrud Gréciano. Strasbourg: Université des Sciences Humaines, 1989. 349–356.

This is a similar article to Rodegem's previous discussion (see no. 4248 above) of the problems that confront international paremiologists due to the lack of terminological consistency. This time the two authors start with definition problems concerning proverbs, proverbial expressions, slogans, apothegms, wellerisms, etc. They also include helpful comments regarding the structure, form, style, and language of such proverbial texts, emphasizing in particular the analogical and normative function of proverbs. A few French examples are cited, and the authors include three charts (pp. 355–356) to help distinguish between the various subgenres that range from true proverbs to so-called pseudo-proverbs.

4252. Röder, Siegfried. "Redensarten aus der Ritterzeit." *Sprachspiegel,* 44 (1988), 47–48.

Röder presents but a short discussion of a few German proverbial expressions from the Middle Ages. He argues that many medieval German phrases refer to the social and political life of the knights. Their metaphors refer often to realia which are no longer understood today, and that is the reason why detailed etymological, historical, and cultural studies are necessary to explain the origin and original meaning of these expressions. Two of the phrases discussed in some detail are "Den Nagel auf den Kopf treffen" (To hit the nail on the head) and "Manschetten vor etwas haben" (To be in a funk about something). Röder also explains that numerous early phrases contain references to old beliefs, customs, and legal matters.

4253. Rodin, Kerstin. *Räven predikar för Gässen. En studie av ett ordspråk i senmedeltida ikonografi.* Uppsala: Almqvist & Wiksell, 1983. 119 pp.

This is an excellent Swedish study of late medieval iconographical representations of the common European proverbial expression "Räven predikar för gässen" (The fox preaches to the geese). Rodin analyzes illuminated manuscripts, architectural decorations, woodcuts, and copperplate engravings (pp. 15–28), but she also studies the appearance of the expression in satirical literature and sermons (pp. 28–35). The section on the meaning and function (pp. 36–45) investigates the social criticism which is symbolized in the expression, and the detailed section on the components of the iconographical tradition (pp. 46–81) deals with the appearance of the expression in animal tales and literature. The last section (pp. 82–91) analyzes sequences of scenes found in England, Germany, and Scandinavia in which the hypocritical fox outwitting the geese is followed by a scene depicting how the duped geese in turn outwit the fox and string him up at the gallows. Many tables, 28 illustrations, and a bibliography (pp. 110–119) are provided, making this study of the relationship of proverbs, iconography, and folk narratives a model to follow. With an English summary (pp. 103–109).

4254. Rogers, Alan D. "Human Prudence and Implied Divine Sanctions in Malagasy Proverbial Wisdom." *Journal of Religion in Africa*, 15 (1985), 216–226.

Rogers begins his study of Malagasy proverbs with the observation that they are of particular value to scholars of anthropology and religion due to the fact that they contain social and cultural information from a time prior to the arrival of the Europeans. Basing his analysis on proverbs that were collected towards the end of the 19th century, Rogers explains that Andriamanitra, the Malagasy God, plays only a small role in the many recorded proverbs. Not only is God seldom mentioned, there are also only a few texts which contain divine sanctions. Most of the proverbs express human prudence and not religious interpretations of social life. They comment on justice, love, truth, courage, fraud, selfishness, hate, etc., and these texts provide valuable ethnographical data concerning the Malagasy society and worldview. The 13 notes (pp. 225–226) include some bibliographical references. See also Lee Haring (no. 3558).

4255. Rogers, Pat. "Tristram Shandy's Polite Conversation." *Essays in Criticism*, 32 (1982), 305–320.

This is a literary proverb investigation starting with some general comments on the use and function of proverbs in 18th century English literature. Rogers discusses some proverbs in the novels of Jonathan Swift (1667–1745) and Henry Fielding (1707–1754) before analyzing in much detail some of the more than 50 proverbs and numerous proverbial expressions contained in Laurence Sterne's (1713–1768) *Tristram Shandy* (1759/67). She cites the proverbial texts in their literary context, she adds philological, historical, and cultural explanations, and she shows how Sterne manipulates proverbial language to suit his stylistic intentions. While he does at times appear to invent his own proverbs based on standard proverbial structures, he does in general accept the proverbs at face value and uses them as colloquial language to add to the realism of his novel. Rogers does not include a proverb index, but she does present convincing contextualized examples.

4256. Rogers, Tim B. "Psychological Approaches to Proverbs: A Treatise on the Import of Context." *Canadian Folklore Canadien*, 8, nos. 1–2 (1986), 87–104.

In this significant review article Rogers presents a detailed analysis of how psychologists have dealt with proverbs during the 20th century. He begins with the important observation that while folklorists study proverbs primarily in their social context, psychologists have unfortunately preferred to deal with proverbs outside of any particular communicative context. He then explains that psychologists began looking at proverbs as indicators of behavior, personality, and certain attitudes. A major area has been the use of so-called psychological proverbs tests used in the testing of intelligence or, especially by psychiatrists, as a diagnostic tool for such mental diseases as schizophrenia. Rogers also refers to studies that have dealt with questions of child development where proverbs are used to establish at what age young children begin to understand metaphors. Proverbs have also been used as slogans by social psychologists in therapeutic communities for alcohol or drug addicts. Finally there are those psychologists who more recently have employed proverbs to investigate modern questions of cognition. The 54 notes contain valuable bibliographical information, and the article in itself presents a superb introduction to the large field of psychological paremiology.

4257. Rogers, Tim B. "The Use of Slogans, Colloquialisms, and Proverbs in the Treatment of Substance Addiction: A Psychological Application of Proverbs." *Proverbium*, 6 (1989), 103–112.

This is a fascinating report on how psychologists and social workers have made use of proverbs in the treatment of substance addiction. Proverbs and proverb-like slogans are displayed on signs and posters in treatment centers for alcoholics and drug addicts as a constant reminder that it is a worthwhile struggle to overcome this addiction in order to live a normal life. Some examples are "No pain, no gain," "No reward for bad behavior," and "You alone can do it, but you cannot do it alone." Such proverbs and slogans are also discussed in group therapeutic sessions where they help to create a common ground for the addicts. While such proverbial texts are only a very small part of the entire therapeutic package, Rogers feels that this new context for proverbs has at least some value in helping people to overcome their addiction.

4258. Rogers, Tim B. "Proverbs as Psychological Theories . . . Or Is It the Other Way Around?" *Canadian Psychology/Psychologie Canadienne*, 31, no. 3 (1990), 195–207 and 215–217 (comments).

In a certain way this significant article is a review of what value psychologists have attributed to proverbs. Stating that proverbs have impressive explanatory and communicative powers, Rogers explains that they have been looked at as theoretical propositions in psychology. In fact, as his table of sampler studies which can be interpreted as empirical tests of the truth value of proverbs shows, such proverbs as "Birds of a feather flock together," "Spare the rod and spoil the child," "Actions speak louder than words," and "You can't teach an old dog new tricks" have all been interpreted as metaphorically expressed psychological theories. Rogers does stress, however, that psychologists must also pay more attention to such matters as contradictory proverbs, the complexity of their meaning, and the importance of the social context in which they are being used. An impressive bibliography (pp. 205–207) and a response by Rogers (pp. 215–217) to commentaries by Ken Dion (see no. 3306), Kenneth Gergen (no. 3473), and Wolfgang Mieder (no. 3930) are attached. English and French abstracts (p. 195 and p. 205) are also provided.

4259. Roggen, Ronald. "'Blind' und 'sehen' in festen Ausdrücken."
      Sprachspiegel, 39 (1983), 53–54.

      This is a short and popular discussion of a number of
      German proverbs and proverbial expressions dealing with
      blindness and vision (seeing), as for example "Liebe macht
      blind" (Love is blind) and "Etwas ins Auge fassen" (To keep an
      eye on something). Examples from the Bible and literature are
      cited, and Roggen shows that many expressions stem from such
      professions as medicine, engineering, printing, etc. The
      onesidedness of some phrases is explained, the wisdom of others
      is put into question, and a few phraseological units are judged to
      be effective metaphors even in modern communicative situations.

4260. Röhrich, Lutz. "Anti-Sprichwörter. Zu einem neuen Buch von
      Wolfgang Mieder." *Muttersprache,* 93 (1983), 351–354.

      Starting with a review of Wolfgang Mieder's first volume of
      Antisprichwörter (1982; see no. 3852), Röhrich adds many
      comments and examples of such anti-proverbs from his own
      proverb archive at the University of Freiburg in Germany. He
      discusses the use of anti-proverbs in newspaper headlines and
      advertising slogans, but he also points out that proverbs are
      varied and parodied through intellectual puns and wordplay. The
      form and structure of these proverb innovations are discussed,
      and Röhrich explains that they are characterized by humor,
      irony, and satire directed at the political, economical, and social
      problems of the modern technological German society. The
      review essay ends with Röhrich's own small collection of anti-
      proverbs as an indication of how widespread they have become.

4261. Röhrich, Lutz. "Prolegomena zu einer Neu-Bearbeitung des
      Lexikons der sprichwörtlichen Redensarten." *Proverbium,* 1 (1984),
      127–152.

      In preparation of a new and much expanded edition of his
      superb *Lexikon der sprichwörtlichen Redensarten* (1973; see no.
      1577), Röhrich offers some prolegomena about the changes and
      additions that will take place in his new lexicon that will be
      comprised of three instead of two volumes. All of the corrections
      and necessary additions mentioned in the many reviews and

letters will be considered, and the number of key-words alone will be increased by about 40%. Many new expressions will be cited for which Röhrich gives a number of examples here. There will be many more bibliographical references at the end of each entry, and much more attention will be paid to foreign language parallels in English, French, etc. More German dialect expressions and proverbial comparisons will be included, and the number of illustrations from medieval woodcuts to modern cartoons will also be largely increased. The very modern scene of graffitis, proverbial aphorisms, slogans, parodies, etc., will be treated in as far as these expressions (often variations of traditional forms) have become commonly known. Here it will also be of much importance to discuss the associative formations of whole strings of new phrases based on one proverb or proverbial expression, and more emphasis will also be placed on the function of these rich materials. Röhrich's comments include an interesting theoretical discussion on proverbial expressions and their relationship to phraseology (pp. 136–148), his basic argument being that his new *Lexikon* will be as inclusive (proverbs, proverbial expressions, twin formulas, proverbial comparisons, wellerisms, graffitis, slogans, etc.) as possible. The new three volumes will also continue to be a diachronic dictionary with philological, folkloric, and cultural emphasis.

4262. Röhrich, Lutz. "Die Welt der alemannischen Sprichwörter." *Einheit in der Vielfalt. Festschrift für Peter Lang.* Ed. Gisela Quast. Bern: Peter Lang, 1988. 434–457. With very small changes also published as "Alemannische Sprichwörter. Form und Funktion." *Europhras 88. Phraséologie Contrastive. Actes du Colloque International Klingenthal-Strasbourg, 12–16 mai 1988.* Ed. Gertrud Gréciano. Strasbourg: Université des Sciences Humaines, 1989. 357–370.

This is a major study of Alemannic and Alsatian dialect proverbs, proverbial expressions, and proverbial comparisons. Röhrich begins with a contrast between the same proverbs in their standard High German and dialect wording, showing that in rare occasions there might be a small difference in meaning. He discusses the form, structure, style, and language of numerous examples, at times also adding English and French parallels. Altogether the texts are interpreted as commentaries on everyday life, but it is interesting to note that quite a few texts have parodistic additions while others can be interpreted as erotic metaphors. Irony and humor play a major role in these examples as well, indicating that proverbs in rural areas are not at all always sacrosanct pieces of folk wisdom. At the end of his article the author presents several groups of phraseological units arranged by such common themes as man and woman (including chauvinistic and misogynous texts), thriftiness and stinginess, scatology, and dairy animals (cow, calf, ox). A valuable bibliography (pp. 456–457, or somewhat expanded pp. 368–370) is attached.

4263. Rölleke, Heinz. "'Dû bist mîn, ich bin dîn'. Ein mittelhochdeutscher Vers in den *Kinder- und Hausmärchen* der Brüder Grimm?" *Fabula*, 23 (1982), 269–275. Also in H. Rölleke (ed.). *"Wo das Wünschen noch geholfen hat." Gesammelte Aufsätze zu den "Kinder- und Hausmärchen" der Brüder Grimm.* Bonn: Bouvier, 1985. 133–141.

A discussion of the popular Middle High German formula "Dû bist mîn, ich bin dîn" (Thou art mine, and I am thine) with special emphasis on its appearance in Jacob (1785–1863) and Wilhelm Grimm's (1786–1859) *Kinder- und Hausmärchen* (2nd ed., 1819). Rölleke explains that this proverbial formula did not appear in the 1812 first edition of the fairy tale "Der König mit dem Löwen," but that Wilhelm Grimm added it to the renamed fairy tale "Die zwölf Jäger" (KHM 67) for the 1819 edition of their *Märchen* collection. The author traces the origin of the expression from the Middle Ages to the Grimms and includes references from Martin Luther (1483–1546) and Jakob Ayrer (1543–1605). See also Karl Hadank (no. 2440), Adolf Hauffen (no. 2449), Friedrich Ohly (no. 2704), and Archer Taylor (nos. 1884 and 1906).

4264. Rölleke, Heinz. "'Wie ein Lämmerschwänzchen'. Zur Herkunft einer Redensart in Grimms Märchen." *Wirkendes Wort*, 32 (1982), 233–234. Also in H. Rölleke (ed.). *"Wo das Wünschen noch geholfen hat." Gesammelte Aufsätze zu den "Kinder- und Hausmärchen" der Brüder Grimm.* Bonn: Bouvier, 1985. 142–144.

In this short article Rölleke is able to show that the German proverbial comparison "Das Herz wackelt (hüpft) wie ein Lämmerschwänzchen" (The heart wags [jumps] like a lamb's tail) as an expression of great joy and excitement was not part of the fairy tale "Das tapfere Schneiderlein" (KHM 20) in the 1812 first edition of Jacob (1785–1863) and Wilhelm Grimm's (1786–1859) *Kinder- und Hausmärchen*. It was added by Wilhelm in the second edition of 1819, who knew it from Christian Weise's (1642–1709) Baroque novel *Die drei ärgsten Erznarren* (1672). This is yet another proof for Wilhelm's stylistic manipulations of fairy tales. Rölleke also cites a later reference of the phrase in Wilhelm Raabe's (1831–1910) posthumous novel *Altershausen* (1912) with specific reference to the fairy tale. For many more proverbial additions to the fairy tales by the Grimms see Heinz Rölleke (no. 4266 below) and Wolfgang Mieder (nos. 3892 and 3896).

4265. Rölleke, Heinz. "Sprichwörtliche Redensarten in Hugo von Hofmannsthals *Jedermann*." *Wirkendes Wort*, 36 (1986), 347–353.

This is a literary investigation of the use of proverbs, proverbial expressions, and proverbial comparisons in the spiritual play *Jedermann* (1911) by the Austrian author Hugo von Hofmannsthal (1874–1929). Rölleke explains that none of the phraseological units in this play are to be found in Hofmannsthal's late 15th century English and 16th century German sources. He himself obviously felt that proverbial language would help to create a more popular and folkloric style that would be appropriate for the moralistic message of the work. Rölleke cites numerous contextualized examples and adds comparative references from other German literary works where possible. He also points out that Wilhelm Grimm (1786–1859) had a similar preference for proverbial texts which he added in later editions of the *Kinder- und Hausmärchen*. Hofmannsthal was an admirer of the Brothers Grimm and their fairy tales, and he might well have been influenced by the many proverbial expressions contained in these folk narratives.

4266. Rölleke, Heinz (ed.). *"Redensarten des Volks, auf die ich immer horche."* Das Sprichwort in den *"Kinder- und Hausmärchen"* der Brüder

Grimm. Ed. in cooperation with Lothar Bluhm. Bern: Peter Lang, 1988. 227 pp.

Rölleke and Lothar Bluhm together with a student team comprised of Beatrix Burghoff, Claudia Kniep, Jutta Rißmann, Achim Hölter, Isabel Oberstraß, Andreas Meier, and Ulrike Marquardt have analyzed all seven editions of Jacob (1785–1863) and Wilhelm Grimm's (1786–1859) collection of *Kinder- und Hausmärchen* (1812/15–1857) in order to establish the appearance of all proverbs, proverbial expressions, and proverbial comparisons in these fairy tales. Rölleke as the major editor of the book begins with a significant interpretative chapter (pp. 11–26) in which he discusses the relationship of folk narratives and proverbial language. He also explains that both Jacob and Wilhelm Grimm added proverbial texts to later editions, but it certainly was primarily Wilhelm who did so with the openly expressed desire to make the tales more traditional and folkloric in tone and style. This is followed by nine chapters (two by Bluhm) in which everybody takes up about 25 fairy tales in chronological order investigating their phraseological units and at what stage of the seven editions they were added. Many historical, philological, and cultural explanations are included, and it becomes clear that the proverbial style of the fairy tales is due primarily to these intentional additions. The original tales, both those from oral and literary sources, definitely did not contain this rich proverbial language. A valuable "Index Proverbiorum" (pp. 215–227) concludes this major textual and paremiological study. See also Wolfgang Mieder's earlier studies (nos. 3892 and 3896) of the proverbial language in the *Märchen.*

4267. Rölleke, Heinz. "'Warteinweil'. Zur Genealogie eines überirdischen Begriffs." *Jahrbuch des Freien Deutschen Hochstifts,* no volume given (1991), 131–138.

Rölleke presents a detailed etymological and historical study of the German proverbial verse "Ein silbernes Wart ein Weilchen, und ein goldnes Nixchen" (A silver wait a while and a golden nothing) which usually is said to children to tell them that they will have to wait for a gift and that there is nothing to be had right now. The author shows that Clemens Brentano (1778–1842) used it in a letter of 1802 and also in his collection of German folk songs entitled *Des Knaben Wunderhorn* (1806/08). However, this fixed phrase that has survived in German folk songs and nursery rhymes is actually much older. Rölleke is able to prove that the word "Warteinweil" (wait a while) and its diminutive form "Warteinweilchen" actually go back to a literary work by Jakob Frey (1520?–1562?). He even cites a possible source in a 14th century German Bible translation. From these early sources it becomes clear that this term refers to a place between heaven and earth where soldiers or people in general have to wait before they are allowed to enter heaven. In its more modern metaphorical meaning it simply refers to the fact that people have to wait for something good.

4268. Roman, Thomas. "Proverbis e locuziones proverbialas en duas ovras da Gion Deplazes *Paun casa* e *La Bargia dil tschéss*: Specia e funcziun." *Annalas de la Società Retorumantscha*, 101 (1988), 7–48.

This is a very detailed literary proverb investigation of Gion Deplazes' (1918–) two Rhaeto-Romanic novels *Paun casa* (1960) and *La Bargia dil tschéss* (1964). Roman begins with a section (pp. 8–15) on the definition of proverbs, proverbial expressions, and proverbial comparisons. The following section (pp. 15–29) deals with the form and structure of proverbs, commenting in particular on the use of rhyme and parallelism. The third section (pp. 29–38) analyzes the function of this proverbial language in its literary context. Many examples are cited to illustrate how proverbs are used in the dialogues and in the prose of the narrator. A short conclusion (pp. 39–40), a useful bibliography (pp. 39–40), and a valuable proverb index (pp. 40–48) without annotations conclude this study of the use and function of phraseological units in the works of a modern Swiss author.

4269. Roos, Eckhard. "Kontrastive Überlegungen zur deutschen, englischen und französischen Idiomatik." *Sprache und Literatur in Wissenschaft und Unterricht*, 16, no. 56 (1985), 74–80.

Realizing that idioms or phraseological units play a major role in foreign language instruction, Roos presents a short theoretical description of such fixed phrases which he illustrates through numerous German, English, and French examples. He starts with a definition of idiomaticity and stresses in particular the fixidity of such phrases. Next he deals with the structure, classification, and metaphorical language of idioms. Roos also includes some comments regarding lexicographical issues, noting that phraseological dictionaries differ greatly in how they register, classify, and annotate idioms. It is argued that foreign language instructors should definitely have a solid understanding of idiomatic structures so that they can teach their students these commonly used expressions. Obviously students who know more than one foreign language will enjoy comparing the similarities or differences of the meaning and metaphors of idioms. A short bibliography (pp. 79–80) is attached.

4270. Roos, Paolo. *Sentenza e proverbio nell'antichità e i "Distici di Catone": Il testo latino e i volgarizzamenti italiani.* Brescia: Morcelliana, 1984. 254 pp.

This is a major philological and historical study of classical Greek and Latin proverbs and sententious remarks. Roos begins his book with a chapter (pp. 11–40) on the origin and nature of these ancient proverbs. This is followed by a large second chapter (pp. 41–186) in which Roos presents discussions of proverbial texts from the works of such authors as Titus Maccius Plautus (250–184 B.C.), Terence (195?–159? B.C.), Marcus Tullius Cicero (106–43 B.C.), Ovid (43 B.C -17? A.D.), Seneca (4 B.C.-65 A.D.), and many others. The third chapter (pp. 187–245) is divided into two major parts: First Roos offers a detailed analysis (pp. 187–231) of the date, possible author, title, structure, sources, and content of the anonymous Latin proverb collection *Disticha Catonis* (11th century). The second part (pp. 232–245) deals with several Italian versions of these *Distici di Catone* for which Roos provides important historical and comparative notes. A solid bibliography (pp. 7–10) and useful name and subject indices (pp. 246–254) conclude this valuable work.

4271. Rooth, Anna Birgitta. "Some Symbols in Bosch's Paintings." *Annales Societatis Litterarum Humaniorum Regiae Upsaliensis*, no volume given (1986), 33–68.

In this significant monograph Rooth investigates the large number of Dutch proverbs and proverbial expressions which Hieronymus Bosch (1450?–1516) illustrated in his paintings. She points out that he was obviously very well versed both in Biblical and folk proverbs, he knew of the relationship of fables and proverbs, and he was particularly interested in the depiction of human characteristics in animal proverbs. While much of this proverbial wisdom appears only in small scenes or mere allusions in his large pictures, there are also such drawings which illustrate one proverb as the major theme, as for example the Dutch proverb "Het veld heeft ogen, het bos heeft oren" (The field has eyes, the forest has ears). Rooth includes 26 illustrations which clearly depict proverbial scenes, and she also provides references to Pieter Brueghel (1520?–1569), Erasmus of Rotterdam (1469–1536), and many other 16th century authors. There are in addition several small sections on how Bosch was especially interested in illustrating proverbs and proverbial expressions referring to bells, eyeglasses, knives, etc. This "proverbial art" is interpreted as a satirical social statement on the part of Bosch. A valuable bibliography (pp. 66–68) is attached, but see also Paul Vandenbroeck (no. 2968).

4272. Roques, Gilles. "'Sans rime et sans raison'." *La locution. Actes du colloque international Université McGill, Montréal, 15–16 octobre 1984.* Eds. Giuseppe Di Stefano and Russell G. McGillivray. Montréal: Editions CERES, 1984. 419–436.

This is a philological and literary study of the French twin formula "Sans rime et sans raison" (Without rhyme or reason). Roques has located 25 references from the 13th century to 1520 in various French literary works, among them those by Guillaume de Machaut (1300?–1377), Eustache Deschamps (1346?–1406?), Christine de Pisan (1365–1429?), and Jean Regnier (1390?–1467). He cites the texts in their literary context and also points out a number of variants. It is shown that this binary formula was indeed very popular in the late Middle Ages in France, but it should be noted that its English equivalent was equally current at that time. For English references see J.W. Rankin (no. 1502).

4273. Rosen, Chaim. "Getting to Know the Ethiopian Jews in Israel by Means of Their Proverbs." *Social Science Information*, 28, no. 1 (1989), 145–159.

Rosen starts with a discussion of the problems that rural Ethiopian Jews have faced in trying to become integrated members of the Israeli society. As immigrants they are confronted with new urban and social challenges, and it will take time for them to deal effectively with their new environment. The author argues convincingly that Israelis could learn a lot about the Ethiopian worldview by paying attention to the traditional wisdom expressed in proverbs. He cites a number of examples to illustrate that Ethiopians are ruled by the social, cultural, and behavioral wisdom expressed in their proverbs. Obviously these proverbs continue to be used among this immigrant group, and Israelis will find it much easier to communicate with the Ethiopians on all social levels by a better understanding of their proverbial beliefs and customs.

4274. Rosenberg, D.M. "*Samson Agonistes*: 'Proverb'd for a Fool'." *The Centennial Review*, 32, no. 1 (1988), 65–78.

This article deals only tangentially with proverbs, but Rosenberg does address John Milton's (1608–1674) play *Samson Agonistes* (1671) as an analysis of the conflict between folly and wisdom. The theme of folly in particular brings to mind the many proverbs about fools and foolishness. As the title of the article suggests, Rosenberg is especially interested in Samson's self-description as being "proverb'd for a fool." It is shown that this statement is an allusion to the Book of Proverbs. Rosenberg also discusses other Biblical allusions to folly in the Old Testament and how these more or less proverbial utterances have become part of Milton's dialogues. See also Laura Knoppers (no. 3694).

4275. Rosenberger, Eva. *Das Pferd in deutschen Sprichwörtern und Redensarten.* M.A. Thesis University of Basel, 1989. 141 pp.

Rosenberger has put together a valuable collection and discussion of those German proverbs which in one way or the other deal with the "Pferd" (horse). Following a short introductory chapter (pp. 4–9) outlining the importance of the horse in German proverbs and proverbial expressions, the author presents a useful second chapter (pp. 10–17) on the history of the horse from classical antiquity to the 20th century. The third chapter (pp. 18–59) begins with an etymological analysis of the various words for "Pferd," and this is followed by an analysis of 25 proverbs which can be traced back to classical, Biblical, patristic, and medieval sources. The chapter concludes with a discussion of the expressions which are contained in major German proverb collections of the 16th century. The fourth chapter (pp. 60–117) analyzes the content of the proverbs, explaining in particular beliefs and superstitions expressed in them. Some concluding remarks (pp. 118–123), useful notes (pp. 124–135), and an impressive bibliography (pp. 136–141) bring this study on the folk wisdom surrounding the horse to a close.

4276. Rosenfeld, Hans-Friedrich. "Georg Christoph Lichtenbergs *Patriotischer Beytrag zur Methyologie der Deutschen* und die niederdeutsche Methyologie der Gegenwart. Ein Beitrag zur Ausdrucksfähigkeit und Bildkraft der niederdeutschen Sprache." *Jahrbuch des Vereins für niederdeutsche Sprachforschung,* 78 (1955), 83–137.

This is an extremely detailed philological analysis of 101 High German and 43 Low German proverbial expressions and proverbial comparisons which the aphoristic writer and science professor Georg Christoph Lichtenberg (1742–1799) published in a small satirical pamphlet with the title *Patriotischer Beytrag zur Methyologie der Deutschen* (1773). After some introductory comments (pp. 83–87), Rosenfeld presents etymological, historical, cultural, and folkloric commentaries (pp. 87–130) for all 144 expressions. He also cites many dialect parallels, making this monograph one of the most complete German collections of fixed phrases concerning drunkenness. Many of the expressions are rather old, and quite a few of them are based on animal metaphors. A useful subject index (pp. 130–131) and a complete word index (pp. 132–137) are included.

4277. Rosenthal, Franz. "The History of an Arabic Proverb." *Journal of the American Oriental Society,* 109, no. 3 (1989), 349–378.

Rosenthal presents an erudite philological study concerning the origin, meaning, and dissemination of an ancient Arabic proverb which may be translated as "Affliction may come from talk" or better yet "Affliction controls talk." He traces it back to the 8th century B.C. and cites numerous references and variants, in each case giving very detailed etymological, syntactical, and metrical comments. The author also explains how this proverb was attached to folk narratives and other stories, always expressing the moral and prudent advice that excessive talk might bring harm to the speaker. The 164 notes contain rich bibliographical materials and additional information. A comparative linguistic table (p. 362) and an English abstract (p. 349) are included.

4278. Ross, Diane M. "Sir Thomas Wyatt: Proverbs and the Poetics of Scorn." *Sixteenth Century Journal*, 18 (1987), 201–212.

This literary proverb investigation studies the use and function of English proverbs in the poetry of Thomas Wyatt (1503–1542). Ross explains that proverbs in lyric poetry prior to the 16th century have usually expressed a moralistic message. In contrast to this didactic tradition, Wyatt incorporates proverbs into his poems as a form of ironic commentary on himself and others. Wyatt associates the proverb not so much with wisdom but rather with foolish behavior. He insults other people by implying that they behave in concert with the common types of behavior summarized in proverbs. His scorn for proverbs is reflected in his visible struggle not to use proverbs to describe his own situations, but as Ross is able to show, sometimes even Wyatt cannot escape acting in accordance with proverbial wisdom. Many contextualized examples are cited to indicate this rather negative employment of proverbs. An English abstract (p. 201) is provided.

4279. Ross, Doran H. "The Verbal Art of Akan Linguist Staffs." *African Arts*, 16, no. 1 (1982), 56–67.

Ross has assembled a most impressive illustrated study of proverbial staffs which are particularly in use among the Akan of Ghana. While proverbs play a major role in oral speech in this

African society, they have also found a very important place in visual arts. Proverbs are always found on the "okyeame poma" (linguist's stick or counselor's stick), a staff of authority used by the principal counselor of the chief. Ross includes 31 illustrations of such proverbial scenes of humans and animals on various staffs, and he also interprets their meaning and function as important traditional wisdom and moral precepts. The article is a fine example for the fact that proverbs should not only be studied as oral or written folk wisdom. There clearly is a strong tradition of proverbs in the visual arts as well. For such proverbial staffs from Ghana see also Kwesi Yankah (no. 4586).

4280. Ross, Ian Campbell, and Noha Saad Nassar. "Trim (-Tram), Like Master, Like Man: Servant and Sexton in Sterne's *Tristram Shandy* and *A Political Romance.*" *Notes and Queries*, 234, new series 36 (1989), 62–65.

In this onomastic study the two authors attempt to explain where the personal name "Trim" comes from which Laurence Sterne (1713–1768) uses in his two novels *A Political Romance* (1759) and *Tristram Shandy* (1759/67). The name originates from the English proverb "Trim tram, like master, like man" which has been recorded as early as 1571. Ross and Nassar explain that Sterne certainly was aware of the proverbial source of this name. In fact, he uses it in the sense of the master-man (master-servant) relationship in his novels. The authors provide contextualized proof of this claim and thus draw attention to the important interrelationship of onomastics, paremiology, and literature.

4281. Rossman, Jeffrey Michael. *Metaphor and Affect: A Study of Metaphorical Thinking and Affective Responsibility in Schizophrenia.* Diss. Adelphi University, 1985. 177 pp.

This dissertation investigates the nature of the disturbance in metaphorical thinking in schizophrenic individuals by making use of a psychological proverbs test. It is shown that schizophrenics suffer from a specific deficit in metaphorical thinking which is independent of the generalized cognitive deficits that accompany schizophrenia. The schizophrenics responded with more literal responses to the proverbial

metaphors than members of a control group. The author
includes an informative chapter (pp. 8–46) reviewing previous
scholarship on metaphor comprehension by schizophrenics. He
also attaches a valuable bibliography (pp. 142–151), and the
actual proverbs test is printed as well (pp. 167–168). The 17
statistical tables provide rich materials to substantiate the fact that
schizophrenics have definite problems in understanding the
abstract or figurative message of proverbs.

4282. Roth, Walter. "Der Bilderreichtum des Siebenbürgisch-
Sächsischen. Versuch einer Analyse örtlicher Redewendungen
und sprichwörtlicher Redensarten von Schäßburg." *Zeitschrift für
siebenbürgische Landeskunde,* 12, no. 2 (1989), 124–130.

Roth presents a collection of proverbs, proverbial
expressions, and proverbial comparisons which he collected
during field research after 1947 among the German settlers of
Schäßburg in Transylvania. He starts his article with some general
comments regarding proverbial language and stresses the fact
that paremiographers and folklorists should continue collecting
proverbs from oral speech even today. The texts are cited in
dialect form with High German texts added for better
understanding. The examples are grouped according to their
metaphors, humor, irony, occupations, localities, etc. Many
historical, etymological, and cultural notes are added, making
this an informative collection and study of the proverbs of a small
dialect region.

4283. Rothkegel, Annely. "Phraseologien in Texten der internationalen
Fachkommunikation." *Europhras 88. Phraséologie Contrastive. Actes
du Colloque International Klingenthal-Strasbourg, 12–16 mai 1988.* Ed.
Gertrud Gréciano. Strasbourg: Université des Sciences Humaines,
1989. 371–378.

This is one of the rare studies that investigates the
phraseological units that appear in scientific and technical
publications. While phraseologists have investigated the
proverbial language contained in literature, newspapers,
advertisments, etc., very little is actually known about the use of
such language in the prose of various occupational fields.

Rothkegel is able to show that such publications contain only a few fixed phrases, and they certainly use proverbs very seldomly. Nevertheless, as her German and French contextualized examples indicate, phraseological units play a significant role in this technical writing. They add some colloquial and metaphorical flavor to a rather dry and straight forward style, and it behooves phraseologists to pay attention to them.

4284. Rothstein, Robert A. "Jews in Slavic Eyes—The Paremiological Evidence." *Proceedings of the Ninth World Congress of Jewish Studies.* No editor given. Jerusalem: World Union of Jewish Studies, 1986. II, 181–188.

Rothstein's article is a comparative study of Slavic proverbs showing the unfortunate anti-Semitism expressed in folk wisdom. The author begins his important article with a short discussion of German and Slavic collections of proverbs dealing with the Jewish people, and he is quick to point out that most of these proverbs express unfair stereotypes, viscious invectives, and hateful slurs. He analyzes a number of standard Polish and Ukrainian proverb collections for anti-Semitic proverbs and shows that they contain misinformation and slanderous comments regarding Jewish appearance, behavior, beliefs, customs, etc. The texts dealing with the Jews as business people and their alleged dishonesty and deceit are particularly distasteful. At the end of his article Rothstein points out that the Gypsies are treated with similar distain in Slavic proverbs. In fact, it is argued that the words Jew and Gypsy are basically interchangeable in these proverbs. The 19 notes include valuable bibliographical information, making this study a necessary reminder of the dangers of proverbial slurs.

4285. Roulon, Paulette, and Raymond Doko. "La parole pilée: Accès au symbolisme chez les Gbáyá 'bòdòè de Centrafrique." *Cahiers de littérature orale,* no. 13 (1983), 33–49.

The two authors discuss a number of "tóó wèn," literally signifying "crushed words" of the Gbáyá 'bòdòè people of Central Africa. They first deal with the various stages a child and adolescent must go through before they can understand orally used "tóó wèn." This is followed by a discussion of their use and social function. The authors also present a definition of these proverbs that are based on a clear binary structure. The two parts of this structure are the basis of a semantic correlation referring to a symbol whose interpretation is at an individual level. Roulon and Doko collected over 300 of these expressions, and they point out that traditional "tóó wèn" can also be changed by a speaker if the conversational occasion necessitates it. The binary structure will, however, always be maintained in such altered proverbs. A small bibliography (pp. 48–49) and an English summary (p. 176) are included.

4286. Roventa-Frumusani, Daniela. "Le proverbe e(s)t énonciation econcée." *Revue Roumaine de Linguistique,* 30, no. 2 (1985), 159–167.

This is a theoretical study looking at proverbs as speech acts. The author starts with some comments regarding standard proverb definitions, and she then argues that they must be looked at from the point of view of semiotics. By means of three charts Roventa-Frumusani shows that a pragmatic approach to proverbs must be based on a detailed analysis of their intertextuality, i.e., proverbs must be regarded as significant speech acts in context. Citing numerous contextualized French examples from oral and written sources, it is argued that proverbs often have an argumentative value. They are used as effective verbal strategies in an argument situation, and they act as signs of traditional wisdom or common experience known to the various participants of such spoken exchange. A short bibliography (p. 167) is attached.

4287. Rozgonyine, Molnar Emma. "A szolasok és közmondasok szövegbe szerkesztése." *Magyar Nyelvör,* 106, no. 3 (1982), 352–356.

Rozgonyine presents a structural analysis of how proverbs and proverbial expressions are integrated into oral or written contexts. She cites many Hungarian examples which illustrate that phraseological units are used within (1) a clause as part of that clause or as an independent clause, (2) a sentence in a clause or subdivided into two or more clauses, and (3) a paragraph. These examples show that so-called fixed phrases may indeed be altered grammatically, lexically, or structurally in order to fit them properly into a speech context. In fact, proverbial expressions are quite often altered in this fashion when being integrated into a communicative situation. Proverbs, on the other hand, will be cited without changes if they are explicitly quoted as independent pieces of wisdom. This is especially the case when they are identified by an introductory formula. But it must be recognized that proverbs can also be changed depending on the situation and the intent of the speaker.

4288. Ruduri, Kwezi. "L'Homme face à la mort, au regard de quelques proverbes rwanda." *Africanistique*, no. 11 (1982), 44–63.

Ruduri analyzes 16 Rwandan proverbs which deal with death and the dead. He cites his African texts with French translations and includes detailed ethnographical notes. Some texts clearly express beliefs and superstitions regarding mortality, while others comment on the possibility of an afterlife. Ruduri also cites proverbs which deal with the fact that all people are equal when it comes to death, and he shows which role God plays in these proverbs that occupy themselves with life coming to an end. The entire anthropological study is a clear indication that the Rwandan people have a distinct corpus of proverbs which is dedicated to death and dying. The same is true for the proverbs of other languages, since human mortality is a universally experienced phenomenon.

4289. Ruduri, Kwezi. "Le thème de l'amitié dans 50 proverbes rwanda." *Africanistique*, no. 3 (1984), 96–126.

In this article Ruduri analyzes 50 Rwandan proverbs which deal with friends and friendship. He cites each text with French translations and equivalents, and he then offers detailed ethnographical notes. Special emphasis is placed on various aspects of friendship, such as trust, support, constancy, honesty, etc. There is also a section in this paper which deals with the problem of false friendships. The article is basically a content analysis of these texts, showing that the feeling of friendship appears to be a universal concern of people everywhere. The value which the Rwandan people from Africa place on friendship is not really that different from that of the French people. The proverbs express very similar ideas and feelings, but they differ in language and metaphors. A short bibliography is attached.

4290. Ruef, Hans. "Understanding Proverbs: Scene Development as a Process of Motivation." *Linguistic Agency University of Trier*, series A, no. 111 (1983), 1–14.

This is a linguistic study of why people in general feel that proverbs are true. Ruef argues that the "truth" of a proverb does not depend on a successful application of it in a context or situation, since informants sense its truth also when directly asked about it. It is shown that the usually perceived gap between proverb-form and proverb-meaning is bridged by the existence of a cognitive process which underlies proverb understanding. Ruef calls this process of comprehending the image of the proverb "scene development." The internal meaning of a proverb is conceived of in terms of a "scene." In order to understand a proverb, its textinternal aspect (scene, image) is brought into connection with its textexternal aspect (meaning, application, situation) by a mental scene development which leads to an understanding of the truth or wisdom of the proverb. Several English examples are cited, and 3 figures as well as a short bibliography (p. 14) are also included.

4291. Ruef, Hans. "Das Sprichwort als Ausgestaltung eines Paradoxons. Zur Geschichte eines deutschen Sprichwortpaares." *Zeitschrift für deutsche Philologie*, 105 (1986), 369–382.

Ruef attempts to explain why the medieval Dutch and German proverb "Hastiger Mann soll keinen Esel reiten" (Hasty man should not ride an ass) also exists in the positive variant "Hastiger (jäher) Mann soll Esel reiten." Citing numerous contextualized references of both the negative and positive variants, Ruef comes to the convincing conclusion that the two counterparts are an illustration of the rather common phenomenon of contradiction among proverbs. In this case, the two texts illustrate the paradox of interpreting the same impatient person differently. The context will decide whether the positive or the negative variant will be cited. References from such standard proverb collections as the Latin *Fecunda ratis* (1022/24) by Egbert von Lüttich (972?–1026?), the Dutch and Latin anonymous *Proverbia communia* (1480, with later printings up to 1497), and Johannes Agricola's *Sybenhundert und fünfftzig Teütscher Sprichwörter* (1534) are included. Ruef also cites various examples from such German authors as Freidank (12th/13th century), Sebastian Brant (1458–1521), Hans Sachs (1494–1576), etc. Short German and English abstracts (p. 369) are attached.

4292. Ruef, Hans. "Zusatzsprichwörter und das Problem des parömischen Minimums." *Europhras 88. Phraséologie Contrastive. Actes du Colloque International Klingenthal-Strasbourg, 12–16 mai 1988.* Ed. Gertrud Gréciano. Strasbourg: Université des Sciences Humaines, 1989. 379–385.

This is an important article dealing with two major paremiological questions. In the first part Ruef investigates what he calls "Zusatzsprichwörter" (augmented proverbs). By this he means standard proverbs to which a few words are added that put the wisdom of the proverb into question. A Swiss German example would be "D'Narre sind au Lüüt, aber nöd so wie anderi" (Fools are also people, but they are not quite like the others). Quite often these additions are introduced by the conjunction "aber" (but), and the added phrases usually express humor, irony or parody. Ruef claims that at least some of these expanded proverbs have become proverbs in their own right, and they should be considered as a subgenre. But he agrees that for those augmented proverbs which have gained no particular currency Wolfgang Mieder's term of "Antisprichwort" (anti-proverb) remains appropriate (see no. 3852). The second part of the article discusses the fact that some of the "Zusatzsprichwörter" are so popular that they are actually part of the paremiological minimum of the German language. Several dialect texts are cited, clearly indicating that paremiologists should pay more attention to these humorous reactions to dry folk wisdom.

4293. Rúke-Dravina, Velta. "Die lettische Phraseologie im Vergleich mit zwei germanischen Sprachen—dem Deutschen und dem

Schwedischen." *Aktuelle Probleme der Phraseologie.* Eds. Harald Burger and Robert Zett. Bern: Peter Lang, 1987. 169–186.

The author investigates the similarities and differences among Latvian, German, and Swedish phraseological units, in particular proverbial expressions, proverbial comparisons, and twin formulas. She points out that there are quite a few fixed phrases that are known in all three languages. These usually go back to classical antiquity or the Bible. Through different processes of loan translations due to historical and cultural contacts there are also groups of expressions which are known only in two languages. But it must not be forgotten that there are also plenty of texts which are current in only one of the languages. Even for those phrases that belong to two or three of the languages, Rúke-Dravina is able to show that they might differ in popularity and in shades of meaning. All of this presents rather vexing problems for lexicographers and translators. A small bibliography (pp. 185–186) is included.

4294. Russell, Daniel. "A Note on Panurge's 'Pusse en l'aureille'." *Études Rabelaisiennes*, 11 (1974), 83–87.

Russell studies the use and function of the French proverbial expression "Avoir la puce à l'oreille" (To have a flea in one's ear, i.e., to be uneasy, suspicious) in François Rabelais' (1494–1553) novel *Le Tiers Livre* (1546). He explains that the main character Panurge actually wears a single golden earring within which is set a black flea. This appears to be an emblematic device based on the common phrase, and it is used by Rabelais as a sign both of Panurge's sexual desire and of an accompanying uneasiness, anxiety, or fear. A few other references regarding this expression in Rabelais' works are cited, and Russell makes clear that it can indeed be interpreted on a sexual level.

4295. Russo, Joseph. "The Poetics of the Ancient Greek Proverb." *Journal of Folklore Research*, 20 (1983), 121–130.

The paper starts with a definition of the proverb and then discusses the structure, content, and context of a number of ancient Greek proverbs which are cited in transliteration and with English translations. Russo deals in particular with such phonetic and structural devices as rhyme, alliteration, assonance, binary and oppositional structure, repetition, and vowel harmony. Many of the texts are also characterized by paradox, irony, and tartness. As an example of some Greek proverbs in context Russo quotes a story out of Herodotus (5th century B.C.) which shows how Gyges is forced to act against the wisdom of his proverbs by the king Candaules whom he subsequently kills. An understanding of the poetics of the Greek proverb should help literary scholars to locate them in Greek literature and thereby bring to light their use and function. The notes include useful bibliographical references.

4296. Ruxandoiu, Pavel. "Iordache Golescu si proverbele romanesti." *Proverbium Dacoromania*, 2 (1987), 18–24.

Ruxandoiu describes a manuscript collection of proverbs from 1845 which was put together by the Rumanian philologist Iordache Golescu (1768?–1848). This is not necessarily a scholarly collection but rather an attempt to assemble as many Rumanian and foreign proverbs as possible. Golescu did not differentiate among Rumanian proverbs and those stemming from other European national languages. It is also not clear which proverbs might have been found in literary works and which texts the author knew from actual folk speech. Altogether Golescu saw his collection as a didactic work which contains moral wisdom in proverbs from many sources and languages. An English abstract (p. 24) is provided.

4297. Rynduch, Zbigniew. "Funkcja przyslow w prozie Andrezeja Maksymiliana Fredry." *Retoryka a literatura*. Ed. Barbara Otwinowskiej. Warszawa: Polska Akademia Nauk, 1984. 153–165.

This is a philological study concerning Andrzej Maksymilian Fredro's (1620–1679) Polish and Latin proverb collection *Przyslowia mow potocznych* (1655). It is shown that Fredro is one of the truly great Polish paremiographers who was not only interested in the proverbs themselves but also in their use and function. He drew attention to their social, political, and moral context, and he also saw their didactic and pedagogical value. While many texts of this collection are folk proverbs, Fredro also included sententious remarks, aphorisms, and maxims. He was influenced above all by Erasmus of Rotterdam's (1469–1536) *Adagia* (1500ff.), and he accomplished a great deal in showing that Polish proverbs could be compared favorably with Latin texts. This early proverb collection is of much importance for historical Polish paremiography. The 27 notes include rich bibliographical information, and a French summary (pp. 164–165) is included.

4298. Ryzhuk, D.A. "Poslovitsy i pogovorki, sobrannye Klimentiem Zinov'evym." *Filologicheskie Nauki*, 6, no. 3 (1963), 188–200.

Ryzhuk reports on a proverb manuscript containing 1600 Ukrainian texts which were collected by Klimentii Zinov'ev (17/18th cnetury). The proverbs were arranged alphabetically and thematically by this collector of the late 17th century. They reflect the cultural and social attitudes of that time, and Ryzhuk is able to show that they comment on class inequalities and other societal conflicts. They also refer to general experience, wisdom that has been handed down for generations, and aspects of normal life, including such matters as work, the family, etc. Numerous examples from this early Ukrainian proverb collection are cited, and the author adds detailed historical and cultural explanations. While some of the texts are clearly indigenous to the Ukrainian language and culture, others are rather common in many other Slavic languages as well. The 14 notes include bibliographical information regarding Ukrainian paremiographical and paremiological scholarship.

S

4299. Sabban, Annette. "'Die dümmsten Bauern haben nicht mehr die dicksten Kartoffeln'—Variationen von Sprichwörtern im und als Text." *Sprichwörter und Redensarten im interkulturellen Vergleich.* Eds. A. Sabban and Jan Wirrer. Opladen: Westdeutscher Verlag, 1991. 83–108.

The author investigates the use and function of German proverbs in newspapers and advertisements, explaining that they are usually employed as variations of the traditional text. Citing numerous examples in context, Sabban indicates that these variations are brought about by the substitution of individual letters or words, by the expansion of the normal text, and through various forms of negation. She also explains that very common proverbs are simply reduced to structural types. An example would be the proverb "Eine Schwalbe macht noch keinen Sommer" (One swallow doesn't make a summer) which becomes the structural pattern "Ein(e) X macht noch kein(en) Y." The two variables can be replaced by almost any noun and the resulting variations can serve as effective headlines or slogans. Some of these innovative texts are in fact "Antisprichwörter" (anti-proverbs), and they serve as attention getting devices or as newly coined proverbial wisdom. A useful bibliography (pp. 107–108) is attached.

4300. Sabban, Annette, and Jan Wirrer (eds.). *Sprichwörter und Redensarten im interkulturellen Vergleich.* Opladen: Westdeutscher Verlag, 1991. 226 pp.

This is a very important essay volume containing 12 contributions by German phraseologists and paremiologists. While the articles are written in German, they almost all deal with proverbs and phraseological units from other languages and cultures as well. The authors and titles are as follows: Irmgard

Simon, "Zum Aufbau eines Sprichwortarchivs: Das Westfälische Sprichwortarchiv bei der Kommission für Mundart- und Namenforschung in Münster" (pp. 13–27); Stanislaw Predota, "Zu den lexikographischen Grundprinzipien des *Kleinen deutsch-polnischen Sprichwörterbuches*" (pp. 28–36); Jarmo Korhonen, "Verbidiomatik Deutsch-Finnisch. Ein Forschungsbericht" (pp. 37–65); Gertrud Gréciano, "Zur Aktivität der Phrasemkomponenten—Deutsch-französische Beobachtungen" (pp. 66–82); Annette Sabban, "'Die dümmsten Bauern haben nicht mehr die dicksten Kartoffeln'—Variationen von Sprichwörtern im und als Text" (pp. 83–108); Ernest W.B. Hess-Lüttich, "Kontrastive Phraseologie im DaF-Unterricht—anhand arabischer und niederländischer Brecht-Übersetzungen" (pp. 109–127); Werner Kummer, "Die Sprüch-Wörter in Wolfgang Teuschls Bibelübersetzung *Da Jesus und seine Hawara*" (pp. 128–138); Winfried Boeder, "Struktur und Interpretation georgischer Sprichwörter aus Chewßuretien" (pp. 139–161); Günther Schlee, "Zur rechtlichen Verwendung von Sprichwörtern bei den Rendille (Nordkenia)" (pp. 162–174); Jan Wirrer, "Anmerkungen zur Sprichwortkultur Madagaskars" (pp. 175–186); Peter Grzybek, "Das Sprichwort im literarischen Text" (pp. 187–205); and Lothar Bluhm, "Sprichwörter und Redensarten bei den Brüdern Grimm (pp. 206–224). The articles deal with such aspects as proverb archives, lexicography, phraseology, variation, translation, structure, law, anthropology, literature, fairy tales, etc. Proverbs are cited from German, Polish, Finnish, French, English, Arabic, Dutch, Georgian, and African languages. For individual annotations see nos. 4380, 4200, 3716, 3510, 4299, 3591, 3746, 3148, 4330, 4571, 3534, 3145.

4301. Sakaoglu, Saim. "Turkish Anecdotal Proverbs." *Motif: International Newsletter of Research in Folklore and Literature*, no. 4 (1982), 4–5.

This is a short investigation of the form and structure of Turkish anecdotal proverbs which consist of a dialogue between two persons. Sakaoglu divides his ten examples into two groups according to the types of communication taking place: proverbs with two-line dialogues and proverbs with three-line dialogues. The proverbs usually start with an opening interrogative sentence, but they might also occasionally end with a question.

The author comments that very little is known about this proverbial subgenre, and he calls for increased historical and structural analysis of such texts. All examples are first cited in English translation followed by the Turkish original.

4302. Salanitro, Maria. "Le pentola che non bolle (Petron. *Satyr.* 38,13)." *Atene e Roma,* 31 (1986), 23–27.

Salanitro studies the origin, history, and dissemination of the classical Latin proverb "Sociorum olla male fervet" which has become proverbial in English as "A pot of comrades boils badly." He cites its earliest reference from the *Satyricon* of the Roman poet and prose writer Gaius Petronius Arbiter (died 66 A.D.). Following an interpretation of the proverb in this work, Salanitro cites a number of later references and shows how the proverb survives today in the modern Italian language and its dialects. The article is a philological study that explains how a classical proverb has survived hundreds of years through written and oral use.

4303. Salveit, Laurits. "Beobachtungen zu einem Sonderfall der Parataxe in deutschen Sprichwörtern." *Aspekte der Germanistik. Festschrift für Hans-Friedrich Rosenfeld zum 90. Geburtstag.* Ed. Walter Tauber. Göppingen: Kümmerle, 1989. 657–670.

Even though the title of this article states that it deals with the problem of parataxis in German proverbs, it is actually an investigation of this syntactical phenomenon in wellerisms. In fact, Salveit begins with a short survey of previous research on wellerisms, citing English examples and pointing out that the term "wellerism" stems from the character Sam Weller in Charles Dickens' (1811–1870) novel *Pickwick Papers* (1837). Salveit argues that while folklorists have studied the content and humor of wellerisms, very little attention has been paid to their form and structure. He cites both High and Low German, Norwegian, and Danish examples to show how the third part of the wellerism, the one that contains the situation in which a speaker uttered a proverbial statement, is connected to the first two parts. He is particularly interested in the German conjunction "da" with the meaning of "then, after that, at that time," etc. It is this small word that usually links the third part of the wellerism to the preceding two elements.

4304. Saly, Antoinette. "Les proverbes dans le *Meliacin* de Girart d'Amiens: Aspect et fonction." *Richesse du proverbe.* Eds. François Suard and Claude Buridant. Lille: Université de Lille, 1984. I, 121–129.

This is a literary proverb investigation of Girart d'Amiens' (13th century) versified epic *Meliacin* (c. 1285). Saly begins her study with a short discussion of the origin and plot of this medieval work. She then states that it contains quite a large number of French proverbs from the Middle Ages. Citing a number of examples in their literary context, she shows how Girart d'Amiens uses proverbs as leitmotifs, how he varies them, and how he employs them as expressions of folk wisdom. For some of the texts Saly provides parallel references from other medieval French authors, and she also refers to French proverb collections as annotations. There is, however, no proverb index.

4305. Samarasinghe, S.G. "The Sinhala Proverb: A Mode of Symbolic Interaction." *Samskrti: Cultural Quarterly,* 17, nos. 1–2 (1983), 59–73.

The author presents a rare glimpse into the nature of Sinhala proverbs from Sri Lanka, citing his examples in the original script, in transliteration, and in English translation. The article begins with a general introduction concerning various definition attempts (pp. 59–62), arguing that Sinhala proverbs in general fit these findings. Samarasinghe then comments on a few Sinhala proverb collections which are in need of being updated and expanded. Next he discusses the form and structure of these proverbs, emphasizing their use of rhythm, verse, and repetition. He also mentions that the content of these proverbs reflects the Sinhala worldview. Proverbs are seen as expressing social norms of behavior, and it is pointed out that they play a major role in verbal communication. A short bibliography (p. 73) is attached.

4306. Sandig, Barbara. "Stilistische Funktionen verbaler Idiome am Beispiel von Zeitungsglossen und anderen Verwendungen."

Europhras 88. Phraséologie Contrastive. Actes du Colloque International Klingenthal-Strasbourg, 12–16 mai 1988. Ed. Gertrud Gréciano. Strasbourg: Université des Sciences Humaines, 1989. 387–400.

Sandig reports on the use and function of German phraseological units that have appeared in short newspaper articles (one to three paragraphs) in the weekly newspaper *Die Zeit.* Journalists often use shortened proverbs or proverbial expressions as attention getting headlines, and within the short texts the fixed phrases are employed to add emotion and folk speech to an intellectual argument. These metaphorical expressions clearly increase the effectiveness of argumentation, and they certainly add authority to what is being discussed. Sandig includes contextualized examples and also adds four short newspaper articles in an appendix (pp. 398–400). A useful bibliography (pp. 397–398) is included.

4307.   Sandig, Barbara. "Formeln des Bewertens." *Europhras 90. Akten der internationalen Tagung zur germanistischen Phraseologieforschung, Aske/Schweden 12.-15. Juni 1990.* Ed. Christine Palm. Uppsala: Acta Universitatis Upsaliensis, 1991. 225–252.

The author treats German phraseological units that evaluate certain human or natural characteristics. Citing numerous idioms, twin formulas, proverbial comparisons, etc., she shows that these fixed formulas of evaluation are either negative or positive. They are used to make emphatic or emotional statements, and they often contain comparatives or even superlatives. Sandig cites examples from German newspapers and illustrates how journalists use such fixed phrases to add expressive language to their journalistic texts. Many times such traditional phrases are also used to manipulate the opinion of the readers through their powerful metaphorical language. A helpful bibliography (pp. 249–252) is attached.

4308.   Sarma, Nabin Ch. "Study of a Few Assamese Proverbs from the Contextual Point of View." *Folklore* (Calcutta), 27, no. 4 (1986), 71–77.

Sarma starts with some comments regarding the importance of knowing the context in which proverbs are being used, and he then discusses a few Assamese proverbs from India. As with most proverb collections, those from the Assamese language have also not recorded them in actual contexts. However, the author is able to provide a context for almost all of his examples since they originated from folk narratives. Sarma cites the proverb first in the Assamese language. This is followed by an English translation, and to this the author has added the tales which illustrate the proverbs in context. It is argued that there is an important relationship between proverbs and folk narratives from which scholars can gain insights into the function of proverbs in early social situations.

4309. Sartor, Mario. "Dichos y refranes de los meses." *Lebende Sprachen,* 29, no. 1 (1984), 27.

This is a short article discussing several Spanish proverbs dealing with various months of the year. Sartor first cites examples from Spain and explains that they refer to certain weather rules or other observations concerning the four seasons and nature in general. While these proverbs continue to be popular in the modern Spanish language, Sartor also points out that they have undergone some changes during the centuries that Spanish has been spoken in the New World. He cites a number of South American variants that illustrate some lexical changes that are due to the new geographical, meteorological, and social environment. While the Spanish language proverbs of South and Central America are quite often identical to those of Spain, some differences do exist, and there are also those proverbs which are indigenous to Spanish speakers of the New World.

4310. Sassen, A. "De verklaring van de uitdrukking 'Iemand een loer draaien'." *Leuvense Bijdragen,* 72, no. 4 (1983), 429–436.

The author investigates the history and meaning of the Dutch proverbial expression "Iemand een loer draaien" (To turn a rag for someone, i.e., to play a trick on someone). He cites several contextualized examples and also reviews previous philological research on this phrase. The difficulty centers around the etymology of the noun "loer" which appears to be a worthless piece of cloth (rag) or rope. Sassen offers new etymological evidence by citing dialect variants of the expression. He also discusses the structural and semantic aspects of the phrase, illustrating that it is very popular among modern Dutch speakers despite its somewhat unsolved linguistic origin.

4311. Saulnier, René, and Henri van der Zée. "La mort du crédit: Image populaire, ses sources politiques et économiques." *Dawna Sztuka*, 2 (1939), 195–218.

This is a major study of the European proverb "Crédit est mort, les mauvais payeurs l'ont tué" (Credit [Giving] is dead, the bad payers have killed him), for which the authors cite primarily French and German references. They explain that broadsheets with illustrations were particularly popular throughout Europe during the 17th century, and they reproduce 7 drawings and etchings which they interpret as satirical commentaries on the politics and economics of the time. Special attention is given to a rare Polish illustration and text from between 1635 to 1650, explaining that this iconographical representation of the proverb also serves satirical and moralistic purposes. See also the other studies by Monique Coppens d'Eeckenbrugge (no. 301), Wolfgang Mieder (no. 3877), Adolf Spamer (no. 1772), and Walter Tobler (no. 1955).

4312. Savenkova, I.E. "Strukturno-semanticheskie preobrazovaniia poslovits i pogovorok v rechi." *Izvestiia Akademii Nauk Turkmenskoi SSR, seriia Obshchestvennykh Nauk*, no. 1 (1989), 48–53.

Savenkova studies the structural and semantic transformations of proverbs and proverbial expressions in modern Russian prose and journalistic writings. She starts her article by observing that so-called fixed phrases are quite often changed once they become contextualized. Several short texts are analyzed, showing that such modifications are based on the exchange of individual words, on merely alluding to traditional proverbs rather than citing them in their entirety, and on the intentional parody of the proverbial wisdom. Savenkova also explains that the meaning of such altered proverbs is obviously changed as well. All of this is a clear indication of how phraseological units can be adapted to modern communicative needs. A very short English abstract (p. 53) is provided.

4313.   Savvina, E.N. "O transformatsiiakh klishirovannykh vyrazhenii v rechi." *Paremiologicheskie issledovaniia.* Ed. Grigorii L'vovich Permiakov. Moskva: Nauka, 1984. 200–222; also in French translation as "Transformations discursives des locutions figées" in *Tel grain tel pain. Poétique de la sagesse populaire.* Ed. G.L. Permiakov. Moscou: Éditions du Progrès, 1988. 114–138.

By means of many Russian examples the author shows and explains the transformation of clichés (i.e., proverbs, proverbial expressions, literary quotations, etc.) in actual language use. Such transformations in modern Russian written and oral language are primarily due to (1) additions (negations, modifications, actualizations), (2) deletions, (3) substitutions, and (4) position changes of lexical elements within the texts. These alterations are discussed on semantic, syntactical, morphological, lexical, and phonological levels. The lexicographical problem of cataloguing such changed phraseological units in a dictionary is also treated. One diagram and a bibliography (pp. 221–222) of primarily Soviet scholarship on such intentional variations of fixed phrases are included.

4314.   Sazdov, Tomè. "Macedonian Proverbs and Sayings." *Macedonian Review,* 14, no. 2 (1984), 214–220.

This is a general treatise on Macedonian proverbs in which the many examples are cited in English translation only. Sazdov points out that there are four major sources for these proverbs, namely (1) traditional wisdom handed down through oral communication since the Middle Ages, (2) condensations of fables and folk narratives, (2) translations from the Bible and other religious writings, and (4) loan translations from the Turks and Greeks. The second part of this short article deals with the content of Macedonian proverbs, stressing that they comment on experience, social relationships, daily life, labor, education, morality, etc. Most of these proverbs are metaphorical, and while some are rather serious and didactic, there are also those texts which express folk humor.

4315. Scattergood, John. "Proverbial Verses in Trinity College Dublin MS 212." *Notes and Queries*, 228, new series 30 (1983), 489–490.

Scattergood reports on a medieval manuscript kept at the library of Trinity College in Dublin, Ireland, which contains three couplets written in three single lines in the Middle English of the mid-fifteenth century. Three English proverbs are contained in these couplets, namely "Cast not away the old until you are sure of the new," "Unknown unkissed," and "Beware of had-I-wist." Scattergood comments on the manuscript and this short text, and he also provides annotations from Bartlett Jere Whiting's superb historical collection *Proverbs, Sentences, and Proverbial Phrases from English Writings Mainly Before 1500* (1968).

4316. Scattergood, John. "'Chaucer a Bukton' and Proverbs." *Nottingham Medieval Stduies*, 31 (1987), 98–107.

In this article Scattergood shows that Geoffrey Chaucer's (1340?–1400) poem "Envoy to Bukton" contains numerous proverbs and proverbial expressions. Since the subject of this Middle English text is marriage, Chaucer delights in quoting misogynous proverbs to give comical and satirical advice. The poem also includes numerous Biblical quotations, making it both a didactic and ironic piece of early English literature. Scattergood provides annotations from Bartlett Jere Whiting's historical collection *Proverbs, Sentences, and Proverbial Phrases from English Writings Mainly Before 1500* (1968), and he also cites several proverbial passages from Chaucer's *Wife of Bath* out of the *Canterbury Tales* (1387/1400) in order to show how well Chaucer was versed in proverbial wisdom about women and marriage.

4317. Schade, Richard E. "'Junge Soldaten, alte Bettler': Zur Ikonographie des Pikaresken am Beispiel des *Springinsfeld* Titelkupfers." *Der deutsche Schelmenroman im europäischen Kontext: Rezeption, Interpretation, Bibliographie*. Ed. Gerhard Hoffmeister. Amsterdam: Rodopi, 1987. 93–112.

This is a fascinating iconographical study of the illustration on the title page of Hans Jakob Christoffel von Grimmelshausen's (1622?–1676) novel *Der seltsame Springinsfeld* (1670). Schade is able to show that this copper engraving is at least in part a depiction of the German proverb "Junge Soldaten, alte Bettler" (Young soldiers, old beggars). In fact, he cites a passage from the end of the second chapter which basically describes this illustration while at the same time quoting the common proverb about young soldiers becoming beggars in old age. The author also includes an engraving from 1631 that illustrates the proverb "Wie gewonnen, so zerronnen" (Easy come, easy go) and argues that both proverbs fit well into the social and military upheavals during the Thirty Years' War. With 10 illustrations and a short discussion of the proverb and its meaning for the entire novel.

4318. Schaffner, Emil. "Spiel mit Wortfügungen und Wendungen." In E. Schaffner. *Es rumpelt und stilzt im Sprach-Spülkasten.* Frauenfeld: Huber, 1982. 92–99.

Schaffner presents a short discussion on modern wordplays with proverbs, proverbial expressions, and literary quotations. He cites German examples from journalistic writings, advertisements, and literature, quoting poems by Bertolt Brecht (1898–1956) and Josef Reding (1929–) as well as aphorisms by Karl Kraus (1874–1936). It is argued that traditional and perhaps archaic expressions are revived through innovative manipulations of their original wording. Through linguistic "tricks" they gain new relevance as formulaic expressions of the political and social concerns of modern Germany. Many examples of such varied phraseological units are discussed, making it clear that "Antisprichwörter" (anti-proverbs) play a major role in modern written communication.

4319. Scheichl, Sigurd Paul. "Feste Syntagmen im dramatischen Dialog. Materialien zur Geschichte eines Stilmittels zwischen Goethe und Kroetz." *Tradition und Entwicklung. Festschrift Eugen Thurnher.* Eds. Werner Bauer, Achim Masser, and Guntram Plangg. Innsbruck: Institut für Germanistik der Universität Innsbruck, 1982. 383–407.

In this literary investigation of the use and function of fixed phrases in German dramatic works Scheichl studies in particular the following authors from the 18th to the 20th century: Johann Wolfgang von Goethe (1749–1832), Friedrich Schiller (1759–

1805), Ferdinand Raimund (1790–1836), Georg Büchner (1813–1837), Friedrich Hebbel (1813–1863), Gerhart Hauptmann (1862–1946), and Franz Xaver Kroetz (1946–). Citing a number of contextualized examples, the author is able to show that phraseological units are a major stylistic element in these German plays. They are used to express feelings and ideas in a colloquial manner, and they certainly present ample proof that the various authors were very much aware of the importance of folk speech in oral communication. The 117 notes (pp. 400–407) contain helpful bibliographical information concerning the integration of proverbial language in literary works.

4320. Schellbach-Kopra, Ingrid. "Parömisches Minimum und Phraseodidaktik im finnisch-deutschen Bereich." *Beiträge zur allgemeinen und germanistischen Phraseologieforschung.* Ed. Jarmo Korhonen. Oulu: Oulun Yliopisto, 1987. 245–255.

The author presents a significant discussion of the Finnish and German paremiological minimum, especially in as far as the establishment of truly current and frequently used phraseological units is of importance in the area of foreign language instruction. She argues that a German studying Finnish would have to know between 300 to 600 proverbs and proverbial expressions in order to master the Finnish paremiological minimum. This number would increase to about 2000–3000 if such other fixed phrases as proverbial comparisons, twin formulas, sententious remarks, etc. were added. Next Schellbach-Kopra analyzes how a phraseological dictionary that serves foreign language students might look like. Such a compilation should include both proverbs and proverbial expressions, be organized according to key-words, provide direct translations and equivalents, and also comment on the stylistic levels of the individual texts. At the end of the article the author also deals with such matters as "faux amis," dialect expressions, origin, phrases based on gestures, and proverb parodies in the form of "Antisprichwörter" (anti-proverbs). A small bibliography (pp. 254–255) is included.

4321. Schellbach-Kopra, Ingrid. "Das Alter im Sprichwort der Deutschen und Finnen—eine kontrastive Betrachtung." *Jahrbuch für finnisch-deutsche Literaturbeziehungen,* 20 (1988), 95–106.

This is a comparative analysis of those Finnish and German proverbs which comment on various aspects of biological age, old people, old things, etc. Citing numerous examples for both languages (with German translations of the Finnish texts), Schellbach-Kopra points out that there are a few proverbs which are identical. However, the indigenous Finnish examples tend to be more serious, didactic, and realistic than the more humorous or ironical German texts. The author includes some historical and cultural explanations, paying special attention to some of the older proverbs and also those recent texts which were coined by the youth culture of today. At the end of the article she includes a list of 50 frequent Finnish proverbs concerning age and a much longer German list of similar proverbs.

4322. Schellbach-Kopra, Ingrid. "Glück und Unglück in Sprichwort und Redensart am Beispiel Finnisch-Deutsch." *Europhras 88. Phraséologie Contrastive. Actes du Colloque International Klingenthal-Strasbourg, 12–16 mai 1988.* Ed. Gertrud Gréciano. Strasbourg: Université des Sciences Humaines, 1989. 401–411.

In this comparative study Schellbach-Kopra deals with Finnish and German proverbs and proverbial expressions whose content is based on the idea of "Glück" (fortune, luck) and "Unglück" (misfortune). She has selected some of the most frequent expressions from both languages, citing the Finnish examples with German translations. Her special interest are those phrases that express in various metaphors the idea of being a(n) (un)lucky person or simply to be (un)lucky. It is argued that there is no particular difference among these German and Finnish texts, but perhaps one could observe that the Finnish examples might be a bit more concrete or realistic. In any case, the examples reflect certain cultural ideas which might be interpreted as expressions of worldview.

4323. Schellbach-Kopra, Ingrid. "Glück und Glas, wie leicht bricht das—'Fortuna' in der finnisch-deutschen Phraseologie." *Finnisch-Ugrische Forschungen,* 49 (1990), 139–168.

This is a somewhat expanded version of the previous article (see no. 4322), once again comparing Finnish and German phraseological units dealing with fortune or luck and to a lesser degree also with those expressions referring to misfortune. Schellbach includes etymological and semantic explanations and treats in particular metaphorical phrases based on the idea of being a(n) (un)lucky person or simply being (un)lucky. She also discusses that these texts do indicate a certain worldview, especially when they express fatalism or refer to superstitions and magic. Some examples of modern "Antisprichwörter" (anti-proverbs) are included, and large lists (pp. 160–166) of texts (with German translations of the Finnish examples) are added at the end of the article. A useful bibliography (pp. 167–168) is attached.

4324. Schellbach-Kopra, Ingrid. "'Ei kiittämistä!'—'Nicht zu danken!' Zur Höflichkeitsphraseologie im Finnischen und Deutschen." *Europhras 90. Akten der internationalen Tagung zur germanistischen Phraseologieforschung, Aske/Schweden 12.-15. Juni 1990.* Ed. Christine Palm. Uppsala: Acta Universitatis Upsaliensis, 1991. 211–223.

In this comparative analysis Schellbach-Kopra treats Finnish and German phraseological units that express the idea of politeness. It is argued that due to the taciturnity of the Finns their language does not have a large number of polite routine formulas. This does not mean that Finns are necessarily less polite than Germans but rather that they express politeness through different cultural patterns. The author includes two lists of such fixed phrases, providing German translations for the Finnish texts. She also reviews the secondary literature on phrases expressing thanks in a metaphorical manner. A useful bibliography (p. 223) is provided as well.

4325. Schemann, Hans. "Was heißt 'Fixiertheit' von phraseologischen oder idiomatischen Ausdrücken?" *Beiträge zur allgemeinen und germanistischen Phraseologieforschung.* Ed. Jarmo Korhonen. Oulu: Oulun Yliopisto, 1987. 23–36.

This is a theoretical article on the concept of fixidity as it relates to phraseological units. Schemann begins with the general observation that it belongs to the definition of idioms and fixed phrases that they be composed of a basic form that does not change. Citing numerous German examples, he shows that there exist logical, semantic, structural, and linguistic levels of fixidity. They all help to identify a certain combination of words as making up a phraseological unit, be it a proverb, proverbial expression, twin formula, etc. While such fixed phrases can be manipulated intentionally for the purpose of humor or parody, their basic form is fixed in wording and meaning.

4326. Schemann, Hans. "Das phraseologische Wörterbuch." *Wörterbücher. Ein internationales Handbuch zur Lexikographie.* Eds. Franz Josef Hausmann, Oskar Reichmann, Herbert Ernst Wiegand, and Ladislav Zgusta. Berlin: Walter de Gruyter, 1989. I, 1019–1032.

In this major review article Schemann discusses a multitude of phraseological dictionaries of various European languages, stressing right at the outset that they differ widely in content, scope, and purpose. Often the titles do not clearly indicate what a particular dictionary does in fact contain, and there exist vast differences regarding the lexicographical treatment of such matters as key-words, meaning, equivalents, stylistic levels, etc. The actual set-up is also quite different, depending on whether the dictionaries are intended for foreign language instruction, general readers, linguists, cultural historians, etc. Most dictionaries fail to include synchronic and diachronic information, and there is also a lack of concern about the function and meaning of the phraseological units in certain contexts. An important international bibliography (pp. 1028–1032) of phraseological collections and scholarly articles on phraseology and lexicographical problems is included.

4327. Scherer, Thomas. *Phraseologie im Schulalter. Untersuchung zur Phraseologie deutschschweizerischer Schüler und ihrer Sprachbücher.* Bern: Peter Lang, 1982. 167 pp.

Scherer presents an interesting analysis of the knowledge, understanding, and use of idioms and proverbial expressions by Swiss school children. Following two short introductory chapters (pp. 1–26) on previous research and the methodolgy of his own field research, Scherer discusses the development of metaphorical comprehension, the understanding of phraseological units in actual speech contexts, and the passive knowledge of such fixed phrases in the third chapter (pp. 27–49). In the fourth chapter (pp. 50–63) he studies their active use in oral and written language, both in their High German form and in the Swiss German dialect. The use and function as well as the stylistic value of such phrases in student essays are investigated in the fifth chapter (pp. 64–88), while the sixth chapter (pp. 89–97) treats the actual knowledge and awareness of these fixed phrases by the students. The seventh chapter (pp. 98–109) analyzes the evalution of phraseological units by the students themselves, while the large eighth chapter (pp. 110–148) contains pedagogical suggestions of how to treat phraseology in language instruction. Some additional comments regarding pedagogical ideas are presented in the ninth chapter (pp. 149–156). Many examples, various proverbs tests to investigate the knowledge of formulaic language (including a test made up of proverb illustrations), statistical tables, an appendix with translations of the dialect expressions, and a useful bibliography (pp. 165–167) are part of this valuable study.

4328. Schick, Ivanka Petkova. "Zum osmanisch-türkischen Einfluß auf die Balkanphraseologie." *Lingua Posnaniensis*, 29 (1986), 23–37.

Schick provides a valuable comparative analysis of how Turkish phraseological units have entered other languages of the Balkans in the form of loan translations. She explains the tremendous cultural influence which the Turks had on the people and languages of Yugoslavia, Rumania, Bulgaria, Albania, and Greece during five hundred years of Turkish rule. She then cites six examples of Turkish proverbial expressions and shows how they survive in various languages on the Balkan Peninsula. Detailed lexicographical, etymological, grammatical, structural, and semantic explanations are included. Schick also argues that most of the Turkish fixed phrases entered the other languages through oral contacts. Equivalent expressions from the Balkan languages are included as well to illustrate the rich tradition of folk speech in this area. A helpful bibliography (pp. 35–37) is attached.

4329. Schievella, Daniel Francis. *Comparison of Cognitive Deficits in Paranoid Schizophrenia and Manic Affective Disorders.* Diss. St. John's University, 1984. 112 pp.

Using Donald R. Gorham's psychological proverbs test (see nos. 557–558), the author attempted to explore the differences between affective disorders (manic) and paranoid schizophrenic groups. A sample size of 30 male paranoid schizophrenics and 30 male affective disorders were diagnosed, and it was found that both paranoid schizophrenic and affective disorder groups displayed similar cognitive deficits. The results of the factor analysis provided evidence for two distinct factors in thought disturbance in both paranoid and affective groups. One factor appeared to be related to measures representing a generalized deficit, while the other distinct factor seemed to be related to a construct of active illogicality. Numerous statistical tables indicating the results of the Gorham proverbs test and several other thought disorder tests are included.

4330. Schlee, Günther. "Zur rechtlichen Verwendung von Sprichwörtern bei den Rendille (Nordkenia)." *Sprichwörter und Redensarten im interkulturellen Vergleich.* Eds. Annette Sabban and Jan Wirrer. Opladen: Westdeutscher Verlag, 1991. 162–174.

This is a fascinating ethnographical study of Rendille proverbs from Kenya. Schlee starts with some general remarks about the Rendille people and explains that proverbs are often used in legal processes. He then presents seven case studies of how these African proverbs are used for the purpose of judicial reasoning. In each case he cites first the Rendille proverb which is followed by a German translation and an explanation of its meaning. Next Schlee offers legal accounts in the original language followed by a German translation which illustrate the proverbs in a speech context. These contextualized examples make clear that proverbs play an important role in solving human problems that require the application of laws. The proverbs function as codified traditional laws and as legal argumentation.

4331. Schlutz, Erhard. "Sprachliche Defizite oder Verdinglichung von Sprache?" *Sprache und Beruf. Zeitschrift für deutsche Sprache und Literatur in Schule, Weiterbildung und Betrieb*, no. 1 (1985), 2–13.

Schlutz discusses linguistic deficits that appear to be present in poorly educated people. He points out that the different German school systems might lead to a neglect of the slower learner who has difficulty in oral and written communication. This failure in proper language acquisition results in feelings of failure and inadequacy. The consequence is an overreliance on generalized language, i.e., metaphors, fixed phrases, formulas, clichés, proverbial expressions, etc. The author cites a number of contextualized examples, and he analyzes in particular the use of the modern proverb "Angriff ist die beste Verteidigung" (Attack is the best form of defense) to indicate how some deficit speakers become linguistically rather aggressive (see pp. 8–9).

4332. Schmid, Annemarie. "Remarques sur le sémantisme de quelques lexies complexes à base de 'mettre'." *Europhras 88. Phraséologie Contrastive. Actes du Colloque International Klingenthal-Strasbourg, 12–16 mai 1988*. Ed. Gertrud Gréciano. Strasbourg: Université des Sciences Humaines, 1989. 413–420.

In this linguistic study Schmid analyzes various French phraseological units that are based on the verb "mettre" (to put, lay, place, set). She explains that the multisemanticity of this verb has resulted in a large number of fixed phrases. While some of them are not necessarily metaphorical, others are clearly used in a figurative sense. Schmid investigates the structure of these verbal phrases and also includes expressions based on the reflexive form of the verb. In addition to explaining the meaning of the fixed phrases, the author also includes contextualized examples that illustrate the wide use and function of this group of phrases. A useful bibliography (p. 420) is attached.

4333. Schmid, Wolf. "Diegetische Realisierung von Sprichwörtern, Redensarten und semantischen Figuren in Pushkins *Povesti Belkina*." *Wiener Slawistischer Almanach*, 10 (1982), 163–195.

Schmid offers a detailed literary investigation of the proverbs, proverbial expressions, and other fixed phrases in the

short stories (novellas) entitled *Povesti Belkina* (1831) by
Aleksandr S. Pushkin (1799–1837). He begins with the
theoretical observation that proverbs in a literary text function
like micro-texts in the longer narrative. He then shows by
numerous contextualized examples how Pushkin has integrated
various phraseological units into five of his stories. It is argued
that many of the characters use proverbs rather incorrectly,
either intentionally or unwillingly misinterpreting their meaning.
The result is a rather innovative use of proverbial language which
is of major consequence for the meaning of the stories in
general. In fact, Schmid speaks of a dialectical interpretation of
these fixed phrases by the reader who obviously will juxtapose the
traditional form of the phrase with the changed version in the
literary text. An important bibliography (pp. 193–195) regarding
Pushkin scholarship is attached.

4334. Schmidt, Margot. "Zwillingsformeln als plus ultra des mystischen
Weges." *Archiv für das Studium der neueren Sprachen und Literaturen*,
223 (1986), 245–268.

This is a very detailed study of the "Zwillingsformeln" (twin
formulas) contained in the anonymous Middle High German
translation *Die siben strassen zu got* (c. 1350) of Rudolf von
Biberach's (13th/14th century) mystical Latin treatise *De septem
itineribus aeternitatis*. Schmidt explains that this medieval mystic
used 253 rather religious binary formulas to express his mystical
experiences and thoughts. Structurally they all follow the pattern
that two words are usually linked by "und" (and). One hundred
nine texts are based on two nouns, 109 on two verbs, 28 on two
adjectives, and 7 on two adverbs. Schmidt cites examples in their
prose context and points out that the two words making up these
formulas are often synonyms of each other. She explains that the
translator has rendered many of these twin formulas quite
literally from the Latin, but there are also those examples which
were either created by the translator or cited from oral folk
speech. A short section (p. 263) on "Drillingsformeln" (triadic
formulas, triads) is included as well, making this study
particularly valuable for the diachronic study of proverbial
formulas.

4335. Schmidt-Radefeldt, Jürgen. "Descriçao semantica e funçoes semanforicas do provérbio." *Estudos de linguistica portuguesa.* Eds. José G. Herculano de Carvalho and J. Schmidt-Radefeldt. Coimbra: Coimbra Editora, 1984. 213–235.

The author begins his article about the meaning and function of proverbs with some general comments concerning their definition, language, and style. This is followed by an analysis of some common structural patterns, the syntax and grammar of proverbs, and the semantics of these traditional texts. Next Schmidt-Radefeldt presents many examples on a comparative basis, usually citing Portuguese, Spanish, French, and German parallels. He explains that most of these proverbs are metaphorical, and it is exactly their figurative meaning which at times needs to be explained, particularly when one considers proverbs of foreign languages and cultures. A useful bibliography (pp. 234–235) is provided.

4336. Schmidt-Radefeldt, Jürgen. "Structure argumentative, reference et contextualité du proverbe." *Stylistique, rhétorique et poétique dans les langues romanes.* Ed. Jean-Claude Bouvier. Aix-en-Provence: Université de Provence, 1986. 87–102.

This article is similar to the previous publication (see no. 4335), but this time Schmidt-Radefeldt stresses French rather than Portuguese and Spanish proverbs, and he also excludes German texts from his comparative examples. Once again he discusses the structure, semantics, syntax, and grammar of proverbs, and he indicates how structural patterns and syntactical aspects have some influence on the meaning of proverbs. Of special interest is, however, the author's discussion of how proverbs are handled in actual speech acts. He analyzes their argumentative nature, the way a speaker uses proverbs as a point of common reference, and the importance of a communicative context for the proper understanding of the meaning of proverbs. A small bibliography (pp. 101–102) is also provided.

4337. Schmidt-Wiegand, Ruth. "Kerbholz." *Handwörterbuch zur deutschen Rechtsgeschichte.* Eds. Adalbert Erler and Ekkehard Kaufmann. Berlin: Erich Schmidt, 1978. II, cols. 701–703.

Schmidt-Wiegand discusses the origin, history, and meaning of the German proverbial expression "Etwas auf dem Kerbholz haben" (To have a lot to answer for) and other fixed phrases based on the noun "Kerbholz" (notched stick, tally). She explains that wooden sticks were used in order to keep track of bills prior to written tallies. Someone who had notches on his "Kerbholz" thus was in debt to someone for a purchase. These wooden tallies were legally binding, being considered legal documents in early German times. The author includes etymological comments and mentions dialect variants of this term from different geographical regions in Germany. Today the proverbial expression is interpreted more figuratively to mean that someone is in trouble. A short bibliography (col. 703) concludes this lexicon article.

4338. Schneider, Angelika. "Verarbeitung von Zitaten und Redensarten." In A. Schneider. *Brecht-Dramen auf Russisch. Problematik der Dramenübersetzung.* Neuried: Hieronymus, 1984. 38–41 and 59–72.

This book chapter deals with the difficulty which translators have encountered in their translation of the German plays by Bertolt Brecht (1898–1956) into Russian. Schneider mentions that it is particularly difficult to translate proverbs, proverbial expressions, Biblical quotations, and "geflügelte Worte" (winged words, i.e., literary quotations). For some fixed phrases there are, of course, precise equivalents in Russian, but the problem is particularly vexing when translators are confronted with Brecht's intentional variation and alienation of traditional proverbs. His proverb parodies often are in the form of "Antisprichwörter" (anti-provrbs) or there are also invented texts which appear to be proverbial. Schneider cites numerous contextualized examples from a number of plays, but many stem from the well-known drama *Mutter Courage und ihre Kinder* (1941). Brecht also played with famous quotations by Johann Wolfgang von Goethe (1749–1832), and once again it appears almost impossible to translate such innovative formulations.

4339. Schneider, Klaus P. "Stereotype und Sprachbewußtsein: Beispiel 'small talk'." *Sprachwissenschaft und Volkskunde. Perspektiven einer*

kulturanalytischen Sprachbetrachtung. Eds. Herbert F. Brekle and
Utz Maas. Opladen: Westdeutscher Verlag, 1986. 140–154.

The author starts his interesting study of the expression
"small talk" with the observation that this "art of talking about
nothing" is of much importance for linguists and folklorists
interested in the average verbal communication and worldview of
people. He explains that the phrase "small talk" in and of itself is
a stereotypical statement due to the fact that it puts a value
judgment on the speech of certain members of society. Schneider
cites some contextualized uses of the term by journalists and such
modern American authors as John Irving (1942–), and he also
includes the findings of the demographic field research that he
conducted about the attitudes that people have towards "small
talk." The amazing result of his statistical survey is that most
people don't see "small talk" that negatively, preferring to look at
it more as a necessary evil in various social situations. A useful
bibliography (pp. 151–152) is attached.

4340. Schnur, Harry C. "The Humanist Epigram and Its Influence on
the German Epigram." *Acta conventus neo-latini Lovaniensis.
Proceedings of the First International Congress of Neo-Latin Studies,
Louvain 23–28 August 1971.* Eds. J. Ijsewijn and E. Keßler.
München: Wilhelm Fink, 1973. 557–576.

While this article deals primarily with the influence of the
Latin epigrammatic writer Marcus Valerius Martialis (38?–101?
A.D.) on Italian humanists and subsequently also on German
authors of epigrams, the examples cited give ample proof of the
relationship between epigrams and proverbs. Schnur shows that
classical proverbs contained in the older epigrams were
translated into German and became proverbial in that language
as well. Texts by Martin Opitz (1597–1639), Julius Wilhelm
Zincgref (1591–1635), Friedrich Logau (1604–1665), and others
are discussed with some references to their proverbial speech.
Schnur also includes an appendix of epigrams (pp. 569–576)
which helps to illustrate that epigrammatic authors enjoyed
playing with the wit and wisdom of traditional proverbs.

4341. Schröter, Ulrich. "Idiomatische Phraseologismen und ihre pragmatischen Funktionen in Luthers deutschen Schriften." *Luthers Sprachschaffen. Gesellschaftliche Grundlagen. Geschichtliche Wirkungen.* Ed. Joachim Schildt. Berlin: Akademie der Wissenschaften der DDR, Zentralinstitut für Sprachwissenschaft, 1984. I, 233–243.

Schröter investigates the use of phraseological units in a number of Martin Luther's (1483–1546) German works. He argues that Luther was very keen on using proverbs, proverbial expressions, proverbial comparisons, and idioms in order to communicate in a colloquial fashion. These fixed phrases serve to add intensification, emotion, and judgment to Luther's vivid and metaphorical style. Schröter also points out that Luther used especially such phrases that contain references to body parts. He did so in order to increase the communicative effectiveness of his sermons, letters, and essays. For additional comments regarding Luther's proverbial style see above all James Cornette (no. 306), Dietz-Rüdiger Moser (no. 1326), and Berthold Weckmann (no. 4542).

4342. Schulte, O. "Spottnamen und -verse auf Ortschaften im nördlichen Oberhessen." *Hessische Blätter für Volkskunde,* 4 (1905), 142–167.

The author reports on the many stereotypical expressions which are in use in the German state of Hesse. He concentrates on those phrases and verses which illustrate the regional ridicule that exists among villages and small towns. It is argued that such "blasons populaires" are not meant to be taken absolutely seriously. Many of them contain good humor and are based on local pride and a delight in puns and wordplay in general. Special emphasis is given to the many proverbial names which are current in the Hessian area to refer to the people of neighboring villages. But Schulte also deals with proverbial expressions and proverbial comparisons which comment about others in the Hessian dialect. As long as these fixed phrases are used for the purpose of humor or irony, they don't necessarily do any harm. However, they can become rather destructive when they exclude others from normal social life.

4343. Schultz, Richard Lee. *Prophecy and Quotation: A Methodological Study.* Diss. Yale University, 1989. 459 pp.

This is a voluminous dissertation on the nature and purpose of prophetic quotations in the Old Testament. Following an introductory chapter (pp. 8–49) reviewing previous literature on prophecy and quotation, Schultz offers a definition of prophetic quotations in his second chapter (pp. 50–103). The third chapter (pp. 105–132) deals with the function of quotations in Egyptian, Mesopotamian, and Ugaritic literature, while the fourth chapter (pp. 133–158) treats prophetic quotations in early Jadaism. The fifth chapter (pp. 159–168) is dedicated to the quotation of proverbial sayings in the Old Testament, arguing that proverbs in the Bible serve as expressions of traditional wisdom and prophetic truths. In the sixth chapter (pp. 169–197) the author looks at the poetics of quotations in Western literature and then presents some new approaches to studying such texts in chapter seven (pp. 199–233). The eighth chapter (pp. 234–329) is then a detailed analysis of the Book of Isaiah for its use of prophetic quotations, several of which are definitely proverbial. A concluding chapter (pp. 330–339), erudite notes (pp. 340–411), and an extensive bibliography (pp. 412–459) bring this valuable study to a close.

4344. Schulze, Carl. *Die biblischen Sprichwörter der deutschen Sprache.* Göttingen: Vandenhoeck & Ruprecht, 1860; rpt. ed. with an introduction by Wolfgang Mieder. Bern: Peter Lang, 1987. 261 pp.

This is a reprint of a major study and collection of the Biblical proverbs in the German language (see no. 1674). Schulze presents 179 proverbs out of the Old Testament in Latin and also includes many German variants from the Middle Ages to Martin Luther (1483–1546) for each proverb. The same method is used for the 117 proverbs out of the New Testament. Wolfgang Mieder as the editor of the reprint has added an extensive introduction (pp. III-LVIII) which is comprised of the following sections: (1) Carl Schulze (19th century) as paremiologist and paremiographer (pp. III-XV), (2) Biblical proverbs (pp. XVII-XXXVI), (3) publications by Carl Schulze (pp. XXXVII, see nos.

1673–1678 and no. 2843 for annotations), and (4) bibliography concerning Biblical proverb collections, general studies about proverbs in the Bible, specific studies of individual proverbs in the Old and New Testament, Martin Luther and the proverb, and proverbs in sermons (pp. XXXVIII-LVIII).

4345. Schulze-Busacker, Elisabeth. "La moralité des fabliaux. Considérations stylistiques." *Epopée animale, fable, fabliau. Actes du IVe Colloque de la Société Internationale Renardienne, Evreux, 7–11 septembre 1981*. Eds. Gabriel Bianciotto and Michel Salvat. Paris: Presses Universitaires de France, 1984. 525–547.

Following her earlier article on the proverbial language of the medieval French fabliaux (see no. 1679), Schulze-Busacker now investigates the relationship between the morality of these texts and the proverbs included in them. She begins with some definition similarities of fabliaux, morality, and proverbs, and she then discusses various stylistic aspects of the integration of proverbial wisdom into these versified texts. It is pointed out that many proverbs are preceded by introductory formulas which clearly identify them as traditional wisdom. Proverbs are without doubt an important rhetorical device to express morality in the often humorous fabliaux. Many contextualized examples are cited, and Schulze-Busacker also includes a valuable annotated proverb index (pp. 541–547) at the end of this literary investigation. The 40 notes (pp. 538–541) contain rich bibliographical information concerning French proverbs of the Middle Ages.

4346. Schulze-Busacker, Elisabeth. "Proverbe ou sentence: essai de définition." *La locution. Actes du colloque international Université McGill, Montréal, 15–16 octobre 1984*. Eds. Giuseppe Di Stefano and Russell G. McGillivray. Montréal: Éditions CERES, 1984. 134–167.

In this valuable article Schulze-Busacker occupies herself with the difficult problem of differentiating between medieval sententious remarks and traditional proverbs. She begins with definition problems and reviews the theoretical opinions of Archer Taylor (see no. 1858), Susanna Schmarje (no. 1648), André Jolles (no. 811), Mathilde Hain (no. 640), Friedrich Seiler (no. 1701), Bartlett Jere Whiting (no. 2059), Samuel Singer (no. 1742), and some others. She then argues convincingly that only diachronic research can establish the difference between these two genres. Above all it is this historical approach which will be able to show how classical or medieval Latin sententious remarks were first translated into the vernacular languages as "literary sentences" which later might have become proverbial through some stylistic adaptations and frequent oral use. Schulze-Busacker includes a number of examples where she traces Latin originals to early French sententious remarks which then became proverbial by the 13th century. References are cited from medieval proverb collections and passages from French literature of the Middle Ages whose contexts show how these sententious remarks became proverbial over time. The 88 notes include very helpful bibliographical information.

4347. Schulze-Busacker, Elisabeth. "Proverbes et expressions proverbiales dans les romans de Chrétien de Troyes." *Chrétien de Troyes et le Graal. Colloque arthurien belge de Bruges.* Eds. Juliette De Caluwé-Dor and Herman Bract. Paris: Éditions Nizet, 1984. 107–119.

In this literary proverb investigation Schulze-Busacker analyzes the use and function of proverbs and proverbial expressions in the medieval works of Chrétien de Troyes (1150?–1190?). She is especially interested in showing how this major author integrates proverbs into his versified epics. Many texts are preceded by introductory formulas which clearly identify the proverbs as traditional wisdom. But there are also those examples which appear in the epic narrative without any particular markers. The numerous contextualized examples cited by Schulze-Busacker show that proverbs definitely are a major stylistic and rhetorical tool for Chrétien de Troyes, who became ever more skillful in integrating proverbial language into his works as he developed as the leading French writer of the Middle Ages. The 43 notes contain useful bibliographical references. See also above all Marcelle Altieri (no. 30).

4348. Schulze-Busacker, Elisabeth. *Proverbes et expressions proverbiales dans la littérature narrative du moyen âge français. Recueil et analyse.* Paris: Librairie Honoré Champion, 1985. 356 pp.

This is without doubt a superb book on the proverbs and proverbial expressions in medieval French literature of the 12th and 13th centuries. Schulze-Busacker begins her study with a short introduction (pp. 9–12) and a first chapter (pp. 13–18) describing the essence and methodology of literary proverb investigations. The large second chapter (pp. 19–155) on the historical survey of proverbial language in French literature of the Middle Ages is divided into three major parts: (1) a discussion (pp. 20–44) of the frequency, introductory formulas, context, and integration of the proverbial texts; (2) an analysis (pp. 44–86) of the use and function of proverbial language in the works of Chrétien de Troyes (1150?–1190?), Gautier d'Arras (1135–1198), Hue de Rotelande (12th century), and the anonymous *Li Proverbes au vilain* (12th century); and (3) additional comments (pp. 86–155) regarding the proverbs in the works of Robert Wace (1100?–1174?), in the fabliaux, and in medieval French literature in general. All of this intriguing information is followed by a large appendix (pp. 157–323) which really is the second half of the book. Here Schulze-Busacker presents an excellent contextualized and annotated proverb index (pp. 167–323) of all the texts which she found in the numerous literary works. This is one of the most scholarly proverb collections in existence, for once citing each text in the literary context and adding historical annotations from Joseph Morawski's *Proverbes français antérieurs au XVe siècle* (1925). A valuable word index (pp. 325–333), a list of the proverbs found in the many fabliaux (pp. 335–349), and an excellent bibliography (pp. 351–354) conclude this seminal study.

4349. Schulze-Busacker, Elisabeth. "Des *Disticha Catonis* en Espagne, Italie et France." *Europhras 88. Phraséologie Contrastive. Actes du Colloque International Klingenthal-Strasbourg, 12–16 mai 1988.* Ed. Gertrud Gréciano. Strasbourg: Université des Sciences Humaines, 1989. 421–430.

In this article Schulze-Busacker treats a number of Spanish, Italian, and French translations and adaptations of the anonymous medieval Latin collection of *Disticha Catonis* that dates back to the third century A.D. She points out that this collection of classical sententious remarks and proverbs became very popular in the Middle Ages of Europe, where it was used for instructional purposes in the schools. The author includes a short discussion of the content of the *Disticha Catonis* and then presents a few vernacular versions. A few comments explaining the importance of these translations for spreading ancient proverbial wisdom throughout Europe are added. A useful bibliography is attached (pp 429–430). See also Ernstpeter Ruhe (no. 2808).

4350. Schulze-Busacker, Elisabeth. "Les *Proverbes au vilain*." *Proverbium*, 6 (1989), 113–127.

The author begins her analysis of the anonymous medieval French work *Li Proverbes au vilain* (12th century) with a short discussion of earlier French proverb collections and a history of this particular manuscript. She explains that it is composed of 280 strophes that usually conclude with a proverb. It is explained that some of these proverbs are based on classical texts, but there are also those examples which clearly show medieval French proverbs. Citing a number of texts in their literary context, the author explains how this work is not only of interest to literary scholars but also to folklorists, cultural historians, and paremiologists. The contextualized proverbs certainly provide insights into the moral and didactic attitudes during the Middle Ages, and they thus represent commentaries on the social and cultural life. The 18 notes (pp. 124–127) contain useful bibliographical information. See also Eckard Rattunde (no. 1508) and Adolf Tobler (no. 1954).

4351. Schumacher, Meinolf. "'. . . ist menschlich'." Mittelalterliche Variationen einer antiken Sentenz." *Zeitschrift für deutsches Altertum und deutsche Literatur*, 119 (1990), 163–170.

This is a philological and literary study of the classical Latin proverb "Errare humanum est" (To err is human) and its medieval variations. Schumacher explains that already Marcus

Tullius Cicero (106–43 B.C.) added an ironic twist to the traditional proverb, and English speakers are aware of Alexander Pope's (1688–1744) adaptation "To err is human, to forgive divine." St. Augustine (354–430) is yet another person who modified this proverb, but it was especially in the Middle Ages that secular and religious writers connected this proverb through additions referring to the devil and the concept of sin. Schumacher cites contextualized references from German medieval authors like Hugo von Trimberg (1230?–1313?), Mechthild von Magdeburg (1207/10–1282/83), etc. These texts illustrate that the classical proverb was used as a loan translation in both its original wording and in religiously or mystically motivated variations.

4352. Schumacher, Robert M. *Factors Affecting Memorial Access to Analogical Similarity.* Diss. University of Illinois at Urbana-Champaign, 1989. 128 pp.

Schumacher's dissertation reports on a psychological study to investigate the memory of analogically similar and superficially similar items. He designed a proverbs test based on fifty unknown Chinese, Persian, Swahili, and Malay proverbs in English translation. Subjects were given a cued-recall task using proverbs that were either analogically or superficially similar. The results showed that repetition increased recall for both the analogical and superficial similarities. At one presentation only, superficially similar proverbs were retrieved significantly better than analogically similar proverbs, but at five repetitions the difference in retrievability decreased substantially. The key issue regarding memorization is thus clearly repetition. A list of the proverbs and the proverbs test (pp. 96–127), 9 statistical tables, and a useful bibliography (pp. 84–90) concerning the use of proverbs for memory testing are included.

4353. Schutt-Kehm, Elke M. "Die Frage nach etwa im Gemälde verborgenen Sprichwörtern." In E. Schutt-Kehm. *Pieter Bruegels d. Ä. "Kampf des Karnevals gegen die Fasten" als Quelle volkskundlicher Forschung.* Bern: Peter Lang, 1983. 132–134.

The entire book represents a detailed investigation of folklore references in Pieter Brueghel's (c. 1520–1569) picture *The Fight Between Carnival and Lent* (1559). The author studies the compositional, formal, and cultural aspects of the many scenes of this picture, and in one small section (pp. 132–134) she also attempts to isolate a few proverbial expressions depicted by the artist. For each expression Schutt-Kehm gives the Dutch text with a German translation and explains their cultural significance as well as their meaning in the picture. A helpful bibliography (pp. 179–187) on the relationship of folklore and art is attached, and there are also 30 illustrations dealing with carnival and lent that are of much interest.

4354. Schwartz, Gerald B. *Thought Disturbances in Mania and Schizophrenia.* Diss. Yeshiva University, 1982. 205 pp.

This dissertation reports on the use of John D. Benjamin's psychological proverbs test (see no. 141) to investigate disturbances in thinking in hospitalized manic depressive patients and a comparison group of schizophrenic inpatients. Manics manifested more inappropriate elaboration, autistic logic, and irrelevance than schizophrenics. The responses of manics were also more abstract than those of schizophrenics. But the schizophrenics manifested more concrete thinking and more "private" language, i.e., neologisms, than manics. Schwartz also includes an analysis of such factors as education and age, the former resulting in excessive verbiage when interpreting the proverbs, and the latter having little effect. Forty-three statistical tables and a useful bibliography (pp. 201–205) are included.

4355. Schwarzbaum, Haim. "Jewish Proverbs and Riddles." In H. Schwarzbaum. *Studies in Jewish and World Folklore* (Berlin: Walter de Gruyter, 1968. 417–424.

Schwarzbaum presents an informative bibliographical review article on Jewish proverbs. He begins with a short discussion of major Hebrew and Yiddish proverb collections, mentioning that many of the ancient proverbs go back to early wisdom literature. A section on the proverbs in the Bible (esp. the Book of Proverbs) and the Talmud is included. Considerable space is allotted to Sephardic proverbs from Spain, notably to Rabbi Santob de Carrión's (14th century) collection of *Proverbios morales* (1345). There are also some special comments on the Yiddish proverbs which were collected by the Polish paremiographer Ignaz Bernstein (1836–1909) in his massive collection *Jüdische Sprichwörter und Redensarten* (1908; see no. 150). Schwarzbaum certainly provides international proverb scholars with rich bibliographical materials to study the fascinating world of Jewish proverbs. The section on the riddles (pp. 423–424) is less inclusive than that of the proverbs.

4356. Schweigert, Wendy A., and Danny R. Moates. "Familiar Idiom Comprehension." *Journal of Psycholinguistic Research*, 17, no. 4 (1988), 281–296.

This psycholinguistic study presents a discussion of the way idioms and proverbial expressions are processed and understood. The authors asked subjects to read a number of sentences containing idioms used either literally or figuratively. Sentences containing idioms used literally required more time than those containing idioms used figuratively. Cued recall was better for idioms used literally than for those used figuratively. These results are interpreted as supporting the so-called "Idiomatic Processing Model" of idiom comprehension, which suggests that the figurative meaning is processed first; only if that one is inappropriate is the literal meaning processed. A short bibliography (pp. 295–296), 3 statistical tables, and an English abstract (p. 281) are part of this study.

4357. Schwingruber, Madeleine. "The Illocutionary and Perlocutionary Acts of the Proverbs in *The Owl and the Nightingale*." *Bulletin de la Section de Linguistique de la Faculté des Lettres de Lausanne*, 6 (1984), 255–265.

Schwingruber's analysis of proverbs in the anonymous Middle English poem *The Owl and the Nightingale* (13th century) does not correspond to most other literary proverb investigations. Instead she uses the findings of speech act theory and attempts to show how the various uses of proverbs in this medieval dialogue can be interpreted as illocutionary and perlocutionary acts. Three diagrams are included to explain the various relationships between the narrator, speaker, and hearer. Schwingruber also cites a number of contextualized examples to illustrate her theoretical points, but she does not provide a proverb index. It is concluded that the proverbs in this work are both a vehicle of superiority and a vehicle of equality due to their function of keeping group identity and group distinction.

4358. Seeger, Reinhart. *Herkunft und Bedeutung des Schlagwortes: "Die Religion ist Opium für das Volk."* Halle: Akademischer Verlag, 1935. 45 pp.

This short monograph contains the history and meaning of the internationally known sententious remark "Die Religion ist Opium für das Volk" (Religion is the opium of the people) which Karl Marx (1818–1883) used in his essay *Zur Kritik der Hegelschen Rechtsphilosophie* (1844). Seeger explains that the idea of comparing religion with narcotics began at the turn of the 19th century. Citing references from Johann Wolfgang von Goethe (1749–1832), Ludwig Feuerbach (1804–1872), Bruno Bauer (1809–1882), Friedrich Engels (1820–1895), etc., Seeger explains how it became ever more popular to refer to religion as a drug. Many contextualized references are cited from philosophical, religious, literary, and sociological sources. But it was Karl Marx who coined the particular quotation that has gained such wide currency today. A name index (p. 45) and many notes containing bibliographical information are included.

4359. Seidl, Helmut A. *Medizinische Sprichwörter im Englischen und Deutschen. Eine diachrone Untersuchung zur vergleichenden Parömiologie.* Bern: Peter Lang, 1982. 406 pp.

This is a significant diachronic and comparative study of English and German medical proverbs. In his introduction (pp. 8–45) Seidl presents the reader with a definition of health proverbs and distinguishes this proverb genre from legal proverbs, weather proverbs, wellerisms, etc. The rest of the book is divided into four major chapters discussing medical proverbs of nutrition (pp. 46–132), proverbs about the human body (pp. 133–206), proverbs regarding various diseases (pp. 207–256), and proverbial advice against disease and for healing (pp. 257–362). Altogether Seidl analyzes 607 texts (235 English and 372 German proverbs) in short essays varying in length from half a page to three pages. Such matters as origin, history, form, language, function, and meaning are treated, and the author also discusses parallel proverbs (75 texts have exact equivalents in both languages) and variants. A large bibliography (pp. 372–391) and German and English subject indices (pp. 392–406) conclude this pioneering investigation. This book is definitely of major importance for the historical study of English and German medical proverbs.

4360. Seifert, Hans-Ulrich. "*Thesaurus proverbiorum medii aevi* (TPMA)." *Proverbium*, 4 (1987), 271–272.

Seifert gives a short report on the so-called *Thesaurus proverbiorum medii aevi*, a major paremiographical project that has been going on in Bern, Switzerland, for about twenty years. Its German title will eventually be *Thesaurus der Sprichwörter des germanisch-romanischen Mittelalters*, and it will contain about 80,000 medieval proverbs from the Germanic and Romance languages. The archive in Bern is based on a 34–volume manuscript which the Swiss paremiologist and paremiographer Samuel Singer (1860–1948; see nos. 1740–1744) assembled during his lifetime. All the proverbs will be cited in their original language with German translations. The texts stem from European literary works from between 500 and 1500, and this wealth of materials will be organized according to key-words. There will, however, also be important "Strukturartikel" (structure articles) that group together those proverbs which are based on the same structure. Work on this large and complex paremiographical project dealing with at least fourteen languages is understandably progressing at a slow pace, but it is the hope of scholars of various disciplines that at least the first volume of this important comparative and international proverb collection might appear in print soon. For two earlier progress reports on the "*Thesaurus Singer*" see Ricarda Liver (nos. 1084–1085) and Ricarda Liver and V. Mumprecht (no. 1086).

4361. Selig, Karl-Ludwig. "Los proverbios españoles de Daniel Georg Morhof." *Estudios sobre el Siglo de Oro en homenaje a Raymond R. MacCurdy.* Eds. Angel Gonzáles et al. Albuquerque/New Mexico: University of New Mexico, Dept. of Modern and Classical Languages, 1983. 327–332.

Selig presents an interesting bilingual list of 21 Spanish and German proverbs which the German scholar Daniel Georg Morhof (1639–1691) included in his philological treatise *Unterricht von der Teutschen Sprache und Poesie* (1682). He explains that Morhof included these Spanish proverbs in his book on the German language to indicate how important the Spanish language had become in Germany during the 17th century due to the Thirty Years' War and Spanish rulers. The texts are provided with annotations from early proverb collections, and Selig also includes a bibliography (pp. 331–332) concerning the life and works of Morhof as well as references to proverb scholarship and collections of that time.

4362. Sellert, W. "'Wo kein Kläger, da ist kein Richter'." *Handwörterbuch zur deutschen Rechtsgeschichte.* Eds. Adalbert Erler and Ekkehard Kaufmann. Berlin: Erich Schmidt, 1978. II, cols. 853–855.

This is but a short note on the German legal proverb "Wo kein Kläger, da ist kein Richter" (Where there is no accuser, there is no judge) from the Middle Ages. Sellert cites medieval German examples and also includes some Latin texts from that time. He argues that the meaning of this proverb can be understood once one realizes that some early judges attempted to enrich themselves by initiating law suits. The proverb negates this possibility, arguing clearly that only an accuser should be allowed to start judicial proceedings. A few bibliographical references (col. 855) to major legal proverb collections are included.

4363. Sellheim, Rudolf. "Eine unbeachtet gebliebene Sprichwörtersammlung. Die *Nuzhat al-anfus wa-raudat al-maclis* des Radiaddin al-'Iraqi (468/1075–561/1166)." *Oriens,* 31 (1988), 82–94.

The author reports that the library in Gotha, Germany, possesses a rare Arabic proverb collection which found its way from Egypt to Europe through the German scholar Ulrich Jasper Seetzen (1767–1811). This enthusiast of the Near East collected over 2000 manuscripts, among them the little-known collection *Nuzhat al-anfus wa-raudat al-maclis* by Radiaddin al-'Iraqi (468/1075–561/1166). Sellheim includes a biographical sketch of Seetzen (pp. 82–84), but the major part of the article is dedicated to a detailed historical and philological analysis of this early collection. The author discusses the life and works of its compiler, and he also gives a clear description of its content with comparative comments regarding other Arabic proverb collections of that time.

4364.   Sellheim, Rudolf. "Vier Miszellen zur arabischen Sprichwörterkunde." *Oriens,* 31 (1988), 353–359.

This article is comprised of four short philological notes regarding Arabic paremiography. Sellheim begins with a discussion (p. 353) of the manuscript history of the early proverb collection *Nubad min Amtal al-Amir* by Abu I-Fadl al-Mikali (died 436/1044). This is followed by a most welcome description (pp. 354–357) of proverb inscriptions on ceramics of the 9th to 11th centuries. Sellheim gives some examples of these texts on plates, bowls, and pitchers, and he explains that the purpose of writing on these dishes was to spread wisdom and to give advice. The third note (pp. 357–358) contains a discussion of Muhammed al-Yusi al-Marrakusi's (1040/1630–1102/1691) proverb collection *Zahr al-akam fi l-amtal wal-hikam.* In the fourth miscellany (p. 359) Sellheim lists a few additions to his major review article on Arabic proverbs (see no. 4365 below). The entire article includes historical, linguistic, cultural, and paremiographical comments by one of the leading scholars on Arabic proverb collections.

4365.   Sellheim, Rudolf. "Mathal." *The Encyclopedia of Islam.* Eds. C.E. Bosworth et al. Leiden: E.J. Brill, 1989. VI, 815–825.

This is a major encyclopedia article on the "mathal" (proverb) or "amthal" (proverbs) of the Arabic languages. Sellheim begins with a discussion (pp. 815–816) of definition problems. This is followed by an analysis (pp. 816–821) of various aspects of Arabic proverbs: relationship with fables and folk narratives, form and structure, currency, poetic language, etc. The third section (pp. 821–824) contains a superb bibliography and description of major Arabic proverb collections. Sellheim cites the authors with precise biographical information, and he provides philological, historical, cultural, and paremiographical information regarding numerous early collections. In the fourth section (pp. 824–825) the author presents a list of modern collections from various Arabic nationalities, but he also includes newer collections of Arabic proverbs which have appeared in different European languages. A bibliography (p. 825) summarizing the paremiological scholarship on Arabic proverbs concludes this extremely important review article.

4366. Sellheim, Rudolf. "Eine fünfte Miszelle zur arabischen Sprichwörterkunde." *Oriens,* 32 (1990), 463–475.

Even though Sellheim chose to entitle this article of considerable length with the modest description "fifth miscellany" (for the first four notes see no. 4364 above), this is actually a major addendum to his significant review article on the "mathal" (see no. 4365 above). The article is filled with philological, biographical, historical, cultural, and paremiographical addenda, making it absolutely essential for the serious scholar of Arabic proverbs. Of particular importance is the section on individual proverbs (pp. 464–465), but the additional remarks concerning Arabic proverb collections (pp. 465–469) is also invaluable. Throughout the article Sellheim has added rich bibliographical references, and this information is of utmost importance for the study of Arabic proverbs and their relationship (through loan translations) with proverbs from other languages and cultures.

4367. Senga, Anikó N. "Correspondences Between Hungarian and English Somatic Proverbia with 'Leg' and 'Foot'." *Ural-Altaic Yearbook,* 59 (1987), 15–33.

The author illustrates the similarites between Hungarian and English proverbs and proverbial expressions referring to such body parts as leg, knee, foot, heel, toe, sole, instep, and corn. These somatic expressions are compared by listing the

Hungarian phrases with English translations in a left column and citing the English equivalents in the right column. While these fixed phrases are not always absolutely identical, it is amazing to see how close the equivalents of these two unrelated languages are. Part of this is due to the fact that some of the texts go back to a common classical or Biblical source, while others have been loan translated later from European languages. There is, of course, today also a notable influence of the English language on colloquial Hungarian speech. Four illustrations indicating the somatic vocabulary of the two languages are included.

4368. Senger, Matthias W. "The Fate of an Early American School Book: Leonhard Culmann's *Sententiae Pueriles.*" *Harvard Library Bulletin,* 32 (1984), 256–273.

Senger discusses the entire history and reception of a very influential school book. It was written by the Nuremberg schoolmaster Leonhard Culmann (1497?–1562; English spelling often Leonard Culman) and published as *Sententiae pueriles* (1540). Many later editions appeared in Germany, and most students learned their Latin by memorizing dozens of the approximately 1200 sententious remarks contained in this volume. Its first edition in England appeared in 1633, and by 1702 it was also published in North America. There is hardly a young American student who did not use this educational text during the 18th century. Many of its *sententiae* were in fact proverbial, and this book played a major role in spreading classical proverbs first in Latin and then as English loan translations in the early colonies. Senger includes a detailed discussion of the organization and content of this book, and he also traces its history as a pedagogical and moralistic tool. See also Charles Smith (nos. 1752–1753) and Matthias Senger's German article (no. 4369 below).

4369. Senger, Matthias W. "Leonhard Culmanns *Sententiae Pueriles.* Zur Sentenz als einer prägenden Denkform vom 16. bis 18. Jahrhundert." *Literatur und Volk im 17. Jahrhundert. Probleme populärer Kultur in Deutschland.* Eds. Wolfgang Brückner et al. Wiesbaden: Otto Harrassowitz, 1985. II, 777–795.

In this article Senger looks at the pedagogical importance of Leonhard Culmann's (1497?–1562; English spelling often Leonard Culman) early Latin school book *Sententiae pueriles* (1540). This book was used not only in German schools but also in Latin schools of England and America. The intent of the book was to teach Latin, but its approximately 1200 sententious remarks from classical authors was also used to make young students aware of moral principles. Senger cites numerous examples, showing that quite a few are in fact proverbial. Since the students had to memorize these *sententiae*, the book was very influential in spreading the proverbial wisdom of classical antiquity first in Latin and later in loan translations. Senger also points out that the students often had to write essays based on these texts in which they explained the ethical value contained in them. References to other proverb collections of the 16th and 17th centuries are included, and Senger explains how most of them were seen as didactic and instructional tools. The 62 notes (pp. 790–795) contain useful bibliographical information. See also Charles Smith (nos. 1752–1753).

4370. Senkoro, F.E.M.K. "Ng'ombe Akivundika Guu: Preliminary Remarks on the Proverb-Story in Written Swahili Literature." *Design and Intent in African Literature.* Eds. David F. Dorsey et al. Washington, D.C.: Three Continents, 1982. 59–69.

The article begins with a discussion of Swahili proverb collections and previous scholarship on this rich African proverb tradition. The author then argues that scholars have not paid enough attention to the use and function of proverbial language in Swahili literature. Senkoro states that there exist numerous short stories and novels which are built exclusively on the essence of a single proverb. Often this text is even cited in the title to make clear from the outset that the story is one of didacticism and wisdom. Citing numerous examples from such writers as J.K. Kiimbila (20th cent.), Shaaban Robert (1909–1962), and others, Senkoro points out that the proverbs are used either as moralistic or satirical-political messages. The proverbs are cited in Swahili with English translations, and the contexts indicate that these authors use the proverbs in a rather traditional and instructional fashion.

4371. Sephiha, Haim Vidal. "Portrait de la société judéo-espagnole ou Dis-moi tes proverbes, je te dirai qui tu es." *Les formes brèves. Actes du colloque international de la Baume-les-Aix, 26–28 novembre 1982.* Ed. Benito Pelegrin. Aix-en-Provence: Université de Provence, 1984. 141–155; also in *Richesse du proverbe.* Eds. François Suard and Claude Buridant. Lille: Université de Lille, 1984. II, 199–209.

This is a general article on the content and themes of Judeo-Spanish proverbs. The author begins with a short history of Spanish Jews and explains that they have a rich proverb tradition. While they have their own proverbs, there are also those texts which show clear influences from the Hebrew, Italian, French, and other languages. Sephiha states that the proverbs deal with life in general, human nature, customs, beliefs, etc. In order to understand the wording and meaning of many of these traditional proverbs, it is necessary to undertake detailed diachronic studies. Many examples are cited, and Sephiha includes historical, cultural, and linguistic explanations. It is also shown that many proverbs are connected to Jewish religious thought and to folk narratives.

4372. Shaked, Shaul. "'Do not Buy anything from an Aramaean': A Fragment of Aramaic Proverbs with a Judaeo-Iranian Version." *Iranica Varia: Papers in Honor of Professor Ehsan Yarshater.* No editor given. Leiden: Brill, 1990. 230–239.

Shaked presents a philological study of a short manuscript from the 10th century which contains an Aramaic proverb with a Judaeo-Iranian translation. He cites both versions in their original languages and includes transliterations as well as English translations. The proverb itself is cited as "Do not buy anything from an Aramaean [Armenian]," and the author speculates as to its origin, history, and meaning. Most of the article deals, however, with the complex linguistic problems of this manuscript. The author has not succeeded in locating this proverb in any of the Arabic proverb collections, but the text does appear to be an early example of a proverbial stereotype from the Near East.

4373. Shalimova, D.V. "Transformatsiia smyslov i znachenii slov pri ponimanii poslovits." *Voprosy psikhologii*, no. 4 (1990), 42–47.

This study by a Russian psychologist is an indication that Soviet scholars are also interested in the theory of proverb comprehension. There have been numerous studies by Western scholars on this question (see in the index under cognition, comprehension, psychology, proverbs test, etc.), and Shalimova now presents similar results. She reports on an experimental study of how the sense or meaning of a proverb is understood. Questions of metaphor comprehension are dealt with, and the author also differentiates between the literal or concrete meaning and the figurative or metaphorical meaning of a proverb. It is argued that a transformation from the concrete to the figurative must take place in order to understand the message of the proverb. A short bibliography (p. 47) is attached.

4374. Shimizu, Kenji. *Goethes Begriff der Weltliteratur.—Japanische Sprichwörter im Kontrast zu deutschen.* Bern: Peter Lang, 1989. 77 pp.

This book is actually made up of two short monographs, the first (pp. 5–43) dealing with Johann Wolfgang von Goethe's (1749–1832) concept of "Weltliteratur" (world literature), and the second (pp. 45–77) comparing Japanese and German proverbs. Shimizu begins with a general history of Japanese proverbs, stating that they originated from three major sources: (1) proverbs from oral speech and indigenous to the Japanese language, (2) proverbs from literary works and from Buddhism, Confucianism, and Taoism, and (3) proverbs loan translated from European languages during the 19th century and afterwards. This is followed by a discussion of the form, structure, metaphors, rhyme, puns, personification, parallelism, irony, etc. of Japanese proverbs. The final part deals with the content of these proverbs, emphasizing the fact that many of them are didactic statements about human life and experience. The Japanese texts are cited with German translations, and many cultural explanations are added.

4375.   Shippey, T.A. "Approaches to Truth in Old English Poetry."
        University of Leeds Review, 25 (1982), 171–189.

> The major part of this article actually deals with what might
> be considered as "truth" in Old English poetry, but there is a
> small section (pp. 173–175) in which Shippey comments on three
> so-called Durham proverbs, a collection of 46 Latin and Anglo-
> Saxon proverbs contained in a Durham Cathedral manuscript
> from the 11th century. The proverbs in modern English are "He
> who means to catch the hare must not care about his horse,"
> "You cannot have your mouth full of porridge and also blow the
> fire," and "The fuller the cup, the fairer you must bear it."
> Shippey provides some etymological comments and also attempts
> to explain the meaning of these texts by adding modern proverbs
> with similar meanings. Regarding the somewhat unclear sense of
> the third text, he feels that it might be similar to Harry S.
> Truman's (1884–1972) proverbial maxim "If you can't stand the
> heat, stay out of the kitchen."

4376.   Sialm, Ambros. *Semiotik und Phraseologie. Zur Theorie fester
        Wortverbindungen im Russischen.* Bern: Peter Lang, 1987. 185 pp.

> Phraseologists and paremiologists not knowing the Russian
> language should be grateful to Ambros Sialm for having written
> this book on phraseology which reviews the important semiotic
> studies by Soviet scholars. In the first chapter (pp. 13–53) the
> author deals with basic aspects of phraseological units, i.e.,
> definition, reproducibility, equivalency, semantics, classification,
> and semiotics. The second chapter (pp. 54–92) investigates the
> lexical and morphemic characteristics of fixed phrases, and the
> third chapter (pp. 93–143) treats synonymy, connotation, and
> idiomaticity. The fourth chapter (pp. 144–172) contains a
> discussion of various theories concerning the questions of how
> and why phraseological units originate at all. Why do people
> repeat fixed phrases like proverbs and proverbial expressions?
> How do they communicate with them? How do they function as
> signs? These and other questions are answered throughout this
> book by referring to leading Soviet scholars and by citing Russian
> examples with German translations. A very important

bibliography (pp. 175–183) listing Soviet phraseological scholarship is included.

4377. Sielicki, Franciszek. "Cechy ludzkie w przyslowiach i powiedzeniach bialoruskich z terenu bylego powiatu wilejskiego." *Slavia Orientalis*, 36, nos. 3–4 (1987), 333–349.

Sielicki investigates the human characteristics expressed in B(y)elorussian proverbs and proverbial expressions. In the first half of the article (pp. 333–342) the author cites 114 examples and explains that their content and themes reflect the culture, attitudes, beliefs, and peasant life of the people of that East European region. In the second part (pp. 342–349) Sielicki presents 106 proverbial comparisons and shows how they refer to certain aspects of normal human behavior and social attitudes. The proverbs were collected in the Wilejski area, and some of the B(y)elorussian texts do indicate some Polish linguistic influence. The 80 notes contain useful bibliographical references to B(y)elorussian and Slavic proverb collections.

4378. Sielicki, Franciszek. "Przyslowia i powiedzenia polskie na Wilejszczyznie w okresie miedzywojennym." *Slavica Wratislaviensia*, 49 (1990), 101–113.

In this article Sielicki studies 136 Polish proverbs and proverbial expressions that were collected between the two world wars in the Wilno (Vilnius) area of today's Lithuania. The rich materials are divided into five groups according to their content: (1) calendar proverbs (i.e., fixed phrases dealing with the weather, saints, planting, etc.), (2) didactic proverbs, (3) humorous fixed phrases, (4) school proverbs (i.e., texts cited for pedagogical purposes), and (5) humorous phraseological units. Historical and cultural comments are included to explain the metaphors and their meaning. Sielicki also refers to the language and form of these traditional texts. The 67 notes include bibliographical information about Polish proverb collections.

4379. Sigelman, Lee. "Is Ignorance Bliss? A Reconsideration of the Folk Wisdom." *Human Relations*, 34, no. 11 (1981), 965–974.

The validity of the proverb that "Ignorance is bliss" was tested through the analysis of the data collected from 600 interviews from the 1974 and 1976 General Social Surveys. An indicator of general intelligence, when correlated with measures of happiness, life satisfaction, and anomia, was found to be significantly related to all three, but only the correlation with anomia was of impressive magnitude. Intelligence was then used as one predictor of psychological well-being in a series of tests. The analyses indicated that intelligence had no independent impact on either happiness or life satisfaction, but that it was a good predictor of anomia. The impact of intelligence on anomia was negative, indicating that even when the effects of all other variables in the analysis were controlled, more intelligent people tended to be less anomic. The result of this study point towards a rejection of the folk wisdom that "Ignorance is bliss." Two statistical tables, a bibliography (p. 974), and an English abstract (p. 965) are included.

4380. Simon, Irmgard. "Zum Aufbau eines Sprichwortarchivs: Das Westfälische Sprichwortarchiv bei der Kommission für Mundart- und Namenforschung in Münster." *Sprichwörter und Redensarten im interkulturellen Vergleich.* Eds. Annette Sabban and Jan Wirrer. Opladen: Westdeutscher Verlag, 1991. 13–27.

This is a report about the archive of Westphalian proverbs, proverbial expressions, and wellerisms at the University of Münster in Germany. The archive was established in 1962, and it is now comprised of approximately 30,000 Low German texts. Simon discusses the questionnaires that were used to collect the many dialect texts from oral sources. The informants were not only asked to supply proverbial texts, but they were also questioned about the context, meaning, and function of this proverbial language. In the second part of the article Simon analyzes the organization of the archive according to key-words, and she outlines the classification system that will be used for a published collection. A useful bibliography (pp. 25–27) is attached. For an earlier report on this proverb archive see Maria Dopheide (no. 366).

4381. Simon, Michael J. "Use of the Proverbs Test in the Assessment of Competency to Stand Trial." *Psychological Reports*, 60 (1987), 1166.

> Even though the Donald R. Gorham's psychological proverbs test (see nos. 557–558) was designed to test for schizophrenia, Simon reports that this test can also be used to assess the competency of criminal defendants to stand trial. The author used the test with 106 subjects, and he concludes that the ability to interpret proverbs properly is a sign that a defendant is of enough mental stability to stand trial. The only problem with using this test is that many criminal defendants might not have the reading skills and/or the intellectual ability to complete the test. It is suggested that one could perhaps administer the test verbally. In any case, this established proverbs test for mental problems appears to be useful in this type of testing as well.

4382. Simonds, Peggy Muñoz. "Sacred and Sexual Motifs in *All's Well that Ends Well*." *Renaissance Quarterly*, 42, no. 1 (1989), 33–59.

> Simonds offers an analysis of the sacred and sexual motifs in William Shakespeare's (1564–1616) comedy *All's Well that Ends Well* (1593). While she mentions some mythological and religious motifs, her major emphasis is without doubt the bawdy language and humor of this play. The author explains how the plot centers around such matters as virginity and matrimony, and the passages that she cites do contain some proverbial language. Above all it is explained (see p. 35) that the proverbial title might actually be a reduced form of the longer English proverb "All shall be well, and Jack shall have his Jill." This proverb certainly is an obvious summary of the plot in folk speech.

4383. Simonin, Vera. "Historie de la classification des phraséologismes dans les pays de l'actuelle Yougoslavie: motivations et réalisations." *Europhras 88. Phraséologie Contrastive. Actes du Colloque International Klingenthal-Strasbourg, 12–16 mai 1988*. Ed. Gertrud Gréciano. Strasbourg: Université des Sciences Humaines, 1989. 431–440.

> Realizing what has happened to the country of Yugoslavia in the 1990s, this article surveying the major proverb collections of the various national, political, and ethnic groups of that part of

Europe is of particular relevance. The author begins with a statement concerning the complex political situation in the area of what used to be Yugoslavia, and she then moves on to discuss major paremiographical publications for the (former) countries of Croatia, Bosnia, Herzegovina, Serbia, and Montenegro. Many paremiographers are cited, among them Ivan Belostenec (1594–1675), Ivo Aletin (1670–1743), Vuk Karadzic-Stefanovic (1787–1864), Djuro Danicic (1825–1882), and Milan Vlajinac (1877–1964). For each paremiographer Simonin mentions the respective proverb collection and its value for diachronic paremiography. A useful bibliography (pp. 439–440) of these collections is attached.

4384.   Simpson, Dean. "The *Proverbia Grecorum.*" *Traditio*, 43 (1987), 1–22.

Simpson reports on the manuscript history and content of a medieval Latin proverb collection entitled *Proverbia Grecorum.* Even though some Greek words appear among its 74 proverbial statements, this collection appears to reflect a Latin rather than a Greek literary tradition. There seems to be no particular reason why the Greeks are mentioned in the title, but perhaps this was done to differentiate this secular collection of wise sayings from those of the Bible. Following a philological and historical analysis of this collection, Simpson presents four medieval documents which have been attributed to belong to the *Proverbia Grecorum.* They are followed by explanatory notes, making this article a valuable study of the sources, manuscripts, and commentaries regarding this small proverb collection.

4385.   Siran, Jean-Louis. "Signification, sens, valeur. Proverbes et noms propres en pays Vouté (Cameroun)." *Poétique*, no. 72 (1987), 403–429; also with slight changes in English translation as "Names and Proverbs among the Vute (Cameroon): Signification, Meaning and Value." *Journal of Folklore Research*, 26, no. 3 (1989), 207–227.

The major part of this ethnographical study deals with names used among the Vute of Cameroon. Only in the last section of his paper does Siran also mention proverbs from this

African people. He explains that they are used to name recurrent phenomena, experiences, and observations. Citing a number of examples in Vute and with French or English translations, Siran differentiates among the following aspects of the proverbial texts: (1) signification (translation), (2) meaning (explanation of the text), and (3) value (in the social context). He concludes that proper names and proverbs serve common goals. They both name someone or something, and while the personal name refers explicitly to someone, the proverb does so metaphorically or figuratively. Two diagrams and a small bibliography (p. 429 and p. 227 respectively) are included.

4386. Sirotkin, V.M. "Prisliv'ia ta prikazki iak dzherelo vivchennia etiko-pravovikh zvichaiv i uiavlen' ukrains'kogo narodu." *Narodna tvorchist' ta etnografiia,* no. 1 (1987), 39–42.

This is a short article studying Ukrainian proverbs and proverbial expressions as traditional statements about the ethics, habits, and customs of the Ukrainian people. The author includes texts from the 17th century to 1917, and he explains that many of them deal in particular with social classes and family relations. Numerous contextualized examples from collections and literary sources are cited. Historical and cultural explanations are included, and the author claims that proverbs can be studied as expressions of worldview. The 20 notes refer primarily to Ukrainian proverb collections, indicating that there exists a long scholarly interest in Ukrainian folk wisdom.

4387. Skara, Danica. "Mjesto i uloga zene u poslovicama hrvatskog ili srpskog i engleskog jezika." *Radovi,* 28 (1988–1989), 117–124.

Skara compares Serbo-Croatian and English proverbs that deal with women, wives, girls, mothers, and widows. She explains that these proverbs about female identity contain traditional beliefs and stereotypes, and she also states that they reflect the worldview of the cultures that produce them. While some proverbs are complimentary towards women, others are definitely misogynous and show that they were coined by men as invectives against women. Skara cites numerous Serbo-Croatian and English examples, illustrating that some texts are in fact identical while others are indigenous to each of the two languages and cultures. Short Serbo-Croatian (p. 117) and English abstracts (p. 124) are included.

4388. Skara, Danica. "Odraz jezicnih i kulturnih doticaja u poslovicama." *Jezici i kulture u doticajima. Zbornik 1. Medunarodnog skupa, Pula 14.-15. 4. 1988.* No editor given. Pula: Pedagoski fakultet u Rijeci, 1989. 282–288.

In this short article Skara makes some general points about the cultural and linguistic contacts that are involved in spreading proverbs from one national language to another. She explains that international proverbs usually go back to classical or Biblical proverbs which subsequently have been translated into many languages. But there are also later borrowings in the form of loan translations among languages and cultures that have come into contact with each other. Skara cites equivalent proverbs from the Latin, Italian, English, and Serbo-Croatian languages which definitely go back to early sources. But the author also includes a few examples which illustrate how the Serbo-Croatian language has become enriched through more recent loan translations of English proverbs. Short Serbo-Croatian and English abstracts (p. 288) are attached.

4389. Skara, Danica. "O specificnostima metaforicnih poslovica s jezicnog i kulturnog aspekta." *Uporabno jezikoslovlje. Zbornik radova s V. kongresa Saveza drustava za primijenjenu lingvistiku Jugoslavije.* Ed. Inka Strukelj. Ljubljana: Zveza, 1989. 342–347.

The author discusses the metaphorical nature of proverbs with special emphasis on Serbo-Croatian and English texts. In the case of classical and Biblical proverbs the metaphors are the same in both languages since these old proverbs were translated directly. However, there are also those proverbs which might express the same idea but have quite different metaphors. Skara explains that this is due to different linguistic and cultural aspects of the two societies. For newer English proverbs which are appearing in the Serbo-Croatian language as loan translations the metaphors are, of course, once again the same. A short English abstract (p. 347) is provided.

4390. Skara, Danica, and Pavao Mikic. "Poimanje kreposti u poslovicama hrvatskog ili srpskog, engleskog i njemackog jezika." *Radovi*, 27, no. 17 (1987–1988), 161–180.

The two authors deal with Serbo-Croatian, English, and German proverbs which comment on such virtues as truthfulness, love, honesty, bravery, wisdom, justice, faithfulness, and hopefulness. It is argued that those proverbs which go back to classical and Biblical sources obviously express identical ideas about these virtues in all three languages. However, there are also those indigenous proverbs which state rules for virtuous behavior that are quite different from one language and culture to another. Skara and Mikic cite numerous examples of all three languages, also including texts which have the same meaning but very different metaphors and structures. A useful bibliography (p. 179) and Serbo-Croatian (p. 161) and English (p. 180) abstracts are included.

4391. Skara, Danica, and Pavao Mikic. "Stari zavjet kao izvor njemacih i hrvatskih poslovica." *Radovi*, 29, no. 19 (1989–1990), 143–166.

In this valuable article Skara and Mikic investigate the Old Testament as a source for German and Serbo-Croatian proverbs. They explain that Biblical proverbs were translated into both languages, and they have remained among the most popular proverbs to the present day. About 30% of the Biblical originals are identical in wording in Serbo-Croatian and German, but the other 70% show certain structural, lexical, and syntactical differences in comparison to the Bible. Altogether 43.3% of the Serbo-Croatian and German Biblical proverbs are identical, indicating a relatively close linguistic and cultural contact between the two societies. The authors include 60 comparative examples, citing the Bible and Serbo-Croatian as well as German loan translations. A statistical table, a helpful bibliography (p. 166), and a Serbo-Croatian (p. 143) and an English (p. 166) abstract are part of this study.

4392. Skorupka, Stanislaw. "Przyslowia a wyrazenia i zwroty przyslowiowe." *Prace Filologiczne*, 32 (1985), 359–364.

The author presents short observations on the definition of such paremiological genres as proverbs, proverbial verses, proverbial expressions, and idioms. He refers to previous definition attempts and then dedicates a few paragraphs to the various subgenres. In each case he discusses such aspects as language, form, structure, style, and poetic devices, and he includes a few Polish examples as well. It is also pointed out that one and the same metaphorical phrase may appear in the form of the four different subgenres. While their metaphors are the same, there will be slight differences in form and meaning. Skorupka illustrates this by several examples and concludes that the various subgenres are clearly interrelated.

4393. Slaveikov, Letko Rachov. "Bulgarskie poslovitsy i pogovorki (Istoriia ikh sobiraniia)." *Letko Slaveikov: Izbrannoe.* Ed. S. Baevoi. Moskva: Khudozhestvennaia Literatura, 1981. 164–208.

This rather general article on Bulgarian proverbs and proverbial expressions was written by Letko Rachov Slaveikov (1828–1895) in 1892 as a commentary on his earlier field research in Bulgaria. Slaveikov includes many autobiographical references and explains how he set out to collect Bulgarian folk speech in the middle of the 19th century. He was particularly interested in recording proverbs that he heard in oral use, arguing that they contain much folk wisdom based on traditional experiences and observations. Numerous examples are cited, and the author includes a few comparative statements regarding Turkish and Macedonian proverbs. While the article has no particular theoretical foundation, it represents an attempt by a teacher and folklorist to record many proverbs current in Bulgaria at that time.

4394. Smith, Charlotte Ann. *A Study of the Relationship Between the Use of Proverbs and Ego Development Levels.* Diss. University of Arkansas, 1982. 83 pp.

Smith argues that proverbs, clichés, and famous sayings (sententious remarks) are a form of verbal habits and represent a valid means for eliciting conscious and unconscious self-referent material. Using a psychological proverbs test developed by

Bernard Bass (see nos. 104–106), the author tested 84 undergraduate and graduate students from the University of Arkansas. The test composed of 131 fixed phrases identified conventional mores, hostility, fear of failure, and social acquiescence. It was concluded that those persons scoring high on these factors are found at the lower levels of ego development. Seven statistical tables, a useful bibliography (pp. 57–63), and a copy of this psychological test (pp. 70–74) are included.

4395. Smith, J.B. "Cockaigne and Lubberland: On the Survival of Some Popular Themes and Forms in English." *Quinquereme*, 5, no. 2 (1982), 226–240.

The author begins his article with the observation that there appears to be a dearth in English tradition of such popular themes as that of "Schlaraffenland" (Land of Cockaigne, or Lubberland). It is argued that this might be due at least in part to the fact that antiquarians and folklorists neglected such themes in the 19th century. This deficiency has now been largely remedied, and folklorists like Smith have located remnants of oral literature in the lore of school children, less well-known descriptions of provincial life, and proverbial expressions. Citing numerous examples in the form of jokes, anecdotes, folk narratives, and proverbial phrases, it is shown that the theme or motif of the Land of Cockaigne or Lubberland is still current today. The 63 notes (pp. 237–240) include helpful bibliographical information.

4396. Smith, J.B. "Of Skinflints and Pinch-Farthings." *Folklore* (London), 95, no. 2 (1984), 177–181.

In this short article Smith offers some comments on a number of English proverbial expressions and proverbial comparisons referring to skinflints and pinch-farthings. He points out that popular phrases about the miserly appear to fall into two main categories. Those in the first category are more or less realistic. They comment on the physical appearance, or, more commonly, on what may reasonably be assumed to be the actual habits of misers. Sayings of the second category are often in the form of hyperbole, and give full rein to the imagination, claiming that in order to indulge his passion the skinflint would perform unlikely or impossible feats—that he would indeed skin a flint. Numerous examples from various English dialects are cited, and Smith provides detailed etymological, historical, and cultural explanations. It is also pointed out that especially those fixed phrases which refer to the miser as having something to do with the devil probably are remnants of longer legends.

4397. Smith, J.B. "A Selection of Proverbial Material from 'Tail Corn'." *Lore and Language*, 4, no. 1 (1985), 68–77.

Smith reports that the British magazine *The Countryman* contained for several decades a column entitled "Tail Corn" which included short, pithy rural sayings as overheard by subscribers with an ear for proverbial language. The author has assembled 55 proverbial expressions and proverbial comparisons as well as 17 proverbs from the issues of *The Countryman* that appeared between 1968 and 1980. He explains that many of these fixed phrases are quite old, but those that have been varied for the sake of a pun or humor certainly exhibit splendid examples of rural variability, creativity, and metamorphosis of traditional folk language and wisdom. Since many of the texts are cited in one of the many English dialects, Smith has attached 70 notes (pp. 73–76) which include etymological, historical, and cultural explanations as well as annotations from major proverb collections.

4398. Smith, Sarah Stanbury. "'Game in Myn Hood': The Tradition of a Comic Proverb." *Studies in Iconography*, 9 (1983), 1–12.

Smith explains that the hood was the most frequently depicted form of male headgear in medieval manuscript illuminations, and the hood is also often cited in literary texts. She cites a number of comical English proverbs and proverbial expressions based on the hood, among them "Two heads under one hood," "To give someone a hood," and "To find (or play) a game in one's hood." All three fixed phrases allude to adultery and hypocrisy in one way or another, as is illustrated by several contextualized examples from Geoffrey Chaucer's (1340?–1400) *Canterbury Tales* (1387/1400). The author also cites an example out of Dante Alighieri's (1265–1321) *Divine Comedy* (1307?/1321?). A section on the depiction of the Flemish proverbial expression "To put a blue cloak on someone" in Pieter Brueghel's (c. 1520–1569) oil picture *Netherlandic Proverbs* (1559) is included as well, the phrase and the illustration referring to adulterous behavior and cuckoldry. With 6 illustrations and 25 notes (pp. 10–12) that contain bibliographical information regarding the relationship among art, literature, and proverbial speech.

4399. Smith, Sidney R. "Ria Stambaugh (1918–1984)." *Proverbium*, 2 (1985), 259–261.

  This is an obituary of the paremiologist and literary scholar Ria Stambaugh (1918–1984) from the University of North Carolina at Chapel Hill. Born in Aachen, Germany, Stambaugh emigrated to the United States and wrote her dissertation on *Proverbs and Proverbial Phrases in the Jestbooks of Lindener, Montanus, and Schumann* (1963). She also published two articles in *Proverbium*, one entitled "Proverbial Material in Sixteenth Century German Jestbooks" (1968), and the other bearing the intriguing title of "Proverbial and Human Corruption and other Distortions of Popular Sayings" (1970). The first article deals with the three authors that are also treated in her dissertation, and the second paper investigates primarily Heinrich von Kleist's (1777–1811) innovative use of proverbial speech. While Stambaugh's speciality was Middle and Early New High German literature, she also taught courses on German folklore and proverbs at the University of North Carolina. For annotations see nos. 1795–1797.

4400. Smith, Sidney R. "John G. Kunstmann (1894–1988)." *Proverbium*, 7 (1990), 255–260.

  In this obituary on a second colleague from the Department of German of the University of North Carolina at Chapel Hill, Smith commemorates John G. Kunstmann (1894–1988) and his work in Middle and Early New High German literature. Kunstmann was born in Australia, went to school in Leipzig, and then earned his Ph.D. with a dissertation on *The Hoopoe: A Study in European Folklore* (1938) at the University of Chicago, where he had the fortune of being a student of Archer Taylor (1890–1973). In addition to his many literary publications, Kunstmann also was an active folklorist with some interest in proverbs. In his paper "'The Bird that Fouls its Nest'" (1939) he investigated the origin and history of the proverb "It is an ill bird that fouls its own nest," and in his article on "And Yet Again: 'Wes das Herz voll ist, des gehet der Mund über'" he studied the Biblical proverb "Out of the abundance of the heart the mouth speaketh" (Matth. 12,34). For annotations see nos. 944–945.

4401. Soler, Maria-Lourdes. *Locuciones idiomáticas en "Buddenbrooks."* Diss. Universidad de Barcelona, 1969. 670 pp.

This is a voluminous and valuable dissertation written in Spanish on the proverbial language contained in Thomas Mann's (1875–1955) novel *Buddenbrooks* (1901), proving once and for all that this intellectual author integrated plenty of folk speech into his prose. Soler begins with a lengthy table of contents (pp. i-xxix) which actually is a detailed index of the expressions discussed in the thesis. Following some prefatory remarks (pp. xxx-xxxviii), the author presents a useful introduction (pp. 1–52) in which she discusses general aspects of proverbial expressions, idiomatic structures, classification of fixed phrases, content and value of phraseological units, and their use and function in literature. The last dozen or so pages (pp. 39–52) deal explicitly with the way Thomas Mann used proverbial phrases in this novel. The rest of the dissertation is divided into several sections that register the various fixed phrases, citing each text in its literary context, adding explanatory comments concerning their meaning, and also providing Spanish equivalents and hints on how to translate them into Spanish. The various sections are as follows: proverbial expressions referring to body parts (pp. 53–128), various other proverbial expressions (pp. 129–225), proverbial euphemisms (pp. 226–243), Biblical phrases (pp. 244–276), twin formulas (pp. 277–398), prepositional phrases (pp. 399–486), adverbial phrases (pp. 487–509), proverbial comparisons (pp. 510–532), adjectival expressions dealing primarily with colors (pp. 533–569), and phrases (pp. 570–613) which are unique to Thomas Mann's own style in this novel. A large bibliography (pp. 614–632) concludes this truly exemplary study of one of Germany's major 20th century writers.

4402. Sommer, Hans. "Schwante dem Schwan etwas?" *Sprachspiegel,* 38 (1982), 85–86.

Sommer offers a short etymological study of the German proverbial expression "Mir schwant etwas" (To have a foreboding). He explains that the phrase refers only to negative events. The verb "schwanen" has nothing to do with the "Schwan" (swan). Instead the expression is based on a linguistic pun that originated among university students. The Latin "olet mihi" (es ahnt mir, i.e., I have a foreboding) was brought in connection with Latin "olor" (swan), and in this form the expression has survived to this day.

4403. Sommer, Hans. "Zu Paaren treiben." *Sprachspiegel,* 41 (1985), 50–51.

In this short etymological study Sommer attempts to explain the origin and meaning of the German proverbial expression "Zu Paaren treiben" (To control someone, to drive someone into a corner). Sommer explains that the German plural noun "Paaren" (pairs) might originally have been "Baren" or "Paren" in the meaning of a post at which one could tie up a horse or a cow. He cites proverbs from Sebastian Franck (1499–1542) and Martin Luther (1483–1546) to support this etymological explanation. The noun might, however, also go back to "Barn" (Latin "pera" = sack, bag) which refers to a fishing net in the shape of a bag. Both explanatory attempts appear to be possible, and it is not absolutely known which one might be the more plausible theory.

4404. Soriano, Marc. "L'enfant du XVIIe siècle à travers les proverbes." *Enfance et littérature au XVIIe siècle.* Ed. Andrée Mansau. Paris: Klincksieck, 1991. 59–65 (=*Littératures classiques,* no. 14 [1991], 59–65).

Citing his many French examples from dictionaries and proverb collections published in France during the 17th century, Soriano investigates how children are being dealt with in these texts. He points out that many proverbs comment on both children and adults together, often indicating that children will be confronted with the same problems of destiny, sin, and work which adults face. There are also those proverbs which deal rather directly with pedagogical matters, and such texts are rather didactic in nature. The worldview of proverbs dealing with children is not particularly kind to childhood or youth. Many of them are so educational and authoritative that they do not seem to allow much space for play and laughter. The psychological goal of these proverbs about children is not to show a carefree and playful life but rather an existence filled with serious concerns for survival in a harsh world.

4405. Sorrell, Paul. "A Collection of Early English Proverbs in Dunedin, New Zealand." *Folklore* (London), 99, no. 1 (1988), 102–109.

The author, a rare book librarian, reports on a copy of John Ray's (1627–1705) important *Collection of English Proverbs* (1670) which a woman brought to him in 1984 in Dunedin, New Zealand. This first edition is in itself a valuable treasure, but its significance is much enhanced due to numerous annotations added by perhaps as many as six different owners of the book from the late 17th and 18th centuries. These additions usually consist of variants of proverbs, proverbial expressions, and proverbial comparisons listed by Ray. Sorrell cites a few examples with some explanatory notes, and he then provides a list of the entire 107 edited texts. He observes that of these variants only 25 have been recorded in standard English proverb dictionaries, making these texts a valuable proverb collection in their own right.

4406. Sorrentino, Antonio. "Folkloristic Structures of Proverbs in the *Tirukkural.*" *Proverbium*, 6 (1989), 129–137.

Referring to the structural theories of Nigel Barley (see no. 86), Alan Dundes (no. 378), and George Milner (no. 1293), the author attempts to delineate the folkloristic structures of some of the proverbs contained in Valluvar's (6th/7th century A.D.) didactic Indian verses published as *Tirukkural.* Citing structural paradigms from the three authors mentioned, Sorrentino shows that these classical Tamil proverbs follow the same patterns.

There are texts which are based on semantic contrastive pairs, some exhibit a symmetrical structure in form and content, others are oppositional, and there are also equational proverbs. Sorrentino presents his examples in the original Indian language with English translations, and he concludes that these basic proverbial structures must exist internationally. Two diagrams and a small bibliography (p. 137) are included.

4407. Soufas, Teresa S. "Calderón's Charlatan of Honor: 'Refranero' Wisdom and Its Condemnation of Gutierre." *Bulletin of the Comediantes*, 38 (1986), 165–176.

This is a literary proverb investigation of Pedro Calderón de la Barca's (1600–1681) play *El médico de su honra* (1635). It is argued that Gutierre, the protagonist of the play, is characterized through his use of proverbs as not being at all honorable. The complaints against unskilled doctors in Spanish proverbs are dramatized by the association that Calderón builds between those inept practitioners of medicine and Gutierre, the metaphorical physician of honor. By basing this figure and the play's discourse on such questionable proverbs, Calderón undermines the honor and nobility of his protagonist and allows the entire society to condemn Gutierre by means of the collective wisdom expressed in proverbs about physicians. Several contextualized examples are cited to support this interpretation. The 18 notes (pp. 171–176) contain useful bibliographical information.

4408. Spaggiari, Barbara. "'Cacciare la lepre col bue'." *Annali della Scuola Normale Superiore di Pisa: Classe di Lettere e Filosofia*, serie III, 12, no. 4 (1982), 1333–1409.

Spaggiari offers a detailed philological study of the classical proverbial expression "To chase (hunt) the hare with the bull" which appears in Petrarch's (1304–1374) works as "Cacciare la lepre col bue." The author begins her richly documented investigation with the observation that the phrase continues to be current in modern Italian, but she shows in particular how it already appears in Greek by Pindar (522?-443 B.C.), Plutarch (46?–120? A.D.), and Saint Gregory Nazianzen (330?-390). The phrase is also present in Latin sources, and it became quite international through Erasmus of Rotterdam's (1469–1536) Latin use of it in the *Adagia* (1500ff.). Many contextualized examples from Greek, Latin, and Italian sources are cited, historical, etymological, and cultural explanations are provided, and the 163 notes include valuable bibliographical information.

4409. Spieß, Gisela. "Die Stellung der Frau in den Sprichwörtern isländischer Sprichwörtersammlungen und in isländischen Sagas." *Proverbium*, 8 (1991), 159–178.

This is a detailed analysis of the role and position of women in Icelandic proverbs. Spieß starts with some general comments concering misogyny in proverbs, and she then investigates various proverbs referring to women, wives, girls, etc. contained in Icelandic proverb collections. There are clearly anti-feministic proverbs in these collections, but as Spieß points out, there are also texts which actually present a positive view of women. As far as proverbs in Icelandic literature are concerned, the author comments on their use and function in the didactic poem *The Havamal* out of the *Edda* (c. 1240) and several of the sagas. She is able to show that the older Germanic proverbs have a rather positive attitude towards women. Later proverbs, those influenced by Christianity, might also contain negative views. But it is definitely true that the worldview about women expressed in Icelandic proverbs is quite complimentary. When more critical proverbs are cited, they are often put into question in the context of the sagas. Numerous contextualized examples with German translations are cited, and Spieß also includes a helpful bibliography (pp. 177–178).

4410. Stanciu, Dumitru. "The Germans in the Romanian Proverbs." *Anuarul Institutului de Istorie si Arheologie "A.D. Xenopol,"* 19 (1982), 95–103.

Stanciu investigates the worldview of Rumanians concerning German settlers which have lived in Rumania for the past seven centuries. Citing over 100 proverbs and proverbial expressions in Rumanian with German translations, he is able to show that the view of the Germans is actually rather positive. While there are some proverbs contained in Rumanian proverb collections which express feelings of resentment, hate, and contempt, there are many more texts which actually show admiration for the German work ethics and other stereotypical character traits. The author draws attention to the fact that his findings are based on proverbial language alone, and he includes valuable bibliographical information in his 12 notes for further comparative studies of the relationship between Rumanians and Germans.

4411. Stanciu, Dumitru. *Proverbul, izvor de cunoastere a gindirii si expresiei folclorice a poporului român. Comparatie cu paremiologia popoarelor balcanice.* Bucuresti: Universitatea din Bucuresti, 1983. 25 pp.

This is an important published summary of Stanciu's doctoral dissertation that deals with many aspects of Balkan proverbs from such languages as Rumanian, Serbo-Croatian, Bulgarian, Albanian, and Greek. The author begins with a review of theoretical paremiology, and he mentions in particular the semiotic and structural work of the Soviet scholar Grigorii L'vovich Permiakov (1919–1983; see esp. no. 1428). He then presents his own thoughts on such matters as proverb definition, structure, form, grammar, style, meaning, etc. Many examples are cited to show the "universality" of these findings concerning Balkan proverbs. Stanciu also points out that the semiotic and structural approach is applicable on a comparative basis for all proverbs of the world. A diagram and structural formulas are included, and a valuable bibliography (pp. 23–25) is attached.

4412. Stanciu, Dumitru. "G.L. Permjakov (1919–1983)." *Proverbium,* 1 (1984), 161–165.

In his detailed obituary for the leading Soviet paremiologist Grigorii L'vovich Permiakov (1919–1983), Stanciu reviews the major publications of this great scholar and shows that his structural and semiotic model includes much more than proverbs. Permiakov's theory of the cliché encompasses such other verbal genres as proverbial expressions, proverbial comparisons, wellerisms, fables, anecdotes, and folk narratives (legends, fairy tales, etc.). For additional obituaries see Peter Grzybek (no. 3522) and Vilmos Voigt (no. 4513). For annotations concerning Permiakov's numerous books and articles see nos. 1424–1433, 2737, and 4145–4155.

4413. Stanciu, Dumitru. "Paremic Universalia." *Cahiers roumains d'études littéraires,* 1 (1984), 79–84.

This significant theoretical article written in English starts with a short review of the structural approaches of Grigorii L'vovich Permiakov (1919–1983; see no. 1428) and Matti Kuusi (1914–; see no. 978) and then presents a comparative paremiological analysis of the proverbs of the Balkan area. Stanciu explains that the fundamental logical schemes of situations in proverbs are: primary structures, derivated structures, compound structures, and the relation of preference. Next the variability of the contents with which these structures may be filled (i.e., thematic variability) and the particularization born from the possibility of modifying the expression (i.e., metaphorization) are studied. By citing Rumanian examples with English translations the author illuminates these mechanisms of producing paremias. He also concludes that it is necessary to connect paremiology with scientific epistemology, choosing as the formal instrument the logic of natural thinking which is part of genetic epistemology. The reconstruction of the semantic or of the thematic field of paremiology must precede any study of the stylistics of proverbs if it is to reach truly theoretical conclusions.

4414. Stanciu, Dumitru. "Rumynskie poslovitsy na balkanakh." *Paremiologicheskie issledovaniia.* Ed. Grigorii L'vovich Permiakov. Moskva: Nauka, 1984. 269–270.

In this short note Stanciu presents a few Rumanian proverbs from the Balkan with Russian translations and discusses their aesthetic structure. He points out that the artistic aspects of proverbs are characterized particularly through metaphors, comparisons, and epithets. Depending on which of these three tropes a particular proverb might or might not employ, Stanciu describes eight structural types. This classification also helps in differentiating proverbs from other fixed phrases. For each type the author includes several examples and argues that more

attention should be paid to the aesthetics of folk proverbs, since
they help to codify indirect and often didactic ideas.

4415. Stanciu, Dumitru. "Points de vue sur la parémiologie structurale."
Proverbium, 2 (1985), 185–232.

This is a major French review article on structural
paremiology by one of the leading Rumanian proverb scholars.
Stanciu begins with some general comments (pp. 186–189)
concerning the theoretical advances of structural analysis in the
case of proverbs, and he then dedicates a major portion of the
article (pp. 189–203) to a detailed evaluation of the structural
and semiotic work of the Soviet scholar Grigorii L'vovich
Permiakov (1919–1983; see esp. no. 1428). This is followed by
some comments on the structural research conducted by Matti
Kuusi (see no. 978), Arvo Krikmann (nos. 923–924), and a few
others. Stanciu reaches the conclusion that there is still much
work to be done, and he argues in particular that structural
analysis alone will not reach definitive answers regarding the
complex nature of proverbs. The 40 notes (pp. 221–227) include
useful references to international scholarship, and an extremely
valuable bibliography (pp. 227–232) of the Rumanian
paremiological accomplishments is attached as well.

4416. Stanciu, Dumitru. "Proverbul si problemele educatiei." *Limba si
literatura*, 1 (1986), 78–87; also in English translation as "The
Proverb and the Problems of Education." *Proverbium*, 3 (1986),
153–178.

The author investigates the traditional and modern
pedagogical value of Rumanian proverbs. He begins with the
observation that proverbs contain much educational value, and
they have certainly always been used as didactic tools in child
raising, in linguistic and religious instruction in schools, and in
teaching about general human experiences. Stanciu cites
numerous Rumanian examples and provides cultural and
psychological explanations. Many of the proverbs deal with such
matters as the mind, wisdom, experience, learning, authority, and
the teacher. Stanciu is convinced that proverbs continue to play a
major role as a pedagogical tool in modern societies, especially

among family members and at school. Proverbs certainly deserve to be taught as part of general education, and since they belong to the common knowledge of basically all native speakers, they are indeed very effective devices to communicate wisdom and knowledge.

4417. Stanciu, Dumitru. "Quelques problèmes de parémiologie comparée: roumaine-bulgare." *Raportui lingvistice, literare si culturale româno-bulgare.* Eds. Laura Fotiade et al. Bucuresti: Universitatea din Bucuresti, 1986. 171–184.

In this comparative article Stanciu deals with the nature, content, and meaning of Rumanian and Bulgarian proverbs. In order to limit the vast number of possible examples, he emphasizes 48 parallel texts from both languages which deal with intelligence (wisdom) and stupidity. It is shown that many proverbs are identical due to common classical origins or loan translations. But even those proverbs which might be different in the two cultures still indicate similar logical structures. Their metaphors might not be the same, but their basic linguistic and logical structures are identical. The examples are cited without French translations, but Stanciu includes explanations of their content and meaning.

4418. Stanciu, Dumitru. "Sinonimie si selectie în proverb." *Proverbium Dacoromania,* 2 (1987), 25–29; and 3 (1988), 2–13.

Taking his cue from the Soviet paremiologist Grigorii L'vovich Permiakov (1819–1983), Stanciu argues that the logico-semiotic level of proverbs helps to explain the interesting phenomena of synonymy and selection in proverbs. He argues that the existence of synonymous proverbs is due to natural thought processes which enable humans to express the same idea (meaning) through different metaphors. The choice of the metaphors clearly depends on the social and geographical environment of the speakers. This also helps to understand the actual selection of a particular proverb from a number of synonymous texts. That proverb which expresses a basic truth with most clarity and brevity together with an effective metaphor and a memorable form will in fact win out over others. Stanciu includes several Ruamnian examples to illustrate this interplay of synonymy and selection. A French summary (p. 29) is attached.

4419. Stanciu, Dumitru. "Patterns of Emergence and Selection with the Proverb (I)." *Proverbium*, 6 (1989), 139–163; also in Rumanian translation as "Modele de generare si selectie în proverb (I)." *Revista de etnografie si folclor*, 36, nos. 3–4 (1991), 131–149.

This is a complex theoretical study by one of the leading Rumanian paremiologists concerning such matters as synonymy, homonymy, and variants of proverbs. Basing his remarks on the logico-semiotic approach of the Soviet scholar Grigorii L'vovich Permiakov (1919–1983), Stanciu deals in particular with synonymous proverbs which he defines as having the same logical structure and similar contents. He has isolated 16 logical structures with four categories of themes yielding 64 subclasses of synonymies. He presents logical formulas for them and cites English examples for the various possibilites. It is also pointed out that not all possible subclasses lead to actual proverbs, since the folk will select only those structures which fit the aesthetics of traditional proverbs. A chart (p. 162) is included, and a second part of this article will appear in *Proverbium*, 9 (1992). The Rumanian translation of the first part contains a French summary (pp. 148–149).

4420. Stanciu, Dumitru. "Prezente românesti în paremiologia universala." *Proverbium Dacoromania*, 4 (1989), 39–41; also in *Revista de etnografie si folclor*, 34, no. 1 (1989), 75–78.

In this important review article Stanciu refers to numerous international proverb collections which include Rumanian proverbs. He is interested in showing that paremiographers have paid at least some attention to the rich proverb lore of Rumania. The article includes references to several proverb collections in English, French, German, etc., thus indicating to international scholars where to find Rumanian proverbs in translation. Those Rumanian proverbs which are included in comparative collections usually belong to the international stock of proverbs having originated in Greek and Roman antiquity or the Bible. But there are, of course, also those smaller collections which include those proverbs which are indigenous to Rumania. Some references to paremiological scholarship on Rumanian proverbs are included as well. A French summary (p. 41) is included.

4421.   Stanciu, Dumitru. "Definitii ale proverbului si zicatorii." *Revista de etnografie si folclor*, 36, nos. 3–4 (1991), 195–197.

This is a compact article citing a numbar of "famous" proverb definitions by Aristotle (284–322 B.C.), Erasmus of Rotterdam (1469–1536), Archer Taylor (1890–1973), Grigorii L'vovich Permiakov (1919–1983), etc. Stanciu also includes the definition attempts by a number of Rumanian scholars, and he explains that all of them have usually dealt with the problem of differentiating between proverbs and proverbial expressions. The author concludes his survey with some of his own comments, stressing the fact that both genres are definitely interrelated as far as language, metaphor, meaning, etc. are concerned. In fact, it is not always clear whether the proverb or the proverbial expression came first in those cases where both genres exist simultaneously. For a similar article in English see Bartlett Jere Whiting (no. 2060).

4422.   Stanciulescu-Bîrda, Alexandru. "Aspecte politico-sociale în proverbele românesti." *Proverbium Dacoromania*, 2 (1987), 7–12; and 3 (1988), 14–22; also slightly expanded in English translation as "Elements of National History Reflected in Romanian Proverbs." *East European Quarterly*, 24, no. 4 (1991), 513–528.

The author presents general comments regarding Rumanian proverbs as expressions of social and political wisdom. He points out that proverbs reflect the attitudes, beliefs, and value system of the people who cite them, and he explains that these proverbs have commented on human existence in Rumania from the Middle Ages to the 20th century. Stanciulescu-Bîrda cites many examples and adds some historical and cultural explanations. He also includes sections on proverbs referring to the use and abuse of power, favoritism, corruption, etc. Altogether the proverbs are seen as commentaries on everyday life and social reality. They also include insightful ideological comments on politics, government, social classes, and basic human behavior. If studied from an historical point of view, these proverbs can be interpreted as commentaries on the national history of Rumania and its people.

4423. Stanciulescu-Bîrda, Alexandru. "Une prestigieuse collection roumaine des proverbes et un grand éditeur: Gheorghe Marin." *Proverbium*, 5 (1988), 167–172.

This is a bibliographical report on a series of collections of proverbs, proverbial expressions, aphorisms, sententious remarks, maxims, etc. under the general editorship of Gheorghe Marin (20th century). The collections have appeared in the Rumanian language since the late 1960s, and the many volumes are grouped together under the general name of "Cogito." While there are many books that deal with Rumanian sayings of this type, Marin has also found editors to put together similar collections from many national languages in translation. Stanciulescu-Bîrda gives precise bibliographical information for close to 50 volumes, and he is definitely correct in his claim that this series of books is an international documentation of proverbs and quotations for general readers.

4424. Stanciulescu-Bîrda, Alexandru. "Préoccupations parémiologiques dans le département Mehedinti (Roumanie)." *Proverbium*, 6 (1989), 207–220.

In this excellent report Stanciulescu-Bîrda describes the truly remarkable paremiological and paremiographical work that has been going on in the district of Mehedenti in the southeastern part of Rumania. The driving force behind this activity has been Constantin Negreanu (1942–1991), one of Rumania's leading proverb scholars who unfortunately died at a very early age. Stanciulescu-Bîrda includes a bibliography (pp. 209–211) of Negreanu's proverb publications, he lists the speakers and the titles of their papers which were presented at two symposia in 1983 and 1986 organized by Negreanu, and he also describes the contents of two issues of the journal *Proverbium Dacoromania* (1984 and 1987) which Negreanu started and edited. Hopefully this exciting and important commitment to national and international proverb scholarship will continue without the remarkable dedication and diligence of Constantin Negreanu. For additional reports on the two Rumanian proverb symposia see C. Negreanu (nos. 3999 and 4006) and Anca Pegulescu (no. 4134).

4425. Stanciulescu-Bîrda, Alexandru. "Proverbele—documente ale originii si continuitatii românesti." *Proverbium Dacoromania,* 4 (1989), 42–44.

A short note on Rumanian proverbs interpreted as early documents of Rumanian thought and language. Stanciulescu-Bîrda cites a few examples and explains that they contain archaic words which go back to the very origin of the Rumanian language. He also shows, however, that early Rumanian proverbs include Latin and Slavic loan words. This is a clear indication how foreign cultures have influenced even the traditional Rumanian proverbs. In addition there are foreign proverbs current among Rumanian speakers which have been loan translated from neighboring cultures. Etymological, historical, and cultural explanations are included for some of the texts which originated during the Middle Ages. A French summary (p. 44) is attached.

4426. Stanciulescu-Bîrda, Emilia and Alexandru. "Boli si remedii în proverbele românesti." *Proverbium Dacoromania,* 4 (1989), 45–46.

The two authors comment very briefly on a few Rumanian medical proverbs, arguing that they contain traditional medical knowledge and beliefs. Most of these texts refer to diseases and their remedies, and they express medical folk wisdom which is based on centuries of observations and experiments. The authors also cite a few texts which mention treatments with various herbs and plants, once again illustrating that folk medicine has a considerable history in Rumania. While these proverbs might not give specific medical advice in the modern sense, they certainly contain valuable general observations about sickness and possible treatment. In fact, there are still plenty of rural Rumanians who adhere to some of this medical advice for some of the common ills.

4427. Stavreva, Svetlana. "Kum problema za opredelenieto na poslovitsite." *Ezik i literatura,* 44, no. 6 (1989), 106–113.

This article deals with the problem of defining proverbs and proverbial expressions. The author begins her study with a review of previous Bulgarian scholarship on this vexing question. She then analyzes such aspects as form, structure, and poetics of Bulgarian proverbs. Numerous examples are cited, and Stavreva attempts to differentiate between the two genres of proverbs and proverbial expressions. She explains that they both might have the same content and metaphor, but their form and meaning will show different degrees of variation. A few examples are cited to indicate the different stylistic, semantic, and functional aspects of these two phraseological subgenres. The 20 notes include useful bibliographical references to Bulgarian paremiological and paremiographical scholarship.

4428. Stedje, Astrid. "Sprecherstrategien im Spiegel der Phraseologie." *Beiträge zur allgemeinen und germanistischen Phraseologieforschung.* Ed. Jarmo Korhonen. Oulu: Oulun Yliopisto, 1987. 91–109.

The author argues that phraseological units represent a certain collective knowledge on part of the speaker. They contain general human experience and require psychological, situational, and cultural competence of the person who uses them. Stedje points out that these fixed phrases are based on conventions and norms, and they are used by the speaker by following certain intentional strategies. Citing many German proverbial expressions, she shows that the value and function of phraseological units depend on the contexts in which they are being employed. In fact, the interpretation and proper understanding of such expressions is made more difficult because of their polyfunctionality and multisemanticity. The speaker uses various strategies to bring the different meanings and functions of a phrase into play, and these will be determined by the context in which the phrase appears. A useful bibliography (pp. 108–109) for considering phraseological units as speech acts is attached.

4429. Stedje, Astrid. "Beherztes Eingreifen oder ungebetenes Sich-Einmischen. Kontrastive Studien zu einer ethnolinguistischen

Phraseologieforschung." *Europhras 88. Phraséologie Contrastive. Actes du Colloque International Klingenthal-Strasbourg, 12–16 mai 1988.* Ed. Gertrud Gréciano. Strasbourg: Université des Sciences Humaines, 1989. 441–452.

Stedje presents some psycholinguistic thoughts concerning German and Swedish phraseological units that refer to getting involved in telling other people how to change or correct their behavior. She cites numerous comparative examples and points out that the use of such corrective phrases is very much dependent on the context in which they are being stated. It is argued that such phrases seem to appear with higher frequency in the German language, and this clearly has something to do with the high value that is placed on behavioral norms in the German society. Nevertheless, there are many fixed phrases of this type which are identical in these two Germanic languages. Their function is usually to ask someone to be more considerate of others, but there are also those instances in which the use of such proverbial expressions means an unwelcome interference in personal freedom of choice. A useful bibliography (pp. 450–452) is attached.

4430. Stedje, Astrid. "Rosen, Lilien und Veilchen sprechen. Zur Semiotik der Blumen in deutscher Phraseologie." *Europhras 90. Akten der internationalen Tagung zur germanistischen Phraseologieforschung, Aske/Schweden 12.-15. Juni 1990.* Ed. Christine Palm. Uppsala: Acta Universitatis Upsaliensis, 1991. 253–264.

This is an informative article concerning the semiotics of flowers, especially roses, lilies, and violets, in German phraseological units. Stedje cites examples from art and literature, drawing primarily from German sources but also including some comparative texts from the Swedish language. She includes detailed comments on the symbolism and folklore surrounding flowers, indicating that women have frequently been compared to flowers in the poetry of Johann Wolfgang von Goethe (1749–1832), Friedrich Schiller (1759–1805), Heinrich Heine (1797–1856), and other poets. The most popular "flower" proverb is "Keine Rose ohne Dornen" (No rose without thorns), and this text has also been a motif in emblems and drawings. The proverbial expressions based on flowers speak a metaphorical language, often symbolizing different aspects of love. A helpful bibliography (pp. 263–264) regarding traditional language and botany is provided.

4431. Steele, Thomas J. "Orality and Literacy in Matter and Form: Ben Franklin's *Way to Wealth.*" *Oral Tradition*, 2, no. 1 (1987), 273–285.

In this article on Benjamin Franklin's (1706–1790) famous essay *The Way to Wealth* (1757) it is pointed out that Franklin used both oral and literary materials to formulate his powerful statement on solid work ethics and virtues. While he might have known some of the many proverbs contained in this essay from oral use, it is well known that he copied most of them from published proverb collections. By doing so, he is actually much more indebted to literacy than orality. He also chose only those proverbs which stressed a life of work and industry, ignoring the many humorous and even suggestive folk proverbs that he found in the English collections. His famous essay might have become proverbial over time, but the proverbs in it are not a true sample of traditional wisdom about human behavior. A bibliography (pp. 284–285) concerning Franklin and folk speech is attached. See also Stuart Gallacher (no. 495) and Patrick Sullivan (no. 4448).

4432. Stegemann, Hartmut. "'Alles palletti'." *Der Sprachdienst*, 28 (1984), 143–144.

A philological and cultural study of the origin and meaning of the German proverbial expression "Alles palletti" (All is saved, all is okay) which probably stems from the Yiddish and goes back to the Hebrew word stem "plt." The word "palletti" is shown to be a mixture of Hebrew and German, having been used by Jewish merchants to indicate that everything was in order as far as goods were concerned at a bankruptcy. In German colloquial speech the expression now has the meaning of "okay," and it does in fact compete with that Americanism in popularity in certain situations. Stegemann also argues that Yiddish is of much importance for the historical study of German proverbial expressions, and he urges philologists and folklorists to increase their interest in the rich Yiddish language. See also Walter Magaß (no. 3803).

4433. Stein, Heidi. "Eine türkische Sprichwortsammlung des 17. Jahrhunderts." *Acta Orientalia Academiae Scientiarum Hungaricae*, 38, nos. 1–2 (1984), 55–104.

This is actually a scholarly reprint of a small Turkish proverb collection which was included in Hieronymus Megiser's (1553?–1618) *Institutionum linguae turcicae libri IV* (1612). Stein discusses the problems which Megiser faced in the 17th century in transliterating the Turkish text into the Latin alphabet. She also discusses possible sources of this collection contained in a book for readers wishing to learn more about the Turkish language. Next she reprints the collection (pp. 59–85) together with Megiser's German translations and philological and cultural explanations. Stein has also added a Turkish-German glossary (pp. 85–100) and a German key-word index (pp. 100–104), thus making this early proverb collection easily accessible to German readers.

4434. Sternkopf, Jochen. "Paarformel vs. verbaler Phraseologismus." *Beiträge zur Erforschung der deutschen Sprache*, 10 (1991), 124–132.

Sternkopf offers a linguistic and structural analysis of German "Zwillingsformeln" (twin formulas). He begins with differentiating this type of expression from other phraseological units, and he then argues that the simplest structure of twin formulas is the one that links two nouns, verbs, adjectives, or adverbs with a conjunction or preposition. It is also pointed out that such twin formulas can be expanded into much more complex proverbial expressions by adding a verb or a comparative element to them, as for example "Haut und Knochen sein" (To be skin and bones) and "Verschieden wie Tag und Nacht" (Different as day and night). Numerous examples are cited fitting certain structural patterns, and the 53 notes include valuable bibliographical information.

4435. Stewart, Susan. "Notes on Distressed Genres." *Journal of American Folklore*, 104 (1991), 5–31.

The author surveys the ways in which a number of oral forms, namely epic, fable, proverb, fairy tale, and ballad, have been "antiquated" and reproduced by literary culture from the late 17th century forward. In creating such "distressed genres," the literary culture attempted to invent a domain of authenticity and originality just as literary culture was itself undergoing dramatic changes in its modes of production and reception. Only a few pages (pp. 17–19) deal with the proverb in an attempt to argue that its time has passed. Referring to Georg Wilhelm Friedrich Hegel (1770–1831) and his thoughts on the fable and proverb, Stewart concludes that the proverb marks the resolution of confusion, the end of history, and speaks with a voice that is both time-honored and superannuated. All of this is seen by Stewart as the irony of a genre worn thin and the proverb's always dubious status within contemporary culture. She even reaches the conclusion that a new proverb would be unimaginable to tradition and that contemporary proverb collections are as obsolete as the interjection of traditional proverbs into conversation. These conclusions are, however, in strong contrast to recent paremiological and paremiographical work. An English abstract (p. 5) and a bibliography (pp. 29–31) are included.

4436. Stitt, J. Michael. "Conversational Genres at a Las Vegas '21' Table." *Western Folklore*, 45, no. 4 (1986), 278–289.

In this article based on actual field research in the Las Vegas, Nevada, gambling casinos, Stitt explains that gambling is a social phenomenon with its own verbal traditions. Concentrating in particular on the card game called "21," he outlines its rules and then cites a number of examples of fixed phrases and superstitions that are used by the players. Certain rules and strategies of the game have become proverbial, as for example "Always split eights against a nine." Such "proverbial" statements are, of course, very much restricted in use to people who know this card game. Nevertheless, the article is an example for the proverbial language of certain groups, something that deserves much more attention by paremiologists.

4437. Stojchev, Petko. "Zhanrova klassifikatsiia, funktsii i vuzpriematelni mekhanizmi pri paremiiata." *Bulgarski folklor,* 14, no. 3 (1988), 17–26.

The author attempts to differentiate among proverbs, proverbial expressions, and maxims, arguing that both their function and content set them apart from each other. The proverb is seen to be an image (metaphor) that contains a judgment reflecting social norms and natural phenomena, the maxim expresses a plan and imposes an imperative on a certain mode of behavior, and the proverbial expression has a commenting function. Stojchev also explains that the action expressed in proverbs is in the past and present, in the maxim it is forthcoming, and in the saying it is in the field of semantic abstraction. The theoretical article includes some comments regarding the function, content, and structure of these three verbal genres. An English abstract (p. 26) is provided.

4438. Stolpe, Herman. "Om konsten att tolka ordoch tänkespråk." *Horisont,* 34, no. 4 (1987), 65–70.

Stolpe presents a rather general discussion of how proverbs and aphorisms are interpreted in different societies and times. He begins with some comments on the use and function of proverbs in Africa, arguing that they play a traditional role in oral communication. Next he discusses the problem of translating the proverbs from one language and culture into another. Often the translations are inaccurate, especially when there are no equivalents in the target language. Stolpe also points out that many proverbs do reflect the social reality of the time when they were coined. But as new historical periods appear, proverbs can also be changed and new ones are placed into circulation. In the last part of the article the author describes modern Swedish proverbs and also mentions the intentional variations of traditional proverbs which Wolfgang Mieder (see no. 3852) has called "Antisprichwörter" (anti-proverbs). Six humorous illustrations are included.

4439. Stone, Judith. "Triumph of the Willies." *Discover,* 9, no. 4 (1988), 80 and 82–83.

This is a popular magazine article attempting to solve the riddle of the origin and precise meaning of the English proverbial expression "To get the willies." Stone includes some etymological speculations on the word "willies," and she then explains the phenomenon of getting the chills or willies when someone scratches a fingernail on the blackboard. A number of variants like "To get the shudders, the whim-whams, the heebie-jeebies, and the juts" are mentioned, and a few contextualized examples from such authors as Harry Graham (1874–1936) and Joseph Heller (1923–) are cited. Stone even includes medical, biological, and neurological explanations for the phenomenon of getting so-called gooseflesh. With 2 humorous illustrations.

4440. Strasser, Gerhard F. "'Wie von der Tarantel gebissen'.: Tarantismus und Musiktherapie im Barock." *Barocker Lust-Spiegel. Studien zur Literatur des Barock. Festschrift für Blake Lee Spahr.* Eds. Martin Bircher et al. Amsterdam: Rodopi, 1984. 245–264.

Strasser gives some detailed comments regarding the German proverbial comparison "Wie von der Tarantel gebissen (gestochen)" (As though someone had been bitten [stung] by a tarantula [bee, hornet]). He deals with the etymology of the word "Tarantel" and also includes various superstitions and beliefs concerning this dangerous spider. He refers to early medical remedies and explains the belief from the 17th century that music might be used for some sort of therapy. Several long quotations from various medical, musical, and encyclopedic sources are cited which comment on how to deal with someone who has been bitten by a tarantula. Two illustrations and 51 notes with rich bibliographical information are included.

4441. Streltsyna, M.S. "K voprosu o tipakh narushenii ponimaniia rechi pri afazii." *Voprosy Psikhologii,* no. 2 (1982), 121–125.

The author studied the comprehension of proverbs in eight aphasic individuals with involvement of the anterior portions of the cortical speech area, six individuals with posterior speech area involvement, and a group of normal subjects. Five proverbs were presented orally and in writing simultaneously with the last word in each proverb omitted. The subjects filled in the blank with one of three words which they could choose from a synonym of the correct word, its antonym, and a word grammatically acceptable within the context of the proverb, but one that made it a concrete or situationally descriptive statement. While the normal subjects made no errors, a qualitative difference in the errors made was observed between the two aphasic groups, the locus of the aphasic involvement interacting with the subjective complexity of the various proverbs. The observed differences are attributed to complex combinations and interactions among psychological, neuropsychological, and linguistic factors. Two graphs and a useful bibliography (pp. 124–125) of Soviet scholarship using psychological proverbs tests are provided.

4442. Strube, Werner. "Zur Geschichte des Sprichworts 'Über den Geschmack läßt sich nicht streiten'." *Zeitschrift für Ästhetik und Allgemeine Kunstwissenschaft*, 30 (1985), 158–185.

This is a philosophical treatise on various theoretical and aesthetic reactions to the Latin proverb "De gustibus non est disputandum" which is current in German as "Über den Geschmack läßt sich nicht streiten" (There is no accounting [disputing] over tastes). Strube presents detailed interpretations of this proverb by such scholars and philosophers as Johann Christoph Gottsched (1700–1766), Georg Friedrich Meier (1718–1777), David Hume (1711–1776), Immanuel Kant (1724–1804), Karl Köstlin (1819–1894), and Gustav Theodor Fechner (1801–1887). It is pointed out that these thinkers deny any particular value to the wisdom of the proverb, since there are some aesthetic principles which go beyond individual tastes. The 121 notes include useful bibliographical information. See also Helmut Walther (no. 4530).

4443. Struever, Nancy S. "Proverbial Signs: Formal Strategies in Guicciardini's *Ricordi.*" *Annali d'Italianistica*, 2 (1984), 94–109.

Struever presents an investigation of Francesco Guicciardini's (1483–1540) collection of maxims entitled *Ricordi* (1512, 5th ed. 1530). She explains that this Italian historian and politician formulated these maxims as aphoristic and proverbial thoughts regarding political, social, and moral aspects of life. It is pointed out that many of his texts are based on proverbs or are critical reactions to traditional proverbial wisdom. His texts can be understood as proverbial signs or strategies to live a useful political and social life. Many of his maxims deal with such aspects as authority, power, social relations, civil interests, political reality, virtue, communal wisdom, etc. Struever cites numerous examples in English translation and interprets them within the larger context of Guicciardini's life and works. The 38 notes (pp. 105–109) contain additional comments and bibliographical information.

4444. Suard, François. "La fonction des proverbes dans les chansons de geste des XIVe et XVe siècles." *Richesse du proverbe.* Eds. F. Suard and Claude Buridant. Lille: Université de Lille, 1984. I, 131–144.

This is a literary investigation of the use and function of medieval French proverbs in nine late *chansons de geste* from the 14th and 15th centuries, the epics being *Hugues Capet* (c. 1358), *Baudouin de Sebourc* (2nd half of 14th cent.), *Le Bâtard de Bouillon* (2nd half of 14th cent.), *La geste de Monglane* (15th cent.), *La geste des ducs de Bourgogne* (c. 1420), *Tristan de Nanteuil* (2nd half of 14th cent.), *Auberon* (c. 1311), *Ogier le Danois* (c. 1335), and *Ami et Amile* (15th cent.). The author presents statistical frequency studies showing that the number of proverbs varies from epic poem to epic poem and that the frequency of proverbs is actually not very high. Most of the texts are introduced with introductory formulas. Suard cites numerous contextualized examples and explains that the proverbial metaphors function primarily as expressions of wisdom and morality.

4445. Suard, François, and Claude Buridant (eds.). *Richesse du proverbe.* Lille: Université de Lille, 1984. I, 163 pp.; II, 275 pp.

These two volumes of paremiological essays by French scholars are of major importance to literary and cultural historians as well as folklorists who are interested in the Middle Ages. The first volume includes 9 articles by the following authors, and they all deal with medieval materials: Anne-Marie Bautier, "Peuples, provinces et villes dans la littérature proverbiale latine du moyen âge" (pp. 1–22); Claude Buridant,

"Les proverbes et la prédication au moyen âge. De l'utilisation des proverbes vulgaires dans les sermons" (pp. 23–54); Juliette de Caluwé-Dor, "Les proverbes de Hendyng" (pp. 55–73); Pierre Demarolle, "Autour de la *Ballade des Proverbes*: Aspects logiques de la poésie de François Villon" (pp. 75–85); Jean-Claude Faucon, "La sagesse populaire au service du roi: De l'utilisation des proverbes par un chroniqueur du XIVe siècle" (pp. 87–111); Eric Hicks, "Proverbe et polémique dans le *Roman de la Rose* de Jean de Meun" (pp. 113–120); Antoinette Saly, "Les proverbes dans le *Meliacin* de Girart d'Amiens: Aspect et fonction" (pp. 121–129); François Suard, "La fonction des proverbes dans les chansons de geste des XIVe et XVe siècles" (pp. 131–144); and Alain-Julien Surdel, "Typologie et stylistique des locutions sentencieuses dans *Le Mystère de S. Didier de Langres* de Guillaume Flamant (1482)" (pp. 145–162). The second volume is comprised of 20 essays which the editors have divided into three sections. The first 11 articles deal with various theoretical and comparative aspects of proverbs: Claudie Balavoine, "Les principes de la parémiographie érasmienne" (pp. 9–23); Fernando Belo, "Analyse des logiques d'un corpus proverbial" (pp. 25–36); Catherine Bloc-Duraffour, "Traitement de la logique des rôles narratifs dans les proverbes italiens" (pp. 37–49); Evelyne Brouzeng, "Stylistique comparée de la traduction des proverbes anglais et français" (pp. 51–60); Pierre Cazier, "Les *Sentences* d'Isidore de Séville, genre littéraire et procédés stylistiques" (pp. 61–72); Charles Guiraud, "Structure linguistique des proverbes latins" (pp. 73–82); Anna Maria Ieraci-Bio, "Le concept de 'paroimia': Proverbium dans la haute et la basse antiquité" (pp. 83–94); Yann Kerdilès, "Les acteurs langagiers dans les proverbes" (pp. 95–105); Bronislawa Kordas, "Quelques problèmes concernant la notion de proverbe en chinois moderne" (pp. 107–113); Hubert Le Bourdellès, " Les proverbes et leurs désignations dans les langues antiques" (pp. 115–120); and Francis M. Rodegem, "La parole proverbiale" (pp. 121–135). The second set of 5 articles deals with the use and function of proverbs in various societies: Raymond Arveiller, "L'univers du vieux Monégasque, d'après les proverbes et dictons" (pp. 139–154); Jean Breuillard, "Proverbes et pouvoir politique: Le cas de l'U.R.S.S. (pp. 155–166); Nicolas G. Contossopoulos, "Les proverbes crétois" (pp. 167–181); André

Gallego, "Pédagogie et parémiologie. L'utilisation des proverbes dans la formation des adolescents au XVIe siècle à l'Université de Valencia" (pp. 183–197); and Haim Vidal Sephiha, "La société judéo-espagnole à travers ses proverbes, ou dis-moi tes proverbes, je te dirai qui tu es" (pp. 199–209). The third part consists of the following 4 essays dealing with proverbs and speech communication: José-Luis Alonso Hernandez, "Interprétation psychanalytique de l'utilisation des parémies dans la littérature espagnole" (pp. 213–225); Monique Gosselin, "De la maxime au proverbe: Fragments du discours sentencieux dans les textes de fiction de G. Bernanos" (pp. 227–243); Monique Joly, "Le discours métaparémique dans *Don Quichotte*" (pp. 245–260); and Alain Juillard, "Discours proverbial et écriture romanesque dans *La Comédie Humaine*. Le cas de *Un Début dans la vie*" (pp. 261–272). For individual annotations of these 29 significant investigations see nos. 3117, 3194, 3212, 3298, 3396, 3594, 4304, 4444, 4449 (first volume); 3088, 3127, 3142, 3175, 3230, 3540, 3630, 3675, 3705, 3773, 4248, 3077, 3162, 3259, 3462, 4371, 3583, 3494, 3647, 3656 (second volume).

4446. Sullivan, Constance. "Gender Markers in Traditional Spanish Proverbs." *Literature Among Discourses: The Spanish Golden Age.* Ed. Wlad Godzich and Nicholas Spadaccini. Minneapolis/Minnesota: University of Minnesota Press, 1986. 82–102 and 160–165 (notes).

Sullivan begins her informative article with the observation that much more work needs to be done by sociolinguists, folklorists, and paremiologists in order to understand the survival of proverbs in the modern Spanish society. In the meantime, much can be learned from how paremiographers and philologists dealt with proverbs during the Renaissance and later centuries. She reviews a number of major Spanish proverb collections and argues that their texts and commentaries include much information regarding the historical and cultural value system. While the proverb collectors were always males, they certainly collected the proverbs from both men and women. Especially the proverbs about women, widows, mother-in-laws, daughters, nuns, whores, etc. say a great deal about social and moral norms and attitudes in former times. Sullivan cites numerous Spanish examples with English translations, and especially in the second part of the article does she deal with the role of women and female gender in these proverbs. The 41 notes (pp. 160–165) contain important bibliographical references.

4447. Sullivan, Margaret. "Bruegel's Proverbs: Art and Audience in the Northern Renaissance." *The Art Bulletin*, 73, no. 3 (1991), 431–466.

This is a superb study of the interrelationship of art and proverbs by an art historian well versed in not only art history but also in folklore and paremiology. Sullivan argues convincingly that folkloristic interpretations have dominated the study of proverbs and proverbial expressions depicted in Pieter Brueghel's (c. 1520–1569) art. Both folklorists and art historians have looked at these proverbs only as sayings of the folk without paying attention to the fact that Brueghel actually addressed a humanist audience in the Low Countries. The relationship between Brueghel's proverbs and the classical past was highly salient for his original audience, and any interpretation of his many proverb illustrations must consider Latin and Greek proverbs as well as those in the vernacular. The author reviews the extensive scholarship on Brueghel's proverb pictures, and she shows in particular how he was doubtlessly influenced by 16th century proverb collections by such humanists as Erasmus of Rotterdam (1469–1536). In fact, the latter's *Adagia* (1500ff.) contains many of the classical proverbs which reappear in Brueghel's art. Sullivan shows this by detailed interpretations of the proverbial expressions contained in Brueghel's *Netherlandic Proverbs* (1559), but she also includes comments regarding the proverb pictures *Big Fish Eat Little Fish* (1557), *The Blind Leading the Blind* (1568), etc. Comments regarding the earlier proverbial art of Hieronymus Bosch (c. 1450–1516), Franz Hogenberg (1538–1590), and others are included as well. There is no doubt that their pictures and those of Brueghel depict classical *and* vernacular proverb lore. The 272 notes are filled with bibliographical references, and Sullivan also includes a useful bibliography (p. 466) of the major scholarship concerning art and proverbs. See also Wilhelm Fraenger (no. 460), Jan Grauls (no. 586), Alan Dundes and Claudia Stibbe (no. 2332), etc.

4448. Sullivan, Patrick. "Benjamin Franklin, the Inveterate (and Crafty) Public Instructor: Instruction on Two Levels in *The Way to Wealth.*" *Early American Literature,* 21 (1986–1987), 248–259.

This is yet another investigation of Benjamin Franklin's (1706–1790) use of proverbs in his famous essay on solid work ethics entitled *The Way to Wealth* (1757). Sullivan argues that Franklin offers proverbial instruction to the public in the simplest, most accessible and memorable form. But while he was a champion and purveyor of proverbs, Franklin also knew that proverbs have a way of acquiring immunity from criticism. Followed blindly and without analysis, proverbs can be dangerous. The many contradictory proverbs show this very clearly, confronting people with conflicting bits of wisdom. Franklin thus warns his readers of the limitations of the proverbs and suggests a cautious application of their wisdom. Citing numerous examples from this essay, Sullivan shows that Franklin talks both positively and negatively about proverbs, but he certainly sees them as a valuable instructional and rhetorical tool. See also Stuart Gallacher (no. 495) and Thomas Steele (no. 4431).

4449. Surdel, Alain-Julien. "Typologie et stylistique des locutions sentencieuses dans *Le Mystère de S. Didier de Langres* de Guillaume Flamant (1482)." *Richesse du proverbe.* Eds. François Suard and Claude Buridant. Lille: Université de Lille, 1984. I, 145–162.

Surdel investigates the use and function of the proverbial language in Guillaume Flamant's (1455?–1510) French mystery play *Ly Mystère de S. Didier de Langres* (1482). He explains that the play contains many Biblical references together with proverbial speech in order to teach morality and virtue. In the middle of the article (pp. 149–151) the author presents a catalogue of all fixed phrases of the play, dividing them according to proverbial allusions, apothegms, aphorisms, proverbial expressions, proverbs, and maxims. He lists all the texts together with the individual speakers of the play. This is followed by some contextualized examples that serve to illustrate how Flamant used this traditional language to add pedagogical insights to his religious drama. The 62 notes (pp. 160–162) contain useful bibliographical references to French medieval proverbs.

4450. Suter, Beat. "Verbale Sprache." In B. Suter. *Graffiti. Rebellion der Zeichen.* Frankfurt am Main: Rita G. Fischer, 1988. 31–49.

Basing her comments on actual field research, Suter describes and interprets German graffiti which she found on city walls. In this chapter she explains that many graffiti are based on proverbs, proverbial expressions, and literary quotations, citing German and also a few English examples. There are two longer sections on the proverbial slogan "Stell dir vor, es ist Krieg, und keiner geht hin" (Suppose they gave a war and nobody came) and the quotation "Cogito, ergo sum" (I think, therefore I am) by René Descartes (1596–1650). Many variations and parodies are cited (see pp. 36–38 and pp. 40–41), of which some might be considered "Antisprichwörter" (anti-proverbs) that comment on the social and political problems of Germany. For the anti-war slogan see Ralf Bülow (no. 3180) and Reinhard Roche (no. 4247), and for the quotation by Descartes see Wolfgang Mieder (no. 3868). With 8 illustrations.

4451. Sverrisdóttir, Oddny Gudrún. *Land in Sicht. Eine kontrastive Untersuchung deutscher und isländischer Redensarten aus der Seemannssprache.* Frankfurt am Main: Peter Lang, 1987. 276 pp.

This is a unique study of many German and Icelandic proverbial expressions that deal with various aspects of the merchant marine. The author begins her study with a theoretical chapter (pp. 11–48) on phraseology, idiomaticity, fixidity, reproducibility, equivalency, and translatability. The major second chapter (pp. 49–201) investigates almost 300 fixed phrases that deal with the ship, boat, deck, keel, flag, sail, rudder, rope, net, harbor, wave, etc. Citing all her comparative examples in their original languages (German translations for the Icelandic texts are provided), Sverrisdóttir adds detailed explanatory notes concerning the origin, history, meaning, and function of the expressions. Equivalents are also included, but it is shown that quite a few expressions are indigenous to the German or Icelandic culture. The third chapter (pp. 202–224) presents some additional semantic comments, while chapter four (pp. 225–242) provides a short history of the merchant marine of both countries. The fifth chapter (pp. 242–258) summarizes the similarities and differences of the proverbial expressions dealing with the sea and shipping of these two Germanic languages. A very helpful bibliography (pp. 259–276) is attached.

4452. Sweterlitsch, Richard. "Reexamining the Proverb in the Child Ballad." *Proverbium*, 2 (1985), 233–256.

The author bases his study of the proverbs in the 305 ballads collected by Francis James Child (1825–1896) on a previous analysis of their proverbial language by Bartlett Jere Whiting (see no. 2064). Having once again analyzed all ballad texts and their numerous variants, Sweterlitsch goes beyond Whiting's study from 1934 which was primarily a catalogue of their fixed phrases. The present author concentrates only on the proverbs and divides the material into three groups: (1) 14 traditional proverbs with numerous variants, (2) 3 mere allusions to proverbs, and (3) 6 variations based on traditional proverb structures. All texts are cited in their ballad context, and the author has also added scholarly annotations from major English proverb collections. Following each group of texts are detailed comments regarding their use and function in these traditional English and Scottish folk songs. Statistical frequency calculations are part of this interpretative study. An important bibliography (pp. 254–256) concerning the appearance of proverbs in various types of songs is included.

4453. Sybesma, Jetske. "The Reception of Bruegel's *Beekeepers*: A Matter of Choice." *The Art Bulletin*, 73, no. 3 (1991), 467–478.

This is a detailed interpretation of Pieter Brueghel's (c. 1520–1569) pen-and-ink drawing *The Beekeepers* (1567/68) which illustrates the Dutch proverb "Dye den nest weet dye weeten / dyen roft dye heeten" (He who knows the nest knows it [has knowledge] / he who robs it has [possesses] it). Sybesma studies this proverb picture in the context of the political and religious conflict in the Spanish Netherlands during the late 1560s. The meaning of this drawing is seen as being deliberately ambiguous because it addresses antagonistic groups of viewers: the Inquisition and Protestants. Although the artist must have been a Catholic, he expresses a veiled condemnation of activities associated with the Inquisition and an even more negative view towwards acceptance of Protestantism. A short discussion of a second proverb picture, Brueghel's *The Bird-Nester* (1568), is included since it depicts the same proverb. With 3 illustrations and 68 notes containing significant bibliographical references for the relationship between art and paremiology. See also Claus Kreuzberg (no. 918).

4454. Syrotinski, Michael Friedrich Joseph. *Reinventing Figures: Jean Paulhan and the Critical Mystery of Literature.* Diss. Yale University, 1989. 269 pp.

Only the first chapter (pp. 13–55) of this dissertation analyzing the literary theories of the French scholar Jean Paulhan (1884–1968) deals with proverbial questions. Syrotinski interprets his early essay on *L'expérience du proverbe* (1913) in which Paulhan describes the way in which he learned to understand and eventually also use Malagasy proverbs while he spent some time on the island of Madagascar. It is shown that Paulhan very early in the 20th century was already speaking of proverbs as a code or sign for naming things. He dealt with such questions as definition, use, function, effectiveness, context, text, signification, syntax, etc. His conclusions are still of importance for modern theoretical paremiology and the theory of oral and written literature. A useful bibliography (pp. 265–269) is attached. For an annotation of Paulhan's original essay see no. 1416.

4455. Szelp, E. "Sprachliche Vergleichung der Sprichwörter und der sprichwörtlichen Redensarten." *Slavica*, 19 (1983), 35–38.

This is a short article on the difference between the two phraseological subgenres of the proverb and proverbial expression. Szelp begins with a discussion of what the four major scholars Karl Friedrich Wilhelm Wander (1803–1879), Vladimir Ivanovich Dal' (1801–1872), Gábor O.Nagy (1915–1973), and Lutz Röhrich (1922–) have had to say about these two related forms of traditional folk speech. Citing a number of German examples, Szelp points out that paremiologists need the help of phraseologists and their linguistic training in order to set up rigid borders (definitions) between these two types of proverbial language. It is not enough to talk only of the fact that proverbs are complete sentences and thoughts while proverbial expressions are mere metaphorical phrases. There are many linguistic criteria that will help to differentiate between them.

4456. Szemerkényi, Agnes. "A parömiologia nehany kerdese." *Nepi Kultura—Nepi Tarsadalom*, no. 9 (1975), 27–35.

Szemerkényi reviews some of the structural and semiotic research by such scholars as Roger Abrahams (see no. 2), Nigel Barley (nos. 86–87), Alan Dundes (no. 378), Matti Kuusi (no. 969), George Milner (no. 1291), Grigorii L'vovich Permiakov (no. 1428), and others for Hungarian readers. While these studies signify major breakthroughs in paremiology, the author argues that some other basic matters need to be addressed, namely definition problems, the use of proverbs in speech acts, meaning of proverbs, lexicographical issues of organizing proverb collections and archives, etc. Paremiologists must involve themselves in all of these concerns if significant advances in the investigation of phraseological units are to occur. A short bibliography (p. 35) and an English abstract (p. 34) are included.

4457. Szemerkényi, Agnes. "A szolasok szemiotikai analizise." *Jel és közösség*. Eds. Vilmos Voigt et al. Budapest: Akadémiai Kiado, 1975. 57–65.

This is a slightly changed Hungarian version of Szemerkényi's previous English article on "A Semiotic Approach to the Study of Proverbs" (1974; see no. 1839). The author presents a review of the structural and semiotic approach to paremiology which was pioneered by the Soviet scholar Grigorii L'vovich Permiakov (1919–1983; see esp. no. 1428). Proverbs are seen as signs of definite situations or of definite relations between things. This system of signs has its roots in human communication, and as signs the proverbs function as moral ideas or regulatory rules of life and behavior in a given society. Szemerkényi argues that paremiologists must also study the syntactical, semantic, and pragmatic aspects of proverbs in actual communicative contexts. Only then can their sociological and psychological significance be properly understood.

4458. Szemerkényi, Agnes. "Közmondas és szolas (proverbium)." *Magyar népköltészet. Magyar néprajz. Folklor I.* Ed. Lajos Vargyas. Budapest: Akadémiai Kiado, 1988. 213–237.

Szemerkényi presents an inclusive essay on Hungarian proverbs and proverbial expressions, beginning her comments with a discussion of various definition attempts regarding proverbs and proverbial expressions. She then treats aspects of the origin, history, meaning, structure, and form of Hungarian texts. Many examples are cited to indicate the use and function of this proverbial language in oral communication and in literary and journalistic writings. Szemerkényi also discusses the major Hungarian proverb collections and analyzes some of the achievements of the national paremiologists. All of this is seen in light of recent international scholarship, making this article a significant contribution to the study of proverbs. It serves Hungarian readers to acquaint themselves with the most important work that has gone on in paremiology during the past two decades. Many bibliographical references are listed at the end of this essay volume by different authors.

4459. Szemerkényi, Agnes. "The Use of Proverbs in Hungarian Folktales." *Proverbium*, 7 (1990), 233–239.

In this article Szemerkényi studies the use and function of proverbs and proverbial expressions in a number of Hungarian folk tales from Transylvania. She is not concerned with the question of whether the proverb or the tale came first. Instead she investigates the intertexuality of these two verbal folklore genres. Citing several contextualized examples in English translation, she explains that proverbial expressions merely add metaphorical language to folk narratives without any major influence on the story itself. However, proverbs take on significant roles at the conclusion of certain tales or as leitmotifs within a single tale. Their function is often to add didactic value to the folk narratives, but they also serve the purpose of expressing traditional wisdom and the social value system of the community. Finally, there are also those folk tales which do not contain any proverbs at all but which appear to be stories exemplifying an obvious proverb.

4460. Szemerkényi, Agnes, and Vilmos Voigt. "A 'hatos' a magyar közmondasokban." *Magyar Nyelvör*, 108, no. 4 (1984), 470–477.

This is basically a Hungarian translation of Szemerkényi's and Voigt's earlier English article on "The Number Six in Hungarian Proverbs" (1980; see no. 1841). The authors start with a general statement concerning the difficulty of defining a proverb. They then analyze a large number of Hungarian proverbs referring to the number "six." In most texts "six" simply means "many," but there are also cases in which this number can take on more figurative meanings. The authors conclude that the meaning of proverbs is based on three factors: (1) the connotations of their individual parts (words), (2) the possibility of changing individual elements (words) of the proverbial structure, and (3) the cultural symbolism contained in the texts. Proverbs and their variants are seen as a semiotic system which can be interpreted only as parts of that system. A useful bibliography (pp. 476–477) is attached.

T

4461. Tabarcea, Cezar. *Poetica proverbului.* Bucuresti: Editura Minerva, 1982. 306 pp.

This is an excellent inclusive study of all aspects of the proverb on an international basis by one of the leading Rumanian paremiologists. Tabarcea has divided his book into two major parts: In the first section (pp. 9–153) he reviews major research in the field of paremiology and devotes detailed comments to such matters as definition, origin, form, content, function, context, and cultural value of proverbs. Most examples stem from the Rumanian language, but Tabercea also includes comparative materials from other national languages. The second part of the book (pp. 154–275) presents semantic, semiotic, stylistic, and structural analyses of proverbs. But cultural and ethnic questions, classification systems of proverbs, proverb collections, and the future for proverbs in the modern Rumanian society are also discussed. Some comments regarding the translatability of proverbs and the problem of finding equivalents in the target language are included as well. Numerous statistical tables and diagrams help to summarize certain parts of this major study. A collection of 267 Rumanian proverbs (pp. 281–289),a useful author index (pp. 299–304), and 440 notes containing important international bibliographical references are part of this major work. A French summary (pp. 291–297) is provided as well.

4462. Tabarcea, Cezar. "Romanian Parallels to the Proverbial Expression 'To Carry Owls to Athens'." *Proverbium*, 3 (1986), 243–252.

Following Wolfgang Mieder's short note on international variants of the classical proverbial expression "'Eulen nach Athen tragen', 'To carry coals to Newcastle'" (1984; see no. 3871),

Tabarcea now presents an inclusive list of Rumanian texts that correspond to the ancient phrase "To carry owls to Athens." He has found the many texts with numerous variants in I.A. Zanne's major Rumanian proverb collection *Proverbele românilor*, 9 vols. (1895/1903). The author cites the Rumanian texts and also includes some English and German equivalents. While these proverbial expressions use different metaphors, they all comment on the fact that someone might be carrying something to a place where there is already an abundance of it. The various texts indicate how a classical phrase has survived in European national languages which have, however, also created their own proverbial metaphors with the same meaning. For additional Irish and Polish variants see Fionnuala Williams (no. 4561) and Stanislaw Predota (no. 4195).

4463. Tamony, Peter. "'Off the Wall' and Its Cogeners." *American Speech*, 57 (1982), 158–159.

This is a short note on the American proverbial expressions "To be off the wall," "To drive someone up the wall," and "To go up the wall." Tamony cites a few contextualized examples out of newspapers and books from the 1960s and 1970s, showing that they all have the meaning of being or going crazy. It is suggested that "To be off the wall" may have its origin in the sport of handball, in which the ball sometimes comes zinging, not off the usual place, the floor, but randomly and unexpectedly, "off the wall." This is then yet another example of the impressive influence that the language of sports has on modern phraseological units.

4464. Tarán, Leonardo. "'Amicus Plato sed magis amica veritas'. From Plato and Aristotle to Cervantes." *Antike und Abendland*, 30 (1984), 93–124.

Tarán offers a detailed philological and historical study of the classical proverb "Amicus Plato sed magis amica veritas" (Plato is dear to me, but dearer still is truth). He is able to prove that it originated with Aristotle (384–322 B.C.) and that it was cited by numerous Greek and Roman authors, a later variant being "Amicus Socrates sed magis amica veritas." The author also mentions that the proverb was known in the Arabic world from which it reached medieval Spain. Little wonder that it finally appeared in the works of Mateo Alemán (1547–1614?) and Baltasar Gracián (1601–1658. Miguel de Cervantes Saavedra (1547–1616) inluded the proverb in his novel *Don Quixote* (1605/1615), and Erasmus of Rotterdam (1469–1536) cited it in his *Adagia* (1500ff.). Many contextualized Greek, Latin, and Spanish examples are presented, showing that this classical proverb has a long history that continues to be alive in the modern vernacular languages of Europe, albeit only in learned circles.

4465. Tarlanov, Z.K. *Ocherki po sintaksisu russkikh poslovits.* Leningrad: Izdatel'stvo Leningradskogo universiteta, 1982. 136 pp.

Following a short introduction Tarlanov begins his linguistic study on the syntax of Russian proverbs with a chapter (pp. 10–23) on compound sentences and their various structural semantic types in the language of these proverbs. The second chapter (pp. 24–69) deals with texts that are based on relative or other dependent clauses, while the third chapter (pp. 70–121) looks at such complex sentences that lack any conjunctions. The short fourth chapter (pp. 122–126) explains some structural types that have an even more complex syntax. Many examples are cited in these chapters to indicate the complexity of some proverbial structures. A major bibliography (pp. 129–135) of linguistic studies by phraseologists from the Soviet Union is attached.

4466. Tatin, Jean-Jacques. "Proverbes et voix du peuple." *Revue des sciences humaines*, 61, no. 190 (1983), 21–30.

This is a short but interesting article dealing with the problem of orality in early proverb collections. Tatin agrees with the general observation that proverbs are the voice of the people, but he wonders about the collecting habits of early paremiographers. Investigating the prefaces of several French proverb collections from the 16th and 17th centuries, Tatin is able to show that the editors or collectors do at times admit that they did not do any field research whatsoever. Instead they have copied from published collections that preceded their own, registering as it were merely written texts. Little wonder that many proverbs of these collections appear to be not very traditional as far as folk speech is concerned. The author recognizes the discrepancy between literacy and orality in these collections and states correctly that some texts do not deserve the label of folk proverb.

4467. Taumoefolau, Melenaite. "Is the Father's Sister Really 'Black'." *The Journal of the Polynesian Society,* 100, no. 1 (1991), 91–98.

The author interprets the meaning of the rather complex Tongan proverb "Ko e 'uli'uli'a mehekitanga" (It is the blackness of a father's sister). She explains that "blackness" in a father's sister really does not matter because a father's sister will always be culturally powerful and high-ranking on account of her birth. This cultural greatness of the father's sister is not explicitily stated in the proverb but it is taken for granted because it is part of the native speaker's tacit cultural knowledge. The proverb, then, does not mean that a father's sister is necessarily "black" or that all father's sisters are "black." Rather, it means that, should circumstances be such that a father's sister is "black" (and it is in such circumstances that the proverb is normally used), that "blackness" would be inconsequential. The cultural greatness of the father's sister is emphasized by the implication that any incidental "blackness" on her part would not detract from her already ample cultural powers. Taumoefolau includes a careful structural analysis of this proverb which serves as proof for the meaning presented here.

4468. Taylor, Archer. "Names in Folktales [and Proverbs]." *Märchen, Mythos, Dichtung. Festschrift zum 90. Geburtstag Friedrich von der Leyens.* Eds. Hugo Kuhn and Kurt Schier. München: C.H. Beck, 1963. 31–34.

This is but a short note concerning the fact that folk tales, proverbs, and wellerisms often contain proper names. Taylor argues that much more attention should be paid to the use and function of names in folk narratives and proverbial speech. He also draws attention to the fact that the ascription of a proverb to a particular person or persons does not mean that it might not have an anonymous beginning. The connection of a name to a proverb is usually just a convenient way of adding some authority to an existing proverb. Taylor makes a good case for the combined study of onomastics and paremiology. For a specialized bibliography of phraseological units containing names see Wolfgang Mieder (no. 1248).

4469. Taylor, Archer. *The Proverb.* Cambridge/Massachusetts: Harvard University Press, 1931; rpt. Hatboro/Pennsylvania: Folklore Associates, 1962; rpt. again with an introduction and a bibliography by Wolfgang Mieder. Bern: Peter Lang, 1985. 381 pp.

This second reprint of Archer Taylor's (1890–1973) classical work on the proverb does not only make this significant book available again to a younger generation of scholars, it also goes far beyond the first reprint of 1962 in that Wolfgang Mieder as its new editor has added an introduction of 48 pages. He starts out with a biographical sketch of Archer Taylor (pp. V-XVII) and then adds an interpretative review (pp. XVII-XXIX) of Taylor's accomplishments as a paremiologist. This is followed by a scholarly appraisal (pp. XXIX-XXXIX) of Taylor's *magnum opus* on the proverb that has influenced paremiologists, folklorists, and scholars from many other disciplines throughout the world. Mieder has also added an inclusive list (pp. XL-LIII) of Taylor's numerous proverb studies, and a photograph of this great master is included as well. For a detailed annotation of Archer Taylor's *The Proverb* (1931) see no. 1858, and for annotations of his many important articles see nos. 1854–1908, 2933–2938, and 4468.

4470. Taylor, Jane H.M. "Poésie et prédication. La fonction du discours proverbial dans la *Danse macabre.*" *Medioevo Romanzo*, 14, no. 2 (1989), 215–226.

Taylor investigates the 62 strophes comprised of a total of 484 lines which accompany the 15th century illustrations of the *Danse macabre* (1425) on a Paris cemetery. She explains that each strophe concludes with a proverb or proverbial expression that summarizes its content. Usually the function of the proverbs is to make didactic and moralistic comments. In fact, the long poem is similar to a religious sermon, using proverbial rhetoric as a persuasive strategy to get people to think about mortality. Several contextualized examples are cited, indicating that the French proverbs work very well for the "Dance of Death" motif depicted in the pictures. They certainly underscore the serious message of the images and the literary text. An annotated list of the 62 fixed phrases (pp. 224–226) is attached.

4471. Teigen, Karl Halvor. "Old Truths or Fresh Insights? A Study of Students' Evaluations of Proverbs." *British Journal of Social Psychology*, 25 (1986), 43–49.

It is a fact that proverbs are often criticized for being contradictory and hence not necessarily true. Teigen's study examines two sets of contradictory proverbs in the form of a psychological proverbs test: one concerned the values or disadvantages of novelty and change; in the other, contradictory pairs were arbitrarily produced through reversals (negations) of a variety of genuine proverbs. Both sets were evaluated by a group of college students for "quality," and by a parallel group for "truth value" and "originality" (novelty). There were high positive correlations between truth and quality ratings, whereas originality tended to be negatively correlated with the other two. Thus truth appears to be the most important criterion of a good proverb. However, truth scores within proverb pairs proved to be uncorrelated, so that a proverbial statement and its negation can both be considered true (or untrue). It is speculated that proverbs may be attractive as traditional (non-novel) sayings capable of being applied to a variety of new situations. An English abstract (p. 43) and a small bibliography (p. 49) are included.

4472. Tekinay, Alev. "Sprichwörter im Deutschen und Türkischen. Eine syntaktisch-semantische Analyse." *Muttersprache*, 94 (1983–1984), 194–202.

This is a comparative analysis of German and Turkish proverbs starting with definition problems and then concentrating on syntactical and semantic questions. The author studies the types of sentences (indicative, interrogative, imperative, and modal sentences) used in proverbs. He then deals with the tense of the proverbs, their formulaic use of relative clauses, and their typical subjects (especially the pronoun "man" [one]). From these syntactical and stylistic considerations Tekinay moves on to the semantic structure and investigates the similarity and difference in the metaphors of German and Turkish proverbs. The author emphasizes that different images of proverbs might have identical meanings, and he argues that the parallels between the proverbs of these two languages and cultures might be due to similar worldviews, loan translations, or common sources like the Bible or folk narratives. Many German and Turkish examples with German translations are cited.

4473. Thompson, Billy Bussell. "Jews in Hispanic Proverbs." *Yiddish*, 6 (1987), 13–21.

The author begins his article with some general statements about anti-Semitism in Spanish proverbs, stating that this type of condemnation of Jews can be found from the Middle Ages to the literary works of Federico Garcia Lorca (1898–1936). The author reviews several Spanish proverb collections and shows that they all include proverbial stereotypes against the Jewish population. This is also true for Spanish writers as Gonzalo de Berceo (1195?–1264?), Lope Félix de Vega Carpio (1562–1635), and others. Miguel de Cervantes Saavedra (1547–1616) appears to be more positive about the depiction of Jews in his novels, and obviously one finds also positive comments about Jews and their proverbs in Rabbi Santob de Carrión's (14th century) *Proverbios morales* (1345). Nevertheless, anti-Semitic proverbs have done their share in the persecution of Jews in Spain, as is amply illustrated by some contextualized examples from collections and literary works.

4474. Thoren, Krista Helene. *Learner and Native Speaker Intuitions for Universal Linguistic Structures in French Proverbs.* M.A. Thesis University of Texas at Austin, 1985. 36 pp.

This is a short psycholinguistic study of 20 French proverb pairs that are based on positive and negative structural features. Thoren designed a psychological proverbs test with which she ascertained the preference of 40 English speakers of French and 20 native French speakers concerning "positive" or "negative" proverb structures. The results show overwhelmingly that positive statements in proverbs are much preferred, and the author concludes that this positive feature must be a universal linguistic structure. One graph, 4 statistical tables, a copy of the test establishing the "positive" preference, and a small bibliography (pp. 32–34) are all part of this unpublished thesis. Some of this work is based on George Milner's theoretical findings regarding evaluative structures of proverbs (see no. 1292).

4475. Tiisala, Seija. "'Ei hätä ole tämän näköinen': Att tolka och oversatta ordspråk och talesatt." *Studier i Nordisk Filologi*, 65 (1984), 289–298.

The author reports on the preparation of a comparative phraseological dictionary that will register Finnish and Swedish proverbs and proverbial expressions. It is pointed out that such a dictionary is very much needed for students who are learning these two languages in Sweden and Finland respectively. Tiisala includes some statistical information concerning translation attempts of fixed phrases by students, indicating clearly that they had extreme difficulties with lexical, morphological, and syntactical aspects. They also faced problems with the proper understanding of the alien metaphors. Only when there are identical equivalents in both languages, i.e. proverbs and proverbial expressions having originated in classical times or going back to the Bible, did the students not have any major problems with translations. Many more such bilingual phraseological dictionaries are needed to aid translators as well as foreign language students.

4476. Tilavov, Bozor. "Svode poslovits Tadzhikskogo naroda." *Paremiologicheskie issledovaniia*. Ed. Grigorii L'vovich Permiakov. Moskva: Nauka, 1984. 270–273.

Tilavov presents an impressive report on the large folklore collecting project that was conducted among 700 informants from 1945 to 1968 in the Tadzhik Soviet Socialist Republic. Five volumes of proverbial materials are ready for publication with Russian and English translations being provided for the Tadzhik language texts. The volumes will include proverbs, regional expressions, archaic and new sayings as well as detailed notes on variants, geographical distribution (maps), collectors, informants, and socio-cultural aspects. This is indeed a significant proverb corpus based on field research which will be of much use for comparative paremiological work. For various other reports by Tilavov on this project see nos. 1939–1944.

4477. Timpunza-Mvula, Enoch. "Nicknaming in Conversational Context Among the Chewa of Malawi." *Folklore Forum*, 17 (1984), 134–142.

The author begins his article with some general comments regarding the importance of names in African societies. He then explains that among the Chewa of Malawi in southern Africa names are used as signs or symbols, and this is particularly true for nicknames. The use of such names becomes a communicative device which is uttered by the speaker for the listener to recall a proverb, a song, or a folk narrative which is related to the name. This nicknaming practice is employed strategically to manipulate social relationships in discourse situations. The nicknames function as a means of social control, warning individuals against the dangers of nonconformity to the norms and values of the society. Citing a number of such nicknames with English translations, Timpunza-Mvula is able to show that they are remnants of or allusions to traditional proverbs, songs, or folk narratives. The article shows clearly that there is a definite relationship between onomastics and paremiology in many African languages.

4478. Tkacz, Catherine Brown. "*The Jew of Malta* and the Pit." *South Atlantic Review*, 53, no. 2 (1988), 47–57.

This is a literary investigation of the use and function of one particular proverb in Christopher Marlowe's (1564–1593) play *The Jew of Malta* (c. 1590, published 1633). Tkacz argues successfully that when the main character Barabas falls into the "pit" Marlowe is alluding to the Biblical proverb "To dig a pit for another and fall into it oneself (Prov. 26,27) out of the Old Testament. A number of parallel sections from the Bible are cited, and the author shows through contextualized examples how Marlowe alludes repeatedly to the traditional wisdom of this proverb which has been loan translated into English and other languages. For a study of other proverbs contained in this important play see Morris Palmer Tilley (no. 2953).

4479. Toporisic, Joze. "Inhaltliche Aspekte der komparativen Phraseologeme in slowenischen Sprichwortsammlungen." *Aktuelle Probleme der Phraseologie.* Eds. Harald Burger and Robert Zett. Bern: Peter Lang, 1987. 291–321.

The author begins his linguistic article on Slovenian proverbial comparisons with a general introduction in which he differentiates between proverbs on the one hand and phraseological units on the other. Next he reviews Slovenian proverb collections and secondary literature dealing with the nature and content of these texts. But the main purpose of this essay is to analyze Slovenian proverbial comparisons and their metaphors, content, structure, meaning, and classification in collections. Toporisic is particularly interested in verbal and adjectival comparisons. Many examples are cited with German translations. The 55 notes (pp. 309–321) contain useful bibliographical information and also many additional Slovenian texts.

4480. Tóthné Litovkina, Anna. *Analiz iazyka vengerskikh poslovits / Russkie ekvivalenty vengerskii poslovitsam.* Diss. Moskovskii gosudarstvennyi universitet, 1985 (=*Proverbium Paratum,* no. 4 [1983–1989]. 1–141). 141 pp.

Tóthné Litovkina analyzes the language of Hungarian proverbs and their Russian equivalents, and she presents significant linguistic data based on many examples as well as 2 graphs and 17 statistical tables. Chapter one (pp. 1–14) includes a statistical analysis of the types of words in these proverbs. The second chapter (pp. 15–18) deals with the origin (age) of these words, and chapter three (pp. 19–32) looks at the semantic fields represented by these lexical items. The very short fourth chapter (p. 33) presents some phonetic features of these Russian proverbs. In the fifth chapter the author considers the various parts of speech that make up these texts, and in the sixth chapter (pp. 40–48) she presents a syntactical analysis of them. The seventh chapter (pp. 49–73) deviates from these linguistic considerations. Here Tóthné Litovkina looks at the use and function of proverbs in the prose works of Kálmán Mikszáth (1847–1910) and the journal *Ludas Matyi*. She also considers the difficulty of translating such contextualized Hungarian proverbs into Russian. A large appendix (pp. 76–126) with a list of the proverbs under discussion, a word frequency dictionary, and a list of proverbs based on repetitive stylistic features is part of this important dissertation. It also includes a valuable bibliography (pp. 127–133) and a long Hungarian summary (pp. 134–139).

4481. Tóthné Litovkina, Anna. "Kisérlet a magyar és orosz közmondasok nyelvi elemzésére." *Magyar Nyelv*, 85 (1989), 58–69; also in English translation as "Hungarian and Russian Proverbs: A Comparative Analysis." *Proverbium*, 7 (1990), 241–254.

This linguistic paper is based on a comparison of 317 Hungarian and Russian proverbs having the same meaning. 151 texts have identical equivalents in both languages, 140 have partical equivalents, and 26 have no equivalents at all. Tóthné Litovkina is able to show that the proverbs of the first group have similar syntactical structures as well as parallel nouns and verbs. The majority of these texts (89% of the Hungarian and 92% of the Russian proverbs) have only 3–7 words, and there is much more synonymy than antonymy in these proverbs. In fact, the existence of outwardly different but semantically the same proverbs is quite common. The author also explains that one can usually find two or more Russian equivalents for each Hungarian proverb. A translator is therefore faced with the difficulty of choosing the most suitable text. One graph and 4 statistical tables are included in this valuable comparative study.

4482. Tóthné Litovkina, Anna. "Zvukovye osobennosti vengerskikh poslovits." *Congressus Septimus Internationalis Fenno-Ugristarum, Sessiones Sectionum Dissertationes, Linguistica*. Eds. Jakab Laszlo et al. Debrecen: CIFU, 1990. 325–330.

Tóthné Litovkina presents a short stylistic and poetic analysis of Hungarian proverbs. She is particularly interested in the frequent use of alliteration, a phenomenon that is also found in proverbs from other languages. The repetition of certain consonants at the beginning of individual words certainly increases the memorability of proverbs. The author also analyzes the alternations or patterns of consonants and vowels in these texts. They are responsible for the rhythm of the poetic language of proverbs. Another stylistic feature is without doubt the repetition of certain words, and finally there is also the frequently used rhyme. All of these linguistic markers together with structural characteristics and metaphors set the proverb text apart from normal speech. Many Hungarian examples are cited with Russian translations and comments.

4483. Trebjesanin, Zarko. "Predstava zene u srpskim narodnim poslovicama." *Psihologija*, 18, nos. 3–4 (1985), 87–102.

This psycholinguistic paper is based on the assumption that the analysis of folk proverbs which concern themselves with women will yield a reliable picture concerning the traditional role of and attitudes towards women. The author has investigated about 12,000 Serbian proverbs, and he has divided those that deal with women into three main groups according to content or theme: (1) the description of women, (2) the attitudes towards women, and (3) the female roles. It is concluded that the proverbs give a fairly coherent view of women, but unfortunately many of the texts are rather misogynous and stereotypical. This is especially the case with those texts that comment on the wife and her behavior. Only the proverbs that deal with the mother deviate drastically from this negative image. Many examples are cited, a useful bibliography (pp. 100–101) is included, and there is also an English summary (pp. 101–102).

4484. Treskow, Irene von. *Mit fremden Federn . . . Suchbilder und Texte zu Sprichwörtern und Redensarten.* Berlin: Benteli, 1983. 36 pp.

This is an interesting art book in which Irene von Treskow (1940–) has illustrated 36 German or common European proverbs and proverbial expressions. They are in fact "Vexierbilder" (search or riddle pictures), since they each hide the animal of the expression that is being illustrated. Each picture is 16x21 cm in size and is accompanied by a page of cultural and philological comments regarding the depicted phrase. These "Suchbilder" (search pictures) include such popular proverbs and fixed phrases as "Einen schlafenden Hund soll man nicht stören" (Let sleeping dogs lie), "Eine Schwalbe macht noch keinen Sommer" (One swallow does not make a summer), "Weder Fisch noch Vogel" (Neither fish nor fowl), etc. Many of the proverb pictures also contain ironic statements on human behavior as expressed in animal metaphors. The end of the book includes solutions to the pictures.

4485. Tung, Mason. "Spenser's 'Emblematic' Imagery: A Study of Emblematics." *Spenser Studies: A Renaissance Poetry Annual,* 5 (1984), 185–207.

Tung investigates the emblematic imagery in Edmund Spenser's (1552–1599) works and argues successfully that his English prose is filled with allusions to Aesop's fables, proverbial lore, and mythological motifs. It is pointed out that Spenser was particularly fond of animal metaphors, and one can certainly find numerous proverbs and proverbial expressions from the animal world in his novels. The animal behavior expressed in such proverbs gives Spenser the opportunity to comment indirectly on human behavior as well. Tung also points out that Spenser enjoyed using the various fixed phrases that center around the Biblical dichotomy of honey versus gall. Many of the proverbs add moralistic messages couched in traditional metaphors that are very reminiscent of emblems. The 35 notes (pp. 199–207) include helpful bibliographical information regarding the interplay of art, literature, and folklore. Several examples are cited, but for a more detailed study of the proverbs in Spenser's works see Charles Smith (no. 1753).

4486. Tupper, Martin Farquahar. *Proverbial Philosophy: A Book of Thoughts and Arguments, Originally Treated. With an Essay on "The Philosophy of Proverbs."* Philadelphia: E.H. Butler, 1852. 276 pp.

While this book by the prolific English writer of prose and verse Martin Farquahar Tupper (1810–1889) is actually a collection of poetic pieces comprised of maxims and reflections (including occasional proverbs) on such matters as humility, pride, wealth, flattery, etc., there is an intriguing introductory essay on "The Philosophy of Proverbs" (pp. ix-xxxvi) that definitely deserves the interest of historically minded paremiologists. Tupper has written an early and inclusive treatise on many aspects of proverbs, among them the problem of definition, the difference between proverbs and proverbial expressions, the form and origin of proverbs, and their didactic function particularly in oral communication. Tupper also deals with classical and European proverbs, explaining that there are international, national, and regional proverbs. Numerous examples are cited from several foreign languages and cultures with English translations. Their content, humor, and worldview are discussed, and Tupper even includes some comments on the relationship of proverbs and folk narratives. This is indeed a readable and informative general essay on the nature of the proverb from the 19th century, and it still deserves at least some attention by proverb scholars.

U

4487. Ugochukwu, Françoise. "Les proverbes igbos d'hier à aujourd'hui: un tour d'horizon." *Cahiers de littérature orale*, no. 13 (1983), 51–65.

This is a study of Igbo proverbs from Nigeria starting with a definition attempt and stressing that they contain ancient oral wisdom which has been passed on from generation to generation. The author differentiates among three levels of interpretation: literal, figurative, and contextual. This is shown by a close analysis of about 25 Igbo proverbs with French translations. Such functions as authority, clarification, education, reproach, criticism, and encouragement are also explained. Their contents express the worldview of the Igbo people and help to understand their cultural and social history and concerns. At the end Ugochukwu mentions the literary use of these proverbs by the African writer Chinua Achebe (1931–) and others, and she also reviews some Igbo proverb collections while calling for more field research for additional collections. An English summary (p. 177) is attached.

4488. Unverfehrt, Gerd. "Christliches Exempel und profane Allegorie. Zum Verhältnis von Wort und Bild in der Graphik der Boschnachfolge." *Wort und Bild in der niederländischen Kunst und Literatur des 16. und 17. Jahrhunderts.* Eds. Herman Vekeman and Justus Müller Hofstede. Erfstadt: Lukassen, 1984. 221–241.

Unverfehrt presents a detailed analysis of the depiction of Christian and secular motifs in European art of the 16th and 17th centuries. He indicates that many grotesque drawings are based on the paintings or sketches of Hieronymus Bosch (1450?–1516). He cites numerous examples of satirical illustrations, and he also explains what Biblical quotations, literary allusions, and proverbs are portrayed in them. A special section (pp. 229–234) is dedicated to the tradition of illustrating the proverb "Big fish eat little fish." The author shows that Bosch already included this proverbial motif in his art, and he then interprets Pieter Brueghel's (c. 1520–1569) proverb picture *Big Fish Eat Little Fisch* (1557) and its numerous adaptations during the time of Brueghel and the 17th century. The paper includes 39 illustrations, of which 8 deal with the "fish" proverb. The 106 notes (pp. 238–241) contain valuable bibliographical information regarding the relationship of art and proverbs. See also Manfred Bambeck (no. 2183), Wolfgang Mieder (nos. 3898 and 3904), and Gerd Unverfehrt (no. 4489 below).

4489.   Unverfehrt, Gerd. "'Große Fische fressen kleine'. Zu Entstehung und Gebrauch eines satirischen Motivs." *Bild als Waffe. Mittel und Motive der Karikatur in fünf Jahrhunderten.* Eds. Gerhard Lamgemeyer et al. München: Prestel, 1984. 268–270 and 402–414.

This is a much expanded version of Unverfehrt's previous discussion of the proverb "Big fish eat little fish." Once again the author shows that Hieronymus Bosch (1450?–1516) started the chain of grotesque and satirical illustrations of large fish eating one or more small fish. There is also Pieter Brueghel's (c. 1520–1569) proverb picture *Big Fish Eat Little Fish* (1557), and this particular drawing was used as the basis for a number of political illustrations during the time of Brueghel and through the 17th century. Especially emblematic artists like Sebastian de Covarrubias Horozco (16th/17th century) and Peter Isselburg (1580?–1630?) depicted this "fish" proverb as a moralistic and political statement. But Unverfehrt also explains that this proverbial motif has remained very popular in modern cartoons and caricatures. The fascinating article contains 29 illustrations with detailed historical and socio-political interpretations, and the 65 notes include important bibliographical references concerning the depiction of proverbs in art. See also Manfred Bambeck (no. 2183) and Wolfgang Mieder (nos. 3898 and 3904).

4490.   Uraksin, Z.G. "Vzaimodeystvie russkogo i tyurkskikh yazykov v oblasti frazeologii." *Voprosy yazykoznaniya*, 31, no. 1 (1982), 107–112.

In this comparative article Uraksin investigates the influence of the Turkic languages on Russian folk proverbs and other phraseological units. It is shown that Russian fixed phrases contain many derivatives from Turkic loan words. It is, however, difficult to establish the influence of Russian phraseological units onto Turkish itself and on other Turkic languages. The Russian contact with the various Turkic cultures and languages differ in chronology and intensity, but obviously they were especially strong in those geographical areas which are closest to Russia. Many historical and modern examples are cited, and the author also shows that journalists and the mass media play a major role in the propagation of Russian words and fixed phrases in the Turkic languages. A small bibliography (p. 112) is attached.

4491. Urdang, Laurence. "Nine Tailors [Make a Man]." *Verbatim: The Language Quarterly*, 12 (1986), 15–16.

A short note discussing the possible origin and meaning of the English proverb "Nine tailors make a man." Urdang cites a number of references from English literature from the early 17th to the 20th century, and he argues that the following two matters might have lead to the formulation of this proverb: (1) tailors were considered worthless fellows who were likely to steal cloth from the bolts given to them by customers; and (2) the proverb "Nine tailors make a man" means that because tailors are worth so little (and are a cowardly lot, besides), it would require nine of them to make up one "real" man—though why nine and not seven or eleven remains a mystery. The proverb certainly is a stereotypical statement that is not used very frequently anymore today.

4492. Urdang, Laurence, and Frank R. Abate. *Idioms and Phrases Index.* 3 vols. Detroit: Gale Research Company, 1983. 1691 pp.

This is a colossal reference work which contains more than 140,000 different idioms, phrases, proverbial expressions, and slang of two or more words which are part of the English language. Every phraseological unit is indexed under each of its key-words, and behind each entry the initials of the dictionary, lexicon, or reference book (altogether 32 of the major reference works of the English language) are given in which the expression can be found. While books relating to English and American slang, idioms, and phrases are included, dictionaries and collections of proverbs are missing. Nevertheless, these three volumes are an invaluable research tool for the study of individual idioms, phrases, and proverbial expressions. Where are the computer-trained paremiologists and paremiographers who will index proverbs and proverbial expressions exclusively from the many printed collections and reference works (especially from those that provide annotations)? Such an index would be of much help for historical and comparative studies. In the meantime the present volumes are a "goldmine" for proverb scholars.

4493.   Uther, Hans-Jörg. "Eulenspiegel und die Landesverweisung (Historie 25,26). Einige Betrachtungen zur Stoff- und Motivgeschichte." *Eulenspiegel-Jahrbuch*, 25 (1985), 60–74.

Uther discusses two of the tall tales included in Hermann Bote's (1460–1520) chapbook *Till Eulenspiegel* (1515). He explains that they are based on traditional concepts of Germanic law, and he argues that they exemplify the role of legal folklore in folk narratives. One of the tales (no. 25) contains the old German legal proverb "Ein ietlicher sol frid haben in seine vier pfele" (Everybody deserves peace and quiet in his/her own four walls). Uther analyzes the use and function of this proverb in this tall tale, and he makes a good case for the importance of proverbs in folk narratives. Historical, cultural, and legal explanations are included. For a more detailed discussion of all the proverbs, proverbial expressions, and proverbial comparisons included in *Till Eulenspiegel* see Wolfgang Mieder (no. 3917).

4494.   Uther, Hans-Jörg. "Machen Kleider Leute? Zur Wertigkeit von Kleidung in populären Erzählungen." *Jahrbuch für Volkskunde*, no volume given (1991), 24–44.

In this article Uther investigates the various roles which clothes of all types (shoes, coats, hats, etc.) play in folk narratives. He cites numerous contextualized examples, and he also includes a small section (pp. 42–44) on tales which could be interpreted as exemplifications of the German proverbs "Das Kleid macht den Mann" and "Kleider machen Leute" (both variants mean: Clothes don't make the man). Uther argues that these tales are usually didactic and moralistic, trying to teach people that outside appearances are not necessarily indicative of the true inner value of a person. He also includes a few literary examples of these proverbs, notably from Thomas Mann's (1875–1955) novel *Felix Krull* (1922). Aphoristic writers like Rudolf Rolfs (1920–) have also parodied these proverbs by changing them into "Antisprichwörter" (anti-proverbs). These examples and comments once again illustrate the important relationship between proverbs and folk narratives.

V

4495. Vandenbroeck, Paul. *Jheronimus Bosch: Tussen volksleven en stadscultur.* Berchem: EPO, 1987. Proverbs esp. pp. 40–41, 100–107, 213–236 (notes pp. 375, 401–405 and 445–454).

This is an important book on various folkloric motifs in the paintings and drawings of Hieronymus Bosch (1450?–1516). Vandenbroeck looks at how this artist bases some of his pictures on such Dutch proverbs and proverbial expressions as "Ene blinde leijdt de ander" (The blind leading the blind), "Het veld heeft ogen, het bos heeft oren" (The field has eyes, the forest has ears), and "Een oog in het zeil houden" (To keep an eye on the sail). He explains these three phrases and includes many historical, cultural, and philological comments (see pp. 40–41 and 100–107). For the first two texts illustrations are included (see ills. 10 and 35), and the notes (pp. 375 and 401–405) contain rich bibliographical information. But there is also a detailed section (pp. 213–236; notes pp. 445–454) in which Vandenbroeck analyzes Bosch's interest in folk language, folklore, and proverbial speech. He argues that Bosch used proverbial expressions and proverbs in order to depict the social and moral attitudes of his age in his proverb pictures.

4496. Vandenbroeck, Paul. "Dits illustrés et emblèmes moraux. Contribution à l'étude de l'iconographie profane et de la pensée sociale vers 1500 (Paris, B.N., ms. fr. 24461)." *Jaarboek van het koninklijk Museum voor Schone Kunsten* (Antwerpen), no volume given (1988), 23–94.

Vandenbroeck describes a fascinating illustrated manuscript of moralistic French verses by Henri Baude (1430?–1496?) which is kept in the National Library of Paris. He investigates the history of this manuscript and points out that it contains sententious remarks, maxims, and proverbs that represent the secular and social thought of the 15th century. He then provides the reader with 32 illustrations accompanied by their didactic verses. Explanatory notes concerning historical, cultural, and philological matters are added. Among the proverb pictures are "Couper la branche sur laquelle on s'appuie" (To cut the branch on which one is sitting), "Jeter des roses aux pourceaux" (To throw roses before swine), and "Réveiller un chien endormi" (To awaken a sleeping dog; i.e., Let sleeping dogs lie). This manuscript is a fine example of how popular the artistic depiction of proverbs and proverbial expressions was during the second half of the 15th century. Hieronymus Bosch (1450?–1516) and later Pieter Brueghel (c. 1520–1569) belong to this iconographic tradition. See also David Heft (no. 696).

4497. Van Lancker, Diana. "The Neurology of Proverbs." *Behavioural Neurology*, 3 (1990), 169–187.

The author begins her significant study with the observation that although psychological proverbs tests have been used in the mental status examination for quite some time, little is actually known about either normal comprehension or the interpretation of proverbs and proverbial expressions. She claims quite correctly that current proverbs tests, as for example the one by Donald Gorham (see nos. 557–558), have conceptual and linguistic shortcomings. The author also mentions that only a few studies have been done to investigate the specific effects of neurological and psychiatric disorders on the interpretation of proverbs. Although frontal lobes have traditionally been impugned in patients who are "concrete," recent studies targeting deficient comprehension of nonliteral language point to an important role of the right hemisphere (RH). Research describing responses of psychiatrically and neurologically classified groups to tests of proverb and idiom usage is needed to clarify details of aberrant processing of nonliteral meanings. Meanwhile, the proverbs test, drawing on diverse cognitive skills, is a nonspecific but sensitive probe of mental status. With 2 illustrations, an English abstract (p. 169), and an excellent bibliography (pp. 182–187).

4498. Van Leeuwen, Raymond C. "Proverbs XXV, 27 Once Again." *Vetus Testamentum*, 36, no. 1 (1986), 105–114.

The author takes yet another look at the Biblical proverb "It is not good to eat much honey" (Proverbs 25,27) which has become proverbial in the English language as "Too much honey cloys the stomach." He reviews previous scholarship on this saying out of the Old Testament. Various Hebrew and Latin versions are cited in context, and it is argued that the insights of this proverb go back to ancient wisdom literature. Detailed philological and theological explanations are included, and Van Leeuwen succeeds in shedding considerable light on this expression. For a previous study and interpretation of this proverb from the Bible see A. Macintosh (no. 2614).

4499. Van Leeuwen, Raymond C. "Proverbs 30:21–23 and the Biblical World Upside Down." *Journal of Biblical Literature*, 105 (1986), 599–610.

Van Leeuwen presents a detailed study of a quadripartite Biblical saying which appears to be based on the motif of the "world-upside-down." The Biblical text is "For three things the earth is disquieted, and for four which it cannot bear: For a servant when he reigns; and a fool when he is filled with meat; For an odious woman when she is married; and an handmaid that is heir to her mistress" (Proverbs 30,21–23). Following philological and historical explanations, the author offers the following translation of the Hebrew original which clearly shows the proverbial reversal of social norms and rules: "Under three things the earth shakes, under four it cannot bear up: Under a servant when he becomes king, and an outlaw when he is filled with food, under a despised wife when she rules, and a maid when she (dis)inherits her mistress." The "world-upside-down" logic of this short text is seen as a humorous but also satirical interpretation of social and cultural upheavals that threaten the status quo of society.

4500. Van Leeuwen, Raymond C. *Context and Meaning in Proverbs 25–27.* Atlanta/Georgia: Scholars Press, 1988. 171 pp.

Drawing from theoretical insights gathered from literary criticism and the anthropological study of proverbs, Van Leeuwen develops a methodology for exposing the structural patterns, poetic techniques, and thematic coherences of the "proverb poem" contained in Proverbs 25–27. In the first chapter (pp. 5–19) he reviews 20th century theological and paremiological research. The second chapter (pp. 21–28) discusses some of the particular problems which these chapters of the Book of Proverbs present to the modern reader. In the third chapter (pp. 29–38) Van Leeuwen presents some heuristic assumptions, and in chapter four (pp. 39–55) he outlines his structural, poetic, and semantic methodology to interpret the many proverbs contained in this section of the Bible. Chapters five to ten (pp. 57–143) contain detailed analyses of these three chapters of the Book of Proverbs, in each case presenting a modern translation and discussing the structures, poetics, and sense of the individual verses. Following a short summary (pp. 145–147), the author presents a valuable bibliography (pp. 149–161), and he also includes a useful index to Biblical passages and other ancient authors and works.

4501. Veit, Veronika. "Farbepitheta und Sprichwörter in mongolischen Epen." *Fragen der Mongolischen Heldendichtung.* Ed. Walther Heissig. Wiesbaden: Otto Harrassowitz, 1987. IV, 101–115.

The author divides her article on the color epithets and proverbs contained in ancient Mongolian epics into two parts. In the first section (pp. 101–109) she discusses the use of colors to describe various characters, animals, dwellings, clothes, food, and nature. Usually the color adjectives simply precede a noun, but obviously such epithets might also be part of proverbial comparisons. The second part (pp. 109–115) contains a small list of Mongolian proverbs in German translations without context or explanations. Veit also includes some comments on Mongolian proverb collections and the use and function of proverbs in these epics. Most of them are used to express wisdom and to add a didactic flavor to the epics. Proverbs contain the worldview of the Mongolian people and are of much use to the scholar in understanding the social and cultural norms of this old society.

4502. Ven, Caspar van de. *Beknopte geschiedenis van de paroemiologie en enige aspecten van de lexicografie van het (dialect)spreekwoord.* Diss. Katholieke Universiteit Nijmegen, 1988. 149 pp.

This is an important dissertation that reviews much of the more recent proverb scholarship for Dutch readers. In chapter one (pp. 3–8) Ven begins with a review of major proverb bibliographies, and this is followed by a discussion of standard Dutch proverb collections in chapter two (pp. 11–18) and of foreign collections in chapter three (pp. 19–28). The fourth chapter (pp. 29–51) reviews the scholarship on the definition of proverbs and the terminology of various subgenres, the fifth chapter (pp. 52–57) describes the international type system of proverbs, the sixth chapter (pp. 58–64) calls for proverb collections from oral sources, literary works, and newspapers, and the seventh chapter (pp. 65–72) describes how a proverb archive should be set up with the help of a computer. In the last two chapters (pp. 73–94) the author analyzes the special problems that might arise with putting together a scholarly collection of dialect proverbs. Lexicographical, orthographical, and classificational aspects are treated in much detail. A useful bibliography (pp. 95–101), a large list of primarily Dutch dialect proverbs (pp. 102–133), and a series of questionnaires (pp. 135–149) to be used during field research to collect dialect proverbs are attached.

4503. Ven, Caspar van de. "De Brabantse spreekwoorden." *Acta Universitatis Wratislaviensis*, no. 1299, *Neerlandica Wratislaviensia*, 5 (1991), 273–299.

This article is basically a revised version of chapters eight and nine of Ven's dissertation on Dutch proverb scholarship (see no. 4502 above). He begins with an analysis of Hein Mandos' (1907–1978) large dialect collection *De Brabantse spreekwoorden* (1988), including a short biographical sketch of Mandos who had collected thousands of dialect proverbs, proverbial expressions, and proverbial comparisons from Brabant in the Netherlands. The article includes useful comments on such matters as classification, orthography, lexicography, etc., and it describes how to do field research to gather dialect texts. Ven also discusses the use of various names in these fixed phrases, and he cites numerous examples to indicate in which way these expressions are typical for Brabant. Altogether this article sets up some basic procedures for the collection and publication of dialect proverbs that are still in use today.

4504. Venier, Martha Elena. "Los proverbios domésticos de Mal Lara." *Actas del IX. Congreso de la Asociacion Internacional de Hispanistas.* Ed. Sebastian Neumeister. Frankfurt am Main: Vervuert, 1989. I, 681–686.

This is a rather general discussion of the Spanish proverbs contained in Juan de Mal Lara's (1527–1571) *La philosophia vulgar* (1568). Venier begins with some comments regarding Mal Lara's interest in folk proverbs even though he clearly was a highly educated humanist. As Erasmus of Rotterdam (1469–1536) before him, Mal Lara values folk wisdom and compares it with the wisdom literature of classical times. Venier cites a number of passages from this work which illustrate that Mal Lara looked at Spanish vernacular proverbs as expressions of social and cultural norms. For a more detailed analysis of this early proverb collection and its relationship to Erasmus' *Adagia* (1500ff.) see F. Sánchez y Escribano (no. 1627).

4505. Verspaandonk, J.A.J.M. *Amsterdam: de koorbanken van de Oude Kerk. Tekst in Duits, Engels, Frans en Nederlands.* Amsterdam: Buijten & Schipperheijn, 1984. Proverbs esp. pp. 12–13, 24–27, 40–43, 58–61, 73–87 and 93–95.

The author begins his informative book on the Oude Kerk (Old Church) with a history (pp. 12–13) of this oldest parish church of Amsterdam from the 13th century. He describes the 36 choir stalls (pp. 24–27) and explains that they all have misericords with religious and secular motifs. Nine of them are based on Dutch proverbs and proverbial expressions, among them "Onder het zeil is het goed roeien" (pp. 40–43; It's good rowing with a sail), "Twee zotten onder een kapioen" (pp. 58–59; Two faces [fools] under one hood), "Hij zit tussen twee stoelen" (pp. 82–84; Between two stools one falls to the ground), and "Met het hoofd tegen de muur lopen" (pp. 85–87; To run one's head against a brick wall). Verspaandonk includes historical and cultural explanations, showing that these wood carvings illustrate folk proverbs that were also registered in early proverb collections. Since the book is written in Dutch, French, German, and English, the author also provides the equivalent proverbs and phrases from these languages.

4506. Veyrenc, Jacques. "Les notions de 'parème' et de 'parémème' (Contribution à la grammaire des proverbes)." *Studies in Ukrainian Linguistics in Honor of George Y. Shevelov.* Ed. Jacob P. Hursky. New York: The Ukrainian Academy of Arts and Sciences in the U.S., 1985. 337–342 (=*The Annals of the Ukrainian Academy of Arts and Sciences in the U.S.*, 15, nos. 39–40 [1981–1983], 337–342).

Veyrenc starts his theoretical article with a detailed discussion of the difference between the two genres of proverbs and proverbial expressions. He explains their stylistic, linguistic, syntactical, and structural differences, but he does realize that both of them usually are based on a metaphor and that some proverbial statements can exist as proverbs and proverbial expressions. In the second part (pp. 339–342) the author discusses recent semantic and semiotic approaches to proverbs, stressing their structural characteristics and the fact that they function as signs in social contexts and human communication. Several Ukrainian examples with French translations are cited to illustrate these points. Some structural formulas are included to show that most proverbs are based on a topic (theme) and a comment.

4507. Vignes, Jean, and B. Boudou. "Proverbes et dits sentencieux dans l'oeuvre de Pierre Gringore." *Bibliothèque d'Humanisme et Renaissance*, 51, no. 2 (1989), 355–392.

This is a literary investigation of the use and function of French proverbs and proverbial expressions in the poems and dramas of Pierre Gringore (1475?–1540?). The two authors analyze the various introductory formulas which Gringore uses to integrate these fixed phrases into his works. Throughout this detailed study they cite numerous contextualized examples, illustrating how the proverbs add wisdom and spice to Gringore's satirical farces. While some texts are employed for obvious didactic and moralistic purposes, there are also many instances in which they add humor and aggressive political or social satire. A special section (pp. 368–372) deals with the proverbs in Gringore's early and ignored collection of *Notables, enseignemen[t]s, adages et proverbes* (1527/28). Here too the proverbs play a dual role in that they are to instruct and also to delight. Unfortunately there is no proverb index, but the 227 notes contain useful bibliographical references to the use of proverbs in late medieval French literature.

4508. Vila Rubio, Nieves. "El refrán: un artefacto cultural." *Revista de dialectología y tradiciones populares*, 45 (1990), 211–224.

Vila Rubio argues that proverbs should be studied from the ethnolingustic point of view as traditional expressions of popular culture. He comments on the nature and content of Spanish proverbs and explains that some proverbs have been used to express certain ideologies. In fact, the author feels that proverbs may be considered as allegories. Following these more theoretical thoughts Vila Rubio also comments on the meaning of proverbs, arguing that a group of proverbs relating to a particular theme will enable the scholar to draw certain conclusions regarding attitudes or worldview. Citing numerous Spanish examples, he illustrates this by discussing the semantic field of marriage in these proverbs. Such texts become indicators of beliefs and cultural stereotypes concerning husband and wife, the family, love, etc., giving the ethnographer much valuable information regarding marital issues in Spain. Short Spanish and English abstracts (p. 224) are attached.

4509. Villalobos, John. "William Blake *Proverbs of Hell* and the Tradition of Wisdom Literature." *Studies in Philology*, 87, no. 2 (1990), 246–259.

This is a literary study dealing with William Blake's (1757–1827) long poem "Proverbs of Hell" which is part of the more extensive work *The Marriage of Heaven and Hell* (1790). Villalobos points out that Blake is reacting to ancient wisdom literature, more precisely to the Book of Proverbs in the Old Testament. Realizing that his Biblical source contains numerous proverbs which are still current today in folk speech, Blake reacts in a satirical and parodistic way to this ancient wisdom. Many of his "proverbs of hell" are in fact "Antisprichwörter" (anti-proverbs) which must have delighted liberal thinkers of his time. Villalobos concludes that the *Marriage* is not at all as discursive or diffuse as scholars have argued. Instead, Blake's strong polemical and satirical intent can best be comprehended if the contexts of Biblical criticism and the creative exfoliations from that tradition are properly understood. See also Randel Helms (no. 2457), and Michael Holstein (no. 2478).

4510. Vladica, Florian. "Posibile corespondente intre proverbele românesti si finlandeze." *Proverbium Dacoromania*, (1988), 37–41.

This is a short article pointing out some equivalent proverbs in the Rumanian and Finnish languages. Vladica starts with a few comments explaining that such parallel texts in two so different languages and cultures are primarily due to the fact that classical and Biblical proverbs were translated into basically all European languages. There have been no major historical and cultural contacts between Rumania and Finland, and for this reason there has been no direct influence of the indigenous proverbs of one country on the other. This is not to say that they might not have proverbs with the same structures and meanings in common, but the metaphors will differ due to other realia being mentioned in them. Many examples in Rumanian are cited to illustrate these points.

4511. Voegtle, Katherine H. *Categorization of Figurative Concepts*. Diss. University of Cincinnati, 1983. 146 pp.

Voegtle reports on a study that examined the role of context in the acquisition and transfer of figurative concepts. During acquisition each subject studied three sentences from each of five "proverb families." Each family contained a proverb, interpretations of the proverb's figurative meaning, and instances or descriptions of events illustrating the proverb's meaning. Instances were either narrow instances (all instances from a given family had similar background contexts) or wide instances (all instances from a family were based on different contexts). The results of this psychological proverbs test indicated that the narrow acquisition context produced poor transfer to cross context instances, but it did not interfere with the transfer to wide instances. Interpretations were the most accurately recognized transfer item, theoretically because they most closely resembled the abstract categorical bases. No overall differences due to acquisition condition were found; possible explanations include the low salience of the context and the subjects' flexible ability to complete proverb understanding using any available family member. Ten statistical tables, a useful bibliography (pp. 109–120), and the proverbs test with instructions (pp. 121–146) are part of this dissertation.

4512. Voigt, Vilmos. "Geflügelte Worte an den sechzigjährigen Lutz Röhrich." *Proverbium Paratum*, 3 (1982), 233–239.

This is a laudatory essay celebrating Lutz Röhrich's (1922–) sixtieth birthday. Voigt acknowledges the accomplishments of this eminent German folklorist and paremiologist, who has also been the valuable director of the Institute of Folklore at the University of Freiburg. The author mentions a number of Röhrich's publications dealing with proverbial matters, and he praises in particular his significant *Lexikon der sprichwörtlichen Redensarten* (1973). Citing a few examples from the two volumes of this lexicon, Voigt shows how reliable its philological, historical, folkloric, and cultural explanations are for German and international scholars. A selected bibliography (p. 239) of Röhrich's paremiological publications is attached, but for annotations of these and others see nos. 1570–1582, 2793–2794, and 4260–4262.

4513. Voigt, Vilmos. "Grigorii L'vovich Permyakov (1919–1983)." *Proverbium*, 1 (1984), 167–173.

In this detailed obituary of Grigorii L'vovich Permiakov (1919–1983), Voigt pays tribute to the outstanding theoretical work which this scholar conducted in the Soviet Union. Voigt presents a touching statement on paremiology being an international science whose active participants are like one family. One of its true masters was without doubt Permiakov who lived and worked in a small town near Moscow. Voigt gives a short biography of this great scholar and reviews his important paremiological publications which include translations, collections, edited essay volumes, and his theoretical masterpieces. For Voigt's bibliography of Permiakov's writings see no. 2976, and for their actual annotations see nos. 1424–1433, 2737, and 4145–4155. For two additional obituaries see Peter Grzybek (no. 3522) and Dumitru Stanciu (no. 4412).

4514. Vorlat, Emma. "'Your Marriage is Going Through a Rocky Patch'. On Idioms in the Lonely Hearts Columns." *Communiquer et traduire. Hommages à Jean Dierickx.* Eds. G. Debusscher and J.P. van Noppen. Bruxelles: Éditions de l'Université de Bruxelles, 1985. 103–108.

Vorlat reports on her investigation of the use and function of proverbs, proverbial expressions, idioms, and familiar quotations in 150 letters to the "Lonely Hearts Column" of three popular British women's magazines and in the answers to those letters. She includes a statistical table that shows the frequency of such phraseological units in these letters by distressed women and psychological counsellors trying to help them. It is shown that this metaphorical language helps people to communicate the complexity of their feelings and emotions. They create a certain linguistic closeness between two women who have never met on a personal basis and endow the counsellor with sufficient authority to perform her counselling task, not only with regard to one particular woman, but for all her readers.

4515. Vranska, Tsvetana. "Bulgarskite narodni poslovitsi s istoricheska tematika v sravnenie s poslovitsite na ostanalite slavianski narodi." *Slavianskaia filologiia. Sbornik statei.* Ed. V.I. Borkovsky. Moskva: Nauk, 1958. III, 334–356.

Vranska presents a comparative analysis of Bulgarian proverbs with those of other Slavic languages, notably Czech, Serbian, Polish, and Russian equivalents. A few Turkish proverbs are cited as well to indicate that some Bulgarian proverbs might in fact be loan translations from the Turkish language. The study is based on about 3000 texts that stem from the 15th to the 18th century. The author is especially interested in the origin and history of these texts, showing that many of them go back to a common origin since they have exact equivalents in several Slavic languages. She also explains that they contain significant references to historical and cultural aspects of this time period. Some of the proverbs express negative stereotypes about other nationalities and ethnic groups, while others also indicate different human and social concerns. The 40 notes include useful references to Slavic proverb collections.

4516. Vredeveld, Harry. "The Motto and Woodcut to Chapter 32 of Sebastian Brant's *Narrenschiff.*" *Modern Language Notes*, 103, no. 3 (1988), 648–651.

This is a short note on the woodcut and its proverbial motto which introduce the 32. chapter of Sebastian Brant's (1458–1521) satirical work *Narrenschiff* (1494). Vredeveld explains that the text contains two German proverbial expressions of futility, namely "Heuschrecken an der Sonne hüten" (To guard grasshoppers in the sun) and "Wasser in den Brunnen schütten" (To pour water into the well). Brant uses these fixed phrases to make the misogynous statement that watching over the faithfulness and purity of women would be as futile as the tasks mentioned in the expressions. Vredeveld also cites medieval Latin sources for the two German sayings. The woodcut is by Albrecht Dürer (1471–1528), and it is indeed a proverb picture illustrating these phrases. For a detailed study of the proverbs in the *Narrenschiff* see Hans Heinrich Eberth (no. 388).

4517. Vredeveld, Harry. "'That Familiar Proverb': Folly as the Elixir of Youth in Erasmus's *Moriae Encomium.*" *Renaissance Quarterly*, 42, no. 1 (1989), 78–91.

Vredeveld presents a detailed philological and interpretative study on a proverb which Erasmus of Rotterdam (1469–1536) might be alluding to in his *Moriae encomium* (1511). While speaking of folly as being the only force that might prevent youth from becoming old too quickly, Erasmus must be paraphrasing a well-known proverb since he introduces his statement with the introductory formula of "that familiar proverb." Vredeveld succeeds in identifying this proverb as being "A merry heart makes life bloom; a sad spirit dries the bones" (Proverbs 17,22).

This Biblical proverb is used by Erasmus in other works with similar comments, and it must certainly have been quite current among the well-educated humanists of Erasmus' age. The 27 notes contain useful bibliographical references.

4518. Vrtunski, Dushko. "O prevodenju poslovitsa u Servantesovom Don Kikhotu." *Mostovi*, 16, no. 63 (1985), 225–228.

This is a short and general article on the use and function of proverbs in Miguel de Cervantes Saavedra's (1547–1616) novel *Don Quijote* (1605/1615). The Yugoslavian author points out that proverbs are being used in the dialogues as well as the narrative portions of this major literary work. They add much folk speech, popular wisdom, and aspects of Spanish worldview to the novel's basic message. A few contextualized examples are cited in Spanish with Yugoslavian translations, but Vrtunski does not refer to the considerable scholarship that exists on the proverbial language of this literary masterpiece. For more detailed studies see Francisco Lacosta (no. 991), Gloria Diaz Isaacs (no. 2317), Margarete Axnick (no. 3081), and Maria Cecilia Colombi (no. 3552).

W

4519. Wacke, A. "Das Rechtssprichwort 'Wer sät, der mäht'." *Juristische Arbeitsblätter*, no volume given (1981), 286–288.

The author investigates the origin, history, and meaning of the German legal proverb "Wer sät, der mäht" (He who sows, mows (harvests). The short article starts with a discussion of laws relating to the growing and harvesting of fruit, vegetables, and grain. Wacker also deals with the issues of land ownership and leasing of land, indicating that there are old Germanic laws that deal with such matters. He then points out that this particular proverb is a rather general statement going back to the Middle Ages. It simply states that the one who plants should also reap the fruits of his labor. While this legal proverb is not part of Germany's offical law books, it is a legal claim based on experience and common sense that survives to this day in oral speech. A short bibliography (p. 288) is attached.

4520. Wacke, A. "'Wer zuerst kommt, mahlt zuerst'—Prior tempore potior iure." *Juristische Arbeitsblätter*, no volume given (1981), 94–98.

Wacke presents a detailed historical analysis of the German legal proverb "Wer zuerst [zu der Mühle] kommt, mahlt zuerst" (He who comes first [to the mill], grinds first; i.e., First come, first served). He points out that this proverb, especially in its shortened general form, is known throughout Europe. It is based on customary law, and it simply expresses the common-sense rule that the person who is first should be served first. Wacke explains that this legal proverb is still applicable in modern society. For example, the German railroad is obliged to transport goods according to this rule. This is also true for certain traffic situations on German roads, especially at bridges where only one car at a time may cross. The 38 notes include helpful bibliographical information. For a valuable monograph on this proverb see Sven Ek (no. 395).

4521. Walcher, Christiane. *Die Frau im deutschen und französischen Sprichwort (ein Vergleich)*. M. A. Thesis University of Vienna, 1983. 146 pp.

This thesis investigates the image of women in German and French proverbs. Citing 891 comparative examples, Walcher comments on the stereotypical and often misogynous view of women in this traditional wisdom. This can be seen from the statements that the proverbs make about young girls, marriage, wives, mothers, old women, widows, whores, etc. The picture is quite similar in those proverbs that mention both men and women. The man is always seen as the dominant person in the marriage, in the home, and in various issues confronting a married couple and the family. Walcher also includes remarks on the metaphorical images relating to women, such as animals, objects, plants, etc. As if that were not enough, it is pointed out that women are quite often compared to or associated with the devil. All of the texts make clear that proverbs have a rather negative view of women, and they most certainly reflect the chauvinistic worldview of the males who coined them in the first place.

4522. Walkley, M.J. "Une allusion au proverbe 'Il ne se tort pas qui va plain chemin' dans *Pathelin*, 284–290." *New Zealand Journal of French Studies*, 10, no. 1 (1989), 52–55.

A short explanatory note concerning an allusion to the proverb "Il ne se tort pas qui va plain chemin" (He does not wrong himself who goes the even [straight] path) in the anonymous *Farce de Maistre Pierre Pathelin* (c. 1461/1469). Walkley cites the contextualized allusion and states that editors of this late medieval French farce have missed its proverbial character. She is able to show that this particular proverb was in common use at that time. The author of this comical play could therefore count on his audience to understand the humorous intent of only hinting at the traditional proverb. Walkley also mentions that this work contains numerous other proverbs and proverbial expressions, making it a rich source for early French proverbial speech.

4523. Walsh, John K. *"El Libro de los doze sabios" o "Tractado de la nobleza y lealtad." Estudio y edicion.* Madrid: Real Academia Española, 1975. 179 pp.

This is a very scholarly edition of the anonymous *El Libro de los doze sabios* (1237/1238), a medieval book of wisdom literature based on classical Greek and Latin as well as Biblical sources. Walsh begins with a valuable introduction (pp. 7–65) in which he discusses the history of the manuscript, previous scholarship relating to it, its structure, date, possible author, sources, and previous editions. The present edition is based on a manuscript from 1502, and its 66 chapters are printed on pages 67–118 of this edition. Walsh supplies 142 detailed notes that explain historical, cultural, and philological aspects of this medieval Spanish work that includes much proverbial wisdom. Lexical variants (pp. 119–140), an appendix (pp. 141–148), and a welcome word index (pp. 149–178) are included.

4524. Walsh, Mary-Elizabeth. *The Role of Imagery and Abstraction in Proverb Comprehension: A Dual-Coding Analysis of Figurative Language.* Diss. University of Western Ontario, 1988. 232 pp.

This is a valuable dissertation on proverb comprehension based on a specially designed psychological proverbs test. In the first chapter (pp. 1–44) Walsh presents a review of previous scholarship on figurative language comprehension, stressing in particular the literal/figurative dichotomy as well as the problems of imagery and abstraction. Chapter two (pp. 46–94) studies the imagery, meaning, and figurativeness of proverbs, while chapter three (pp. 95–104) analyzes the imageability, comprehensibility, and interpretability of proverbs. In the fourth chapter (pp. 105–117) Walsh includes an analysis of concrete and abstract interpretations of proverbs, and the short fifth chapter (pp. 118–122) summarizes what has been said thus far. Chapter six (pp. 123–148) looks at proverb interpretations as memory cues, especially concrete/abstract differences in cued recall. The seventh chapter (pp. 149–178) does the same as the previous chapter but uses randomly selected interpretations as recall cues. In the eighth chapter (pp. 179–198) the author summarizes all of her findings in a more general discussion. Two figures, 15 statistical tables, a solid bibliography (pp. 199–208), and appendices (pp. 209–232) including various proverbs tests are part of this study.

4525. Walther, Helmut. "'Bucklige Verwandtschaft'." *Der Sprachdienst,* 26, nos. 11–12 (1982), 180–181.

Walther attempts to explain the origin and meaning of the German proverbial expression "Bucklige Verwandtschaft" (Hunchbacked relative or kinship; i.e., distant relatives). He reports on 15 possible meanings which were submitted as answers to a contest regarding this fixed phrase by the Society of the German Language (Wiesbaden). No absolute agreement could be reached, but it seems plausible that the phrase refers to distant relatives who are perceived as being of secondary importance. This is also indicated by the often ironical use of the expression in oral speech. The short essay is a clear example of the multiple meanings that a proverbial expression can take on once folk etymology gets a hold of it in an attempt to find explanations of archaic words contained in it. See also Rudolf Dunger (no. 3339).

4526. Walther, Helmut. "'Er grient wie ein Oktoberfuchs'." *Der Sprachdienst,* 26, nos. 9–10 (1982), 139–140.

A short etymological investigation of the German proverbial comparison "Er grient wie ein Oktoberfuchs" (He smiles [grins] slyly or craftily like a fox in October) and its variant "Er freut sich wie ein Oktoberfuchs" (He is happy like a fox in October). Walther explains that these fixed phrases originated in the dialect of Berlin, but he also cites variants from other German dialects. He explains that a fox is usually thought of as being a cunning and smart animal. The noun "Oktober" probably refers to the season in which the fur of the fox is least appealing and therefore adds extra weight to this proverbial comparison. The word "Oktoberfuchs" is also applied to people of red hair who have traditionally been associated with negative characteristics in

folklore. Concerning the beliefs and superstitions about red hair
see Wayland Hand (no. 659) and Hans Niedermeier (no. 1357).

4527. Walther, Helmut. "'Hände besehen gibt Streit'." *Der Sprachdienst*,
29, nos. 5–6 (1985), 84–85.

The author attempts to explain the meaning of the German
proverb "Hände besehen gibt Streit" (Looking at each other's
hands will result in a quarrel). He points out that there is an old
belief which claims that if two people look at each other's hands,
they will soon have a serious quarrel. There is, however, also the
belief that if they were to look quickly at their feet, then the
quarrel could be avoided. Walther feels that this proverb is based
on the former belief in magical powers, and he is correct in
stating that this phrase is in fact more a superstition than a
proverb. It is an excellent example of how superstitions and
beliefs are formulated on the basis of proverbial structures.

4528. Walther, Helmut. "'Jägerlatein'." *Der Sprachdienst*, 30, no. 6
(1986), 167–168.

This is a short comment on the German proverbial
expression "Das ist Jägerlatein" (That is hunters' Latin) that can
be traced back to the early 19th century. Walther explains that
the term "Jägerlatin" was originally used to refer to the
specialized language that German hunters have developed over
the past few centuries. Their hunting vocabulary is so alien to the
general population that it appears like "Latin" to them. But
hunters are also known to tell rather exaggerated tales about
their successes, and it is this unrealistic bragging which is now
associated with the meaning of this proverbial expression.
"Jägerlatein" has become synonymous with telling tall tales.

4529. Walther, Helmut. "'Nobel geht die Welt zugrunde'." *Der
Sprachdienst*, 30, no. 5 (1986), 159.

In this note Walther explains the meaning of the German
proverb "Nobel geht die Welt zugrunde" (Nobly [stylishly,
extravagantly] the world will cease to be). He shows that it stems
from the 19th century and cites early references from Prussia and
Berlin. The actual source is still not known, but it certainly has

gained common currency in Germany as proverb collections and quotation dictionaries show. Walther points out that the proverb is usually used in an ironical or satirical way, basically arguing that someone who lives beyond his/her means will go down in style, go bankrupt, wind up in ruin, etc.

4530. Walther, Helmut. "'Über den Geschmack läßt sich nicht streiten'." *Der Sprachdienst*, 31, no. 4 (1987), 113.

The author points out that the popular German proverb "Über den Geschmack läßt sich nicht streiten" goes back to the classical Latin proverb "De gustibus non est disputandum" (There is no accounting [disputing] over tastes) which was translated into many European languages. Walther also explains the linguistic problem of the possibility of three plural forms for the German noun "Geschmack" (taste). While the proverb is usually cited using the singular noun, some people prefer to use the plural. Both "Geschmäcke" (with umlaut) and "Geschmacke" are possible, but the third variant "Geschmäcker" adds a certain irony to the proverb in an actual speech act. See also the longer article on this proverb by Werner Strube (no. 4442).

4531. Walther, Helmut. "'Dein Wort in Gottes Ohr'." *Der Sprachdienst*, 35, no. 5 (1991), 166.

Walther reports on the answers which members of the Society of the German Language (Wiesbaden) submitted regarding the question of the possible origin of the proverbial expression "Dein Wort in Gottes Ohr." Most of them refer to the Biblical passage "Denn er [der Herr] neigte sein Ohr zu mir; darum will ich mein Leben lang ihn anrufen" (Psalm 116,2; Because he [the Lord] has inclined his ear unto me, therefore will I call upon him as long as I live). Other Biblical passages as well as a possible Yiddish source are mentioned. Walther also cites literary references from such authors as Gotthold Ephraim Lessing (1729–1781), Friedrich Rückert (1788–1866), and Emanuel Geibel (1815–1884), but they are not exact duplicates of the phrase under discussion. The meaning of the expression appears to be that even though one does not believe a particular statement uttered by someone, one wishes that it might become true by divine intervention.

4532. Walton, George W. "Bunyan's Proverbial Language." *Bunyan in Our Time.* Ed. Robert G. Collmer. Kent/Ohio: Kent State University Press, 1989. 7–34 and 200–202 (notes).

In this literary proverb study Walton investigates the use and function of English proverbs and proverbial expressions in the works of the religious writer John Bunyan (1628–1688). He begins with some general comments on the definition and tradition of proverbs in the 17th century, and he then shows that Bunyan valued proverbs as expressions of experience and wisdom. They function as a stylistic device to add folk speech to the didactic works of this moralistic writer. At the end of the article is a special section (pp. 26–34) that deals with the integration of proverbs in *The Pilgrim's Progress* (1678/80). Many contextualized examples are cited, and Walton provides detailed comments regarding both the folk and Biblical proverbs. The 28 notes (pp. 200–202) contain useful bibliographical references to the study of proverbs in literature. See also Walton's dissertation on this subject matter (no. 2025).

4533. Wander, Karl Friedrich Wilhelm. *Das Sprichwort, betrachtet nach Form u. Wesen, für Schule u. Leben, als Einleitung zu einem großen volksthümlichen Sprichwörterschatz.* Hirschberg: Zimmer, 1836; rpt. with an introduction by Wolfgang Mieder. Bern: Peter Lang, 1983. 312 pp.

This is a reprint of Karl Friedrich Wilhelm Wander's (1803–1879) significant study on the proverb from 1836 which marks the beginning of modern paremiology in Germany. The book discusses German proverb collections and their organization, definition problems, various proverbial genres (commonplace, quotation, maxim, proverbial expression, etc.), the difference between proverbs and proverbial phrases, as well as their origin, use, function, form, content, and meaning (see no. 2028 for a more detailed annotation). Wolfgang Mieder has added a long introduction that includes a discussion of Wander's life and works (pp. i-xii), an account of his paremiographical and paremiological activities (pp. xii-xxiii), and an analysis of this early study on proverbs (pp. xxiii-xxxvi). A bibliography (pp. xxxvii-xxxxiii) of Wander's proverb publications and of secondary sources about him is also provided, and at the end of this reprint Mieder has added name, subject, and proverb indices (pp. 211–247). For Wander's publications and their annotations see nos. 2028–2029 and 2988–2993. See also Klaus Dieter Pilz (no. 1461).

4534. Wandruszka, Mario. "Contraintes instrumentales et liberté créatrice." *Europhras 88. Phraséologie Contrastive. Actes du Colloque International Klingenthal-Strasbourg, 12–16 mai 1988.* Ed. Gertrud Gréciano. Strasbourg: Université des Sciences Humaines, 1989. 453–458.

In this short article Wandruszka points out the constraint and the creativity that literary translators feel when rendering the phraseological units of a novel, drama, or poem into another language. Choosing Patrick Süskind's (1949–) German novel *Das Parfum* (1985) as his example, the author shows by means of contextualized examples how English, Italian, and French translators have dealt with various fixed phrases. For some of the older classical or Biblical proverbs and proverbial expressions the translators were able to find exact equivalents in the target languages. However, in those cases where the target languages had only partial or nor equivalents at all, the translators had to be quite liberal and creative in their translations. Often the proverbial metaphors are lost, and there are also occasions where the translators simply do not express the same meaning by choosing a phraseological unit that has a different metaphor.

4535. Wandruszka, Mario. "Sprache aus Bildern." In M. Wandruszka. *Die europäische Sprachengemeinschaft: Deutsch-Französisch-English-Italienisch-Spanisch im Vergleich.* Tübingen: A. Francke, 1990. 51–76.

This is a comparative article on the use and function of metaphorical language (i.e., proverbs, proverbial expressions, and idioms) in Robert Musil's (1880–1942) Austrian novel *Der Mann ohne Eigenschaften* (1930/42), Patrick Süskind's (1949–) German novel *Das Parfum* (1985), Golo Mann's (1909) autobiography *Erinnerungen und Gedanken: Eine Jugend in Deutschland* (1986), and Gabriel Garcia Márquez' (1928–) Spanish novel *El amor en los tiempos dol cólera* (1985). Wandruszka is particularly interested in how various Dutch, French, Spanish, English, and Italian translators have dealt with the translation of these phraseological units. Numerous contextualized examples are cited, and the author shows the difficulty of translating fixed phrases for which the target languages have no equivalents. He also points out the challenge of translating traditional proverbs which have been intentionally varied by the literary authors. The same difficulty arises for the translators when being confronted with phrases that express certain elements of worldview. Quite often translators have to be quite imaginative and creative in rendering such idioms into a foreign language.

4536. Ward, Donald. "The Wolf: Proverbial Ambivalence." *Proverbium*, 4 (1987), 211–224.

Taking his lead from Wilhelm Grimm's (1786–1859) essay on *Die mythologische Bedeutung des Wolfes* (1856), Ward discusses the etymological, historical and cultural reasons for the ambivalent view of the wolf in German proverbs. Already Grimm had pointed out that the wolf is seen both negatively and positively by the folk. Ward cites numerous examples that show the wolf as a bloodthirsty killer, an evil foe, and a dangerous enemy. But he also explains that the name of the wolf is used quite positively in German personal and geographical names. From time to time he is also seen in a positive light in proverbs. It is thought that these more complimentary images go back to Germanic times when the wolf was looked at as a noble, courageous, and mythological creature. The author concludes his valuable article by the general observation that much of folklore is based on such ambivalence (notice, for example, the figure of the Pied Piper of Hamelin). The 41 notes (pp. 221–224) include useful bibliographical information.

4537. Ward, Donald. "Wayland Debs Hand (1907–1986)." *Proverbium*, 4 (1987), 255–261.

This is a touching tribute by Ward to his former teacher and much admired colleague Wayland Debs Hand (1907–1986), who passed away unexpectedly in October of 1986 on his way to the national meeting of the American Folklore Society in Baltimore, Maryland. Ward gives a short biographical sketch, and he praises Hand in particular for his untiring work on a unique archive of beliefs and superstitions that occupied him for almost five decades. Ward is now carrying on the work of his mentor, and the first volume of the *Encyclopedia of American Popular Beliefs and Superstitions* will appear in 1993. Ward also includes some anecdotes and personal memories concerning this giant of American and international folklore. It might also be pointed out here that the fourth volume of *Proverbium* (1986) was a "Festschrift" in honor of Wayland Hand. He died about twenty hours before I could present him with this volume in recognition of his major contributions to folklore scholarship. For annotations concerning Hand's paremiological publications see nos. 658–662 and 2442–2443.

4538. Waterhouse, William C. "The Case of the Persian Proverb." *The Baker Street Journal: An Irregular Quarterly of Sherlockiana*, 40, no. 3 (1990), 135–136.

Waterhouse tries to solve the question whether there really does exist a Persian proverb "There is danger for him who taketh the tiger cub, and danger also for whoso snatches a delusion from a woman" which appears in Sir Arthur Conan Doyle's (1859–1930) *The Adventures of Sherlock Holmes* (1892). Having checked without success in standard Persian proverb collections, the author decides that Doyle made the proverb up himself. Even though the proverb is registered in Selwyn Gurney Champion's collection *Racial Proverbs: A Selection of the World's Proverbs* (1938) as a Persian proverb, Waterhouse contends that it is not a traditional proverb. Instead, it is very likely that Champion found it in Doyle's work and that he took it for an authentic text.

4539. Webster, Sheila K. "Women, Sex, and Marriage in Moroccan Proverbs." *International Journal of Middle East Studies*, 14 (1982), 173–184.

Based on 93 proverbs selected from Edward Westermarck's collection *Wit and Wisdom in Morocco* (1930; see no. 2056), the author discusses three aspects of Arabic proverbs that deal with women, sex, and marriage. There are first of all those sexual proverbs which refer to intercourse, homosexuality, bestiality, male autoeroticism, and incest. The proverbs of the second group dealing with marriage comment on such matters as honesty, desirability of a spouse, age, family, morality, etc. In the third group the proverbs express misogynous views and claim a natural inferiority of women. Many stereotypical and anti-feministic examples are cited with detailed cultural and historical explanations that include comments on worldview. Two tables and a helpful bibliography (pp. 183–184) conclude this ethnographical study.

4540. Webster, Sheila K. *The Shadow of a Noble Man: Honor and Shame in Arabic Proverbs.* Diss. Indiana University, 1984. 222 pp.

This is a significant dissertation on aspects of shame and honor expressed in Arabic proverbs. Webster begins with a chapter (pp. 1–23) on Arabic oral literature, culture, and proverb collections. In the second chapter (pp. 24–48) she provides detailed comments on the historical, cultural, religious (Islam), and geographical aspects of the Arab world. Chapter three (pp. 49–113) discusses such matters as definition, origin, structure, context, style, meaning, and ethnography of Arabic proverbs. The fourth chapter (pp. 114–139) presents a cross-cultural analysis of honor and shame in proverbs, notably feelings about honor and women as well as honorable behavior. The fifth chapter (pp. 140–178) looks especially at Arabic proverbs of honor and shame, dealing with such concerns as the family, women, generosity, hospitality, etc. In the sixth chapter (pp. 179–197) Webster discusses the meaning of her examples in the cultural and communicative context. An appendix (pp. 179–197) includes a list of 105 proverbs on honor and shame in Arabic and with English translations. A valuable bibliography (pp. 210–22) is attached as well.

4541. Webster, Sheila K. "Arabic Proverbs and Related Forms." *Proverbium*, 3 (1986), 179–194.

Webster offers a solid review article on various aspects of Arabic proverbs. She begins with the observation that oral literature and proverbs in particular have long played an important role in classical Arabic and also in the modern dialects. As wisdom literature proverbs are used as powerful rhetorical devices, and they also serve didactic and religious (Islam) purposes. The author reviews some of the early Arabic proverb collections and also comments on more modern bilingual compilations with special emphasis on English language editions. Some of the major scholarship is mentioned, and Webster deals in much detail with Robert Barakat's informative *Contextual Study of Arabic Proverbs* (1980; see no. 82). A useful introductory bibliography (pp. 192–194) to the rich field of Arabic paremiology and paremiography is included.

4542.   Weckmann, Berthold. "Sprichwort und Redensart in der Lutherbibel." *Archiv für das Studium der neueren Sprachen und Literaturen*, 221 (1984), 19–42.

This important article deals with the German proverbs and proverbial expressions in Martin Luther's (1483–1546) Bible translation. Weckmann starts with definition problems and then gives a detailed account of German proverb collections up through the age of the Reformation. He also treats Luther's own collection (c. 1530; see Ernst Thiele, no. 1917) and the reformer's views of proverbial speech. This is followed by a statistical analysis of the proverbs in the Bible including the marginal notes. The rest of the paper discusses the history of a few proverb translations up to Luther's version, including the proverb "Wes das Herz voll ist, des gehet der Mund über" (Matth. 12,34; Out of the abundance of the heart the mouth speaketh). Weckmann also analyzes some religious texts which might have been coined by Luther and which have become proverbial. It is argued that Luther used and liked proverbs because of their understandability (comprehensibility) and their authority which made them effective traditional statements in his work as a church reformer. The 139 notes include valuable bibliographical information. For the proverb cited above see also John Kunstmann (no. 945), William Kurrelmeyer (no. 2567), Wolfgang Mieder (no. 3862), and Timothy Nelson (no. 4015).

4543. Wehse, Rainer. "Parodie—eine neue Einfache Form?" *Festschrift für Lutz Röhrich.* Eds. Rolf Wilhelm Brednich and Jürgen Dittmar. Berlin: Erich Schmidt, 1982. 316–334 (=*Jahrbuch für Volksliedforschung*, 27–28 [1982–1983], 316–334).

Starting with a discussion of André Jolles' concept of "Einfache Formen" (Simple Forms; see no. 811)), Wehse argues that the parody might be considered as belonging to these forms that include such genres as the legend, riddle, joke, fairy tale, proverb, etc. He gives a definition of parody and then presents numerous German examples which are in current oral use. For each of these texts he explains what genre is being parodied, what the context is, etc. Parodies of famous literary quotations, folk songs, children's rhymes, prayers, slogans, and also proverbs (esp. pp. 326–328) in the form of "Antisprichwörter" (anti-proverbs) are included. Valuable bibliographical references can be found in the 23 notes. There is a definite need for more theoretical work on the part of folklorists and paremiologists regarding such modern parodies of traditional verbal communication.

4544. Weigelt, Sylvia. "Predigt als Flugschrift—untersucht am Beispiel der Zehntenschrift von Otto Brunfels." *Wissenschaftliche Zeitschrift der Friedrich Schiller Universität Jena*, Gesellschaftswissenschaftliche Reihe, Sprachwissenschaftliche Beiträge, 34, no. 1 (1985), 91–96.

Weigelt analyzes various rhetorical devices in the polemical pamphlet *Vom Pfaffenzehnten* (1524) by Otto Brunfels (1488–1543). As a radical church reformer and friend of Martin Luther (1483–1546) he fought against various ills of the Catholic Church, and he employed numerous German proverbs and proverbial expressions for his satirical attacks. Weigelt cites a number of contextualized examples and shows that they are effective weapons in the verbal fight against religious abuses. Using such colloquial folk speech, Brunfels also was assured that his German readers could follow his emotional and aggressive arguments. The entire pamphlet is written in the style of a moralistic sermon, and it is filled with Biblical quotations and folk proverbs. German, Russian, and English abstracts (p. 96) are attached. See also Wolfgang Pfeifer (no. 1449) and Marinus van den Broek (nos. 3164–3170) for other such proverbial authors of the Reformation period.

4545.   Weininger, Simon. "Parallele Sprichwörter." *Proverbium,* 3 (1986), 231–232.

This is a short research report by the Israeli scholar Simon Weininger who is preparing a large collection of parallel proverbs from 23 languages, among them the major European languages including classical Latin. The collection will include 650 texts and their parallels. On the average Weininger will list 6–7 equivalents, but there are also those proverbs that have equivalents in up to 14 languages. The book will appear in two versions: the one for the market in Israel will add literal Hebrew translations for all the texts, while the other will add German and English translations to gain a wider readership. At this date (Oct. 1992) the collection has not been published yet. It will doubtlessly be of much value to international proverb scholars.

4546.   Weng, Jianhua. *Der Mensch und sein Körper in deutschen Phraseologismen.* M.A. Thesis University of Würzburg, 1990. 191 pp.

Weng studies numerous German proverbs, proverbial expressions, and proverbial comparisons that refer to various parts of the human body. In the first chapter (pp. 1–15) she introduces the importance and high frequency of somatic phraseological units. Chapter two (pp. 15–48) treats their form, fixity, polysemy, metaphors, and meaning, while the third chapter (pp. 49–62) analyzes syntactical and lexical aspects. In the fourth chapter (pp. 63–82) Weng attempts a semantic classification of these fixed phrases, and in the fifth chapter (pp. 83–129) she explains their use and function in literature and newspapers. It is here where she also discusses how they are varied in oral speech and in literary texts. In chapter six (pp. 130–161) the author deals with the origin of such somatic expressions, mentioning in particular aspects of body language, gesture, and mimicry. The seventh chapter (pp. 162–181) offers a comparative analysis of German and Chinese somatic phrases, and the bibliography (pp. 184–190) contains important references concerning body parts as part of proverbial language.

4547. Wenliang, Yang. "Chinesische und deutsche idiomatische Redewendungen. Kontrastive Betrachtungen." *Muttersprache,* 101 (1991), 106–115.

This is a comparative analysis of Chinese and German phraseological units. Wenliang begins with definition problems and then explains the form and structure of proverbs and proverbial expressions. It is observed that there are many similarities between the fixed phrases of these two languages and cultures. Some of them have identical equivalents due to common sources such as the Bible, fables, and literary works from classical or more modern times. In that case the proverbs were loan translated using the same metaphors and linguistic structures. In the case of indigenous origins, the texts contain quite different metaphors while their meaning might be the same. The author includes many examples and cites the Chinese texts with German translations. Three comparative tables are provided, and the 17 notes include useful bibliographical information.

4548. Werbow, Stanley N. "'Es ist nicht (so ganz) ohne'. Aufstieg und Fall einer Redewendung. Ein Beitrag zur historischen Phraseologie." *Opitz und seine Welt. Festschrift für George Schulz-Behrend.* Eds. Barbara Becker-Cantarino and Jörg-Ulrich Fechner. Amsterdam: Rodopi, 1990. 561–568.

The author starts with a detailed etymological description of the German preposition, adverb, and conjunction "ohne" (without). He then explains that the fixed phrase "Es ist nicht (so ganz) ohne" (It is not [entirely] without) can have a positive and negative meaning that is depended upon the context in which it is employed. It dates back to 1540, was used by Martin Luther (1483–1546), and became particularly popular during the age of the Baroque in the 17th century. At that time it was used frequently in literary works, and it was also included in the early dictionaries of that time. The phrase is quite often used in an ironical tone, and it is then when it takes on the metaphorical meaning of someone being quite a person to reckon with, i.e. not at all a person who is lacking in something. Werbow includes additional comments regarding the lexicographical history of the phrase in modern dictionaries.

4549. Werlen, Iwar. "Vermeidungsritual und Höflichkeit. Zu einigen Formen konventionalisierter indirekter Sprechakte im Deutschen." *Deutsche Sprache*, 11 (1983), 193–218.

Werlen states that politeness can be regarded as an interpersonal avoidance ritual which in addition to certain gestures is also expressed through formulaic language. Citing numerous German examples, the author shows that the modal verbs "dürfen" (to be allowed to), "wollen" (to want to), "mögen (möchten)" (To like [would like] to), "müssen" (to have to), and "können" (to be able to) are used quite idiomatically to create various types of phraseological units that add politeness to a speech act. Often this is also accomplished by using certain fixed expressions in conditional phrases, in the subjunctive mood, and as a question. Such conventional and formulaic language is employed primarily to avoid direct confrontation, the indirect fixed phrase being able to state things without coming across as being aggressive or impolite. A useful bibliography (pp. 216–218) and short German and English abstracts (p. 193) are provided.

4550. Werner, Jürgen. "'Arbeit überwindet alles'." *Zeitschrift für Phonetik, Sprachwissenschaft und Kommunikationsforschung*, 41 (1988), 387–388.

A short philological note establishing the classical Latin source of the German proverb "Arbeit überwindet alles" (Work conquers all). Werner explains that this text appears in Latin as "Labor omnia vincit" in the *Eclogues* (37 B.C.) of Virgil (70–19 B.C.). It is also pointed out that the same author refers to the variant "Omnia vincit amor" (Love conquers all) in the same literary work. The German text thus appears to be a loan translation from the Latin original. In an addendum to this note by Werner Neumann, it is shown that the monk Notker Labeo (950?–1022) cites the Latin proverb "Omnia uincit [sic] amor" in one of his Old High German texts. Werner also includes some comments regarding the word order and grammatical form of this old proverb that are due to certain metrical restrictions in Virgil's hexameters.

4551. Wescher, Paul. Die 'Verkehrte Welt' im Bild. Ihre Geschichte und Bedeutung." In P. Weber. *Gesammelte Aufsätze zur Kunst*. Ed. Frank Otten. Köln: Böhlau, 1979. 3–33.

This is a major study on the iconographical history of the proverbial motif of "Die verkehrte Welt" (World-upside-down). Wescher begins with depictions of animals acting as humans from ancient Mesopotamia, and he traces this old motif all the way to medieval fables and to those of Jean de La Fontaine (1621–1695). German, French, and Italian literary references are cited, but the author studies in particular how such artists as Pieter Brueghel (c. 1520–1569), Cornelis Saftleven (1607–1681), David Teniers II (1610–1690), Pier Leone Ghezzi (1674–1755), Francisco de Goya (1746–1828), and others have illustrated this motif. Many of the illustrations contain references to proverbs and proverbial expressions dealing with animals, especially with the fox, wolf, ape, etc. Early woodcuts as illustrations of books are discussed as well, and Wescher interprets this iconographical tradition as an indicator of indirect political and social satire. The article is richly illustrated by 33 pictures from early to modern times, and a useful bibliography (pp. 32–33) is included as well.

4552. Wexelblatt, Robert. "The Proverbs of Klaren Verheim: A Note from the Editor." *San Jose Studies*, 10, no. 1 (1984), 97–104.

Wexelblatt prints 130 proverbial aphorisms by Klaren Verheim (1935–1966), who was born in Vienna, studied musicology at Columbia University, became a businessman in New York, and who was killed tragically while crossing a street in that city. In a short note (pp. 103–104) Wexelblatt makes some comments on the content of these short texts of which many are based on proverbial structures in the form of "Antisprichwörter" (anti-proverbs). He points out that they refer to music and art, to certain ethical convictions, the family, political life, etc. The small collection of aphorisms was given to Wexelblatt by Verheim's sister. There are no other poetic publications by him, but these texts certainly show an intellectual mind at work who enjoyed puns and wordplays with traditional proverbs.

4553.   Wheeler, Everett L. "'Polla kena tou polemou'—The History of a Greek Proverb." *Greek, Roman and Byzantine Studies*, 29, no. 2 (1988), 153–184.

This is a very detailed philological and historical study of the origin and dissemination of the Greek proverb "Polla kena tou polemou" (Many empty [fruitless] things in war, Many futilities in war, War is full of false alarms). Wheeler points out that the earliest written reference appears in Thucydides (460?-400 B.C.). Aristotle (384–322 B.C.) also used this saying, but it was Polybius (205?–125? B.C.) who called it a proverb for the first time. In addition to these and other Greek sources Wheeler also cites Latin references from Marcus Cato (234–149 B.C.), Marcus Tullius Cicero (106–43 B.C.), Plutarch (46?–120? A.D.), and many others. Many contextualized examples are quoted in Greek and Latin without English translations to illustrate how this piece of wisdom about war was handed down through written sources in the form of many variants. The author also refers to numerous classical proverb collections, and his 96 notes contain rich bibliographical information.

4554.   Wiedemann, Ulrike. "Zu einigen Aspekten der Bestimmung und konfrontativen Untersuchung satzwertiger Phraseologismen (Phraseotexteme) des Russischen und Deutschen auf der Grundlage slawistischer und germanistischer Forschungsergebnisse." *Wissenschaftliche Zeitschrift der Pädagogischen Hochschule Karl Liebknecht* (Potsdam), 30 (1986), 328–333.

The author presents a comparative analysis of Russian and German proverbs and proverbial expressions. She begins with a review of recent theoretical distinctions between these two genres, and she points out that there are cases where the same metaphor might be expressed as a proverb and as a proverbial phrase. She also comments on the fact that proverbs are not as rigidly fixed as scholars have claimed. Once proverbs are contextualized, they can be changed in order to fit different semantic and syntactical situations. At the end of her article

Wiedemann discusses the problem of equivalency between Russian and German phraseological units. For those that have common classical or Biblical sources there exist identical equivalents. Some have also been loan translated from German or Russian into the other language. But there are, of course, also those indigenous texts for which there are only partial or no equivalents at all in the target language, causing any translator particular problems. A small bibliography (p. 333) is attached.

4555. Wienker-Piepho, Sabine. "Sozialisation durch Sprichwörter: Am Beispiel eines anglo-amerikanischen Bestsellers." *Proverbium*, 8 (1991), 179–189.

Wienker-Piepho investigates the proverbial contents of a small best-seller by Michele Slung (20th cent.) entitled *Momilies: As My Mother Used to Say* (1985). This is a little book filled with proverbs and pseudo-proverbs, but as Wienker-Piepho correctly points out, even those "invented" texts might already be proverbial in the family of the author or other small groups. There is no reason why "Antisprichwörter" (anti-proverbs) might not become proverbial once they get accepted and reach a larger geographical distribution and currency. The book probably became so popular because it contains traditional and innovative pieces of wisdom relating to the frustrations of modern life. They express social wisdom and behavioral advice, but some of these texts are also meant as humorous or satirical comments about today's society. They also express certain stereotypical beliefs about human nature and comment on social rules and attitudes.

4556. Wiese, Ursula von. "Aus Namen werden Begriffe [Johann Balhorn]." *Sprachspiegel*, 41 (1985), 51.

A short note on the interrelationship of onomastics and paremiology. The author explains the origin of the German proverbial expression "Etwas nach Johann Bal(l)horn verbessern" (To correct something like Johann Bal[l]horn, i.e., to make something worse by attempting to correct it). The phrase refers to the printer Johann Balhorn (1530–1603) from Lübeck, Germany, who was known for making changes in the new editions of books which were not at all improvements or which were even incorrect. The German language also has two verbs based on this name with the same meaning as the fixed phrase, namely "verballhornen" and "verballhornisieren." Von Wiese explains that the spelling with the double "l" might have come about in order to avoid confusion with the adjective "verbal" (verbal). The double letter also shortens the preceding vowel and thus reflects the pronunciation of the name more accurately.

4557. Wilcke, Karin, and Lothar Bluhm. "Wilhelm Grimms Sammlung mittelhochdeutscher Sprichwörter." *Brüder Grimm Gedenken.* Ed. Ludwig Denecke. Marburg: N.G. Elwert, 1988. VIII, 81–122.

The two authors report on the discovery of a manuscript by Wilhelm Grimm (1786–1859) that contains on 29 pages his own Middle High German proverb collection that he assembled between 1832 and 1852. Most of the texts were taken from Freidank's (end of the 12th century to 1233?) medieval book of ethics entitled *Bescheidenheit* (1215/30) which Grimm edited in 1834. But he also found proverbs in the long epics by Heinrich vom Türlein (12th/13th century), Hugo von Trimberg (1230?– 1313?), and other medieval authors. Wilcke and Bluhm print the entire collection for the first time, and they provide detailed annotations. The article also includes a discussion of Grimm's work on the *Bescheidenheit,* including comments on the importance of folk proverbs in this work. A key-word index (pp. 117–121) of the proverbs and 26 notes (pp. 121–122) with bibliographical references are attached. For further studies on Grimm's interest in medieval proverbs see Günter Eifler (no. 392), Samuel Singer (no. 1742), and Wolfgang Mieder (no. 3892).

4558. Wilhelm, Albert E. "Robert Frost's Proverbial Promises: Indian Responses to *Stopping by Woods.*" *Motif: International Newsletter of Research in Folklore and Literature,* no. 4 (1982), 7.

A short comment on the proverbial nature of the last stanza of Robert Frost's (1874–1963) poem "Stopping by Woods on a Snowy Evening" (1923). Wilhelm explains that the popular American lines "But I have promises to keep, / And miles to go before I sleep" are often quoted in India as well, most likely because they were a favorite quotation of Jawaharlal Nehru (1889–1964). A few references are made to where the author found the well-known quotation in India, for example adorning the hallway of a public school and as a headline in a news magazine. This American poetical quotation has indeed become proverbial due to its common knowledge and use among the population.

4559. Williams, Fionnuala. "Of Proverbial Birds and Beasts." *Sinsear*, 5 (1983), 127–132.

In this article the leading Irish paremiologist Fionnuala Williams presents a description of the many animal sayings that are part of the large "Schools' Collection" of Irish folklore materials that were collected during the 1930s with the help of school children (see Williams, nos. 2089 and 3014). Of the 122,500 proverbs, proverbial expressions, proverbial comparisons, triads, etc., about 15% refer to domestic and wild animals. Some of the more popular animals are the dog, horse, cow, hen, pig, cat, wolf, fox, etc. Only three animals that do not inhabit Ireland are mentioned, namely the camel, lion, and elephant. The animal metaphors usually reflect human characteristics and behavior, and they also indicate that they originated in a rural community. Williams includes 2 statistical tables (pp. 131–132) to differentiate the frequency of certain animals being mentioned in Irish and Swedish phraseological units.

4560. Williams, Fionnuala. "'Bachelors' Wives and Old Maids' Children'—A Look at the Men and Women in Irish Proverbs." *Ulster Folklore*, 30 (1984), 78–88.

Williams investigates a large number of Irish proverbs from the "Schools' Collection" (see Williams, nos. 2089 and 3014) that refer to men and women, matrimony, the family, and human relationships in general. Numerous examples are cited, and for those texts in Irish the author does provide English translations. It is pointed out that these proverbs deal with certain attitudes and stereotypes, but they are also based on experience that has been gained over a period of many centuries. The proverbs refer

to marriage, beauty, money, work, etc. There are also those texts
which are clearly misogynous, and some of the anti-feministic
texts indicate unfair comments regarding the behavior of women.
Some of these texts are hopefully decreasing in use today, but
they do show general attitudes concerning the stereotypical roles
and views of men and women in the older Irish culture and
society.

4561.   Williams, Fionnuala. "'Eulen nach Athen tragen'—Versions from
Ireland." *Proverbium*, 3 (1986), 253–256.

A short note listing a number of Irish proverbial expressions
with the meaning of doing something that is absolutely
unnecessary and superfluous. The classical phrase is "To carry
owls to Athens" (in German: "Eulen nach Athen tragen"), and
the common English variant is, of course, "To carry coals to
Newcastle." The latter fixed phrase is also known in Ireland, but
Williams is able to show that the expression "To throw apples into
the orchard" is used with much more frequency. She lists a few
variants from the counties of Monaghan, Louth, and Cavan, and
a few linguistic and cultural explanations are added concerning
these texts from the "Schools' Collection" (see Williams, nos.
2089 and 3014). For some additional German, Polish, and
Rumanian variants of this proverbial motif see Wolfgang Mieder
(no. 3871), Stanislaw Predota (no. 4195), and Cezar Tabercea
(no. 4462).

4562.   Williams, Fionnuala. "Triads and Other Enumerative Proverbs
from South Ulster." *Ulster Folklife*, 34 (1988), 60–67.

In this article Williams reports on so-called enumerative
proverbs from the south Ulster counties of Cavan and Monaghan
that are part of the "Schools' Collection" of folklore materials
(see Williams, nos. 2089 and 3014). While she cites a few duads
and tetrads, it is especially the triads that have gained
considerable popularity in Irish proverbial tradition. A triad is a
proverbial statement in which three things with a common
characteristic are grouped together, two examples being "Beware
of a bull's horn, a dog's tooth, and a mule's hoof" and "There are
three kinds of men who do not understand women—young men,

old men, and middle-aged men." The author discusses the possible origin of such texts as well as their meaning and metaphors, and she explains that many of them are based on shorter proverbs and proverbial expressions. An annotated list of 24 triads (5 in Irish) is provided, and Williams makes special references to individual fixed phrases that might have been the root of these longer triads.

4563. Williams, Fionnuala. "An Irish Threshing Proverb." *Folk Life*, 28 (1989–1990), 41–45.

This is a detailed note on an Irish proverb in the form of a tetrad which lists four essentials for good flail thrashing: "A hand-staff of holly, A souple of hazel, A single sheaf, And a clean floor." Williams cites a number of variants in Irish with English translations from the "Schools' Collection" (see Williams, nos. 2089 and 3014) and published Irish proverb collections. She also includes etymological and cultural explanations of these texts that were collected during the 19th and 20th centuries. Williams concludes her comments with the observation that this rather specific proverb could not be used metaphorically, and since its advice refers to practices of thrashing that are basically not used any more, the proverb has now lost its usefulness in popular speech. The 18 notes (pp. 44–45) contain helpful bibliographical information.

4564. Williams, Fionnuala. "Irish Versions of Some Proverbs Found in Scots." *Review of Scottish Culture*, no. 6 (1990), 53–60.

Williams notes the obvious fact that England, Ireland, and Scotland have many proverbs in common. However, due to the historical and cultural links between Ireland and Scotland, there are also some proverbs known only in those two countries. The author discusses five of these, namely "A bonny bride's easy (soon) buskit" (i.e., A bonny bride is soon busked, and a short horse is soon whisked), "An aal (i.e., old) fiddle plays sweetest," "It'll be dry on Friday tae dry the priest's sark" (i.e., It will be dry enough on Friday to dry the priest's shirt), "It's aye kent the mullert (miller) keeps fat hogs but naebody kens faa feeds them" (i.e., It's known that the miller keeps fat hogs but nobody knows whose meal feeds them), and "There's aye a weet an slippery steen at ilky body's door" (i.e., There is always a wet and slippery threshold at everybody's door). The author includes detailed etymological and cultural explanations, she provides variants from numerous Scottish and Irish proverb collections, and she cites useful bibliographical references in the 66 notes (pp. 58–60).

4565.   Williams, Fionnuala. "Survey of 'It's All Double Dutch to Me'." *Proverbium*, 8 (1991), 203.

A very short note in which Williams asks international paremiologists for help in finding variants of the proverbial expression "It's all double Dutch to me" with the meaning that something is incomprehensible. She explains that this phrase is quite common in Ireland, while the similar expression "It's all Greek (or Chinese) to me" is heard less frequently. The note is published in English and in French, and the hope of the author is to find fixed phrases that might use names of other languages to indicate something that is hard or impossible to understand. A very popular German equivalent is "Das kommt mir spanisch vor" (That is Spanish to me). For this phrase and its origin and history see Edwin Zeydel (no. 2138).

4566.   Williams, Fionnuala. "'To Kill Two Birds with One Stone': Variants in a War of Words." *Proverbium*, 8 (1991), 199–201.

In this note Williams shows how the English proverbial expression "To kill two birds with one stone" was adapted to a political statement in the form of graffiti painted on two walls in Belfast, Ireland. They read "3 die with one Stone" and "3 dead with one Stone" and refer to a certain Michael Stone, who on March 16, 1988, killed three people at a funeral at Belfast's Milltown cemetary. The graffiti appeared after this incident and are interpreted as a grim political statement concerning the violence in Northern Ireland. The terrible boast contains a pun based on the assailant's last name, and this innovative use of the proverbial expression unfortunately has caught on among some parts of the population who have raised Stone to a "cult figure" after he was sentenced to thirty years' imprisonment. The article includes 2 illustrations of this hateful proverbial graffiti.

4567. Williams, George Walton. "Shakespeare Metaphors of Health, Food, Sport, and Life-Preserving Rest." *Journal of Medieval and Renaissance Studies*, 14, no. 2 (1984), 187–202.

Williams investigates various plays by William Shakespeare (1564–1616) for their inclusion of metaphors about health, food, sport, and rest. He explains that Shakespeare enjoys using metaphorical language, and there is no doubt that much of it is based on proverbs, proverbial expressions, and proverbial comparisons. Numerous contextualized examples from such tragedies and comedies as *The Comedy of Errors* (1593), *The Merchant of Venice* (1597), *As You Like It* (1599), *Julius Caesar* (1599), and *Macbeth* (1605) are cited. It is pointed out that Shakespeare was well versed in medical proverbs, that he had much knowledge about food and its proverbial lore, and that he also was keen in using metaphors relating to various types of sports. It is exactly this proverbial language with its metaphors which makes Shakespeare's plays so appealing to viewers and readers. The 37 notes include useful bibliographical information.

4568. Williams, Harry F. "French Proverbs in Fifteenth-Century Literature: A Sampling." *Fifteenth-Century Studies*, 5 (1982), 223–232.

The author begins with some general comments regarding early French proverb collections. He also mentions some of the later and major collections, and he argues that many more literary works need to be investigated for proverbial materials in order to make such historical collections more complete. The second part of the article includes a short discussion of the use and function of proverbs and proverbial expressions in Martin Le Franc's (died 1461) long epic *Champion des dames* (1440/42). A few contextualized examples are analyzed regarding their meaning and function. Williams also includes an annotated list of 52 proverbs (pp. 228–232) to indicate not only the wealth of proverbial texts in this literary work, but also to encourage paremiologists to study other authors of the 15th century for their use of proverbial language.

4569. Wilson, Edward. "An Aristotelian Commonplace in Chaucer's *Franklin's Tale.*" *Notes and Queries*, 230, new series 32 (1985), 303–305.

A short philological study of the possible origin of the proverb "Nature forms (does) nothing in vain" to which Geoffrey Chaucer (1340?–1400) alludes in his *Franklin's Tale* of *T h e Canterbury Tales* (1387/1400). Wilson relates that Aristotle (384–322 B.C.) was quite fond of this proverb. The same is true for Boethius (475?-525). A few contextualized examples of the proverb in the writings of these two authors are cited and discussed. Wilson adds some additional references and also indicates that major proverb collections have registered additional sources. There is no doubt that Chaucer knew this proverb and that he made use of it in English at an earlier date than what some historical proverb collections would have us believe.

4570. Winton, Alan P. *The Proverbs of Jesus. Issues of History and Rhetoric.* Sheffield: Sheffield Academic Press, 1990. 236 pp.

This is a major study of the wisdom literature contained in the synoptic gospels. Following some introductory comments Winton discusses in chapter one (pp. 13–29) various aspects of wisdom in the gospels, looking in particular at Jesus as a wise man who draws on traditional wisdom literature. The second chapter (pp. 31–57) deals with the classification, definition, and structure of the proverbs of Jesus, and the third chapter (pp. 59–98) investigates their use and function as an effective rhetorical device. The fourth chapter (pp. 99–125) interprets this proverbial wisdom as part of the Kingdom of God, and the fifth chapter (pp. 127–140) returns one more time to a detailed analysis of the function of Jesus' proverbs in the synoptic gospels. The sixth and last chapter (pp. 141–167) discusses the significance of this proverbial wisdom from a theological point of view. Many contextualized Biblical examples are cited throughout this valuable study. Detailed notes (pp. 169–213), an inclusive bibliography (pp. 215–225), a useful index of Biblical references (pp. 227–232), and an index of authors (pp. 233–236) complete this new and important study of the proverbs in the New Testament.

4571. Wirrer, Jan. "Anmerkungen zur Sprichwortkultur Madagaskars." *Sprichwörter und Redensarten im interkulturellen Vergleich.* Eds. Annette Sabban and J. Wirrer. Opladen: Westdeutscher Verlag, 1991. 175–186.

This is a rather general study of a number of Malagasy proverbs from the island of Madagascar. The author begins with a few historical and cultural comments, and he then presents numerous examples in Malagasy with German translations. He includes ethnographical and cultural explanations which help to understand the meaning of these proverbs. A content analysis is presented, and Wirrer points out that the texts include comments on experience, life, marriage, attitudes, etc. The author also mentions that some of these texts refer to rituals and superstitions, and he shows that the inhabitants of Madagascar have a rich tradition of folk speech. For a more detailed study of Malagasy proverbs see Lee Haring (no. 3558).

4572. Wooldridge, Terence R. "La locution et les premières dénominations de 'locution' dans le métalangage dictionnairique français." *La locution. Actes du colloque international Université McGill, Montréal, 15–16 octobre 1984.* Eds. Giuseppe Di Stefano and Russell G. McGillivray. Montréal: Éditions CERES, 1984. 437–449.

Wooldridge presents an historical and lexicographical study of how French dictionaries have dealt with the term "locution" (proverbial expression). He begins with a glance at some modern dictionaries, but his major interest is directed towards language dictionaries of the 16th century. He cites many examples, in each case quoting the definition and the examples which these early lexicographers included in their large volumes. There are also some examples in which these scholars have defined the "locution" by contrasting it with the "proverbe." At the end of the article (pp. 448–449) the author includes a comparative table of the different definition attempts. Many of them are quite similar, indicating how these diligent lexicographers built on each other as ever more dictionaries appeared in France.

4573. Workman, Mark E. "Proverbs for the Pious and the Paranoid: The Social Use of Metaphor." *Proverbium*, 4 (1987), 225–241.

Beginning with a discussion of Peter Seitel's view of proverbs as social metaphors (see no. 1704), Workman presents a literary investigation of the use and function of a few proverbs in three novels. He starts with some comments on Chinua Achebe's (1931) African novel *Things Fall Apart* (1959). This is followed by interpretative remarks concerning the Russian proverbs in Feodor Mikhailovich Dostoevsky's (1821–1881) novel *The Brothers Karamazov* (1879/80). At the end of his article Workmann also takes a look at Thomas Pynchon's (1937–) integration of American proverbs into his novel *Gravity's Rainbow* (1973). A few contextualized examples are cited from each work, and the author is able to show that all three authors employ proverbs as effective rhetorical devices that reflect social, cultural, and religious attitudes. See also G.A. Levinton (no. 3781).

4574. Wörster, Peter. "'Polnische Wirtschaft'." *Der Sprachdienst*, 28 (1984), 93–95.

The article explains that the German proverbial expression "Polnische Wirtschaft" (Polish household or state of affairs) dates back to the 18th century when Western travellers, writers, and civil servants observed the economic, political, and social chaos that ruled in Poland. The first literary reference can be found in a letter dated 1785 by Johann Georg Forster (1754–1794). The fixed phrase is also known in French (économie polonaise) and in Czech (polska hospodarka). Wörster mentions that the Poles have the ironical expression "Polska nierzadem stoi" (Poland exists because of a disordered household) which ridicules the chaotic situation and the stereotypical slurs about it by foreigners. The short essay concludes with the statement that such national slurs must be understood in their historical context and that they should be used with care (if at all). See also Bernhard Stasiewski (no. 2906) and Uwe Förster (no. 3439).

4575. Wotjak, Barbara. "Ansatz eines modular-integrativen Beschreibungsmodells für verbale Phraseolexeme (PL)." *Europhras 88. Phraséologie Contrastive. Actes du Colloque International Klingenthal-Strasbourg, 12–16 mai 1988.* Ed. Gertrud Gréciano. Strasbourg: Université des Sciences Humaines, 1989. 459–467.

Wotjak presents a linguistic study of German phraseological units, emphasizing various types of verbal phrases. She points out that phraseologists need to look at such factors as content, structure, context, syntax, and meaning. Only if all of these aspects are investigated will a better understanding of the use and function of fixed phrases be reached in oral and written communication. The author cites numerous examples to show that phraseological units are indeed complex language forms. She also discusses lexicographical problems, stating that much more uniformity is needed in the preparation of general and phraseological dictionaries. Some comments regarding the importance of phraseological units in foreign language dictionaries and in the instruction of foreign languages are included as well. The 12 notes (pp. 466–467) contain useful bibliographical references.

4576. Wotjak, Barbara. "'Der Gag heiligt die Mittel?' Modifikationen und Vernetzungen von Sprichwörtern im Text." *Sprachpflege*, 38, no. 9 (1989), 125–129.

This is a short article commenting on the intentional variations of traditional proverbs that result in so-called "Antisprichwörter" (anti-proverbs). Wotjak cites many German examples and shows that these modifications are usually based on a humorous wordplay or pun. She explains that popular proverbs are reduced to mere proverbial structures in which one or two nouns are exchanged at will. The result are parodies, satirical statements, and ironic commentaries on various aspects of modern existence. Sometimes the exchange of one letter or one word suffices to give the proverb a completely new meaning. Such innovative play with proverbs has become particularly popular in newspaper headlines, advertising slogans, and graffiti. For a large collection of such anti-proverbs see Wolfgang Mieder (no. 3852).

4577. Wotjak, Barbara. "'Wo der Hund begraben liegt'. Modifikationen und Vernetzungen von kommunikativen Formeln im Text." *Sprachpflege*, 39, no. 3 (1990), 65–69.

In this article Wotjak investigates modern modifications of phraseological formulas that are used as traditional greetings, to express politeness, to swear, to make a comment, etc. Many of these formulas are in fact proverbial, and due to their frequent use they lend themselves well to innovative wordplays and puns. The author cites many German examples, explaining that they are quite popular in newspaper headlines, in advertising slogans, and in graffiti. The traditional texts are reduced to certain structural formulas whose major components, usually one or two nouns, are varied in order to make a satirical or humorous comment. Such parodies of popular expressions are a clear indication that linguistic play has become a widespread phenomenon in oral and written communication.

4578. Wotjak, Gerd. "Zur Bedeutung ausgewählter verbaler Phraseologismen des Deutschen." *Zeitschrift für Germanistik*, 2 (1986), 183–199.

This linguistic article deals with the meaning of German phraseological units. Wotjak is especially interested in verbal phrases, and he classifies them into several types. This is shown by a number of structural formulas and 6 tables that indicate various semantic and functional aspects of these fixed phrases. The author also deals with such matters as meaning, context, structure, and syntax, always indicating that phraseologists must look at all of these aspects in order to gain a proper understanding of the use and function of phraseological units in oral and written communication. Most of his examples are common proverbial expressions that certainly find frequent use in the modern German language. They should definitely find a more comprehensive inclusion in general dictionaries, and lexicographers need to be more precise in indicating their meaning, use, and stylistic level. A useful bibliography (p. 199) for theoretical studies on phraseological units is attached.

4579. Wotjak, Gerd. "Übereinzelsprachliches und Einzel-sprachspezifisches bei Phraseolexemen." *Europhras 88. Phraséologie Contrastive. Actes du Colloque International Klingenthal-Strasbourg, 12–16 mai 1988.* Ed. Gertrud Gréciano. Strasbourg: Université des Sciences Humaines, 1989. 469–483.

Wotjak begins his linguistic and theoretical article with a review of recent scholarship on phraseological units, and he also presents a definition of such fixed phrases. He then argues that proverbial expressions are linguistic signs which can be studied by analyzing their structure, syntax, context, and meaning. Numerous German examples are cited, and Wotjak explains how these phrases can have literal and figurative meanings. Much depends on how and in which context they are being used. The difficulty of specifying a particular meaning of a fixed phrase also creates a vexing problem for lexicographers of general and foreign language dictionaries. Much work remains to be done by phraseologists before all the semantic and classificatory problems of phraseological units are solved. A helpful bibliography (pp. 481–483) is provided.

4580. Wulff, Michal [sic]. *Das Sprichwort im Kontext der Erziehungstradition. Dargestellt am Beispiel deutsch-jüdischer Sprichwörter.* Frankfurt am Main: Peter Lang, 1990. 317 pp.

This is a valuable book on the educational importance of proverbs for German Jews. Wulff begins her study with a general chapter (pp. 9–47) on proverbs in which she deals with definition problems, other proverbial genres, function, worldview, and national character as illustrated by proverbs. The second chapter (pp. 49–65) analyzes the interrelationship of proverbs and education during the 19th and 20th centuries, and the third chapter (pp. 67–149) describes the commitment to education of the Jews in Germany from the Middle Ages to the present day. Chapter four (pp. 151–171) contains introductory remarks concerning the Yiddish language, and the major fifth chapter (pp. 173–293) includes a detailed content analysis of German Jewish proverbs dealing with such aspects as God, ethics, the Talmud, Jewish identity, human relations, family, the world at large, and the Jewish existence as such. Wulff cites 478 Yiddish proverbs with German translations and provides detailed historical, cultural, linguistic, and ethnographical explanations. The entire book shows that the Jewish people have always placed a very high value on traditional education, and proverbs certainly play a major role in this pedagogical goal. An excellent bibliography (pp. 297–317) is attached.

4581. Wyk, E.B. van, and Melanie J. Bushney. "Linguistiese eienskappe van spreekwoorde in Noord-Sotho." *South African Journal of African Languages*, 9, no. 3 (1989), 127–133.

The authors explain that North Sotho proverbs from South Africa often contain linguistic structures or exhibit features which either do not occur in ordinary language usage or occur with a markedly lower frequency, and therefore appear to be ungrammatical. Some of these deviations from regular grammar include deletion of certain lexical components, certain adjectival and verbal changes, more frequent use of the conditional mood, etc. Research on poetic language has shown that many, but not all, of these peculiarities are also typical of poetry. Wyk and Bushney conclude that poetic language and proverbs are both conservative forms of linguistic usage which tend to perpetuate archaic structures. Proverbs, being formulaic expressions, are more likely to undergo irregular forms of deletion than poetry. Regular usage, poetic usage and proverbs, therefore, constitute a continuum in which grammatical irregularities occur increasingly in direct relation to their formulaic nature. Many North Sotho examples with Afrikaans translations are discussed along these linguistic lines. A useful bibliography (p. 133) as well as English and Dutch abstracts (p. 127) are included.

X

4582. Xhagolli, Agron. "Les dictons populaires albanais et leur caractérisation." *Lettres Albanaises*, 11, no. 2 (1988), 164–176.

This is a general article on various aspects of Albanian proverbial expressions. The author begins with some comments regarding the definition and difference of proverbs and proverbial expressions. He then goes on to explain their form, structure, meaning, metaphors, and context, arguing that all of these must be considered when paremiologists study the use and function of proverbial language in oral and written communication. Xhagolli also points out that many proverbial expressions go back to folk narratives, fables, and anecdotes. A discussion of various classification systems is part of this study, in particular those that group fixed phrases according to the alphabet, meaning, content, and structure. Finally, Xhagolli also mentions that Albanian proverbs and proverbial expressions reflect the worldview of the Albanian people. Only a few examples in French translation are cited, and the small bibliography (p. 176) contains little information regarding Albanian proverb collections and scholarship.

Y

4583. Yankah, Kwesi. "The Proverb and the Western-Educated African: Use or Neglect?" *Folklore Forum*, 15 (1982), 143–158.

In this article one of the leading African paremiologists analyzes the oral use of proverbs among 160 African students enrolled at Indiana University in Bloomington, Indiana (USA). Yankah discusses field research methods and comments on a number of proverbs which he observed being used in a natural context and which he asked informants to comment upon. All examples are cited in English translation, and Yankah adds some remarks concerning the difficulty of translating African proverbs into a European language. Having presented eight contextualized proverbs Yankah concludes that the use of proverbs among the Western-educated Africans is rather limited. This is felt to be a disadvantage when students return to their native lands where traditional proverbial wisdom is held in high esteem. A short bibliography (pp. 157–158) on African proverbs and their usage is attached.

4584. Yankah, Kwesi. "Toward a Performance-Centered Theory of the Proverb." *Critical Arts*, 3, no. 1 (1983), 29–43.

The article starts with a solid review of previous scholarship on the contextual study of proverbs, and the author then states that the creativity and recreativity of proverb performance has not been studied in enough detail. Yankah points out that proverbs are dynamic survivals and that they can best be understood from a linguistic, aesthetic, and contextual study of their performance. A clear model for the structure of proverb performance is presented: discourse, cognition, selection (of a fitting proverb), application, discourse. These constituent units of proverb performance are sequentially ordered, and they are explained by Yankah by means of convincing examples of Akan proverbs from Africa with English translations as well as texts from other cultures. The element of proverb foregrounding which separates proverb performance from the normal automatized discourse is also discussed, stating in particular that the use of a proverb is an artistic performance. The 56 notes (pp. 41–43) contain valuable bibliographical references.

4585. Yankah, Kwesi. "Do Proverbs Contradict?" *Folklore Forum*, 17 (1984), 2–19.

Many scholars have dealt with so-called contradictory proverbs and Yankah reviews some of their findings. He then argues that the problem of contradictory proverbs exists primarily because scholars study them out of context. If one deals with proverbs only as a concept of a cultural fact or truism, contradictions are easily found in any proverb repertoire, but once the proverbs are in contextual usage the claimed truth in a proverb is irrelevant. The author uses his distinction between proverb concept and proverb in context to show that such contradictory proverb pairs as "Out of sight, out of mind" and "Absence makes the heart grow fonder" will lose their contradiction once their meaning is understood by the various situations in which they might be used. Proverbs in discourse are not contradictory, and their apparent contradiction stems from looking at them without a context. A useful bibliography (pp. 17–19) and Akan, English, Somali, Maori, and Chinese examples of "contradictory proverb pairs" are included.

4586. Yankah, Kwesi. *The Proverb in Context of Akan Rhetoric.* Diss. Indiana University, 1985. 455 pp. Now published with a slightly different title as *The Proverb in the Context of Akan Rhetoric. A Theory of Proverb Praxis.* Bern: Peter Lang, 1989. 313 pp.

This is an invaluable dissertation that has now also been published as a book. In chapter one (pp. 9–25) Yankah presents a cultural and ethnographical view of the Akan people of Ghana in Africa. Chapter two (pp. 27–51) reviews theoretical proverb scholarship, stressing in particular the importance of performance, context, and rhetorical function of proverbs. The third chapter (pp. 53–69) describes how the author collected his contextualized texts by means of field research, and the fourth chapter (pp. 71–116) analyzes various aspects of proverbs in the Akan society, for example the use of proverbs among elders, their effectiveness in oratory, their indirection, their use in folk narratives, their visual appearance on cloth, gold weights, spokesman staffs, and umbrella tops, their use on drums, etc. In the fifth chapter (pp. 117–152) the author looks at traditional proverb performance, and in the sixth chapter (pp. 153–181) he shows how native speakers are also quite creative in their proverb usage. Chapter seven (pp. 183–213) discusses the origin, authorship, and novelty of more recent indigenous proverbs, chapter eight (pp. 214–245) looks at the rhetorical use of proverbs in the judicial process, and chapter nine (247–260) investigates actual proverb praxis, i.e. discourse, performance, cognition, selection, and application. An appendix (pp. 261–300) lists all 72 contextualized proverbs in the African original with English translations (the texts in the nine chapters are cited only in English). A valuable bibliography (pp. 301–313), several diagrams, and 4 illustrations are included.

4587. Yankah, Kwesi. "Proverb Rhetoric and African Judicial Processes. 'The Untold Story'." *Journal of American Folklore*, 99 (1986), 280–303.

This is a slightly revised version of the eighth chapter (pp. 214–245) of Yankah's dissertation and book on Akan proverbs from Ghana in Africa (see no. 4586 above). He reviews previous scholarship on the use of proverbs in the judicial process and argues that scholars have exaggerated the power of this traditional wisdom. Proverb rhetoric is effective only when it is matched by a comparable control of facts, evidence, and compliance with customary law. A proverb's rhetorical force can hardly be separated from the efficacy of the argument it embellishes. Yankah proves this point by citing several contextualized proverb performances that he collected during field research. English translations are added to the Akan texts, and Yankah shows how traditional proverbs and legal arguments work hand in hand in the Akan judicial system. A useful bibliography (pp. 302–303) and an English abstract (p. 280) are included. See also John Messenger (no. 1200) for the use of proverbs in the Nigerian courts.

4588. Yankah, Kwesi. "Proverb Speaking as a Creative Process: The Akan of Ghana." *Proverbium*, 3 (1986), 195–230.

The article is a revised version of the sixth chapter (pp. 153–181) of Yankah's dissertation and book on Akan proverbs from Ghana in Africa (see no. 4586 above). The author claims that paremiologists have not paid enough attention to the creativity in actual proverb performance. He argues that proverbs are not as rigidly fixed as has been suggested. Citing numerous contextualized examples in the Akan language with English translations, Yankah shows a considerable creative variability of proverbs when they are used in a speech act. Innovative introductory formulas as well as truncation, elaboration, or intentional manipulation of proverbs can be found quite frequently in the oral use of this traditional wisdom. All of this has much influence on the meaning of the texts, and quite often such changes bring about a desired ambiguity. Proverbs are not at all static once they enter the dynamics of actual usage in a certain context. The 52 notes (pp. 224–230) contain helpful bibliographical references.

4589. Yankah, Kwesi. "Proverbs: Problems and Strategies in Field Research." *Proverbium*, 6 (1989), 165–176.

Yankah discusses the problems that field researchers have faced in collecting proverbs. He reviews some of the basic methodologies, among them direct elicitation from informants, proverb competitions, proverbs through stories, hypothetical situations, and the recall technique. He argues convincingly that all of these methods are forced and unnatural, claiming that the best way to collect proverbs is with the help of a tape recorder when the informant (any speaker) is not even aware of his/her speech being recorded. This is without doubt the ideal scenario, but it also results in hours of tape recordings that often have but very few or no proverbs at all in the texts. Yankah is, of course, correct in maintaining that such audio tapes record the actual proverb performance in its entirety. But one could go one step further and argue that the most perfect way to collect proverbs in actual communicative acts would be with the video recorder. After all, certain gestures also play a role in the actual utterance of a particular proverb. Yankah includes a few contextualized examples of Akan proverbs with English translations that he collected in Ghana, Africa. The 20 notes (pp. 175–176) include some useful bibliographical information.

4590. Yankah, Kwesi. "Proverbs: The Aesthetics of Traditional Communication." *Research in African Literature,* 20, no. 3 (1989), 325–346.

This is a comprehensive article on African proverbs with special emphasis on Akan proverbs from Ghana which are cited with English translations. Yankah reviews previous scholarship and explains the high esteem that African people have for proverbial wisdom. Proverbs are to be found everywhere, even as slogans on vehicles or on textiles (cloth). But obviously they are used most frequently in oral communication. The author explains the importance of the social context for a proper understanding of proverbs, and he includes a special section on the use of proverbs in the judicial process. Proverbs are even cited as rhetorical statements during board games, and they are today quite effective devices in modern political rhetoric. Yankah claims that proverbs still play a much more important role in the African societies than those of Europe or North America. A solid bibliography (pp. 344–346) concludes this valuable survey article.

4591. Yassin, Mahmoud Aziz F. "Spoken Arabic Proverbs." *Bulletin of the School of Oriental and African Studies—University of London,* 51 (1988), 59–68.

The author argues that the most fruitful approach to the study of Arabic proverbs is provided by a functional and linguistic approach. He begins with a short review of previous research and then discusses various functions of proverbs in oral contexts. Numerous examples are cited in Arabic with English translations, showing that they express attitudes, experience, social norms, moral imperatives, etc. The major part of the essay deals with the form and structure of these texts. Yassin analyzes such aspects as repetition, rhyme, alliteration, assonance, reduplication, ellipsis, contrast, and parallelism. It is argued that this variety in form and function is very characteristic of Arabic proverbs that also makes them so difficult to translate into other languages.

4592. Young, Kathleen E., and Elizabeth L. Mapplebeck. "Proverbial Sayings." *A Folklore Sampler from the Maritimes with a Bibliographical Essay on the Folktale in English.* Ed. Herbert Halpert. St. Johns/Newfoundland: Memorial University of Newfoundland Folklore and Language Publications for the Centre of Canadian Studies, 1982. 117–137.

This book chapter begins with a richly annotated collection of 60 proverbs, wellerisms, proverbial expressions, proverbial comparisons, proverbial exaggerations, and proverbial rhymes that were collected in the Maritimes of Canada. The texts (pp. 117–129) represent a fine example of proverbial materials collected during field research in Newfoundland and other provinces. The second part of the article (pp. 129–137) is a bibliographical essay relating to the various proverbial genres mentioned. It is stated that there is a definite paucity of Canadian proverb collections. What is needed are major collections that register the various proverbial genres in actual speech contexts. In the meantime this bibliography lists primarily general and regional proverb collections that were published in England and the United States.

Z

4593. Zemb, Jean-Marie. "Des atomes et des molécules." *Europhras 88.
Phraséologie Contrastive. Actes du Colloque International Klingenthal-
Strasbourg, 12–15 mai 1988.* Ed. Gertrud Gréciano. Strasbourg:
Université des Sciences Humaines, 1989. 485–493.

Zemb presents a rather general discussion of phraseological
units as "minima semantica." The philosophical essay begins with
some comments concerning the "minima naturalia" which are
described as consisting of atoms and molecules. The author feels
that fixed phrases might be considered in a similar fashion as
making up a semantic minimum in the whole area of possible
sentences. They are formulaic statements that have survived from
generation to generation, and they are ready to be employed at
any moment as traditional semantic units. The fact that they
contain metaphors, that they are based on certain structures, and
that they can be used repetitively in different contexts makes
phraseological units to basic communicative devices. A short
discussion of the possibility of establishing dictionaries that
contain the most universal proverbs and proverbial expressions is
added at the end of the essay. This would go along well with
Grigorii L'vovich Permiakov's (1919–1983) idea of so-called
paremiological minima (see no. 2737).

4594. Zemke, John Max. *Critical Approaches to the "Proverbios morales" of
Shem Tov de Carrión.* Diss. University of California at Davis, 1988.
408 pp.

This dissertation on Santob de Carrión's (14th century)
medieval Spanish proverb collection *Proverbios morales* (1345)
includes a critical review of the entire scholarship on this
significant work. Zemke starts with an introduction (pp. 1–28)
concerning the life, works, and manuscripts of this Jewish author,
and he then discusses in chronological order the reactions to the

Proverbios morales from the 14th century to the present day. It is pointed out that references made to this work by 14th and 15th century writers emphasize the ethical content, didacticism, and orality. From the 18th century until the present, the predominant interpretative approach has been historical reductionism. Since the 20th century an important minority of scholars has also compared its poetic content with Arabic apothegmatic compendia, Biblical and Rabbinic literatures, and folkloric wisdom, thus identifying the varied source materials integrated into the *Proverbios morales.* Modern linguistic and poetic analyses have isolated the prevalence of Hebrew prosody and traditional poetic techniques, especially parallelism. In the conclusion (pp. 248–254) it is argued that further research on the work's literary tradition, social functions, and structural and poetic organization may develop adequate responses to issues of medieval semantics. The 761 notes (pp. 255–348), the inclusive bibliography (pp. 349–381), and the helpful subject index (pp. 382–408) add to the high value of this study. See above all also Theodore Perry (nos. 4157–4160).

4595. Zemke, John Max. "A Neglected Fragment of Shem Tov' *Proverbios morales." La Coróonica.* 17, no. 1 (1988–1989), 76–89.

Zemke reports on a little known fragment of Santob de Carrión's (14th century) Spanish proverb collection *Proverbios morales* (1345) that is contained in a 15th century manuscript entitled *Libro del regimiento de señores.* Detailed philological and comparative notes are provided, and the author includes a reprint of this manuscript which corresponds to stanzas 222 to 226 of Santob's work. Zemke also includes comments regarding other issues about the reception of Rabbi Santob de Carrión's moralistic proverb collection during this early period of Spanish history. He notes in particular that this work by a Jewish writer continued to be known despite of the Spanish Inquisition. The 25 notes (pp. 86–89) contain useful bibliographical references.

4596. Zholkovsky, Alexander. "Deriving Poetic Structure: A Somali Proverb." In A. Zholkovsky. *Themes and Texts. Toward a Poetics of Expressiveness.* Ithaca/New York: Cornell University Press, 1984. 99–111.

This book chapter represents an abridged English version of Aleksandr Zholkovskii's (Russian spelling of his name) earlier Russian article on the poetic structure of a Somali proverb (see no. 2133). The proverb under discussion is "Caano aan fiiqsi loo dhamin iyo hadal aan fiiro loo odhan feedhahaaga ayyay wax yeelaan" (The milk that one does not drink in sips and the words that one speaks without attention harm your ribs; or simply: Gulped milk and careless words harm your ribs). The author analyzes the poetic devices used in this proverb, and he also comments on its structure, meaning, and theme. Problems of augmentation and variation are discussed as well, and a diagram is provided to illustrate how various expressive devices work together to give the proverb its poetic structure. See also Zholkovsky's article on the intersection of linguistics, paremiology, and poetics (no. 2132).

4597. Ziejka, Franciszek. "'Polegaj jak na Zawiszy'." *Pamietnik Literacki*, 75, no. 1 (1984), 145–180.

This is a major historical study on the origin, dissemination, meaning, and use of the Polish proverbial comparison "Polegaj jak na Zawiszy" (To rely [depend] on someone as on Zawisza). The author points out that this fixed phrase refers to the great Polish national hero Zawisza Czarny (1370?–1428) who won a major battle in 1410 at Grunwald against the Teutonic knights (see pp. 147–154 for a biographical sketch). The earliest recorded reference to this expression stems from 1561, but Ziejka is able to show how Zawisza became a legendary hero in various folk narratives and chronicles (see pp. 154–160). The remainder of the article discusses various literary and journalistic references from the 16th century to the present day. Of particular interest is that this patriotic hero was depicted in Jan Matejko's (1838–1893) famous painting of the "Battle of Grunwald" (1878) and that he plays a major role in Henryk Sienkiewicz's (1846–1916) novel *Krzyzacy* (1900) that deals with the Teutonic knights in Poland. The 84 notes contain important bibliographical references to many Polish proverb collections that have registered this well-known and frequently used proverbial comparison.

4598. Zimin, V.I., and M.S. Kharlitskii. "Etimologicheskii aspect v opisanii frazeologii i paremii." *Bulgarskaisa rusistika.* no. 2 (1990), 55–61.

The two authors treat various etymological aspects of Bulgarian phraseological units. It is pointed out that many of the older fixed phrases contain archaic lexical and grammatical elements which make them difficult to understand today. There are quite a few proverbial expressions and proverbs whose general meaning is known to native speakers but who are not able to explain certain words or the historical realia behind the metaphors. Zimin and Kharlitskii cite a few examples and illustrate how etymological research can help in trying to establish the precise meaning of individual words of fixed phrases and also their entire meaning. As long as the basic meaning remains understood, people will continue to use such phraseological units. However, very obscure expressions will eventually drop out of use. A small bibliography (p. 61) is attached.

4599. Zuluaga O. [sic], Alberto. "Empleo de locuciones y refranes en *La consagración de la primavera,* de Alejo Carpentier." *Aspekte der Hispania im 19. und 20. Jahrhundert. Akten des Deutschen Hispanistentages 1983.* Ed. Dieter Kremer. Hamburg: Helmut Buske, 1983. 97–112.

This is a literary proverb investigation of Alejo Carpentier's (1904–) Spanish novel *La consagración de la primavera* (1978). The author begins with some general comments on the use of proverbial expressions and proverbs in modern literature, and he then proceeds to show that Carpentier employs phraseological units quite frequently. They function primarily as descriptions and characterizations of various protagonists. This metaphorical language also adds elements of folk speech to the novel, thus enabling its author to give an authentic picture of the social situation depicted in the novel. Numerous examples are cited in their narrative context, and Zuluaga adds some interpretative comments regarding their effectiveness as a literary device. A useful bibliography (pp. 111–112) is attached, but there is no proverb index.

NAME INDEX

Those scholars whose publications are annotated in alphabetical order in this bibliography are not listed here. However, second or third authors of any particular entry are included. This index registers all names mentioned in the titles of the bibliographical entries and in the annotations. All numbers refer to the entries and not to pages.

Abate, Frank R. 4492
Abraham a Santa Clara 3904, 3911
Abrahams, Roger 4456
Abrams, Clara 3433
Abu I-Fadl al-Mikali 4364
Acca, Bishop 3084
Achebe, Chinua 3035, 3066, 4064, 4122, 4487, 4573
Adalberg, Samuel 4197
Adams, Abigail 3898
Adams, John 3898
Adelung, Johann Christoph 4113
Agel, Vilmos 3588
Agricola, Erhard 3955
Agricola, Johannes 3070, 3159, 3225, 3481, 3696, 3840, 3872, 3901, 4017, 4291
Aichinger, Ilse 3929
Aiiad at-Tantavi, Mukhammed 3772
Aimeric de Peguilhan 4167
Akhmed, Madikha Makhmud Reda 3772
Al-Harizi 4158
Albee, Edward 3849
Alemán, Mateo 4464
Ambrose, Saint 3898, 3904

Anders, Günther 3933
Andersch, Alfred 3597
Anderson, Izett 3765
Andreesco-Miereanu, Ioana 3062
Angenot, Marc 3308
Anikin, V.P. 3524, 3529
Apperson, G.L. 3981
Aquinas, Saint Thomas 3838
Arany, Janos 4102
Arbiter, Gaius Petronius 4302
Archilochus 3980
Arcipreste de Hita 3583
Aristophanes 3051, 3274
Aristotle 3264, 3269, 3512, 3630, 3773, 4421, 4464, 4553, 4569
Ashley, Leonard 3247
Astel, Arnfrid 3584, 3933
Athanasius, Saint 3630
Auden, W.H. 3902
Augustine, Saint 3269, 3898, 3904, 4091, 4351
Augustus 3838
Ausländer, Rose 3929
Avianus, Testus Rufius 3246
Ayckbourn, Alan 3484
Ayrer, Jakob 4263

SUBJECT INDEX

This index is based on the key-words in the titles of the bibliographical entries and also refers to the subjects and concepts in the annotations. Some of the larger entries such as "bibliography," "collection," "literature," and "proverbial expression" have been broken down into national, ethnic or subject categories. The most important international bibliographies are listed under "bibliography (general)." All numbers refer to the entries and not to pages.

4051, 4111, 4125, 4130, 4140,
4147, 4157, 4158, 4161, 4183,
4205, 4207-4210, 4213, 4215,
4219, 4230, 4235, 4241, 4242,
4246, 4252, 4254, 4255, 4261,
4266, 4273, 4276, 4282, 4293,
4321, 4322, 4326, 4350, 4353,
4364, 4365, 4371, 4374, 4378,
4389, 4391, 4396, 4397, 4408,
4416, 4422, 4428, 4432, 4445,
4446, 4460, 4461, 4467, 4476,
4484, 4487, 4493, 4495, 4496,
4499, 4501, 4504, 4505, 4515,
4523, 4536, 4539, 4540, 4561,
4563, 4564, 4571, 4573, 4580,
4585, 4586
cultural historian 3195, 4326,
4350, 4445
cultural literacy 3173, 3834, 3884
cultural loading 3622
cultural text 3535, 3785
culture 3066, 3123, 3171, 3172,
3174, 3192, 3260, 3290, 3292,
3294, 3307, 3336, 3342, 3355,
3416, 3419, 3427, 3459, 3474,
3476, 3517, 3535, 3536, 3578,
3583, 3585, 3600, 3601, 3622,
3629, 3634, 3639, 3661, 3674,
3704, 3757, 3769, 3778, 3780,
3787, 3810, 3824, 3831, 3834,
3842-3844, 3874, 3933, 3966,
3967, 3976, 3989, 4005, 4024,
4034, 4041, 4042, 4045, 4046,
4048, 4052, 4059, 4064, 4078,
4115, 4122, 4134, 4135, 4142,
4148, 4163, 4165, 4190, 4193,
4194, 4198, 4199, 4216, 4225,
4232, 4239, 4243, 4246, 4298,
4300, 4321, 4335, 4366, 4377,
4387, 4388, 4390, 4417, 4425,
4435, 4438, 4451, 4472, 4486,
4490, 4508, 4510, 4540, 4547,
4560

cuneiform tablet 3049, 3050,
3052, 3053, 3724
cup 4375
currency 3046, 3073, 3086, 3140,
3209, 3218, 3265, 3428, 3465,
3523, 3603, 3639, 3640, 3643,
3669, 3768, 3813, 3830, 3837,
3855, 3880, 3920, 3926, 3948,
3989, 4170, 4188, 4195, 4219,
4232, 4245, 4250, 4358, 4365,
4517, 4529, 4555
curriculum 3173, 3398
curse 3118, 3304, 3601
curtain 3860
custom 3168, 3349, 3355, 3440,
3443, 3497, 4068, 4111, 4252,
4273, 4284, 4371, 4386
cut 3987
cute 3247
Cuttack 3968
cutworm 3922
Czech 3345, 3351, 3537, 3580,
3581, 3620, 3641, 3969, 4123,
4515, 4574
Czechoslovakia 3918, 4205
Czechoslovakian 4209

dactylic 3322
daisy oracle 3903
Dalila 3694
Dallas 3152
dance 3056, 4213, 4470
Dance of Death 4470
danger 4538
Danish 3557, 3608, 3662, 3686,
3734, 4065, 4094, 4123, 4303
Danse macabre 4470
Darwinism 3060
date 3308
dative 3711
day 3275, 3458, 3465, 3830, 4434
dead 4288

4154, 4176, 4177, 4197, 4201,
4210, 4215, 4230, 4248, 4251,
4326, 4355, 4358, 4360, 4388,
4415, 4420, 4423, 4424, 4458,
4461, 4462, 4486, 4502, 4512,
4513, 4537, 4538, 4545
internationality 3161, 3869
interpretability 3728, 4524
interpretation 3062, 3132, 3150,
3158, 3173, 3193, 3200, 3223,
3268, 3271, 3311, 3331, 3333,
3337, 3388, 3402, 3442, 3476,
3477, 3487, 3491, 3534, 3550,
3561, 3563, 3583, 3604, 3606,
3658, 3659, 3672, 3697, 3763,
3766, 3780, 3783, 3809, 3841,
3898, 3903, 3913, 3919, 3984,
4004, 4024, 4025, 4050, 4053,
4058, 4073, 4119-4121, 4144,
4160, 4182, 4207, 4333, 4354,
4428, 4442, 4487, 4497, 4511,
4524
interrogative 3109, 4014, 4301,
4472
intertextuality 3222, 3554, 4109,
4286, 4459
interview 3043, 3433, 3472, 3627,
3639, 3766, 3768, 3968, 3975,
3976, 4021, 4379
intonation 3541, 3834
intoxicated 3424
introductory formula 3165, 3194,
3208, 3252, 3343, 3353, 3396,
3436, 3489, 3628, 3703, 3705,
3826, 3839, 3917, 4017, 4030,
4167, 4168, 4170, 4231, 4287,
4345, 4347, 4348, 4444, 4507,
4517, 4588
invective 3283, 3480, 3595, 3902,
4284, 4387
invention 4255
Iowa 3248
Iran 3078

Iraq 4173
Iraqi Jew 3080
Ireland 4559, 4561, 4564, 4566
Irish 3048, 3329, 4061, 4559-4564
Iron Curtain 3860
ironic 3085, 3208, 3251, 3293,
3296, 3811
irony 3073, 3097, 3852, 3854,
3868, 3912, 3935, 3936, 3989,
3992, 4001, 4033, 4035, 4039,
4181, 4220, 4225, 4246, 4260,
4262, 4282, 4292, 4295, 4316,
4321, 4342, 4351, 4374, 4484,
4525, 4529, 4530, 4548, 4576
Islam 3078, 4165, 4540, 4541
Israel 3321, 3569, 3782, 4014,
4273, 4545
Israeli 3565, 3566
Istanbul 3321
Istrian 4224
Italian 3038, 3091, 3142, 3152,
3161, 3213, 3228, 3237, 3257,
3265, 3282, 3291, 3327, 3333,
3395, 3410, 3482, 3514, 3717,
3760, 3790, 3798, 3808, 3843,
3844, 3980, 3986, 4044, 4045,
4065, 4098, 4099, 4184, 4185,
4186, 4192, 4270, 4302, 4340,
4349, 4371, 4388, 4398, 4408,
4443, 4445, 4534, 4535, 4551
Italy 3607, 3609, 3760, 3843, 3984,
4192

Jack 3680, 4382
Jamaican 3765
Janosik 4208
January 3680
Japanese 3241, 3903, 3962, 3967,
4069, 4097, 4101, 4104, 4374
jazz 3248
Jerusalem 3043
jestbook 4399
Jesus 3182, 3599, 4570

Low German 3626, 3725, 4021,
    4276, 4303, 4380
Luba 3392
Lubberland 4395
Lübeck 4556
luck 4322, 4323
Ludas Matyi 4480
Luganda 3112
Lugbara 3279
lunch 3113, 3660
lyric 3603, 3614, 3736, 4166, 4278
lyrical 3255, 3454
lyrics 3910

Mac 3247
Macedonia 3310, 4173
Macedonian 3443, 4314, 4393
mackerel 3330
Madagascar 3558, 4454, 4571
Madison (Wisconsin) 3518
madness 4064
Madras 3601
Madrid 3137, 3264
magazine 3075, 3181, 3202, 3205,
    3334, 3701, 3742, 3755, 3851,
    3852, 3857, 3859, 3916, 3937,
    4231, 4397, 4514, 4558
Maghreb 3079
magic 4124, 4204, 4207, 4323
magical 3304, 3440, 3693
maid 4499, 4560
maize 3467
Malagasy 3558, 4254, 4300, 4454,
    4571
Malawi 4477
Malay 4352
male 3321, 3627, 3638, 3694
Maltese 4104
man 3224, 3568, 3795, 3882, 3884,
    3897, 3990, 4046, 4048, 4074,
    4089, 4224, 4244, 4262, 4291,
    4446, 4521, 4560, 4562
"man scal ..." 3795

management 3468
Manchester Cathedral 3648
manipulation 3185, 3287, 3321,
    3324, 3331, 3449, 3470, 3518,
    3550, 3573, 3591, 3740, 3758,
    3759, 3849, 3858, 3867, 3887,
    3906, 3935-3937, 3946, 3949,
    4020, 4059, 4179, 4233, 4255,
    4307, 4318, 4325, 4588
mankind 3120
Mannheim 3819
manuscript 3068-3070, 3084,
    3115, 3137, 3139, 3160, 3212,
    3231, 3246, 3264, 3270, 3303,
    3313, 3400, 3518, 3552, 3599,
    3601, 3616, 3640, 3779, 3817,
    3846, 4012, 4090, 4128, 4150,
    4157, 4184, 4242, 4253, 4296,
    4298, 4315, 4350, 4360, 4363,
    4364, 4372, 4375, 4384, 4398,
    4496, 4523, 4557, 4594, 4595
Maori 4585
map 3064, 3155, 3806, 4051, 4101,
    4141
Marcolf 3290, 3652
Mari 4104
Maria 3986
Marianne 3519
Maritimes 4592
marker 3073, 3926, 3996, 4054,
    4062, 4347, 4446, 4482
marketing research 3572
marriage 3077, 3085, 3570, 3658,
    3822, 3958, 4067, 4068, 4244,
    4316, 4508, 4521, 4539, 4560,
    4571
marry 3658, 3698
Mars 3957
Marxism 3937
Maryland 3220, 3231
mass market 3807
mass media 3075, 3123, 3134,
    3151, 3181, 3185, 3192, 3261,

4229, 4236, 4240, 4258, 4261,
4286, 4325, 4346, 4411, 4415,
4419, 4437, 4442, 4445, 4451,
4500, 4506, 4508, 4513, 4554,
4578, 4579, 4586
theory 3204, 3306, 3473, 3521,
3522, 3597, 3612, 3663, 3930,
4039, 4154, 4238, 4258, 4357,
4376, 4412, 4454, 4584
therapeutic 3113, 4024
therapy 4256, 4257
Thesaurus Singer 4360
thin 3890, 3963
thing 3559, 3561, 4074, 4499
think 3868, 3888, 3890, 4450
Third Reich 3331
thorn 3890
thought 3158, 3193, 3226, 3241,
3442, 3562, 3563, 3606, 3783,
3907, 4000, 4051, 4119, 4120,
4159, 4223, 4236, 4329, 4354,
4418, 4425, 4486
thrashing 4563
three 3289, 4562
threshold 4564
Thresor de Sentences Dorées (Le) 3302
throng 3330
thunder 3828
Tibetan 3688
tiger 4070
Till Eulenspiegel 3917, 4042, 4493
time 3261, 3458, 3570, 3981, 3987,
4031, 4083, 4097
tip 3776
Tischchen deck dich 3896
title 3134, 3160, 3207, 3215, 3216,
3301, 3309, 3439, 3623, 3849,
3883, 3888, 3894, 3910, 3917,
3933, 3935, 4023, 4112, 4186,
4370, 4382
toad 4070, 4080
toe 4367
toilet 3424, 3831

tomato 3992
Tongan 4467
tongue 3328
"tóó wèn" (crushed words) 4285
toponym 3422, 3424
topos 3328, 3697, 3838, 4175
tortoise 4080
touch 3171
tourism 3461
town 4111, 4342
Towneley Plays 4034
trade 3164, 3334, 3770
tradition 3062, 3072, 3156, 3174,
3393, 3498, 3555, 3644, 3772,
3787, 3812, 3813, 3857, 3860,
3902, 3903, 3920, 3968, 3976,
4076, 4161, 4173, 4328, 4370,
4384, 4398, 4532, 4571
traditional 3044, 3061, 3063, 3097,
3146, 3151, 3207, 3208, 3218,
3224, 3230, 3238, 3241, 3258,
3269, 3279, 3286, 3296, 3381,
3398, 3433, 3434, 3449, 3461,
3478, 3500, 3513, 3544, 3568,
3569, 3572, 3573, 3579, 3588,
3594, 3596, 3628, 3639, 3641,
3659, 3661, 3673, 3681, 3682,
3699, 3704, 3707, 3719, 3753,
3755, 3758, 3769-3771, 3782,
3794, 3797, 3835, 3836, 3854,
3882, 3885, 3887, 3893, 3894,
3896, 3902, 3906, 3907, 3912,
3918, 3929, 3932, 3934, 3935,
3946, 3953, 3959, 3967, 3971,
3977, 3979, 3982, 3988, 3989,
3997, 4003, 4008, 4016, 4017,
4021, 4025, 4029, 4067, 4071,
4075, 4078, 4087, 4095, 4117,
4122, 4126, 4131, 4141, 4142,
4145, 4166-4168, 4170, 4174,
4179, 4181, 4185, 4205, 4208,
4209, 4221, 4233, 4242, 4246,
4261, 4266, 4273, 4279, 4286,

PROVERB INDEX

The proverbs and proverbial expressions listed here refer to publications concerned with individual proverb studies. They are grouped according to languages and key-words and are quoted for the most part in their original languages. English translations for each text are provided in the actual annotations.

African

The cunning *bird* is caught with plantain fibre, 3836

The *monkey* says that but for its eyelids, it would have been very handsome, 3379

Proverbs are the palm-oil with which words are eaten, 3066

If a *woman* prepares a bad meal, she will say it is the one to her taste, 3379

Akkadian

The *bitch*, in its being in a hurry, gave birth to blind (puppies), 3051, 3080, 3980

The man who seized the tail of a *lion* sank in the river. He who seized the tail of a fox was saved, 3054

Anglo-American

Absence makes the heart grow fonder, 3698, 4585

Last but not least, 3888

A *leopard* does not change his spots, 4098

Life is just a bowl of cherries, 3910

Lightning never strikes twice in the same place, 3338

It is not as easy to get the *lion's share* nowadays as it used to be, 3219

Like *lips*, like lettuce, 3325

Live within compass, 4087

He (She) *loves* me, he (she) loves me not, 3903

There is no (such thing as a) free *lunch*, 3113, 3660

Semper Fi, *Mac*, 3247

Holy *mackerel*, 3330

A *man* does not live by bread alone, 3882

A *man* shall not be too soon afraid nor too soon pleased, 3069

Every *man* likes his own thing best, 4089

It is not good for *man* to be alone, 3568, 3990

That is why a *man* leaves his father and mother and is united to his wife, and the two become one flesh, 3568, 3990

Marry in haste, repent at leisure, 3658, 3698

Trim tram, like *master*, like man, 4280

The real *McCoy*, 3247

It's five *minutes* to twelve, 3919

Slow as *molasses* running uphill in January, 4039

Arabic

Affliction controls talk, 4277

Affliction may come from talk, 4277

The *bitch* in her hurry whelps blind pups, 3080

The *cat* in her haste kittens blind kittens, 3080

Aramaic

Do not buy anything from an *Aramaean* (Armenian), 4372

Burmese

There are three kinds of *mistakes*: those resulting from a lack of memory, from lack of planning ahead, or from misguided beliefs, 3124

Czech

Polska *hospodarka*, 4574

Dutch

Once an *ass*, always an ass, 3690

Ene *blinde* leijdt de ander, 4495

De strijd om be *broek*, 3847

To fill in the ditch after the *calf* has drowned, 3251

To put the blue *cloak* on someone, 4398

Though a *donkey* go to school in order to learn, / He'll be a donkey, not a horse, when he does return, 3690

Big *fish* eat little fish, 3251

Met het *hoofd* tegen de muur lopen, 4505

Twee die aan een *krakeling* trekken, 3576

Iemand een *loer* draaien, 4310

Dye den *nest* weet dye weeten / dyen roft dye heeten, 4453

Een *oog* in het zeil houden, 4495

Het achterste *paar* krijgt de krakelingen, 3576

Hij zit tussen twee *stoelen.* 4505

To swim against the *stream,* 3251

Het *veld* heeft ogen, het bos heeft oren, 3093, 4271, 4495

De *vos* geeft zangles, 3847

De *wolf* hoedt de schapen, 3847

The *world* turns on someone's thumb, 3251

Onder het *zeil* is het goed roeien, 4505

Twee *zotten* onder een kapioen, 4505

Estonian

Haukuja *koer* ei hammusta, 3729

To chew a *reed,* 4065

Loodetuul on *taeva* luud, 3729

French

Un *ange* passe, 3099, 3508

N'être pas sorti de l'*auberge*, 4171

Couper la *branche* sur laquelle on s'appuie, 4496

Aller à *Brion* bijer le cul de la vieille, 3297

Il ne se tort pas qui va plain *chemin*, 4522

Réveiller un *chien* endormi, 4496

Conte à dormir debout, 3624

Crédit est mort, les mauvais payeurs l'ont tué, 3593, 4311

Ci a grant *courtoisie*, 4156

Porter la *culotte*, 3593, 3802

Si m'aist *dex* (Se *dex* m'ait), 4073

Mon petit *doigt* m'a dit que . . ., 4171

Qui *dort* dîne, 4236

Économie polonaise, 4574

Donner le *feu* vert à quelqu'un, 3288

Honi soit qui mal y pense, 3552

Marianne, 3519

De bonne *mère* prent la fille, 3817

Retour à la *nature*, 3923

Avoir son *panier* percé, 3390

German

Greek

Haitian

Hebrew

A *bird* of the air shall carry the voice, 3566

Do not trust the *gentiles* even forty years in the grave, 3565, 3566

Hungarian

He who cannot speak *Arabic*, should not speak Arabic, 4098

Nem minden *arany*, ami fénylik, 4101

The *child* of seven nurses is always blind, 4099

Out of a *dog* there will be no lard, 4098

Every *Gypsy* praises his own horse, 4099

Kosarat *kap*, 3133

You may repeatedly throw dry *peas* to the wall, they will not stick, 4099

Irish

To throw *apples* into the orchard, 4561

A bonny *bride*'s easy (soon) buskit, 4564

It'll be *dry* on Friday tae dry the priest's sark, 4564

An aal *fiddle* plays sweetest, 4564

A *hand-staff* of holly, / A souple of hazel, / A single sheaf, / And a clean floor, 4563

Beware of a bull's *horn*, a dog's tooth, and a mule's hoof, 4562

There are three kinds of *men* who do not understand women—young men, old men, and middle-aged men, 4562

It's aye kent the *mullert* (miller) keeps fat hogs but naebody kens faa feeds them, 4564

There's aye a weet an slippery *steen* at ilky body's door, 4564

"*Walk* straight, my son," as the old crab said to the young crab, 3048

Italian

Il povero *Codro*, 3038

Cacciare la *lepre* col bue, 4408

Avere il *marchese*, 3291

Cercar *Maria* per Ravenna, 3986

Moglie et buoi dei paesi tuoi, 3228

Quando la *montagna* ha il cappello / o valligiano prendi l'ombrello, 3760

Quando il *monte* ha la cappa / presto aspettati la burrasca, 3760

Latin

Omnia vincit *amor*, 4550

Dulce *bellum* inexpertis, 3556

Cacatum non est pictum, 3126

Cogito, ergo sum, 3868, 3888, 4450

Ex abundantia *cordis* os loquitur, 4015

Cucullus non facit monachum, 3157

Bis *dat*, qui cito dat, 3387

In *dubio* pro reo, 3607, 3609, 3984

Errare humanum est, 4351

De *gustibus* non est disputandum, 4442, 4530

Labor omnia vincit, 4550

In eadem es *navi*, 3933, 4136

Necessitas non habet legem, 3501

Nomen est omen, 3122

Oleum in auricula ferre, 3745

Sociorum *olla* male fervet, 4302

In mare quid *pisces* quid aquas in flumina mittas? / Larga sed indiguis munera funde locis, 3084

Amicus *Plato* (Socrates) sed magis amica veritas, 4464

Aut *regem*, aut fatuum nasci oportet, 3695

De spinis *rosas*, de terra aurum, 3036

Sub *rosa* dicere, 3291

Veni, vidi, vici, 3938

In *vino* veritas, 3918

Latvian

All is not *gold* that glitters, 3657

To carry *owls* to Athens, 4462

Russian

Delo mastera boitsia, 3469

Gol kak cokól, 3361

To make a *mountain* out of a molehill, 3203

U semi *nianek* ditia bez glazu, 4147

Valit' cherez *pen'* kholodu, 3357

The other *side* of the coin, 3203

Slovo—ne vorobei, 3235

Kak v *vodu* gliadel, 3359

Zhizn' prozhit'—ne pole pereiti, 3784

Slovakian

Kto liha medzi otruby, prichodi *svini* pod zuby, 3966

Somali

Gulped *milk* and careless words harm your ribs, 4596

Spanish

Al buen *callar* llaman Sancho, 3253